Social and Personality Development

An Evolutionary Synthesis

Perspectives in Developmental Psychology

Series Editor: Michael Lewis
Rutgers Medical School
University of Medicine and Dentistry of New Jersey
New Brunswick, New Jersey

ASSESSMENT OF YOUNG DEVELOPMENTALLY
DISABLED CHILDREN
Edited by Theodore D. Wachs and Robert Sheehan

COGNITIVE DEVELOPMENTAL AND CHILD
PSYCHOTHERAPY
Edited by Stephen R. Shirk

THE DIFFERENT FACES OF MOTHERHOOD
Edited by Beverly Birns and Dale Hay

FATHERING BEHAVIORS
The Dynamics of the Man–Child Bond
Wade C. Mackey

PSYCHOLOGY OF DEVELOPMENT AND HISTORY
Edited by Klaus F. Riegel

SOCIAL AND PERSONALITY DEVELOPMENT
An Evolutionary Synthesis
Kevin B. MacDonald

Social and Personality Development

An Evolutionary Synthesis

Kevin B. MacDonald

California State University-Long Beach
Long Beach, California

Plenum Press • New York and London

Library of Congress Cataloging in Publication Data

MacDonald, Kevin B.
  Social and personality development: an evolutionary synthesis / Kevin B.
MacDonald.
      p.   cm. — (Perspectives in developmental psychology)
  Includes bibliographical references and index.
  ISBN 0-306-42891-1
  1. Socialization. 2. Social psychology. 3. Personality in children. 4. Parent and child.
I. Title. II. Series.
HM131.M23   1988   88-25364
303.3′2 — dc19   CIP

© 1988 Plenum Press, New York
A Division of Plenum Publishing Corporation
233 Spring Street, New York, N.Y. 10013

Printed in the United States of America

To my mother

Preface

This volume is an attempt to integrate the theory and data of social and personality development within a modern evolutionary framework. The various chapters are not meant to be read in isolation from one another but rather are intended to form an integrated whole. There is thus a great deal of cross-referencing between chapters and to some extent they all stand or fall together. This also suggests that the accuracy (or usefulness) of a particular chapter cannot be judged until the book is comprehended as a whole.

Chapter 1 deals with the theoretical foundations of this enterprise, and the focus is on the compatibility of mainstream approaches within the field to a modern evolutionary approach. Chapters 2–4 concern what I view to be the fundamental proximal mechanisms underlying social and personality development. Chapter 2, on temperament and personality development, is particularly central to the rest of the volume because these processes are repeatedly invoked as explanatory concepts at later points in the volume.

If the theory of temperament is one central pillar of the volume, Chapter 5, on family processes, is the other. The perspective developed there on the evolution of the family is central to much of the discussion in Chapter 6 on aggression and sex differences as well as the discussion of the development of altruism in Chapter 8. Chapter 5 is the first chapter to emphasize modern evolutionary theory and the remaining chapters continue and expand this perspective in several of the central areas of social development, including moral reasoning (Chapter 7) and the wider context of human development (Chapter 9).

This work culminates a long process of attempting to develop a unified account of social and personality development based on evolutionary theory. It draws on a wide range of theory and data, and I have benefited from the help of a great many individuals in trying to put it together. None of this would have been possible without the help of Ross Parke. The time I spent at the University of Illinois on a postdoctoral fellowship and the discussions we had exposed me to a great many ideas that have found their way into this book.

Since coming to California State University-Long Beach, I have also benefited greatly from conversations with Robert Thayer on the subject of personality, and his work is a major part of the theory developed in the Appendix to Chapter 2. The other major influence in the areas of temperament and personality development has been Mary K. Rothbart. The more I thought about these issues and my own data, the more I realized that she had developed a theory which was powerful enough to incorporate the central data on personality development and was yet simple enough to incorporate into an adaptationist account of personality. Her critical comments on Chapter 2 and several other chapters are greatly appreciated. I would also like to thank Virginia Douglas for her critical reading of Chapter 2 and for her encouragement in the area of the linkages between the theory of temperament and conceptualizing clinical diagnoses.

One of the main purposes behind the book is to integrate modern evolutionary theory with the data and theory of developmental psychology. In this endeavor I have benefited greatly from the help and encouragement of William Charlesworth, a true pioneer in the area of applying models and ideas deriving from evolutionary biology to the area of child development. His work is responsible for the prominence in this volume of thinking in terms of resources as being fundamental to an evolutionary approach. This aspect of the book has also benefited from the work of sociobiologically oriented researchers on child development, including Jerome Barkow, Robert Burgess, James Chisholm, Patricia Draper, Henry Harpending, Dennis Krebs, Jeffrey Kurland, Charles Lumsden, Nancy Segal, Martin Smith, and Glenn Weisfeld. I have tried to feature their work and integrate it with the other areas of social and personality development. Another source of help in this area has been Michael McGuire whose critical readings of earlier versions of several of the chapters were very helpful. I would also like to thank Richard Lerner, who has given me the opportunity to develop several of the ideas presented here and whose work in the area of plasticity and early experience parallels my own work.

Finally, thanks of another kind must be given to my wife Susan who has patiently put up with several relocations and the need to adjust her own academic career to mine. Her encouragement has been indispensable. My children, Joshua and Geoffrey, also deserve a great deal of credit, since they have served as unwitting case studies in my ongoing attempt to understand temperament and personality. It has been said that every parent with more than one child believes in the importance of temperament, and I am no exception.

KEVIN B. MACDONALD

Long Beach, California

Contents

*Social and
Personality Development*

Theoretical Considerations

I. INTRODUCTION

The purpose of this volume is to develop an evolutionary account of human social and personality development. In the past evolutionary theory has been quite restricted in its application within developmental psychology. Evolutionary accounts have been influential in the area of attachment and in the area of dominance relations among peers, and there is an increasing emphasis on biologically based mechanisms such as temperament and genetic variation. Still, the role of biology is quite fragmented and in some areas of social and personality development there has been no influence at all of biological models.

The reason for the patchy influence of evolutionary thought in the science of human development is at least partly historical. The mainstream influences within the field have derived from the long behaviorist tradition in British and North American psychology and from the more recent work of Piaget. However, perhaps even more crucial has been the inability of evolutionarily derived thinking to provide meaningful hypotheses in some of the central areas of social development. If evolutionary thinking did shed some light on social dominance, it certainly did not appear to shed any light on friendship or on moral development. Moreover, in some areas, such as the development of aggression, evolutionary thinking was extremely primitive and easy to dismiss outright. No reasonable person could entertain seriously the idea that aggressive urges build up until they are released or that aggression is "instinctive," whatever that might mean.

The thesis here is that recent advances in evolutionary thought enable a more complete evolutionary account of human development to be given. These new theoretical advances allow for a highly integrated account of human development in evolutionary terms, an account that is able to incorporate cross-cultural and historical data as well as data derived from a wide variety of paradigms within developmental psychology. It is an account that is able to address problems that have not been placed in an evolutionary perspective before, such as moral development and altruism, and, it is hoped, provide more sophisticated accounts of other areas, such as family influences, aggression, and sex differences in behavior. Ironically, it is an account that gives a large role to the environment in shaping human behavior.

The foregoing might be summarized by the statement that the study of human

1

development will greatly benefit from the influence of recent evolutionary biology. The second major purpose of this volume is to suggest the converse of this statement, that is, that recent evolutionary accounts of human behavior will benefit greatly from a consideration of the proximal mechanisms studied by developmental psychologists. The rise of a powerful adaptationist theory in evolutionary biology has led many to hope that great strides could be made in the social sciences by applying this framework to human behavior. However, progress has been slow and controversy has arisen because quite often the practitioners of human sociobiology have not been interested in the proximal mechanisms studied by other disciplines, particularly psychologists. A major part of the present endeavor, then, will be to show that by considering in detail these proximal mechanisms it is possible to provide a more convincing evolutionary account of behavior.

In the present chapter some of the central theoretical issues in human development will be discussed. The purpose will be to show how modern evolutionary theory relates to the other theoretical traditions in the area of social and personality development. In addition, an important goal is to show how an integrated account of development is possible, an account that is quite contrary to the rationalist philosophy of science and the resultant "world view" theory of scientific theories and research. However, it is necessary first to describe this perspective and then contrast it with a modern version of philosophical realism, which is much more compatible with an evolutionary perspective.

II. Philosophical Issues and World Views

A. Rationalist Philosophers of Science: Kuhn, Lakatos, and Lauden

Scientists usually begin their research with a general idea of where to look for a cause or which associations are important, and this is often derived from their theoretical perspective. Indeed, it is quite common to suppose that it is theoretically impossible for anyone, scientists included, to look at the world except through theoretical lenses of some sort. Thus, the philosopher of science Thomas Kuhn (1962) proposed that "facts" are not simply out there waiting to be discovered, but are relativized to the *paradigm* or *world view* that the scientist adopts. Observation then becomes a highly theory-laden enterprise, so that the fact that a scientist believes, for example, that individuals are fundamentally passive recipients of environmental input would actually determine the experiments that he or she conducted and what he or she saw in analyzing data. For example, if a Freudian and a behaviorist looked at the transcript of a psychoanalytic session, the former might interpret the dialogue as showing how the analyst is reinforcing certain responses in the patient, while the latter would interpret the responses of the patient as showing the subconscious motivation of behavior.

In the view adopted by Kuhn, even standards of accuracy and measurement depend greatly on the paradigm accepted by the scientist. For example, the Freudian in the above example might be perfectly satisfied that the statements made by the patient about his or her childhood are not only accurate, but also constitute proof that subconscious motivations exist, while the behaviorist would continue to doubt the validity and veracity of these statements until a "scientific" experiment (i.e., one that the behaviorist accepts as valid) can allay the behaviorist's doubts.

Within this perspective, scientists adopt their particular world views for a number of different reasons, but clearly it is not accurate to say that they adopt them on the basis of the objective facts. Instead, the different world views are held for *preempirical* reasons, which really amount to sociopolitical reasons. Adopting a world view is more like adopting a religion or a political affiliation than it is a matter of plugging into the nature of reality or even an approximation of reality. Although scientists may be quite objective while working within their world view, the differences between world views are not open to empirical verification. The "facts" of one world view are the fictions of another world view, and since no one can really be sure that nature is uniquely reflected in his or her world view, there is no way to be certain that one's world view is correct.

Indeed, rival world views are *incommensurable* according to Kuhn. That is, there is no way independent of a world view to appraise scientific procedures as good or bad, no neutral standpoint from which to evaluate rival world views. As Aronson (1984) points out, this quite clearly leads to an extreme relativism in which it is impossible to argue that one world view is more accurate than another. Moreover, within this perspective it is not possible to suppose that scientists are somehow getting closer and closer to the truth about reality. Although progress might be said to occur within a world view as various findings accumulate, there is no way within this perspective to argue that in fact these findings are due to the nature of some underlying reality.

Kuhn's work has been extremely influential in the philosophy of science, but subsequent work has attempted to provide a more rational account of the scientific endeavor than provided by Kuhn while still holding to his basic philosophical assumptions. One important attempt in this direction was that of Lakatos (1970). Lakatos described research programs as a succession of theories that coexist in competition with each other. At the core of the research program is a set of assumptions that are relatively immune from experimental refutation, although this set of beliefs may change as the research program develops. Within the research program a better theory is defined as a theory that can both accommodate the findings explained by its predecessor and also explain anomalous findings and generate new predictions, which can then be confirmed. Research programs themselves are judged by whether they are progressing, that is, continuing to develop new theories and new verified predictions. Research programs that are not able to do this are degenerating and eventually they exhaust themselves as scientists start to look for a new research program. Eventually a new research program is developed that defeats the previously held program and the cycle continues.

Lakatos thus provides a rational manner of evaluating theories within a research program (explanation of empirical findings and verified predictions) as well as evaluating research programs themselves (degenerating versus progressive). However, he shares with Kuhn the idea that there is no way of knowing if these theories actually describe reality or even an approximation of reality.

Lauden (1977) has continued the evolution of the rationalist perspective in the philosophy of science. For Lauden science is a problem-solving activity, where the solution of problems is often only approximate and is completely independent of the truth or falsity of the research tradition. Scientists work within research traditions, which have a large number of specific theories characteristic of them as well as a variety of metaphysical and methodological commitments. Theories within a research tradition are often inconsistent and in competition with each other. While these individual theories are testable, the research tradition is not directly testable and does not provide detailed answers to specific problems. Research traditions, however, can be objectively evaluated:

> A *successful research tradition is one which leads, via its component theories to the adequate solution of an increasing range of empirical and conceptual problems.* (Lauden, 1977, p. 82; italics in original)

Again, there is no claim that a successful research tradition is true or an unsuccessful one false. Moreover, the core elements of the research tradition, while nonrejectable at a particular time, change as the research tradition develops.

In summary, the progression from Kuhn to Lauden involves an increased emphasis on providing rational ways to choose between world views or research traditions. Whereas for Kuhn the acceptance of a world view is an irrational process and world views are fundamentally incommensurable, for Lauden the acceptance of a research tradition is a rational process grounded in scientists' appraisals of the relative progress of different research traditions in solving problems. Although these appraisals are rational, they are not dependent on the truth of the research tradition, so this group of philosophers of science remain relativists with respect to this question. As all of our observations are necessarily theory-laden, we can never uncover nature as it really is in order to compare our theories against it.

B. Three Research Traditions in Developmental Psychology

Perhaps the greatest source of support for the relativist ideas of Kuhn, Lakatos, and Lauden has come from their interpretation of the history of science as well as their interpretation of disagreements within developmental psychology. According to the relativist perspective, developmental psychology has been and is beset with theoretical fragmentation and lack of consensus on basic issues: scientists seem to put on their theoretical lenses and thereafter are unable to see the situation in the same way as someone with a different set of lenses. Most textbooks begin with a litany of theories and the student is led to believe that any one of the theories constitutes a valid approach to studying development, however incompatible it may be with the other theories. Reflecting these basic disagreements, Overton and Reese (see Overton, 1984; Overton & Reese, 1973; Reese & Overton, 1970) have argued that fundamentally incompatible world views or research traditions strongly influence the construction of scientific theories and the empirical research derived from these theories. They argue that there are two fundamental world views or research traditions within developmental psychology: mechanism and organicism. The mechanistic model views the child as a passive recipient of external forces. These external forces are accidental in the sense that their occurrence is contingent rather than part of the inherent organization of the organism. Development occurs by the addition of discrete elements, so that there is continuity over age in the types of behavior shown by the child. Older children are just larger editions of the same basic elements, not qualitatively different organisms.

An example conforming to the mechanistic world view within human development would be that of classical behaviorism. Older children differ in their reinforcement history, but not in any qualitative way from younger children. Explanation of behavior in-

volves reducing behavior to discrete relationships between antecedent stimuli and consequent behavior. These relationships are purely contingent, since they depend on the
unique experience of each organism rather than the common structural features of the
organism.

The organismic world view, on the other hand, views the child as a living, organized
system. Rather than the passive view of the child implied in the mechanistic approach, the
child is seen as active in structuring its environment. Children of different ages are said to
be characterized by qualitatively different structures, which are part of their inherent
organization rather than their contingent experience. Since there are qualitative differences between ages, development is said to be discontinuous: A child at a different
stage of development does not simply possess more or less of the same type of thing a
child at a different stage possesses. Rather, the child possesses qualitatively different
structures, much as the development of a butterfly is discontinuous with the development
of the caterpiller. In addition, here one has a goal or common endpoint to development,
namely the attainment of the structures characteristic of adults. The classic example of an
organismic viewpoint within developmental psychology would be Piaget's theory of
cognitive development.

Recently Lerner and his colleagues (e.g., Lerner & Kauffman, 1985) have elaborated
a contextual world view and claim that it represents a significant research tradition within
developmental psychology. Contextualism differs from organicism in that there is no
postulation of a goal or final endpoint to development. Contextualists view development
as being influenced by a wide variety of nonnormative life events, ranging from sociopolitical conditions to events in the microenvironment of the child. Rather than the
organicist emphasis on internal principles of organization or the mechanistic emphasis on
external events, contextualists emphasize a transactional or reciprocal model of the relation between organism and environment. The organism influences the environment and
the environment influences the organism. Although there is no goal or typical endpoint to
development, Lerner and Kauffman (1985) characterize the contextualist position as
implying a probabilistic course for development. Development is thus systematic and
directional, but not deterministic. Moreover, because development is probabilistic, plasticity is postulated as a general feature of the organism.

C. An Alternate Perspective: Philosophical Realism

The rationalist philosophy of science described above is clearly dominant as a philosophical account of the area of developmental psychology (see, e.g., Overton, 1984).
However, such an account is intuitively nonappealing within an evolutionary perspective.
Evolutionary biologists implicitly believe that the account they give of the origin and
transformation of species is a more or less *true* account of real processes that occurred to
real organisms over an immense period of time on Earth. They believe in the reality of
genetic variation, the importance of certain macromolecules with a very definite structure
that influence such disparate phenomena as the reproductive physiology of lions and the
wing morphology of bees, and that something very much like the present conception of
natural selection resulted in the diversity of plants and animals. This implicit realism
suggests that whatever else one might say about the history of biological science prior to

the mid-19th century, at that time the essential truth about the natural world was discovered. This is not to say that evolutionary science has not developed since that time, but only that more recent versions of evolutionary theory have come progressively closer to the truth about the natural world. When this perspective is applied to human behavior, the recent *discoveries* of evolutionary theory are aptly described as "the greatest intellectual advance of the century" (Alexander, 1987, p. 3).

It is apparent, then, that the evolutionary perspective developed here cannot coexist comfortably with a rationalist philosophy of science. Philosophical realism is, however, a viable intellectual alternative to the inevitable relativism of the rationalist perspective. Philosophical realists such as Aronson (1984) propose that there are entities that underlie the observable data of science, entities that account for the lawlike phenomena observed by scientists. Contrary to Kuhn, Lakatos, and Lauden, Aronson accepts an approximation view of the scientific endeavor. Scientific progress means a closer approximation to a true description of nature:

> How else can we *explain* why our new theories give better predictions, lead to an improved overall technology except that all of these things resulted from theories that give a better description of nature, i.e., theories that are getting closer to the truth? Otherwise, why should we believe that these things are even an indication of scientific progress? One thing is certain: they can not be explained by the values and commitments of the scientific community, as if a change in the latter can automatically bring about better predictions and technology. Without the notion of truth, then, I wonder how one can believe that "scientific development is, like biological, a unidirectional and irreversible process." (Aronson, 1984, pp. 129)

Aronson proposes that explanation occurs when the number of independent phenomena is reduced. In developmental psychology, for example, if one could show that a Piagetian approach was consistent with or reducible to an information processing approach, there would be a reduction in the total number of independent phenomena to be explained. As a historical example, early in the century there was a debate between proponents of the particulate and blending theories of inheritance. This debate eventually subsided when experimental data indicated that blending could be accounted for in a model that assumed particulate Mendelian entities (genes), and the field was unified in a manner that remains unchallenged today. By proposing these entities, it was possible to develop lawlike relationships that were impossible previously, and subsequent research has discovered the chemical nature of these entities and continued to refine the lawlike relationships to which they conform. Thus, the theoretical entities of one age become part of the furniture of the universe to the next. Similarly, in the present book it is argued that cognitive-developmental, social-learning, and evolutionary approaches are compatible and capable of yielding a unified theory.

According to Aronson, theories make claims about which objects exist and about the relations between these objects. The modern realist position does not repudiate the idea that scientists always view the world through theoretical lenses. It thus cannot be characterized as "naive realism." In agreement with the claim of the rationalists described above, there is no claim that the scientist is able to obtain an unvarnished view of reality. However, the claim is that there is a reality to be described and explained and it is this reality that results in the regularities observed by the scientist. The modern realist thus expects that over time there will be theoretical convergence as scientists come closer to the true nature of reality. This is an important empirical prediction of the realist philosophy of science and it is a central theme of this volume.

Finally, it should be pointed out that the realist perspective, whether true or false, is the guiding faith of most scientists. As Gray (1982) notes in his discussion of theories and methods in the study of behavioral inhibition:

> The close relation between method and theory noted above must make us suspect that none of the hypotheses advanced so far can be completely correct, for a successful theory transcends method. But it is probable that each method has led research workers closer to some aspect of the truth. (Gray, 1982, pp. 113–114)

This point of view clearly conflicts with that of Overton and Reese, described above, since these authors propose that psychology is characterized by fundamentally incompatible world views, which cannot be synthesized. One of the purposes of this book is to give an integrated account of social and personality development from a realist philosophical perspective. Such an approach must argue that different theoretical perspectives within developmental psychology are compatible accounts, which approximate a true description of real members of our species. In the following sections of this chapter, several general theoretical issues will be raised, followed by a beginning attempt to develop a realist integration of the theoretical diversity of developmental science. In the following chapters, this theme will reemerge as a unifying feature of the volume.

III. GENERAL THEORETICAL ISSUES

A. The Nature–Nurture Problem

The nature–nurture controversy has given rise to some of the most heated debates in the history of developmental psychology. Historically, the field shifted from the extreme genetic determinism of Arnold Gesell in the 1930s and 1940s to the pervasive environmentalism of the 1950s and 1960s. At the present time, the pendulum is swinging back toward an appreciation of biological factors in human development, but the emphasis is now on how both biological factors and environmental factors are important.

1. Models of Nature–Nurture Interrelationships

One way to think about these relationships is to develop several models of how biological and environmental factors can be related and then see if there are any data that conform to the models. By proceeding in this manner it is not necessary to assume that any one model is correct for thinking about the development of behavior. Thus, it could be that the development of language is best described by one model and physical growth is better described with another model. The development of one child's peer relationships may be describable with one model, while those of another child are better described with another model.

When scientists think about the relation between nature and nurture they have in mind a continuum between complete determination by the environment and complete determination by the genes. In between there can be interactions between biological and environmental factors. In the following, four types of models will be described, but it should be emphasized that the models should be seen as part of a continuum, so that they grade into each other. (See MacDonald, 1986a,b, for a discussion.)

The first model to be described postulates complete environmental determination of the differences in a population. The environment is conceived as an independently exist-ing force, which acts on a passive organism to produce differences among individuals. The individual does not influence the environment and the environment does not have different effects on individuals depending on what the individuals are like to start with. A good example that would conform to this model would be a conditioning experiment in which some individuals learn a fairly simple task because they are exposed to appropriate relationships between the stimuli and some do not learn the task because they are not so exposed. In such a case we can imagine that all the variation between the groups is accounted for by whether or not they observed the relationships between the stimuli. Differences among individuals in the two groups, such as genetic differences affecting differences in IQ, do not affect the outcome, because the task is a fairly simple one to learn. Moreover, we can imagine that the individuals in the study did not affect their environment, as would be the case if some individuals managed to influence the way the experiment was conducted by being extremely distracting or irritating to the experimenter. Differences due solely to environmental contingencies are undoubtedly important in social development and many examples will be given throughout this book.

A second model describes the relation between organism and environment as one of weak interaction (Lerner, 1986). In this model, as in Model 1, the environment is conceived of as an independent force acting on a passive organism, but here the environ-ment does not affect all individuals in the same way: "different strokes for different folks." For example, Henderson (1970) showed that some genetic strains of mice that had very low scores on a maze test if they were reared in a deprived environment profited greatly by being reared in an enriched environment. Other strains of mice did not profit as much from the change in environments, while some strains profited even more. As a possible example in the area of human social development, Thomas, Chess, Sillen, and Mendez (1974) found that middle-class families made strong efforts to get their infants to maintain a rhythmic sleep schedule. As a result, some infants who were arhythmic to start with had a difficult time and some developed problem behaviors later.

A third type of model describes the relationship between organism and environment as a strong interaction (Lerner, 1986) or as consisting of transactions (Sameroff, 1975). In this model the organism influences its environment and the environment influences the organism. These reciprocal organism–environment transactions result in a chain of causes. Recent research has uncovered many examples where individuals influence their environments. In the study by Thomas et al. (1974) mentioned above, there was some evidence that the arhythmic children seemed to have some effects on their parents, who reported high levels of stress, anxiety, and anger. Another example comes from the case of child abuse. Several studies have shown that premature babies are more likely to be abused than are full-term infants (Klein & Stern, 1971). These premature infants are much more likely to be irritable and unresponsive to their parents and may influence their parents' behavior. MacDonald (1986b) pointed out that children are more likely to affect and provoke unusual reactions from their environments when they are rather extreme on a temperamental dimension. As will be discussed extensively in Chapter 2, it is the child who is unusually irritable or active who tends to elicit extreme environmental responses such as child abuse from its parents.

In addition, Scarr and McCartney (1983) argue that as children get older they are better able to actively structure their environment. When children are young they are much more at the mercy of their environment. Their parents are vastly more powerful than they are and can arrange the environment in a manner that the children cannot control. When a child reaches adolescence, however, it is much more able to choose its own environment, and parents are consequently less able to exert control. It should be noted, however, that this active ability to structure one's environment may not result in strong effects on the child if there is less plasticity in the child's behavior as the child gets older. In Chapter 4 it will be argued that this is indeed the case. Moreover, in Chapter 9 contextual influences on development will be discussed, indicating that in some cultures adolescents are effectively prevented from choosing their own environments and indeed are probably less able to choose their environments than they were earlier in their life.

A fourth type of model minimizes the importance of the environment in the development of behavior. Behaviors conforming to this model may be termed well-buffered or canalized, because normal environmental variation is not translated into variation in behavior. Scarr (1976) argued that Piagetian sensorimotor intelligence in infants is canalized because it occurs in all human cultures and occurs even despite wide variations in rearing conditions. In the area of social development, it is quite possible that some of the basic social skills of children are highly canalized. Thus, all infants eventually move from parallel play with no mutual awareness to more complex, reciprocal forms of play (Hartup, 1983). Although the social environment may speed up or slow down the acquisition of these skills, it is reasonable to suppose that they will show up in any case in a wide range of normal human environments.

It is important to realize that saying that a behavior is well-buffered or canalized is not to deny that the environment is important in the development of behavior, but only that environmental variation is not important. The development of the social and cognitive skills of infancy may be highly dependent on the environment, but virtually any normal human environment may be sufficient to develop these skills, so that environmental variation is not important in understanding the development of these behaviors.

Second, it is also necessary to emphasize again that the four models are not meant to be mutually exclusive, but simply list the various possibilities of organism–environment relations that a given behavior may exhibit. Clearly, not all behaviors can be viewed as well-buffered or canalized, and, as will be seen in the following sections, there are some cases where the individual influences the environment much more than in other cases. Consistent with the realist philosophical perspective described above, each model is viewed as an empirical possibility, which may or may not be true of a particular behavior. Thus, Piagetian sensorimotor intelligence may be well-buffered, but IQ may not be, and some individuals influence their environments much more than others do. Unlike the world-view perspective typical of the rationalist philosophical approach, there is no commitment here to one model for all behaviors or all individuals.

2. Behavioral Genetics As a Model of the Nature–Nurture Problem

Recently there has been a great upsurge of interest within developmental psychology in the importance of genetic variation in understanding how people differ from one another in their cognitive and social behaviors. The methodology of behavior genetics provides a very compelling model of the potential ways in which genes, environments, and their interactions affect behavior.

Behavioral geneticists attempt to find the relative importance of genes and environment for the determination of individual differences in populations. Thus, they are not concerned with understanding the universal features of behavior, but rather with understanding the reasons that individuals differ from each other. Moreover, the results of the analysis describe the features of an entire population of individuals, not one individual, and as such the results may not apply to other populations or accurately reflect the relative contribution of genes and environment in a particular individual.

Behavioral genetic research has generally found that the effects of genes are often pleiotropic, that is, one gene has an effect on many different behaviors or phenotypes.[1] For example, if mice are selectively bred for their activity in an open field, it is found that there are almost no albino mice in the high-active lines, while such mice are quite common in the low-active lines. Here the single gene responsible for albinism affects the pigmentation of the eye and this in turn affects performance in the open field test by making the eye more sensitive to light (DeFries, Hegmann, & Weir, 1966).

Behavioral geneticists have also found that, although there are sometimes important effects of single genes, for the most part complex human behaviors are influenced by a large number of genes, each with a small, cumulative effect. This state of affairs is termed *polygeny*. In fact, no single gene has ever been found to be responsible for any complex behavior, although sometimes genetic mutations affecting a small number of individuals can have major effects. As a result, behavior genetic research on complex human behavior has been forced to use the indirect methods of quantitative population genetics in order to determine the relative influence of genetic and environmental factors. These quantitative methods essentially assume that a behavior is influenced by a large number of genes each with a small positive or negative effect on the phenotype. By using statistical analysis of data on large populations of individuals in which the effects of genes and environment can be disentangled, behavioral geneticists are able to determine the relative importance of each in producing the observed variation in a particular population.

In terms of the four models described above, behavioral genetic methods can find pure environmental influences uncontaminated by genetic similarities (Model 1). Such a result would be indicated if, for example, adopted individuals resembled their adoptive families and showed no resemblance to their natural parents. This represents a major methodological advance, because much of the socialization literature consists of observations or interviews of parents and their children. These subjects share both genes and environment, so that it is impossible to tell from these studies the relative importance of either.

It is important to realize, however, that a major effect of the adoptive environment can occur independently of any significant correlations between adopted children and their adoptive parents. This is because there may be a large average effect of an adoptive environment on the adopted children that is not reflected in correlations between adopted children and their adoptive parents. For example, Scarr and Weinberg (1976) found that black children adopted into white middle-class homes showed a large increase in IQ over what would have been expected if they had remained with their natural parents. This large average increase is completely independent of either the correlations between natural

---

[1]A phenotype refers to the observable properties of an individual's traits, and contrasts with a person's genotype, which is his or her genetic constitution. A phenotype is the outcome of both genetic and environmental processes.

parents and their adopted-away children or the correlations between adopted children and adoptive parents. This is so because the magnitude of a correlation coefficient is completely independent of the mean of the populations being correlated. To put it another way, the large average effect of adoption does not depend at all on finding an association such that the brighter adoptive parents have the brighter adoptive offspring. As a hypothetical example related to social behavior, adoption into a middle-class home may have a large average effect such that the adoptive children are less aggressive than would be expected if they had remained with their natural parents, but it still might not be the case that the less aggressive adoptive parents have the less aggressive adoptive children. Indeed, the correlations with the natural parents may be much higher than those with the adoptive parents. Nevertheless, there is a large average effect of the middle-class environment that is not reflected in the strength of these correlations.

Evidence supporting weak interacton (Model 2) can also be provided by an adoption study. Measures of genetic propensities derived from biological parents can be compared to environmental measures in adoptive homes in order to determine whether a particular behavior only occurs in particular genotype–environment combinations. Statistically, a weak interaction would thus show up in a behavioral genetic analysis as a significant genotype–environment interaction term. It should be noted that for cognitive behaviors there is little evidence for such interaction (Plomin, DeFries, & Loehlin, 1977). As Scarr and McCartney (1983) point out, the great majority of environments, especially therapeutic environments, affect nearly everyone in the same way. We would be very surprised if adoption into a middle-class environment or an enriched curriculum would actually result in lower IQ scores for a significant number of children. Since, all things being equal, more rather than less intelligence is presumably a good thing, it is fortunate that this is the case, since it allows us to devise environmental manipulations that will be quite likely to benefit virtually all children. However, this may not be the case with personality and social development. As will be seen in Chapter 2, there is little reason to suppose that there has been natural selection for one type of personality.

Evidence supporting strong interaction (Model 3) can be derived from an adoption study by finding active or evocative genotype–environment correlations. If, for example, the genetic propensities of adopted children cause their parents to react differently to them, this will show up as a correlation between the genetic characteristics of the child and their adoptive environments. This is the case, provided that the adoptive homes were not selected on the basis of the behavioral characteristics of the children, as happened in some of the earlier adoption studies.

Evidence supporting an independent effect of the genes is provided in an adoption study by data showing that despite adoption to an environment created by nonrelatives, the child still resembles the biological parent. If there is no effect at all of the adoptive environment, then the environmental variation sampled in the study is not important for variation in the behavior, an example of the canalization of behavioral development (Model 4). The environment may be important for the development of the behavior, but environmental variation is not important in producing variation in the behavior.

These considerations emphasize the fact that behavior genetic methodology is addressed to finding the sources of individual differences in populations. If a behavior is universal to all members of a species, such as some of Piaget's stages or the stages of moral development proposed by Kohlberg, behavioral genetic methods cannot be used.

Moreover, behavior genetic methodology cannot analyze genetic commonality between individuals. It may well be the case that most of the genes affecting behavior are common to everyone rather than showing variation among individuals. It is these common central tendencies of human behavior that are so important to the ethological, sociobiological, and cognitive-developmental theories described below. Finally, it should be noted that because behavior genetic studies are restricted to a given population, they study only the effects of present environments, not the effects of the best possible (or worse possible) environments. In order to perform a good adoption study, one must try to sample as much as possible of the normal range of environments and argue that the environments sampled are representative of those found in the population as a whole. The results say nothing about the relative importance of genes and environment in any one individual, but instead are an average for all of the individuals in the population. It will be shown that many therapeutic and pathological environments depart radically from the average expected environment in a population, so that the effects of these environments are not addressed by a behavioral genetic study. Moreover, if a new educational intervention were developed that would make everyone equally sociable and if this treatment were given to everyone, then all the old estimates of the relative influence of genes and environments would have to be discarded. Even if in the presently studied populations there is a large effect of the genes in producing variation in social behavior, this might not be the case in the future.

These points can be easily seen by examining a basic formula for the degree of genetic determination of behavior: Heritability $= V(g)/[V(g) + V(e)]$. This formula indicates that the heritability of the behavior is equal to the variance due to genetic sources $V(g)$ divided by the total phenotypic variance, which is the sum of the variance due to genetic sources plus the variance due to environmental sources $V(e)$. As the variation due to the environment decreases, the degree of genetic determination must increase. Therefore, if everyone receives the same effective environment, the only source of variation remaining will be the genes. For example, 300 years ago there was probably a great deal of environmental variation in nutrition, which caused variation in height, so that heritability was low. In a modern, affluent industrial society there is very little malnutrition, so that the heritability of height is much higher, and almost all of the variation in height that we see is due to genetic variation, that is $V(e)$ is very low.

These considerations, along with the point made above that there may be large average effects of environments that are not reflected in the patterns of correlations between relatives and nonrelatives, are particularly important for thinking about cross-cultural variation in environments. As indicated in Chapters 5, 6, 8, and 9, some cultures appear to have adopted quite extreme methods of socialization, characterized by parent–child aloofness and rejection of children or by state intervention in the socialization process. These extreme methods of child rearing may have quite important effects on development when comparing children between cultures, that is, there is a large average effect of culture. However, since all members of the society encounter substantially the same environment, a behavior genetic study performed within the culture would conclude that the variation within the society for a particular social behavior is due almost entirely to genetic variation. The effect of mean differences in the environments characteristic of the different cultures cannot be captured by the behavior genetic methodology.

Finally, some mention should be made regarding the relationships between behavior genetics and evolutionary theory. Behavioral geneticists have in general shown little interest in the adaptiveness of behavior. Behavior genetics is a methodology, not a theory of how genes influence adaptive behavior. It can be used with the same facility to study the inheritance of intelligence, presumably an adaptive trait, as to study the inheritance of television-watching patterns, presumably not an important aspect of evolutionary pressures on human populations. Moreover, behavioral genetic methodology does not shed light on the structure of the biological traits underlying a behavior, so that other methods must be used to discover the traits that have actually been subject to natural selection. For example, in Chapter 2 it will be suggested that Undersocialized Aggressive Conduct Disorder involves extremes on three temperamental traits. A behavioral genetic study using individuals with this phenotype might show heritability, but would not disentangle the relative influence of genes on each of these traits.

It should also be noted that the relationship between behavior genetics and evolutionary theory is bidirectional. Evolutionary biology will have an influence on the design and interpretation of behavioral genetic studies. For example, Segal (1988) points out that rather than viewing twins as individual pair members living in individual environments, a sociobiologically influenced twin study emphasizes how genes affect the interaction between members of groups depending on the degree of their genetic relatedness. Thus, identical twins are expected to behave differently toward each other than do fraternal twins. They are expected to have quite different affective interactions, etc., not simply because genetic similarity results in similarity in behavior, but because genetic similarity affects the degree of common interests in a twin pair. Traditional behavioral genetic research views twins as individual pair members whose scores are correlated and compared with other groups with different degrees of genetic relatedness. Rather than studying the sources of variation of altruism in a population viewed as consisting of independently existing individuals subjected to independently existing environments, the focus shifts to studying how the genetic relatedness of the individuals in a particular context influences altruism.

Similarly, a sociobiological perspective would propose that adoptive parents would treat their adopted children differently from their biological children because of the importance of genetic overlap as a consideration in parental investment. This type of discriminative parenting would thus result in a nonshared environmental source of variation between adopted and nonadopted siblings within a family, tending to make them less like each other than are biological children reared in the same family. As a concrete example of this tendency, several studies have shown that child abuse is more common when parents are not biologically related to their children (Burgess, Garbarino, & Gilstrap, 1983; Daly & Wilson, 1981). This form of discriminative parenting would thus result in an underestimate of the typical effects of a common rearing environment in adoption research utilizing comparisons of scores of related and unrelated children reared in the same family, but would not bias estimates in studies where two or more adopted children are studied in each adoptive family. However, even in studies utilizing two adopted children within the family, parents may discriminate between children on the basis of phenotypic resemblance, since it is expected that parents will favor children who resemble them in some way. This is an aspect of genetic similarity theory (Rushton, Russell, & Wells, 1984) and is discussed more fully in Chapter 8. Clearly, there may well be qualitatively and quantitatively different discriminative parenting occurring in adoptive homes than occurs in homes composed only of biological offspring, so that the assumption of a comparable common rearing environment in these cases is highly questionable.

Moreover, it is quite reasonable from an evolutionary perspective to suppose that the parenting environment in the case of monozygotic twins would be more similar than in the case of dizygotic twins because of differing degrees of phenotypic resemblance between parents and offspring in the case of dizygotic twins as well as differences in sex and perhaps even reproductive value. In Chapter 8, data gathered by Smith (1988) indicating that parents in fact feel closer to children whom they phenotypically resemble are discussed and it is quite reasonable to suppose on the basis of these data that parents provide more affective and material resources to such children. The problem of the differential environmental influences in the case of monozygotic and dizygotic twins has long plagued twin research (Plomin & Daniels, 1987) and these evolutionary considerations indicate that the problem will not go away. As indicated in Chapters 5, 6, and 8, the theory of discriminative parenting deriving from evolutionary theory not only provides a large number of hypotheses relevant to interactions among biological and nonbiological relatives, but is also highly relevant to the interpretation of nonshared environmental influences discovered in behavioral genetic studies.

Behavioral genetic research will be an important part of this volume, but will remain secondary to the main issues. Throughout this book there will be mention of epigenetic rules that influence social interaction, and genetic variation in these rules will be important to the argument. Moreover, the theory of cultural evolution proposed by Lumsden and Wilson (1981) requires estimates of heritability of the epigenetic rules that bias human learning and culture in order to carry out this program of research. For example, behavior genetic studies have already been performed on behaviors that are of particular interest to evolutionary biologists, such as the work of Rushton, Fulker, Neale, Nias, and Eysenck (1986) showing important genetic variation for altruism and aggression. However, it will be apparent throughout that an evolutionary approach to human development involves far more than applying behavioral genetic methodology to phenotypes considered interesting in sociobiological theory. Rather than attempting to show that certain human behaviors are influenced by genes, the present endeavor will have as its central premise that much of the research performed in radically divergent theoretical paradigms can be integrated within an evolutionary framework. Genetic variation is of peripheral rather than central concern, therefore, in this volume.

B. Continuity

Continuity refers to the connectedness of development and is one of the most important questions addressed by developmental theory and research. Indeed, as indicated above, the world views of mechanism and organicism differ radically on their view of continuity. Essentially we want to know to what degree the experiences and mental structures that are present at one time in a child's life continue to exert an influence later. Lerner (1986) refers to two types of continuity, descriptive continuity and explanatory continuity. Two behaviors observed at different ages are descriptively continuous if they can be described in the same manner. For example, some of the behavior of a shy 5-year-old might be described in the same way as that of a shy adolescent. Both may be afraid of new things and have only a few friends. On the other hand, other types of behavior may not be describable in the same way at two different ages: the shy adolescent may worry a great deal about dating, while such behavior is absent from the 5-year-old.

Explanatory continuity refers to sameness in the variables used to explain behavior or the structures underlying behavior at two different ages. Explanatory continuity in personality would occur, for example, if the same genes that affect shyness at one age also affect shyness at a later age. Explanatory continuity would also occur if shyness in a child at a later age was due to environmental events that occurred early in life. If there is a qualitative change in behavior, as proposed by the organicist world view, there is a lack of explanatory continuity in development. The new behavior is explained not by early events or structures, but by later events and structures.

Kagan (1980, 1983) showed that in general philosophers and scientists have assumed that explanatory continuity is characteristic of human development. We tend to approach development as if there must be some continuity between ages, and I suspect that most developmental psychologists would leave the profession if they really thought that what they were studying was necessarily irrelevant to how adults behave. Imagine what the extreme form of a noncontinuity position would be like: Children would be seen as being constantly in flux, just as the Greek philosopher Heraclitus conceived all of reality. Just as Heraclitus compared the world to a river that is constantly changing, so that one can never put one's finger in the same river twice, so the extreme version of lack of continuity would suppose that the scientist studying a child can never study the same child twice. The structures inside the child are constantly changing and old structures are simply discarded rather than incorporated into new structures. Taken to the extreme, it would not matter how one treated the child at any point in development, because the child at age 18 years is unconnected to the child of age 3 or age 10 or age 17 years or, indeed, yesterday.

On the other extreme is the viewpoint that there is a strong thread running through development. Structures inside the child, such as the child's temperament and the genes underlying temperament, continue to exert influences on the person. Or early experiences at the hands of caretakers continue to influence the child's behavior completely independently of later environments. Taken to its extreme, this viewpoint would suppose that people are unalterable as they become older.

Another quite different view of continuity has been developed by theorists working in the organismic tradition (Langer, 1970; see also Werner, 1957). For these writers, the essential problem is to understand how an organism can change in a qualitative manner and yet retain its individual identity. Langer (1970) proposed that discontinuity occurs as the result of change from a relatively global state into a more differentiated state. Continuity occurs because earlier states and abilities are continuously being hierarchically subsumed under those that develop later (Lerner, 1986). Such a position allows for continuity in the face of qualitative change. This interpretation of the continuity–discontinuity issue may be applicable to certain issues in development, and, for example, Lerner (1986) uses this as a model for continuity–discontinuty in conceptual development.

Nevertheless, it is important to realize that this conception of continuity is not at all parallel to the one developed earlier. Fundamental to the previously defined idea is the notion of the connectedness of the processes and structures of development. The concept of progressive subsumption under hierarchically structured categories is far too narrow a conception of continuity and would leave out much that the term is usually (and usefully) considered to apply to. For example, such a conception would not be applicable to the data on the continuity of cognitive development from infancy presented by Bornstein and Sigman (1986), the behavioral genetic approach of Plomin and DeFries (1985), or the data on early experience and cognitive development (MacDonald, 1986c; see also p. 19). In the Bornstein and Sigman work, the issue is the continuity or discontinuity of processes underlying intelligence in childhood. The hierarchical structure of behavior does not appear to be a necessary feature of the proposed analyses: The decrement and recovery of attention may be fundamental features that show explanatory continuity, that is, continuity of underlying process, throughout childhood. The behavioral genetic data indicate that there are genes that affect variation in cognitive and personality processes quite early in life and continue to affect them throughout childhood (Plomin & DeFries, 1984). Finally, the early-experience literature, summarized on pp. 131–137, clearly indicates that in some cases intensive environmental stimulation can have long-lasting effects on behavior, effects best construed as indicating that the early environments resulted in effects on processes internal to the child that are then continuous with later development. In none of these cases is the hierarchical structure of behavior a feature of the analysis.

These results indicate that the model of Werner and Langer is inapplicable to a broad range of developmental phenomena usefully viewed as exhibiting continuity. In the following, continuity will be used in the sense of explanatory continuity (Lerner, 1986) and, consistent with the realist philosophical perspective described above, continuity will be regarded as an empirical question, which can be decided on the basis of experimental data, rather than as an attribute of competing world views. The evidence for these ideas will be presented in the final section of this chapter.

C. Plasticity, Sensitive Periods, and the Intensity of Environmental Stimulation

Another set of theoretical issues revolves around the plasticity of behavior. Plasticity refers to the ability of the organism to be affected by environmental influences. From a developmental perspective it is important to ask whether a child is equally susceptible to environmental influences at all ages or whether there are changes during development in how susceptible a child is to environmental stimulation, that is, whether there are age differences in *relative plasticity*. If, for example, it is easier to influence children when they are young than when they are older, it would make sense to begin therapeutic programs as early as possible. And if the child's early years were particularly important in shaping later development, then it would behoove parents and society to be particularly concerned with this period in a child's life.

Most of the debate on the questions surrounding relative plasticity have centered on the question of the importance of early experience. The belief that early experience is somehow more important than later experience goes back a long way in the history of philosophy, at least as far as Plato and certainly including the great empiricist philosopher John Locke. Within 20th century psychology the belief in the importance of early experience derives from two main sources: the work of Freud and research on animals. Although the influence of Freud has dwindled within developmental psychology, animal research showing age differences in relative plasticity has continued to be influential. The great animal ethologist Konrad Lorenz first noticed the importance of early experience when he raised some geese from the time of their hatching to adulthood. These animals had never seen an adult goose and they treated Lorenz as if he was their mother. Everything went smoothly until it was time for the geese to mate, at which time, instead of being attracted to their own species, these animals attempted to mate with humans. Lorenz termed the process by which these animals came to prefer a particular species as a mate *imprinting* and viewed it as a special form of learning.

One property of imprinting that made it special was the fact that there seemed to be a limited time period when the environmental stimulus had its greatest impact. This time period was called a *critical period* because it was believed that whatever behavior was formed during this period could not be reversed by later experience; that is, if the animal was imprinted to humans, it was not possible to change the animal so that it preferred its own species. Recently, however, scientists have abandoned the use of the term "critical period" and adopted the term "sensitive period" or have spoken of relative plasticity to indicate that, although it may be difficult to change behavior after the sensitive period, it is usually not impossible. The usage of the term "sensitive" period thus is consistent with the idea that, although the environment may be more effective in changing behavior at some ages than at others, there is no age beyond which the environment has no effect. Such a usage is consistent with a great many studies of early experience in animals. For example, Immelmann (1972) found a period of maximum sensitivity for mate preference in the Zebra Finch lasting from 13 to 40 days of age, but reversal of the effects of environmental stimulation could occur much later if the birds were exposed to their own species for a prolonged period.

This example is an illustration of the fact that one feature of the environment that often appears to be relevant to whether later experience will exert an effect can be termed its *intensity* (see MacDonald, 1985, 1986a,b). Environments differ greatly in their power to affect an organism and one dimension that appears to affect this power is the degree to which it departs from average levels of stimulation. For example, handling mice during a sensitive period results in their being less emotional later in life when they are placed in an open field situation. These effects on emotionality can be obtained at an age that is past the peak period of sensitivity if the intensity of the stimulation is increased. Thus, Denenberg (1964) found that giving increasing amounts of electric shock to the mice could overcome the declining plasticity of the mice and have an effect on open field behavior well after the period of peak sensitivity. These considerations suggest the general principle that highly intensive environmental stimulation can compensate for or overcome the declining plasticity of the organism, so that environments can have effects long after the period of peak sensitivity.

Powerful, intensive environments can be beneficial to the child or they can be quite detrimental. As is shown in Chapter 4, there is a tendency for children who are subjected to extremely pathological environments early in life to be affected later on in life. Nevertheless, there is also a tendency for children to benefit from highly stimulating, affectively positive environments. Recent writers (Lerner, 1984; MacDonald, 1985) have commented that behavioral plasticity is a two-edged sword. Plasticity is highly beneficial to humans because, on the one hand, it allows behavioral change in situations where one's present behavior is maladaptive. On the other hand, it also allows for the possibility that some environments will have deleterious effects on people. In addition, if indeed there is a decline in plasticity as people become older, it is quite possible that the deleterious effects of early environments will be difficult to erase later in life. The fact that the modification of human behavior has given rise to a huge industry with often dubious success shows quite clearly that in general behavior is not very easily changed. In fact, in many ways it would be better if behavior were less subject to environmental perturbations. Child abuse would be impossible and one could ignore one's children completely without worrying that they might not turn out right. However, for better or worse, it is quite clear that plasticity is with us to stay. The hope must be that we can devise sufficiently powerful environments to take advantage of whatever plasticity individuals have in order to encourage adaptive behavior.

As a concluding point on intensity, it may well be that one aspect of the evolution of social behavior in the primates is that social interactions are increasingly characterized by social interactions of high stimulus intensity. Mitchell (1981) showed that there is a general tendency for increasingly intensive play interactions as one moves from the Prosimian families to the Old World monkeys and apes. These findings suggest that one aspect of social evolution is the increasing ability to process and find reward value in highly intense social interactions, particularly among males. The interactions of more advanced animals are thus generally characterized by more intense stimulation, stimulation that is both affectively arousing and affectively valenced. In the ensuing chapters evidence will be provided for the importance of temperament in mediating the subjective response to variation in the intensity of environmental stimulation and for the importance of both the intensity of stimulation and its affective valence as general features of social development.

1. Early Experience and Behavior: The Sample Case of Intelligence

Although this volume is principally concerned with social and personality development, the large number of studies using IQ as a dependent variable illustrate well the power of the approach outlined above (see MacDonald, 1986a, for a fuller treatment). First, both animal and human studies indicate age-related differences in plasticity. For example, Forgays and Read (1962), studying rats, found that exposure to an enriched environment from days 21 to 42 after birth had a greater effect on maze learning than did exposure from days 0 to 21 or during 21-day periods after day 42. Similarly, in a study of children, Dennis (1973a) found that children adopted prior to age 2 years had a higher IQ and a higher rate of mental development than did children adopted after this age, with these effects being particularly clear after age 4 years. McKay, Sinesterra, McKay, Gomez, and Floreda (1978) found that children treated with 9-month enrichment sessions benefited most when the treatment was started early. These results are consistent with those from adoption studies, which generally indicate that early adoption into middle-class environments has a more beneficial effect on IQ than does later adoption.

The role of the intensity of environmental stimulation in both animal and human studies is also quite impressive. In a classic study with rats, Forgays and Forgays (1952) found graded effects of enriched environments depending on the degree of complexity of seven different enriching conditions. Bennett (1976) constructed an enriched environment in which survival of the animals depended on their being able to make their way through complex mazes and barriers. These ''superenriched'' animals were superior in their maze performance even to animals reared in standard enriched environments and much superior to the animals reared in nonenriched conditions. Regarding human studies, several studies have shown graded effects on IQ depending on the degree of stress suffered by the child early in life (Sigman, Cohen, & Forsythe, 1981; Winick, Meyer, & Harris, 1975).

These results clearly indicate the importance of age-graded differences in relative plasticity and the importance of the intensity of stimulation in producing the effects of early experience. However, the usefulness of this model as a general model for early experience remains controversial (see, for example, Kagan, 1986; Skolnick, 1986; Wachs, 1986). One of the most pressing problems with which such a model must deal is the multidimensionality of environmental influences in human development. This is particularly clear in the area of cognitive development (Wachs, 1986; Wachs & Gruen, 1982), but such a result may well also apply to social development. The animal literature relied upon in building the model has used a simple enrichment–deprivation paradigm in attempting to document the importance of environmental influences. In the literature on human cognitive development, Wachs and Gruen (1982) documented the effects of a host of environmental influences on cognitive performance, ranging from variation in the amount of floor space children have in which to play, to the amount and kind of verbal interaction. On the other hand, the studies that clearly support the biologically derived model tend to use IQ as a dependent variable and far coarser measures of the environment, such as social class or a broad-based cognitive intervention, what Wachs (1986) terms the first stage of research on the environment. These measures are analogous to the enrichment–deprivation paradigm used in the animal literature and the results obtained are quite similar. Future studies using the biologically derived model will have to use more fine-grained measures of the environment, but there is every reason to believe that such studies will be rewarded: The results described above using IQ as a dependent measure and coarse measures of environmental variables indicate that there must be some set of environmental variables that behave in the manner predicted by the biologically derived model. That is, given the success of the model in describing the results of the environmental deprivation and enrichment literature as well as the results indicating that such a model also applies to environmental variation within the normal range (MacDonald, 1986c), it must be possible in principle to develop a more fine-grained description of the variables that affect the development of IQ. Since IQ remains an extremely important tool in predicting success within society, such research is of great importance.

2. Relative Plasticity, Intensity of Stimulation, Continuity, and the Nature–Nurture Question

The theoretical issues that have been defined up to this point are related to each other, and these relationships will be further discussed in the concluding section of this chapter and related to the issue of the usefulness of world views in developmental psychology. As a preview, however, it should be noted that continuity will be a feature of development in cases where early environmental events continue to influence later development. If it can be shown that there is declining plasticity as children get older, then early environmental events, especially if they involve intensive stimulation, will exert a disproportionate influence on later development (MacDonald, 1986a). Intensive environmental events will also tend to have their effects independently of the characteristics of the organism, that is, they will tend to affect everyone in much the same manner (MacDonald, 1986b). Thus, intensive environmental stimulation will often be an example conforming to Model 1 described above, since the results are completely determined by the environmental events. Since these environmental events act fairly independently of organism characteristics, the source of continuity observed is reasonably believed to be processes internal to the child, not a result of organism–environment transactions or a continuing environmental influence.

Finally, as will be seen in Chapter 4, intensive environmental stimulation is often a characteristic of therapeutic environments. These environments may not be particularly common in the normal range of environments sampled by behavior genetic studies and thus their possible effects on children are ignored in behavioral genetic research. Behavioral genetic research presents a partial picture of the effects of actually existing environments on children, but does not tell us what is possible.

IV. EVOLUTIONARY THEORY AND THE THEORETICAL TRADITIONS OF SOCIAL DEVELOPMENT

This section will describe contemporary evolutionary approaches to social development as well as integrate this body of theory with social learning theory and cognitive-developmental theory. Although these theories have often been construed as being fundamentally inconsistent with each other, it argued here that it is possible to integrate this theoretical diversity into a fundamentally evolutionary approach to social development.

A. Ethological Theory

Ethological approaches to the study of human behavior derive from the first wave of evolutionary thinking on behavior. The main influences in this body of theory were Konrad Lorenz and Niko Tinbergen and the main focus of the original research was the behavior of invertebrates and less advanced vertebrates. Behavior was viewed as the result of natural selection and as being adaptive for the animal, although adaptation at the individual and group levels was not an issue in this research. Moreover, perhaps because they studied the behavior of relatively simply animals, the original ethologists came to view animal behavior as quite often being rigidly controlled by the genes. They used the term "instinct" to describe these genetically controlled behaviors and emphasized what might be termed the releasing role of the environment, that is, particular features of the environment simply released the instinctive behavior. For example, upon seeing the red coloring of another male stickleback fish, the aggressive behavior of the animal is released. The behaviors that most interested ethologists were the species-typical behaviors that occurred in more or less the same form in all members of a species.

This body of theory has influenced thinking about human behavior, but it has become clear that human behavior cannot be modeled rigidly on the behavior of invertebrates and the lower vertebrates. The main tendencies during the evolution of behavior include an increased plasticity of behavior and increased information processing and learning capabilities of animals. These properties result in an important role for environmental variation in the the production of adaptive behavior, and allow the animal to adjust its behavior rapidly to ongoing circumstances rather than react to the environment in the rigid, stereotypical fashion typical of many lower animals. These properties are most highly developed in humans and the most influential ethological theories of human behavior have succeeded in taking them into account.

The best example of a modern ethological theory of behavior is provided by Bowlby (1969, 1973) for human attachment behavior. This theory will be considered in more detail in Chapter 4, but for the moment it is important to note the following features of the theory:

1. Like the traditional ethologists and contemporary evolutionary theorists, Bowlby emphasizes the adaptativeness of attachment.[2] Within the adaptationist perspective, attachment behaviors are viewed as having evolved as a response to particular environmental stresses, what Bowlby called the environment of evolutionary adaptedness. The idea that behavior generally is adaptive is a crucial aspect of the present treatment, and its intellectual basis is discussed below.

2. Rather than describing behavior as rigidly programmed and instinctive, Bowlby argued that there are biological predispositions to respond affectively to particular environmental events. The cognitive–affective evaluation of these events can then result in a variety of motor behaviors, such as crying or crawling toward the attachment figure. Because the affective consequences of these events are biologically based rather than the result of learning, they act as ''natural clues'' for the child's affective response. Examples would include the child's affective evaluation of contact comfort from its mother (positive affective response) or the absence of the mother (negative affective response). Another term for genetic systems that bias behavior in particular directions is *epigenetic rules* (Lumsden & Wilson, 1981) and this usage will be followed here. These biases and constraints include not only the affective processing rules mentioned above, but a wide variety of ''predispositions in what an individual responds to and in what he or she learns, and constraints upon what he or she can learn that are not merely limitations of capacity'' (Hinde, 1987, p. 63). Hinde reviews evidence for a wide variety of such predispositions and constraints in both animals and humans, including the nature of the sensory/perceptual apparatus, motor patterns, motivation, and learning (see also Lumsden, 1988).

3. Bowlby also developed the idea of an evolutionarily expected environment. He proposed that humans are programmed to expect particular types of environments, so that departures from these environments are associated with negative affective response and the potential for pathological effects due to the environment. Thus, children are biologically predisposed to form attachments to caretakers and the theory predicts that if there is no opportunity to form such attachments or if long-term separation from attachment figures occurs, there will be a tendency for maladaptive behavior or at least dysphoric

---

[2]In evolutionary biology a behavior is adaptive if it makes the organism more fit to survive and reproduce in comparison to other members of the same species (Wilson, 1975). As used here, the idea of adaptation has no implications regarding the extent to which the behavior is under genetic control, its degree of plasticity, etc. Thus learning and information processing capabilities are important human adaptations, and learning a particular skill which resulted in greater biological fitness for the individual would be an example of an adaptive behavior. Other aspects of adaptation which are peculiar to the human situation are discussed in Chapter 5.

behavior. Thus, the theory is consistent with strong effects of the environment on behavior.

4. Bowlby also emphasized the importance of cognitive, affective, perceptual, and motor systems for attachment. Attachment is viewed as a goal-corrected system that becomes increasingly flexible with age. Rather than characterizing attachment as a rigid, instinctive, and stereotyped behavioral system, it is seen as the result of a complex interplay of behavioral systems that is able to provide a graded response to environmental events.

5. Finally, attachment in infancy is viewed as having long-range effects on a variety of adaptive behaviors, ranging from cognitive style and peer relationships to patterns of attachment throughout the life span.

Following the lead of Bowlby, the ensuing chapters will emphasize theories that include flexible biological mechanisms that interact with cognition and social learning in order to produce adaptive behaviors. It should be noted here that one of the biggest problems of the ethological approach is to provide strong evidence for the genetic basis of certain behaviors and responses to the environment. This is the case because ethologists, like contemporary evolutionary thinkers and cognitive-developmentalists, are interested in species-typical behaviors, what might be called the central trends in human behavior. As indicated above, behavioral genetic methods are well suited to finding genetic variation influencing behavior, but are not equipped to uncover genetic commonality underlying behavior. In fact, most genetic influences on behavior are probably common to everyone, since the great majority of genes within a species and often between closely related species are common to all members of the species. For example, the genes of humans and chimpanzees are almost indistinguishable (Hrdy, 1981). The result is that indirect arguments, often involving comparison to other species, must be used. This lack of a powerful methodology is a drawback to evolutionary approaches to the study of human development, but one that often can be overcome by careful consideration of the evidence.

B. Contemporary Evolutionary Theory

In the past two decades, among the important developments in the field of evolutionary biology has been a body of work that can be subsumed under the term *sociobiology*, in accord with Wilson's (1975) synthesis of this material, but it is important to realize that the field of human sociobiology is a developing one with much diversity and, as with any new field, a great deal of disagreement. The presentation that follows will describe the historical roots of human sociobiology as well as some of the more recent trends. Since this field is relatively unfamiliar to developmental audiences compared to the other theoretical viewpoints described here, a fuller treatment of the theory will be provided.

Although sociobiology came to fruition in the 1970s, it was preceded by several important developments in the 1960s. G. C. Williams (1966) argued against group-selectionist arguments current at the time (Wynne-Edwards, 1962) and proposed instead that instances of apparently self-sacrificing behavior were the result of individual self-interest. In Williams' view, natural selection thus operated at the level of the individual rather than the group, as envisioned by previous evolutionary theorists. The basic idea here is that it is difficult to conceptualize how individuals who are truly altruistic will be able to compete in evolutionary terms with individuals who are selfish. Think of an altruistic animal that, instead of feeding its own offspring, decides to give all the food it can gather to a selfish animal who raises its own offspring. The result of this state of affairs is that the altruistic individual will not leave any genes for the next generation, while the selfish individual will. If the trait of altruism is influenced by the genes of the animal, those genes will soon disappear, while those of the selfish animal will spread. Even if the individual's altruism results in the group being better off than some other group, within the group there will always be a tendency for selection against altruism. Although there has been a great deal of theoretical and empirical work in this area in the last two decades, recent discussions of these issues (e.g., Alexander, 1987) have left unchanged William's central conclusion that true altruism is not likely to evolve.

The second major influence with regard to the study of social evolution derives from William Hamilton (1964), who developed the idea that individuals could maximize their fitness not only by maximizing the number of their own offspring, but also by extending aid to their genetic relatives. This is the case because relatives share a certain percentage of genes as a result of their descent from the same individuals. Thus, parents and children share one-half of their genes, as do brothers and sisters. With second-degree relatives, such as aunts and uncles, individuals share only one-fourth of their genes, and with more distant relatives they share correspondingly fewer genes. Imagine an individual who has a choice between having two children of his or her own or helping a sibling raise four more of its children than it would have been able to raise without the help. From a genetic point of view it should not matter which alternative was chosen, since the result of either choice would be an equal representation of the individual's genes in the next generation. Help given one's relatives is often called *kin selection,* and is the evolutionary explanation for why parents give resources to their children and why humans and many other animals form kinship groups to defend important resources. These themes will figure prominently in this volume.

As in the case of cognitive-developmental theory and ethology, recent evolutionary theory describes what are hypothesized to be the central tendencies of human behavior. From the perspective described above, it is expected that humans will tend to be self-interested and that they will tend to provide more help to their relatives than to non-relatives. This point of view is clearly relevant to the development of prosocial behavior and moral development and will be discussed more fully in Chapters 7 and 8.

It is important to note here, however, that simply because these traits are predicted by the theory does not imply that these traits are "instinctive" or "genetically determined." In fact, there is no implication at all as to how these behaviors develop. The theory tells us nothing about the relative influence of genes or environment or the relative plasticity of these behaviors. Sociobiologists distinguish between what are called *ultimate causes* and *proximal causes.* Proximal causes are the actual mechanisms underlying the behavior, such as genes, hormones, or social learning. By understanding the proximal mechanisms we can understand the degree of plasticity found in the behavior and how to change the behavior if we want. Ultimate causes are the reasons why the behavior evolved in the first place, that is, why it was adaptive in evolutionary history. The ultimate causes of selfishness and helping one's kin are provided by Williams and Hamilton, but the proximal mechanisms are provided by developmental psychologists.

1. Adaptationism

The focus on ultimate causes brings up the problem of adaptationism. Evolutionists propose as a fundamental principle that via the process of natural selection organisms tend to become better adapted to their environments. When an evolutionist seeks the ultimate cause of a behavior, the type of answer sought is one that specifies why such a behavior might have been adaptive in the phylogeny of the species. Thus, Bowlby's (1969, 1973) ethological theory of attachment proposed that attachment evolved because it provided a proximal mechanism whereby the infant would remain close to the mother and thereby avoid predators. In later chapters adaptationist hypotheses will be explored in several areas important to developmental psychology, including parent–child interactions, prosocial behavior, and moral reasoning.

Nevertheless, it is fundamental to an evolutionary approach that behavior need not always be adaptive. Evolution is an ongoing process, so that there is continuing natural selection against maladaptive behavior. The general finding of a good fit between organism and environment is an empirical proposal which is well grounded in theory. It is not a law of nature. Individuals who fail to reproduce, whether because of personal preference, physical malady, psychiatric disturbance, or economic necessity are still being selected against. Recent work in the area of human sociobiology (Barkow, 1986; MacDonald, 1988a) has emphasized ways in which behavior can be maladaptive, but this work has been performed within a fundamentally adaptationist framework. For example, within a psychological perspective, maladaptive behavior can occur for a variety of reasons, despite the fact that there are central tendencies for humans to behave in a self-interested manner and to help relatives. These include the following:

1. *Genetic variation.* Genetic variation within the human population appears to be an important factor resulting in increased likelihood of a variety of debilitating and maladaptive physical and psychiatric conditions. There is overwhelming evidence for genetic variation underlying the vulnerability to schizophrenia (Gottesman & Schields, 1982) as well as evidence that this disorder results in low rates of fertility (Price, Slater, & Hare, 1971; Reed, 1971; Slater, Hare, & Price, 1971) and downward social mobility (Dunham, 1965; Goldberg & Morrison, 1963; Turner & Wagenfeld, 1967).

2. *Secondary effects of sociobiologically predicted central tendencies.* Sociobiology predicts that conflicts of interest will be extremely important in human relationships and one consequence of this state of affairs is that some individuals may incur decrements in adaptiveness as a result of the behavior of others. Thus, in Chapter 5 a theoretical model of divorce is developed involving differential strategies of male–female reproductive behavior which lead to decrements in adaptive behavior in children. There is no implication in the theory that the children do not attempt to maximize their own opportunities in life, only that the context of their development has been altered for the worse.

3. *Cultural change resulting in maladaptive consequences for formerly adaptive behavior.* Population genetic theory indicates quite clearly that natural selection tends to be a rather slow process. Human culture and the environment can change very quickly, so

that there is a possibility that epigenetic rules that were adaptive at one time may be maladaptive later. This is particularly the case with humans, whose epigenetic rules presumably originated in the prolonged prehistoric phase of our evolution and have yielded a culture that is changing at an explosive pace. For example, in Chapters 5 and 8 I will argue that changes in economic conditions resulted in massive shifts in family structure and the socialization of children, so that the environments that had previously resulted in adaptive behavior no longer did so.

4. *Social controls*. Social controls include a wide variety of social sanctions that serve to control the behavior of the individual. Such controls range from laws and penal sanctions for robbery or assault to subtle controls exercized by a group in order to ensure conformity to dress standards. One important aspect of these controls from a sociobiological standpoint is that social controls on individual behavior can be effective independent of an individual's genotype. Thus, independent of one's intelligence or any other phenotypic characteristic one can be forced to be a slave; or an individual who is nonaltruistic can be forced to pay taxes that support others. Moreover, as illustrated by the slavery example, social controls can result in decrements in the adaptiveness of behavior: The person who is a slave may be forced to provide resources to others rather than use them in ways he or she might prefer. Social controls are extremely important in understanding human behavior, especially in the economically advanced societies, and often can have important effects on child development. Social controls affecting family structure and the socialization of children are discussed in several chapters of this book, particularly Chapters 5 and 9.

5. *Pathological environmental influences*. The existence of pathological environmental influences is entirely consistent with an evolutionary approach, and we have already seen that the ethological theory of attachment provides for important adaptive and maladaptive environmental influences on development. Recently McGuire and Troisi (1987) have developed a theory of how environments lacking in appropriate resources, including especially what one might term affective resources, such as the concern and respect of others, can result in pathological behavior, and in Chapter 9 the instability of environmental resources will be explored as a contextual variable in human development. In addition, I have already commented on the idea of human plasticity as a double-edged sword. This idea implies that environments can have pathological influences as well as therapeutic influences.

6. *Developmental constraints*. A particularly important source of a lack of correspondence between an adaptationist optimum and actual behavior is peculiar to a developmental approach. Evolution has presumably adapted children for life under the protection of the family, so that parents are a buffer between the child and the world. Thus, the limited cognitive capacities of the child or a too generous altruism would be highly disadvantageous if the child had to compete with adults for resources. Thus, the skills of the child will often appear relatively incompetent and far from ideal. For example, in Chapters 6 and 7 we note that children's resource acquisition behavior with their peers and their ability to generate objectively persuasive examples of moral reasoning often fall short of the adult ideal. Nevertheless, their behavior in these situations remains self-interested and is thus consistent with evolutionary theory. It is as if they are doing the best they can, given their relative lack of competence. The situation is analogous to thinking about adaptiveness in the context of individual differences in ability. For example, because of

individual differences in IQ, some individuals are handicapped in the pursuit of resources and their behavior is thus relatively maladaptive. This difference in biological fitness clearly in no way prevents an evolutionary analysis. The following chapters will attempt to show that developmental differences in competence do not vitiate an evolutionary analysis.

In sum, an adaptationist hypothesis is an empirical proposition, which is open to reasoned discussion. Alternative hypotheses, including the possibility that the behavior is maladaptive, can be reasonably considered and data can be marshalled to support the various alternatives.

2. Reductionism

The approach adopted in this book is explicitly nonreductionistic. Reductionism refers to the belief that all of behavior can be explained by the principles of some more basic science, in this case evolutionary biology. This would be the case if all of human behavior could be explained as being due, for example, to the self-interest of individuals. Recent theorizing in human sociobiology has emphasized the importance of nonreducible contextual variables in accounting for human behavior. These contextual variables are *emergent* in the sense of Lerner (1986): They possess properties that are not predictable on the basis of the properties of their constituent parts. Particularly prominent in this book will be discussion of the variable of social controls. As indicated above, social controls are means by which the behavior of individual humans is controlled and influenced by others. The nature of these social controls is the result of group processes and is not predictable from knowing the behavioral tendencies of individuals.

Individuals cannot always do what they want, because of the laws, rules, and customs of the societies in which they live. These controls act to constrain behavior so that it often becomes impossible to predict whether individuals will behave in an adaptive manner. It is crucially important to realize that these social controls can have effects that are egalitarian or antiegalitarian. In our own society there are many laws that help subsidize poor people and in many socialist countries such laws are even more prominent. Thus, sociobiology can make no political predictions and does not have any political implications. The sociobiological thesis that individuals tend to be self-interested does not ensure exploitation and oppression, but does imply that social controls regulating human interactions will be an extremely important aspect of public policy.

3. The Importance of Resources

In the above exposition of evolutionary theory it has been necessary to introduce the idea of resources. Despite the clear importance of resources to an evolutionary-ecological approach to behavior, it is only recently that Charlesworth (1988) has shown that the central issues of human development can be seen within this framework. Within this perspective children may be thought of as resource acquisition devices. A concern for resources has not been a prominent aspect of evolutionary views of human development. For example, despite the concentration of ethological research on topics such as social dominance, there has been very little emphasis on the idea of resources at all in evolutionary treatments of human development. Charlesworth (1988) traces the idea that access to resources is fundamental to adaptation back to Darwin, and notes that resource acquisition and distribution are fundamental aspects of all human societies. Organisms have evolutionarily based needs and a variety of mechanisms that they utilize to satisfy these needs. Because resources answer human needs, they are often the object of goal-directed behavior, so that a variety of cognitive processes are important analysanda in an evolutionary framework. Charlesworth also notes that competition over resources is important in human societies and involves a large number of the processes studied in the area of social psychology, such as group dynamics, conformity to group pressure, attitude change, and the general field of social exchange theory. These considerations indicate that Charlesworth's approach provides a framework for thinking about a wide range of issues in human development, and in the present volume, virtually all of the topics covered are in some way importantly related to resource acquisition and control. Thus, sexual competition over reproductive resources is basic to the treatment of family interaction (Chapter 5) and aggression (Chapter 6). Social dominance relations involve the control and distribution of resources (Chapter 6), as does the entire area of altruism (Chapters 7 and 8). Chapter 9 details how contextual variables influence resource control in human societies. At various points the importance of information (e.g., via modeling) and affective resources as aspects of socialization will be discussed. The approach of Charlesworth thus has tremendous integrative potential as a framework within which to view virtually all of the interesting problems within social development.

4. Summary and Conclusion

Modern evolutionary theory will be part of a two-pronged approach to the data generated by developmental psychologists. The first level of analysis involves determining how the data conform to the predictions made by evolutionary theory. This approach is at the level of ultimate evolutionary explanations, and there is no implication regarding the proximal mechanisms involved (e.g., the extent to which learning is important). For example, in Chapter 6 the data on sex differences in development are first examined with respect to their conformity to evolutionary theory and, independently, data are then reviewed on the relative importance of temperament, socialization, and so on. The former part of this enterprise is successful if either of the following two propositions are true: (a) the results of the study reviewed indicate that significant proportions of variance are in conformity with predictions made by evolutionary theory, or (b) the theory allows for the integration of a large amount of previously disparate data. As Hinde (1987) notes, the integration of facts is a prime criterion for the acceptance of evolutionary hypotheses, and philosophers of science (e.g., Aronson, 1984) have long noted that one criterion of a more powerful theory is the ability to integrate previously unrelated sets of data. A crucial test of the power of a theory, then, is the range of predictions it can make and the sheer amount of data that it is able to integrate.

If either of these propositions is supported, then there is good evidence to believe that the behavior in question is adaptive; that is, that the behavior is functionally related to biological fitness in present environments or in Bowlby's environment of evolutionary adaptiveness. This proposition can then be further supported by evidence that engaging in the behavior actually increases biological fitness in present cultures or did so during human evolutionary history. Such data are desirable but are not essential in order to provide a rational choice regarding the question of whether the behavior is adaptive. The realist perspective described above implies that improvement in our theories results from a closer fit between the theory and the real objects of scientific study, but does not imply that the choice of the best theory must be on the basis of incontrovertible, "proven" facts. Rather we choose theories on the basis of their power to explain and integrate previously disparate phenomena, and clearly there is no theory which can come close to the power of evolutionary theory in this regard. In other words, it is not enough to simply show that an evolutionary hypothesis may not be true. In order to provide a convincing case for abandoning the evolutionary hypothesis, one must also show that some other competing theory offers a more powerful integration of the data. Acceptance of the null hypothesis on the basis of the possibility that the evolutionary theory may be incorrect is to commit theoretical suicide.

For example, consider the general findings from evolutionary anthropology that there is a positive association between reproductive success of males and the control of resources. This hypothesis flows naturally from evolutionary theory and there is a great deal of support for it (see Chapter 5). These findings support the hypothesis that control of resources functions to facilitate reproductive success in males, and in the absence of a more powerful theory it is rational to accept this hypothesis. The hypothesis is well integrated with a theory which applies to a host of phenomena in nonhuman species and, as we will try to show throughout this volume, to incredibly diverse data sets in the social sciences.

One could provide alternative explanations for these findings, but the explanations would be relatively *ad hoc* and unconnected to any wider set of data. Thus one could propose that a high level of sex drive just happens to correlate with success in entrepreneurial activities in the way that brown hair goes with blue eyes. Or one could propose that these two types of success are merely the product of one trait which is exhibited both sexually and in the marketplace. One need not be causally related to the other and one (success in controlling resources) need not function in the service of the other (reproductive success). Such *ad hoc* hypotheses are entirely possible but completely unconvincing. They amount to little more than the glorification of the null hypothesis.

The second level of analysis is an attempt to understand the proximal mechanisms underlying both the general tendency for conformity to the theory and for important exceptions to the theory. As indicated above, the proximal mechanisms may include cognitive processes underlying flexible responses to environmental contingencies, biological propensities such as temperament, the epigentic rules which constrain and bias behavior, or they may involve relatively unconstrained social learning. In Chapter 9, cultural mechanisms that occur beyond the level of the individual are emphasized. In all of these cases attention must be paid equally (or perhaps more so) to the mechanisms underlying maladaptive behavior and behavior that departs from evolutionary predictions. Thus, much attention is paid in subsequent chapters to the finding that in Western societies there is no positive association between reproduction and control of resources.

Contemporary evolutionary theory at this time is just beginning to have an impact on research and thinking about human development. Developmental psychology has been slow to be influenced by evolutionary theory, partly because human development is far removed from theorizing derived from modern population genetics. It will become clear, however, that this body of theory integrates a great deal of previously obtained data within an evolutionary framework and makes some significant developmental hypotheses. It is the main purpose of this volume to illustrate the utility of this approach as a general framework for social development.

C. Evolutionary Biology and Social Learning Theory

Contemporary social learning theory is the direct descendant of philosophical empiricism and the behaviorist tradition in British and North American psychology. As a continuously evolving theory it has been influenced by the cognitive revolution in psychology and, as described in Chapter 5, it is quite possible to integrate social learning theories of cultural transmission with evolutionary theory. Basically, social learning theorists such as Bandura (1977) emphasize external sources of information in influencing behavior. The environment is seen as providing rewards and punishments for behavior as well as providing models whose behavior can be imitated. In addition, the environment sometimes provides direct instruction in how to perform particular behaviors. On the basis of these sources of information the child is able to generate *response–outcome contingency rules,* which can then be used to choose the desired behavior.

It is important to realize that social learning theory is not a competitor with an evolutionary approach to behavior. An evolutionary account of behavior must accept the role of the environment in shaping human behavior in adaptive ways. As has been emphasized by many writers (e.g., Skinner, 1971), the ability of organisms to adjust their behavior according to its consequences is of overwhelming adaptive value. By not being constrained by a rigid genetic program organisms are able to react quickly and adaptively to a wide range of subtly different situations. Sociobiological views of social learning (Barkow, 1986; Lumsden & Wilson, 1981; MacDonald, 1984, 1987a, 1988a; Pulliam & Dunford, 1980) essentially agree that social learning is an important means of cultural transmission. These writers also emphasize, however, that social learning can have effects on Darwinian fitness, as occurs when individuals profit (or lose) by imitating the behavior of other individuals or cultures. From an evolutionary perspective, culture evolves in much the same way as genes do, by the selection of adaptive variants. For example, a new and successful method of warfare would be expected to diffuse quickly throughout an area, because cultures that did not themselves adopt it would soon be subjected by those that did. This is not to state that social learning is always adaptive, and examples of culturally based maladaptive behavior will be discussed throughout. Like plasticity in general, learning is a two-edged sword. The very quickness and flexibility of learning can also lead to poor choices and our epigenetic rules have not changed quickly enough to ensure adaptive learning at all times. Cultural inertia also occurs, and learning can be retained long after it has ceased being useful or adaptive (Barkow, 1986).

Although learning can occur without reinforcement, social learning theorists have also emphasized that behavior itself is strongly influenced by rewards and punishments. That an organism would be designed to behave in such a manner comes as no surprise from an evolutionary point of view, since it clearly implies that behavior is generally performed out of self-interest. Indeed, without an ultimate-level theory such as that provided by evolutionary biology, this fundamental principle of behaviorism must remain as a sort of unexplained first principle. Indeed, many social learning theorists (e.g., Gelfand & Hartmann, 1982) have had difficulty accepting the idea that behavior can be self-sacrificing and truly altruistic for this reason. Consistent with the essential principle that behavior indeed tends to be self-interested, much of the discussion in the ensuing chapters will be premised on the idea that individuals often base their behavior on rough cost–benefit decisions.

Although an evolutionary account emphasizes the adaptiveness of behavior and its flexibility, it also proposes that there are biologically based influences on human learning. As indicated above, these epigenetic rules influence what an organism learns and what it finds rewarding. Thus, animal behaviorists have shown that learning is constrained in many species in ways that are quite adaptive. For example, Garcia, Hankins, and Risiniak (1976) showed that rats avoid food that makes them ill after one or at most very few exposures. In the present volume epigenetic rules that affect the reward value of social stimulation will be crucial to the discussions in Chapters 2–6 and 8. Although the considerations that lead to this perspective will be provided in later chapters, the essential idea is that the universe of stimuli that humans are biologically predisposed to find rewarding is not confined to metabolic needs such as food, shelter, and water. The ethological perspective, sketched above and detailed in later chapters, proposes a wide array of primary reinforcers for human social behavior.

A second theme of this volume relevant to social learning, particularly emphasized in Chapter 5, is the idea that these evolutionarily derived, nonmetabolic, social reinforcers have a strong effect on social learning. In particular, social learning theorists have proposed that several characteristics of the model facilitate social learning, including the warmth, power, similarity, and competence of the model (e.g., Mischel, 1976). The evolutionary framework suggests that these characteristics of the model are effective because they represent epigenetic rules that have resulted in adaptive behavior in the human evolutionary past. The emphasis in Chapter 5 is on showing that warmth within the family not only promotes cohesiveness, but also facilitates the transmission of culture by making parents more attractive models. The facilitative effect of the power, competence, and similarity of the model may well also be the result of epigenetic rules affecting modeling and, in any case, these have clear effects on adaptive behavior.

D. Evolutionary Biology and Cognitive-Developmental Theory

Jean Piaget was a biologist by training and his theory very strongly reflects this influence. The organismic theory of development associated with Piaget is essentially a biological analogy, with the internal structure of the organism structuring its interactions with the environment. Development is teleological and its goal is an adaptive level of adult functioning, that is, increasing competence and understanding of oneself and one's social and material environment.

One of the aspects of Piaget's theory and the cognitive-developmental tradition generally that is congruent with an evolutionary approach is the theory of motivation. Motivation is conceived as intrinsic to the child. From this point of view, the motivation to engage in cognitive interaction with the external world does not depend exclusively on a continuous stream of reinforcement, but often results instead from the properties of the child's nervous system. The child is viewed as biologically endowed with an interest in novel stimuli, or stimuli that are relatively complex or surprising or lead to uncertainty in the child's mind. Indeed, many of the aspects of stimuli that make the child want to engage in cognitive interactions with the environment are also very important in producing affective responses in children during parent–child interaction and are fundamental to social development as well as cognitive development. An infant does not need to be rewarded in order to persist in making movements that result in intriguing stimulation or to interact in pleasurable ways with its parents. Indeed, the circular reactions that Piaget found to be characteristic of infancy often involve repeated movements followed by positive affective response when the effects of the movements are observed. As Flavell (1985) points out, if one wants to understand the motivation for information processing, imagine how evolution would have designed an optimal learning device. Such a device would not depend on extrinsic reinforcements, which may or may not be forthcoming from the environment. It is far more efficient to program the motivation into the child in order to make it a "self-starter." As described in Chapter 4, a similar conception makes sense out of the motivation of much of children's social behavior.

The cognitive-developmental point of view has always emphasized the role of the environment in the development of cognitive structures. In Piaget's model of cognitive development, progress occurs when the child is forced to alter its cognitive structures in order to accommodate the information coming from the environment. Nevertheless, the environment is conceived in a very different manner in cognitive-developmental theory than it is in social learning theory. In the latter the environment is viewed in a very fine-grained manner. The environment consists of a host of reinforcing events and imitatable people, and the effect of the environment is to make individuals different from one another. Social learning theory is thus a theory of the origin of individual differences.

Cognitive-developmental theory, on the other hand, views the environment in a much less fine-grained manner. The environment consists of general features, such as the properties of people and objects, which are experienced by anyone living in our world (Kohlberg, 1969). As a result, development will be substantially the same for everyone in any culture or historical era. Indeed, it makes excellent evolutionary sense for the organism to be designed so that its basic capabilities are not subject to the whim of uncertain environments (McCall, 1981; Scarr & McCartney, 1983). Instead, the basic processes of cognitive development seem to depend on very general features of the environment (Kohlberg, 1969) and thus are not dependent on a narrow range of environmental contingencies, which may or may not occur (Kagan & Klein, 1973; MacDonald, 1986a,b; Scarr & McCartney, 1983). Such a perspective is entirely consistent with the idea that the environment has an important influence on individual differences (MacDonald, 1986a; also see pp. 36–38 in this volume).

In recent years the status of a strong stage theory of cognitive development has become controversial. Research has tended to show more continuity in cognitive development in children rather than the qualitatively different stages proposed by Piaget (Gelman & Baillargeon, 1983; Flavell, 1985). Nevertheless, the viewpoint adopted here is that a theoretical approach emphasizing the universal features of social development and the common achievements that distinguish one age from another is an essential element in a complete description of social development. Such a theory could postulate that these broad features of social development are not the result of subtle differences in environments that vary among individuals, but are instead the result of features of the environment that are common to virtually everyone, if indeed the environment is important at all.

From an adaptationist perspective, these general features of the environment that are essential for basic cognitive functioning may be considered an evolutionarily expected environment; that is, these environments are those minimally necessary to sustain basic human competence. As such, they are common to all human cultures, and any culture that did not provide this minimal environment would necessarily have ceased to exist long ago.

Correspondingly, the organismic structural attributes that are essential for incorporating these environmental influences constitute species-wide genetic invariance. Such genetically invariant structures are analogous to the genetically based species-typical behaviors studied by ethologists. This genetic invariance is the human ethogram, the epigenetic rules that make us distinctively human. As indicated above, behavoral geneticists have often noted that most of the genetic influences on behavior are common to all members of the species. These influences, among other things, make us quite different from other species: No matter how stimulating one makes the environment of a chimpanzee, it will never write interesting poetry or understand the second law of thermodynamics. In the terms of the previous discussion, such behavior would conform to the well-buffered model of behavioral development, since it appears in all members of the species across wide environmental variation.

Although accepting the importance of species-wide central tendencies in human development is an essential aspect of an evolutionary theory, there is no need to accept some of the views of cognitive-developmentalists regarding the endpoints of development. As indicated above, recent evolutionary theory proposes that there will be a strong tendency for human behavior to be self-interested, a proposition that conflicts with the Kohlbergian idea that moral development proceeds in the direction of increasingly selfless reasoning and behavior. An evolutionary theory is consistent with increasingly complex cognitive processing which enables high-level moral reasoning to occur, but is not consistent with the idea that human development proceeds toward ever greater selflessness. These ideas are discussed at length in Chapter 7.

In addition, recent evolutionary theory proposes that the rational, scientific construction of the social and nonsocial world proposed by cognitive-developmentalists is only half the picture. As Krebs, Denton, and Higgins (1988) point out, cognitions about the world are likely to be self-serving, acting to manipulate one's own and others' beliefs about the behavior of self and others, often by means of deception or self-deception. Thus, in Chapter 3 evidence will be discussed indicating that people sometimes manage their self-esteem by manipulating their cognitions regarding their own behavior and the behavior of others, often by deceiving themselves, and in Chapter 7 the self-serving and self-deceptive cognitions commonly occurring in moral reasoning will be discussed.

V. THEORETICAL FRAGMENTATION OR INTEGRATION?

One of the impressions generated in students by textbooks in developmental psychology and social development is that these areas are beset with conflicting theories of virtually everything. The student is given the idea that there is eternal war of all against all in this theoretical potpourri and that no one ever wins or loses. As indicated above, this general perspective has been given intellectual sanction within developmental psychology by Reese and Overton (1970), who argue that the different theories and models within psychology derive from different basic assumptions or world views about which there can be no rational basis for resolving disagreements.

Without denying that there may indeed be some fundamental disagreements between these theoretical approaches that are quite difficult to resolve empirically, there is little reason to suppose that contemporary developmental psychology is adequately described in terms of incommensurable world views or research traditions. Many contemporary theories as well as historically important theories are difficult at best to pigeonhole in the manner required by the world-view perspective. For example, Beilin (1984) points out that contemporary information processing models have some mechanistic properties as well as some structuralist properties usually associated with the organismic world view. Classical Freudian theory posited a high degree of internal structure and stages of development, suggesting an organismic classification, but the child was also seen as a relatively passive recipient of the socialization practices of its parents, a perspective suggesting the mechanistic world view. Beilin (1984) also points out that the recent history of developmental psychology indicates convergence of theories and is not well described by the world-view perspective of Overton and Reese. We have seen that the convergence of theory is an important empirical prediction of philosophical realism, whereas the world-view perspective of Overton and Reese must predict that convergence is impossible.

Indeed, many of the historically important battles within psychology are best interpreted as disagreements between rival theories that are commensurable, that is, there are empirical means of deciding between them. For example, Barker and Gholson (1984) show that the long rivalry between cognitivist and behaviorist positions in psychology essentially hinged on the results of key experiments. The ascendency of one of the other of these perspectives within the scientific community did not involve an irresolvable dispute between world views that allowed no communication between rival camps, but was rather an empirical question. The final result has been a blending of viewpoints that earlier were seen as incompatible with each other (Beilin, 1984). A similar example within developmental psychology has been the controversy surrounding the question of whether cognitive development is best viewed as stagelike or more continuous. As indicated above, there is growing doubt that changes in cognitive systems after infancy are as qualitative or stagelike as believed by Piaget. The interesting point here is that this change in scientific opinion occurred as the result of experimentation: The data generally indicated that the difference between younger and older children could be better characterized as the difference between a novice and an expert rather than as the difference between qualitatively different types of children (Flavell, 1985). Rather than reflecting a nonempirical world-view issue between incommensurable paradigms, the question was decided in an empirical manner on the basis of experimental data.

Similarly, empirical work in the area of cognitive and social development has been guided by the belief among scientists that the issue of continuity is an empirical question. Thus, Kagan (1980, 1983) rejects the importance of continuity because he believes that the available data do not warrant this inference. Sackett, Sameroff, Cairns, and Suomi (1982) provide an extensive discussion of methodological issues surrounding continuity, with the implication that it is possible to devise studies that will settle the issue. Bornstein and Sigman (1986) provide alternative models for cognitive continuity and evaluate them by their congruence with empirical studies. Finally, the behavioral genetic literature strongly suggests that there is genetic continuity between childhood and adulthood for intelligence (Plomin & DeFries, 1985). Behavioral genetic methodology allows for an empirical test of the explanatory continuity of behavior.

In attempting to argue for the plausibility of their model within developmental psychology, antirealists typically cite instances where there have been enormous changes in scientific opinion or instances where the issues are unsettled, complicated or highly controversial. For example, Scarr (1985) characterizes family research of the 1950s and 1960s as attempting to show the pathology of the single-parent family, whereas more recent research, inspired by the women's movement, is focussed on showing that women are able to fill a variety of occupational roles and attempts to find strengths in single-parent families. She also discusses unsettled, highly complex questions in which there are large numbers of highly intercorrelated variables, such as whether low levels of lead poisoning lower a child's IQ and whether parental management techniques affect intellectual and emotional development.

These types of examples in no way constitute an argument for relativism and can be very plausibly accounted for within a realist perspective. A realist account of the change in scientific opinion regarding the talents of women, for example, could propose that previous views were simply incorrect and that their incorrectness has been demonstrated by the present successes of many women in a variety of fields. Similarly, scientists at one time believed that the earth was at the center of the universe, and Plato (a reputable scientist of his day) believed that the true elements of the material world were two different right triangles from which God made form and number. These views are simply false and changes in scientific opinion away from such views do not at all imply the truth of relativism or preclude the possibility of genuine progess in science (i. e., coming closer to a true picture of reality).

A realist account is thus compatible with the idea that ideology can sometimes have an effect on scientific perceptions. As indicated in Chapters 4 and 9 of this volume, individuals often use ideology in order to advance their self-interest and improve their self-esteem, and there is no reason to suppose that scientists are immune to these tendencies. Nevertheless, to suppose that developmental psychology is adequately characterized as an ever-changing kaleidoscope of political ideologies is an oversimplification. Political ideologies are important in psychology, but, as seen by the examples discussed above, the history of psychology is not adequately characterized as merely a social construction of reality: Issues tend to be decided on the basis of empirical findings and changes in scientific opinion tend to follow changes in empirical findings. Although there will always be individuals whose personal ideologies prevent them from even attempting to find out how the world works, there is no reason to suppose that this is an adequate characterization of more than a small minority of scientists.

Secondly, the realist can argue that complex studies of highly intercorrelated variables, such as the lead poisoning and parent–child interaction examples, do indeed result in genuine (not just consensual) progress. Old unidirectional, univariate models have been replaced by multivariate, bidirectional models because the former cannot account for the data. In the realist perspective this is viewed as a genuine advance, because such models are a better approximation of reality.

This modern complexity thus can be seen as a sign of real progress and this is the case even if there is indeed a sort of uncertainty principle governing developmental psychology. For example, Scarr (1985) argues that field studies attempting to show causality tend to be hopelessly confounded, whereas well-controlled laboratory studies tend to be of doubtful applicability to the real world. First, even if such an uncertainty position were true, it in no way implies that a realist criterion of truth and scientific progress is incorrect and certainly does not imply that relativism is true. Secondly, our view of the nature of children tends to be built up gradually from a variety of empirical studies rather than on the basis of completely unconfounded superexperiments. Simple unidirectional, univariate models are shown to be inadequate by studies focusing on temperament and genetic variation. Laboratory studies show that some mechanisms are highly plausibile candidates for explaining the development of real children. Studies where individuals have been exposed to extreme environments sometimes admit no other conceivable causal explanation and often suggest similar processes in less extreme cases. Finally, it is argued in this volume that historical and cross-cultural studies can also shed light on developmental mechanisms.

In this perspective scientific knowledge about human development is a rich web of theory and empirical data deriving from a variety of studies and theories. The picture which emerges is not dependent on any one unconfounded study but is rather a pattern which emerges when the pieces of the puzzle are evaluated as a whole. For example, the discussion of the development of aggression in Chapter 6 relies on laboratory studies of humans and animals, observational and correlational studies of aggressive children, the theory of temperament (which itself is linked to a vast body of theory and data, including behavioral genetic data), cross-cultural and historical studies, as well as basic evolutionary theory, especially the evolutionary theory of sex. Similarly, Parke (see Parke, Mac-Donald, Burks, Carson, Beitel, Bhavnagri, & Barth, in press) notes that the experimental study of directionality in parent–child interactions and peer social competence can be explored with a variety of techniques, including assessing parents behavior across different children and assessing child behavior in response to different parental behaviors. Interventions in which behaviors of adults or children are systematically modified through training or instruction are also useful, but longitudinal studies that explore the emergence of both parent-child and peer systems are also required. These studies would at the very least, shed light on this area, eliminate particular hypotheses, and result in a very sophisticated, reasonable answer to the direction of effects issue.

These considerations are reinforced by the difficulty antirealists have of even presenting their point of view without lapsing into the language of realism. It is difficult indeed to expunge the language of realism from one's writing, and Scarr (1985), for example, notes that:

> The truth about this world [of parent–child interaction] cannot be simulated by the isolation of single variables, because parent and child characteristics have nonadditive effects on each other. Bright parents have intellectually responsive children and provide a more stimulating rearing environment for them, and the children evoke and generate for themselves more intellectual stimulation than less bright children. (Scarr, 1985, p. 62)

The implication is clearly that the truth about parent–child interactions is more accurately portrayed by the more complex contemporary models. As a further example from many other possible ones, Scarr notes that the results of research indicate that "improving mothers' discipline and control techniques will not dramatically improve children's language skills" (p. 57), clearly a claim about the real nature of parents and children.

Finally, the emphasis on complicated examples from the frontiers of research distracts attention from the many things which one would have to be literally a lunatic to deny. Although the question of whether small amounts of lead affect IQ is a difficult one, the question of whether large amounts of lead have such an effect (like the question of whether there are such things as genes or whether the earth moves around the sun) is proved beyond question. As Scarr states, ''(e)veryone agrees that lead in large doses is not good for children'' (p. 50). Such a claim is undoubtedly true and reflects the way things work in the real world, not merely scientific agreement. Moreover, it is important to realize that such statements are not trivially true but are the results of genuine scientific advance. The vast majority of human history was spent in ignorance of the existence of genes or of the results of lead poisoning. By focusing on the presently difficult and the controversial, one fails to note the many things that we do know. We may not know the fundamental nature of matter (yet), but we do know a great many things, including (I think) a few things about children's psychological development, and we certainly have a better (truer) idea of the real nature of these things than Plato had, or than was the case even up to the late 1960s.

The discussion in this volume therefore emphasizes the integration and consistency of the major theoretical perspectives in the study of social development, with major theoretical disagreements open to empirical testing. Rather than interpret one point of view as correct or all as equally correct but nevertheless incompatible, the usefulness of particular theories for particular aspects of social development will be stressed. No one theory is adequate to explain all of social development, but individual theories and combinations of theories are much better able to explain particular aspects of development than are others. To claim, for example, that some aspect of cognitive development is well-buffered, whereas some other aspect is highly dependent on passively experienced environments is a perfectly reasonable empirical claim, not a matter of embracing two different world views.

One major way in which the theories and methods discussed differ is in whether they are interested in the explanation of individual differences or developmental universals. As reflected in the above discussion of cognitive-developmental theory and as pointed out originally by McCall (1981), there are two aspects to development, one emphasizing individual differences and the other emphasizing the universal features of development. A researcher interested in individual differences is impressed with the subtle behavioral differences among children of the same age. A researcher who emphasizes developmental universals emphasizes the similarities among children of the same age and notices the broad trends of development. It is as if the former researcher looks at development with a microscope in order to recognize the relatively slight differences among children of the same age, while the latter looks at development with a telescope from a distance in order to recognize the main trends that distinguish 3-year-olds from 10-year-olds.

McCall points out that different mechanisms may well underlie these two quite different phenomena. The theories and methods described above differ greatly in whether they are concerned with individual differences or central tendencies. Social learning theory, behavioral genetic methodology, and the theory of plasticity and environmental influence are primarily interested in understanding how individuals differ from one another as a function of their specific learning experiences, their genes, and other environmental influences. In particular cases one or another of these influences may be most important. For example, the long-range effects of certain severe stresses during infancy are probably best conceived in terms of the early experience paradigm. The stressful events do not involve social learning and, since they are outside the normal range of environmental variation, genetic variation may not be particularly relevant. On the other hand, to take an extreme example, normal genetic variation and early experience are presumably not important for learning to write one's name or how to how to cook scrambled eggs.

On the other side of the coin are cognitive-developmental theorists, ethologists, and sociobiologists who are more interested in the central trends of human development, although each of these theories emphasizes different central tendencies. Cognitive-developmentalists emphasize the similarity of reasoning processes within a particular stage and across cultures, while ethologists emphasize the child's need for an attachment object or tendencies to respond to parental stimulation with affective arousal, and sociobiologists emphasize the importance of self-interest and helping relatives.

The perspective of the fundamental compatibility of these theoretical approaches is consistent with the compromise between the world views of mechanism and organicism proposed by Overton (1984). Overton notes that the organicists are impressed with the constancy and universality of development, while those attracted to the mechanistic perspective stress variability and individual differences in behavior. Although not abandoning the emphasis on the universal trends of development, researchers can nevertheless focus on contingent explanations for why individuals differ from each other in, for example, their rate of attaining behaviors. The formal type of explanation favored by organicists is thus compatible with the contingent explanations of the mechanists.

Such a perspective implies the abandonment of the idea that incompatible research traditions are an inevitable aspect of developmental psychology. Overton (1984) is uneasy with his proposed synthesis because it entails abandonment of some of the key suppositions of the mechanistic research tradition, namely the idea that behavioral development is strictly continuous and the idea that behavior can be reduced to elementary units. Since Overton accepts the relativism characteristic of the rationalist philosophers of science whose work he champions, he can accept the possibility that fruitful research traditions proposing two quite different and incompatible types of children could peacefully coexist, even if these research traditions propose ontologies which are radically incompatibile with each other.

Aronson's (1984) focus on ontology is particularly relevant here: without some such compromise one becomes committed to the possibility of an ontology in which there exist literally two (or more) sets of objects which are incompatible with one another. That is, the set of objects proposed by the mechanistic world view is incompatible with the set of objects proposed by the organismic view. This is a highly metaphysical point of view, a point of view which, I think, it is impossible to even conceive as true. This does not, of course, mean that it is false or that we know it is false, but it does mean that we cannot conceive how it could possibly be true.

However, from the perspective of philosophical realism, described above, this synthesis makes very good sense. The synthesis is attractive because it essentially proposes that there is one set of objects (children) which developmental psychology is attempting to describe. The existence of such a set of objects is not only conceivable but reflects the common sense not only of practicing scientists but also of everyone everywhere. In this perspective, developmental psychology is making progress because it is coming closer to true descriptions of children. Progressively more satisfactory theories result from being better able to incorporate all of the data generated in empirical studies, and this occurs because the set of ontological objects studied by the data gatherers of developmental psychology continues to give a consistent set of signals. As theory becomes more sophisticated, it is able to incorporate these signals into a coherent account of development. As progress is made, it is predicted that theoretical integration will occur as scientists realize that their theories offer compatible descriptions and explanations of this universe of objects. As Aronson (1984) points out, the mistake of rationalism is to ignore the feedback provided by the objects of scientific study.

Besides the fact that some theories are best thought of as applicable to individual differences or central tendencies of behavior, there are ways in which these theories can be integrated. Bowlby's theory of attachment, described above, includes provision for the importance of cognition and learning as well as for biologically based predispositions. Moreover, I have already noted many relationships between evolutionary theory and social learning theory and cognitive-developmental theory.

The recent emphasis on contextual factors in human development is also consistent with an evolutionary approach. Developmentalists have become more aware of the importance of contextual factors in human development (e.g., Bronfenbrenner, 1979; Lerner & Kauffman, 1986). Development is seen as embedded in a rich web of interactions among different levels of analysis. For example, events occurring at the level of the entire society, such as an economic depression, affect family interaction patterns and these in turn affect child development. As indicated in the discussion of contemporary evolutionary theory, contextual variables constitute an irreducible element of evolutionary thinking. Contextual variables will be emphasized throughout the following chapters, but will be of particular importance in Chapter 9.

Finally, the fruitfulness of a synthesis between world views or research traditions in developmental psychology can also be seen by examining the issue of active versus passive organisms and the issue of continuity. The world view of organicism posits that the child is an active participant in its development, while the mechanistic world view posits the child as a passive recipient of environmental stimulation. In our discussion of developmental models of the nature–nurture relationship, it was noted that in two of the models the child is the passive recipient of environmental stimulation, while in the third model characteristics of the child are quite influential in determining the outcome of organism–environment interactions. MacDonald (1986b) proposed an empirical dimension ranging from very intensive environments and passive organisms to relatively weak environments and active organisms. As indicated above, intense environmental stimulation tends to have predictable effects independent of the charactistics of the child, whereas children with unusual temperaments or other characteristics tend to have large effects on their environments. Thus, the active–passive organism dichotomy need not be seen as an irresolvable world-view issue, but can be seen as an empirical dimension descriptive of children.

Regarding the issue of continuity, I have already noted that researchers tend to view continuity as an empirical issue. Here it is argued that, like the active–passive dimension described above, some aspects of continuity can be understood as empirical issues resulting from the study of the effects of experience on behavior. According to the world-view perspective, one either accepts the mechanistic world view of development as the continuous addition of responses with no qualitative changes or one accepts the organicist world view, which proposes qualitatively distinct stages of development. However, the review of the literature on relative plasticity suggests that continuity will tend to occur when very powerful environments act on organisms at a time when there is a high degree of relative plasticity, especially if there is declining plasticity after the environments have their effect. This implies that rather than viewing continuity or lack of continuity as a general feature of a behavioral system, these phenomena will constitute an empirical dimension along which individuals differ depending on the specific environments to which they are exposed.

For example, the IQ of individuals exposed to extremely deleterious early environments and no remediation may well exhibit explanatory continuity throughout development. Other individuals exposed to remediating later environments may show lack of explanatory continuity. Continuity versus noncontinuity thus emerges not as a model issue of incommensurable world views, but as an empirical dimension that describes individual children. The continuity of a behavior such as IQ, considered apart from continuity in particular individuals, is thus reduced to statements about the generality of continuity in individuals. If the great majority of individuals in the population exhibit continuity of IQ, one would then be justified in speaking of IQ as continuous. If not, one would be more accurate in restricting statements regarding continuity to particular individuals.

To conclude this section, in the following chapters there will be an attempt at theoretical integration and compromise whenever possible. In a sense we should be biased in favor of finding examples of integration and theoretical consistency. After all, individuals from these diverse research traditions are really studying the same thing, that is, they are all studying the behavior of the young of a single species in all their normal and abnormal environments. At the very least it would be a worthy aesthetic ideal to attempt a true integration of the field of social development.

CHAPTER 2

Temperament and Personality Development

Most discussions of *temperament* begin with Allport's (1961) definition:

> Temperament refers to the characteristic phenomena of an individual's emotional nature, including his susceptibility to emotional stimulation, his customary strength and speed of response, the quality of his prevailing mood and all the peculiarities of fluctuation and intensity of mood, these phenomena being regarded as dependent upon constitutional make-up and therefore largely hereditary in origin. (Allport, 1961, p. 34)

Temperament is therefore a stable attribute of an individual. It involves aspects of the individual's response to stimulation, and is biological in origin.

I. THEORIES OF TEMPERAMENT

A. The New York Longitudinal Study (NYLS)

The pioneering work on children's temperament has been performed by Stella Chess and Alexander Thomas (e.g., Thomas & Chess, 1977, 1986; Chess & Thomas, 1984). This study has followed the development of 133 middle- and upper middle-class subjects from early infancy to early adulthood. On the basis of interview material, these researchers developed nine categories of temperament, as follows:

1. Activity level: the extent of motor activity during daily interaction with parents, sleeping and waking, and so on.
2. Rhythmicity: the regularity of body functions, sleep/wake cycle, etc.
3. Approach/withdrawal: the nature of the child's reaction to new situations.
4. Quality of mood: the amount of pleasant, joyful behavior.
5. Intensity of mood: the energy level of the response, whether positive or negative.
6. Distractibility: the extent to which extraneous stimuli interfere with ongoing behavior.
7. Persistence/attention span: persistence in the face of obstacles.

8. Sensory threshold: the intensity level of stimulation needed to evoke a response.
9. Adaptability: change in response to new or altered situations (unlike approach/ withdrawal, this category records the degree to which the child is able to alter the response after, for example, initially withdrawing from it).

These nine categories were then combined into three constellations on the basis of qualitative judgment and factor analysis, as follows:

1. Easy temperament: rhythmic, high approach, predominantly positive mood with mild to moderate intensity and quick adaptability.
2. Difficult temperament: arrhythmic, high on withdrawal responses to new situations, relatively frequent negative mood of high intensity, and slow adaptability.
3. Slow-to-warmup temperament: high on withdrawal to new situations with mild to moderate intensity and slow adaptability.

Thomas and Chess (1984, 1986) adopt an interactionist approach to thinking about how temperament affects adjustment. One of the major sources of influence on this point of view is the work of the animal behaviorist Schnierla (1957). Schnierla questioned the view of some of the classical ethologists such as Lorenz that development was under strict genetic control. Schnierla pointed to studies showing the complex interplay of environmental and organismic events during the development of even the most "instinctive" types of behavior. This "fusion" of organism and environment made a strict distinction between instincts and learning useless. Applied to temperament, this leads to the view that behavior is affected by biological influences underlying temperament, but that this influence is constantly fused with environmental influences. In particular, Thomas and Chess emphasize the "goodness of fit" between the child and the environment, that is, the consonance or dissonance of the properties of the environment, particulary the demands and expectations of the parents, with the subject's temperament and other characteristics. For example, Thomas and Chess (1986) describe the optimal reactions of the parents of a child with difficult temperament as involving labeling the behavior of the child as "lusty" and as showing patience when the child rejects new situations. The parents did not blame themselves for the child's behavior, but generally supported each other in dealing with their difficult child. In such a case there is no expectation that the child will become poorly adjusted, while if the parents react to the child with impatience and frustration, there is a greater likelihood that the child will have problems.

The work of Chess and Thomas is historically important because it is really the first overall system for studying temperament. The results of the work have been criticized for a number of reasons, most recently by Buss and Plomin (1984). They point out that factor analyses of temperament questionnaires do not yield the nine dimensions of temperament described by Chess and Thomas, but resemble in important ways the dimensions discovered in their own work, described below. They argue that the concept of difficult temperament is well established from a variety of sources, but see this concept as reflecting essentially the dimension of emotionality in their theory. The idea of goodness of fit is said to be intuitively appealing, but with little concrete data to support it. In support of the goodness-of-fit-model, Thomas and Chess (1986) describe data showing that high activity in children is considered stressful by parents in a Puerto Rican sample, but not the main sample studied in the NYLS. In addition, Super and Harkness (1981) found that night wakening is perceived as more stressful in American samples than in Kenyan samples. However, the Lerners and their colleagues (Lerner, Lerner, Windle, Hooker, Lernerz, & East, 1986) failed to find evidence that congruences between the child's actual temperament and the attitudes of parents, teachers, and peers regarding the difficulty of interacting with individuals with that temperament can explain more variance than simple knowledge of the child's temperament.

B. The Theory of Rothbart and Derryberry

Rothbart and Derryberry (1981) provided a comprehensive theory of temperament involving differences in *reactivity* and *self-regulation*. Reactivity refers to how the individual responds to environmental changes, while self-regulation refers to processes such as approach/withdrawal that modulate reactivity. The response systems involved in reactivity include the following:

1. Motor activity or activity level.
2. Vocal activity in response to stimulation.
3. Facial expressions used in communication, such as brightness and openness of the eyes.
4. Emotional activity.

This last category refers to the qualitative tone of the reaction and can be positive or negative. All of these systems show variability along several intensive and temporal dimensions of measurement, including the threshold of response, the intensity of response, the latency of the response, the rise time of the response (how long it takes to get to peak intensity), and the length of time it takes to recover from a peak response.

The organism is not simply a passive responder to the environment, and Rothbart and Derryberry propose several ways in which the child regulates its level of stimulation by increasing, decreasing, maintaining, and restructuring stimuli (see also Rothbart & Posner, 1985). These activities include approach and avoidance behaviors (similar to the approach/withdrawal dimension of Thomas & Chess, 1980), attention, and self-stimulating and self-soothing. For example, a child can maintain attention toward a stimulus that is arousing or withdraw its gaze entirely, or a child can suck its thumb in order to calm itself down after being distressed.

Rothbart and Derryberry also propose specific structures in the nervous system underlying these behaviors and response systems and propose that constitutional variation will characterize each point of the system. Moreover, there will be variation among modalities in how an individual reacts to stimulation: for example, some individuals may react strongly to bright lights and not to loud noises. Finally, there will be developmental variation due to the maturation of all of these systems and variation among individuals in how fast they develop. With development, new forms of reactivity and self-regulation become functional. For example, early in development the excitatory systems of the brain predominate, while later in the first year forebrain inhibitory processes assume more importance.

The authors emphasize the importance of the various aspects of reactivity and self-regulation to virtually all aspects of social behavior in children. The theory essentially deals with how children react to and regulate stimulation from their environment, and it will be a major theme of this volume that these characteristics are indeed fundamental to understanding social development in children. At this stage much research remains to be done to verify the relative importance of individual variation on all of these dimensions and behaviors, but the overall framework is intuitively quite appealing, and, indeed, as we shall see, differentiation into a dimension of reactivity and a dimension of self-regulation is common to other theories of temperament and personality.

C. The Theory of Buss and Plomin

Buss and Plomin (1984) define temperaments as "inherited personality traits present in early childhood" (p. 84). The theory focuses on broad traits that are operative in a wide variety of situations from childhood to adulthood, rather than the multiplicity of dimensions and behaviors considered by Rothbart and Derryberry (1981). They adopt an evolutionary approach and review data indicating that the dimensions of temperament that they find evidence for also show heritability in a variety of other species, including chimpanzees, dogs, and mice.

Buss and Plomin (1984) propose three basic dimensions of temperament: emotionality, sociability, and activity. Emotionality refers to the tendency to become upset easily and intensely. An emotional person is relatively likely to become highly aroused as a result of the stimulation and the stresses of life and such individuals are relatively difficult to soothe after being aroused. This tendency to become aroused easily is hypothesized to be the result of an overactive sympathetic nervous system. Distress is the first sign of emotionality and appears at birth. During the first year of life this primordial emotion of distress differentiates into fear and anger, and children high in emotionality are likely to be labeled as difficult by their parents: They are easily distressed or angered and difficult to soothe.

Sociability refers to "the tendency to prefer the presence of others to being alone" (Buss & Plomin, 1984, p. 63). Sociable people enjoy the stimulation of being with other people. Social interchange fundamentally involves reacting to the stimulation provided by another individual. People are seen as a source of novel and unpredictable stimulation, which results in arousal in the individuals with whom they are interacting. This arousal has reward value (presumably intrinsic; see Chapter 3) and it is this reward value that drives social interaction forward. For example, as shown in more detail in Chapters 3–5, interaction with parents is highly arousing as well as highly rewarding to children: Simply gazing into the eyes of its mother is highly arousing to an infant. Buss and Plomin suggest that the highest stimulation occurs when an individual initiates a social interaction with others, especially in a leadership role or by actually intruding into the privacy of others. Sociable people are more reinforced by social stimulation and therefore seek it out more.

Activity refers to the tempo of behavior. A highly active person is "in a hurry" all of the time and likes to keep busy. Activity does not involve discrete responses, but describes the style of behavior.

The emphasis in the theory of Buss and Plomin on the importance of genetic variation for temperament has been quite influential in developmental psychology. One of the advantages of the theory is that it can be tied to influential theories of adult personality (see pp. 46–48). As in the theory of Rothbart and Derryberry (1981), Buss and Plomin describe dimensions of temperament that essentially affect how the individual reacts to stimulation (emotionality) and how the individual regulates the stimulation he or she receives (sociability).

D. The Theory of Goldsmith and Campos

Goldsmith and Campos (1982) view temperament in infancy as consisting of stable dimensions of individual differences that affect the behavioral expression of emotion. They accept the list of intensive and temporal parameters proposed by Rothbart and Derryberry (1981) and state that it is variation in these parameters that constitutes variation in temperament. The dimensions of temperament are themselves a group of observable behaviors, which are explicitly tied to the various affective states of the child: For each emotion there is a corresponding temperament dimension of behavior. The authors list 19 dimensions of temperament, corresponding to 19 different affects or relations between affects. For example, the emotion of happiness is associated with a temperamental dimension of smiling and laughter; the balance between positive and negative affect in a novel situation is associated with the temperamental dimension of approach/withdrawal. All children have these dimensions (behaviors), but children vary in the intensive and temporal parameters that affect their emotional behavior.

E. Integration of Theories

These theories of temperament differ in several important ways. Only that of Buss and Plomin (1984) is explicitly grounded in evolutionary theory and this is the only theory that requires a heritable basis for temperament. It is also the broadest of the theories, focusing on only three very broad dimensions rather than the multiplicity of dimensions implicit in the other theories. The theories also differ in the degree to which they are explicitly tied to physiological and neurophysiological processes, with the theory of Rothbart and Derryberry being the most explicit and that of Goldsmith and Campos insisting on describing temperament only at the behavioral level.

Despite these (and other) differences, the theories all agree on the centrality of arousal and the self-regulation of stimulation emanating from the environment. Goldsmith and Campos (1982) are least explicit regarding the exact relations here, but they strongly emphasize the close relation between emotions, which clearly involve arousal, and temperament. The distinction provided by Rothbart and Derryberry (1981) between the reaction to stimulation and self-regulation of stimulation seems basic. As indicated above, Buss and Plomin's trait of emotionality is essentially a trait measuring reactivity (albeit to negative environmental events), while their trait of sociability measures the manner in which a child regulates its level of (social) stimulation. The dimensions of Thomas and Chess (1980) consist of several that involve these two basic dimensions of temperament,

including approach/withdrawal, sensory threshold, intensity of response, and adaptability, and Buss and Plomin (1984) comment on the strong correlations between several
of the dimensions used by Thomas and Chess and their own dimensions.

Moreover, the work of Kagan and his colleagues (Kagan, Reznick, & Snidman,
1986), while not comprising a complete theory of temperament, clearly involves the
reactivity dimension and quite possibly the self-regulation dimension. They studied what
they view as a type of behavior strongly influenced by temperament, the inhibition of
behavior in the presence of the unfamiliar. Children characterized as extremely inhibited
withdraw from unfamiliar situations, become extremely quiet, and are very hesitant to
approach an unfamiliar peer. Uninhibited children, on the other hand, show no signs of
timidity in an unfamiliar situation and readily approach an unfamiliar peer. Physiological
evidence (summarized below on pp. 58–59) indicates that inhibited children have very
intense sympathetic nervous system reactions to unfamiliar situations, and Buss and
Plomin (1984) point out that such a situation is congruent with the idea that inhibited
children are high in their trait of emotionality. The fact that inhibited children tend to
withdraw from unfamiliar situations and social stimulation suggests the importance of
stimulus regulation in their behavior (i.e., that they are low in sociability).

Further support for viewing temperament as fundamentally concerned with reactivity
and the self-regulation of stimulation emanating from the environment comes from the
areas of adult personality and animal research. Animal research with rodents has indicated
two separate factors of emotionality and exploratory behavior (Whimbey & Denenberg,
1966). Rats placed in an open field testing apparatus differed in their exploratory tendencies and, independently, in their tendency to exhibit emotional responses to the testing
situation, as assessed by defecation rates while in the open field. In addition, MacDonald
(1983b, 1987b) found evidence for a dimension of reactivity to stimulation as well as a
dimension involving the degree of attraction to other animals and humans. These dimensions are thus identical to the emotionality and sociability dimensions of Buss and Plomin
(1984). Similarly, Suomi (1987) found that monkeys show variation in the temperamental
trait of emotionality. These monkeys react strongly to stressful situations as a result of
their temperament, but their personality is also affected by rearing conditions.

Regarding the connection with adult theories of personality, both Rothbart and
Derryberry (1981) and Buss and Plomin (1984) linked their theories to the theories of
Eysenck (1982) and Zuckerman (1983). Such a link is theoretically attractive because it
suggests continuity between the dimensions of childhood temperament and those of adult
personality. There is considerable evidence for stability of individual differences in temperament into adulthood as well as for heritability of the basic dimensions of temperament
in both children and adults (see below).

Eysenck (1967) proposed a model of adult personality based on three factors: introversion–extraversion, neuroticism–stability, and psychoticism; the former two have been
related to similar dimensions in children. Individuals high on the extraversion scale are
viewed as being in a low basal state of cortical arousal, so that they behave in ways that
tend to increase their level of arousal. Extraverts are said to seek out stimulation, and, as
Buss and Plomin (1984) emphasize in describing their trait of sociability, other people are
a prime source of stimulation. The factor of introversion–extraversion thus implies the
self-regulation of behavior and includes Buss and Plomin's dimension of sociability

interpreted as a tendency to seek arousing social stimulation (see pp. 49–51 for an alternate interpretation).

Sensation seeking and impulsivity are other traits related to extraversion (Eysenck, 1983; Fulker, 1981; Zuckerman, 1983) and also involve the self-regulation of behavior. Individuals high on sensation seeking enjoy novelty, danger, excitement, and new experiences and are easily bored. Although Buss and Plomin (1984) argue that sensation seeking does not qualify as a temperament because there is no evidence of its heritability prior to age 4 or 5 years, this may be due to lack of appropriate tests prior to this age, and the conceptual similarity and sharing of genetic variance later in life suggest that sociability, extraversion, and sensation seeking are all closely related traits involving variation in the tendency to approach environmental sources of stimulation. Indeed, there is evidence for variation in stimulus-seeking behavior shortly after birth: Korner (1971) found that restless, active, noncuddly babies seek out new stimulation and react with pleasure to surprising events, while, on the other extreme, infants who are relatively inactive tend to avoid novel stimulation.

The other factor of adult personality suggested by Eysenck (1982) is that of neuroticism, and Buss and Plomin (1984) suggest that this is related to their trait of emotionality measured in children. They point to evidence that neuroticism essentially measures reactivity to environmental stresses. Rothbart and Derryberry (1981) also relate their idea of reactivity to similar dimensions found in adult models of personality, although in their view emotionality is physiologically complex rather than a unitary trait. Thus, Rothbart (1986) notes that the intercorrelation among the various aspects of reactivity accounts for only about 40% of the variance in infants. The concept of "strength of the nervous system," deriving from Pavlov and incorporated into several modern theories of personality, is essentially a measure of reactivity or sensitivity to stimulation (emotionality in the terms of Buss & Plomin, 1984). Individuals with weak nervous systems tend to have low thresholds of reacting to stimulation, as indicated by their having a low threshold to auditory stimulation (Sales, Guydosh, & Iacono, 1974; Goldman, Kohn, & Hunt, 1983). Such individuals also tend to have an overactive sympathetic nervous system, that is, a system that responds intensely to rather low levels of stimulation. Thus, Buss and Plomin (1984) suggest that Kagan's behaviorally inhibited children are high on emotionality as indicated by their autonomic reactivity in unfamiliar situations.

This general theoretical perspective thus suggests a two-factor model of temperament in children and personality in adults, consisting of independent factors of reactivity (emotionality, neuroticism, sensitivity to stimulation) and the self-regulation of stimulation emanating from the environment (sensation seeking, sociability, extraversion; see Figure 1). Following Rothbart (1986, 1987), it is proposed that these dimensions are not unitary, but consist of a group of overlapping, intercorrelated traits, which nevertheless account for a significant proportion of variance in adults and children. This model corresponds essentially to Eysenck's (1982) model for adults and is highly congruent with the theory of Rothbart and Derryberry (1981), which emphasizes a self-regulatory system in children in addition to a dimension of reactivity or strength of the nervous system. This reactive dimension, unlike emotionality as used by Buss and Plomin (1984), but in agreement with Rothbart (1986), is here viewed as an index of general reactivity rather than confined to negative reactivity as indexed by the emotions of fear and anger.

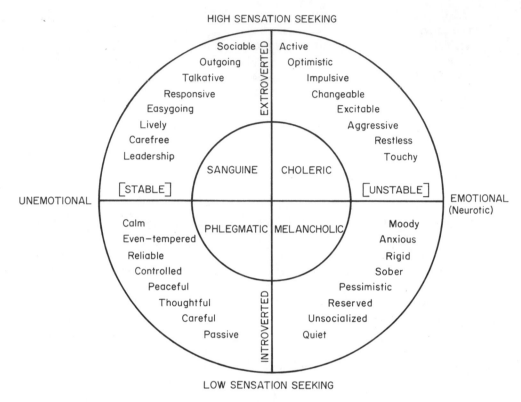

FIGURE 1. Modified representation of Eysenck's (1982) dimensions of personality. The horizontal dimension is a reactive dimension, while the vertical dimension is a self-regulatory dimension.

Eysenck (1982) notes the congruence of his scheme of personality to the four dimensions of personality proposed by the ancient Greeks (see Figure 1). In this scheme melancholic individuals are viewed as high in emotionality and low in sociability, a category similar to shyness as described by Buss and Plomin (1984). ''Choleric'' children are high in both emotionality and stimulus seeking. Children high in sociability and low or moderate in emotionality would be labeled ''sanguine'' in the ancient Greek terminology, while children low in both these dimensions would be labeld ''phlegmatic'' (Eysenck, 1982).

In the Appendix to this chapter a more detailed theory is provided, which implies that the dimensions as proposed by Eysenck must be altered somewhat. However, as argued there, the more detailed theory is essentially compatible with the dimensions as broadly described here. The theory described in the Appendix is therefore not essential to the main arguments in this chapter or later in the book.

II. SELF-REGULATION AS SENSITIVITY TO REWARDS, WITH AN EMPHASIS ON THE POSITIVE SOCIAL REWARD SYSTEM: EVIDENCE FOR A THIRD PERSONALITY DIMENSION

The preceding discussion of the vertical axis in Figure 1 suggests a cluster of interrelated traits that affect the extent to which one is attracted to sources of environmental stimulation. One interpretation of these traits, that of Eysenck (1967), is that an individual high on this axis seeks a high level of cortical arousal and thus approaches environmental stimulation that acts to correct a low basal level of arousal. Extraverts are less sensitive to environmental stimulation and therefore approach highly stimulating environments, which they perceive as pleasurable. Introverts, on the other hand, avoid highly stimulating environments because they become overaroused in these environments and this results in dysphoria and avoidance. Extraversion and sensation seeking are thus interpreted as seeking high levels of arousal because such arousal is pleasurable and tends to correct a basal state of underarousal, whereas introversion is characterized by very high basal levels of cortical arousal and avoidance of exciting, high-intensity stimulation.

This interpretation of the traits related to the vertical axis in Figure 1 is controversial. For example, Zuckerman (1983) points out that sensation seekers use drugs that suppress the central nervous system (CNS), such as alcohol, barbiturates, and heroin, as well as drugs that stimulate the CNS. The arousal theory described above would suggest that they would use only CNS stimulants. Zuckerman also points out that the biochemicals most closely associated with sensation seeking, such as monoamine oxidase, are found mostly in the subcortical areas of the brain (i.e., the limbic system), rather than in the cortex as predicted by Eysenck's theory. Moreover, the phenomena associated with sensation seeking, such as sexuality and strong emotional response, are also found in the limbic system. Zuckerman also notes the results of a study (Carrol, Zuckerman, & Vogel, 1982) that showed that both high- and low-sensation seekers performed and felt better with amphetamine, whereas the optimal-level-of-arousal theory predicts that only the high-sensation seekers would do so.

Further criticism of the optimal-level-of-arousal idea of Eysenck was put forward by Gray (1981), who noted that anxious individuals are highly sensitive to punishment, but not to reward. This difference is compatible with his theory, described on pp. 63–65 in the Appendix, which postulates separate systems of sensitivity to punishment and sensitivity to reward, but is not predicted by Eysenck's theory. Finally, as described more fully in the Appendix (see p. 73), both of Eysenck's proposed dimensions are reactive dimensions and biological measures of these two types (cortical and autonomic) of reactivity are significantly correlated. They are thus not appropriate as the biological bases of two independent dimensions of personality.

In place of the optimal-level-of-arousal theory, both Zuckerman and Gray propose that sensation seeking as well as related traits such as impulsivity, extraversion, and sociability involve the sensitivity to reward (Zuckerman, 1983; Gray, 1982; Gray, Owen, Davis, & Tsaltas, 1983). Individuals high in sensation seeking are viewed as very sensitive to rewards, and the behavior of these individuals is self-regulated in order to bring them a maximal amount of the rewards to be gained from their own social behavior. Such a view is consistent with the present perspective that central, autonomic, and somatic reactivity and the regulation of arousal are the essence of the traits underlying emo-

tionality, whereas sensation seeking is a self-regulatory dimension comprising physiologically distinct systems concerned with variation in sensitivity to the limbic reward systems.
It is thus a self-regulatory system in which individuals regulate their own behavior in order
to obtain rewards.

Such a position need not deny that the regulation of arousal itself often has motivating properties. For example, if stimuli are too intense and the individual becomes overaroused, there would be motivation to avoid the source of stimulation. However, the
reward theory does imply that the biological basis of human motivation is far more
complex than the rewards involved in seeking or avoiding arousal (see Appendix). Indeed, the regulation of arousal theory would seem to imply that the only aspect of the
reward relevant to its attractiveness is the degree to which it arouses the individual, so that
highly stimulating activities, such as sexual behavior, sky diving, parent–child and peer
physical play, socializing at a party, or falling in love would be completely interchangeable as long as they provided similar levels of arousal. This is a very impoverished
biological theory of human motivation. It will be argued throughout this volume that a
modern ethological theory is compatible with a very rich set of biologically given human
motivators.

The biological basis of the reward system involved in sensation seeking is hypothesized by Zuckerman and Gray to be in the limbic system and other subcortical structures
rather than in the cortical arousal-regulating system, since these structures have been
shown to support self-stimulation in studies with animals. In such self-stimulation experiments, electrodes are implanted in areas of the brain, particularly the median forebrain
bundle, and the animal allowed to self-administer stimulation to the brain. High rates of
self-stimulation are believed to indicate that the area in question is a reward site. Stein
(1983) summarizes evidence that reward centers can be found in a variety of areas of the
rat brain and that several different neurotransmitters are utilized at the different sites.

This picture of the biological basis of the traits associated with sensation seeking is
very attractive from an evolutionary point of view. As is shown in Chapter 3, one of the
prime functions of the emotions is to motivate behavior. Individuals are attracted to
behaviors that they find rewarding and the mechanism underlying this attraction is that
these behaviors stimulate the reward centers in the brain. Thus, an individual who is high
in sensation seeking is strongly attracted to the rewards involved in, for example, risk-
taking behavior or vigorous rough and tumble play (see Chapter 3), while an individual
low in sensation seeking does not find such behavior as rewarding. Gray and Zuckerman
thus essentially propose a dimension of individual differences in which individuals are
more or less motivated to attain the rewards that certain types of behavior bring them.
From an evolutionary perspective, these behaviors tend to be adaptive, although the
extremes of variation in this dimension may result in maladaptive behavior.

The reward systems underlying behavior and especially those underlying social
behavior are certain to be a major area of interest in the years ahead. As indicated in
Chapter 3, one of the main differences between the ethological view of social behavior
and the views derived from classical behaviorism is that the former is consistent with a
wide variety of biologically given motivations. From this perspective it is reasonable to
suppose that not only the behaviors associated with sensation seeking, but also those
involved in parent–child interactions and other aspects of social interaction, are intrinsically motivated due to natural selection for specific reward centers in the brain. As

Zuckerman (1983) points out, the sex difference found in sensation-seeking behaviors, in which men are found to be higher in these traits than women, is highly consistent with evolutionary theory. As is discussed more fully in Chapter 5 and especially in Chapter 6, the evolutionary theory of sex predicts that males will be risk takers and be highly motivated by sexual gratification. Males have also been found to engage in far more rough and tumble play than females (see Chapter 3), while females appear to be more responsive to positive social reinforcers, such as those involved in caretaking and those involved in the affective side of sexual relationships (see Chapter 6). These hypothesized, biologically based sex differences in sensitivity to reinforcers may be mediated by testosterone, because testosterone appears to be associated with variation in sensation seeking. Other reinforcers may not show a sex difference, as is suggested by the trait of sociability as defined by Buss and Plomin (1984).

Thus, in the present volume the rewarding aspects of social behavior will be stressed, particularly what we term the positive social reward system. It is proposed that this set of social rewards exists in addition to the set of rewards involved in sensation seeking and, indeed, may constitute a third dimension of temperament. Unlike the set of behaviors influenced by sensation seeking, it is proposed that the positive social reward system underlies the cohesiveness of human social organization. It accomplishes this function by making the behaviors involved in human familial relationships pleasurable to the participants, so that individuals seek out experiences, such as an intimate relationship, that provide this stimulation. It is a major theme of this volume that the social reward system is crucial to understanding virtually all of the central issues in social development. In Chapter 4 the ethological theory of attachment is stressed, particularly the ideas that certain classes of environmental stimulation act as "natural clues" by producing positive or negative evaluations on the part of the baby. Secure attachment is seen as an affective bonding that results in increased sensitivity of the positive social reward system. In Chapter 5 the construct of parental warmth is interpreted as consisting of stimuli that are intrinsically reinforcing to the child and in Chapter 6 the importance of the positive social reward system for aggression, peer relations (especially friendship), and sex differences is stressed. Finally, in Chapter 8 it is argued that the socialization of altruism involves the facilitation of the positive social reward system.

One way to conceptualize the reward systems is to suppose that there are many independent dimensions of personality corresponding to the set of independent reward systems in the brain, all of which are independent of the reactivity (emotionality) dimension described above. In this view, Figure 1 should be amended to include a variety of vertical dimensions corresponding to the different social and nonsocial rewards characteristic of humans, some of which may be moderately correlated with each other. Each dimension is conceptualized as a dimension of individual differences in the reward value of a particular type of environmental stimulus, ranging from sexual gratification and vestibular stimulation to nurturance and love. In this view an individual could be high in sensitivity to the rewards involved in, for example, rough-and-tumble play, but low in sensitivity to the rewards of nurturance, and so on for a very large number of independent dimensions. In this view the reward system is thus inherently multidimensional, although there may be moderate correlations among some of the reward systems, such as those among Zuckerman's (1979) subscales of sensation seeking.

A second way of conceptualizing the reward systems in humans is to simplify the data and propose that there are really essentially two independent reward systems, one corresponding roughly to Zuckerman's idea of sensation seeking typified by an attraction to the stimuli involved in thrill seeking, risk taking, rough-and-tumble play, or sexual behavior, and the other consisting of the positive social reward system underlying such positive social behaviors as warmth, nurturance, and love. These systems would consist of two physiologically distinct systems of interrelated traits, one (sensation seeking) comprising a phylogenetically ancient system underlying a set of primitive appetitive behaviors, while the other is a phylogenetically more recent system underlying the affective basis of human social cohesion, particularly human family relationships. In this view, therefore, there would be three dimensions of personality: emotionality, sensation seeking, and positive social reward.

There is much to reccomend this point of view. First, Eysenck and Eysenck (1976) developed a third personality dimension, which is independent of extraversion and neuroticism and clearly taps qualities that suggest unresponsiveness to positive social rewards: Individuals high in psychoticism are impersonal, cold, lacking in empathy and concern for others, and generally are unconcerned about the rights and welfare of others (Eysenck, 1982). Royce (1973) also presented evidence from a large number of factor-analytic studies of personality that there are three superfactors corresponding roughly to Eysenck's dimensions.

The view that personality fundamentally involves three dimensions corresponding to emotionality, sensation seeking, and positive social reward also receives support from recent work by Cloninger (1987). Cloninger notes that factor analysis is useful because it can show the number of dimensions of personality, but by itself cannot show the correct rotation of the dimensions in space. This task requires evidence from empirical studies designed to show how each dimension is rooted in a different biological system or how a particular interpretation of the dimensions can provide a simplified theory to explain variation in some meaningful set of social behaviors. Cloninger (1987) proposes that by adopting a three-dimensional theory of personality one can create a dimensional theory of psychiatric classification. Such an integration is much more intellectually satisfying than the categorical systems typical of traditional psychiatric classifications, such as the *Diagnostic and Statistical Manual-III* (American Psychiatric Association, 1980), and integrates much better with the data on human development reviewed in this volume.

Cloninger's three dimensions of personality are clearly quite similar to the three dimensions proposed here. *Novelty seeking,* like Zuckerman's idea of sensation seeking adopted here as one dimension of personality, is a dimension involving approach tendencies toward novel stimulation and potential nonsocial rewards as well as the avoidance of boredom and monotony. These tendencies are mediated by positive feelings such as exhiliration. This dimension corresponds to the dimension of sensation seeking described here, but unlike the present notion of sensation seeking, it includes the characteristic of excitability. Excitability is viewed here as an aspect of the reactive dimension of emotionality. Cloninger's dimension of *harm avoidance,* like emotionality as here conceived and like Gray's concept of anxiety (Gray *et al.,* 1983), is a reactive dimension involving a tendency to respond intensely to signals of punishment or frustration, and such individuals are characteristically cautious, tense, and behaviorally inhibited. The present concept of emotionality is, again following Rothbart (1987) and consistent with the work of Kagan and his colleagues (Kagan *et al.,* 1986; Reznick, Kagan, Snidman, Gersten, Baak, &

Rosenberg, 1986), a broader concept involving reactivity to a variety of types of social and nonsocial stimulation. Nevertheless, harm avoidance and emotionality as conceived here are clearly dimensions that influence an individual's emotional reaction to environmental events. Cloninger's third dimension is termed *reward dependence,* and involves intense responsiveness to rewards, particularly those of social approval, love, and nurturance. This dimension is here termed the positive social reward dimension and appears to be the same as Eysenck and Eysenck's (1976) concept of psychoticism. Cloninger shows that by assuming three independent dimensions, one can provide a classification system incorporating the vast majority of adult psychopathological categories. Individuals who are extreme on any one dimension will have a corresponding tendency for maladaptive behavior, and the various combinations of the three dimensions yield a rich network of possible psychiatric diagnoses.

The usefulness of such a three-dimensional approach will be apparent in several of the discussions of this volume and fits well with multivariate statistical studies of childhood psychiatric disorder. For example, many of the descriptors of psychiatric classifications reviewed by Quay (1986) in his review of statistical approaches to psychiatric classification involve these dimensions. Thus, children diagnosed as exhibiting Undersocialized Aggressive Conduct Disorder appear to be high on the sensation-seeking dimension (e.g., attention seeking, shows off, boisterous, noisy), low on the positive social reward system (e.g., uncooperative, resistant, inconsiderate, stubborn, negative, refuses directions, untrustworthy, dishonest, lies, destructive), and high on emotionality (e.g., irritable, "blows up" easily, temper tantrums; see Chapter 6 for further discussion). Children diagnosed as exhibiting Socialized Aggressive Conduct Disorder appear to be more attracted to the social rewards of group membership and are thus quite possibly higher on the positive social reward system (e.g., is loyal to delinquent friends, belongs to a gang). Children with the syndrome of Anxiety–withdrawal–dysphoria would appear to be high in emotionality (e.g., hypersensitive, easily hurt, anxious, fearful, cries frequently, easily flustered or confused) and low in sensation seeking (e.g., shy, timid, bashful). The Schizoid–unresponsive syndrome contains items indicative of being low on the positive social reward system (e.g., cold and unresponsive, withdrawn, likes to be alone) and low on sensation seeking (e.g., shy, timid, bashful, lack of interest; see Appendix). The Motor overactivity syndrome appears to involve emotionality (e.g., excitable, cannot wait), sensation seeking (e.g., impulsive), as well as the trait of activity described as an independent dimension of temperament by Buss and Plomin (1984; see above) (e.g., restless, overactive, overtalkative, squirmy, jittery). Besides these syndromes described by Quay (1986), it is argued in Chapters 3 and 6 that hyperactive children are high in emotionality and high in sensation seeking, a situation that accounts for the strong overlap between hyperactivity and Undersocialized Aggressive Conduct Disorder in statistical analyses (Hinshaw, 1987; Quay, 1986).

The dimension of positive social reward (the present terminology), psychoticism (Eysenck & Eysenck, 1976), or reward dependence (Cloninger, 1987) is clearly of the utmost importance for an evolutionary account of development. This is so because it is this system that mediates social cohesiveness as well as the forces of social dispersion that figure so prominently throughout this volume. It is a system with major effects on the development of family relationships, as well as altruism, empathy, and aggression, and there appear to be strong sex differences in this system. It is too soon to determine whether the reward system is multidimensional, with a large number of independent social rewards and nonsocial rewards, or whether it is essentially two-dimensional (sensation seeking and the positive social reward system), but the present evidence clearly points to a two-dimensional approach as explaining a significant proportion of the variance in psychiatric diagnosis, and therefore this view must be favored.

Although the specific considerations leading to the view that the positive social reward system is crucial to an understanding of the central issues of development will be discussed in later chapters, two general points should be made. The positive social reward system is an environment-expectant genetic system (MacDonald, 1984); that is, it is a system that essentially programs for the affective response to events that occur in the environment. It is thus a highly contextually sensitive system, because it is responsive to the cues available in the environment. Its "traitness" lies in its being a disposition to respond to environmental events, and in this it is quite unlike a trait such as height, which, although it may be influenced by environmental forces, is not essentially involved in reacting to the environment. Moreover, the response to the environment is an affective, evaluative response that can vary greatly even within short periods of time rather than a very slowly changing response that can often be measured by relatively permanent physical changes in the organism (e.g., changes in height). In Chapter 4, the contrast between attachment viewed as an environment-expectant biological system and as a system of biological traits relatively independent of the environment is considered.

A second crucial question that emerges within this perspective is the degree to which the social reward system is an environmentally programmable system, that is, the extent to which variation in sensitivity to various social rewards can be influenced by the environment. The perspective developed throughout this volume is that it is possible to produce significant variation in this system by manipulating environmental stimulation during development. The evidence for this point of view involves an interpretation of the early-experience literature in the area of social development (Chapter 4) together with the cross-cultural literature on socialization (Chapter 5, 6 and 8), as well as contextual influences on socialization (Chapter 9). In attempting to develop a model of how these environmental influences might work, one possible analogy is the work on brain stimulation in rodents mentioned briefly in Chapter 1. In this model early environmental stimulation is relatively efficient at elaborating specific neural systems associated with cognitive abilities such as maze learning in rats. The neural systems become more complex as the result of increased growth and density of nerve fibers, and a variety of correlative physiological changes occur in the system. The analogy here then would be that early, affectively positive stimulation would result in the progressive elaboration of the neural basis of the positive social reward system, making individuals more sensitive to the rewarding behaviors of others. Experiencing an environment rich in events that stimulate the positive social reward system, such as those involved in secure attachment (Chapter 4) or parental warmth (Chapter 5), leads to an increasing abundance of synapses, and the system becomes increasingly sensitive to such events, that is, they become more subjectively pleasurable and rewarding. As a result of this increased sensitivity, individuals are more likely to seek out sources of positive social interaction with others and perform behaviors toward others that result in these others providing socially rewarding experiences to them, what might be termed affective reciprocity. This is essentially the mechanism proposed for the socialization of altruism discussed in Chapter 8 and variations of this mechanism occur throughout the volume.

Another aspect of this model is that although elaboration by environmental events is possible, there is also a well-buffered central tendency for humans in general to find similar behaviors rewarding. As described in Chapter 1, animals and children who are deprived of environmental stimulation nevertheless are able to perform some cognitive functions, so that cognitive functioning is in some ways a well-buffered system. Similarly, for social development some levels of social behavior may be well-buffered (see Chapter 4 for a more detailed discussion), and in particular the positive social reward system may in part be well-buffered. This would suggest that even in the absence of socialization such as the warm, sensitive caregiving discussed in Chapters 4 and 5, which would tend to elaborate the social reward system, the reward system would exist at a rudimentary level, just as some levels of Piagetian intelligence develop even in the most deprived environments (MacDonald, 1986a). Finally, there may be genetic variation in sensitivity to social rewards and the extent to which the positive social reward system is susceptible to environmental programming. Behavior genetic data on the heritabilty of Eysenck's trait of psychoticism indicate that there is genetic variation for this trait (Fulker, 1981). Nevertheless, it is the thesis of this book that the social environment can have a very large main effect on the positive social reward system.

Regarding the conceptualization of the neural and neurochemical bases of the positive social reward system, Panksepp and his colleagues (Panksepp, 1986) provided data from rats strongly implicating opioids in both the negative emotions of separation and the positive social emotions involved in social support. Administration of morphine decreased separation distress and naloxone increased it. He views these results as indicating that the level of morphine influences the level of positive affect. Panksepp (1986) proposes that decreases in opioids occur as a result of the loss of social support, while return of social support activates opioid systems and restores positive affect.

The environmental socialization influences described in Chapters 4–6 and 8 may be conceptualized as elaborating these systems. For example, the sex differences between males and females discussed in Chapter 6 would then be viewed as resulting from different levels of elaboration of the physiological systems underlying positive social reward due to a combination of socialization influences as well as differences in base levels of these systems (i.e., in the well-buffered aspect of the positive social reward system described above). Such elaboration would result in greater sensitivity to social rewards and a greater tendency to seek them out and a corresponding tendency to be more negatively affected by the loss of social rewards. Early experience would be particularly important for this elaboration, but in view of the model of plasticity described in Chapter 1 and the data on attachment described in Chapter 4, sufficient plasticity occurs later in life for significant effects to occur.

Overall, in light of the interactions among the three dimensions of personality proposed here, there is the suggestion that the trait of emotionality will be intimately connected to the socialization of the positive social reward system as well as the reward systems underlying sensation seeking. Although I have argued that emotionality and the self-regulatory social reward systems are genetically independent systems, they are intimately associated within any one individual. Thus, a person high on emotionality will tend to overreact to rewarding (or punishing) stimulation, especially if this stimulation is of high intensity. A considerable body of animal research indicates that rewarding or punishing stimuli tend to result in general, nonspecific arousal as well as the elicitation of a variety of behaviors (Carlson, 1986; Falk, 1972; Koob, Fray, & Iversen, 1976). Events that are intensely rewarding are thus also likely to be highly arousing. Similarly, individuals who are high on behavioral inhibition become highly aroused to the threat of punishment (Gray, 1982). (See the Appendix for a discussion of the relations among rewards, punishments, and arousal.) Here the implication is that in attempting to have an impact on the positive social reward system it is necessary to take into account the emotionality of the child. The progressive elaboration of the social reward system may thus depend not only on providing affectively positive stimulation, but on also providing it in a manner that is not overarousing to the child. As a further example, in Chapter 3 the interrelationships between emotionality and the rewards involved in rough and tumble play are discussed. Clearly there are important implications for clinical intervention here.

III. BIOLOGICAL AND ENVIRONMENTAL INFLUENCES ON TEMPERAMENT

A. Behavioral Genetic Research

Buss and Plomin (1984) present evidence from a variety of twin studies indicating that the dimensions of activity, sociability, and emotionality are heritable. Twin studies based on parental report consistently show higher correlations for identical twins than for fraternal twins. Correlations between twins for personality measures generally are lower than for general cognitive abilities, but the amount of difference between monozygotic and dizygotic twins is about the same, about .20 (Scarr & Kidd, 1983). However, estimates of heritability based on parental ratings of their twin children are considerably higher than those based on other types of behavioral genetic analysis (Scarr & Kidd, 1983), due in part to the tendency for the behavior of fraternal twins to be viewed as quite dissimilar (Buss & Plomin, 1984). Buss and Plomin (1984) argue that this "contrast effect" of the fraternal twins may be due to the behavior of the twins themselves, since this effect appears even when independent observations of each twin are made by trained observers.

Observational studies offer stronger support for the heritability of emotionality, activity, and sociability (EAS), since they are not based on parent reports, but on independent observations of each twin. Buss and Plomin (1984) interpreted several items of the Bayley scales used by Matheny, Dolan, and Wilson (1976) as assessing EAS traits and concluded that there was evidence for their heritability in the first 2 years of life. Although temperament is not very stable in infancy, Matheny (1983) provided evidence that the patterns of change found over this period were partially due to genetic factors: the profiles of change of the identical twins were more similar than the profiles generated by the fraternal twins.

Data from an adoption study (Plomin & DeFries, 1985) show little relationship between biological or adoptive parents and infants. These low correlations could be due to low stabilities of the measures used or to the fact that different genes affect temperament in infancy than affect similar measures of adults. The authors conclude that individual differences in temperament in infancy are unpredictable and unpredictive. However, they argue that there is considerable genetic continuity between infancy and adulthood, that is, some of the same genes that affect variation in temperament in infancy also affect variation in adult temperament.

Scarr and Kidd (1983) conclude their review of the developmental literature on the heritiability of personality by noting that "most of the variance in personality measures is not accounted for by either genetic differences or environmental differences *between* families" (p. 418; see also Plomin & Daniels, 1987). The environment provided by a family thus does not serve to make siblings like each other. This is an important finding, since many theories of socialization have assumed that parents provide an environment that would have predictable effects on all their children, so that differences between children would be due essentially to differences in their family environment that they share with other family members. Rather, the environmental differences affecting variation in personality appear to be peculiar to individual family members.

As indicated by the review by Plomin and Daniels (1987), there is little agreement on how to conceptualize these nonshared environmental influences and what systematic sources of nonshared variation exist, if any. One important source of hypotheses for such nonshared influences is evolutionary biology (Buss, 1987). As described in Chapter 5, the theory of discriminative parenting predicts that parents will distinguish among their children on a variety of dimensions, including sex, birth order, reproductive value, and phenotypic resemblance to themselves, and this will result in sources of nonshared environmental variation.

However, despite the general finding that most of the environmental variation is not a function of general effects of the family, it is possible that in particular cases there may indeed be environmental effects that would serve to make all family members alike. The behavioral genetic data are essentially averages of large samples and can be understood as reflecting the average situation in the population. Thus, in particular cases family environments may indeed result in differentiating all the children within the family from children reared in other families. As discussed in Chapter 1, one would expect this to be the case where the family was characterized by relatively extreme environments, such as highly rejecting or abusive environments. In such a case, if all the children in a family were so treated, one would expect a large main effect resulting in pathological behavior in all the children as a function of their family environment. Such environments would function to make the children more like each other and less like children reared in other homes. This type of consideration also applies to thinking about cross-cultural data: As is shown in Chapters 5, 6, and 8, it is quite possible that extreme environments have been used to socialize children adaptively in some cultures. These environments would effectively make the average child reared in one culture different from a child reared in another culture, but this difference would not necessarily be reflected in between-family variation in any particular culture. Further discussion of behavior genetic issues relevant to family influences is given in Chapter 5.

Finally, since I am proposing links between child and adult personality, it is relevant to describe findings on the heritability of sensation seeking, emotionality, and psychoticism in adults. Fulker (1981) reviewed studies of the Eysenck Personality Questionnaire and concluded that extraversion, neuroticism, and psychoticism are all highly heritable. Moreover, as concluded by Scarr and Kidd (1983), the environmental variance that was important was not related systematically to families, but was specific to individuals. In addition, the relationship between the traits of extraversion and sensation-seeking was explored and it was found that a common constitutional basis accounted for these traits. Similar results are described by Eysenck (1983).

B. Proximal Biological Correlates of Emotionality and Sensation Seeking

Kagan and his colleagues (Garcia-Coll, Kagan, & Reznick, 1984; Kagan *et al.*, 1986) studied autonomic reactivity, here considered to be an aspect of emotionality, in behaviorally inhibited children. Behaviorally inhibited children respond to unfamiliar visual and auditory stimulation with higher and more stable heart rates. This physiological response is part of a general bodily response to unfamiliarity, which involves a variety of biological systems, including the hypothalamus, the pituitary and adrenal glands, the reticular activating system of the brain, and the sympathetic nervous system. They propose that following exposure to unfamiliarity, the hypothalamus is stimulated to affect one or more of the following systems: (a) the secretion of ACTH from the pituitary and cortisol from the adrenal gland; (b) the discharge of the reticular activating system, which results in arousal and increases in muscular tension; and (c) the discharge of the sympathetic nervous system, which results in a higher and more stable heart rate and pupillary dilation. Behaviorally inhibited children are characterized as having a low threshold for the activation of this system. Reznick *et al.*, (1986) suggest that these differences may result from genetic differences in the neurotransmitter epinephrine in the central nervous system.

The research of Rothbart and Derryberry (1981; see also Rothbart, 1986, 1987) indicates that the trait of emotionality is physiologically complex and is really a group of interrelated traits affecting arousal regulation. These traits consist of variation in the reactivity of the central nervous system and the autonomic nervous system as well as somatic sources of reactivity. For example, central influences on arousal involve both excitatory processes and inhibitory processes, with the latter appearing later in development (Rothbart & Derryberry, 1981; Rothbart & Posner, 1985). After childhood both types of processes appear to decline in their responsiveness, so that older adults both show longer latencies to react to stimulation and are less able to inhibit emotional responses when confronted with highly arousing stimulation (Woodruff, 1985). Older adults are thus particularly prone to deleterious effects of highly stressful stimulation, since once aroused they are less able to inhibit their arousal.

Another system that appears to be involved in the regulation of arousal is the septohippocampal system. Gray (1982) emphasizes the role of the septohippocampal system in behavioral inhibition in animals, but also argues for an increasing role of the prefrontal cortex in humans. Antianxiety drugs lower the arousal that occurs when punishment is anticipated or when confronting novel environments and result in a decrease in behavioral inhibition (see Appendix). Taken together, these considerations suggest that despite sharing a considerable amount of common variance, several different measures of reactivity would be useful for measuring individual differences in emotionality (Rothbart, 1986).

Rothbart and Posner (1985) review developmental studies of self-regulation. They note that the basic emotional processing of reward and punishment begins early in infancy. At around 7–9 months of age there is an increasing sensitivity to punishment and the onset of behavioral inhibition. In addition, a number of studies (reviewed by Zuckerman, 1983) indicate that sensation seeking reaches a high point in young adulthood and declines with age. These changes, which also appear to coincide with increases in emotionality in adolescence (see Chapter 6), are associated with increases in gonadal hormones at this time, a finding that is consistent with a large sex difference for sensation seeking in which males are higher on this trait than females (see Chapter 6). Another physiological characteristic common to both extraversion and sensation seeking is that individuals who are high in sensation seeking and extraversion are low in the enzyme monoamine oxidase (MAO). In both humans and monkeys low MAO is related to high levels of social activity and agonistic behavior. Although a definitive model of the physiology of the regulation of arousal or the sensitivity to reward has yet to emerge, these findings do point to the presence of a biological basis for these dimensions in children.

C. Cross-Cultural Research and the Effects of Powerful Early Environments

Cross-cultural research on temperament attempts to ascertain whether there are population differences in temperament and to relate these differences to various aspects of culture and adaptation. The pioneering work in this field was performed by Daniel Freedman (see Freedman, 1974, for a review), who studied newborn infants prior to the time when they could have social contact with their mothers. Freedman and Freedman (1969) found that Chinese-American infants differed from European-American infants on dimensions that tapped excitability/imperturbability, with the Chinese-American infants being less excitable and more imperturbable than the European-American infants. The Chinese-American infants were less labile, habituated more readily, and were more easily soothed, all behaviors suggestive of lower emotionality in the terminology used here. These differences continued into the school years, with the Chinese-American children continuing to show little intense emotional behavior. (See also p. 70.)

Freedman (1974) expanded this work to include other groups derived from the Oriental gene pool, including Japanese and Navaho infants. The combined scores of the three Oriental groups (Chinese-American, Japanese, and Navaho) again indicated differences in emotionality, and Freedman concluded that the differences are accounted for by differences between the Caucasian and Oriental gene pools.

Recently Chisholm (1983) replicated the findings of Freedman (1974) for the Navaho. Navaho infants are quieter and less labile and irritable than Caucasian infants, a dimension clearly related to emotionality. Rather than ascribing the differences to gene-pool differences as Freedman does, however, Chisholm shows that a cluster of variables relating to the mother's age, parity, and blood pressure is significantly related to infant irritability. This suggests that the infant's prenatal environment may influence irritability. In particular, the high maternal blood pressure could result in damage to the placenta and result in higher irritability in the child by damaging the fetal neuroendocrine system. Several studies have shown that variation in maternal blood pressure is related to neonatal irritability (e.g., Korner, Gabby, & Kraemer, 1980). This prenatal environment may be influenced in turn by variation in the mother's genetic makeup, but this is presently unknown. One environmental possibility proposed by Chisholm for the generally lowered irritability of Navaho infants is that there is less stress in Navaho culture, resulting in generally lower blood pressure. Navaho males who have left the reservation have higher blood pressure than reservation males, including males who intend to leave (Alfred, 1970). Thus, the hypothesis of gene-pool differences between groups is not supported. However, there is genetic variation for both infant temperament (Buss & Plomin, 1984) and maternal blood pressure (Kass, Rosner, Zinner, Margolius, & Lee, 1977), so that individual variation in irritability is apparently affected by genetic variation.

Other cross-cultural research has focused on behavioral inhibition. Kagan, Kearsley, and Zelazo (1978) found that Chinese-American infants were more behaviorally inhibited than Caucasian infants. The former infants were consistently more inhibited in a laboratory setting during which unfamiliar visual and auditory events were presented. In addition, Chinese-American infants showed more fear in these unfamiliar situations as well as more distress when separated from their mothers. Like many other behaviorally inhibited children, they exhibited a high and stable heart rate in response to these threatening situations. As adults, Chinese psychiatric patients are more likely to show symptoms of anxiety and panic than European or American groups (Kleinman, 1982).

Other possible environmental sources of variation in constitutional differences in the temperamental dimension of emotionality include very intense, powerful events that occur prenatally and/or as a result of prematurity. The research involving the handling paradigm with rodents described in Chapter 1 as an example of the effects of early experience supports the idea that moderately stressful perinatal events decrease emotionality later. However, extremely stressful events in infancy have the opposite effect, resulting in later maladaptive behavior (Hutchings, 1963), and there is evidence that several abnormal environments can increase reactivity to stimulation in humans. Thus, prematurity and especially extreme prematurity is associated with hypersensitivity to stimulation (Field, 1982; Goldberg & DeVitto, 1983). These infants show far more negative affect during interactions with their parents due to the difficulty of providing stimulation at an optimal level of arousal. During face-to-face interaction with their parents, these infants often avert their eyes when their parents attempt to make eye contact, because they are so easily overaroused. Goldberg and DeVitto (1983) find that parents of premature infants respond to this hypersensitivity as well as their babies' lack of responsiveness by more intrusive forms of stimulation despite the fact that there is much less positive affect on the part of both parent and child during the interactions than occur in normal children. Crnic, Greenberg, Ragozin, Robinson, and Basham (1983) found that this tendency for higher levels of parental stimulation and infant irritability and gaze aversion continued throughout the first year.

The findings regarding prematurity are excellent examples of the importance of powerful, intensive environmental influences during development, in this case affecting a temperamental dimension. In such cases the child is best viewed as a passive recipient of environmental adversity rather than an active creator of environments (MacDonald, 1986b; see also Chapter 1). Parents of premature babies appear to use highly intense, intrusive environments in an effort to facilitate development, an effort that is quite possibly adaptive even though it is accompanied by negative affect on the part of the baby (Goldberg & DeVitto, 1982).

These studies suggest that the environment, particularly intense and powerful early environments, can have important effects on emotionality. Regarding the other two dimensions of temperament suggested earlier, I have already provided a model for environmental effects on the positive social reward system, and evidence for important environmental effects on this dimension is described in Chapters 4–6 and 8. I am aware of no evidence for the importance of the environment on sensation seeking, but this possibility will be discussed in Chapter 3 in the context of a discussion of parent–child physical play.

D. Temperament and Adaptation

The finding of relatively low correlations within biological and adoptive families (Scarr & Kidd, 1983) suggests that the genetics of temperament and personality is quite different from the genetics underlying cognitive abilities, where there are quite high correlations within natural families. In other words, knowing that two individuals are related is much less of a clue about their personality than it is about their intelligence. These findings suggest that in the area of temperament natural selection has not operated in a directional manner in order to produce an ideal personality type that would be adaptive in a particular culture or in all cultures. The finding of genetic variation in all cultures suggests instead that a wide range of personality and temperament types may be adaptive in particular contexts. Variation in personality may be beneficial, so that the ideal adaptive strategy for a parent would be to have several children with somewhat different personalities. Such a situation would be less likely for intelligence, where, all things being equal, it would be better to have intelligent children. Consistent with this, Super and Harkness (1986) point out that there may be discontinuities in the adaptive niche for temperament: children in a Puerto Rican sample in New York (Thomas & Chess, 1977) were well adjusted during preschool when few demands were made on them. However, when they entered school and demands for regularity increased, there was an increase in behavior problems.

One important possible explanation of these findings is that it reflects less of a role of additive genetic variation to temperament, that is, a lesser role for genes that contribute in a similar manner to a temperament phenotype independent of the other genes a person has. Lykken (1987) notes that even very small genetic differences may result in qualitative differences between individuals and account for the relatively low correlation between dizygotic twins compared to those for monozygotic twins.

While variation may be adaptive, it is also the case that extreme temperaments are quite possibly maladaptive. From an adaptationist perspective the trait of emotionality can be considered as a group of interrelated systems that affect the organism's monitoring of and reaction to the environment. Individuals high on emotionality will be highly vigilant and be able to muster great energy in response to even relatively slight perturbations or crises in their environments. At its maladaptive extreme such an individual would overreact to even the slightest disturbance in the environment and even the most benign environment would be stressful. A person low on emotionality would become excited only in the presence of great danger or overwhelming sensory stimulation. At its maladaptive extreme, such a person would ignore or fail to react sufficiently to counteract even deleterious environmental events. As a result of this situation it is expected that natural selection will act in a stabilizing manner, with both extremes having a tendency to be maladaptive.

Similarly, with regard to sensation seeking, it is argued in Chapter 6 on adaptationist grounds that males especially should be inclined to take risks and in general overvalue possible rewards as compared to possible punishments, while females would be expected to be more cautious. However, at its extreme such behavior becomes foolhardy and dangerous, and many more young males die as a result of accidents and violence than do older males or females (see Chapter 6). At the other extreme, however, individuals may so overvalue the possible dangers of taking risks that opportunities are lost. Again, unlike the case with intelligence, both extremes are maladaptive, so that natural selection against the extremes and the development of nonadditive genetic mechanisms are expected.

IV. The Stability of Temperament

Buss and Plomin (1984) explicitly require that behaviors reflecting temperament be stable. Stability is assessed in longitudinal studies, with the same or conceptually similar measures being used at different ages. The issues surrounding stability are grouped around the following propositions:

1. *Stability is greater if more extreme individuals are used in the analysis.* If there is indeed a biological underpinning of temperament, as seems likely, one would expect that individuals who are most extreme on the dimension will tend to remain relatively extreme when assessed later. On the other hand, individuals in the middle of the temperament distribution will be more likely to change their score relative to others. This is at least partly due to the fact that there is relatively little difference between these individuals to start with and, given that there is some plasticity in human development, they will rather easily change their rank ordering on the temperamental dimension. Similarly, the effects of early experience are most apparent when individuals have been subjected to extreme environmental events, which place them at the extreme ends of measured behavioral dimensions (MacDonald, 1986b; see also Chapter 1).

Some of the most convincing evidence for the stability of temperament comes from studies that restricted themselves to the extremes of the temperamental dimension. For example, Kagan and his colleagues (Kagan et al., 1986; Reznick et al., 1986) followed samples at the extreme ends of the dimension of behavioral inhibition and lack of inhibition to the unfamiliar between the ages of 21 months and 5½ years. At the later age 78% of the children remained in their original category. In addition, heart rate and the stability of heart rate at age 5½ years were also predictable from these indices at 21 months. Ten of the 13 children with high and stable heart rates at the two ages had a variety of fears, including fear of the dark and large animals, and were characterized by several types of medical symptoms, including allergies, irritability, and constipation. Kagan et al. (1986) also review studies indicating that these behavioral styles can persist into adulthood, with inhibited males choosing intellectual careers and uninhibited males choosing traditional masculine occupations.

2. *Stability increases with age.* It was argued in Chapter 1 that plasticity in behavior declines gradually during development. This implies that there will be increasing stability in temperament at later ages because the child will be less susceptible to changes induced by the environment. Recent reviews of the stability of temperament and personality are consistent with this interpretation. McDevitt (1986) found a trend for increasing stability, so that by age 7 years almost three-fourths of the reliable variance was stable, compared to very negligible relationships found within the first year. Buss and Plomin (1984) came to a similar conclusion regarding the EAS traits, with sociability reaching a correlation of .69 between 9 and 12 years of age. Finally, Moss and Susman (1980) drew a similar conclusion for personality studies of children and Costa and McCrae (1980) pointed to the very high stability of adult personality.

3. *Stability is greater if more global constructs are used.* Recent reviews (Buss & Plomin, 1984; McDevitt, 1986) found greater stability in cases where global assessments of personality were used. At the opposite extreme are laboratory assessments of a particular behavior in a particular situation. For example, Reznick *et al.* (1986) found much higher stability when the individual measures of behavioral inhibition were combined into a global score. McDevitt (1986) concluded that temperament is found to be more stable to the extent that the analysis is less specific, less contextual, and less situational. A similar finding accounts for the lack of predictability of discrete behaviors in mother–infant interaction compared to the predictability found by attachment classification (Sroufe, 1979a).

4. *Conclusion: stability and continuity.* These results indicate important stability of temperament and personality during childhood, increasing steadily into adulthood. The overall picture also strongly suggests continuity of underlying process. Particularly convincing are the results of behavioral genetic studies indicating a common genetic basis of some aspects of temperament from childhood to adulthood (Plomin & DeFries, 1985). In addition, the work of Kagan *et al.* (1986) indicates that a similar set of biological responses underlies behavioral inhibition throughout early childhood. They report that stability and continuity are observed even though the parents are worried about their children's behavior and often try (with some success) to change it. If indeed there is declining plasticity during childhood, one would expect that the biological processes underlying temperament would be increasingly resistant to change at later ages, that is, more likely to show continuity within that individual.

V. APPENDIX

A. A More Detailed Theory

The theory of temperament developed above must be considered to be a rough approximation of an adequate theory of temperament. In the following it is maintained that both emotionality and sensation seeking are much more complex than would be suggested by the proposal of two unitary dimensions. The purpose is to describe some of this complexity as well as to show why a theory of two independent dimensions follows from it as a useful first approximation.

The dimension of sensation seeking is much more complex than suggested by a unitary dimension. First, there appear to be several correlated dimensions of sensation seeking corresponding to Zuckerman's subscales of sensation seeking. As indicated in Chapter 2, these dimensions can be seen as a group of intercorrelated dimensions involving sensitivity to rewards. Secondly, and more important to the present discussion, there is evidence that there are independent dimensions of sensitivity to reward and sensitivity to punishment. This theory has been persuasively presented by Gray (1981, 1982; see also Gray et al., 1983) and recently Rothbart (in press-a) has argued for a similar conceptualization. Gray proposes that the dimension of anxiety involves essentially the sensitivity to signals of uncertainty or anticipated punishment, whereas the dimension of impulsivity is characterized by great sensitivity to rewards, thus yielding two independent dimensions of personality. The biological bases of these two dimensions are the median forebrain bundle (impulsivity) and the septo-hippocampal system (anxiety) respectively.

The reason why the single dimension of sensation seeking proposed in this chapter offers a useful approximation to the more complex reality is that the extreme types proposed by such a theory are the most unbalanced types, that is, individuals who are high in sensitivity to reward and low in sensitivity to punishment (extremely impulsive), or low in sensitivity to reward and high in sensitivity to punishment (extremely behaviorally inhibited). Other combinations tend to fall in between these extremes so that these two extreme types approximate a single dimension ranging from impulsivity and sensation seeking to caution and inhibition (see Figure 2). Thus an individual who was high on both sensitivity to rewards and sensitivity to punishments would neither be as impulsive as someone high on impulsivity and low on behavioral inhibition, nor as cautious as an individual who was high on behavioral inhibition and low in impulsivity. This theory predicts several interesting intermediate types. Particularly interesting would be the individual who was high on both of these dimensions. Such an individual would therefore be strongly appetitive but also strongly motivated to inhibit behavior in order to avoid punishments—thus avoiding the extremes of foolhardiness.

The hypothesis that there are two independent dimensions corresponding to Gray's dimensions of sensitivity to rewards and sensitivity to punishments makes excellent biological sense and results in a number of predictions, described below. It is intuitively plausible because the proposed biological bases of these dimensions are anatomically separate areas of the brain. Moreover, from an adaptationist standpoint, individuals who are high on both sensitivity to reward and sensitivity to punishment would appear to represent a very adaptive compromise so that it is easy to visualize natural selection acting to make these two sensitivities independent systems. As indicated above, such a person would be strongly appetitive and yet easily inhibitable and therefore not foolhardy. It is difficult to see the adaptiveness of being low on both of these dimensions, but it will be argued that this situation may characterize some clinical populations.

In any event, because the independence hypothesis is testable, and because these two dimensions can nevertheless be usefully approximated by a single dimension of impulsivity–caution (thus not violating the observed three-factor structure of personality), there is every reason to adopt it as a reasonable hypothesis. Indeed, Rothbart (in press-a) summarizes a wide range of data which strongly supports this hypothesis. Observations of infants reveal an approach dimension that is independent of the inhibition dimension and that occurs across conditions of high- and low-stimulus intensity. There was stability of individual differences in approach but not inhibition in the age range 6.5–12.5 months.

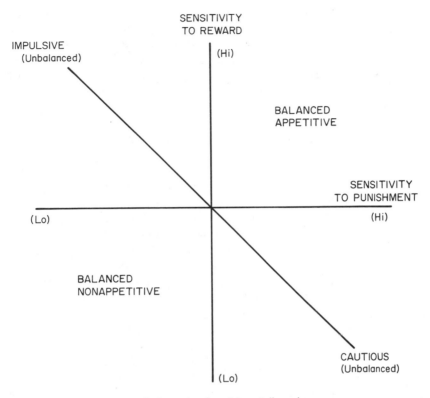

FIGURE 2. Reward and punishment dimensions.

Rothbart also reviews studies indicating different physiological substrates to approach and avoidance responses, with the former mediated by dopaminergic systems and the later by seratonergic systems. These data strongly implicate two independent systems underlying sensitivity to rewards and punishments, respectively.

As well, the dimension of emotionality described in Chapter 2 is not a unitary dimension. Factor-analytic research on arousal has identified two phenomenologically different types of arousal, termed by Thayer (1978, 1986) energetic arousal and tense arousal. Energetic arousal is characterized by adjectives such as energetic, lively, active, vigorous, and full-of-pep, and occurs when the subject is alert and energetic. Tense arousal on the other hand is characterized by adjectives such as tense, clutched-up, fearful, jittery, and intense and is accompanied by muscular tension. Other researchers on activation and mood have used terms such as positive and negative affect to describe Thayer's dimensions of energetic and tense arousal (e.g., Watson & Tellegen, 1985), and Thayer (1985) notes that energetic and tense arousal are moderately correlated at moderate levels of mood intensity. Similarly, in the developmental literature Rothbart (1986) has identified positive and negative reactivity as aspects of reactivity. Positive reactivity is characterized by behaviors such as smiling, laughter, and high activity, whereas negative reactivity includes fear and distress to limitations.

These two types of arousal are intimately related to the two self-regulatory dimensions. The arousal produced in response to signals of anticipated punishment is central to Gray's theory and we have noted in this chapter that arousal is also a concomitant of rewarded behavior. It is proposed that the arousal produced during anxiety is of the tense variety. Indeed, the adjectives used by Thayer (1987) to describe tense arousal read like an exact description of anxiety—clutched up, tense, fearful, and anxious. An anxious individual also has a high level of muscular tension. Consistent with this perspective, one of the effects of antianxiety drugs is to relax the muscles (Gray, 1982). The paradigmatically anxious person, having received a signal that punishment is about to occur, is tensely waiting and scanning the environment for possible means of avoiding the punishment. Behavior is inhibited and phenomenologically there is a feeling of tension. This is reflected in increased muscular tension.

The arousal produced by reward on the other hand is theorized to result in energetic arousal or positive reactivity. Again, the adjectives used by Thayer to describe energetic arousal describe someone who is in an affectively positive mood (peppy, lively, vigorous), as would occur if the person had just been rewarded. In Chapter 3 it is argued that parent–child physical play involves highly rewarding stimulation that is also energetically arousing.

Positing a unitary dimension of emotionality may serve as an adequate first approximation of this underlying complexity because both energetic and tense arousal are characterized by high levels of excitation. An individual who is highly reactive is prone to either energetic or tense arousal depending on whether the behavioral inhibition system or the reward system is being activated. Thus highly reactive individuals who are also highly cautious are expected to respond to novelty and threats of punishment with tense arousal whereas highly reactive impulsive individuals respond to the anticipation of reward with high levels of energetic arousal. A single unitary dimension of emotionality thus serves as an adequate first approximation for this underlying biological variation.

This perspective predicts that there will be some individuals who are highly sensitive to anticipated punishments and rewards respectively who are nevertheless not highly reactive. Recently Kagan, Reznick, and Snidman (1987) have shown that behavioral inhibition is independent of physiological measures of emotionality, as predicted by the present model. Within their group of behaviorally inhibited children (defined by their behavioral responses to novel stimulation) there is a group who respond with high and stable heart rate and a group that responds with a low and variable heart rate. In terms of the present model, the former group is high on emotionality, the latter is low on emotionality, and both are high on behavioral inhibition. Similarly, within the category of behaviorally uninhibited children there is a group with high emotionality and a group with low emotionality. In addition, evidence indicates that some highly impulsive, reward oriented children are extremely reactive to stimulation (hyperactive children) (see p. 104). On the other hand, Quay (1985) notes that some severe conduct-disorder children, a group that is highly impulsive and reward-oriented, are hypoarousable as indicated by the galvanic skin response test.

Thus, by distinguishing between emotionality and both sensitivity to rewards and sensitivity to punishment as separate dimensions, it is possible to develop a theory that is consistent with the factor-analytic work on the structure of personality. Moreover, the resulting theory retains a dimensional view of the biological variation underlying these phenomena rather than proposing qualitative categories as do Kagan et al. (1987). From an evolutionary perspective the adoption of a continuous trait approach is far more intuitively appealing than a qualitative approach, because polygenic traits, such as those presumably underlying personality and intelligence, tend to result in continuous distributions.

B. Arousal and Reward

This theory posits four separate physiological processes: sensitivity to rewards, sensitivity to punishments, energetic arousal, and tense arousal. The reward and punishment centers are postulated to be systems physiologically distinct from the arousal systems, but it is clear that arousal *per se* has rewarding and punishing aspects. Thus energetic arousal is pleasant and tense arousal is aversive, and it is expected therefore that individuals would seek and avoid these subjective feelings, respectively. An individual who knows he or she is about to be punished waits tensely and is motivated to alter his or her aversive feeling by avoiding the punishment. Nevertheless, the aversive feeling he or she is attempting to avoid is not the same as the aversively felt tense arousal, and this is crucial to Gray's theory of the behavioral inhibition system. Gray provides data showing that the antianxiety drugs do not impair the effectiveness of unconditionally punishing stimulation. Their action is on the individual's response to threatened punishment. Gray's work shows clearly that these drugs have the effect (among others) of decreasing arousal and muscular tension.

On the other hand, a person anticipating a reward awaits with energetic arousal (and perhaps a subjective feeling of hope), but this positive feeling is not the same feeling that occurs when the person is actually rewarded. Thus, the eager anticipation with which one awaits a good dinner is not the same as the pleasure involved in eating it. If the present theory is correct and as the animal data described in this chapter indicate (see p. 56), the rewards involved in eating the dinner will also be accompanied by energetic arousal. However, in this case there will be two separate sources of positive feelings, one the result of energetic arousal and the other the result of stimulating the reward centers involved in gustatory pleasure.

These points are consistent with Gray's (1982) idea that there are three physiologically distinct reinforcement systems, one involved in reward and nonpunishment, one in unconditioned punishment, and one in behavioral inhibition. In the first case (reward), it is proposed that the physiological basis is the median forebrain bundle and that stimulation of this area results in pleasure and also results in energetic arousal. Reward stimulation and energetic arousal then combine (perhaps additively) to result in a pleasant feeling. In the case of anticipation of the reward, the only reinforcing event is the feeling of energetic arousal, and this is phenomenologically and physiologically quite different than the feelings occurring while actually being rewarded, as actual reward involves also the stimulation of the median forebrain bundle reward centers.

In the case of unconditioned punishment, it is proposed that an analogous pain center is stimulated, resulting in aversive tense arousal as well as pain. In the case of behavioral inhibition, it is proposed that the aversive feeling is produced only by arousal resulting from the anticipation of the punishing event, that is, tense arousal. In this case, therefore, it is the aversiveness of tense arousal itself that is the sole motivating affect. Thus, as in

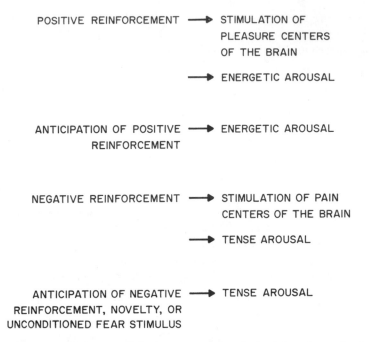

FIGURE 3. Proposed relationships among reinforcements, arousal, and stimulation of reward and punishment centers.

the case of rewards, there are two independent motivating affects that combine in the presence of actual punishment (tense arousal plus pain), whereas only one is present in the anticipation of the negative event (tense arousal). (See Figure 3 for a summary of all of these relationships.)

C. Implications for Learning Processes

Conditionability has always been central to Eysenck's theory of extraversion–introversion (E–I), so it is instructive to review the evidence on conditionability. Following Gray's (1982) logic, individuals who are high on impulsivity should be easy to condition with rewards because of their attractions to the rewards involved, although if they are high on caution they should be easy to condition to punishment because of their sensitivity to punishment. This point is crucial to Gray's theory and is also predicted by the theory developed here. Gray (1982) cites considerable evidence in favor of this viewpoint (see also Rothbart, in press-a).

However, by proposing two independent dimensions of sensitivity to rewards and sensitivity to punishments, the present theory also predicts that individuals who are high on both dimensions should be easily conditionable in general, whereas individuals low on both should be difficult to condition in general. Because emotionality is viewed as independent of impulsivity–caution, it should have no effect on conditioning (but see pp. 73–74). For example, two individuals who are equally sensitive to punishment are predicted to learn equally well by the threat of punishment independent of their emotionality, but if the person is highly emotional he or she will in addition be very tense and anxious while learning it. Similarly, two individuals who are very impulsive will be equally conditionable by rewards, but if one is more emotional than the other, there will also be an accompanying excitement and energetic arousal. Gray notes that, consistent with the present perspective, the results of Pavlov and his Soviet followers indicate no association between conditionability and strength of the nervous system (i.e., emotionality).

Moreover, studies of conditioning of hyperactive children are highly congruent with this perspective. In Chapter 3, it is argued that hyperactive children are high on both impulsivity-sensation seeking and emotionality. They are thus expected to be very strongly attracted to rewards during conditioning experiments and they are expected to become very emotionally aroused by the rewards and their anticipation. Douglas (1985) found exactly these results. Hyperactive children were often so interested in obtaining rewards during learning experiments that they became extremely excited and climbed all over the desk to get into the drawer where the rewards were kept and often seemed unaware of the contingencies required in order to earn them. Douglas (1985) notes that hyperactive children respond impulsively in learning experiments and tend to seek immediate gratification and stimulation. However, as predicted by Gray's theory, because hyperactive children are very sensitive to rewards, there is no difference between hyperactives and control children on continuous reinforcement schedules. Performance during partial reinforcement, however, is deficient, because many responses are unrewarded. Loss of reward often provokes very strong emotional response, and during extinction the performance of hyperactive children returned to baseline much more quickly than did that of normal children. The behavior of these children thus suggests very strong attraction to rewards and immediate gratification as well as strong emotionality. As predicted, their arousal is of the energetic variety.

Other clinical data which can be incorporated into the theory of temperament derive from studies of primary sociopaths. For example, Schmauk (1970) found that these individuals had very low anticipatory arousal, anxiety, and avoidance learning under conditions in which incorrect choices were followed by shock or negative feedback. However if money is taken away for incorrect choices, the subjects scored approximately the same as normals. These individuals thus conform to the profile of a highly impulsive person—low on sensitivity to punishments and high on sensitivity to reward.

D. Predictions Resulting from the Theory

1. The strongest correlates between biological measures and the vertical dimension of Figure 1 will be with impulsivity, not extraversion–introversion (E–I); sociability will be even less correlated. This follows because the extremes of the dimension are an imbalance between sensitivity to rewards and sensitivity to punishment, that is, impulsivity versus caution. As a result Eysenck's factors are incorrectly placed, and should be rotated approximately 30 deg to the right so that they run through impulsivity. The rotation of the factors in space is an important aspect of any theory because various phenotypic classification schemes are consistent with each other. As Gray (1981) states:

> The decision where to place factor dimensions in space is a theoretical one: it is to play a hunch it
> is here, not there, that the causal influences will be found. (p. 250)

Once the mechanism is understood at the physiological level it is possible to provide a very strong rationale for the proposed configuration. This, in fact, is the motivation for the search by Eysenck and others to find this biological substrate. In Gray's (1982) critique of Eysenck, he states that impulsivity is indeed the strongest correlate of biological studies of extraversion, that E–I is less correlated, and that sociability is not correlated at all. The findings for sociability are as predicted because sociability is even more to the left of the biological basis of personality than is E–I.

2. *It is predicted that there will be a negative correlation between measures of everyday feelings of tension and degree of impulsivity.* This is the case because cautious individuals will tend to react with tense arousal in response to everyday stresses and strains. However, the correlation between everyday energetic arousal and impulsivity should be substantially higher. This is because the impulsive person will actively seek out rewarding environments and will become at least moderately aroused by them even if low on emotionality, whereas cautious individuals will not be attracted to situations that would tend to result in arousal at all, because the arousal they tend to feel is aversive tense arousal. Only when subjected to situations such as dangers or novelty that are beyond control or the result of great need will the cautious person be found to be aroused. Such a person should exhibit a great deal of active and passive avoidance to these situations.

In laboratory situations where one can control the types of stimulation presented, it is expected that the correlations will be the same, that is, given a sample of individuals who are high on impulsivity and normally distributed on emotionality these individuals should exhibit energetic arousal in response to a given level of rewarding environmental stimulation in proportion to their degree of emotionality. Similarly for a highly cautious sample normally distributed with respect to emotionality, there should be a response of tense arousal proportionate to the novelty or danger of the stimulation. These predictions are supported by findings reported by Rothbart (in press-b) in which children who approach novel stimulation quickly tend also to smile and laugh more, whereas those who are fearful tend to be more likely to be highly susceptible to discomfort and negative reactivity.

These predictions are also compatible with the data on cross-cultural variation in temperament described in Chapter 2. Asians are higher on behavioral inhibition than Caucasians and as a result exhibit more anxiety and tense arousal than Caucasians. Caucasians are lower on this dimension and thus are more likely to exhibit excitation and energetic arousal in response to unfamiliar events. This suggests that the temperamental difference between Asians and Caucasians is not a difference in emotionality but rather represents only a difference in behavioral inhibition. Caucasians will appear more excitable than Asians not because they are more emotional but because, since they are lower on behavioral inhibition, they are more prone to energetic arousal.

3. *It is predicted that in a sample of highly emotional individuals who are normally distributed with respect to impulsivity-caution, individuals who are highly cautious will respond with tense arousal at a much lower level of intensity of stimulation than highly impulsive individuals.* However, there is some level of stimulation at which even individuals who are high on impulsivity will react with tense arousal. Such levels may not be reached in laboratory experiments with ethical controls on human-subject research.

This prediction is validated by patterns of sex differences in the emotional tendencies of boys and girls. Buss and Plomin (1984) note that girls are much more inclined to fear whereas boys are more inclined to anger. We have noted that the trait of sensation seeking is heritable and that boys are much higher on this trait than girls (see also Chapter 6). Thus it is expected and found that highly emotional girls are much more likely to react to novelty and danger with fear, anxiety, and tense arousal, whereas boys are more likely to respond with energetic arousal and behaviors indicating a lack of behavioral inhibition.

4. It is predicted that in a sample of individuals low on emotionality who are normally distributed with respect to impulsivity-caution, there will be a trend similar to that described previously for highly impulsive individuals to react with tense arousal at higher levels of stimulus intensity than cautious individuals. However, the intensity of stimulation required to produce a similar level of arousal in this sample is predicted to be much higher than in the sample described in Prediction 4. That is, because such individuals are less emotional they will require a higher level of stimulation to reach tense arousal at a similar level of impulsivity-caution.

5. It is predicted that impulsive individuals will be easily conditionable by rewards whereas cautious individuals will be predicted to be easily conditionable by punishments. (See pp. 68–69 for the evidence that this is the case.)

6. It is predicted that emotionality will be uncorrelated with conditionability. (See p. 69 for the evidence that this is the case.)

Several predictions follow from the suggestion that sensitivities to rewards and punishments are independent dimensions rather than the single dimension proposed in the simplified system:

1. It is predicted that there should be a group of individuals who are as sensitive to rewards as highly impulsive individuals and as sensitive to punishment as highly cautious individuals—the hi-hi group. It is also predicted that there is a group of individuals who are neither sensitive to rewards nor sensitive to punishments—the lo-lo group. These groups should be indistinguishable with respect to their scores on impulsivity-caution, and indeed their intermediacy on this dimension is the reason impulsivity–caution is usefully viewed as a single dimension of personality. However, there should be a major difference between these groups regarding their conditionability. Whereas the lo-lo group should be difficult to condition using either type of reward, the hi-hi group should be highly conditionable to either rewards or punishments. This proposition follows the logic of Gray in deducing Prediction 6 above.

2. It is predicted that hi-hi individuals who are also high on emotionality (the hi-hi-hi group) will be particularly prone to both energetic and tense arousal. This follows because the high emotionality of these individuals makes them very reactive to environmental events of a rewarding or a punishing kind, and thus susceptible to high levels of energetic and tense arousal. The hi-hi-lo group would be equally conditionable and equally intermediate on impulsivity–caution, but would be much less reactive in general.

3. The theory also predicts that there will be a group of individuals whose reward systems remain relatively unelaborated but who are nevertheless highly emotional (the lo-lo-hi group). This group would appear to be a rather strange group of individuals who would be expected to be very emotional but with little apparent reason for being this way. That is, their emotionality would not be an aspect of strongly appetitive behavior. Although the emotionality of an individual who is strongly in pursuit of a reward or intensely seeking to avoid punishment is an easily understandable phenomenon, the behavior of an individual such as that described above would seem bizarre and unmotivated. It would be difficult to shape the behavior of such an individual by normal sources of motivation, either positive or negative, so that the individual would not easily conform to social standards. Such an individual would be little attracted to sexual behavior or, as a child, rough and tumble play, and not find social relationships of any kind rewarding.

The other type of lo-lo group would be similarly unmotivated but not given to high reactivity and emotional outbursts (the lo-lo-lo group). Such individuals would be expected to be similarly unmotivated as the lo-lo-hi group, but in addition it is expected that such individuals would be very flat affectively. Cloninger (1987), whose work is discussed in this chapter, suggests that the schizoid personality is characterized (in the present terminology) as low in impulsivity and low in emotionality, but does not distinguish between sensitivity to rewards and punishments.

Overall, the lo-lo group are hypothesized to be particularly likely to be represented in psychiatric populations and I would suggest that this constellation of traits is characteristic of various types of schizophrenia depending on how the individual stands on the traits of emotionality and positive social reward. As indicated above, Cloninger (1987) describes individuals who are low in emotionality and low in impulsivity as schizoid, and he describes individuals who are high on emotionality and low on impulsivity as obsessional. An obsessive person, however, is presumably very sensitive to threatened punishment, so that this would not be identical with the lo-lo-hi individual proposed here.

One might propose that lo-lo individuals would be particularly difficult to socialize no matter where they stood on the positive social reward dimension with the result that they would not elicit positive social interactions with their caretakers. Given the proposed susceptibility to environmental influence for this dimension, it would be expected that such individuals would also tend to be relatively detached and unattracted to warmth and nurturance.

E. Conclusion

The above theory is consistent with an essentially three-factor theory of personality (impulsivity–caution, emotionality, and positive social reward), while at the same time providing a much greater degree of richness. The theory is very closely tied to particular physiological systems and thus provides a rationale for a particular rotation of the factors discovered in factor analytic personality research. Moreover, the theory makes a great many predictions, many of which have already been confirmed and many of which are not at all the same as those predicted by other theories. In the framework of philosophical realism discussed in Chapter 1, it is hoped that the theory is a little closer to the truth about personality, but whether or not this is so will be determined by the results of future empirical studies.

It should also be noted that the theory is able to provide an intuitively plausible account for many of the findings that have been used to support Eysenck's present theory. As described in Chapter 2, Eysenck (1967, 1982) based his theory of personality on the proposition that introverts have higher levels of cortical arousal and thus seek to avoid stimulation, whereas extraverts have low levels of this arousal and thus seek higher levels of stimulation. This optimal level theory of E–I predicts that introverts should be relatively easily overaroused by stimulation and thus tend to avoid it, whereas extraverts should be much more difficult to overstimulate. Eysenck claims considerable success in showing that these relationships exist. For example, Eysenck (1982) describes data indicating that introverts condition better under conditions of low-stimulus intensity, whereas extraverts condition better under high-stimulus intensity. In the former case, high-intensity stimulation brings introverts beyond their optimal level of arousal, although in the latter case such stimulation brings extraverts closer to their optimal level of arousal.

In this chapter reasons were provided for supposing that the theory of optimal level of arousal is inadequate as a theory of extraversion. It is interesting to note that Eysenck's theory of the biological basis of extraversion–introversion really supposes that introverts are more reactive than extraverts. Eysenck (1982) cites Pavlov's law of transmarginal inhibition as a physiological basis for supposing that in situations of high-stimulus intensity introverts will develop more inhibition and thus more aversion to the stimulus. In terms of the present theory and in conformity with Pavlov's idea of the strength of the nervous system, the relative excitation–inhibition in response to a given level of stimulation is a defining feature of reactivity, and this idea implies an optimal level of stimulation that would differ between individuals depending on their reactivity. In this volume, the idea of an optimal level of stimulation will be essential to the discussion of physical play in Chapter 3. It is interesting that Eysenck's dimension of neuroticism is clearly also a reactive dimension, differing only in the proposed physiological systems thought to be reactive. Whereas E–I depends on differences in the optimal level of stimulation for pleasant cortical arousal, neuroticism refers to balance or imbalance in the autonomic nervous system, also a system that reacts more or less strongly to environmental stimulation.

In a recent critique of Eysenck's theory of personality, Thayer, Takahashi, and Paul (1988) note that physiologically the autonomic arousal system underlying neuroticism and the cortical arousal system proposed to underlie E–I are interdependent (Duffy, 1962), and indeed Rothbart (1987) notes that they are highly correlated. These two types of arousal reactivity are thus totally inappropriate as the foundations of a theory of independent dimensions of personality, and the theory developed here combines both of these aspects of arousal into a general notion of reactivity (emotionality)—Pavlov's strength of the nervous system—as does that of Rothbart (1987). The other dimension, as indicated above, involves sensitivity to rewards and punishments, and is physiologically independent of the arousal dimension of emotionality.

It is an important corollary of the theory developed here that emotionality strongly interacts with impulsivity–caution and that this interaction yields the categories of individuals described by Eysenck's E–I. Emotionality as proposed here is an activation system for behavior which is physiologically independent of the limbic reward and punishment systems but in addition has its own motivating properties (see p. 67). Thus, an individual who is highly cautious and also highly emotional is strongly motivated to avoid the possibly negative results of risky behavior, but in addition is prone to high levels of anxiety (tense arousal) in anticipation of punishment. He or she is thus doubly avoidant of risk and novelty. Consistent with this idea, Kagan et al. (1987) found that among their behaviorally inhibited children, those who were high on emotionality were the most behaviorally inhibited.

The most cautious individuals are thus expected to be highly emotional, but, in addition, the most impulsive individuals are expected to be low on emotionality. This follows because an extremely impulsive individual, if also highly emotional, will tend to become overaroused relatively easily. This is expected to result in an increase in tense arousal, which will tend to dampen ongoing behavior because of its aversiveness. Such a person would be expected to show ambivalent behavior—highly attracted to rewards, but also finding the pursuit of those rewards more costly in affective terms. In Chapter 3 the physical play of hyperactive and sociometrically rejected children is characterized as closely resembling this description, as there are high levels of both approaching stimulation and withdrawing from it with expressions of overarousal. A less-emotional, impulsive person would not find this level of stimulation overwhelming and would thus continue the pursuit of reward with a feeling of energetic arousal. Consistent with this interpretation, Quay (1985) notes that adolescents diagnosed as exhibiting severe conduct disorder, a group that is highly impulsive and reward-oriented, are hypoarousable as indicated by the galvanic skin response test.

These two extremes of individuals will thus act according to Eysenck's optimal-level-of-arousal theory of E–I; that is, highly extraverted individuals will be low on emotionality and strongly seek rewards. Because they are low on emotionality, they will not become overaroused when pursuing rewards or when being rewarded, and their behavior will be interpretable as seeking a higher level of cortical arousal—Eysenck's conceptualization of the classic extravert. The other extreme will be individuals who are highly cautious and also highly emotional. Their behavior will be interpretable as seeking lower levels of cortical arousal—Eysenck's conceptualization of the classic introvert. Thus, Eysenck's conceptualization of E–I in interpretable within the present framework, despite the fact that this framework involves a reinterpretation of both of Eysenck's dimensions.

It is an important point that the physiological basis of personality need not coincide with the psychometric extremes of the distribution. This was also implied in the analysis of the reward and punishment systems described above. In this case the psychometric extremes were simply the most unbalanced individuals, not the ones who were higher on either trait considered separately, and this will be the case whenever two dimensions interact as closely as these two dimensions are proposed to do. The above analysis implies a similar synergistic effect in the case of emotionality and impulsivity–caution.

The theory described here clearly begins with a theory of the biological basis of personality and then works upward to explain some of the phenotypic variation that is found. There are many advantages of such a method, not the least of which is that the two proposed dimensions are highly congruent with an adaptationist account of personality (see "Temperament and Adaptation" on pp. 61–62). This is especially clear in the case of impulsivity-caution where sex differences in accordance with evolutionary theory are particularly marked (see Chapter 6). Because sex is such an important differentiating factor in human evolution, it is highly likely that the biological basis of this personality difference is the crux of a real focus of natural selection and thus constitutes a fundamental personality dimension. Given a theory that is soundly based in specific brain structures and interactions as well as one that makes sense in adaptationist terms, there would be theoretical justification for performing nonorthogonal rotations of the dimensions derived from factor analysis. The present theory implies that the extremes of phenotypic im-

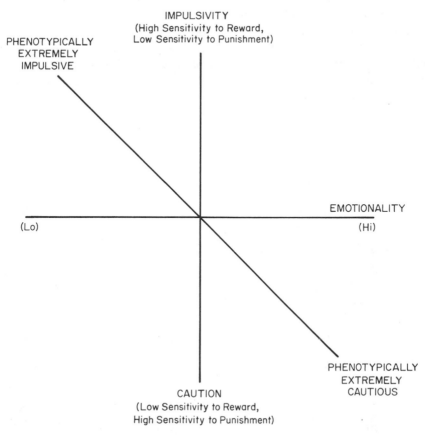

FIGURE 4. Relationships among emotionality and extremes of phenotypic impulsivity and caution.

pulsivity–caution will not be orthogonal to the emotionality dimension (see Figure 4). Also, because an interaction between emotionality and impulsivity–caution is proposed, the phenotypic extremes of impulsivity–caution will not be a simple reflection of the underlying biological trait of impulsivity–caution. Indeed, it might be argued that it is far more rational to develop a theory of the biological basis of personality and then construct personality tests and rotate factors than it is to construct personality tests and then look for biological underpinnings. In the latter case, if the construction is incorrect, the search for biological underpinnings will be futile, and there is no other means of determining the truth of the theory. And there is always the danger that one will attempt to achieve the simplicity of adopting orthogonal factors when nature may have other things in mind. If one starts with a theory of the biological basis of personality, on the other hand, a clear, principled factor structure in the psychometric test should result, a factor structure that accurately reflects the underlying biology. If the theory is incorrect, this clear, theoretically expected factor structure will not occur and the empirical predictions made on the basis of these tests will not be confirmed. Thus there is a clear sense in which theory construction is ultimately confirmable or disconfirmable. From the realist philosophical perspective, these constant interactions between theory and data collection are thus not incompatible with the idea that eventually the truth will emerge: Inadequate theories simply cannot explain all of the data (as appears to be the case with the theories of both Eysenck and Gray). Good theories do a better job because they more adequately reflect the state of what is going on out there.

The Development of the Emotions

In their review of the literature on socioemotional development, Campos, Barrett, Lamb, Goldsmith, and Stenberg (1983) point out a dramatic change in the *Zeitgeist* concerning the importance of emotion in understanding behavior. Whereas the study of emotion held considerable importance in the early part of this century, by 1970 there were very few references to emotion in standard reference works in the area of developmental psychology. Moreover, the only interest in emotion that occurred at all was in cases where emotions were used as dependent variables to measure some cognitive or perceptual process. For example, one way to determine the cognitive capabilities of infants is to observe the "smile of assimilation" shown in response to discrepant schemas (Kagan, 1971). In recent years, however, the study of emotion has generated a number of new theories, and there is a large mass of data on the functions of emotion in the social behavior of children as well as on developmental changes in the emotions.

I. THEORIES OF EMOTIONAL DEVELOPMENT

A. The Theory of Carrol Izard

Izard (1971, 1972, 1977, 1984) has proposed a strongly biological theory of the emotions. Izard proposes that there are ten fundamental emotions: interest, joy, surprise, distress, anger, disgust, contempt, fear, shame/shyness, and guilt. Each emotion has a neurophysiological, an expressive, and a phenomenological component. The expressive component, especially facial expression, is particularly important, since it is feedback from the facial expression that provides stimulation to the brain that is necessary for subjective emotional experience. The neural mechanisms for both emotional expression and emotional experience are regarded as innate and primarily determined by maturational processes. Moreover, the emotions emerge as they become adaptive in the life of the child.

Much of the evidence for Izard's hypothesis of the innateness of emotion comes from cross-cultural research demonstrating that the basic emotions can be recognized from facial expressions without any information on the context of the expression. In these studies, photographs of individuals with particular emotional expressions are shown to subjects, who are then asked what emotion is being experienced by the person in the photograph. Using these methods in a sample of literate cultures, Ekman, Sorenson, and Friesen (1969) found that the emotions of happiness, sadness, surprise, fear, anger, and disgust were reliably identified. Even more impressively, it was found that adults in nonliterate cultures could identify these emotions, with the exception that fear and anger were not distinguished from each other, although they were distinguished from the others. The fact that these basic emotions can be observed in infancy is also strong evidence for a strong biological basis for emotional expression.

Consistent with his general deemphasis on the cognitive aspects of emotions, Izard believes that each emotion is characterized by a unique feeling state, which serves the function of motivating behavior. Unlike Kagan, Izard argues that the basic emotions result in subjective feelings that are the same throughout the life span: Even though the events that elicit emotions change radically as a result of cognitive development, the anger felt by an infant ''feels'' the same as the anger felt by an adolescent. The eliciting events for emotions can range from highly innate connections, such as the ''natural clues'' of Bowlby (1969; see also Chapter 4), to a wide variety of learned associations. As the child gets older and is able to use symbolic processes, the roles of perception and cognition become increasingly prominent.

Regarding the central question of the ways in which these biologically based emotions interact with cognition, Izard states that until the acquisition of short-term memory in infancy there need be no cognition at all for emotions to occur. The biologically preprogrammed emotional expressions simply occur as the result of what Izard terms *affective processing*. For example, infants between 1½ and 5 months of age will smile in response to the face of adults indiscriminately. Although the infant must be able to discriminate facelike from nonfacelike objects, there is no need for comparison or matching of the perceptual input to some standard. These latter activities are clearly cognitive, but during early infancy the expression of emotions is better described by what Bowlby (1969; see also Chapter 4) refers to as ''natural clues,'' that is, innate connections between certain stimulus events and affective states. Izard argues that it would be odd indeed, considering the adaptive and motivational roles of the emotions, if the baby really was unable to experience the motivational aspect of its subjective feelings even if it could not represent the feelings cognitively.

Despite the deemphasis on the importance of cognition in analyzing the emotions of infants, Izard argues that at later ages the expression of emotions comes to be more under voluntary control and is achieved by controlling the superficial musculature of the face. Cognitive control of emotional expression is thus possible, as individuals are able to give the appearance of having an emotion without really having it. However, since feedback from the facial musculature is believed by Izard to result in emotional experience, there is a tendency for individuals who are giving the appearance of having a particular emotion to actually feel that emotion.

Izard also argues, along with Zajonc (1980) and Bower (1981), that emotions and cognition are separate, independent systems, with affective processing often occurring prior to cognitive processing. For example, there is evidence that being in a particular emotional state has a variety of effects on cognitive processing. Subjects who have been induced to be happy will tend to perform differently on cognitive tasks, and selectively attend to, learn, and remember different types of information (see Izard, 1984, for a review). Thus, in an experiment that addresses many of the concerns of Izard's theory, Laird, Wagener, Halal, and Szedja (1982) showed that individuals instructed to manipulate their facial muscles in patterns that mimic emotional expressions were better able to recall passages from a text that was similar in emotional tone to the induced expression; i.e., individuals mimicking angry expressions were better able to recall information from an angry passage than from a happy one. The fact that emotions can influence cognition and occur prior to cognition does not deny that often cognition will influence emotions and occur prior to the emotions.

B. The Theory of L. Alan Sroufe

Sroufe (1979b) begins his presentation with a discussion of the inadequacies of a learning theory of emotional development. Learning theories are said to be insufficient to account for the fact that babies show rage when their heads are restrained, since there is no pain, and thus no negative reinforcement, involved. In addition, wariness to unfamiliar faces and the initial instances of separation protest are said to be inexplicable on a learning view, since this wariness occurs even in the absence of any actual negative experiences with unfamiliar people. Moreover, learning theories are inadequate in accounting for instances of positive affect in general. As emphasized by the ethological view of attachment and the emotions presented in Chapter 4 and in this chapter (see pp. 97–98), there is no reason to suppose that the behaviors of parents that make infants happy acquire their ability to do so as a result of some the prior reinforcement history of the pair. For example, infants do not enjoy games of peek-a-boo because their mothers feed them after playing a game. Instead, Sroufe describes mother–infant interaction as based on reciprocity and synchrony rather than reinforcement. Finally, Sroufe describes the work of Ainsworth and her colleagues (see e.g., Ainsworth, 1974) indicating that contingent response to crying is associated with reduced crying, rather than with increased crying as a reinforcement theory would predict.

Sroufe also criticizes drive-reduction theories and energy-distribution theories deriving from psychoanalysis as similarly unable to account for positive affect. These theories posit that there are internal, endogenous sources of energy, which are constantly building up and requiring release. Thus, Freud believed that the libido was an internal source of sexual energy, which was constantly building up and seeking expression in self-gratifying types of behavior. This energy could be repressed by the ego or by parenting practices. Similarly, the classical ethologists conceived of aggression as resulting from the buildup and release of an action-specific energy, which was released when triggered by the environment. These views have been discredited in a number of ways, but they are especially inappropriate as an account of emotional development. Sroufe notes that the laughing that occurs during social games such as physical play cannot be analyzed as reducing tension, but occurs when arousal is already high. Moreover, as will be shown in Section II of this chapter, rather than always attempting to reduce arousal and tension, infants often actively seek out sources of highly arousing stimulation. In addition, the child, rather than gradually building up an internal tension that is awaiting release, is often the relatively passive recipient of parental attempts at stimulation. Rather than conceive of the child as an internally regulated energy machine, it is far more appropriate to conceive of it as an active stimulus seeker and potential responder to appropriate stimulation.

Purely cognitive models of emotional development are criticized by Sroufe as insufficient to account for developmental data on attachment and positive affect in general. For example, as will be shown in Chapter 4, Bowlby's (1969) theory of attachment postualtes that behavior in the Strange Situation is activated when the value of the set point is exceeded. If the mother strays beyond this point, attachment behaviors are triggered in the baby. However, the value of the set point changes over time and is a function of the sensitivity and responsiveness of the caregiver. There is no purely cognitive account of how developmental changes in the set point can occur, and Sroufe and Waters (1977) propose instead that changes in felt security, an affective concept, mediate these developmental changes. The purely cognitive theory of Mandler (1975) is also rejected because it postulates that emotion is the result of an interruption of plans. Although such a conception can account for some emotions, there is no obvious way in which such a theory can account for the positive emotions that occur during social games or when viewing a sunset.

Regarding the important question of the relation between affect and cognition, Sroufe argues that these notions are inseparable, that indeed there can be no noncognitive theory of emotion. Cognitions such as those involved in the recognition of individuals, the concepts of causality, object permanence, and intentionality are necessary conditions for the occurrence of emotions. Affect also influences cognition, however, and Sroufe suggests that an infant first learns many cognitive concepts in a highly affectively charged context; for example, becoming angry could crystallize the relationships among the concepts of self, object, and obstacle.

Sroufe proposes that feelings as well as information are required in attempting to account for changing sensitivities found in the Strange Situation. The same external information may be given new meaning because of the affective experience with which the information has been associated. If the infant's mother does not return, the original protest may give way to despair and finally to detachment without any change in the external information. What has changed is the affective evaluation of this information.

In addition, Sroufe proposes the necessity of a tension construct to account for emotional behavior in infancy. Both tension fluctuation and the cumulative buildup of tension are required. The buildup of tension is proposed as a fundamental process underlying the negative emotions. The rage that an infant experiences when its head is restrained is thus the result of gradually built up, unreleased tension. Similarly, infants attending to a visual stimulus often become highly distressed because they cannot disengage from the stimulus, again due to the gradual increase in tension. If the tension is released, the infant shows positive affect.

In addition to the idea of the cumulation of tension, Sroufe proposes that a concept of tension fluctuation is required to account for positive affect. The termination of an unpleasant situation for an infant is often associated with a positive affective display. Laughter and smiling are viewed as involving a buildup and release of tension, with the former involving a more rapid fluctuation than the latter.

Sroufe argues that the tension aroused by the event is not merely the result of stimulation *per se,* but is the result of the infant's *engagement* of the event. In other words, the infant does not merely respond to the event, but is cognitively aroused by it.

There is a transaction between the infant and the event, and the infant's active engagement of the event makes possible the tension produced. Infants actively seek a moderate amount of tension and the positive emotions are the result of tension fluctuations, with no particular amount of tension being necessarily aversive.

Sroufe's account is basically cognitive, because it postulates the interpretation or evaluation of the stimulus as a necessary condition for emotion. A given level of stimulation can be interpreted as positive or negative, with the direction of the effect determined by contextual factors. Thus, if the baby is tickled in the familiar surroundings of home, the stimulation may be evaluated positively, while if it occurs in an unfamiliar laboratory situation, the stimulation will be evaluated negatively. Within this framework, Sroufe proposes that the caregiver could promote growth by developing tolerance in the child for higher levels of tension so that even fairly high levels of tension are positively evaluated.

For Sroufe, then, emotions are at the center of social development:

> In an important way, understanding emotional development is understanding the development of the zestful, affectively expressive child, who enjoys and is a source of enjoyment for others, who seeks out sources of gratification and pleasure using personal and environmental resources, and who generally moves toward its experience, as well as understanding the child who is retreating from affective contact with the environment, being unable to cope with the tensions inherent in such contact. (Sroufe, 1979b, p. 508)

This remark indicates the close association between the theory of emotions and the theory of temperament. As indicated in Chapter 2, temperament involves centrally the reactivity to stimulation as well as the self-regulation of stimulation that is perceived as rewarding.

C. The Theory of Campos and Barrett

Campos and Barrett (1984) characterize emotion as having three features: (a) Emotions are regulators of social and interpersonal behavior; (b) emotions regulate the flow of information and influence the responses of the child; (c) the basic emotions, such as anger, joy, surprise, sadness, and fear, are genetically "hardwired," that is, they are highly canalized expressions of basic biological processes. Like Izard, then, they consider the production of emotions as well as their decoding in others to be uninfluenced by social learning.

However, the elicitation of emotions and their quality are profoundly influenced by the cognitions of the individual, and particularly important are cognitions referring to the goals of the child. Following Roseman (1979), they view individuals as monitoring the relationship between events and goals, and the outcome of this process results in an emotional reaction. For example, if a child goes to the store to buy some candy and finds on reaching the store that it has lost its money, the child would exhibit a negative emotional response. Campos and Barrett refer to the cognitions relating the present situation to the goal of the child as *appreciations,* and emphasize that appreciations add something beyond mere knowledge of the goal of the person and the input received from the situation. Some of these goals, however, especially in the human infant, may be prewired genetically rather than result from social constructions. Moreover, like Izard (1977), they propose that although the goals that elicit a particular emotion may change throughout development, particular relations between goals and emotions may be unchanging, leading to the existence of what they term a ''core of affective continuity across the lifespan.'' For example, anger in an infant may be elicited by an obstacle to some very concrete goal, while in an adolescent the goal may be symbolic. In both cases the frustration of not being able to attain one's goal results in anger and this feeling has the same phenomenological ''feeling'' at both ages.

D. The Theory of Jerome Kagan

Kagan (1984a) uses the term *emotion* to refer to the interrelationships among external events, cognitive appraisals, and internal feeling states. He disputes the notion, so central to biological theories of emotion such as that of Izard (1978), that there is a discrete set of emotions that are biologically more fundamental than others. He points out that many cultures have emotions that they consider to be even more fundamental than those given importance by Western psychologists. For example, the emotion of enlightenment was highly valued by 13th-century Buddhist monks. Basic emotions, such as those described by Izard (1978), are pragmatically important in dealing with encounters with the world, but there is no sense in which they are more basic than other emotions.

Kagan emphasizes the context in which internal feelings are evaluated. Like many cognitive theorists of emotion (e.g., Schacter & Singer, 1962; Schacter, 1964), Kagan emphasizes that our cognitions ''frame'' how we interpret a particular feeling state. Thus, a headache can be evaluated as a symptom of anxiety or as a symptom of sadness and this label will determine what emotion we may be feeling. Moreover, the labels we use for our internal feeling states are really constructs that reflect a very loose covariation among external events, cognitive appraisals, and internal biological states. Emotion words are not like words such as ''tree'' that refer to a discrete material entity, but are arbitrary classifiers of combinations of external events, appraisals, and states. However, despite the general cognitive flavor of the theory, Kagan does distinguish between emotions, which require cognitive evaluations, and *feeling tones,* which do not. The latter are said to be typical of the first 4 months of life, when it is likely that the infant does not cognitively evaluate its feelings. Although they may often appear to be the same as real emotions, such as anger, because of the lack of evaluation they are not classified as emotions. Thus, for Kagan it is a logical truth rather than an emipirical truth that emotions involve cognitive evaluations.

This perspective on emotion, contrary to that of Izard (1978) and that of Campos and Barrett (1984), denies any developmental continuity to emotions as well as any cross-cultural generality. Since the cognitive appraisal of a particular event will change as the child becomes older and thus more cognitively sophisticated, so will the experienced emotion change. Similarly, different cultures will have vastly different ways of categorizing feelings, so that, for example, one culture (the Ifaluk of the Caroline Islands) classifies emotions by their incentive conditions (actions of others versus one's own thought processes), while another culture (our own) classifies emotions in terms of their intensity and whether they are evaluated positively or negatively. Kagan notes, however, that such a position is counterintuitive because it would suggest that people from different cultures would experience a different feeling state when confronted with a coiled snake. However, he proposes that within a particular class of feelings, in this case that of fear, there may be subtle differences among cultures due to differences in how the experiences are evaluated. Moreover, in keeping with this relativistic approach, Kagan argues that a scientist working within a culture can never be certain that instances of an emotion in two different children really feel subjectively the same to the children experiencing them. Even if the children use the same term to describe their feelings, this does not imply that in fact they have the same feelings. Thus, self-report data on emotions cannot tell us if two subjects really are experiencing things in the same manner.

Kagan states that the goal of science is to find lawful associations between the external incentive events and responses of the child. These response classes in turn reflect some internal emotional state. To the extent that a scientist finds regularities between the external incentive events and responses of children, there will be justification for speaking of a generalized emotional state in children in these circumstances. Thus, if a variety of circumstances reliably give rise to a certain facial expression (e.g., fear) as well as a typical vocal response and perhaps the cessation of play, there is justification for the scientific use of an emotional construct that refers to these coherencies. However, the scientist cannot be certain that in fact different children really feel the same way when these regularities occur, and the labeling of the emotion as fear in this case is quite arbitrary.

E. The Theory of Lewis and His Colleagues

Lewis and his colleagues (Lewis & Michalson, 1983; Lewis, Sullivan, & Michalson, 1984) postulate five major components for the emotions: (a) *Emotional elicitors* are the events or situations that impinge on the emotion receptors of the organism. (b) *Emotional receptors* are the pathways within the CNS that mediate between the emotional elicitors and changes in the physiological and cognitive states of the organism. (c) *Emotional states* refer to the physiological changes in the organism when an emotion is experienced. (d) *Emotional expressions* are the behavioral manifestations of the emotion, such as facial expressions. (e) *Emotional experiences* refer to the subjective feelings and evaluations of the person having the emotional experience. These subjective experiences can be strongly influenced by previous social experiences.

A central issue addressed by Lewis and his colleagues is the relation between emotion and cognition. Lewis *et al.* (1984) present three possible relationships and data that conform to them. First, emotion may occur as a result of cognition. This point of view is common to many cognitive theories of the elicitation of emotion. For example, Arnold (1960) and Lazarus (1982) propose that emotions result from cognitive appraisals that essentially evaluate stimuli according to their perceived effects on the individual's well-being. For example, if an individual evaluates a situation as indicating that he or she will shortly be run over by a train, he or she will evaluate this situation negatively and have the emotion of fear. Another type of cognitive theory posits that discrepancies between external stimuli and internal schemas result in an emotional response. Thus, Kagan (1974) argues that infants confronting a discrepant event will react with a decreased heart rate and an inhibition of motor activity. If the infant is unable to assimilate the event, fear may result, but if the event is easily assimilated, the infant may show boredom. Thus, the emotion that results is the consequence of the infant's cognitive processing of the stimulus. Lewis *et al.* (1984) point out that the mechanism whereby these cognitive events result in emotion is unknown, but they make the reasonable suggestion that in many cases the connection is prewired into the nervous system. Thus, discrepancies between stimuli and schemas, failure to assimilate, and the acquisition or violation of an expectation could result in an emotion "through their direct effect on as yet unspecified receptors" (Lewis *et al.*, 1984, p. 269). Indeed, it is difficult to imagine any other mechanism for the general tendency to react emotionally to these types of events independent of specific content. On the other hand, in some cases the specific content of the event may be important and the emotion produced as a result of a previously learned association: The fear that a child shows when seeing an adult who has abused him or her would not be due to a discrepancy between stimulus and schema, the failure to assimilate, or a violation of expectation, but rather to specific past experiences with that adult.

Cognitions can also influence emotional expression, as would occur if a person was attempting to deceive another by feigning an emotion or by concealing inappropriate emotions. Moreover, cognitions can affect emotional experience. For example, Mandler (1980) proposes that the interruption of an ongoing activity results in arousal and that the interpretation of this arousal results in specific emotions. Thus, anger might result if an individual believes another person is responsible for the interruption, whereas joy may result if a goal is attained.

The second type of relationship between emotion and cognition is that emotion is an antecedent of cognition. In addition to the types of examples provided by Izard (1984) (see above), Lewis *et al.* (1984) point out that individuals often engage in activities in order to be able to experience the emotion that goes along with the activity, much as a skydiver engages in that activity because of the thrills that are anticipated. Although the emotion follows in time the behavior that results in it, it is the expectation of the emotion that drives the behavior in the first place. Many of the emotions that motivate behavior in this manner are presumably unlearned, as is argued below in the case of the affective responses occurring during physical play between parents and children. Some, such as doing well in an exam, are undoubtedly learned. It should be pointed out, however, that in these cases it is not really the emotion that results in the cognition, but rather the expectation of having the emotion that results in cognitive processes that lead to action and hence the desired emotion.

Lewis *et al.* (1984) then propose that the two linear models of the relation between emotion and cognition described above are inadequate and propose a third model in which emotion and cognition are intricately woven together, a process they term the cognitive–emotional fugue. In this model, they conceive of behavior as occurring in a continuous stream with a variety of cognitive and emotional processes preceding and following each other. In real sequences of behavior they argue that this fuguelike process is a better representation of what is occurring rather than simply emphasizing a small part of the sequence and finding instances where the first or second model applies. Lewis *et al.* provide support for their model by showing that infants show a variety of emotions during a learning task and that these emotions are intricately linked with cognitive processing. Some emotions occur prior to learning and some after, but emotions are displayed throughout the entire process. They argue that the question of precedence does not really apply here and they reject linear models of the relationships between emotion and cognition. Instead, emotions and cognitions "chase" each other in a continual stream of behavior.

F. Summary of Theoretical Positions

The various theoretical positions described above will be discussed by presenting and contrasting their viewpoints on two central issues:

1. *The relationship between emotion and cognition.* All of the theories agree in supposing that cognitive processing can result in emotional reactions. That the reverse is also possible is emphasized by Izard, Lewis and his colleagues, as well as Sroufe, although in the case of Sroufe, as with Kagan, cognition remains a necessary condition for emotion. To some extent the issue here is a matter of definition: Kagan refuses to classify what infants experience as an emotion, because they are held to be incapable of cognitive appraisals, using instead the term "feeling tone." Izard acknowledges that recognition may be involved in producing emotions even in infancy, but he points to the lack of more sophisticated cognitive processing, such as comparisons between stimuli and standards, to argue that it is really a type of affective processing that is occurring. Sroufe, on the other hand, apparently regards recognition as sufficiently cognitive to warrant the general principle that there can be no noncognitive emotions at all.

Several of the theories postulate that in some cases at least there may be biologically programmed affective consequences of particular incentive events. This is certainly true of the theories of Izard and of Lewis and his colleagues, and the remark of Campos and Barrett that there may be biologically programmed goals of the organism also suggests this. Such events are the basis of the ethological theory of attachment described in Chapter 4 and are typical of many of the events occurring during physical play, which is analyzed in detail in the next section of this chapter. In such cases cognitions are certainly of minimal importance, perhaps not even requiring recognition for the occurrence of emotions, so that at the very least it is reasonable to posit a gradation in which some emotions require considerably more cognitive processing than others. Thus, more sophisticated emotions such as grief and embarrassment, which require quite sophisticated cognitive processing, occur only relatively late in development, whereas an emotional response to loss of support or contact comfort could occur even without the infant realizing anything at all about why it feels the way it does. In the latter type of case, there would be no need for recognition of any specific environmental event relevant to the context of the emotional response, nor would concepts of causality, object permanence, or meaning be required. Cognitions are often sufficient to produce emotions, but are not necessary in general. Whether one refuses to label feelings that occur as the result of minimal or no cognitive processing as emotions is a definitional matter without much scientific interest. Further issues in the relations between emotion and cognition are discussed in Chapter 6 in the context of the development of aggression.

2. *The biological basis of emotional expression and experience.* There is a clear conflict between Izard and Kagan regarding the existence of a set of biologically based emotional expressions as well as a set of unique subjective feeling states that are specific

to these emotions. The position of Izard regarding the biological basis of emotional expression is strongly supported by the cross-cultural evidence cited above as well as the predictable occurrence of basic emotions in human infants. There is good theoretical reason to restrict the notion of basic emotions to those emotions that are indeed universal in humans, whether or not these emotions are particularly valued by a particular culture. By accepting the theory of evolution one is able to defend the idea that some emotions are more basic than others: Certain emotions, such as fear, anger, or joy, are the result of natural selection on all human populations, and certain emotions, such as enlightenment, are highly culturally specific.

In accord with evolutionary theory, it is also highly unlikely that the subjective, affective feeling accompanying the basic emotions differs in any very significant way between individuals or between cultures. By the nature of the situation it is not possible to provide experimental data to test the hypothesis that when person A feels angry he or she feels the same as person B does when he or she is angry, any more than it is possible to test whether your pain feels the same as mine. Nevertheless, the importance of species-wide physiological processes involved in the production of pain and emotion certainly suggests an essential similarity here within the bounds of any relevant genetic and environmental variation. Since subjective feelings act to motivate behavior, there is at least as much reason to suppose that subjective feelings associated with particular emotions result from natural selection for species-wide physiological processes as there is to suppose this in the case of emotional expressions. Neither a relativist such as Kagan nor an absolutist such as Izard can prove their cases, but certainly it is far more reasonable on the basis of evolutionary theory to accept Izard's position with the proviso that a certain amount of variation in subjective feelings accompanying emotions may well occur. As Kagan seems to suggest with regard to fear of snakes, there may be a small amount of variation produced by cultural variation (or, I would suggest, genetic variation) around a strong, biologically based central tendency to experience a qualitatively similar emotion of fear in response to a coiled snake.

Finally, it should be pointed out that from a modern evolutionary perspective the strong connection between facial expression and phenomenological feeling proposed by Izard is not expected except perhaps for infants. Sociobiological theory emphasizes the importance of deception and even self-deception in human interaction (Krebs et al., 1988; Trivers, 1985). The natural world is replete with examples of animals providing false information to others, and it is quite clear that natural selection is not a seeker of truth, but a wily manipulator of information. Izard's proposal, on the other hand, implies that emotions are essentially veridical communications about the person's inner feeling state. Such a function makes sense with regard to infants, since it is generally in the interest of caregivers to provide for the needs of infants. As a result, deception is not likely to be a major aspect of the emotional behavior of infants. Even here, however, it would not be surprising from an evolutionary perspective to find that infants were able to learn to produce emotional cues in the absence of genuine feelings, which resulted in their obtaining valued resources from parents who were unwilling otherwise to provide these resources. Indeed, many parents are convinced that this is the case. As children grow older, and certainly with regard to adults, there is every reason to expect that individuals will attempt to hide their true feelings as well as attempt to manipulate others by feigning emotional states. As an example, Lewis and Michalson (1983) provide the case of a young child who falls down but does not begin crying until in the presence of a parent. We also expect children to develop an increasingly sophisticated ability to detect such attempts to hide and fake emotions.

On the other hand, it is interesting that such deception is much more difficult if the emotion is very intense and this may well reflect a primitive tendency for the strong connection proposed by Izard between facial expressions and feelings. Perhaps reflecting this, we are more likely to believe that an individual is truly feeling a certain way when the behavioral signs are intense and especially if the emotion makes sense in terms of some environmental event, such as an open wound or winning the lottery. We are least likely to believe that a person is feeling what is being signaled if the emotion is incompatible with the person's self-interest, presumably the origin of the expression "crocodile tears." Clearly, emotions have the communicative function proposed by Izard, but there is no reason to propose a one-to-one relationship.

II. PARENT–CHILD INTERACTION AS AN EXAMPLE OF EMOTIONAL PROCESSES IN DEVELOPMENT

A. The Emotional Content of Parent–Child Interaction

In this section, certain types of parent–child interaction will be described and placed in a theoretical perspective and comparisons and contrasts will be made with the theories described above. The behaviors of concern here are derived from observational analyses of parent–child interaction, an area described as interaction theory by Maccoby and Martin (1983). Interaction theory is not so much a theory as it is an area of interest. Interactionists are interested in the dynamics of social interaction, the ebb and flow from moment to moment of social interaction. From the perspective of this chapter, the emotions are essential to understanding the ebb and flow of social interaction. Emotions are regulators of social interaction and the regulation of affect thus becomes an absolutely essential social skill. Unlike social learning theorists, researchers who study these interactive processes are not concerned with identifying reinforcing contingencies or punishments. Interactionists study circular processes that occur during social interaction and the conceptualization of these processes. The child is necessarily viewed as an active participant in these interactions, as influencing the environment and being influenced by it, but this influence is the influence that naturally occurs during a conversation, not necessarily any long-term effects on the child's personality or the adult's behavior. Indeed, one of the important questions arising from this research is the extent to which there are long-term effects of variation in early interaction patterns.

The great majority of research in this area has been performed on mother–infant interactions. The basic technique is the observation of mothers and infants interacting in natural surroundings or in situations in which the behavior of the mother is manipulated. One of the essential findings is that the mother–infant interaction is characterized by a delicate "dance" of affective modulation (Stern, 1977). The infant is viewed as an active stimulus seeker whose goal in these playful interactions is "to be with and enjoy someone else" (Stern, 1977, p. 71), or to "maintain a relational state that is evaluated positively"

(Tronick, 1982, p. 3). These interactions involve the provision of stimuli, which are attended to with interest and allow for the buildup and fluctuation of excitement so that affectively positive experiences result. Brazelton, Koslowski, and Main (1974) also document the fluctuating, cyclic nature of early mother–infant interaction. Interactions typically build to a peak of excitement followed by a period of gaze aversion or withdrawal on the part of the infant when the interaction becomes too intense. In the view of Brazelton *et al.* (1974), the most important rule for maintaining interaction is that the mother "develop sensitivity to her infant's capacity for attention and his need for withdrawal—partial or complete—after a period of attention to her" (p. 59). Thus, in very young infants attention to the mother is arousal inducing, and successful interaction requires sensitivity on the mother's part.

Stern (1977) explicitly adopts an optimal-level-of-arousal point of view regarding the reactions of the infant:

> [T]o keep things in an optimum range, the stimulus events cannot be too weak, or too powerful, or too simple or too complex, or too familiar or too novel. Successive events cannot be too repetitive or attention is lost and excitement falls below the optimal range; affect becomes neutral. On the other hand, successive stimuli cannot be too drastically dissimilar or the infant will not be able to engage them cognitively. (Stern, 1977, p. 72)

Optimal-level-of-arousal theories have a long history in psychology, starting with Wundt (1893). Recently the work of Berlyne (1960, 1966) has called attention to the role of arousal in play generally, but for purposes of this discussion his ideas will be restricted to social play between parents and children.

The essential idea is that social play involves stimulus-regulating behavior. There is an optimal level of stimulation at which the child is comfortable. Below this level the child will seek stimulation from the environment. Above this level the child will withdraw from the stimulation if it is too intense. In parent–child play the source of stimulation is an adult who can control the level of stimulation given, and one essential role of the adult is to regulate the arousal level of the child. The mother and infant can be conceptualized as an affect regulatory unit (Tronick, 1982). The mother responds to the affective signals of the infant and the infant in turn responds to the signals of the mother.

A similar account is given by Field (1982), who also emphasizes that the degree of arousal that is pleasurable to infants is a function of the rest–activity state that the infant is in as well as differences due to clinical conditions, such as prematurity with respiratory distress, Down syndrome, or autism. The discussion of temperament in Chapter 2 also suggests variation in the sensitivity to stimulation: A highly emotional infant would be one who reacts very strongly to relatively low levels of stimulation, whereas an infant who was very low on emotionality might appear to be hyporesponsive.

Several studies have documented what happens when there is a breakdown in this pattern of communication. Cohn and Tronick (1982) conceptualize the mother–infant interaction process as involving a set of rules that regulate affective displays. The principal rule is that the affective display must be appropriate to its context. If the display is not appropriate, the partner will attempt to alter it, and if this is not successful, there will be a complete reorganization of the behavior of the partner. For example, Tronick, Ricks, and Cohn (1982) instructed mothers to behave in a depressed manner with their infants, i.e., with no animation or positive affect. The infants appeared to attempt to reinstate the normal behavior of the mother and, failing this, they became increasingly negative themselves. This procedure was quite stressful to the infants and many cried steadily. Although normal patterns of interaction were restored, it was initially quite difficult to do so. Variations in the pattern of these mother–infant interaction styles is also related to attachment classification. Tronick *et al.* (1982) reported that when mothers were instructed to provide a blank face the reactions of infants obtained at 6 months of age were systematically related to attachment classification at 1 year of age, with securely attached infants engaging in more positive attempts to elicit a response from the still face. These results are interpreted as agreeing with the general finding that sensitive maternal caregiving is associated with secure attachment, but, in addition, emphasize the importance of competent affective regulation to attachment classification.

Although most of the work on affect regulation has been done by infancy researchers, there is evidence that affect regulation continues to be an important facet of parent–child interaction long after infancy. Particularly noteworthy is physical play between parents and children. Physical play includes activities such as tickling, wrestling, and chasing young children and is most typically carried out by the father (Lamb, 1977a,b; Power & Parke, 1983; MacDonald & Parke, 1984) and commonly occurs long after infancy. In a recent survey, MacDonald and Parke (1986) found that physical play peaked in early childhood and gradually declined with age, especially for girls, but remained at significant levels even between adolescents and their parents. This type of play involves arousal regulation in parents and children. Children often react with intense positive affect to the physical stimulation provided by their parents, but overarousal and attempts by the child to regulate the stimulation provided by the parent are common.

In addition, there are associations between the amount of physical play between parents and their preschool children and the social competence of children with their peers. MacDonald and Parke (1984) found that children who engaged in more physical play with their parents and exhibited more positive affect during these play sessions were more popular with their peers. Moreover, MacDonald (1987c) found that in a sample of boys of age 3–5 years neglected children tended to have low levels of physical play and affective displays with their fathers compared to both popular and rejected children. As described more fully on pp. 102–103 rejected children differed from popular children by becoming overstimulated more often and by avoiding stimulation more, results that may well be due to temperamental differences between these two groups. Nevertheless, at this stage of research it is also possible that the parents of some rejected children may contribute to the overstimulation observed because they are insensitive to the affective cues of the children.

In conclusion, interactionist research provides a framework for understanding dyadic interactions between parents and children. This framework integrates well with important issues of emotional development, temperament (Chapter 2), parent–child interactions (Chapter 5), and quite possibly attachment (Chapter 4). The framework emphasizes the affective side of parent–child interactions far more than do social learning or attributional approaches. The main difficulty with the approach is demonstrating whether characteristics of the parents or of the child carry the most weight in producing important social outcomes. Nevertheless, the thesis that maladaptive parent–child interaction patterns are the basis of later pathology is certainly plausible, given the possible connections between early interaction patterns and attachment classification. In addition, several studies have shown that the mother–infant interaction patterns of children who later became psychotic were highly abnormal. For example, Massie (1982) describes the case of Joan, who was diagnosed as autistic at 12 months of age. At 4 months of age the child's interaction with her mother was characterized by the mother turning away from the attempts by the child to engage in smiling face-to-face interactions. The child would then turn away and cease smiling, and her reactions became increasingly dysphoric as time went on. Although it is not possible to rule out biological characteristics of the child, the results suggest that in some cases lack of maternal responsiveness may indeed lead to psychopathology.

Additional mention should be made of the special role of fathers in initiating games with children that are relatively highly stimulating. Clarke-Stewart (1978) found that children are more responsive, more excited, and more interested in play initiated by their fathers than by their mothers and chose fathers over mothers as a playmate in a choice situation. These results indicate that children generally highly value the high-intensity stimulation provided by fathers. There is a parallel here with other primate species. Parke and Suomi (1981) find that in primate species where there are interactions between adult males and infants, the interactions are playful. Even in species where such interactions are infrequent, play is still the most common type of nonaggressive behavior observed. Moreover, male–infant interactions, including play, are highest among monogamous species, especially those species that mate for life and live in nonextended family groupings. From an evolutionary perspective, these circumstances suggest that high levels of paternal investment in their offspring, as indicated by monogamy, are associated with higher levels of play. As described in Chapter 5, there is good reason to believe that there was a prolonged phase of human evolution in which monogamous, nonextended nuclear families were the norm. Under these circumstances the evolutionary basis of father–child interactions, involving relatively high levels of stimulation, was developed. One possible evolutionary basis for this style of play is the general male–female difference in sensation seeking. As indicated in Chapter 2, a dimension of self-regulation involving the relative degree of seeking stimulation is a basic personality trait in humans. There is a major sex difference in this trait, with males being generally higher than females for stimulus seeking (Zuckerman, 1983). Males thus would be expected to seek relatively high levels of stimulation in their interactions with their children and also provide higher levels of stimulation. The general finding that this dimension of personality is heritable (see Chapter 2) as well as the cross-species evidence presented here thus suggest a biological system that predisposes males to initiate and enjoy high-stimulus interactions with their children. Clearly there is a great deal of plasticity in this system, since in some cultures father–child interactions are quite distant (see Chapter 5). Congruent with the primate evidence discussed here, these cultures tend to be nonmonogamous and are characterized by extended-family type of social organization (Katz & Konner, 1981). However, there does appear to be a biological bias toward this type of interaction.

It is clear from the above that emotions function as regulators of behavior in the context of parent–child interaction. Campos et al. (1983) propose that emotions generally function as regulators or organizers of social behavior as well as regulators of cognitive processing. A particularly clear example of the former is the phenomenon of social referencing. Klinnert, Campos, Sorce, Emde, and Svedja (1983) found that infants crawling across a visual cliff apparatus tended to look to their mother for information on whether it was safe or not. Particularly important was the affective expression of the mother: If the mother exhibited a fear face, infants did not attempt to crawl across the apparent cliff, while if the mother showed a happy face, the infants were very likely to cross over.

B. A Theory of Affect Regulation in the Context of Parent–Child Interaction

It remains to provide a theoretical framework for this style of interaction, and a beginning will be made by discussing the theory of play in the context of evolution. Any theory of play must take account of several general findings in the natural history of play. The five following propositions are derived from Robert Fagen's (1981) encyclopaedic work on play in animals:

1. Play is ubiquitous among the mammals and clear cases occur among many bird groups. Play occurs among the marsupial as well as the placental mammals and even among the monotremes, those very ancient and odd organisms. This indicates that play is phylogenetically ancient and most likely that it evolved independently in several different lineages. This also suggests that whatever function(s) play has, it represents a very important adaptation. Moreover, it also indicates that functional explanations of play must propose that play solves some very general problems of adaptation rather than problems peculiar to, for example, social species.

2. Increased levels of play are associated with increased brain size, and particularly increased cortical size. For example, the bird species with the highest level of cortical development (macaw, raven, and many raptors) are also the species with the highest levels of play, and the differences between mammals and marsupials and within mammals reflect this generalization. This trend toward increased levels of play apparently reaches its pinnacle in humans, where children left to their own devices do little except play, and many people continue to show aspects of playfulness far into adulthood.

3. Although play among adults occurs in a variety of species, play occurs much more frequently among young animals. The general trend is for play to decrease as animals get older and to be replaced by behavior which is of immediate functional value for survival.

4. There is good evidence for the training hypothesis of the function of play. This hypothesis goes back at least to Plato, and it is the only one which is strongly supported by modern investigations. Fagen summarizes data showing that physical exercise increases aerobic capacity and that play and exploration are the only behaviors known to mediate the differential patterns of dendritic growth and branching in animals subjected to enriched versus deprived environmental rearing conditions. These experiments have effectively ruled out a variety of nonplay experiences as explaining these results, including observational learning, nonplayful training, operant conditioning and group living. Interestingly there is evidence for differences in relative plasticity in the trainability of physical capacity which are exactly analogous to those described in Chapter 1 as a general feature of cognitive and social development: Eriksson (1972) found that although adult men gained the same amount as 11–13-year-old boys by a physical-training regime, the

training affected different systems in the boys than in the men. The author concluded that prepubertal training for physical capacity was optimal and that greater adult capacity could be obtained if training was begun earlier in life.

Furthermore, the types of play animals engage in seem related to the types of activities the animal will engage in as an adult. Among species such as carnivores where adults engage in fighting or predation, there are high levels of play fighting and few sex differences in play. On the other hand in species where males fight and females do not, quite often the play of males is focused on fighting whereas that of females appears to be training for predator avoidance. In our own species as well as many other primates, the play of males is more vigorous and oriented toward fighting than that of females, a difference that reflects adult differences in aggression (see Chapter 6) and physical capacity.

5. There are costs as well as benefits to play. Play requires high amounts of energy, and field observations have often shown that play can result in injury or even death. (I myself spent a few weeks in a neck brace after being blind-sided by a 10-year-old boy during a wrestling bout, and minor injuries are fairly common among children engaged in rough and tumble play with parents or peers.) Even more telling is the finding that play drops off when animals are sick or hungry, and Fagen provides evidence that play tends to occur in the absence of factors which threaten the animal's immediate well-being.

These considerations suggest that play is a very central aspect of adaptation in many animals, one intimately related to the idea of plasticity as discussed in Chapter 1. Several writers have noted a trend in evolution toward the evolution of animals with less rigid, stereotypical behavior and responses to the environment (see Lerner, 1986, for a review). Many of the species studied by the classical ethologists were on the stereotypical end of this continuum, and it is not surprising that the resulting theory emphasized such concepts as sign stimuli, releasers and fixed-action patterns. Primitive animals tend to respond in stereotypical ways to a highly delimited number of incentive stimuli. For example, the swollen belly of a female stickleback fish triggers stereotypical courtship behavior in males, and the appearance of another male or the reflection of a male in a mirror is enough to elicit aggressive responding in male fighting fish.

These primitive, stereotypical programs are quite useful but they can easily be fooled, and, more importantly, they are minimally sensitive to subtle variation in environmental contingencies. Because of these limitations, the trend in evolution has been toward increased plasticity and flexibility in dealing with environmental contingencies. Play would appear to be an integral part of this process. During play an animal places itself in a position to learn about a large array of environmental contingencies. Rather than attempting to design an animal that will be able to make an increasing number of stereotypical responses to an increasing number of environmental contingencies, the animal is programmed to discover and respond to environmental contingencies.

Moreover, and this is crucial to the concept of play, rather than depend on passively experiencing and learning from a large number of contingencies, the organism is programmed (as Piaget recognized) to actively seek out information on environmental contingencies. This active seeking out of contingencies is the very essence of many types of play. Play with objects involves exploration and manipulation of objects with a view to understanding what they can do. Animals and children eventually get bored with simply exploring a new object unless the object has some source of rewards other than its simply being new. Think of how difficult it would be to program by means of releasers and fixed-action patterns all of the contingencies that a child can come to understand from exploring a set of construction toys. The same is also the case with play fighting: Rather than rigidly program the enormous number of subtle feints, holds, and bites that are the optimum responses to the stimuli provided by the other animal, the animal is programmed to seek out rough and tumble play and during this play it is able to learn what works best. The fighting behavior of such advanced animals as carnivores is thus likely to be far more subtle and complex than is typical of, for example, fish or insects, and this is indeed the case.

Play and plasticity are thus intimately connected to each other. If there were no plasticity, there would be no reason to engage in play, and the decline in play during adulthood is an important prediction of this perspective. In this perspective development is a time when the organism is able to learn the way the world works, while in adulthood the animal reaches a point of diminishing returns and increased cost as play behavior results in resources being diverted from efforts at reproduction and other vital activities.

As a further point related to the interplay of plasticity and play, development is also a time when the animal's brain can be selectively programmed to respond to differing requirements in the animal's environment. The early-experience literature indicates that experience during times of plasticity can effectively alter the structure of the brain so that resources are devoted more to one competence than another. As an extreme example, cats reared in chambers with vertical stripes become specialized for vertical perception and even lose some of the ability to observe horizontal bars (Hirsch & Spinelli, 1971; see Lerner (1984) for further examples). These processes result in increased specialization, as environments which are particularly salient during development are more influential in producing the structure of the brain. By programming the animal to seek out a large variety of environmental stimulation (i.e., by programming the animal to play) the animal will develop neural structures that are maximally responsive to the salient features of its environment.

As indicated above, much of the species variation in play patterns reflects differences in adult behavioral ecology. In conformity with these findings, social species are expected to exhibit more social play, as a crucial aspect of their future environment will be other members of their own species. In support of this, Fagen notes:

> In at least nine mammalian taxa . . . the tendency of young to play *together*, with body contact and in closely interacting groups is apparently associated with the sociality (group size, group permanence, average physical closeness, "cohesion," or degree of cooperation) of adults. (Fagen, 1981, p. 346)

Because humans are highly social animals, it is expected that social play will be very important in our species, and the discussion that follows emphasizes parent–child play patterns.

It should be noted that the general finding that decrements in play occur during adulthood is far from universal, and continued play during adulthood may well be highly functional for some species. There would appear to be two general situations in which play would evolve during adulthood. The first is that there may be selection for relatively high levels of plasticity throughout the lifespan. From an evolutionary perspective, humans appear to be neotenous, that is, there is a tendency for juvenile features, including plasticity, to remain present during the period of reproductive competence (Gould, 1977). One aspect of human neoteny is the tendency for humans to continue to play during adulthood. However, corresponding to the declining plasticity proposed in Chapter 1, play is less common in human adults than among children. This adult playfulness is quite possibly functional because playful adults tend to be more inventive and more exploratory in their behavior. We have already noted that the effects of deprived environments in producing behavioral rigidity and stereotypy in rats appear to be mediated by the suppression of play, and Rubin, Fein, and Vandenberg (1983) summarize research indicating that playful experience with objects facilitates both convergent and divergent problem-solving in children.

Fagen (1981) also recounts several anecdotes of scientific discovery, ranging from Einstein to Kekule (the discoverer of the benzene ring), suggesting that these scientists made their discoveries by playful transformations of ordinary occurrences. Playfulness is also often assumed to be an aspect of artistic invention, and Fagen recounts several incidents from the life of Samuel Johnson, the 18th-century British essayist, that are particularly illustrative of the playful spirit among some adult humans. For example:

> During a walk with his friends, the Langstons, Johnson came to the top of a very steep hill and announced that he wanted to take a roll down. The Langstons tried to stop him. But he said that he had not had a roll for a long time, and taking out of his pockets his keys, a pencil, a purse, and other objects, lay down parallel at the edge of the hill and rolled down its full length, turning himself over and over till he came to the bottom. (Fagen, 1981, pp. 354–355)

When the incident occurred, Johnson was 55 years old.

The second reason why play may continue among adults is that adults often provide play partners for their offspring. This is true in many species of primates, carnivores, and ungulates, and in my own observations of wolves, adult play with the cubs was extremely common, usually consisting of prolonged wrestling and chasing bouts. Parent–child play among humans is very common. As with play in general, parent–child physical play declines as parents get older, an effect that is independent of the age of the child (Mac-Donald & Parke, 1986).

I emphasize the idea that play is essentially an active system in the sense that it results in the animal actively seeking information from the environment. This active aspect of play implies that play is intrinsically motivating, which is extremely important for the conceptualization of several aspects of human play. This motivating function seems to involve affect, that is, the subjective pleasure obtained by participation in playful activities. The organism also is often quite aroused during playful activities, and it is this affective motivation, often occurring in a state of arousal, which is responsible for the active, stimulus-seeking aspects of play.

The literature related to these issues has been developed by Berlyne (1960, 1966), Ellis (1973), Schultz (1979), and Fein (1981), and although the paradigm has been exploration and play with objects, some aspects of this theoretical framework are applicable to parent–child physical play. Some of the features of this theoretical approach are as follows:

1. Play involves stimulus-regulating behavior. There is an optimal level of stimulation at which the child is comfortable. Below this level the child will seek stimulation from the environment. Above this level the child will withdraw from the stimulation if it is too intense, or seek to reduce uncertainty by specific exploration of the source of the

uncertainty. In parent–child physical play the idea of an intermediate level of arousal as being sought by the child is useful. The source of stimulation for the child is here a person who can control the level of stimulation given, and arousal-regulating actions on the part of the child are a common feature of parent–child physical play. Thus, the child is often seen telling the parent to stop tickling or the child sets up rules for the parent's behavior in order to provide the parent with guidelines on the level of acceptable stimulation. Alternatively, the child will often elicit stimulation from a parent, sometimes more than the parent wants to give. The parent, however, is an active participant in the process, and often initiates or terminates physical play with the child, so that there is a level of complexity found in parent–child physical play that is not found in play with objects.

The maintenance of an optimal range of such stimuli requires complex and subtle ability on the part of the parent to regulate the quantity and timing of appropriate stimulus events. The work of Brazelton *et al.* (1974) and Stern (1977), described above, clearly documents the subtle ability required on the part of the parents to keep the stimulus events in the optimal range. The parent must also be aware of the many contextual factors that will affect the child's reactions to a particular stimulus, a point made particularly by Sroufe and Waters (1977). Thus, whether or not the child is hungry, tired, or in an unfamiliar situation will affect how he or she reacts to the particular affectively arousing stimuli.

Because there are two participants in the playful interactions considered here, it is not appropriate to view play as motivated solely "by the need to elevate the level of arousal toward the optimal" (Ellis, 1973, p. 110) on the part of either one of the participants. As Sroufe (1979b) points out regarding emotional development in general, parent–child physical play need not be seen as a drive or drivelike phenomenon in which play results from the needs of the child's or adult's CNS. What often happens is that the adult will attempt to engage the child in these activities independently of the child's expressing a desire to do so, although the child may also elicit play from the parent. The difference is between a theory that posits that children are stimulus-deprived in much the same way that people who are hungry seek to eat, and a theory that suggests that some play occurs as a result of a parent's intentional actions and need not be dictated by the needs of the child. Analogously, one can offer a child a treat even though he or she does not need it and did not actively seek it. The results may nevertheless be pleasurable, and in the case of parent–child physical play, the pleasure may depend on the competent regulation of the child's affect by the parent. Thus, parent–child physical play need not be seen in the context of stimulus deprivation. The environment is not an inanimate collection of stimuli with the organism constantly seeking an optimal level of arousal, but rather consists of another person with attitudes, expectations, and a sense of what constitutes appropriate interactions. The occurence of parent–child physical play is thus largely independent of the arousal-producing aspects of the environment and arousal ceases to be a necessary motivating condition of play, but is nevertheless a salient aspect of it.

2. Berlyne (1960) lists several sources of arousal: intensity of stimulus, emotional reactions, and the collative variables, including such attributes of stimuli as novelty, degree and suddenness of change, surprise, incongruity, complexity, and uncertainty. These sources of arousal are probably all present in physical play and indeed Berlyne includes as a paradigmatic example the case of an adult tossing a child in the air. This process may involve uncertainty, suddenness of change, surprise, novelty, and intensity of stimulus. If the stimulus is too intense, fear and an aversive reaction will result, while if

the uncertainty created is only mildly arousing, the experience will be viewed as pleasurable.

3. This body of theory has made specific proposals regarding the relationship between positive affect and arousal. Berlyne (1960) states that moderate degrees of arousal are sought if they are promptly followed by relief: "Such slight and transitory jumps in arousal will become pleasurable as a consequence of the drop in arousal that quickly terminates them" (p. 199). This theory is very similar to that of Sroufe (1979b), described above, in which tension is seen as building up and it is only when tension is being dissipated that positive affect occurs. Negative affect is seen as the result of the unbroken buildup of tension. However, Berlyne also discusses evidence from electrical stimulation of the brain in cats suggesting that moderate amounts of stimulation are pleasurable *per se,* and Schultz (1979) and Berlyne (1971) discuss evidence that pleasure may accompany both increases and decreases in arousal.

The view of the biological basis of temperament and personality presented in Chapter 2 (see especially the Appendix to that chapter) suggests a theory that incorporates all of these influences on the expression of positive affect and its relation to stimulation and arousal. First, consistent with the suggestion of Berlyne, it is proposed there that there are specific reward centers in the brain, which are stimulated during physical play. The pleasure deriving from this stimulation is part of what makes physical play so attractive to children. Moreover, this proposal is consistent with the idea that children who are strongly attracted to physical play tend to be extraverted (see pp. 102–106). In the terminology of Chapter 2, they tend to be very sensitive to the rewards involved in physical play.

Second, it is proposed that the arousal that occurs during physical play can be rewarding *per se,* but that overstimulation results in arousal that is negatively evaluated. This proposal depends on the discussion of tense and energetic arousal in Chapter 2. Energetic arousal (or positive reactivity in Rothbart's (1987) terms) occurs as a result of excitation processes and is evaluated positively. During physical play the child tends to be pleasantly aroused, partly as a result of the fact that the stimulation of the reward centers itself results in excitatory arousal (see Chapter 2). However, if the stimulation is too intense, inhibitory processes are triggered and the child feels aversive tense arousal and withdraws from the source of stimulation. Such a theory predicts that children who are high on stimulus seeking and also high on emotionality will show high levels of approach and withdrawal behavior during physical play—approaching because of their attraction to the rewards involved in physical stimulation, and withdrawing because their high emotionality results in a tendency to develop aversive tense arousal as a result of the stimulation.

Such a position would be consistent with the fact that during physical play there are often prolonged sequences of positive affect lasting for up to several minutes as the result of continuing physical stimulation. In such cases it is not the drop on arousal that is evaluated positively, but simply the reward value of the stimulation and the energetic arousal *per se.* During such sequences there may be slight fluctuations in the degree of positive affect, but there are no periods when the child is not positively aroused by the continuing stimulation.

Thus, although tension fluctuation is certainly present in many cases of positive emotion, there is little reason to suppose that fluctuation itself is a necessary or sufficient condition for positive emotion. Besides the existence of periods of prolonged positive affect resulting from continuing stimulation described above, there are also instances of acute tension increase that are evaluated positively, as when a baby sees its mother. Moreover, a fluctuating process of tension modulation may well lead to negative affect if the stimulus is too intense, and overstimulation is a common occurrence during physical play, especially for certain groups of children (see pp. 102–103). Moreover, the negative affect occurring during physical play is not reasonably viewed as the culmination of unrelieved tension, but as something that can occur very quickly as the result of momentary overstimulation.

These considerations pose a major problem for Sroufe's (1979b) theory and result from the overemphasis of the role of cognition in the production of emotion. As will be argued below, the hedonic tone of the affective interchanges involved in parent–child physical play is the result of a complex interaction among cognitive factors and aspects of the stimulus, such as intensity. Only by considering aspects of the stimulus as being able to affect emotional response independent of the child's cognitive engagement with the stimulus can one account for the fact that often during a play bout that consists of a fluctuating flow of generally positive arousal there can also be overarousal and negative affect. In the present theory this is often due to changes in aspects of the stimulus interacting with the child's temperament rather than any change in the "playframe" of the encounter or any changes in the child's cognitive engagement with the event.

This is not to say that a drop in arousal cannot also be pleasurable. In Chapter 2 and in the above the pleasurable effects of excitation and the aversive effects of tense arousal are emphasized, but there is reason also to suppose that large decreases in arousal are accompanied by pleasure as well. Thus, free-falling parachutists report feelings of euphoria after landing safely. In the context of physical play, however, this process is expected to occur after the physical play is over and the participants pleasantly exhausted rather than as an important part of the play process itself.

1. Intrinsic Motivation: The Interplay of Biology and Cognition

As indicated above, play in general is viewed as intrinsically motivated (Rubin, Fein, & Vandenberg, 1983). The idea of intrinsic motivation is familiar to developmentalists because of its central role in Piaget's theory of cognitive development (Flavell, 1985). Such a view fits well with recent views of the child as an active participant in its development (e.g., Bell, 1968; Lerner & Busch-Rosenagel, 1981; MacDonald, 1986b; Parke & Collmer, 1975). In the case of physical play, the source of the intrinsic motivation presumably involves the affective response to physical stimulation, which can vary in intensity, as well as the affective response to stimuli that are perceived as surprising, novel, incongruous or leading to uncertainty (Berlyne, 1960, 1966).

The hypothesis that physical play is intrinsically motivated is important, but requires elaboration. In the following a theory of the motivation of physical play involving a complex interplay between biological and cognitive factors will be presented. On the biological side, many of the stimuli that occur during physical play, such as those resulting from tickling or being tossed in the air, and that are within the range of the optimal level of arousal of the individual are viewed as intrinsically reinforcing, that is, they act as unlearned elicitors of positive affective response by affecting emotion receptors in the child. As such, these elicitors have the same theoretical status as the "natural clues'' described by Bowlby (1969) as essential to an ethological analysis of attachment (see Chapter 4). From the standpoint of the literature on emotion, these unlearned elicitors have the same theoretical status as the startle response to loud noises or the arousal induced by falling. The view that elicitors such as these may result in affective response as a result of innate programming is common to many theories of emotion, including those of Mandler (1975), Izard (1978), Lewis and Michalson (1983; see also Lewis & Saarni, 1985), and Campos and Barrett (1984). For example, Mandler (1975) suggests that sudden loss of support or sudden loud noises may well result in emotional behavior and experience as a result of innate programming. Similarly, Lewis and Michalson (1983) propose that fear of strangers in infants may be biologically programmed and describe ''non-developmental elicitors,'' such as startling noises and the sight of food when hungry, which have emotional consequences throughout the individual's life.

Despite the virtually universal agreement that prewired response tendencies exist, there is no adequate integration of these unlearned elicitor–receptor connections with cognitive factors and socialization experiences in the development of complex emotional states. In order to appreciate the role of cognition in the context of parent–child physical play, it is necessary to consider the development of positive emotions in general. Sroufe (1979b) characterizes early infancy as a period when cognitive processing has minimal importance in affective responses. Prior to the third month the smile occurs solely as a result of CNS arousal, without the psychological processing of the stimulus content. As they get older, infants react with laughter to ''physically vigorous, intrusive stimulation,'' but it is only in the latter part of the first year that cognitively mediated events, including especially incongruity, are able to elicit laughter. Sroufe states that at this point the meaning of the event to the infant becomes the dominant mode of producing laughter.

This analysis of the increasing importance of cognition applies also to physical play, with the proviso that physically intrusive stimulation continues to be of central importance. During early infancy there is presumably very little if any cognitive processing in the child's enjoyment of physical stimulation. However, as the child gets older, cognitive factors become of increasing importance. A father who approaches a child with a ''monster'' face, grabs and tickles the child implicitly assumes a variety of cognitive processes in the child that ''frame'' the interaction, in the sense of Bateson (1956). For example, the child must recognize that the approaching person is, despite the facial expression, not intending harm, but intends only to have fun. Since the person is the father and thus familiar, the child has a variety of expectations about what will happen in the interaction, expectations that would be absent if the man were a stranger. If a play frame is established, these cognitive processes function as what one might term ''enablers,'' in that they allow the physical characteristics of the stimulus to determine the affective result. Thus, if the father proceeds to physically overstimulate the child in this context, the affect will be negative and there will be attempts by the child to regulate the parent's behavior. If the child is optimally stimulated, positive affect will result and the child may well attempt to elicit more such behavior on the part of the parent.

If the play frame is not established, the cognitions of the child determine completely the affective result of the stimuli provided by the parent, and I term these cognitions *determiners*. If the adult is not recognized as familiar, but rather as a threatening stranger, there will be a qualitative change in the interaction such that any stimulus occurring as the result of the interaction will be perceived as aversive, with the degree of aversion determined by a variety of factors, one of which is presumably the intensity of the physical stimulus. In this case the subjective feeling resulting from the interaction is determined almost exclusively by the cognition that the adult is fearsome.

The important point is that the fact that cognitions *can* be of overriding importance does not mean that in the ordinary course of parent–child physical play they *are* the determining factors resulting in the affective response. In most cases the play frame of the interaction results in the possibility that the emotional response will be determined largely by the physical stimulation encountered—the play frame allows for the possibility of a strong association between the physical stimulation and the affective quality of the response.

In addition, cognitive factors are crucial in producing the affective arousal associated with the collative variables described by Berlyne (1966). The collative variables, proposed by Berlyne (1966) as aspects of stimuli that elicit emotional responses, and which certainly occur during physical play, clearly involve some sort of cognitive processing. The affective expression of a child being swung in the air may well be due at least in part to a feeling of uncertainty as to how the episode will end. Such experience may also contain elements of novelty and surprise.

In a sense, however, there is a negative role for cognition in many of the examples of emotional arousal resulting from the collative variables, since the degree of affective arousal produced by stimulation that results in uncertainty or surprise is higher in cases where the stimuli depart most from expectations and presently held schemas (Lewis & Goldberg, 1969). By definition, unfamiliar, novel, incongruous, discrepant, and unexpected stimuli are those that the organism has not yet assimilated cognitively. Thus, the emotion appears to result from the fact that the stimulus has not been cognitively assimilated, a process studied extensively by Kagan and his colleagues. For example, Kagan (1984a) reviews research indicating that infants have emotional reactions to stimuli that they have difficulty assimilating and proposes the term "vigilance" for this emotion. In addition, Lewis and Michalson (1983) note that stimuli that produce emotional response often have a fast rise time, suggesting that the emotional response occurs because there is inadequate time for the stimulus to be cognitively processed: The sudden appearance of even familiar stimuli often results in emotional arousal. Sudden, surprising, and unexpected movements are commonly observed during physical play and result in emotional responses in children. Part of the fun is not knowing exactly when the stimulation will occur or exactly what the stimulation will be. Since the play frame has already been established, there is an expectation on the part of the child that the events will not in general be aversive, so that the child is even more likely than otherwise to react to these stimuli with displays of positive affect.

Thus, cognitions are central to many examples of physical play, but they coexist along with intrinsically rewarding physical stimulation. Moreover, these cognitions themselves appear to result reliably in intrinsically rewarding subjective affective response (i.e., energetic arousal or positive reactivity) if the arousal induced is within the optimal range. In the same manner that according to Piaget, the discovery of an effect that is contingent on a child's actions is intrinsically rewarding to the child, affective arousal induced by surprise, incongruity, or uncertainty is an important intrinsically rewarding aspect of physical play. As Lewis *et al.* (1984) point out, the fact that cognitions such as these tend to result in an emotional response independent of the specific content of the stimuli strongly suggests that these connections are biologically prewired. From an evolutionary viewpoint, it makes sense to design an organism in such a way that novel, unassimilated, or unexpected stimuli arouse the organism and cause the organism to attempt to reconcile the stimuli with presently held schemata: Such stimuli may have highly beneficial or highly detrimental effects on the organism.

Figure 5 is a schematization of these relationships. It depicts several factors and their interrelations as follows: On the parent side there are three types of stimuli: (a) Stimuli such as the facial expression and verbalizations of the parent that are intended to indicate that the interaction is performed in a "play frame" (Bateson, 1956). For example, a father may approach the child with a "monster" face and say he is going to get the child, but the child will know that the father is just pretending. (b) Stimuli calculated to result in the collative variables described by Berlyne (1961, 1966). These would include characteristics such as surprise, novelty, incongruity, and suddenness of change. (c) Physical manipulations of the child, such as tickling or swinging in the air.

On the child's side there would be the following factors: (a) Cognitive processing required to realize that the interaction was done within a play frame, such as the ability to

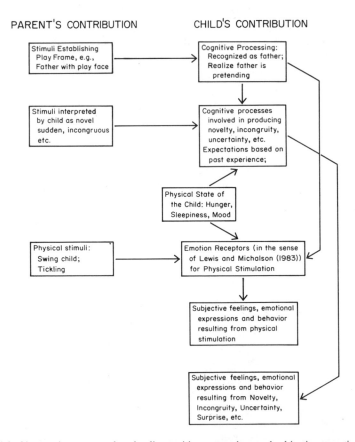

FIGURE 5. Model of interactions among the stimuli, cognitive processing, and subjective sensations involved in physical play.

recognize the father and realize that he is pretending. (b) Cognitive processing that interprets the behaviors of the father as surprising, novel, incongruous, or sudden and results in subjective affective feelings, emotional expressions, and behavior. (c) Emotion receptors that are sensitive to the physical stimulation of the parent and, when stimulated, result in subjective affective feelings, emotional expressions, and behavior. (d) Moods, that is, whether the child is hungry, sleepy, or unhappy for some other reason. The child's mood is seen as affecting how it reacts to all the other types of stimulation: For example, if the child is in a bad mood, all physical stimulation may be aversive and playful overtures by the parent may be rejected.

As indicated above, establishing that the interaction will be done in a play frame is extremely important here. If the child interprets the situation as a nonplayful incident, as would happen if the adult were an intrusive stranger, then none of the other stimuli provided by the adult will result in a positive affective experience even though these same stimuli would result in such an experience with a familiar person. Once the play frame is established, however, it is the features of the stimuli themselves that result in affective response of the child. Once the play frame is established, then the biologically based predispositions to respond with positive or negative affect to the stimuli provided by the parent come into play. Cognition thus sets the stage, but once the stage is set, biological connections between stimulus and affective response assume central importance. As argued above, there are good reasons to suppose that both the physical manipulations involved in physical play as well as the novelty, suddenness, etc., of the parent's actions achieve their affective results in the child because of biological predispositions on the child's part.

There are presumably also feedback loops connecting the subjective experience of the child with the cognitive processes relevant to emotional expression. Positive experiences in physical play with a parent may result in expectations about what the parent will do and perhaps enable a higher level of physical stimulation and a greater degree of uncertainty and surprise to be perceived as pleasurable. These interactions also may lead to the conception of the parent as a source of pleasure, and thereby affect the whole range of parent–child interaction and identification. Finally, these interactions may result in expectations as well as specific skills involved in social interaction in general (see below for a further discussion of specific skills that may be involved in parent–child physical play).

C. The Socialization of Emotions in Parent–Child Physical Play

Flavell (1985) states that in order to understand Piaget's theory of cognitive development, one need only ask how evolution would design a child as an optimal learning organism. In the present case, we ask how evolution would design an organism that is similarly predisposed to interact socially. Although individual differences are important (see below), there is a central tendency for children to respond with affective arousal to many of the typical behaviors of parents. As indicated above, these involve physical stimulation behaviors as well as behaviors perceived as novel, incongruous, or surprising. The valence of these subjective experiences depends partly on the constitution of the child, but also depends critically on the sensitivity and skill of the parent as well as the willingness of the parent to engage in these behaviors. Thus, in understanding the socialization of the emotions involved in physical play it is necessary to consider both the contribution of the parent and the contribution of the child. At present the relative contributions of parent and child to variation in physical play are unknown, but the following will describe several possible sources of variation. From a theoretical point of view, however, there is presumably wide variation in the relative contributions of parents and children, depending on the idiosyncracies of particular cases. For example, children with extreme temperaments are expected to have a very large impact on the character of parent–child physical play, whereas in cases where both the parent and child are unexceptional there is expected to be a more balanced contribution from each (MacDonald, 1986b; see also Chapter 1).

1. Possible Child Contributions to Individual Differences

Regarding the contributions of the child, emphasis should first be given to a point discussed above, the intrinsic nature of the motivation involved in physical play. Children are best thought of as being biologically prepared to respond with affective arousal to many of the behaviors of parents, including those involved in physical play. Regarding the variables affecting individual differences among children in response to physical play, there is ample evidence that boys engage in more intense physical games with their parents (and peers) than do girls, especially activities such as wrestling (MacDonald & Parke, 1984, 1986). In addition, as indicated above, the age of the child is an important variable affecting both the amount and the intensity of physical play.

Variation among children in the affective response to these types of stimulation may also be mediated in part by the temperament of the individual. The research on temperament in childhood summarized in Chapter 2 indicates variation in a dimension of reactivity to stimulation, termed emotionality, as well as two self-regulatory dimensions. One extreme of these self-regulatory dimensions defines highly impulsive, reward sensitive individuals who are prone to sensation seeking, while the other extreme is defined by individuals who are highly cautious and sensitive to punishment. There is evidence which can be interpreted as indicating that both of these dimensions affect parent–child physical play.

Specifically, MacDonald (1987c) found that sociometrically popular children engaged in significantly more physical play than did rejected children and both of these groups engaged in more physical play than did neglected children. The largest differences, however, were between the neglected children and the other two groups. Similar findings occurred for ratings of positive affect during the play sessions. The results for physical play and the affective measures indicate not only that neglected children engage in less of the affectively arousing type of stimulation characteristic of physical play than do the rejected and popular children, but that neglected children are less likely to approach stimulation during the physical play sessions. These findings are consistent with the idea that neglected children are lower on the trait of sensation seeking than are popular or rejected children.

However, despite the indication that popular children engage in more physical play and show more positive affective expressiveness than do rejected children, the data indicate that the play sessions of rejected children are characterized by more overstimulation and avoidance of stimulation than is the case with popular children and their parents. The interactions of the rejected children were characterized by alternately approaching and then withdrawing from the source of stimulation. Since the rejected children were characterized by higher levels of overstimulation than were the other groups and since withdrawal from stimulation often coincided with expressions of overstimulation on the part of the child, it seems reasonable to suppose that the withdrawal from stimulation was motivated by the child's being overstimulated. As a result of this tendency toward over-stimulation, the play sessions of the rejected children were less uniformly affectively positive than were the sessions of the popular children. The data on physical play are thus consistent with the theory of temperament described in Chapter 2: That theory predicts that there will be a group of children characterized by high levels of both sensation seeking and emotionality who will tend to show high levels of both approach and with-drawal during physical play.

Other aspects of the MacDonald (1987c) study, as well as recent extensions of this research, have indicated that abnormalities in the regulation of affect are characteristic of hyperactive children. The data described above also indicated that rejected children scored higher than either popular or neglected children on nine of the ten scale items of the Conners Abbreviated Symptom Questionnaire (Conners, 1973). Since in this study the rejected children engaged in high levels of physical play and had several other charac-teristics of hyperactive children, such as poor peer relations, the results suggest an overlap between hyperactive and sociometrically rejected children and that both types tend to seek highly stimulating environments.

In addition, MacDonald (1987d) reported that clinically referred hyperactive children engage in very high levels of physical play with their parents, especially their fathers, as well as with their peers and older children. The play sessions indicate very high levels of affective arousal. Although there may be some overlap in individual cases with unselected children, it is clear that these levels are on the average much higher than in unselected populations. Moreover, interview material indicates that these children seek out this style of play from their environment, often asking parents or older siblings to engage in physical play. The interviews also indicate that parents characterize their children as tending to engage in dangerous activities, such as riding bicycles in a reckless manner or climbing on roofs, and that they often worry that they will act in a reckless and impulsive manner that could endanger them. Parent and teacher reports on the EAS Temperament Survey (Buss & Plomin, 1984) indicate that these children are characterized as highly extraverted, scoring low on items such as shyness. These data are highly congruent with the idea that hyperactive children are high in the temperamental characteristic of stimulus seeking described in Chapter 2.

Other data also suggest that hyperactive children are high in sensation seeking. Brimer and Levine (1983) found that hyperactives sought auditory stimulation more than normals did and propose that the high level of activity seen in these children is a result of an abnormal need for sensory stimulation. Fiedler and Ullman (1983) found that hyperac-tive boys were more curious than normal boys, a finding that could be interpreted in terms of stimulus seeking. Medication with methylphenidate decreased the level of curiosity, but the hyperactives still remained more curious than normal boys. In addition, Zentall and Zentall (1983) synthesized a large body of work within the framework of optimal-level-of-arousal theory that points in this direction. Hyperactive children "behave as though normal levels of stimulation were insufficient'' (p. 453). The increased activity, vocalization, and even aggression characteristic of hyperactive children are interpreted as being engaged in because they increase visual, auditory, and kinesthetic input. (The relationship between hyperactivity and aggression is discussed in Chapter 6.)

More evidence for this interpretation of the behavior of hyperactive children comes from studies indicating that they behave relatively normally in highly stimulating environments and more poorly in very boring tasks, such as ones requiring vigilance (Kaspar, Millichap, Backus, Child, & Schulman, 1971; Minde, Lewin, Weiss, Lavigueur, Douglas, & Sykes, 1971; Stewart, 1970; Zentall, 1975, 1977, 1980). A very boring stimulus environment results in these children seeking out stimulation from aspects of the environment not relevant to the task at hand or engaging in self-stimulation.

Second, the data indicate that hyperactive children are hyperreactive to stimulation, that is, high on the temperamental trait of emotionality. First, I have already commented on the overlap between the categories of hyperactive and rejected children. In the Mac-Donald (1987c) study it was noted that rejected children had higher levels of overstimulation as well as withdrawal from stimulation during the physical play sessions. These findings are consistent with the idea that rejected, and, by extension, hyperactive children are hypersensitive to stimulation and become overaroused during physical play sessions. Similarly, many of the hyperactive children are hyperreactive to stimulation. During the physical play sessions there are high levels of screaming and avoidance of stimulation, as well as instructions to the parent to stop engaging in particularly arousing practices such as tickling. In some cases the child screams and begins to avoid the parent even before the parent has actually touched the child. Parents sometimes comment that they are hesitant to engage in physical play with their child, even though the child requests it, because the child gets out of control during the physical play and/or cannot calm down afterward. During physical play the child often becomes overexcited and continues to engage in behavior that the parent finds objectionable, such as hitting or kicking, even after attempts at discipline on the part of the parent. In addition, the child often continues to elicit physical play after the sessions are over and the parent can only terminate this type of activity with great difficulty and often with tears and tantrumlike behavior on the part of the child.

In addition, interview material as well as the results of the Buss and Plomin (1984) EAS Temperament Survey performed by both parents and teachers indicate that these children are considered to be highly emotional. They are characterized as "wearing their emotions on their sleeve" and as crying a great deal. One perceptive parent characterized his daughter as "having a problem with stimulation" because she consistently over-reacted to stimulation of all types. Moreover, although not true of all the highly emotional hyperactive children, it is not uncommon for these parents to describe their children as generally hyperresponsive to stimulation. Some of these children are characterized as overreactive to spicy foods, new situations, bright lights, the labels on clothing, etc.

In concluding this section, one might speculate that variation in parent–child physical play could itself be one source of environmental variation in temperament. As noted above, Sroufe (1979b) proposes that parents engaging in affectively arousing play with infants may foster the development of tension tolerance. Physical play between fathers and their children involves the provision of extremely high levels of affectively arousing stimulation. Thus, it could be that by providing the child with high levels of affectively arousing stimulation in a sensitive manner (that is, not overarousing the child), it would be possible to increase the level of stimulation at which the child is comfortable. Fogel (1982) points out that when individuals are consistently exposed to high levels of stimulation, they develop coping mechanisms so that the situation becomes less arousing to them: "The infant's ability to remain engaged with the mother during a period of optimal arousal may be a developmental achievement that begins with becoming overwhelmed by intense positive arousal, and culminates with the ability to control the level of arousal through tension-release mechanisms" (p. 35). Thus, the child would be expected to become less sensitive to stimulation as time goes on and thereby become lower on emotionality as defined in Chapter 2.

Although parents may contribute to tension tolerance in the child, it may well be that part of this increased tolerance to higher intensity of stimulation is the result of maturational processes. For a young infant, simply gazing into the mother's face often leads to overarousal, and many of the typical activities that occur during physical play, such as swinging the child around or tossing it in the air, would be much too arousing. As children get older they are able to respond positively to much higher levels of stimulation typical of physical play, and still later, as adolescents, they enjoy roller coaster rides and loud music. In Chapter 6, evidence is discussed indicating that sensation seeking peaks in young adulthood and declines thereafter.

Besides influencing the temperamental trait of emotionality, engaging in physical play with a sensitive, responsive adult or peer may well result in greater skill in the regulation of affect. We have seen that the regulation of affect is a fundamental social skill and is a ubiquitous feature of parent–child and presumably peer social interaction. Physical play provides an arena in which the child could be made more aware of his or her emotionality and encouraged to monitor his or her levels of arousal so that overstimulation and overexcitement do not occur. Parents of extremely emotional children could also be trained to be more aware of overstimulation in the child and taught to lower their levels of stimulation, much as Field (1982) advocates for the parents of premature children.

It is also reasonable to infer that parent–child physical play may influence temperament by making children more sensitive to the reward value of the affectively arousing stimulation provided by the parents. In Chapter 2, it was argued that the biological basis of impulsivity-sensation seeking involves sensitivity to rewards. Although the emphasis there was on the idea that genetic variation has an important role in influencing variation on this trait, it is quite possible that repeated stimulation of these reward centers would result in greater sensitivity to rewards. Such a model would be parallel to the model of environmental influences on the positive social reward system: Repeated stimulation of these reward centers results in increased sensitivity to these rewards. This possibility would suggest that physical play would be contraindicated as a form of therapy for hyperactive children, because it would tend to make them even more reward oriented than they already are. Alternatively, engaging in supervised physical play may have very salutary effects for such children if the physical play is tied to training in affect regulation as suggested above. Moreover, because physical play is so rewarding to these children, it often results in the child being in a good mood. As suggested by MacDonald (1987c), because physical play is so rewarding to many children, it may have a generally beneficial effect on parent–child relations by causing the parent to be generally viewed in a positive manner. As such, physical play may be viewed as one aspect of the parental behaviors that make up the concept of parental warmth. In Chapter 5, evidence is reviewed indicating that parental warmth is associated with a variety of positive outcomes in children in our society.

These considerations would also suggest that increasing the amount of physical play may be an effective form of therapy for behaviorally inhibited children: By continually exposing them to the rewarding stimulation found in physical play they would become more sensitive to these rewards and the relative balance between sensitivity to reward and sensitivity to punishment would shift in the direction of the former. Clearly a great deal of research remains to be done on the possible therapeutic effects of the physical play paradigm. This research has the promise of shedding light on basic processes by which the environment influences temperament and the regulation of affect.

2. Possible Parental Contributions to Individual Differences

Regarding the possible contributions of the parent, there is evidence that as parents get older they are less willing to participate in physical play, even after controlling for the age of the child (MacDonald & Parke, 1986). The lowered levels of physical play are congruent with data indicating that parenting styles become more androgynous (i.e., less sex-specific) as parents get older and result in the possibility that age is an important source of variation among parents in the degree to which they engage in physical play with their children. Even more important than age, however is the often replicated effect of sex of parent described above, with men engaging in much higher levels of physical play than women. Other sources of variation in the degree to which parents engage in physical play presumably include contextual variables such as amount of leisure time, economic stress on the family, and type of job.

Parents may also differ in the extent to which they are sensitive to the affective cues of their children. We have seen that the physical play sessions of sociometrically rejected and hyperactive children tend to be characterized by overstimulation and approach–withdrawal behavior. Future research should address the question of whether there is important variation in the sensitivity of parents to the affective cues of their children during physical play and whether there are general personality differences among parents which are associated with the extent of physical play. Parents who are insensitive to the affective cues of their children may chronically overstimulate or understimulate their children with the result that the play situation is aversive to the child. Such a situation may well contribute to a generally negative parent–child affective tone with effects that go far beyond the immediate play context. Conversely, a sensitive parent and a correspondingly positive affective tone in the parent–child interaction could affect the general affective tone of the parent–child relationship in a positive manner.

Regarding possible variation in personality, individuals relatively high on the trait of sensation seeking (Zuckerman, 1979) would be expected to seek high levels of stimulation in interaction with their children, while individuals who are low on this trait would be expected to enjoy quiet games with their children. In this regard, it is interesting that men generally score higher on tests of sensation seeking than women (Zuckerman, 1979; see also Chapter 6) and, as indicated above, there is a peak of sensation seeking in young adulthood, findings that parallel the general findings that men engage in physical play more often and more intensely than do women and that there is a decline in physical play among parents as they become older.

3. Conclusion: The Functions of Physical Play

Our earlier discussion of play in animals suggested that play has important adaptive functions and that these effects are made possible by high levels of plasticity during development. The finding that high levels of parent–child physical play occur in popular children (MacDonald & Parke, 1984; Parke, MacDonald, Beitel, & Bhavnagri, 1988; MacDonald, 1987c) suggests that physical play performs a socializing function in children, possibly related to affecting the skills involved in the regulation of affect. In this perspective physical play would be proposed to influence popularity by having a beneficial effect on reactive and self-regulatory processes which are central to social competence. Moreover, we have suggested that parent–child physical play may be an aspect of parental warmth and thus associated with cohesive familial interactions.

Other research by Parke and his colleagues (Parke et al., 1988; Parke, MacDonald, Burks, Carson, Beitel, Bhavnagri, & Barth, in press) suggests that physical play is related to emotional decoding and encoding skills. Ability to decode emotional expressions was positively associated with sociometric status and with teacher ratings of popularity. In addition, the emotional expressions of popular children were more easily decoded by nonfamilial observers, indicating that their emotional expressions were clearer. Further investigation revealed that there were positive correlations between father's physical play and daughter's ability to correctly discriminate emotional states, and there was a similar trend for boys.

Taken together, these results indicate a rich set of interrelationships between parent–child physical play and the development of social competence with peers. However, as the results with rejected and hyperactive children (MacDonald, 1987c) indicate, differences in temperament and perhaps the relative sensitivity of parents to the affective cues of their children may also strongly affect the behavior of children in physical play sessions. High levels of physical play *per se* are not expected to be associated with social competence, and high levels of overstimulation and approach–withdrawal behavior during physical play are associated with sociometric rejection and hyperactivity.

The proposed socialization function of physical play is consistent with the animal literature and research in peer rough and tumble play, but there is the additional suggestion that physical play involves practice for fighting and is associated with dominance among children, at least as children approach adolescence. Humphreys and Smith (1987) observed rough-and-tumble play in children aged 7, 9, and 11 years. Rough-and-tumble play was predominantly nonaggressive in nature and the partners were significantly more liked by each other than average at each age. By age 11, the initiators of rough-and-tumble interactions were seen by classmates as significantly stronger than the partner and, despite this disparity in strength, they were more similar in strength than would be expected by chance: "Eleven-year-olds seemed to prefer partners who were weaker, but not much weaker, than themselves" (p. 208). As indicated in Chapter 6, boys tend to interact with other boys near them in the dominance hierarchy, so that these interactions may well be an aspect of dominance relationships.

The authors interpret these results as suggesting that for younger children rough and tumble play has a social affiliative function. Younger children also use rough-and-tumble play as a mechanism to practice fighting, but the serious practice of fighting skills occurs later. The fact that the older children choose partners of similar strength is especially suggestive of this function. Neill (1976) found that in 12–13-year-old boys rough and tumble was more like serious fighting, and often involved hostility and aggression. However, playful rough and tumble remained more common than hostile rough-and-tumble play even at this age, even though it became rougher as the children approached adolescence. Fagen (1981) has noted that play fighting in animals tends to become more intense and serious as the animals approach adulthood.

Pellegrini (1987) also suggests that rough-and-tumble play may function to teach children to differentiate between playful and aggressive episodes. This function is similar to the emotional encoding and decoding hypothesis for parent–child physical play described above. Beyond learning to differentiate these episodes, children may well learn how far they can go in play-fighting without provoking an angry or aggressive response in another child. This function of rough and tumble may well be first apparent in parent–child physical play, as fathers are often seen telling their children how far they can go without causing pain. Such a function is also suggested in the rough-and-tumble play among wolf cubs: by receiving negative responses from injured animals the animals appear to gradually learn to inhibit their biting during play fighting.

The relationships between peer rough-and-tumble play and aggression are undoubtedly complex. The research described above suggests that as children become older peer rough and tumble play tends to become rougher and more a part of the serious business of dominance interactions. It thus would not be surprising to find that popular children, especially boys, tend to engage in fairly high levels of this activity, and this appears to be the case. However, the data on parent–child physical play also suggest that hyperactive and rejected children engage in high levels of physical play, and both of these groups are highly prone to aggression (see Chapter 6). Again, high levels of physical play *per se* are not expected to be related to popularity with peers. Physical play which leads to aggression and which is characterized by relative inability to regulate one's affect is expected to be aversive to other children and the evidence is that rejected and hyperactive children are prone to having exactly these deficits.

Finally, more emphasis should be given to thinking about the role of positive affect during the physical play sessions. This response is particularly obvious in parent–child physical play with younger children. In observing videotapes, the proposed function of practice for fighting seems to be almost completely submerged to just having fun. Particularly noteworthy is the common presence of tickling behavior on the part of the parent. It is difficult to imagine how this ubiquitous behavior is related to future fighting skill. Yet tickling often forms the entire basis of very prolonged parent–child play bouts. Parents will grab the child and tickle him or her, then release the child who gleefully avoids the parent but then returns almost immediately to receive more of the stimulation.

The function of this very intense positive affective response of the child remains a mystery. Among other animals only chimpanzees, our closest relatives, engage in tickling games, and this behavior is very common among them. If tickling were essential for play fighting, it is difficult to understand why its distribution among animals should be so limited. Tickling games could facilitate father–child bonding in humans, but such a role is not indicated among chimpanzees, as chimpanzee males have no role at all in rearing offspring. Indeed, female mating is promiscuous, so that the biological father is unknown. Moreover, the examples of male–infant tickling games provided by van Lawick-Goodall (1971) ended with the infant's mother "rescuing" the infant from the game, even though the infant was obviously enjoying it. However, mother chimpanzees also play tickling games with their infants, so that a generally positive effect on improving social ties within the group is a strong possibility. Indeed, it is difficult to avoid the conclusion that the provision of such intensely pleasurable stimulation to a child would result in the child viewing the person providing this stimulation in a positive light. This is the basis for the suggestion made above the parent–child physical play is an aspect of parental warmth and a factor underlying social cohesiveness in these species. The factors underlying social cohesiveness in human societies are the subject of Chapters 4 and 5.

III. The Development of the Emotions

A. Emotions in Infancy

Sroufe (1979b) describes the development of three specific affect systems in infancy: pleasure–joy, wariness–fear, and rage–anger. For each of these systems, there is a general tendency for an increasing importance of the cognitive abilities of the infant, a trend from undifferentiated, un-self-conscious feeling, what Kagan would term a "feeling tone" (see above), to the existence of highly specific emotions instigated by cognitively appraised external events.

1. *Pleasure–joy.* The system of pleasure–joy begins in the neonatal period with endogenous smiles, which are the result of CNS modulation of arousal during REM sleep. Later, within the first 2 months, the smile can be elicited by gentle stimulation, at first when the infant is drowsy, and later when the infant is fully awake. Sroufe notes that the smile is typically elicited only after the level of stimulation goes beyond a hypothetical threshold and then only occurs after the peak of arousal, that is, as the infant is relaxing during the decline in arousal. Around the third month the infant smiles as a result of recognizing and psychologically processing the content of the stimulus. If the infant is presented with visual stimulation repeatedly, smiling occurs as a result of the infant's being able to assimilate the event to its previous schema of the event. Sroufe emphasizes that it is the infant's psychological *engagement* with the event that produces the smile rather than the smile being purely the result of stimulation *per se*. The occurence of laughter is similar to that of smiling, but requires a steeper gradient of tension release than does the smile, that is, there is a greater buildup of tension, so that during relaxation there is a more intense release of emotion.

The occurrence of joy involves a further degree of cognitive processing than mere recognition or psychological processing of an event. The emotion of joy occurs when the infant is able to assess the meaning of an event in relation to itself, and this occurs around the seventh month of life. The infant is now able to derive positive emotions as a result of fairly sophisticated social games, such as peek-a-boo. Later, in the second year the infant is able to have a sustained feeling of joy, what Sroufe terms *elation,* which can occur in response to a general situation, such as entering a room full of toys or having access to a large box of cookies.

Thus, in general, the development of the positive emotions during infancy is characterized by an increasing cognitive sophistication and a gradual shift from a sole dependence on unprocessed stimulation to the importance of meaning in producing positive emotions. The discussion of physical play presented above, however, indicates that there is a continuing importance of pure stimulation not only in infancy, but throughout childhood. As children develop, they are apparently able to experience positive emotions via a much broader set of incentive events as a result of increasing cognitive sophistication, but this fact need not be seen as indicating the complete demise of physical stimulation as an important incentive event for positive affect throughout childhood.

2. *Wariness–fear.* Sroufe traces the fear response to early instances in which infants appear to become "stimulus-bound" while looking at objects. In the second month of life the infant will look at an object for a prolonged period, seemingly unable to become disengaged, until finally a negative emotional response occurs. The content of the event is unimportant here, but in the fourth month infants will become distressed at the sight of unfamiliar events, especially the face of an unfamiliar person, that they cannot assimilate to their presently held conceptual schemas. This latter incidence of wariness does involve more cognitive processing and is a clear case of an emotional response. Kagan (1984a) also gives great importance to distress aroused by unfamiliar events, which first occurs between 4 and 10 months of age, but argues that it is not necessary to suppose that this fear response derives from any developmentally more primitive form of distress.

The next phase in development according to Sroufe occurs when the infant is actually able to place an event in a negative, threatening category. The vast majority of infants 10–12 months of age will show a fear response to strangers, a response that is particularly common if the stranger is intrusive, as would occur if the stranger immediately picked up the child without becoming familiar with the child first (Sroufe, 1977). Moreover, if the intrusive stranger picks the child up a second time, the child will show the emotional response even sooner than the first time, indicating that it is not merely lack of assimilation to presently held schemas that is occurring, but rather the recognition of an event that is appraised as threatening. At times the negative category for an event may be the result of conditioning, as would occur if a child developed a fear of doctors because of the shot that a doctor had given it.

Kagan (1984a) also emphasizes the fact that fear may result when stimuli depart from expectations, as, for example, if a 7-month-old infant is presented with a disfigured face. Similarly, Hebb (1946) showed that chimpanzees reared with other chimpanzees developed a strong fear of a picture of a chimpanzee head without a body, while animals reared in isolation showed no such fear. The former animals would appear to have developed the fear as a result of a violation of their expectation as to what a proper chimpanzee should look like, and similar fears may develop in children.

There is compelling evidence that some of the developmental changes in fear responses are biologically based. It has already been noted that fear is one of Izard's (1978) basic emotions and is seen in all human cultures and indeed in many mammalian groups. Moreover, there is evidence that some of the releasing stimuli for fear are innate. Sackett (1966) studied infant rhesus monkeys who were isolated from birth to 9 months of age and were presented with pictures of other infants and adults as well as a picture of an adult with a threatening expression. The infants spontaneously showed a fear response only to the adult with the threatening expression and the highest frequency of this response occurred between approximately 2 and 3½ months of age. In addition, many writers on human emotions (e.g., Gray, 1971, 1982) have noted that humans are far more likely to develop fears of things that have been dangerous and threatening in our evolutionary past than of far more dangerous things that have recently appeared. Thus, people tend to develop phobias of snakes and spiders, open places, and heights rather than of far more dangerous things such as guns, knives, and automobiles that have recently become available. The developmentally predictable fear of strangers that occurs in the latter part of the first year must be seen in a similar light, as due to natural selection for an adaptive response to a potentially dangerous situation.

The data of Sackett clearly suggest a biologically based timetable for the development of fear in monkeys and there is evidence for a similar timetable in humans. Human infants show a maximum fear reaction to strangers at approximately 8 months of age whether reared in Uganda (Ainsworth, 1963), on a Hopi Indian reservation (Dennis, 1940), or in middle-class America (Sroufe, 1977). There is also evidence that this response is tied to physiological changes in the infant: Emde, Gaensbauer, and Harmon (1976) showed that in the latter part of the first year in humans and at similar developmental points in a variety of other species there is a major developmental shift in EEG patterns that is associated with the onset of true fear reactions as well as changes in heart rate patterns such that the heart rate increases in response to the presentation of threatening events. Finally, Plomin and DeFries (1985) showed that the onset of fear is more similar in identical twins than in fraternal twins.

These considerations indicate that there are strong, biologically based central tendencies to develop the emotion of fear as well as to show species-wide patterns of development of this emotional response to particular types of stimuli. This of course does not imply that the learning of specific fears as a result of conditioning and specific negative experiences is unimportant. Nor does this imply that cognitive processing is unimportant in the development of some fears. The work of Hebb (1946) and similar work with humans described above (Kagan, 1984a) show that fears may occur when stimuli violate expectations. Nevertheless, as Sroufe (1979b) points out, the development of fear of strangers is unlikely to be due to a simple violation of expectation, but rather results from actively categorizing the stranger in a negative category: The second presentation of an intrusive stranger results in fear even sooner than did the first presentation.

3. *Rage–anger.* As in the case of pleasure–joy and wariness–fear, Sroufe distinguishes between rage, which can occur in the newborn, and anger, which requires intentionality and occurs only after 6 months of age. Anger occurs when an infant responds negatively to a particular event and thus requires more cognitive sophistication, such as attributing the predicament to a particular cause. More sophisticated manifestations of anger, such as defiance and aggression, are said to occur only in the second year and require a stronger, more mature concept of self. Kagan (1984a) notes that anger often results from the disruption of a goal-directed activity, and speculates that from an evolutionary perspective it might be adaptive for an infant to establish a resistant response to such events rather than simply acquiesce to the occurrence of interruptions. Such a child would tend to react assertively to such interruptions, a response that might serve it well in competing for social status later in life.

In the second year the trend toward the development of emotions that require more sophisticated cognitive processing continues. Kagan (1984a) notes especially the existence of depression following prolonged absence of the caretaker, an emotion that involves the ability to recall the presence of a caretaker that is no longer present. Emotions such as pride and performance anxiety, which involve the comparison of one's present or future behavior to a standard, also occur in the second year. Kagan hypothesizes that such emotions would be evolutionarily adaptive because they would inhibit aggression among siblings because such aggression would violate an adult standard. That such aggression could have important adaptive implications is illustrated by a case (albeit rare) in which a 30-month-old infant killed his 22-month-old playmate. Kagan also notes the development of guilt well after the second year, at about age 4 years, with the delay being due to the need for further cognitive maturation required to realize that another action was possible.

B. Emotions in Childhood and Adolescence: The Importance of Cognitions and Resources

The theme that continuing cognitive sophistication is required for the development of new emotions is continued into childhood and adolescence. Kagan (1984a) notes that children begin to evaluate themselves in comparison to other children on such qualities as intelligence or athletic skill and develop emotions such as insecurity, confidence, jealousy, and envy. Unlike the 2-year-old, older children need not attend to a specific action of another as a standard, but can evaluate themselves with respect to a general disposition of another person. Emotions resulting from the increased analytical ability of adolescence also occur, as when a teenager becomes distressed by the lack of rational foundation for religious beliefs.

The general picture is thus one in which increased cognitive competencies drive the development of new emotions, which overlay the primitive emotions that are directly linked to facial expressions and go back to early infancy. These shifts are essentially due to the incentive events for these new emotions becoming increasingly complex interpretations of reality. From an adaptationist view and reflecting the importance of resources in such a view (Charlesworth, 1988), it is expected that specific emotions will be associated with specific aspects of resource control and distribution. This general perspective can be integrated with the views of several theorists of emotion who have stressed the importance of goals to the elicitation of emotion (Campos *et al.,* 1983; Mandler, 1975; Roseman, 1979). Emotions motivate as well as result from evaluations of resource-directed behavior. Thus, positive emotions such as joy and pride often occur when a child is succeeding or has succeeded in obtaining resources, while frustration, anger, or sadness occur as a result or in anticipation of losing or failing to obtain the resource. Thus, Elder (1974) shows that negative affective evaluations and emotional distress were common among middle-class families who suffered economic hardship during the Depression and such negative emotional reactions are an everyday occurrence among children in response to loss of resources. Anticipation of obtaining a resource, and regret for lost opportunities for obtaining a resource, would also result in emotions. Resources may be material objects that satisfy needs, but the needs involved may also relate to affective resources, such as friendship (Charlesworth, 1988).

The evolutionary perspective suggests the commonsense result that very valuable resources, for example, resources essential to survival, would be associated with the strongest emotions: Losing the family farm is likely to result in a more intense emotion than losing a football game. For the reasons described in Chapters 4 and 5, relationships that involve attachments are also expected to be associated with intense emotions, and in Charlesworth's terms this is because important affective resources are involved. In many cases the relative importance of the resource can be predicted by evolutionary theory, so that one can make specific hypotheses regarding the degree of emotional reaction. Thus, Smith (1988) and Segal (1988) show that bereavement patterns are influenced by the reproductive value of the deceased as well as the degree of genetic relatedness of the bereaver to the deceased (see Chapter 8 for a detailed discussion of the importance of the degree of genetic relatedness in affecting emotional reactions affecting altruism).

Besides the importance of the perceived value of the resource and the importance of these resources in adaptation, the evolutionary perspective suggests that the risk to oneself or to one's relatives or allies incurred in the activity should be importantly related to the intensity of the emotional reaction. This principle reflects the importance of costs as well as benefits in evolutionary-ecological theory. That risky behavior is associated with high emotional intensity is well known. High-stakes gambling, if one cannot afford the possible losses, is extremely exciting and the reward value of this excitement (for sensation seekers) is the reason gambling is so popular. One of the most interesting aspects of this phenomenon from an evolutionary perspective is the sex difference in risk-taking behavior discussed in Chapter 6. As indicated there, risk-taking behavior is affected by the temperamental trait of sensation seeking and there are evolutionary reasons for expecting this trait to be higher in males. The trait of emotionality would also be expected to influence one's arousal level in a situation with risks to the self. Other aspects of riskiness that would be expected to influence the intensity of the emotion include the probability of a given result and the related quality of degree of expectedness, and Roseman (1979) includes these dimensions as dimensions related to goals associated with different emotions.

Emotions such as self-esteem that arise from the self-evaluative process are also indirectly related to resource-directed behavior. High self-esteem occurs for the most part when one is getting on well, that is, when one is (roughly) engaging in adaptive interactions with the environment. This is reflected in the dimensions of self-esteem proposed by various writers. For example, Harter (1983) suggests that competence, power, virtue (the feeling of being morally correct), and acceptance by others are dimensions of self-esteem. With the exception of moral virtue (but see below and especially Chapter 8), it takes little imagination to relate these dimensions to resource control. Thus, individuals who have power over others (resources) feel good about themselves and are thereby motivated to continue this situation or increase their power. Individuals without power have low self-esteem, which is a negative affective state, and are thereby motivated to change things, a change that would also be adaptive. As an example directly relating resource possession to self-esteem among children, Elder (1974) found that during the Depression economically deprived adolescents were rated by their mothers as being more self-conscious and susceptible to "hurt feelings" than were nondeprived children. In addition, economic deprivation was associated with a higher incidence of worrying, crying easily, and angering easily. The self-image of deprived girls was especially affected, quite possibly due to restrictions on their clothes-buying. These findings clearly implicate the importance of resources for self-esteem as well as the importance of contextual effects on resource availability. These findings are discussed further in Chapter 9.

Another evolutionary aspect of self-esteem is the possibility that it involves self-deception. Krebs *et al.* (1988) review evidence indicating that people sometimes engage in self-serving attributional biases in order to protect their self-esteem, including their self-image as a person of high moral rectitude. These data are placed in an evolutionary perspective by noting that this behavior involves self-deception. Evolutionary theorists have noted that a species that is able to detect its own lies may benefit from not being conscious of them (Trivers, 1985). Therefore the self-evaluative emotion of high self-esteem can occur even in the presence of self-interested motivations related to resource acquisition and control. This type of self-deception, which clearly results in a feeling of moral virtue or recittude, is a prominent aspect of moral reasoning and is discussed further in Chapters 7 and 8. Krebs *et al.* review studies showing that individuals who feel good about themselves tend to behave adaptively whether or not this feeling is due to their having distorted reality. They have more perseverence and more self-confidence. By thinking that they are right or that they are special, even if this is not true, they induce positive mental states and physical health. Thus, Alloy and Abramson (1982) found that depressed people make attributions that are not flattering to the self, but these attributions are also more valid than those of people who are not depressed. Denial that one has a serious disease or is at risk during surgery is also associated with good outcomes (Goleman, 1986). As Krebs *et al.* point out, it is not the validity of a belief that is acted on by natural selection, but the adaptiveness of the behaviors to which the belief gives rise.

These considerations raise the issue of the relationships among personal ideology, self-esteem, and adaptation. In Chapter 9, ideology is introduced as a contextual variable in sociobiological theory, intimately bound up with social controls, developmental contexts, and biological fitness. It is appropriate here, however, to note that one role of ideology is to make people feel good about themselves. Individuals without resources, competence, or power, three of the dimensions of self-esteem, are able to adopt ideologies that attribute these conditions to circumstances beyond their control or to the behavior of others, independent of the truth or falsity of these attributions. Krebs *et al.* note that, in conformity to sociobiological theory, the attributions of the causes of behavior are often self-serving, and clearly an ideology such as that described above can be an important aspect of self-serving political change. As indicated in Chapter 9, however, ideology is a very poorly behaved variable and variation in personal ideology can occur that is quite independent of the adaptiveness of the behaviors it justifies.

Finally, it should be noted that people's attempts at self-understanding do not always involve self-deception. Krebs *et al.* also stress that it is quite often adaptive for humans to develop a sense of themselves and the world that corresponds to reality, just as the realist philosopher of science claims that the scientist is attempting to do. Such a perspective can be found in cognitive-developmental approaches to self-understanding (e.g., Damon & Hart, 1982). Goleman (1987) also notes several examples where self-deception is radically maladaptive, as, for example, when the citizens of Pitcher, Oklahoma failed to heed an engineer's warning that the town was about to collapse and many died as a result. Denial of the reality of child abuse or parental alcoholism can lead children to label these behaviors in more socially acceptable ways and thereby prevent adaptive changes. Goleman notes that psychotherapy often involves a realistic confrontation of these problems.

In Chapter 1, it was noted that although there is a central tendency for the proximal mechanisms underlying behavior to result in adaptive behavior, there are many instances in which this is not the case. A nonreductionistic sociobiology as proposed here accepts the adaptiveness of behavior as an empirical problem and proposes that the adaptiveness of behavior is a central tendency, not a preempirical dogma or law of nature. Moreover, it is clear that not all goals that become invested with significant emotion are adaptive or that one's emotional reactions to attaining or losing them are adaptive. As Campos *et al.* (1983) point out, many goals are idiosyncratic or even neurotic. Nevertheless, it is clear that one's most intense emotions tend to occur as a result of resource-directed behavior in which the consequences to one's life or other aspects of one's successful adaptation to the world are highly significant and that generally these emotions facilitate adaptive behavior.

While agreeing therefore that cognitive processes are increasingly important in eliciting emotions, it clearly does not follow that one is not able to give an evolutionary, adaptationist account of these matters. Moreover, it does not follow that the biologically based natural incentive events emphasized as important in eliciting emotion in this chapter as well as in Chapters 4–6 and 8 become of decreasing importance in development. It is an important thesis of the perspective developed here that biologically based associations between incentive events and emotional responses continue well beyond infancy without important cognitive evaluations. For example, in Chapter 5 it is argued that the affective response of a child to the behaviors of a parent labeled warm and affectionate continue to exert influence well beyond infancy and that this connection between child response and adult behavior is best viewed as a biologically facilitated connection, as described in the present chapter for the case of the stimuli that are effective in physical play. In this perspective there are strong associations between these types of parental interactions and adaptive behavior in children, including social learning and the transmission of culture, friendship formation, and the socialization of aggression and morality. As a result, the importance of biologically based connections between parental behaviors and the affective responses of children may actually increase with development.

CHAPTER 4

Social and Biological Events in Infancy and Their Relevance for Later Behavior

It is incumbent on anyone writing a book on social development from an evolutionary perspective to write a chapter on attachment. Indeed, it is probably correct to state that the area of attachment theory and research has constituted the most visible triumph of an evolutionary approach within developmental psychology. There will be no attempt to review the research literature on attachment; instead I focus on some specific issues deriving from the concerns stated in Chapters 1 and 2. The purposes of this chapter are as follows: (a) to describe John Bowlby's theory of attachment and present it as a paradigm of a modern evolutionary theory of a developmental system; (b) to consider the question of the adaptiveness of attachment in the light of contemporary evolutionary theory; (c) to relate attachment to the theory of temperament described in Chapter 2; and (d) to address several of the theoretical issues raised in Chapter 1, namely the importance of early experience, the relative plasticity of social development, and the continuity and stability of behavior.

I. ATTACHMENT IN EVOLUTIONARY PERSPECTIVE

A. *The Ethological Theory of Attachment*

Theory and research on attachment have assumed a central place in our conceptualization of social development and seem to many to hold the promise of answering some of the fundamental questions of social development. If the claims of some attachment researchers are correct, adult affective relationships, adjustment with peers, and a variety of other attributes of the older child and adult can be traced back to the behavior of the infant with its mother in an unfamiliar situation.

The ethological theory of attachment has become the dominant theoretical perspective guiding research in the area of social relationships in infancy. This theory has been developed chiefly by Bowlby (1969, 1973), and several of the basic propositions of the theory were discussed in Chapter 1. The most basic way in which the ethological theory of attachment differs from previous theories is in the rejection of the secondary drive theory of attachment. Both Freudians and learning theorists argued that the infant's tie to its mother is based on the mother's role in satisfying the primary drives of the infant, especially the drive of hunger. It was believed that as a result of the repeated association between the gratification of hunger and the presence of the mother the child would be classically conditioned to view the mother in positive terms and seek to interact with her even when she was not providing nourishment. This tendency to seek out the mother as a result of the association of the mother with gratification was termed a secondary drive because it was produced as a result of learning the association between the presence of the mother and the satisfaction of the basic primary drive of hunger.

The secondary drive explanation of the process by which an infant develops an affective bond with its caretaker was called into question by the results of animal research, particularly the work of Harry Harlow (see Harlow & Harlow, 1965). In a famous experiment, Harlow housed infant monkeys in a situation where they received nourishment from a surrogate mother made out of wire mesh. The room also contained a surrogate mother covered with soft terrycloth. The secondary drive theory predicted that the monkey would become attached to the wire mesh surrogate, but in fact the monkey sought comfort and security with the soft terrycloth surrogate. The straightforward interpretation of these results is that the contact comfort provided by the terrycloth surrogate is intrinsically rewarding to the infant monkey. The attractiveness of the surrogate does not depend on its having satisfied a more basic need. Several similar studies have been done with dogs. For example, Igel and Calvin (1960) found that dog pups preferred a cloth surrogate to a wire surrogate independent of feeding. The study of Tizard (1978) of orphanage-reared children (described below) also indicates that providing children with an environment with proper nourishment and stimulation is not sufficient to prevent behavior problems. The author interprets these findings as indicating that the lack of a one-to-one attachment relationship resulted in these problems.

The results of studies such as this have important implications. The secondary drive approach attempted to build a theory of the motivation of human behavior out of a small number of biological drives, such as that of hunger, absolutely necessary for survival. Beyond these few drives human behavior derived from learned associations based on the contingencies surrounding the satisfaction of these drives. The animal research described above essentially implies that the list of biologically given motivations must be expanded, and this view of a highly variegated reward system is basic to the perspective developed in Chapter 2. The ethological theory proposes that many behaviors of the mother are intrinsically reinforcing to infants. The child does not enjoy the contact comfort it receives from its mother because the mother feeds the baby and changes its diapers, but because the baby is programmed to respond positively to this stimulation. Bowlby also suggests that absence from the mother in an unfamiliar situation is intrinsically fear-inducing. Again, the infant does not need to have a history of negative consequences occurring during the mother's absence in order to respond negatively to the situation, and its crying functions to bring the mother back. In Chapter 5, it is similarly argued that the parent behaviors classed as warm constitute such a set of intrinsically rewarding behaviors.

The basic view of the baby proposed here can be likened to a machine with a variety of buttons that can be pressed by the parent or other environmental events. Some of these buttons result in a positive affective response (e.g., contact comfort, smiling, gentle tickling) and some in a negative response (e.g., mother absent, parent hostile). The wiring underlying these responses is built into the machine rather than being dependent on prior learning experiences involving the provision of food or other basic survival needs.

Moreover, as in the treatment of emotion in Chapter 3, there is no implication within the ethological theory of a drivelike state that builds up, like hunger, until it is satisfied. The theory simply posits that the child is biologically predisposed to process certain types of environmental events in a positive or negative manner, but there is no implication of an internal state that builds up until it is satisfied or released. The positing of drivelike states as the basis of motivation is common not only to older learning theory, but is also common to Freudian theory and classical ethology. For Freud, instinctual sexual energies build up within the child and have to be released or repressed. For the classical ethologist, such as Konrad Lorenz, aggressive energy builds up within the animal until it is released by an appropriate environmental event or simply results in aimless aggressive behavior, termed *vacuum behavior* by the classical ethologists. It is a major step forward in developing a biological theory of motivation to be able to dispense with drive states as sufficient to form the basis of a biological theory of motivation.[1]

The presence of this relatively extensive repertoire of biologically prepotent affective responses to environmental stimulation does not imply that learning is irrelevant or nonexistent. A parent who consistently pushes the positive buttons is likely to have a child who develops a scheme of its caretaker as sensitive, responsive, and a source of pleasure. This scheme is the result of learning what to expect from the environment and developing schemas that reflect that experience.

The cognitive side of attachment is also very important to Bowlby and he draws extensively on control systems theory to describe the dynamics of the attachment relationship. Although infants generally attempt to attain proximity with their attachment figure, the degree to which they do so depends on a variety of internal and external circumstances. For example, if there is a stranger present or the child is in unfamiliar surroundings, there will be increasing attempts to maintain contact. Or if the child is tired and irritable it may be more likely to be distressed by the absence of its mother. The child behaves as if there is a set point, such that if the caretaker goes beyond it or if the set point itself is altered by the presence of strangers or unfamiliar surroundings, then the attachment behaviors of the child are triggered. The system works much like a thermostat, which is programmed to raise the temperature if the set point is exceeded. The child attempts to retain a feeling of security in the face of a variety of changing internal and external conditions. Attachment is thus a highly flexible response to changing environmental conditions, not a rigid set of stereotyped responses.

Bowlby also places attachment in an adaptive context. He proposes that as human

---

[1]This is not to state that the drive theory of socialization is completely inapplicable, at least for some species. Bacon and Stanley (1963) found that the attraction of dogs to humans had drivelike properties: Animals deprived of all but visual contact with humans approached humans more quickly than did animals not so deprived. Moreover, Stanley and Elliot (1962) found that dogs became socialized to humans even if the humans behaved passively rather than actively interacted with the animal. Thus, the attraction of dogs to humans not only does not depend on the human providing positively reinforcing contingencies such as food, but does not appear to depend on providing reinforcements of any kind.

groups developed into free-ranging savannah dwellers it was very important for the infant to retain proximity to the mother. As a result, there was natural selection for behaviors that facilitated proximity, and behaviors such as crying and smiling perform this function in human infants. The social signaling between mother and infant and the responsiveness of the mother to these signals are adaptive because they ensure proximity of infant to mother as well as efficient response to the changing needs of the infant. Moreover, the mother is also biologically predisposed to engage in caregiving responses that are appropriate responses to the care-eliciting behavior of the infant.

This evolutionary scenario is a reasonable one, but it is probably incomplete. Predation may be involved, but the proposed role of attachment as generally underlying human familial affective relationships suggests that other evolutionary pressures were involved as well. As is described in more detail in Chapter 5, there is reason to suppose that there has been natural selection in favor of nuclear family structure. Another adaptationist explanation of attachment and its consequences, then, is that the attachment system provides the cohesive bonding mechanism that facilitates the prototypical human social structure. Avoidance of predation is ill-suited to account for a system that according to several theorists (see pp. 126–130), provides prototypes for all future affective relationships. The alternative hypothesis is that human family structure was facilitated by the evolution of the reinforcers described in the attachment literature. At an ultimate level these reinforcers resulted in ties between the parents (greater paternal investment) and between parents and children (greater parental investment), as well as facilitated kin-directed acts of altruism (see Chapters 7 and 8).

A further reason supporting this perspective is that attachment behaviors occur in a large number of primate species but there is little evidence that attachment in many of these species results in affective bonding later in life or in the intimate, affectively valenced familial relationships characteristic of many human societies (see Chapter 5). Attachment behaviors are common among the nonhuman primates and serve to keep the infant close to the mother during a period in life when the infant is completely helpless, dependent, and highly subject to predation. Attachment among the primates is thus intimately connected to the survival of offspring, but in the vast majority of these species the close family ties and adult attachments characteristic of humans in many societies are not present. For example, the rhesus monkey so often studied in nonhuman research on attachment is highly promiscuous in its mating habits and shows no paternal care (Snowdon & Suomi, 1982). Monogamy occurs relatively frequently among the primates compared to other mammals, but still represents only about 18% of primate species (Hrdy, 1981). Indeed, the sexual behavior of the females of many primate species is quite promiscuous. Hrdy (1981) notes a common pattern in which female primates engage in sexual relationships with many males and proposes that this behavior is adaptive because:

> The uncertainty which inevitably surrounds paternity favors any female able to plant a seed of doubt. Even if a male is not a sufficiently probable progenitor to induce him to invest directly in an infant by caring for it, if he has mated with that female, it is unlikely that he could rule out completely the possibility that he fathered subsequent offspring. (Hrdy, 1981, p. 153)

In addition to the pattern of female promiscuity, another common pattern is that of a male and a harem of females. Monogamy and affectively based pair-bonding are definitely in the minority among primate mating systems.

Far more likely than the predation hypothesis is the possibility that the evolution of human attachment as an affective system related to later pair bonding is due to natural selection for monogamy. (The reasons for proposing that natural selection for monogamy is an important factor in human evolution are deferred until Chapter 5.) In this perspective the ubiquitous primate system of mother–infant attachment is viewed as a pre-existing system that became modified to function as a proximate mechanism of affective bonding underlying monogamy. As is demonstrated in Chapter 5, from the perspective of evolutionary theory monogamy is closely linked with increased levels of paternal investment. One might suppose then that the mother–infant attachment relations of monogamous species would involve more of what we would describe as love and affection, whereas among nonmonogamous species the attachment relations would be limited to physical care and protection. The love and affection of monogamous species would predispose individuals to form pair bonds later in life and thus facilitate monogamy. However, other pair-bonding mechanisms apart from affection may well occur in different monogamous primates, and the fact that monogamy appears sporadically in eight different primate families ranging from the relatively primitive prosimians up to humans is highly compatible with a variety of proximal mechanisms underlying pair-bonding in primates. The point is that in humans the existence of such affective bonds later in life is an important aspect of our social biology and is crucial to a discussion of family relationships (see Chapter 5).

Bowlby's ethological theory of attachment is heavily dependent on evolutionary theory. However, as indicated in Chapter 1, evolutionary theory has changed greatly since Bowlby's work, particularly by emphasizing differences in genetic self-interest in human relationships. Recently Lamb, Thompson, Gardner, and Charnov (1985) reassessed the adaptationist strand of attachment theory from the standpoint of contemporary theory. They point out that evolutionary theory predicts that parents will care for their children because children share their parents' genes and are their parents' means of propagating their genes to the next generation. Following Trivers (1974), they point out that there will be tradeoffs regarding how much resources should be invested in offspring or between different offspring. Parents may have to choose which offspring to invest in, so that behaving insensitively to a particular offspring may be adaptive to the parent. Moreover, it is expected that the behavior of the parents will change as a function of the developmental status and other characteristics of the child. In addition, Lamb et al. reject the idea of the "environment of evolutionary adaptiveness" advocated by Bowlby (1969, 1973) in favor of the view that behavior will involve flexible responses to current ecological conditions.

The idea that adaptive parent behavior often involves discrimination between offspring in the apportionment of resources is quite valid and is discussed by Smith (1988) and in several chapters below. Parenting is quite often not sensitive and responsive, and in Chapter 5 it will be argued that the cross-cultural patterns in these behaviors fits an adaptationist model. The rejection of the idea of the environment of evolutionary adaptiveness is more troublesome. Several sociobiological theorists have emphasized the possibility that natural selection could result in biological systems that become maladaptive in particular contexts at some later time (Alexander, 1979; MacDonald, 1984; see also Chapter 1 in this volume). For example, a natural tendency to be altruistic to those with whom one is reared might be adaptive in the context of small societies composed of relatives, but maladaptive in a large industrial society where one is raised with many nonrelatives (MacDonald, 1984; see also Chapter 8).

There is reason to believe that such a situation exists in the case of attachment. According to Bowlby, the environment-expectant genetic systems underlying attachment evolved in the prolonged prehistoric phase of human evolution. Under these conditions the parental behaviors associated with secure attachment came to result in positive affective response on the part of the child—the evolution of Bowlby's "natural clues." The enormous ecological shifts that have occurred since that time have not changed the biology of attachment. Infants still respond positively to sensitive, responsive caregiving, but the adaptive context has changed completely. The history of these changes will be described in more detail in Chapter 5, but the point to be noted here is that these changes may be considered to involve alterations in the environment provided by the parents, not alterations in what constitutes the biologically expected environment. From the standpoint of the infant it would still prefer to be treated with sensitivity and responsiveness: That is a part of its biology. That is the way it responds affectively to these behaviors of the parents. Unfortunately, the ecological context has not always made it adaptive for parents to provide this type of environment to children.

The situation is completely analogous to the case of the biological predisposition to respond with subjective pleasure to the taste of sweetness and recent changes in the environment that can result in maladaptive behavior involving sugar. As described by Barash (1987), the predisposition to respond with subjective pleasure to the taste of sugar is adaptive in evolutionary history because it is adaptive to eat natural foods containing sugar: Such foods are high in nutrition and calories. In a modern industrial society the ready availability of refined sugar along with our biologically based sweet tooth can result in health-threatening obesity and tooth decay. The sweet tooth remains, but the environment in which it evolved has vanished.

There is evidence that major changes in the way parents treat children can occur quite quickly in human history, too fast to be due to natural selection acting on genetic variation. For example, Lumsden and Wilson (1981) showed that the minimum time for a genetic change affecting human culture would be approximately 1000 years, and yet a major change in familial affective interactions occurred in less than 300 years in Western Europe (see also Chapter 5). Thus, the environment-expectant nature of the attachment system allows for quick, flexible responses to environmental events, but change in the biologically expected environment presumably takes much longer, and apparently has not occurred.

These comments, of course, reflect the view that attachment is indeed an environment-expectant genetic system in the sense of Chapter 2. If, instead, attachment is overwhelmingly influenced by some temperamental trait internal to the child and strongly influenced by the genes, then these speculations are moot. In such a case one would have to suppose that phenotypic variation in attachment classification and hence later behavior was adaptive, so that variation continues to be found in the population. The fact that there is indeed a great deal of cross-cultural variation in parental behaviors presumably related to attachment classification and that this variation tends to be adaptive suggests that the environment-expectant view may be correct (see Chapter 5 for a more detailed discussion). The environment-expectant point of view could, of course, be supplemented with the view that there is some variation in the internal characteristics of the child that affect but do not determine attachment status.

B. Attachment as an Environment-Expectant Genetic System versus Attachment as a Trait

Attachment research has moved into a mature state in which attachment status is increasingly seen as being affected by a number of variables, including not only the behavior of the mother as originally proposed, but also possible temperamental factors as well. These sources of variation can be interpreted as implying different biological mechanisms. The ethological tradition of Bowlby and the great majority of researchers in attachment have postulated that variation in the environment provided by the caregiver results in variation in attachment classification. In this view, the biology of the situation is captured in a postulated innate need for attachment and what have been termed environment-expectant genetic systems underlying the affective responses of the baby (see Chapter 3). Children are programmed to respond affectively to environmental variation in the sensitivity and responsiveness of their parents. Their attachment classification and the way in which they form relationships with other people are products of this environmental variation.

The view that temperament is important, however, hypothesizes that there are factors internal to the child that produce variation fairly independent of the environment. Environment-expectant genetic systems are very flexible and can change rapidly to meet new contingencies and in Chapter 5 it will be argued that much of the cross-cultural variation in parent–child interactions results from environmental variation interfacing with these environment-expectant genetic systems. Internal temperamental factors are perhaps not as flexible and in any case do not involve a valenced evaluation of environmental stimulation. However, making the reasonable assumption that they are not all-powerful in creating the phenotype, one can see them as interacting with environment-expectant genetic systems to influence the phenotype.

The importance of both types of biological system is a consistent theme throughout this book. The state of the research in the area of attachment remains unsettled regarding the relative importance of these two types of biological systems, but there is persuasive evidence for the importance of both. Regarding temperament, there is evidence that the trait of emotionality described in Chapter 2 is important (Kagan, 1984b). Both Ainsworth, Blehar, Waters, and Wall (1978) and Grossman, Schwan, and Grossman (1985) found that A babies react least emotionally in the Strange Situation, with C babies being the most emotional.[2] These results are broadly consistent with the results of Thompson and Lamb (1984), who found that A babies and two subclasses of B babies were less emotional than C babies and the other two subclasses of B babies. These results consistently

[2]There are three categories of attachment, termed secure (B babies), avoidant (A babies). and resistant (C babies). Assessment of attachment is based on the behavior of 10–24-month-old babies in the Strange Situation (Ainsworth & Wittig, 1969), a procedure that subjects the infants to gradually increasing amounts of stress as a result of the unfamiliar laboratory setting, an unfamiliar female experimenter, and two brief separations from the parent. Secure infants become upset when the parent leaves, but are happy to see her or him return and eagerly seek contact with the parent. Avoidant infants typically ignore the parent when the parent returns after the separation episodes, and seem relatively nondistressed when the parent leaves. The resistant infants are ambivalent in their reactions to the returning parent: They both seek contact with the parent and angrily reject it when the parent offers it. They are very distressed when the parent leaves and remain distressed after she or he returns.

portray C babies as more emotional than A babies, with B babies tending to be intermediate but variable. Although the differences in emotionality are assessed well after birth and can thus possibly be due to different patterns of mother–infant interaction within these groups, the fact that emotionality does have a genetic base (see Chapter 2) does suggest a role for a stable characteristic of the baby in producing attachment classification that is independent of the behavior of the mother.

Other studies have attempted to assess the infant shortly after birth and associate characteristics of the infant with later attachment classification. Studies of this nature are relatively immune from the possibility that the infant has been affected by the sensitivity or insensitivity of its caregiving. The results from this group of studies have been mixed (Lamb et al., 1985), but several studies have found quite striking associations among early assessments of temperament, later environments, and attachment classification. Particularly interesting is a study by Miyake et al. (1985). These researchers studied Japanese infants and their mothers by assessing temperament in the newborn period and attachment at 12 months of age. Temperament was assessed by observing the reaction of the baby to interruption of sucking produced by removing the nipple. This dimension of temperament measures the threshold of distress and is quite possibly the same as the dimension of emotionality described above and in Chapter 2. In agreement with the results described above, C infants cried significantly more than B babies during the Strange Situation. (There were no A babies in this study, a result that the authors attribute to temperamental differences between Japanese and American babies as well as the tendency of Japanese mothers to maintain close physical proximity with their infants.) In addition, the babies classified as resistant were found to have cried more as neonates in response to the interruption in sucking, although they took longer to begin crying. Moreover, despite the fact that not all irritable babies turned out to be resistant, there was a significant tendency for the resistant babies to be more irritable than secure babies when assessed at 1 and 3 months of age, and they reacted more strongly (emotionally) to the presence of strangers at 7.5 months.

Despite the clear role for constitutionally based temperamental factors in this study, the authors emphasize that the behavior of the mother interacts with the temperament of the child. Of 10 infants who were irritable in the first 3 months of life, 3 eventually became B babies. The behavior of the mother that appeared decisive was labeled ''intrusiveness'' and measured the tendency for the mother to interrupt the ongoing activities of the baby. If the baby was temperamentally calm, intrusiveness had no effect, whereas if the baby was irritable, there was an increased likelihood that the baby would turn out to be a C baby. These results then suggest that the temperament of the baby and the behavior of the mother interact to produce attachment classification, and some attachment researchers believe that any temperamental configuration can be overcome with appropriate mothering (e.g., Sroufe, 1985). Nevertheless, it is reasonable to suppose that it will be difficult to form a secure attachment with babies who are extreme on a temperamental dimension such as emotionality. MacDonald (1986b) showed that in a variety of developmental contexts individuals who deviate markedly from the average are much more likely to influence their environments than are individuals in the middle range.

Recently, Belsky and Rovine (1987) provided further evidence for the importance of emotionality in attachment classification, data that are quite consistent with the previous reports. They report data on subclassifications of attachment status indicating that B3 and

B4 babies are temperamentally similar to C1 and C2 babies in being high on emotionality. On the other hand, B1 and B2 babies are like A1 and A2 babies in being relatively low on emotionality. The authors interpret the data as indicating that temperament does not determine security of attachment, since a highly emotional infant can be either securely or insecurely attached. Nevertheless, a highly emotional infant who is insecurely attached will be resistant rather than avoidant and one who is securely attached will be a B3 or B4 rather than a B1 or B2. These data thus point to the importance of both temperament and the social environment in attachment behavior and appear to be an important synthesis of previously incompatible positions. Similarly, Smith and Noble (1987) found that B3 and B4 babies were more likely to score higher on withdrawal in ratings of temperament as well as be distressed in the presence of a stranger in the home.

These data indicating the importance of the social environment on attachment status agree with a large body of research suggesting such an influence (e.g., Ainsworth *et al.*, 1978). The early studies indicating the importance of the social environment have been extensively criticized by Lamb *et al.* (1985), but the results of similar studies are consistent with the idea that a harmonious relationship between caregiver and infant is associated with secure attachment (Lamb *et al.*, 1985). Moreover, there is some indication of differences between the mothers of A and C babies. Ainsworth *et al.* (1978) found the mothers of A babies to be more compulsive and rigid than the mothers of C babies. Belsky, Rovine, and Taylor (1984) found that mothers of A babies were engaged in more reciprocal interaction with their infants than were the mothers of the other groups, with mothers of C infants interacting the least. These researchers view reciprocal interaction as an aspect of caregiver sensitivity.

These associations are generally not very strong (Lamb *et al.*, 1985), and in the absence of behavioral genetic research that would shed light on the relative contribution of genes and environment, it is impossible to know the relative contribution of the child and parent to these findings. Perhaps the clearest evidence for the role of the parents comes from studies of maltreated infants. Schneider-Rosen, Braunwald, Carlson, and Cicchetti (1985) studied maltreated infants at 12, 18, and 24 months of age. These infants experienced various forms of maltreatment, including physical injury (33%), emotional mistreatment (48%), and physical neglect (75%). At 12 months 29% were classified in the A attachment classification, 29% in the B group, and 42% in the C group, compared to 11%, 67%, and 22%, respectively, in control groups of children from similar socioeconomic circumstances. There was a trend in the data for an increase in the percentage of A babies and a decrease in the percentage of C babies at the later ages, so that by 24 months of age 46.5% were classified as A, 32% as B, and 21.5% as C. These results show a much higher percentage of insecurely attached babies than in the control groups as well as a tendency for there to be relatively more A babies at later ages. The authors interpret this as consistent with the idea that abused babies are increasingly able to "cope with the inconsistent and problematic nature of the relationship with the caregiver" (Schneider-Rosen *et al.*, 1985, p. 206).

In addition, there was less stability of attachment in the maltreated groups. Although approximately 30% of the children in the study were classified as securely attached, there was a tendency for children to move from being securely attached to being insecurely attached. The reverse process also occurs, however, and the authors propose that a variety of enduring and potentiating factors may affect attachment classification. Enduring factors include such things as the personality of the mother (e.g., high on hostility or affectionate) and the temperament of the child (e.g., irritable or easy-going). Transient factors include temporary features of the family situation, such as stressful life experiences and marital harmony. These factors can affect attachment classification in a positive or negative manner and are able to compensate for one another. As a result, although there is little empirical confirmation of the model, the authors suggest that the effects of child abuse may be ameliorated by other compensatory factors and result in secure attachment. It is also possible that some children are relatively immune from the effects of even rather extreme environmental variation. Using the terms of Chapter 1, their behavior is well-buffered from the effects of the environment. In any case, the data on child maltreatment and attachment strongly suggest that maltreatment has the general effect of increasing insecure attachment.

C. Issues in the Predictive Validity of Attachment

One of the crucial issues in attachment research is how to conceptualize the connections between early behavior in the parent–child relationship and later behavior in a variety of different contexts. The most influential view is derived from the writings of Bowlby (1969, 1973) and is represented in the recent literature by Sroufe (1983), Bretherton (1985), and Main, Kaplan, and Cassidy (1985). Although Sroufe does believe that later environments can have important effects on behavior, he proposes that the early interactions with the parents have their effects on later behavior because the child develops a cognitive prototype or "internal working model" of later relationships by forming expectations and attitudes concerning his parents. This prototype is then carried forward and affects the child's expectations and attitudes "concerning the availability and likely responses of others and the outcome of his/her own efforts to cope with stress" (Sroufe, 1983, p. 45). This proptotype can then be seen in a variety of developmental contexts. For example, the infant whose parent is not responsive during times of intense emotional arousal may cope with arousal in later life by withdrawing.

The cognitive theory of the mechanism whereby early relationships affect later behavior is consistent with much of the data. This internal working model clearly has affective as well as cognitive aspects (e.g., Main et al., 1985), although the former are generally not treated in detail. We have seen that there is evidence that the social environment is crucial in determining attachment classification, and the above-mentioned attachment theorists maintain that the environment works by affecting the cognitive representations of others in the working model.

However, the social environment may also affect the child's affective responses to others in a more direct manner, by programming the positive reward system as suggested in Chapter 2. In such a view one source of continuity and predictive validity in attachment behavior is an affective one, which is subject to elaboration during the early years. This process involves the elaboration of specific neural systems involving the opioid neurotransmitters. The long-range effects of attachment behavior would then be due in part to the effects of the affectively salient events occurring in parent–child interactions on the elaboration of the positive social reward system. In this view the relationships of securely attached infants to their parents are characterized by warmth and love and as a result the child develops increased sensitivity to such environmental rewards. Later, in the presence of peers such a child remains highly sensitive to positive social rewards from others and behaves in such a way as to receive such rewards from other children, thus establishing affectively based friendships (Chapter 6) and cohesive marriages (Chapter 5). Such a child would also be more empathic and less aggressive (see Chapters 6 and 8 for a discussion of the relations between parental warmth and empathy, prosocial behavior, and aggression) and thus likely to be regarded as generous and helpful by his or her peers.

The thread of continuity here is provided not solely by a cognitive prototype, but by an increased disposition to find the positive behaviors of others reinforcing and to elicit these behaviors in others. This is not to deny that the behaviors of parents would not have effects on the child's cognitive representations. Since the parental behaviors that result in secure attachment are highly pleasurable to the child, a securely attached child may well look at the world as a pleasant place wherein people tend to be nice. The expectations of such a child would be quite different than those of a child who is consistently abused, for example, or treated insensitively or neglectfully.

The effects of the social environment on the positive social reward system would tend to be relatively enduring and resistant to change compared to a cognitive prototype that would be responsive to frequent shifts in the behavior of others. The enduring and self-sustaining nature of the link between early relationships and later behaviors is a feature of all of the ethologically based theories of attachment, but if this link is essentially a cognitive link, one must propose a very special type of cognitive prototype to account for the effects of attachment, one quite different from those proposed by cognitive psychologists studying event schemata (Mandler, 1979) or generalized event representations (Nelson & Gruendel, 1981). Clearly, the unique aspect of this cognitive representation calls for some type of biological explanation (Main et al., 1985), and the elaboration of the positive social reward system would be one important possibility. By invoking the idea of the opioid systems underlying the positive social reward system described in Chapter 2 one can provide a biological basis for continuity in attachment behaviors over the life span and provide an especially compelling account of the negative emotions occurring during loss of the attachment figure: The loss of an attachment figure is the loss of someone who is an important source of the positive stimulation to which the positive social reward system is sensitive. It is difficult to conceive how an internal working model of human relationships would result in such a sense of loss. Individuals literally become addicted to the positive stimulation provided by others, so that the loss is experienced as a highly negative event. Indeed, Panksepp, Siviy, and Normansell (1985) liken the social dependence characteristic of attachment to opioid dependence: The administration of opioids is intrinsically rewarding to humans and animals and their withdrawal results in severe distress.[3]

---

[3]The theory presented here regarding the source of continuity in attachment behavior is incomplete. The theory accounts for adult variation in attachment behaviors by proposing the elaboration of specific reward centers but does not account for the negative, dysphoric behavior shown by children exposed to parenting that departs from Bowlby's evolutionarily expected environment. These negative affective reactions may well also have longterm structural effects on the child that are independent of the lack of elaboration of the positive social-reward system. These effects are poorly conceptualized from a biological perspective, but the positing of a cognitive template underlying the effects of such negative interactions is little more than proposing a theoretical entity to explain the results. In Chapter 6, it is proposed that aversive stimulation during development predisposes animals and humans to aggression, and clearly in the case of animals there is no reason to propose a cognitive mechanism for these effects. Further research into the biological substrate of long-term effects of aversive stimulation during development is called for.

This proposed account of the mechanisms underlying the continuity of attachment can be related to the view that attachment represents a psychobiological attunement (Field, 1985; Reite & Capitanio, 1985). Field (1985) proposes that individuals in an attachment relationship provide meaningful stimulation to each other and modulate each other's arousal with the result that when the source of stimulation is removed there is a negative, dysphoric reaction involving a biphasic response of agitation and depression. Such a model has the advantage of applying to a considerable body of data in rats (Hofer, 1987), subhuman primates (Reite, 1985), and children (Field & Reite, 1984) indicating that disruptions in mother–infant interaction result in physiological arousal to the infant.

As indicated in Chapter 3, there is good evidence that the regulation of arousal is a crucial aspect of parent–child interaction, intimately associated with temperament. These affectively arousing stimuli are often highly pleasurable to the child, and we have suggested that by stimulating the child in this manner the child may come to view the parent as a source of rewards. Moreover, in Chapter 2 it is suggested that interactions between emotionality and the positive social reward system are an important possibility. In particular, intensely emotional infants, such as premature babies, are described as having interactions with adults which tend to be more affectively negative than interactions with normal babies. Pleasurable, affectively arousing stimulation then may well be intimately associated with attachment and with the construct of parental warmth, which is the focus of discussion in Chapter 5. In this view, the provision of pleasurable stimulation is the very essence of love and affection.

Nevertheless, we have emphasized the positive social reward system as a system which is independent from the systems underlying the regulation of affect and arousal in general. The positive social reward system is viewed as sensitive to a much more specific type of stimulation than is suggested by the view that attachment simply involves attunement and the modulation of arousal. For example, the stimulation involved in parent–child physical play is not viewed as directly relevant to the positive social-reward system, although it is related to the regulation of affect and arousal and it does result in positive stimulation for the child. In the theory developed here human attachment is a fairly unique system, one which serves a crucial additional function compared to attachment in rats and many other primate species: It functions to facilitate warmth and affection between bonded adults and between adults and their children and the primary behaviors that stimulate this system are behaviors associated with nurturance in humans—sensitivity, responsivity, and, most importantly, warmth and affection. The earlier discussion of adaptationist theories of attachment is relevant here: Rats and rhesus monkeys may have attachment relationships, but there is no reason at all to suppose that they fall in love. The theory of a specific system related to affection and nurturance is necessitated both by the idea that human attachment is fundamentally related to the evolution of monogamy in humans (see pp. 120–121 and Chapter 5) and to the theory of temperament as involving independent dimensions of reactivity, self-regulation and positive social reward developed in Chapter 2.

Finally, another reason for supposing that predictive validity and continuity are at least partly due to the continuity of a biologically based social reward system is that this would enable a theoretical integration between attachment theory and many other areas in developmental psychology. Such a concept would be the biological basis of parental warmth discussed in Chapter 5 and related to many adaptive behaviors both cross-culturally and within contemporary industrial cultures in that chapter and in later chapters. By emphasizing the affective side of the linkages between parent–child attachment behavior and later development one can provide a wide-ranging evolutionarily based synthesis of the data, whereas without this emphasis the present research on attachment cannot be well integrated into these other aspects of social development.

It is important to note in this context that many of the characteristics separating securely and insecurely attached children involve affective dimensions (see also p. 89). Connell and Thompson (1986) showed that infants' emotional reactions during the Strange Situation are more consistent across episodes and less contextually sensitive than the pattern of social interactions. Moreover, emotional expressiveness during the Strange Situation is more predictive of later behavior with the mother than are social interactive behaviors. One interpretation of these results is that during parent–child interactions the child becomes more sensitive to the reward value of positively valenced parental behaviors and in addition learns affect-regulatory skills. The relative sensitivity to social rewards and ability to competently regulate one's affect would be quite specific skills and are quite different from a cognitive prototype of how others may be expected to behave. As described in Chapters 2 and 3, the regulation of the affective state of the child is a fundamental aspect of parent–child interaction as well as interaction with peers. Thus, instead of a cognitive representation, the child simply may be more skillful at regulating its own and others' affective expressions. The importance of the positive social reward system for later functioning will be emphasized throughout.

Other indications of the importance of affect as an aspect of variation in attachment classification come from data on the predictive validity of attachment status for interactions with peers. For example, Pastor (1981) found that children found to be securely attached between 12 and 18 months were more sociable and more oriented to peers than were insecurely attached children when assessed at 23 months of age. When assessed at 4–5 years of age (Sroufe, 1983), the B children were higher in social competence, popularity, and empathy. Regarding the issue of differences between A and C children, Sroufe (1983) reported that at age 4–5 years A and C children could be reliably grouped into theoretically derived categories that clearly implicate the importance of affect. The avoidant children tended to be placed in the categories of "hostile," "isolated," and "disconnected," while the resistant children tended to be grouped in the categories of "impulsive" and "helpless." Other methods of analyzing these data yielded similar results. Finally, in an especially interesting study, Sroufe, Schork, Motti, Lawroski, and LaFreniere (1984) found that children who were securely attached as infants were more affectively expressive (in a positive way) and were more "fun to be around" than children who were insecurely attached as infants.

These results are consistent with the idea that an important aspect of the continuity of attachment behavior and the source of much of its predictive validity is (in addition to the continuity of the temperamental trait of emotionality) the relative degree of the elaboration of the positive social reward system. Another characteristic of the attachment system is important to mention here. Bowlby stressed the monotropic nature of attachment, that is, the tendency for it to be focused on one individual or at least a hierarchy of individuals (Bowlby, 1982). Although subsequent studies have indicated that infants can become attached to several individuals, there is no question that affiliative relationships are highly discriminative. As Bowlby indicated, when a strong affiliative relationship such as attachment is built up with an individual, the person becomes highly vulnerable to loss of that person, with such loss being accompanied by strong negative affect and depression (see Chapter 6 for a discussion). The social reward system is thus prone to becoming highly person-specific regarding the individual(s) who are able to be the source of social rewards. In terms of the model described in Chapter 2, the opioid system of the brain is highly vulnerable to the loss of specific individuals.

D. Attachment as a Developmental Task

One indication of the power of modern evolutionary theory is its ability to incorporate theories derived from quite disparate scientific traditions. An excellent example is Charlesworth's (1988) evolutionary interpretation of developmental task theories such as those of Erikson (1968) and Havighurst (1972). Charlesworth emphasizes the idea that from an evolutionary perspective reproduction is a vital task and that the prereproductive years serve to provide the individual with skills necessary to function adaptively as an adult. Charlesworth also notes that developmental task theories emphasize the idea that success on any one task is contingent on success at earlier tasks. Erikson proposed that secure attachment, what he would term "basic trust," is such a developmental task, and he believed, with many attachment theorists (e.g., Sroufe, 1979a), that success on this task prepares one for all later developmental tasks.

Another interesting aspect of Erikson's developmental tasks from an evolutionary perspective is the affective quality of many of the proposed stages. Erikson essentially delineates a series of basic issues in adaptation, and individuals who pass through the crisis on the positive side not only are viewed as adapting well to their society but, as an indication of this adaptive success, they regard their lives in affectively positive terms. Thus, infants who begin their lives with mistrust have an unhappy infancy. Individuals who are characterized by identity diffusion are clearly behaving maladaptively and also are characterized by affective dysphoria. Individuals who are unable to develop intimate relationships are, in Erikson's terms, not only less likely to reproduce, but also less likely to be happy than individuals who are able to do this. Generativity and ego integrity are also accompanied by positive self-evaluation. Indeed, the opposite of ego integrity is despair, clearly a negative affective state, and Erikson notes that individuals often engage in rationalization in order to achieve the positive affective state of ego integrity.

Two types of analyses previously discussed here are relevant. First, in Chapter 3 it was noted that positive emotions such as those involved in self-esteem generally accompany adaptive interactions with the environment. Thus, an individual who is being generative by successfully engaging in economically viable activity and biologically reproducing or an individual who can review his or her life without developing despair is able to have positive self-evaluations. To live one's life on the negative side of Erikson's stages is to live a very unhappy life indeed. It was noted in Chapter 3, as it was by Erikson, that these evaluations may involve rationalizations and self-deception.

Second, in the present chapter the analysis of the affectively valanced stimulation involved in secure attachment implied that individuals respond with positive affect to stimulation that was adaptive in our evolutionary past. The fundamental plausibility of

Erikson's theory derives similarly from this very commonsense proposal of a link between adaptive behavior and positive affect.

These are two different sources of positive affect, one deriving from present adaptive interactions with the environment, the other deriving from biologically based predispositions for affective response to particular types of environmental stimulation. I have already cast doubt on the idea that the latter type of affective response will necessarily be associated with present adaptation. Insecure attachment and hostile parenting do appear to be quite adaptive in many cultures and these phenomena will be a major concern of the chapters to follow. In these cultures adaptive socialization is not directed at producing basic trust, and successful reproduction is achieved without the expectation of intimacy in family relationships, an essential task of young adulthood according to Erikson. Positive affect and adaptation are effectively decoupled. I shall also argue that identity achievement, proposed by Erikson to be the essential task of adolescence, is a culture-bound phenomenon. These considerations imply that there is no universal set of developmental tasks that can be specified in the manner attempted by Erikson.

The only universal developmental task, as Charlesworth (1988) has pointed out, is reproduction. The genetic predispositions as well as the learned skills necessary to achieve reproductive success will vary markedly among cultures, as will the nature of adaptive environmental influences and their affective consequences to the individual.

II. Aberrations in Attachment and Later Behavior

The previous section discussed the possibility that early attachment classification is causally related to later behaviors. In this section data from animals and humans are discussed in order to determine under what conditions early events might affect later behavior. Studies on attachment performed on individuals who have been adopted or institutionalized will be described. These data describe disruptions in attachment or lack of attachment, but do not include assessments in the Strange Situation, so that their relevance to the studies described above is unclear. However, the data do conform reasonably well to the predictions made by the ethological theory of attachment and they do indicate strong influences on later behavior.

These studies raise a number of important theoretical questions. Particularly important are the questions of the importance of early versus later environments in producing later behavior, the question of whether there are changes in the relative plasticity of the child, and the question of what types of environments appear to have the most effect. Regarding the last question, it should be pointed out that the great majority of the studies considered here involve what may be termed extreme environments. Most children are not reared in orphanages or subjected to physical insults at the time of birth. These environments are therefore not typical of the great majority of children and in deriving conclusions one must be aware of this fact.

The studies summarized here can be considered as tests of the ethological theory of attachment. The ethological theory of attachment posits that major deviations from the "environment of evolutionary adaptedness" will result in pathological behavior in children. If such deviations occur, it is expected that children will react negatively and that if the environment is not altered to better conform with the biological predispositions of the child, maladaptive behavior will result.

A. Animal Studies

One very influential source of evidence on the long-range effects of major deviations from species-typical environments has been studies on monkeys and canids. Harry Harlow and his colleagues (Harlow & Harlow, 1969) performed classic studies with rhesus macaques showing that isolation for the first 6 months of life had profound effects later in life. The animals were often indifferent to other animals, engaging in vacant staring, stereotypical movements, and self-clutching. However, they also engaged in "suicidal aggression" against older animals and, if they became mothers, they abused their infants. Later it was found that some species of monkeys do not show ill effects of early isolation: Sackett, Ruppenthal, Fahrenbruch, Hold, and Greenough (1980) found that isolated individuals of a different species of macaque, the Crab-eating macaque, were indistinguishable from nonisolated monkeys. Similarly, wolves and dogs that are isolated after the first few weeks of life until between 4 and 6 months of age tend to be minimally affected by the experience (MacDonald & Ginsburg, 1981; MacDonald, 1985). These animals show all the normal behavior of canids and seek social companionship. However, several studies have shown that isolated animals tend to be less aggressive and dominant than normally reared animals.

These results show that there is genetic variation among species in the degree to which social behavior is buffered. The social behavior of the Crab-eating macaque fits the model of well-buffered behavior described in Chapter 1, while that of the rhesus shows more plasticity. In fact, later studies by Suomi and Harlow (1972), Novak (1979), and Cummins and Suomi (1976) showed that the isolated rhesus could be rehabilitated significantly if they were housed with young animals. These young animals clung to the older isolates and elicited play, but the rehabilitation was not complete: The male isolates still did not engage in the double-foot-clasp mount essential for mating. The fact that some behaviors of these animals fail to change even after extensive attempts to rehabilitate them shows that early experience is sometimes important independent of later environments. On the other hand, some aspects of normal social behavior seem to be completely unaffected by social isolation even in the rhesus monkey: Ruppenthal, Arling, Harlow, Sackett, and Suomi (1976) found that some aspects of maternal behavior in isolated females were entirely normal, while other aspects were grossly deficient.

The socialization of dogs to humans shows both the long-range effects of early experience as well as the importance of age when the experience occurs. Freedman, King, and Elliot (1961) exposed dogs to humans for 2-week periods between 3 and 14 weeks of age. Dogs that were removed between weeks 5 and 7 were the most socialized to humans when tested at 16 weeks of age, with animals who were exposed to humans either very early (weeks 3–5) or very late (weeks 14–16) the least socialized. These results indicate a sensitive period for the socialization of dogs to humans: At certain ages dogs are far more susceptible to this environmental influence than they are at others.

The animal literature does not yield any general principles regarding the importance of early experience in development (MacDonald, 1985). There is variation among species and for different behaviors within a species in the importance of early experience, later experience, and the degree of genetic buffering of behavior. These differences imply that the degree of plasticity of behavior is under natural selection, so that plasticity itself must be viewed as a biological adaptation with a genetic basis. For some animals and some behaviors there has been selection for a great deal of plasticity and a major role for environmental variation in producing adaptive phenotypes. For others, the uncertainty of environmental programming has been eliminated in favor of the more reliable means of genetic control. By adopting the route of greater plasticity an animal is better able to alter its behavior according to current circumstances, but is more likely to be negatively affected by major deviations from the expected environments. As described in Chapter 1, plasticity is thus a two-edged sword (Lerner, 1984; MacDonald, 1985).

B. Human Studies of Orphanage Rearing and Adoption

One of the most influential studies showing the importance of early attachment relationships was performed by Tizard (1978). Previous studies of orphanage-reared children had generally found profound differences associated with such rearing, but the results were criticized because the studies were performed in very inadequate orphanages. The deleterious effects of orphanage rearing may have been due not to deficiencies in attachment, but, for example, to the fact that the orphanages did not provide enough stimulation (Casler, 1968). Tizard (1978) studied children in an institution that was highly stimulating but had a policy that discouraged close relationships between staff and children. Moreover, there was a great deal of staff turnover, so that there was no opportunity to form a close relationship with one adult. In fact, by the age of 24 months, the average child had been looked after for at least 1 week by 24 people. The children were adopted into normal homes between the ages of 2 and 4 years, and when these children were followed up at age 8 years, about one-half the sample showed behavioral abnormalities as rated by their teachers when compared to a sample of normal working class children. These abnormalities included being more restless, irritable, and quarrelsome, telling lies, being resentful of correction by their teachers, displaying indiscriminate affection, and having poorer ratings by their teachers for socialization with other children. Particularly interesting was the finding that the children exhibited a superficial overfriendliness or extreme shyness to adults, including strangers who entered the classroom. At the same time these children had fewer friends among their peers than the contrast group, and were less popular and more aggressive toward their peers. The finding that children who do not develop normal attachments show indiscriminate affection ("disinhibition") was also reported by Wolkind (1974) in a study of children admitted to an institution before age 2 years.

These differences occurred despite the fact that the adoptive parents of the children spent more time with their children than did control parents, and played with them and helped them more. Although the parents did not evaluate their adopted children as negatively as the teachers did, they also commented on the attention-seeking behavior and indiscriminate overfriendliness that these children exhibited toward adults.

There is evidence that simply being in an ophanage does not necessarily lead to poor adjustment if the child has an adult figure with whom to form an attachment. Wolins (1970) found that a good adjustment in the orphanage was associated with a "warm, close relationship" with adults or older children inside the institution, and Pringle and Bossio (1960) found that the children were much better adjusted if they formed a relationship with an adult outside the institution. Taken together these studies show that institutional rearing is compatible with a good outcome if the emotional needs of the child are met in the institution.

Adoption of a child often involves the severing of an attachment relationship and there is evidence that later adoption is associated with problems of adjustment (Pringle & Bossio, 1960). For example, Kadushin (1970) studied the outcomes of children adopted well after infancy and found that, although their parents were satisfied with the adoption, the children often seemed set in their ways and exhibited separation anxiety as well as the superficial overfriendliness indicated in the studies by Tizard and Wolkind. Moreover, there was evidence that the poorer adjustment was associated with later adoption. These results are consistent with the idea that as children get older they are less able to make major changes in their attachments, and are thus consistent with a theory of declining plasticity of social behavior.

More evidence for a sensitive period for the effects of separation comes from studies of hospitalization (Douglas, 1975; Quinton & Rutter, 1976). Long and repeated hospitalization was associated with troublesome behavior, delinquency, and unstable job patterns in adolescence. Moreover, a sensitive period when the child is most susceptible to these effects was indicated: Children who had been separated between 6 months and 3 years were most affected.

Although these studies indicate important long-range effects and age-dependent differences in plasticity during development, it is certainly not true that all individuals who are subjected to these environments are similarly affected. For example, in the Tizard study, less than 70% of the sample exhibited behavior problems, so that other factors must be involved in some children. These may include genetic factors and intensively therapeutic later environments, but there is some indication that relatively unaffected children had received less exposure to pathological early environments (MacDonald, 1985). For example, Kadushin (1970) found that a good relationship with the natural mother was associated with good adjustment after adoption and the studies of Wolins (1970) and Pringle and Bossio (1960) show that adequate relations with adults can ameliorate the effects of institutional rearing.

These results suggest that there can be graded effects of the environment, depending on the degree of departure from normalcy. Further evidence for such a graded effect of the severity of environmental stressors comes from work on the effects of prenatal and perinatal events on later behavior. Werner and Smith (1982) found a direct relationship between the severity of perinatal stress and the proportion of children rated as below average in social (and intellectual) development at 20 months of age. At 10 years of age, there was less difference between stressed and unstressed groups, but the severely stressed infants were still quite below the performance of the less stressed groups and this continued to age 18 years. At age 18 years, the moderately stressed group had three times the rate of serious mental problems and, for girls, twice the rate of pregnancy.

C. Conclusion

These results generally show the importance of powerful early environments in producing long-lasting effects on human behavior and indicate that there is differential plasticity in human behavior depending on age. The former conclusion must be restricted, however, to the powerful, extreme types of environment studied here. There is no indication from these studies that normal environmental variation studied, for example, in samples of middle-class children, is similarly important for later behavior. However, normal environmental variation may continue to exert influence if the child becomes less plastic at later ages, and this appears to be the case.

The conclusion that individuals are less plastic as they become older is derived from studies involving extreme environments, but is presumably generalizable to all children and would predict minimally that individual differences in personality would become more stable as children get older. This is in fact the case. Moss and Sussman (1980) reviewed longitudinal studies of personality and found greater stability at later ages. Similarly, within a life-span perspective, Costa and McCrae (1980) consistently found that personality in adults remains quite stable. It would appear from these data that indeed there are formative years in personality development, and they occur during early childhood. Regarding the studies of attachment classification, these findings would be consistent with findings such as those of Thompson, Lamb, and Estes (1982) of relative instability in infancy, but would imply that as the child gets older it is less vulnerable to environmental perturbations that would alter attachment status.

I have introduced the notion of the degree to which environments vary from normal environments in a deleterious direction. Is there any evidence that some environments are extremely beneficial? Presumably the environments designed by clinicians for therapy are intended as such environments, and there is evidence that interventions can be effective for children in orphanages particularly if they begin early. For example, Flint (1978) substantially reversed the decline in social behavior in a group of institutionalized children with a program emphasizing a very high ratio of adults to children and individual attention of adults to children. It is particularly noteworthy that the therapeutic program included the provision to the children of highly affectively arousing stimulation from adults, including physical play (see Chapter 3). Such environments may be "supernormal" in their ability to effect therapeutic change in the individual. Despite the fact that there appears to be declining plasticity in the child as it grows older, highly stimulating, affectively salient therapeutic environments may be able to have major beneficial effects on behavior (MacDonald, 1985). This example illustrates how the intensity of environmental stimulation can overcome declining plasticity, as emphasized in the theory of sensitive periods (see Chapter 1).

Is there any evidence that some of the basic social skills of humans are well-buffered from the effects of even extreme environments? Such skills do exist, but they have not been well studied, since the emphasis has always been on pathology. Dennis (1973) studied the cognitive development of children reared in a very inadequate orphanage in Lebanon. Although little mention was made of the social skills of these children when they became adults, they did show many basic social competencies. Many of the females as adults became caretakers for the younger children and despite severely depressed IQs of

about 50 they were able to function competently. These competencies presumably included being able to carry on conversations and perform menial labor. Very few become
married, however, illustrating an effect on biological fitness, and mental problems were
common.

The relevance of these data to some of the theoretical points made in Chapter 1
should be reemphasized. The perspective of philosophical realism adopted there suggested that whether the child is an active elicitor of stimulation or a passive recipient of
such stimulation and whether behavior is continuous are empirical questions rather than
irresolvable aspects of incompatible world views. Clearly there are some instances when
the child is the passive recipient of very intensive, powerful stimulation. In such cases the
stimulation would tend to have similar effects on any child, so that the individual characteristics of the child are fairly irrelevant and the child can be considered the passive
recipient of environmental stimulation. Just as virtually all children would benefit from
being raised in a stable middle-class family rather than being reared in an impoverished
single-parent family, virtually all children will be negatively affected by extremely
abusive or neglectful environments or environments without attachment figures independently of their temperament or any other personality characteristic that they may have. In
less extreme circumstances, the individual characteristics of the child will be important in
eliciting environments.

Regarding the question of continuity, in cases where a child is subjected to relatively
extreme early environments there will be a tendency for strong threads of continuity
between the later behavior of the child and the influence of these early intensive and
powerful environments. On the other hand, in a sample of children subjected to average
levels of stimulation in normal environments, the individual characteristics of the child
will have a much larger impact and later experiences may well be crucial in producing
variation. Thus, external stresses impinging on the caregiver–infant relationship would be
expected to result in less stability. Intensive environmental stimulation is especially likely
to bring about discontinuities in development and in this case the expectation is that
attachment classifications will be stable in the absence of intensive environmental
perturbations.

Besides the evidence described above suggesting greater continuity for individuals
subjected to extreme environments, results consistent with this formulation have been
found within the Strange Situation paradigm. Waters (1978) studied a sample ranging
from lower middle class to upper class with some indication of stability of paternal
employment, residence, and marital status during the study. The great majority of the
attachment classifications (96%) remained stable over the course of the study (12–18
months of age). Far less stability is shown in studies where the sample experiences stress
and changing life circumstances. For example, Vaughn, Egeland, Sroufe, and Waters
(1979) found that in a lower income sample the stability was only 62%. Moreover, the
severity of stress was associated with infants changing from secure to either of the
insecure classifications. Similarly, Thompson, Lamb, and Estes (1982), studying a middle-class sample, found that maternal employment and the onset of regular nonmaternal
care were associated with instability of attachment. The stresses encountered by the
sample in this study were clearly far less traumatic than those encountered by the lower
class sample, and there was no general tendency for these stresses to be associated with a
switch to insecure attachment. Rather, these mild stresses in the middle-class sample

resulted in the dyad "renegotiating" their attachment relationship, with some changing from insecure to secure and some the reverse.

Whether or not an individual child is subjected to the extreme early environments or intensively beneficial later environments is an empirical question. Moreover, the finding of much greater stability at later ages is also an empirical finding and suggests greater continuity at later ages. Thus, it is incorrect to regard the questions of whether the child is active or passive and the question of continuity versus discontinuity as preempirical, philosophical issues. They are questions on which it is quite possible to provide empirical data, to come to reasonable conclusions, and to make real progress.

Finally, and perhaps most importantly, it is necessary to connect this discussion to the discussion of the positive social reward system described previously. In Chapter 2 it was suggested that the positive social reward system was programmable by the environment. The data reviewed above can be explained by supposing declining plasticity of the positive social reward system during development and the importance of affectively salient stimulation in programming the status of this system during development. This interpretation assumes the correctness of the affective rather than the cognitive interpretation of the data on the predictive validity described in Section I of this chapter. Essentially it proposes that affectively positive stimulation during development facilitates the elaboration of the positive social reward system and that with development there is declining plasticity of the organism, so that it becomes more difficult to elaborate the system later in development. This perspective would suggest that increasing the intensity of affectively positive stimulation later in development would be of therapeutic value in correcting for a deficient positive social reward system.

Parent–Child Relationships and the Transmission of Culture

The parent–child relationship has always assumed a central place in developmental theories of socialization. If the environment is important in social development, then the individuals with the largest potential impact on children would arguably be the parents. Parents begin interacting with the child from birth and, because of their relatively greater power, they are able to control much of the daily life of the child, especially in the early years. As the child becomes older there is more exposure to other possible environmental influences, but even exposure to these factors is often influenced by the parents, as when a parent chooses the child's school or neighborhood. Moreover, if children are increasingly less susceptible to environmental influences as they become older, it is quite possible that their reaction to the wider world and their choice of a niche in the world is influenced by their early interactions with their parents, so that the later environment has relatively little effect on them.

These ideas suggest the possibility that parents can have major effects on their children, but in recent years the trend has been to be quite skeptical of this point of view. In a very influential paper, Bell (1968) pointed out that studies of socialization based on correlations between parents and their children could be interpreted either as indicating that the parent caused some effect in the child or that children actively structure their environment. We have already seen evidence that a child's temperament can have important effects on the style of parent–child interactions and we have explored parent–child interactions involved in attachment (Chapter 4) as well as the structure and importance of affect regulation between parents and children (Chapter 3). Moreover, as mentioned in Chapter 2, recent behavioral genetic research has shown that the environmental influences do not appear to act in such a way as to make children in the same family like one another and different from children in other families. In the following the traditional research on family environmental influences is described and placed within an evolutionary perspective.

I. GLOBAL PARENTING STYLES

Researchers in the area of parent–child relationships have attempted to relate stable characteristics of the child with stable characteristics of the parent. The goal of the research has been to find ways in which differences in families are systematically related to differences in how children behave. In general the research has been conceptualized as a unidirectional system in which stable differences in parents cause differences in children, so that any child reared by a given set of parents would be affected by them in a similar manner. As described below, recent work has also emphasized the role of the child in affecting parental behavior and has questioned the idea that parents have broad, generalized effects on their children.

A. Dimensions of Parenting and Their Correlates

One of the remarkable things about research in this area is the degree of agreement reached by different researchers working with different samples and different research techniques over the last 30 years. Schaefer (1959) analyzed several previous studies and concluded that there were two basic dimensions of parenting. The first dimension is that of *warmth–hostility,* and on the warm end consists of high affection, positive reinforcement, and sensitivity to the child's needs and desires, with the low end consisting of the opposite types of behaviors. The second dimension is a control dimension and reflects the degree to which parents restrict the child's freedom or impose duties and demands for mature behavior. These basic dimensions were also found by Becker (1964), and Baldwin (1955) also found a warmth–coldness dimension.

Recently, Maccoby and Martin (1983) argued for two basic dimensions very similar to those of Becker (1964), but summarized recent data showing a very different pattern of associations for the parenting styles. The first dimension in the Maccoby and Martin scheme is that of high demandingness and control, while the second reflects the degree to which parents are accepting, responsive, and child-centered. These two dimensions give rise to four basic types of parenting.

Authoritarian parenting, as described by Maccoby and Martin (1983), consists of an unbalanced state of affairs in which the child is expected to obey without question the edicts of the parent. There is no negotiation or bargaining with the parents and the parents tend to apply an absolute set of standards to the behavior of the child. In an early set of studies, Baldwin (1948, 1949) found that children of authoritarian parents tended to be low in social interaction with peers and subordinate to them in social status. Such children were highly obedient, but tended to be low on spontaneity, affection, curiosity, and originality. Boys with authoritarian parents have also been shown to have low self-esteem (Coopersmith, 1967), and several studies have shown an association between authoritarian child-rearing and aggression (see Chapter 6 for a more detailed discussion of family influences on aggression). In Baumrind's (1971, 1977) work, boys with authoritarian parents are particularly likely to be low in cognitive competencies and to withdraw from social contacts.

Indifferent–uninvolved parents tend to "minimize the costs in time and effort of interaction with the child" (Maccoby & Martin, 1983, p. 48). In evolutionary terms, these parents are low in parental investment. They keep the child at a distance and tend not to monitor the behavior of their children or set standards of conduct. Egeland and Sroufe (1981a,b) found that psychologically uninvolved mothers had infants with severely disturbed attachment relationships and deficits in a variety of social and cognitive areas at 2 years of age. Martin (1981) also found that mothers who responded to their infant's level of activity rather than their own previous level of activity tended to have compliant and secure children when assessed at 42 months of age.

A report by Pulkkinen (1982) found that parents who scored low on attributes such as knowing the child's whereabouts and interest in school events tended to have children who were less responsible, less achievement-oriented, and less socially competent. In addition, they were characterized by aggressive outbursts, less interest in school, and delinquent behavior. Similarly, Hogan and Kitigawa (1985) found that teenage childbirth was more common in cases where parents reported low supervision of dating behavior.

Maccoby and Martin (1983), following Baumrind (1967), characterize the *indulgent–permissive* pattern of child-rearing as involving a generally accepting and responsive attitude toward the child and as avoiding the imposition of controls and restrictions on the child's behavior. Baumrind (1967) found that children reared by indulgent parents were immature and lacked impulse control and self-reliance. In a later study, Baumrind (1971) found that at 4 years of age children with indulgent parents were dependent and lacked social responsibility. A follow-up (Baumrind, 1977) indicated that these children were low on cognitive and social agency.

The *authoritative–reciprocal* pattern of parenting (Baumrind, 1971; Maccoby & Martin, 1983) is characterized by fairly high levels of control by the parents, but with open communication, negotiation, and reciprocity in setting limits. The affective tone of the parent–child interactions in the samples studied by Baumrind was generally warm and accepting. The children of authoritative parents tend to be high on the social and cognitive competencies described above. In addition, Maccoby and Martin (1983) review evidence that such children tend to be independent, self-confident, socially responsible, and capable of controlling aggression.

B. Bidirectional Processes and Nonshared Environmental Effects

The implicit model in all of the above work is that different parenting styles result in a major source of between-family variation in the behavior of children. In other words, we would expect that authoritative parents will have the effects described above on any children that they socialize. However, there is reason to doubt this claim. Studies that utilize more than one child per family have provided little evidence that children reared in the same family resemble each other to any significant extent in personality, whether biologically related or not. For example, Loehlin, Horn, and Willerman (1981) found a correlation of .05 for pairs of biologically related siblings and .04 for adopted siblings. Scarr and Weinberg (1976, 1978) found an average sibling correlation of .19 for biologically related siblings and .01 for unrelated siblings. Thus, a prolonged common rearing environment and even a considerable genetic overlap do not yield a substantial degree of resemblance. Given that the personality measures include traits resembling those described above as resulting from parenting styles, such as sociability and social agency, these results suggest that parents of a particular type cannot be generally characterized as having an average effect on their children. As Scarr and Kidd (1983) conclude, "there seems to be little role for the common experiences of rearing in the same family" (p. 419).

The finding that environmental influences within families are nonshared is a major discovery of behavior genetic methodology, and, as described in Chapter 2, there is no accepted theory for the source of this environmental variance. Indeed, it is quite possible that the source of nonshared environmental variance is mediated genetically, as implied by Scarr's theory (e.g., Scarr, 1987) that genetically different children evoke different environments. Nevertheless, the cross-cultural and historical research on socialization described below and in Chapters 6 and 8 fits well with the view that the dimensions of parenting are as described by traditional research and it is argued on pp. 152–155 that the data strongly suggest that the source of influence is from parent to child. Moreover, even if between-family variation in socialization influences does not exist in our society, it is nevertheless quite possible that the dimensions of parenting have been accurately discovered by the one-child-per-family type of research that has been used to support these dimensions. Thus, Daniels, Dunn, Furstenberg, and Plomin (1985) found that differences in parental treatment as perceived by both parents and children were associated with differences in their adjustment. Consistent with the traditional perspective, warm family relationships were associated with better psychological adjustment. Moreover, children who saw themselves as having more of a role than their sibling in family decisions were better adjusted psychologically, suggesting that they perceived their environment as less controlling.

Thus, the question of whether affective and control dimensions really affect children is independent of whether all children in the family receive these influences. The idea that family environmental influences function as a source of between-family variation in children's behavior was never really essential to family research. Moreover, even if Scarr's (1987) evocative theory of nonshared environments is correct, this does not imply that the dimensionalization of environmental influences is not as described above. Nor does it imply that simply because a child evokes its own environmental influences, possibly for genetic reasons, that those influences are any the less environmental influences. In retrospect the mystery is why anyone should have supposed that each child in the family would be subject to the same environment. Indeed, the theory of discriminative parenting deriving from evolutionary biology implies just the opposite (Smith, 1988; see below and Chapters 6 and 8). Nevertheless, since there are systematic family influences in development, it is proposed here that cultures are able to program adaptive phenotypes by engineering socialization contingencies. The argument for this perspective follows.

II. THE FAMILY AND THE SOCIALIZATION OF CHILDREN IN EVOLUTIONARY AND HISTORICAL PERSPECTIVE

The literature described above indicates that an evolutionary theory of parent–child interactions must take account of the two dimensions of parenting revealed by descriptive studies, place these dimensions in a cross-cultural and historical context, and provide a rationale for viewing the dimensions as causal factors in producing variation in children's behavior. However, before discussing these issues, an even more fundamental aspect of parenting from an evolutionary perspective must be discussed, the idea of parental investment.

Basic to a modern evolutionary-ecological view of parenting as put forward by Trivers (1974) is the idea that there are costs and benefits associated with reproduction. For example, the parents of many bird species must invest large amounts of time and energy in their offspring, chiefly by building nests, getting adequate food, and protecting the young birds from predators. Parents benefit from all this effort by being able to reproduce successfully. There is a great deal of variation in the degree to which different species invest in their young, but even more important, it is expected that within a species there will be conflicts of interest over how much each parent should provide and how much each offspring should take. If the parents invest too much in one individual, that one individual may be very well adapted to its environment, but the parents will have to restrict their total reproductive output to fewer individuals than they could have reared with less investment per offspring. Moreover, there is a potential conflict between the mother and father, since each would ideally prefer to have the other invest more in the offspring. Among mammals, males especially have a strong motivation to avoid investing large amounts in one offspring or even the offspring of one female, since one male is potentially able to impregnate many females. Because of the very high costs of pregnancy and lactation, females cannot similarly benefit from reproducing with a large number of males.

The organization of this section will reflect the tension between what one might call centripetal and centrifugal tendencies within the human family. Centripetal tendencies are forces that make the family a cohesive social structure and result in adaptive levels of investment in offspring. Included here are the proximal affective bonding mechanisms, including the dimension of parental warmth derived from the descriptive studies of the previous section. These mechanisms are viewed as tending to make the family a cohesive social unit, and in the following the historical and cross-cultural context of their expression will be described, especially with regard to how they influence development. Centrifugal tendencies are forces that pull the family apart and result from conflicts of interest over the amount of investment in offspring.

A. Centripetal Tendencies within Families and the Context of Development

It is a basic thesis of this volume that the nuclear family form of social organization is a fundamental human adaptation. Lovejoy (1981) argues that increased parental investment is a prime mover in human evolution. He notes a trend within the primates toward increased length of preadult developmental phases. For example, chimpanzees, a species with whom we share over 98% of nonrepeated DNA, have a prereproductive period of approximately 10 years, and are still carried by their mothers as late as 5 or 6 years of age. Lovejoy notes that this trend toward increased parental investment is necessarily accompanied by increased longevity, as individuals must remain alive for longer periods in order to replace themselves in the population. Prolonged preadult development is also associated with greater plasticity, and we have seen previously that early human development is generally characterized by higher levels of plasticity than later in life.

This strategy of producing relatively few offspring with a high investment of time and energy in each one, what ecologists term K-selection, comes at a very high price. Human babies are totally helpless and even older children require high levels of parental care. The resources available for parental investment can be maximized by requiring ever greater levels of maternal care, but Lovejoy argues that human evolution is also characterized by tapping into an enormous pool of previously underutilized resources, that of the hominid male. Males who cooperated in the provisioning of food and care for their biological offspring would have a higher rate of reproductive success, because their assistance would result not only in increased protein and calories for the mother and offspring, but also a shorter period between births.

An essential aspect of this strategy of increased male parental investment is monogamy. Lovejoy proposes that by concentrating his parenting resources in the offspring of one female males were able to maximize the numbers and survivorship of their offspring. In return for this provisioning of resources monogamy provides the male with the confidence that he is indeed the biological father of the offspring and that he is not being reproductively exploited by providing resources to offspring that are not genetically related to him.

This theory of the evolution of the human family is of profound importance for conceptualizing human social development. It is a theory which can integrate the findings on human evolution, as Lovejoy shows, and it is also consistent with anthropological descriptions of the most primitive extant human societies. Moreover, the general idea that monogamy be viewed in terms of increased paternal investment is consistent with a large body of theory and data in evolutionary ecology on the correlates of monogamy (e.g., Kleiman, 1981; see also Chapter 6).

From an evolutionary perspective, then, the idea that the nuclear family is the basic form of human social organization implies a high level of paternal investment in offspring. Rather than diluting his reproductive energies by mating with several females, the nuclear family social organization implies that the father invests highly in the offspring of one female. As a result it is expected that proximal mechanisms fostering male–female as well as parent–child social bonding will evolve. Mechanisms such as continuous sexual receptivity and concealed ovulation have been proposed by sociobiologists as proximal mechanisms underlying human social cohesion (see, e.g., Alexander, 1979). These mechanisms essentially make it in the interest of the male to maintain close contact with the female not only during mating, but long after mating occurs in order to ensure his paternity. Relatively less emphasized by sociobiologists are affective bonding mechanisms, which have been a major area of interest to psychologists. It is an important thesis of this volume that affective bonding mechanisms are an important proximate cause of cohesion in human social organizations.

As illustrated in Chapters 2 and 4, the ethological analysis of parent–child affective ties involves a biologically based predisposition to respond with positive or negative affect to particular nonrandom classes of parental behaviors. In the present chapter, it is necessary to expand this type of analysis to cover the broader context of parent–child affective relationships. In particular, parent–child warmth, found in the previous section to be a consistent dimension of the parent–child relationship, can be seen as an example of this type of environment-expectant biological system. Thus, in the ethological view, parental warmth consists of a broad group of behaviors that the child is biologically predisposed to perceive in an affectively positive manner.

There are two reasons for accepting this point of view (MacDonald, 1984, 1987a):

1. The inadequacy of the secondary drive theory of the origin of parent–child affective ties during infancy strongly indicates the existence of social reinforcers that are independent of parents simply physically maintaining their children or providing other nonsocial reinforcers. Warm parenting can thus be considered as a continuation of the types of behavior necessary for a secure, nonanxious attachment, thus forging a link between research on attachment described in Chapter 4 and the present concern with the affective dimension of parenting indicated in studies with older children. There is no reason to suppose that an entirely different system occurs after infancy.

2. The ethological theory proposes that natural selection has resulted in biologically based reinforcers specific to social behavior and responsible for the persistence cross-culturally and historically of an affective dimension of parent–child interaction. The parent–child interactions classed as warm thus constitute a nonrandom collection of parental behaviors with consistent within-culture and cross-cultural correlates. The fact that it is possible to set up laboratory procedures involving social reinforcers that will reliably result in a positive affective response in children (e.g., Cichetti and Sroufe, 1978) as well as the fact that it is possible to describe such a dimension cross-culturally and historically strongly suggest the species-typical nature of these behaviors. In other words, from the child's point of view the behaviors of parents labeled as warm are subjectively pleasurable and this is true cross-culturally and thus independent of the contingencies imposed by particular cultures.

B. Familial Affective Relationships in Cross-Cultural Context

As indicated in Chapter 1, one goal of the present effort is to provide an integrative account of development, that is, one that is able to incorporate data gathered in a number of theoretical contexts. Aronson (1984) points out that the ability of a scientific theory to provide a coherent explanatory account of previously unrelated or unexplained phenomena is the hallmark of a good theory and it is contended here that only sociobiology, of all the theories available to developmental psychologists, is able to provide such an account of the cross-cultural data on socialization. Cross-cultural developmental psychology has either attempted to find universals, of which there are very few interesting ones, or has simply cataloged variation with no attempt at an explanatory scheme for why these patterns make sense. Recent evolutionary theory is able to provide such a scheme and in addition it is contended that the results shed light on developmental mechanisms studied in contemporary industrial societies, which are the focus of the vast majority of contemporary research.

In the following, two general types of constructs will be utilized to develop a theory of cross-cultural and historical variation in socialization practices. The first construct derives immediately from an evolutionary approach and consists of the central tendencies in behavior predicted by evolutionary theory. These central tendencies are insufficient to result in a powerful theory of this variation, but it is argued that by invoking a variety of contextual variables it is possible to provide such a theory.

1. Sociobiologically Predicted Central Tendencies

As described in Chapter 1, central tendencies or the universals of development reflect one of the two main realms of developmental theory, the other being that of individual differences. Here the idea of central tendencies refers not necessarily to the commonalities of development, but to the theoretically expected outcomes of development. These central tendencies predicted by sociobiological theory constitute average expected levels of certain types of behavior, and are consistent with the idea of variation around that average. Analogously, developmentalists study average differences in mental ability as a function of age and these averages may be conceived as consisting of a mean and a standard deviation, as in the concept of IQ. Evolutionary theory predicts that on the whole individuals will tend to be self-interested rather than truly altruistic, that this self-interest will often be manifested by attempts to aid genetic relatives, and that males and females will have vastly different reproductive strategies.

The emphasis in the present section will be on the sociobiologically predicted central tendency for males and females to pursue strongly divergent reproductive strategies. As described more fully in Chapter 6, it is a major finding of evolutionary biology that parenting often involves large differences between the sexes in the amount of time and energy invested. Typically, males invest far less time and energy in the parenting effort than do females, with the result that individual females become a relatively scarce resource compared to males. As a result, sexual competition among males for access to this resource occurs, with the consequence that some males are far more successful than others. Thus, there tends to be higher variation in reproductive success among the males than among females and, since for males mating involves relatively little cost, males tend to be rather indiscriminate maters, while females are much more discriminating.

These apparently primitive trends toward sex differences in reproductive strategy can be modified by natural selection. For example, the great majority of bird species (but relatively few mammals) are monogamous. In such species there is a tendency for equal investment between the sexes and such species tend to be morphologically quite similar as well. The work of Lovejoy (1981), described above, along with evidence of the social structure of hunter–gatherer groups indicate an evolutionary trend toward monogamy among humans. This would indicate natural selection among humans for greater investment by the male and a corresponding diminishing of the differences between males and females in their investment in the offspring of a particular mating.

The second ultimate biological source of sex differences is really a corollary of the above discussion. Among mammals the sex difference in reproductive strategy has resulted from morphological traits that effectively result in males having much higher reproductive capacities than females. A male can sire children by a large number of females, but, due to the requirements of a prolonged pregnancy and lactation for females as well as the enormous physical strain that this entails, females do not similarly benefit from mating with a large number of males. It is thus quite often in the interest of males to attempt to mate with many females, and among humans the great majority of preindustrial societies in fact practiced polygyny (males having many wives), whereas polyandry (females having many husbands) is exceedingly rare. This sex difference results in the expectation that there will be a central tendency for males to engage in polygyny when the context permits.

2. Contextual Variables

One of the central difficulties of developing an evolutionary approach to human social behavior is that of attempting to account for cross-cultural variation. One technique has been to develop theories in which genetic variation occurring between cultures influences cultural choice (Lumsden & Wilson, 1981). Such an approach may be likened to an individual differences approach within psychology (MacDonald, in press), since it is proposed that cultural variation can be explained by biological variation. The approach developed here proposes instead to account for a significant proportion of the variance in human social and family structure by invoking biological uniformity (i.e., central tendencies) in conjunction with contextual variation.

The notion of a contextual variable is familiar to developmentalists as a result of work by Bronfenbrenner (1979) and Lerner (e.g., Lerner & Kauffman, 1986), but this idea has not received the attention it deserves in an evolutionary theory of humans. It is proposed here that contextual variables are essential to an evolutionary account of human social organization. Ironically, despite utilizing the idea of sociobiologically predicted central tendencies as an essential construct, this view is compatible with a high degree of plasticity in human social organization. Human social organization is seen as able to react quickly to changing contextual conditions, so that although self-interest and sex differences in reproductive capacity remain as theoretical bedrocks of the theory, there is no limitation on the form of human social organization. Mating structures and variation in resource control, the two most central concerns from an evolutionary perspective, are fundamentally the result of context interacting with sociobiologically predicted central tendencies, not well-buffered behavioral phenotypes.

The first contextual variable considered here is economic production. Human societies may be graded according to the amount of economic production per individual (Goody, 1976; Sahlins, 1974). In these terms hunter–gatherer societies are the least productive of human societies and this low level of production must be viewed as essential to the early (and by far the longest) stages of human evolution. At a somewhat higher level of production are primitive agricultural and pastoral societies, and the highest productivity among traditional societies was reached by advanced agriculture typical of the nation-state level of political organization.

This increasing production is an essential prerequisite for increased levels of male sexual competition (MacDonald, 1983a). This is the case because at higher levels of economic production it becomes ecologically possible for individual males to control more than one female. The relatively low levels of economic production characteristic of the great majority of human evolution thus effectively inhibited sexual competition and pressures for high paternal investment led to the evolution of epigenetic rules facilitating monogamy.

However, at higher levels of economic production the reproductive strategies of males and females are expected to strongly diverge. Polygyny becomes an increasingly attractive strategy for males as individual males are able to support or control the production of several wives. As predicted by these considerations, van den Berghe (1979) describes data indicating an association between increasing economic production and polygyny in a cross-cultural sample, and such a relationship is implied in the work of Draper and Harpending (1988) and Blain and Barkow (1988). These writers note the association between low levels of resource base and monogamous mating practices and for a tendency toward polygyny with increasing levels of production. As expected, the culmination of this trend occurs in the highly advanced agricultural economies of Eurasia, where extremely intensive polygyny resulting in massive differences in male reproductive success occurred in many societies (Dickemann, 1979).

As economic production becomes more advanced, human social organization becomes more extensive. The monogamous type of social organization existing in the least productive economies implies a high degree of decentralization of social structure. Kinship is important in these societies, but with increasing economic production families become immersed to a much greater extent in kinship relations that reach far beyond the nuclear family (Sahlins, 1974). Sahlins (1974) notes that the conflict between the household and more extensive kinship relations is the fundamental dilemma of these more advanced societies. In sociobiological terms, this cleavage between household and wider kinship results from increasing genetic distance as one moves beyond the nuclear family to immersion in extensive kinship relations. Extended kinship relations become essential for obtaining and defending important resources and individual males are forced to give up the autonomy of the independent economic family unit in order to compete more successfully as part of a larger kinship organization.

This changing context of human evolution has important effects on development described in this chapter and several other sections of this volume. As a first attempt to describe these developmental effects, the literature on adolescent reproductive rituals will be examined. Economic production is crucial to the analysis of the cross-cultural literature on reproductive rituals performed by Paige and Paige (1981). They note that societies with relatively low levels of production are characterized by extensive reproductive rituals for girls. Fathers attempt to maximize the chances of an attractive marriage for their daughters by forming temporary political alliances to gain support against possible seducers and to assure a proper marriage by advertising the economic success of the girl's family. In a politically decentralized society the father is unable to rely on extensive kinship relationships to protect his interests and in their absence he relies on reciprocal obligations forged by these rituals.

As societies become more economically productive and males become more integrated with an extensive network of genetically related kin, the father can depend on these kinship relationships to promote his interests in his daughter's marriage. As a result, there is no need for large reproductive ceremonies. Moreover, since there is increased sexual competition in these societies, the economic value of the daughter to the father increases and economic payments to the father's family (termed bridewealth) are a prerequisite of marriage. The protection bestowed by the large kinship group functions, therefore, to ensure that the girl will command the best possible bridewealth as well as ensure that she will marry an economically productive male (Dickemann, 1981). Individual economic success by a male not only ensures his own ability to have several wives and large numbers of children, but also allows him to purchase wives for his sons when they mature.

Data on male initiation rites can also be incorporated into this perspective. As indicated above, beyond the lowest levels of economic production extensive kinship networks function to control resources. These kinship networks are essentially solidary groups of males with overlapping genetic interests. However, despite the strong genetic overlap in these groups, the large size of the groups ensures that conflicts of interest will be an important feature of these societies. Some males are much more closely related than others and there is considerable variation in economic success. As a result, and quite unlike the situation in societies organized around the economically independent nuclear family, individual males must integrate themselves into this wider community of fairly distantly related individuals. Male reproductive rituals thus take on a relatively hostile atmosphere in these societies, becoming more like "rites of submission," which function to show allegiance to the tribal elders (Paige & Paige, 1981). Individual self-interest and the epigenetic rules underlying nuclear family social organization thus constitute a centrifugal tendency in human evolution and male reproductive rites are an effort to overcome these tendencies in the interests of group solidarity. Whereas in less economically productive societies male initiation rites are affectively positive and attended only by very close relatives, in these more productive societies there is an atmosphere of anxiety and hostility as boys are integrated into a group where fissioning along the lines of individual genetic self-interest is always a possibility (see MacDonald, 1987a, for a more detailed discussion).

A second contextual variable importantly related to family structure and functioning is that of social controls. Independent of what one would ideally want to do, the behavior of individuals can be controlled by others to a greater or lesser extent. As described in Chapter 1, social controls consist of a wide variety of cultural practices, which attempt to channel the behavior of individuals and can range from brute force or ostracism to various types of social disapproval, as might occur when one contravenes a fairly minor social convention. Social controls are systematically related to variation in economic production: At relatively low levels of economic production the decentralizing force of the nuclear family prevents high levels of social control, but as indicated above in the discussion of male initiation rites, the extended kinship group attempts to exert significant levels of control on its members. As described below and especially in Chapter 9, at the highest levels of economic production kinship ties tend to weaken, but the possibility of even greater means of social control exist—the nightmare of George Orwell's *1984*. Social controls thus become an extremely important contextual variable for thinking about human social structure and human development in these societies.

Particularly important here are social controls regulating family life. The previous discussion might lead to the conclusion that as societies became more productive, there would be ever higher levels of sexual competition and polygyny. However, social controls are able to regulate human reproduction in a manner that is completely independent of individual self-interest. For example, postrevolutionary China instituted severe controls on families, requiring them to have only one child. Whereas traditional Chinese society allowed males to have as many wives and concubines as they could afford, the new regulations were egalitarian to an extreme probably never before attempted by any society.

The present thesis is that social controls supporting monogamy are crucial to understanding Western family relationships. In evolutionary terms these controls may be viewed as egalitarian institutions, which effectively inhibit male sexual competition. As a result of these social controls differences among males in resource acquisition could not be translated into the massive differences in reproductive success possible in societies allowing polygyny. These controls have been successful, as indicated by the fact that in contemporary industrial societies there is little evidence for an association between resource acquisition and reproductive success (Vining, 1986), whereas such an association in traditional societies has been well established (Barkow & Burley, 1980; Dickemann, 1979; MacDonald, 1983a). The only indication that wealth is positively associated with fertility in contemporary America is the finding by Essock-Vitale (1984) that the very wealthiest Americans (mean net worth greater than $230,000,000) have a slightly larger average number of children than the population average (3.1 versus 2.7). This relatively small difference is miniscule compared to what could (and did) occur in polygynous societies, where a male with this much wealth could have easily supported dozens of children.

This view contrasts strongly with the approach of Freud (1930/1961), since Freud viewed Western sexual repression as the result of the primeval Oedipal situation, although Freud appeared to realize the egalitarian function of sexual repression to some extent (see MacDonald, 1986c, for a discussion).

In any case, historians such as Stone (1977) have described extensive social controls on marriage and sex that occurred in historical periods in England, particularly during the Puritan era. These controls functioned to strictly regulate family life in accordance with Christian ideology. In the United States, laws reinforcing monogamy have been present since colonial times, and have resulted in the repression of polygamy as practiced by the Mormon church.

The account given above of human family structure differs in several important ways from the account given by Alexander (1979, 1987). Alexander sees a general tendency for socially imposed monogamy to occur as groups reach the nation-state level of organization. Such monogamy is adaptive because it results in more social unity within societies in the face of external threat. There are, however, difficulties with this position:

1. Rather than finding an empirical trend toward monogamy with increasing production, the general trend is that with increased production and its concomitant social complexity polygyny *increases*. As Alexander (1979, 1987) himself points out, there is an increase in polygyny from bands to chiefdoms. Moreover, as in the societies described by Dickemann (1979), the classical Eurasian civilizations were decidedly polygynous and the intensity of the polygyny practiced by the dominant males involved was far higher than could occur in less productive societies (MacDonald, 1983a). As a general feature, these societies were highly stratified, with large gaps between social classes in the control of resources, including women.

2. The Western European type of family structure is unique and not part of a general trend toward monogamy in highly productive agricultural societies. As Alexander notes, this form of social organization has been extraordinarily successful and has spread by conquest to other parts of the world. The origins of this unique pattern thus become an extremely important historical question. Alexander's suggestion that this type of organization evolved because of its effects on intragroup cooperation is an interesting one, and in Chapter 9 it will be argued that this is the origin of monogamy in ancient Sparta. Nevertheless, this is only one possibility for the origins of European monogamy. Herlihy (1985) and Gies and Gies (1987) emphasize the importance of Christian religious ide-

ology, and MacDonald (1983a) describes the battle between ecclesiastical and secular authorities over the issue of monogamy in medieval Europe. There is no indication from these accounts that socially imposed monogamy resulted from cooperation against external pressures. Rather, there was continuous pressure from high-ranking males to engage in polygyny as had been common in the tribes that settled in Europe after the fall of the Roman Empire (see also Gies and Gies, 1987). The conflicts that occurred may well have been over the politics of ecclesiastical versus secular political control rather than an egalitarian response to an external threat. In any case, the rarity with which socially imposed monogamy has occurred in the highly productive traditional cultures of the world suggests that the pull of individual self-interest is very difficult to overcome.

C. Familial Affective Relations in Evolutionary Perspective

The foregoing provides a contextual account of variation in family structure (monogamous versus polygynous) and social structure (society structured around the economically independent nuclear family versus society structured around extended solidary groups of related males). These structural relationships within the family are associated with variation in familial affective relationships. Correlational data indicate that societies characterized by the economically independent nuclear family have affectively warm parent–child and husband–wife relations (e.g., Blain & Barkow, 1988; Draper & Harpending, 1988; MacDonald, 1984, 1987a; Weisner, 1984). As indicated above, they are also characterized by relatively low levels of economic production and sexual competition.

In terms of the preceding discussion and in agreement with anthropological opinion (e.g., Lee, 1979), it is proposed that the economically independent nuclear family is the primitive form of human social organization and that warm affective relationships functioned as a proximal mechanism of social cohesion. As societies become more economically productive, larger groups with higher levels of male sexual competition tend to occur, with the result that the independent family unit becomes enmeshed in extensive kinship networks. The resulting tension between the individual and the group as well as the emergence of a situation in which socialization for aggression is adaptive (see Chapter 6) are reflected by increasingly hostile intrafamilial affective relationships and the male initiation rites characteristic of these societies (Paige & Paige, 1981). Affective means of social cohesion are replaced by social controls which exist beyond the family, and relationships within the family become severely strained as each male strives to integrate himself into the wider network of kin, often in competition with his own family members. Paige and Paige (1981) state that "Every man is a potential head and, therefore, also a potential traitor to his lineage. In the words of an Arab proverb 'I against my brother; I and my brother against my cousin; I, my brother and my cousin against the next village; all of us against the foreigner' " (p. 128). This passage indicates the affective strains associated with such a social system. Notice also that there is a greater likelihood of cooperation with another person to the extent that the other person is genetically related to oneself. This is an example of kin selection as predicted by sociobiological theory: Individuals are expected to help others to the degree that they are genetically related.

I agree then with Paige and Paige (1981) that in societies based on extensive kinship relations the source of military and economic power is also the potential or actual opposition: Without a higher level of centralized political control feuds are endemic. The polygynous family structure that results from increased levels of sexual competition depends much more on the economic power of males than on affective bonding and the generally distant affective atmosphere is adaptive in a society in which conflicts of interest and feuding are far more salient. Thus, Katz and Konner (1981) found that fathers tended to be closer to their children in cultures "where combinations of polygyny, patrilocal residence, the extended family, or patridominant division of labor are absent" (p. 203). Violent and hypermasculine behavior are associated with father distance, and Bacon, Child, and Berry (1963) found father distance associated with violent crime and extremely punitive disciplinary measures with children. Aloof husband–wife relationships are also associated with polygyny and military activity on the part of the husband (see also Whiting & Whiting, 1975). These findings suggest strongly that socialization of adaptive phenotypes related to aggression and altruism can occur, and these themes are explored further in Chapters 6, 8, and 9. Anthropological case studies are provided in the Appendix (p. 169) that illustrate these ideas.

D. Implications for Developmental Mechanisms

There are three theoretical reasons to suppose that the environment is crucial in producing cross-cultural variation in behavior. First, as argued in several chapters of this book, many of the mechanisms involved in human social behavior are environment-expectant. Thus, the ethological theory of attachment described in Chapter 4 and the general analysis of parent–child affective interactions in Chapter 3 and the present chapter propose that these systems program for the affective response to expected environmental variation, so that it is reasonable to suppose that environmental variation can affect variation in adaptive phenotypes.

Second, given that the affective systems underlying family cohesion are environment-expectant systems, it is expected that highly intensive stimulation would facilitate the production of extreme phenotypes (MacDonald, 1985, 1986a,b; see also Chapter 1). The interpretation of the literature on early experience in the areas of both cognitive and social development indicates that environments that depart significantly from the culturally prescribed norm are relatively more likely to have major effects on development (see Chapters 1 and 4). When this perspective is applied to the cross-cultural literature, this suggests that cultures are able to effectively program individual development in adaptive ways by providing extreme socialization environments. Anthropologists (e.g., Konner, 1981; Weisner, 1984) have noted that there is a much broader range of environmental variation cross-culturally than within any one culture. A good example of this phenomenon is the practice of weaning infants from breast-feeding. In American samples the range of weaning is highly curtailed compared to a cross-cultural sample, where weaning into early childhood is not uncommon.

The important conclusion here is that it is not possible to make a general conclusion about the role of family environments on the basis of studies of one particular culture. It was noted above that behavioral genetic studies have failed to find systematic sources of between-family environmental variation within industrial cultures. Compared to a cross-cultural sample, however, there is good reason to suppose that the environments sampled are relatively homogeneous. These findings do not preclude a major average effect of family environment due to the modal type of parent–child relations prevailing in a particular society. Analogously, in Chapter 1 it was noted that adoption studies often indicate a large average effect of adoption of children from lower-class families into middle-class families (Scarr & Weinberg, 1976). This large average effect of adoption is independent of the correlational patterns between biological and adoptive relatives in an adoption study: The average effects of differences in parenting style between cultures may not be related to individual differences among children in the same family within a particular society but may still be an important source of between-society environmental variation (see also Chapter 9 for a discussion of context effects on behavior genetic studies).

Third, Lumsden and Wilson (1981) have suggested that significant genetic change underlying cultural change could occur in as little as 1000 years. This implies that if significant cultural variation can occur in a period of time which is significantly shorter than 1000 years there is evidence that the change was not mediated by changes in gene frequencies. Historical evidence (e.g., Stone, 1977), reviewed below, indicates clearly that major changes in familial interaction patterns have occurred much more quickly than 1000 years and there is no evidence of massive natural selection driving this process. These considerations suggest that this cultural shift was the result of a major alteration in rearing environments, and in the ensuing chapters it will be argued that environmental variation underlies a considerable portion of the cross-cultural variation in aggression and prosocial behavior.

Chapters 6 and 8 examine in detail the evidence for associations between familial affective interactions and aggression and prosocial behavior, respectively. As a preview, it should be noted that these studies have generally shown that warm familial interactions are positively associated with measures of prosocial behavior and negatively associated with aggression, while cold, hostile, and rejecting familial interactions have the opposite associations. Thus, these variations in affective tone seen cross-culturally may well have important effects on adaptive behaviors in these societies. The perspective developed above can be summarized as follows: Economically intermediate societies characterized by extensive kinship relations and high levels of sexual competition will tend to have cold, hostile interpersonal relations and there will be socialization for aggression and exploitative social relationships. On the other hand, societies at the lowest level of economic production are characterized by independent nuclear families, affectively warm intra-familial interactions, and socialization that favors adaptive imbalances of resource flow between close relatives and lack of aggression.

E. The Family and Adaptation in Contemporary Society

Over the last several hundred years there has been an increasing importance in European societies of nuclear family social organization and a corresponding decline in the importance of extended kinship relationships. This shift has been accompanied by an increasing emphasis on the importance of affective ties in family relationships. Stone (1977) finds that prior to the 17th century an atmosphere of deference, psychological manipulation, and aloofness characterized family relationships and he notes that close parent–child relationships were uncommon. Moreover, most children left home between the ages of 7 and 14 in any case, so that much of their rearing was performed by others who would have little interest in providing an affectively positive atmosphere. Warm husband–wife relationships were also quite rare, and married life was "brutal and often hostile" (p. 117). Personal choice of a spouse presumably promotes the importance of affective ties in marriage, but this practice was not typical among the landed classes, and especially in the upper classes, because of the vital reproductive importance of keeping property in the lineage.

A trend toward warmer familial relationships becomes apparent in the period from 1640 to 1800, a trend accompanied by personal choice of a marriage partner. Warm parent–child relations appeared first in the middle classes and later became more common among the other social classes. The ideology of child rearing was much influenced by John Locke, whose idea of the *tabula rasa* is well known to psychologists. Locke clearly believed in the importance of experience (and early experience), and advocated relationships of love and friendship between parents and children (Borstelmann, 1983). During this period, children were increasingly viewed as individuals and their interests taken more into account, as indicated by the appearance of children's literature. Children were no longer expected to practice old customs of deference, such as kneeling or doffing the cap in the presence of the parent. Children stayed at home longer and many of the brutal practices characteristic of public education declined.

These trends can be viewed as indicating higher levels of parental investment in children. Gillis (1981) notes that there was more concern for children, as parents attempted to take advantage of increasing chances for upward social mobility by increasing the level of investment in children. Increased schooling can be seen as an aspect of this trend toward increased parental investment and the modern idea of adolescence as a period of prolonged sheltering from adult responsibilities was inaugurated. As Kagan (1979) notes, increased education and child-oriented means of child rearing are likely to produce instrumental competence and thus upward social mobility. These child-oriented means of child rearing include importantly an emphasis on warm parent–child relationships to the point that in the present period such relationships are taken to be the norm and are strongly buttressed by public policy and scientific opinion. From a sociobiological perspective the prominence of this type of relationship stems from the decline in extended family relationships, lower levels of sexual competition (monogamy), and the consequent greater sexual egalitarianism within the family. These relationships are culturally adaptive because of their association with upward social mobility and instrumental competence. In this view the epigenetic rules underlying familial affective interactions retain considerable importance in affecting adaptive behavior in contemporary societies.

The idea of variation in levels of parental investment corresponding to ecological contingencies is a familiar one to biologists. The ecological idea of K- and r-selection implies a continuum between few offspring and high parental investment to many offspring and little parental investment in each one. In a highly competitive environment it is maladaptive to have many offspring with little investment in each one, since none of the offspring will do well. Viewed in this perspective, the increased investment characteristic of parents in industrial societies is a trend toward a K-selection situation in which increased investment in offspring is adaptive due to an increasingly competitive situation in which upward mobility is a possibility. Unlike the situation with regard to the biological data, however, there is no indication that engaging in high levels of parental investment actually results in higher long-term reproduction in humans. Greater affluence at all levels of society and particularly the imposition of social controls resulting in increased survivorship and state support of poor parents have largely freed reproduction from the very tight economic constraints of previous ages. Personal ideologies, such as voluntary restraints on fertility and those involving the relative importance of family and career, have also assumed great importance, despite the fact that they are presumably reproductively maladaptive (see Chapter 9 for a discussion of maladaptive ideologies). Thus, there is much less of a connection between resources and reproduction than in traditional societies.

These findings imply that familial affective relationships are sensitive to historical, contextual forces and have a complex history that is far from unidirectional. The perspective developed here proposes that warm affective ties were crucial in the prolonged early phases of human evolution and functioned to facilitate the pair bonding and cohesiveness of family units. Economic independence and high levels of paternal investment were characteristic of these families. Increased levels of economic production placed severe stresses on this primitive type of social organization, however, and it gave way ultimately to social organization based on extensive kinship relationships. In these intermediate groups social relationships are profoundly affected by increased levels of competition for resources, particularly sexual resources, and affective relations tend to be cool and distant or hostile. Corresponding to increasing genetic distance among the members of the society, there are individual conflicts of interest and a generalized predisposition toward altruism is maladaptive (see Chapter 8 for a detailed description).

Perhaps ironically, the demise of the extended family type of social organization has seen a return to familial relationships based on these epigenetic rules and modern research indicates that these familial affective relationships remain important in the development of a great many behaviors with implications for adaptation in contemporary society. For example, there is considerable evidence that affectively toned familial interactions are implicated in "a very wide range of problems" (Conger & Petersen, 1984) in adolescence and indeed throughout childhood, including psychiatric disorders (Hetherington & Martin, 1979, 1986). In addition, the general tenor of much of the attachment literature described in Chapter 4 suggests that socially desirable behaviors such as social popularity and ego resilience are associated with responsive, sensitive caregiving and thus presumably affectively positive environments.

In the terminology of Chapter 2, warm parent–child interactions facilitate the elaboration of the positive social reward system and thus make the individual more sensitive to the positive social rewards to be obtained by nurturant, loving interactions with others. Many of these behaviors affected by the positive social reward system presumably have important implications for adaptiveness in any society. In the final section of this chapter several behaviors will be discussed in which there are complex interactions among social learning and familial affective relationships.

Finally, the parent–child affective dimension appears to be an important moderator of contextual influences in development, including peer influences, school influences, and media influences, and in Chapter 9 the importance of the parent–child relationship will be discussed with reference to its role in mediating these contextual influences. In this perspective, the evolutionarily derived epigenetic rules perform a continuing vital function in the socialization process, even in the presence of a vast array of modern institutions that form an entirely novel evolutionary environment.

III. CENTRIFUGAL TENDENCIES WITHIN FAMILIES AND THEIR EFFECTS ON CHILDREN

A. *Adaptation in Contemporary Societies*

One of the difficulties of providing an evolutionary account of human behavior is that there are theoretical reasons for supposing that humans are pulled in different directions by contradictory evolutionary forces. Chapters 7 and 8 examine the contradictory pulls of mechanisms underlying self-interest and altruism. In the preceding I have emphasized the cohesive forces in human evolution as affective mechanisms that tend to keep families together and facilitate high paternal investment. However, I have also noted that the different reproductive strategies of males and females combine with contextual variation in economic production to militate against the economically independent nuclear family and propel the male into more extensive kinship relationships. Both the centripetal forces underlying family cohesiveness and the centrifugal forces favoring dispersal are highly adaptive in particular contexts and in the present section these centrifugal forces will be further examined by considering how they operate in a modern industrial society.

One of the difficulties faced by an evolutionary account of human behavior has been the difficulty of providing a meaningful conceptualization of adaptation in contemporary industrial societies. In the above discussion of social controls it was noted that there is little evidence for a relation between resource control and reproduction in modern societies. Social controls have resulted in lowering the variance in reproductive success among males and have made difficult the testing of adaptationist hypotheses in terms of biological fitness. This is not to say that human behavior has been entirely divorced from biological fitness in these societies. Debilitating psychiatric disorders such as schizophrenia have been shown to be associated with lower fertility (Price *et al.*, 1971; Reed, 1971; Slater *et al.*, 1971) and downward social mobility compared to the social status of biological fathers (Dunham, 1965; Goldberg & Morrison, 1963; Turner & Wagonfeld, 1967).

In addition to using biological fitness (fertility) as a dependent variable in sociobiological analysis, there are reasons for using social class and upward and downward mobility as dependent variables. From an evolutionary perspective the control of resources is of fundamental importance (e.g., Charlesworth, 1988), and social class is thus viewed as an index of resource control. Many studies have shown that in traditional societies there is a strong association between resource control and fertility for males (Betzig, 1986; Dickemann, 1979; Hartung, 1976; Hill, 1984; Irons, 1979). Therefore, the logic is that if there were no social controls on reproduction there would in fact be a strong association between resource accumulation and fertility for males. In the language of the philosophy of science (e.g., Aronson, 1984), such a proposition is termed a contrary-to-fact conditional, that is, a statement of the form, "If X were the case (but it is not), then Y would occur.'' Such statements are important features of scientific theory because they make claims about what would happen if certain events were to take place. For example, psychological theory and data support the contrary-to-fact conditional that if a child from an abusive environment were to be adopted into a middle-class home, its IQ would subsequently be found to be higher than if it had remained in the abusive environment. Such a contrary-to-fact conditional would remain true even if adoption were not a current social policy, and similarly in the case of social controls on marriage. These considerations justify an interest in the determinants of social class status in contemporary societies from a sociobiological perspective.

Another way to view the situation is to note that social controls may prevent a strong association between resource acquisition and fertility, but not affect the proximal mechanisms underlying resource-directed behavior. Thus, even if removed from its ultimate rationale, resource-directed behavior is expected to remain an important human concern. As predicted by such an assumption, sociologists studying relationships between social class and child development (e.g., Elder, 1974) assume (and find) that individuals attempt to maximize their social class status, resist downward social mobility, and experience downward social mobility with a large measure of dysphoria.

Finally, it will be argued below that high socioeconomic status facilitates certain types of sociobiologically predicted behavior even within industrial societies. Males who have acquired a high level of material resources are able to mitigate the negative effects of divorce on their children and are thus able to engage in these behaviors with much less decrement in the adaptiveness of their children than can poor males.

B. Divorce in a Sociobiological Context

I have already provided a sociobiological rationale for supposing that the reproductive strategies of males and females are markedly different. Given social controls on polygyny and in the absence of social controls on divorce, it is expected that males will divorce one woman in order to marry a younger woman. Males remain reproductively competent longer than females, and older, economically well-off males are expected to remain attractive to younger women. On the other hand, older, poor women are least likely to benefit from divorce, because they have little or no reproductive value and generally must increase their relative share of parental investment after the divorce. In a society such as contemporary America in which women tend to have fewer marketable skills than men, it is expected that divorce will lower the socioeconomic position of women more than it will that of men. This effect would not occur in a culture in which the male contributes little to the maintenance of women and is thus an example of the importance of contextual variation in human development. From an evolutionary perspective divorce implies a lessening of paternal investment and it is predicted that there will be negative effects on the adaptive behavior of children.

This perspective implies the following: (a) Divorce should tend to lower the economic position of women and children more than it does that of men. (b) Divorced women should take longer to remarry and remarry less often than men. (c) Children should react very negatively to divorce. The negative feelings of the child result, in an ultimate-level sense, from the anticipated decrement in adaptiveness resulting from divorce. Moreover, guilt resulting from sympathy with the negative feelings of the child could result in the father remaining with the family. (d) The decrements resulting from divorce will be significant, but not devastating. If even minimal functioning in children required the continued presence of a father, it would be expected that divorce would always be pathological behavior by the male and thus relatively unlikely even in the absence of social controls on divorce.

These decrements in adaptiveness are seen as nonoptimal behavior of offspring secondary to the adult male's engaging in sociobiologically predicted behavior. The result of this behavior is to create a context for the child's development that is less than optimal from the point of view of the mother and child. However, there is no implication that the children do not attempt to maximize their own adaptiveness. The decrements can be seen within the context of parent–offspring conflict as well as parent–parent conflict regarding the appropriate level of investment in offspring (Trivers, 1974). Finally, it should be emphasized that the above propositions are propositions about general trends in the data, not about particular instances. Like any other theory, sociobiological predictions are put forward as explaining a significant amount of variance.

Regarding the first two assertions, women do indeed have a longer average duration of divorce before remarriage than men and a lower incidence of remarriage than men (U.S. Census, 1978, as reviewed in Mackey, 1980). These results are particularly true for older women: 76% of divorced women up to age 29 remarry, while only 32.4% remarry between the ages of 40 and 49 and only 11.5% between 50 and 75. In addition, males tend to marry women who are younger than themselves, results suggesting a greater fertility for divorced men than for divorced women. Moreover, divorce tends to result in economic decrements for women, part of the recent "feminization of poverty." Child support requirements have tended to be poorly enforced, and, in about half of the cases reported in the 1975 census, amounted to less than 10% of the income of divorced women. Alimony is also present in only a small minority of divorce cases: 1975 U.S. Census data indicate only 4% of 4.5 million divorced women received alimony. The result is that female-headed divorced families tend to experience downward social mobility and are more likely to be impoverished than prior to the divorce (Hetherington, 1979; Ross & Sawhill, 1975; Wallerstein & Kelley, 1980), a result that is in part due to women having fewer marketable skills and less training than men. In the Wallerstein and Kelley (1980) study the downward mobility of women and children, often involving a move to less desirable neighborhoods, was much more severe and much more permanent than that experienced by men: Five years after the divorce, "with few exceptions the women were poorer than they had been in their first marriages and appeared likely to remain so" (p. 185).

There is also evidence that children react very negatively to divorce. Hetherington (1979) describes children as feeling anger, fear, depression, and guilt following the divorce of their parents. Wallerstein and Kelly (1980) found that only 10% of the children welcomed the announcement of a divorce, and most reacted with anger or apprehensiveness. Over 75% opposed the divorce and many engaged in emotional appeals designed to prevent the divorce.

Finally, there is evidence for decrements in adaptiveness in the children of divorce. One of the controversial aspects within the literature on the effects of divorce on child behavior is whether the effects of divorce are mediated by father absence or by the negative home environment prior to or after divorce. These questions regarding proximal mechanisms are important, but are irrelevant here, since the concern is solely with the ultimate question of the adaptiveness of the behavior and the decrease in paternal investment, whether this decrease in investment (including lack of affective investment) has most of its effects before or after the divorce. There is little question that negative associations with the behavior of children occur concomitantly with divorce, but the issue of long-term pathological effects is more difficult to document. Negative effects are found less often for girls than for boys, who show continuing problems in the home as well as in the school with teachers and peers—problems characterized as aggression and noncompliance (Hetherington, 1979; Hodges, Buchsbaum & Tierney, 1983; Hodges & Bloom, 1984). Guidubaldi, Cleminshaw, Perry, and Mcloughlin (1983) found significant performance decrements in a random sample of elementary school children from divorced families compared to intact families. Hetherington, Camara, and Featherman (1983) found a decrement associated with divorce on standard tests of intelligence and achievement even after controlling for socioeconomic status. Wallerstein and Kelly (1980) found a wide range of outcomes after 5 years, with outcome associated with a variety of factors. School performance was adversely affected for two-thirds of the children, but at the 5-year follow-up there was less evidence of problems, with three-fifths of the sample doing average or better work.

Regarding emotional adjustment, Wallerstein and Kelly (1980) found that 5 years after the divorce over one-third of the children were "consciously and intensely unhappy and dissatisfied with their life in the postdivorce family" (p. 211). Thirty-seven percent of the children were described as moderately to severely depressed, and the depression manifested itself in behaviors such as "chronic, intense unhappiness (at least one child with a suicidal preoccupation), sexual promiscuity, delinquency (drug abuse, petty stealing, some alcoholism, breaking and entering), poor learning, intense anger, apathy, restlessness and . . . a sense of intense emotional deprivation" (p. 211). Several studies have found that boys in mother-headed households tend to be more antisocial, impulsive, delinquent, and rebellious against adult authority (Guidubaldi *et al.*, 1983; Hetherington, Cox, & Cox, 1982). Father absence has been shown to be associated with disruption of sex-typing in boys, especially preadolescent boys (Hetherington, 1966; Huston, 1983). Father absence also disrupts relations of adolescent girls with males: Hetherington (1972) found that adolescent daughters of divorced families were sexually precocious and inappropriately assertive in their interactions with men. These findings on the importance of fathers for daughters' sexual behavior fit well with the cross-cultural evidence and the data on teenage pregnancy indicating a major role for the father in regulating the sexual behavior of the daughter (MacDonald, 1987a; see also below).

Finally, divorce often leads to remarriage on the part of the mother, so that her children are reared by another man. These men do not share a similar genetic interest in the offspring of their new wife and the development of affective bonds between them and their stepchildren is expected to be difficult. Evolutionary theory thus predicts that aberrations of parenting such as child abuse should occur at a high rate by stepparents than by biological fathers, and there is considerable evidence that this is the case (Burgess *et al.*, 1983; Daly & Wilson, 1981). These data show that there are often long-term psychiatric impairments for the children involved. Even apart from the extreme case of child abuse, Hetherington (1987) noted that as a general phenomenon stepparents invest less in their stepchildren than do biological fathers. As noted in Chapter 1, this type of differential parenting could be an important source of nonshared family environmental variation in behavioral genetic adoption studies utilizing natural and adopted children reared in the same family.

It should also be noted that a divorcing male can lessen the decrement in adaptiveness to his children by providing for his children economically and perhaps even by making his ex-wife attractive as a marriage partner by providing her with sufficient resources that his children will have a male figure in the home. This is clearly the option of a wealthy male and once again illustrates the importance of social class and the control of resources in a sociobiological analysis. In a society in which polygyny is officially proscribed, a wealthy male can, via serial polygyny, have children by several women and minimize the economic and psychological decrements associated with divorce. Less wealthy males can engage in similar behavior, but must be prepared to accept relatively larger decrements accruing as a result of decreased paternal investment.

Supporting these contentions, Wallerstein and Kelly (1980) found that downward social mobility was less common for women in the upper and upper-middle classes and also found that poor psychological outcome in children was associated with economic distress. In addition, Hodges, Wechsler, and Ballantine (1979) found that divorced children from families of higher socioeconomic status showed fewer psychological problems than those from families of lower socioeconomic status. Finally, it should be noted that in addition to economic support, divorced fathers appear to be able to effect better outcomes in their children by maintaining a good relationship with the child after the divorce (Guidubaldi *et al.*, 1983), that is, by maintaining a fairly high investment in their offspring.

Finally, it is relevant to mention here that secular trends in the ease of divorce have had a large impact on the incidence of divorce. These trends constitute a contextual effect on child development involving variation in the social controls affecting sexual relationships, and these contextual effects will be examined more closely in Chapter 9. It is only recently that the divorce rate in the United States has reached epidemic proportions, increasing from 2 per 1000 individuals in 1940 to over 5 per 1000 in 1980, a change accompanied by decreasing legal strictures and such innovations as no-fault divorce laws (Adams, Milner, & Schreph, 1984). Strong prohibitions on divorce remain in some countries, such as Ireland, and historically such controls were very strong in England (MacFarlane, 1986). The economic effects of divorce have prompted women's groups to support social controls affecting the economic consequences to men who engage in divorce, including the enforcement of child support laws and making the ex-husband's professional degree and future earnings part of the divorce settlement.

These trends show that contextual variation in social controls can have important effects on sociobiologically predicted male sexual behavior and thus also affect the socialization of children. As is often the case with social controls, the fact that they apply to broad classes of individuals indicate that they are relatively insensitive to genetic variation or to the self-interest of particular individuals. As such they constitute a truly irreducible contextual element in the sociobiological analysis of behavior (see Chapter 9 for a further discussion of social controls).

IV. AFFECTIVE RELATIONSHIPS WITHIN THE FAMILY AND THE TRANSMISSION OF CULTURE

One of the themes of this chapter has been the importance of familial affective relationships in facilitating a variety of behaviors in children. Thus, compliance in children appears to be facilitated in cases where the mothers freely express positive emotion during laboratory play sessions (Hatfield, Ferguson, & Alpert, 1967) and show emotional involvement with their children (Martin, 1981). In addition, Maccoby and Martin (1983) also suggest that the degree to which families have shared goals is related to the level of warmth in the family.

These examples suggest what Maccoby and Martin (1983) describe as "the time-honored concept of warmth and identification" (p. 72). There has indeed been a long tradition within developmental psychology that proposes that an affectively positive parent–child relationship results in the child's adopting the attitudes and/or behaviors of the parent, that is, identifying with the parents. Within the social learning tradition, there are considerable data that the warmth or nurturance of the model facilitates the learning and production of responses (Bandura, 1969; Mischel, 1976). For example, Bandura and Huston (1961) found that children who had spent 15 minutes interacting with a warm, attentive model imitated more of the model's behavior in a free play session than did children who interacted with a cold, abrupt model. Hetherington and Frankie (1967) found that children of parents who expressed very warm, positive attitudes about them were more likely to imitate their parents in a play session in the home.

From the standpoint of the ethological theory of familial affective relations described above, this situation represents an interaction between social learning and biologically based affective interactions. Moreover, there is every reason to suppose from the standpoint of evolutionary theory that one of the most important tasks of parents is to transmit cultural values to their children. Cultural practices are often a vital component of biological fitness in human societies: Failure to adopt the social and religious ideology of the society or failure to learn the technology available to the society could well result in decreases in reproductive capability. Affectively warm parent–child interactions would tend to facilitate the adoption of parental attitudes and values and result in a conservative mechanism for the transmission of culture. Such a mechanism may well have been adaptive within the context of primitive human social organization, where there were no social or economic controls or valuable resources that could be transmitted from parents to children. Under such circumstances cultural continuity cannot be assured either by parental power to manipulate the reproductive chances of their offspring by their control over resources or by centralized political controls on young people. Under such circumstances parental control over the cultural choices of their children would be greatly facilitated by affectively positive familial relationships.

Interactions between familial affectively toned relationships and social learning are implicated in the literature on parent versus peer sources of influence, discussed in Chapter 9. In the present chapter several other behaviors in which the parent–child relationship appears to have adaptive implications are discussed. One particularly interesting set of behaviors is that subsumed under the idea of identity formation. From an evolutionary perspective identity formation affects parent–child transmission of culture. By identifying with the attitudes and ideologies of their parents, children learn behaviors with a great deal of adaptive significance. The thesis here is that this process is influenced by social learning processes in which attitudes and ideologies are transmitted from parents to children. This mechanism of cultural transmission would result in children adopting the values and attitudes of their parents, but the transmission of these ideologies and values is also importantly influenced by familial affective interactions. As the theory described above indicates, a warm, nurturant relationship with the model facilitates the adoption of the modeled behaviors and attitudes.

Studies of identity formation have indicated four different identity statuses (Marcia, 1966, 1967) as follows:

1. *Identity-diffused* subjects have not experienced an identity crisis or made any commitment to a vocation or set of beliefs.
2. *Foreclosure* subjects have not experienced an identity crisis, but have made commitments that they have accepted from other individuals, usually parents, without question.
3. *Moratorium* subjects are in a state of crisis and are actively searching for values, but have yet to find a set of values to which they are committed.
4. *Identity-achieved* subjects have experienced crises, but have resolved them, so that they now have a personal commitment to a set of beliefs or occupation.

The social learning theory described above suggests that warm familial relationships should facilitate the adoption of parental values with little conflict on the part of the child, and this prediction is confirmed. Matteson (1974) found that foreclosures participated in a "love affair" with their families. Muuss (1982) summarized evidence indicating that foreclosures are very close to and feel highly valued by their parents. Degree of control is intermediate, neither too harsh nor too limited, and such individuals perceive parents as accepting and supportive. Further support for this perspective comes from Marcia and Friedman (1970), who found that foreclosure women had high self-esteem and were low in anxiety, and from a review by Marcia (1980), who summarized a variety of studies showing that the foreclosure females are well-adjusted.

Another prediction of the ethological–social learning theory is that as parent–child interactions become more negative, there is less identification with parental values and more conflict and questioning of parental values. This also appears to be the case. Moratorium and identity-achieved individuals are described as ambivalent toward their parents, that is, as both accepting and rejecting (Marcia, 1980; Muuss, 1982). In Marcia's theory, moratorium is a necessary condition for the occurrence of identity achievement, so that we expect and find that individuals in both of these categories describe their parents in ambivalent terms, although identity achievers appear to have less ambivalence toward their parents and view them more positively. This finding is presumably due to the adoption by identity achievers of a more accepting attitude toward their parents after the struggle of identity achievement. During the moratorium period, however, there is a more negative relationship.

The ethological–social learning theory predicts that very negative parent–child relationships will lead to minimal identification with the values and ideologies of the parents, and this is indeed the case with identity-diffused subjects. Parents of such individuals are described as "distant, detached, uninvolved and unconcerned" (Muuss, 1982; see also Marcia, 1980) and such individuals appear not to accept the values of their parents. There is even evidence that identity-diffused individuals are at risk for psychopathology. Several studies have found identity-diffused subjects to be relatively isolated (e.g., Orlofsky, Marcia, & Lesser, 1973), and we have already seen that affectively negative parent–child relations are associated with a variety of poor outcomes in children.

I have suggested that during human evolutionary history warm parent–child interactions were most adaptive because they reliably resulted in children acquiring the cultural beliefs of their parents. I also noted in several places that the environment can rapidly change, so that a mechanism that is adaptive in Bowlby's "environment of evolutionary adaptiveness" may not be adaptive in highly altered circumstances. This may well be the case with identity formation in modern industrial societies. Compared to the primitive forms of human social organization that characterized humans throughout most of their history, individuals of all social strata in a modern, pluralistic society have many more choices available and observe a very wide variety of life-styles, belief systems, and occupational possibilities. The university in particular is designed to provide a wide range of intellectual challenges to traditional beliefs and attitudes, and the great majority of subjects for the experiments on identity formation are university students. Cultural change in modern societies occurs at a very fast pace compared to traditional societies and initiating or participating in novel ideas and practices is often highly rewarded. Under such circumstances the confusion and anxiety characteristic of moratorium and the earlier histories of identity-achieved individuals may be quite adaptive and this is supported by the available research. Identity-achieved individuals are relatively autonomous (Orlofsky *et al.*, 1973) and high-achievers (Orlofsky, 1978; Marcia & Friedman, 1970). On the other hand, identity diffusion appears to be a maladaptive response and is associated with psychopathology.

These results suggest that the idea that warm parent–child interactions are most adaptive in a modern industrial society may need reevaluation. The data suggest that the most negative parent–child interactions are indeed associated with pathological outcomes in children, but that milder forms of parental ambivalence may actually be adaptive for many individuals in a rapidly changing society where innovation is highly prized. Nevertheless, it is probably premature to dismiss the idea that warm parent–child relationships foster adaptive identificatory behavior in children. Mortimer and her colleagues (Mortimer, 1976; Mortimer, Lorence, & Kumka, 1982) found a strong tendency for sons to choose an occupation similar to that of their fathers' along the dimensions of autonomy and function. This tendency was increased if the father and son had a close relationship and the father had a prestigious occupation. From an evolutionary perspective, identification is expected to be facilitated if the model controls large amounts of resources, and this is a common finding in social learning studies (Bandura, 1969). Moreover, one might well suppose that in cases where the father did not have a prestigious occupation, the father may not have encouraged the son to emulate his choice of occupation.

V. GENERAL EFFECTS OF DECREMENTS IN PARENTAL INVESTMENT AND AN EVOLUTIONARY ANALYSIS OF PARENTAL CONTROL

A. *Effects of Decreases in Parental Investment*

Although the case of divorce, described above, is a particularly attractive example of how the developmental literature on families can be placed in a sociobiological perspective, it can be viewed as a special case of the general phenomenon of the developmental effects of decrements in parental investment, which can occur for any reason. The general case of the single-parent family, whether created by divorce, choice of single-parenthood, or the death of a spouse, thus represents a situation that can be viewed as likely to result in a decrease in the psychological and material resources available to the child. For example, Dornbusch *et al.* (1985) found that mother-only households were associated with a variety of deviant behaviors in adolescents, as well as with lower levels of parental control of adolescent decision-making. The measures of deviance included contact with the law, arrests, and truancy. One of the areas of parental control that is quite likely to suffer in single-parent families is control over a daughter's sexual behavior. MacDonald (1987a) suggested that one of the primary roles of the father in human evolution is the control of daughters' sexual behavior. Single-parent families are predicted to be much less effective in regulating girls' sexual behavior, and this appears to be the case. Teenage pregnancy is strongly associated with a variety of negative outcomes to both parent and child, including lack of upward social mobility. Recent evidence collected by Surbey (1987) suggests that father absence may even affect the physical development of the daughter by accelerating menarche. In conjunction with the findings on the sexual behavior of the daughters of divorce discussed above (Hetherington, 1972), these results indicate major effects of father absence on the physiology and sexual behavior of girls.

Simply having two parents in the family does not guarantee high levels of investment in children. Indeed, the general parenting style labeled "indifferent–uninvolved" by Maccoby and Martin (1983) would appear to be characterized by relatively low levels of parental investment and a variety of pathological outcomes in children. From an evolutionary perspective such indifferent–uninvolved parenting is expected to be particularly likely in reconstituted families in which one parent is not biologically related to the child. Recently Steinberg (1987) found that susceptibility to antisocial peer pressure was higher in families with a stepparent, and the author argues, on the basis of other studies (e.g., Berndt, 1979), that there are significant associations between responses in hypothetical antisocial dilemmas and actual behavior. As indicated above, Hetherington (1987) found that stepparents are less likely to invest in their stepchildren. Stepparents are less likely to be willing or able to exert control over their stepchildren and, in addition, the affective strains placed on divorced and reconstituted families and the lack of strong affective ties with the stepfather may also be causally related to sexual abuse, child deviance, and a greater influence of peer pressures compared to parental values. Thus, Daly and Wilson (1981) and Burgess *et al.,* (1983) show that child abuse occurs more frequently when the parent is not biologically related to the child.

Nor does having two biological parents in the family guarantee equally high levels of investment in each offspring. As indicated at the beginning of this chapter, evolutionary theory predicts that parents will be highly discriminating regarding the extent of their investment in each child. One particularly salient example of this phenomenon is related to parental distribution of resources to children. As Charlesworth (1988) notes, the study of resource acquisition is fundamental to an evolutionary approach to development, and parents can control the amount of resources that their offspring receive. As a result, in societies beyond the most rudimentary level of economic production parents are able to have profound effects on the reproductive success of their offspring. For example, parents via the practice of primogeniture are able to concentrate their wealth in the next generation by effectively disinheriting later born sons. Older sons will tend to reproduce sooner than younger sons and by concentrating the wealth in the next generation the father prevents the gradual dissolution of resources into progressively smaller holdings. Such practices are likely to be particularly important in societies where polygyny is possible, since by investing heavily in a male offspring a parent can facilitate the son's acquisition of females. Investment in daughters is expected to be at a lower rate, since the reproductive capacity of a daughter is limited relative to that of a son. Nevertheless, by providing a dowry to a daughter, a father can ensure the social status of his grandchildren, so that in many societies dowry competition, in which fathers essentially compete with each other to purchase sons-in-law, is intense (Dickemann, 1981). Dickemann (1981) shows that the practices of dowry competition and primogeniture were common in the traditional civilizations of Eurasia.

Both dowry competition and primogeniture were common in traditional European societies. Stone (1977; see also Gillis, 1981) points out that the landed classes in Reformation England were forced to restrict the claims of younger sons in order to keep the property intact. Younger sons married far less often and were often forced to seek careers in the military and the clergy with far lower remuneration. Dowry payments to daughters are also a form of resource distribution, and fathers would often place daughters in nunneries to avoid this drain on their resources. The percentage of the daughters of squires and above remaining unmarried rose to 25% between 1675 and 1799 and similar percentages held for younger sons. Even in the lower classes the prospects of marriage were intimately tied to the ability to inherit property.

Such inequities in resource distribution and the strong associations between resource acquisition and reproduction undoubtedly caused a great deal of friction among family members. Such inequities in resource distribution conforming to evolutionary predictions continue in contemporary societies. In a Canadian study of probated wills, Smith, Kish, and Crawford (1987) found that wealthier decedents favored male offspring, whereas the less wealthy favored females. This follows evolutionary predictions because in the sexually competitive societies in which humans evolved, females will tend to reproduce even without controlling large amounts of resources, whereas the reproductive efforts of males will be greatly aided by resource control (Trivers & Willard, 1973; see Chapter 6). Wealthy decedents gave twice as much to their sons as to their daughters, whereas poorer decedents gave twice as much to daughters as to sons.

I have suggested that parent–child affective relations offer a mechanism that facilitates the transmission of cultural values to offspring. In societies where such inheritance is possible and crucial to reproductive success, parents would be able to exert considerable control over their offspring's behavior by manipulating the possibility of inheritance. In such cases affective relations would be relatively unimportant.

Several other studies (reviewed by Smith, 1988) indicate the importance of discriminative parenting in two-parent families. One important variable here is the reproductive value of the offspring, defined as the relative likelihood of future reproductive success. As reflected in the practice of primogeniture discussed above, older children have a higher reproductive value than younger children, and this is the case because, all things being equal, they will tend to reproduce sooner and require fewer resources to reach reproductive age. (Reproductive fitness is affected not only by the number of children, but by the timing of their birth: Parents who have their children at an early age and successfully rear them will outreproduce those who wait and have the same number of children, since they will have grandchildren sooner.) Children who are defective or sickly can be predicted to have a lower reproductive value as well, so that evolutionary theory predicts that parents will provide fewer resources to them, especially in times of scarce resources.

Consistent with these predictions, Daly and Wilson (1984) found that the killing of children as well as child abuse are much more common with regard to younger than to older children. Daly and Wilson (1981) also note that child abuse is more common when the child is born prematurely or has congenital defects, mental retardation, or emotional disturbance. Data that especially implicate characteristics of the child are those showing that increased child abuse occurs more commonly in cases where the child has a severe handicap, such as spina bifida or Down syndrome. Moreover, the parents of institutionalized handicapped children are relatively more likely to abandon their children or visit them infrequently.

Parental bereavement at the loss of a child also shows the importance of discriminative parenting. Littlefield and Rushton (1986) found that parents grieved more for healthy children than for unhealthy children and more for older than for younger children, although the latter finding only appeared after controlling for the age of the parents. These examples suggest that discriminative parenting regarding resources is a source of nonshared environmental influence on development. Parents may have quite different patterns of affective and material investment in offspring, depending on the characteristics of children hypothesized to be important by evolutionary theory.

B. Parental Control as an Aspect of Parental Investment

In the present chapter, I have emphasized the importance of the affective side of parent–child interactions and provided an evolutionary framework for thinking about this dimension of parent–child interactions. However, the data described above and in the first section of this chapter suggest that the dimension of parental control is another aspect of parental investment. These data indicate that low levels of parental control, especially when it suggests parental indifference or inability to control children, is an index of low parental investment. From this perspective parental monitoring of children and the time and energy required to do so constitute an important part of parental investment. This point of view has been elaborated by Draper and Harpending (1988), who place the cross-cultural literature on parenting in an evolutionary perspective. They describe two basic strategies, the "dad" strategy, characterized by high levels of parental investment, and the "cad" strategy, characterized by low levels of parental control and socialization by peers.

Although the developmental literature derived from contemporary industrial societies indicates a variety of negative outcomes for this style of parenting, Draper and Harpending emphasize that low levels of psychological investment in offspring may be adaptive in the traditional societies where it is found. Indeed, the same correlates described above for the affective side of parenting exist for this control dimension; that is, societies at the middle level of economic production, with polygyny and socialization for aggression, are characterized by generally low parental investment. Although the correlations with the affective dimension have been emphasized here because of their power to incorporate the large developmental literature on the correlates of the affective dimension of parenting, this perspective suggests that a greater attention to the control dimension is warranted. A synthetic viewpoint would propose that both the affective and the control dimensions are independent aspects of parental investment and that they may affect development independently and synergistically. For example, Jessor and Jessor (1974) found that adolescents with a relative absence of deviant behaviors (including drug and alcohol use and sexual activities) were more likely to have parents who successfully transmitted an ideology that disapproved of these behaviors and who exhibited both a reasonable degree of control over their children (e.g., monitoring school performance and activities) and had an affectionate relationship with them.

Teenage pregnancy is another phenotype that illustrates the relationships between the dimensions of parenting and adaptive behaviors. Teenage childbirth is particularly interesting from a sociobiological viewpoint, because teenage women who have children tend to have very high rates of fertility as well as a conspicuous lack of upward social mobility (Ooms, 1981). Although the phenomenon is a complex one and has been approached from a variety of perspectives, there is evidence for the importance of familial interaction patterns in teenage childbirth. Several studies have shown the importance of the affective quality of the mother–daughter relationship and husband–wife relationship as a predictor of teenage pregnancy (Abernathy, 1974; Fox, 1981; Inazu & Fox, 1980; Lewis, 1973). Teenage pregnancy is also more common in female-headed households (Barglow, Bornstein, Exum, Wright, & Visotsky, 1968; Kantner & Zelnick, 1973; Roebuck & McGee, 1977), suggesting that adaptiveness, construed as upward social mobility, but not fertility, is negatively affected by the lack of paternal investment. Thus, Hogan and Kitigawa (1985) found that teenage childbirth was much more common in cases where the parent of the teenager reported low supervision of dating behavior.

The fact that low levels of parental control can be characterized as low parental investment and as a causal factor in developmental outcomes with negative consequences in contemporary society does not imply that very high levels of parental control are beneficial. As indicated in Section I of this chapter, authoritarian parenting, characterized by very high levels of control and lack of reciprocity, has correlations with a variety of negative characteristics of children in contemporary societies. Historically, this pattern of parenting was more common prior to the 18th century in the West and the question of the adaptiveness of this style of parenting is complex. In Chapter 8 the negative effects of this style of parenting on the socialization of altruism and its adaptive history will be emphasized. As suggested there, it is quite possible that extreme levels of parental control are aversive to children for much the same reason that negative affective relationships are: Children are biologically predisposed to view such parental behaviors negatively.

From an evolutionary perspective conflicts between the interests of parents and children are expected (Trivers, 1974). Although tipping the balance in favor of the parent is presumably adaptive for both parent and child because of the parent's greater knowledge and experience, total control by the parents without any reciprocity, especially if extended into later childhood and adulthood would be inconsistent with the logic of parent–offspring conflicts of interest as elaborated by Trivers (1974). Children would thus be expected to view such an unbalanced arrangement negatively, just as individuals tend to view victimization in any exploitative relationship negatively. In Chapter 8 the role of the emotions in motivating individuals to avoid and terminate exploitative relationships is emphasized, and in the present case authoritarian parenting is viewed as evoking a strong negative emotional response for much the same reason. The authoritative pattern of parenting described by Baumrind is clearly a compromise that reflects the legitimate interests of both parents and children. Attribution theorists (e.g., Lepper, 1981; Lepper, Greene, & Nisbet, 1973) have emphasized that children are much more likely to comply with parental wishes if they are able to attribute the cause of their behavior to their own volitions rather than as the result of external pressure. These findings indicate the extent to which children resist the control of others and are seen here as reflecting an evolutionarily based need for minimal reciprocity even in such an unbalanced relationship as that of parent and child.

Another source of the negative affective reaction to authoritarian parenting may be that authoritarian parents are by definition cold and hostile. The developmental literature indicates that quite high levels of parental control are tolerated by children without strong negative reactions if they are accompanied by parental warmth. Maccoby and Martin (1983) call attention to the possible role of the affective side of the parent–child relationship in mediating the effects of parental discipline and control. The evolutionary logic sketched above is consistent with this perspective, but does suggest that extreme levels of control will be resisted. It is predicted that at these extreme levels an independent effect of the control dimension will be found even in cases where parents have warm relationships with their children. In fact, since parental warmth is highly reinforcing to children, while very high levels of control are aversive, children in such a situation would be expected to be quite conflicted and ambivalent about their parents. Further research is required to investigate these predictions.

There would appear to be an analogy between the social controls described above, which act at the level of the social group, and parental control within the family. In both cases, the control results from the elementary fact that the behavior of individuals can be controlled by others. Since parents, especially of young children, are physically and mentally superior to their children, it is not surprising that they tend to exercise this control. As in the case of social controls, parental control may act independently of the genetic characteristics of the controlled children, so that there would be a main effect of parental control independent of the individual characteristics of the child. This main effect of parental control may not make children in the same family alike in some way, but may be an important environmental influence nevertheless, especially in extreme cases where very high levels of control are applied. As in the case of social controls, it is expected that parental controls may be subject to rapid historical changes due to a variety of contextual features. In Section II it was argued that historical variation in the affective side of parent–child interactions occurred too quickly to be due to natural selection, and a similar argument holds for the control dimension. Authoritarian parenting styles are much less common today than even 100 years ago, so that historical variation in parental control is unlikely to be due to natural selection. In many ways, therefore, both social controls and parental control behave like the environment-expectant genetic systems emphasized throughout this volume: They are highly flexible and able to change quickly depending on the contingencies of particular environments.

VI. APPENDIX

The purpose of this appendix is to present in some detail two anthropological case studies which illustrate some of the themes of this chapter as well as some of the other chapters in this volume. The first ethnography examined here was written by Levine and Levine (1966) as part of the classic Six Culture Studies of Child Rearing Series. The Levines provide an ethnography of Nyansongo, a community of the Gusii tribe in Kenya. The Gusii are a clan-type society based on the extended family at the intermediate level of economic production. Since the ethnography is over 20 years old and much may have changed in this period, the past tense will be used. Following the discussion of the Gusii is a discussion of the !Kung based on the observations of Lee (1979, 1982), Silberbauer (1981), and others. The !Kung are hunter–gatherers and thus represent prototypical human social organization. The discussions are centered around several propositions derived from sociobiological theory.

A. Social Structure and Child Rearing among the Gusii in Evolutionary Perspective

1. *Sexual competition among males was a highly salient characteristic of the society.* Polygyny was the ideal form of marriage among the Gusii, and the great majority of children were reared in polygynous households. Males with four or five wives were not uncommon, and some wealthy elders had up to 11 wives and scores of children. Large numbers of both wives and children were actively sought by males.

The mechanism by which males acquired females was by purchasing them by means of bridewealth. Bridewealth gave the husband exclusive sexual rights to the female and was paid to the father of the bride. Brides were expensive. For example, it took the entire pay of a plantation worker for over 3 years to purchase one female, so that males without sisters often had a difficult time marrying. That women were in some sense the ultimate resource is indicated by the fact that when a neighboring tribe, the Kipsigis, had a famine, they sold the Gusii some of their females, who then became wives of Gusii males.

Sexually competitive species of animals often show much greater variability among males than among females in reproductive success (see Chapter 6). This is reflected in the finding that among the Gusii there was more variability in age of marriage for males than for females. A poor male would be unable to marry until he was 20 or 30 years old and his reproductive success would thus tend to be much lower than the son of a wealthy man who married in early adolescence. Girls tended to marry at the same age, however, and their reproductive capacity was much lower and thus showed less variation than that of the males.

Despite the commonness of premarital sexual relations at the time of the ethnography, there appear to have been fairly strong sanctions against fathering illegitimate offspring. These social controls had the effect of reinforcing the strong connections among male resource control, male reproductive success, and paternity confidence. The girl's value to the father in obtaining bridewealth was clearly compromised by illegitimate pregnancy, and as a result there were a number of social controls aimed at preventing this. An illegitimate birth was extremely disgraceful and the girl was forced to name the father before giving birth. If the father was from a different clan, the family would often attempt to recover damages in a lawsuit. If the father was within the clan, he was stigmatized by the event. Apparently the controls over female sexual behavior were more stringent in times past: The Levines note that prior to modern times warriors protected their sisters from violation. This intense vigilance of young girls in order to protect their value on the marriage market is the basis of the theory of Paige and Paige discussed in this chapter.

Another aspect of the sanctions against premarital sexual behavior was that illegitimate children had low social status in the household into which the woman eventually married, and the amount of bridewealth commanded by the girl was lowered by the illegitimate birth. Adultery was also rather severely punished. Before the British outlawed it, killing of the adulterous male by the offended husband was considered justifiable homicide, and economic sanctions against the offending male paid to the husband still occurred.

2. *Sexual competition among the females was directed at advancing the interests of their own children relative to the other children within a polygynous marriage.* Clearly there is a great deal of hostility and competition within the polygynous marriage system. Secondary wives brought with them a great deal of dissension and hatred, and women often attempted to prevent secondary marriages, sometimes successfully. Thus, in Nyansongo there were two monogamous males whose wives dominated them and prevented them from acquiring further wives. Once a man had two or more wives he was in a much better political position with any one of them, since he could punish one wife by temporarily abandoning her, while in a monogamous marriage the wife could also effectively punish the husband by withdrawing from him.

Many of the disagreements within the marriage had to do with the apportionment of resources among the wives and the children. Thus, a woman complained if she felt that the husband was favoring one wife or the children of one wife compared to her or her children. The resources that were closely monitored included gifts and money, education, and bridewealth for a son. Since children were greatly desired, the number of children was a prime focus of competition among females and the source of a great deal of animosity within polygynous families. Since the husband was in a superior political position, the hatred of the wife was directed at the co-wife: "Such ill feeling among the co-wives is the price of polygyny" (Levine & Levine, 1966, p. 24). The wives were also jealous because the younger wives were preferred over the older ones and they attributed many of their own problems, most notably barrenness, to the witchcraft and sorcery of co-wives.

Within the household, resources such as cattle and land were associated with a particular wife, so that, for example, if a woman had a son and a daughter, the bride-wealth obtained from the daughter's marriage would be reserved for the woman's sons. If the husband used the cattle associated with one woman to obtain a bride for himself, he incurred a debt to the woman. Reflecting the principles of kin selection, women were clearly interested in using this resource for their own sons rather than for purchasing another bride for the husband.

This competition within the household extended also to sons. They were often unwilling to give gifts to their fathers, because they feared that they would be used for the bridewealth of another son. However, mothers and sons were extremely loyal to one another, clearly a result of their commonality of genetic interest. Whereas the father's interest was diluted among his several sons by different women, the interest of a mother was exclusively focused on her own children:

> This reciprocal protectiveness is a recognition of their common fate, for a son acquires his share of the patrimony through rights established by the mother and her daughters, while a mother gains helpers in her daughters-in-law and is dependent on her sons and their wives when she is old and feeble. (Levine & Levine, 1966, p. 29)

3. *The acquisition of wealth was essential to males for success in sexual competition.* Evolutionary theory emphasizes the importance of control of resources as essential to variation in reproductive success (see this chapter and Chapters 1 and 6). Among the Nyansongo there was a clear relationship between resource control and reproductive success. Simply put, men with large numbers of cattle could afford large numbers of wives for themselves and their sons:

> A Nyansongo man desires land, cattle, and money partly for the prestige that accrues to him. The size of his herds and number of his wives are visible signs of his affluence. The extent of a particular individual's wealth is a complex function of his father's wealth, the number of heirs with whom he had to share his father's wealth, the number of his daughters whose marriages bring in cattle and his own personal efforts to acquire property through work and trade. In general, a man is fiercely jealous of a neighbor who is slightly richer, deferential to one who is richer, and fearful of the jealousy of those who are poorer. Wealthy men were respected and poor men despised: indeed, the term for "poor man" was an insult in the Gusii language. (Levine & Levine, 1966, p. 11)

The Levines note that the wealthy did not share with their neighbors, but used their wealth to dominate them: "The poor man's property belongs to the rich man" (Levine & Levine, 1966, p. 11) and "The property of the monogamist is owned by the powerful man" (p. 70) were Gusii proverbs. Wealthy men often claimed the property of poorer individuals and nothing could be done to prevent this apart from appealing to a higher authority, a possibility presumably not present before the colonial era.

Interestingly, rich men were not able to confer much hereditary wealth on the next generation because, since they had many wives and therefore many sons, their property became highly diluted. As a result, the individual success of males in sexual competition remained more strongly tied to personal characteristics than in more economically advanced societies, where property was often concentrated in the next generation via the practice of primogeniture (see this chapter).

I have noted that exploitation of poor males by the rich was a common aspect of Gusii life, but reciprocity was also a common characteristic of their economic life. Thus, the women in neighboring homesteads cooperated in agricultural work on a strictly reciprocal basis. The name of such groups was *egesangio*, meaning "an equally shared thing," and each woman kept strict account of her own contribution and that of the other women. Reciprocity and exploitation are discussed in Chapter 8 in the context of the theory of moral development. There is no evidence at all for any behaviors remotely resembling altruism among the Gusii, a conclusion that fits well with the material on the socialization of altruism in Chapter 8.

4. *There was strong evidence for kin selection among the Gusii.* The Gusii viewed themselves as descending from a common ancestor. They were a patrilocal clan society and political allegiance was a function of genetic distance between the males of the clan. The social organization was composed of units of increasing size and thus increasing genetic distance among the males. When a man died, his property went to his sons first, and if he was without sons, it went to his brothers. If an entire group was wiped out, the property went to the nearest set of relatives. Widows were also inherited by the brothers of the deceased—the institution of the levirate. When the interests of a lineage were threatened, individuals grouped together on the basis of their degree of genetic relatedness. Although military forays were less common during the 1950s (when the data were gathered) than earlier, due to the British administration of the area, lineage groups still combined in lawsuits against other lineages: "In general, a lineage unit of any order tends to act as a unit only when its interests are endangered by outsiders" (Levine & Levine, 1966, p. 31). Clearly, self-interest and commonality of interest based on degree of genetic relatedness was a highly salient feature of Gusii life.

The importance of genetic relatedness could also be seen with the methods of social control. The male head of the homestead had a great deal of power within the homestead, but if there were serious crimes, he would bring in an older brother or a closely related elder to adjudicate. Close relatives also adjudicated disputes within a lineage, but if the dispute was between distantly related individuals, then the group of elders would be expanded to the minimum size necessary to include both of the disputants.

Kin selection can also be seen in the nepotistic behavior of the chief who was appointed by the British. This man is described as having 14 wives and as being the wealthiest man in the district. While in office, he had enriched his kinsmen and employed many of his relatives as personal servants. This chief also benefited greatly from new economic development, which he controlled, and he "has favored members of his family and lineage, and to a lesser extent people of his subclan and clan, in the allocation of shops, jobs, and loans . . . He has used this influence on behalf of the selection of his own kinsmen and in barring persons of subordinate or 'adopted clans' . . . from access to economic advantage" (Levine & Levine, 1966, p. 106). Thus, the provision of economic benefits for some individuals as well as the obstruction of others was a direct function of the degree of genetic relatedness.

5. *Military defense and aggression was an important part of the ecology of the Gusii.* I have emphasized, following Paige and Paige (1981), that societies at the intermediate level of social organization tend to be constantly feuding and competing with other clans. This pattern clearly pertains to the Gusii. The Gusii themselves were subdivided into large "descended" clans, which had been in the area since its settlement, as well as smaller, "adopted" clans, many of which were refugees from conflicts with other clans. These adopted clans must be viewed as losers in competition with other clans and as having been incorporated on unfavorable terms into the new area. The Levines note that the descended

clans were dominant to the adopted clans. Paige and Paige (1981) also note in their comments on clan societies that weaker clans become absorbed on unfavorable terms by more successful clans, so this appears to be a general pattern.

Gusii clans feuded with each other, engaging in prolonged spear fights and the abduction of women as well as the cattle used to purchase wives. Marriage was exogamous, so that wives came from other clans within the Gusii. This practice resulted in something of a damper on intraclan hostilities, but they continued nonetheless. They also engaged in war with non-Gusii neighbors, such as the Kipsigis, and the focus of this warfare was in at least some cases territorial. Thus, it is noted that the various Gusii tribes would combine militarily against the Kipsigis and that they had lost a piece of land to them. However, land apparently was abundant among the Gusii until recent large increases in population, so that land is now a source of conflict much more than in the past.

The Gusii homestead was a military unit with the sons under the command of their father. Wealthy men with many wives and many sons thus commanded much more military power and were able to dominate their poorer neighbors. As clans became larger they tended to fission into smaller clans, which then became enemies, a prominent theme in the discussion of this type of social structure by Paige and Paige (1981; see also Chagnon, 1979):

> The leader at every level was faced with the problem of maintaining order among conflicting segments, using his power to induce people to submit their disputes to him and the lineage elders rather than settling them by force . . . Above the local groups, social control was only achieved when a leader arose who was not only acknowledged as wealthier and more powerful than anyone else in the area, but who also was willing to use severe physical punishments of offenders to maintain respect for his judicial authority. (Levine & Levine, 1966, p. 71)

6. *Gusii society was characterized by pronounced relationships of dominance and subordination.* Another feature of Gusii behavior that conforms well to evolutionary expectations was the general authoritarianism of the society. I have characterized the lowest levels of human social organization as relatively egalitarian in their relationships, and this is certainly true of the !Kung described below. At the intermediate level of social organization characteristic of the Gusii, social relationships were far from egalitarian, but there is none of the institutionalized social structure characteristic of politically centralized states that is able to ensure the stability of hierarchical relationships.

Gusii society was thus an authoritarian society in the sense of there being "a general tendency to structure relationships in terms of dominance and submission, unquestioning obedience to a strong leader, and dependence on powerful individuals for the attainment of goals such as law enforcement and social mobility" (Levine & Levine, 1966, p. 184). Powerful men were expected to (and did) control and exploit less powerful individuals for their own personal advantage.

7. *Familial and nonfamilial relationships were lacking in warmth.* This proposition and the following relate more directly to developmental psychology because they involve the socialization of children. Children were greatly desired by the Gusii and parents tended to have as many children as possible. Apart from the obvious ultimate genetic reasons, boys were desired because of their importance in increasing the military power of the father and his lineage. Girls were also highly desirable because of the system of bridewealth.

The theoretical perspective developed in this chapter suggests that parent–child relationships in a society such as the Gusii will be characterized by lack of warmth. This was indeed the case. Infants were given a great deal of physical care, but there is little indication of mother–infant affection. The typical mother is described as nursing the infant "mechanically, without looking at the child or fondling him, and she often continues conversing with the other women and older children" (Levine & Levine, 1966, p. 122). "It is rare to see a mother kissing, cuddling, hugging, or cooing at her child" (p. 126). Mothers tended to remain aloof from their infants unless attending to their physical needs. Older children, who often acted as caretakers to the infants, were sometimes seen interacting affectionately with their charges, but their behavior was inconsistent and quite often the stimulation they provided was perceived as aversive by the child.

Later in childhood mothers typically did not respond to minor hurts with nurturance, and half responded by scolding the child for crying and stated it was the child's fault. In addition, children were often beaten severely for eliciting nurturant behavior: "Nyansongo mothers have little patience with children who make excessive demands for attention and support" (Levine & Levine, 1966, p. 145). In addition, mothers of older children (aged 3–8 years) did not show overt affection for their children by, for example, fondling them or interacting with them playfully.

Whereas warmth was not characteristic of the mother–child relationship, children were expected to be deferential and obedient to their parents. Conformity to adult values and wishes was ensured by the economic power fathers had over their sons. Thus, unlike the situation proposed in this chapter as characteristic of nuclear family social organization, acceptance of adult values was not facilitated by affective epigenetic rules, but by economic power over sons and the threat of physical punishment. Sons were forced to depend on their fathers to accumulate the cattle used for bridewealth and the land they cultivated, as well as his good will, which would influence the son's reputation in the community even after the father's death.

The outcome of this socialization process was a suspicious, mistrustful adult without a great deal of warmth, nurturance, or affection for others. When together, there was a "slight feeling of distrust" (Levine & Levine, 1966, p. 77), and a very high rate of paranoia, backbiting, and litigiousness was characteristic. Social interactions even between equals were described as ambivalent or lacking in interest, and even joking tended to be abusive and threatening. In Chapter 6, it is pointed out that peer relationships in this type of society tend to be hostile, and this was certainly the case among the Gusii. Also reflecting the generally negative affective tone of the society, there were very high rates of both homicide and rape among the Gusii. For example, an "extremely conservative estimate" indicated that the rate of rape among the Gusii was almost four times higher than in the United States at that time.

Even marriage relationships were devoid of tender touching and positive emotional display. Men did not discuss important matters with their wives and they did not spend much time together. I have already noted the tendency for hostility and competition between co-wives and between the children of different women within the same family. Mothers often encouraged hatred on the part of their children toward the children of other co-wives.

8. *Specific socialization for aggression involving the provision of aversive events during childhood was highly characteristic of the Gusii.* In Chapter 6, evidence is discussed indicating that aggression is facilitated by providing aversive events during devel-

opment. Since aggression was such a highly adaptive behavior among the Gusii, it is not surprising to find that aversive events were characteristic of the socialization process. For example, traditional feeding practices included force-feeding of gruel to very young infants by holding the infant's mouth open, closing off the nasal passages, and forcing the food into the mouth. The child would be forced to eat the food in its attempt to inhale air. This practice was presumably quite aversive to the child.

Weaning was conceptualized by the Gusii as a painful process, one in which greater severity by the mother resulted in a quicker, smoother acceptance by the child. The methods used included putting bitter substances on the nipples, slapping the child, burning the arms with a caustic liquid, and ignoring the child's cries, clearly experiences that are aversive to the child. Moreover, even though the negative response of the infant appeared to reflect a feeling of emotional abandonment rather than any nutritional deficiency caused by weaning (all infants were fed solid foods from a very early age), there was no attempt to replace the nurturance of nursing with some other affectionate behavior.

Physical punishment was used at an early age in order to obtain compliance. For example, 22 of 24 mothers reported caning their young children (2–3 years old) when they showed dependence behaviors after the birth of a sibling. As an example, consider the following incident, in which a mother (Nyaboke) is attempting to leave her 2-year-old son (Manyara) with a co-wife:

> As Nyaboke left, infant in her arms, to visit a neighbor . . . , Manyara began to run after her . . . Nyaboke chased him back to the homestead, a stick in her hands. Manyara was crying hard, but his mother threatened him with the stick and told him to sit down and wipe his nose with a leaf. He did so but continued bawling violently. Nyaboke struck him across the legs several times, then picked up the infant and began to walk away again. As Manyara again began to follow, the co-wife threatened to tie him up with some rope and, when this did not work, beat him on the feet with a stick. He continued screaming and trying to follow Nyaboke, who had turned around and come back again. She beckoned Manyara to come to her, and when he did, she caned him sharply on the legs. The co-wife pushed him into his mother's hut once more and locked the door as Nyaboke went off for good. Locked in the hut, Manyara continued screaming his mother's name. (Levine & Levine, 1966, pp. 134–135)

Physical punishment of young children occurred for other reasons as well, particularly for crying. Another normative event that usually brought out physical punishment was toilet training, which began typically shortly after the second birthday. The speed of the toilet training was directly related to the severity of punishment: When mothers desired quick toilet training, it was accomplished by more severe punishment.

Physical punishment, particularly caning, continued to occur at later ages as the principal method of control of children aged 3–6 years (along with promoting fear) and was a normal response to requests for aid, prolonged crying, and aggression. In conformity with the discussion of sex differences in aggression in Chapter 6, boys fought more than girls and were therefore punished more often for it. Thus, they were the recipients of more aversive stimulation during development than were girls. All mothers reported caning their children for crying and if the child did not stop it was severely beaten. At later ages mothers used food deprivation to ensure compliance and extreme deviations were referred to the father for severe physical punishment. Finally, adolescent reproductive rituals, discussed further below, included the provision of a great deal of pain, including genital mutilation and hazing.

9. *Behavior among the Gusii was strongly sex-differentiated.* In Chapter 6, it is hypothesized that sex differences are most salient in societies, such as the Gusii, with a high degree of sexual competition. In conformity with the discussion in Chapter 6, boys were far more aggressive than girls. Parents used physical punishment against children's aggression, but they behaved differently, depending on who was fighting. Fighting between brothers was frowned on less than between nonrelatives because in the latter case there was the possibility of a lawsuit. Also, in conformity with the discussion in Chapter 6, although neither sex could be described as even moderately affectionate, girls and women are said to be more affectionate than men.

Gusii wives were expected to be obedient and deferential to their husbands. Wives had to serve their husbands and wife-beating was a common and socially accepted practice. The behavior of adults was highly sex-typed, with activities such as food preparation, cultivation of fields, and child care the exclusive province of women and caring for cattle and military activity the province of men. Fathers were not involved at all in child-rearing activities during infancy and were only rarely seen holding the baby or having any physical contact with it.

10. *Gusii initiation rites conformed to the theoretically expected patterns.* The theory of adolescent reproductive rituals described in Chapter 5 implies that the initiation rites of the Gusii should conform to the pattern typical of extended family organization. This is generally the case. First, the initiation rites of boys, occurring at around 10–12 years of age, included a significant amount of aversive stimulation. Boys were treated roughly by older, initiated boys who sponsored them in the circumcision ceremony. Circumcision itself occurred under the hostile gaze of older boys and men and they "aim spears and clubs at the boys head, shouting continuously through the operation that he will be killed if he moves or shows signs of pain" (Levine & Levine, 1966, p. 180). The boy was then led away by his classificatory brothers, who sang songs concerned with aggression against neighboring tribes. During seclusion the boy was hazed by older boys, including being made to eat caustic or nauseating substances and being beaten for refusing. Beatings occurred for a variety of other reasons as well. Upon completing the ceremony the boy was considered to be able to bear weapons and go on raids against other groups.

Conforming to the generalizations discussed in this chapter, the ceremony was dominated by individuals who were not close relatives of the boy, and parents and other close relatives were precluded from witnessing it. Initiation for the boys was a matter of integrating them into the wider network of male kinsmen. Significantly, the boys stayed away from their parents' households during the period and engaged in activities such as hunting and theft with their agemates, whereas the girls remained within the mother's house.

The Gusii appear anomalous in that, contrary to the generalizations described in this chapter, there was a reproductive ritual for girls. However, it is clear that the ritual was not at all like the rituals described as typical of societies with lower levels of economic production. Here there was no effort on the part of the father to promote his daughter as a good marriage partner and to prevent seduction as proposed by Paige and Paige to be the pattern in reproductive ceremonies of societies with low levels of economic production. Initiation of girls occurred at 8–9 years of age, while marriage did not occur until several years later. Moreover, marriage among the Gusii was exogamous, so that, far from advertising the girl to potential mates, the clan into which she would marry was not even present and was probably viewed as an enemy. Also, girls were economic assets to the father among the Gusii, so there was no necessity for the father to advertise them to eligible males. Indeed, fathers played no discernible role in the initiation of girls among the Gusii.

The principal ceremony of girls' initiation involved clitoridectomy. The operation was painful and was followed by sexually uninhibited celebration by the adult women, which was avoided by men. The girl was then secluded for a month in the mother's house, during which time the father was kept from entering. The Levines comment that the entire ceremony appeared to have had less to do with the girls than with the older women, who used the occasion to engage in prohibited sexual interests and hostility toward males. It should be remembered that married women were brought in from other clans that were often enemies of their husband's clan, and the marriage ceremony and even the manner of sexual intercourse contained elements of hostility and the intentional infliction of pain on the woman by the man.

Thus, even though there was a reproductive ritual, the results are quite consistent with the theory of Paige and Paige. There was no obvious function for it apart from providing an excuse for revelry on the part of the other women, who were indeed very oppressed by this social system, as indeed they are by all social systems based on sexual competition (see Chapter 6). The clitoridectomy may have functioned to lessen female interest in sex in a society where the control of female sexuality within marriage by husbands is of paramount importance, and this makes excellent evolutionary sense. Indeed, the Levines comment that women did not acknowledge enjoying intercourse and some apparently genuinely found it painful.

Overall many of the central features of Gusii society conform well to evolutionary predictions. The Levines note the continuity between childhood and adulthood among the Gusii regarding authoritarianism, emotional restraint, and sexual antagonism. They propose that childhood experiences are important influences on adult development, and the perspective developed in this chapter agrees with this. However, genetic variation involving, for example, the positive social reward system may also be involved. Finally, it will be very interesting to follow the development of African family patterns both in Africa and in black communities in Western countries following prolonged exposure to Western influences emphasizing egalitarian social controls on sex, monogamy, and warm parent–child interactions. Such studies will be important tests of the hypothesis of the plasticity of family structure argued for in this chapter.

B. Social Structure and Child Rearing among the !Kung in Evolutionary Perspective

The theory of the family described in this chapter as well as the theory of aggression presented in Chapter 6 proposes that the societies representing the most primitive level of human social organization are the hunter–gatherers and that this social organization is the primeval human social organization. This is a mainstream viewpoint in anthropology and is explicitly stated by Lee (1979) in the introduction to his book on the !Kung:

> Peoples who live by hunting and gathering . . . are among the few remaining representatives of a way of life that was, until 10,000 years ago, a human universal. Basic human social forms,

language, and human nature itself were forged during the 99% of human history when people
lived in hunting and gathering camps. (Lee, 1979, p. 1)

As indicated by the following, the social organization and child rearing typical of the
!Kung stand in marked contrast to those of the Gusii described above:

1. *Sexual competition was not a salient feature of the society.* Unlike the Gusii, there
was no institution of bridewealth among the !Kung. Females were, however, relatively
scarce, so that the bride and the parents of the bride were able to be choosy when selecting
a husband. Typically, the prospective husband lived with the wife's family for a period of
time (termed "bride-service"), during which he was encouraged to remain with the
wife's group. The prime criterion for a girl's family in deciding to accept a man as a son-
in-law was that he be a good hunter and be willing to live with them for a considerable
period so that he could provide them with meat. In a sense this is similar to bridewealth
described above for the Gusii, since the prospective husband must be willing to provide
the girl's family with some economic benefit. However, there is an enormous difference
here, since there is no way in which such a male could provide a similar economic benefit
to a large number of families and thus accumulate a large number of wives. The ecology
of the situation tends to produce monogamy because, unless a man was an extraordinarily
good hunter, he could not provide enough meat to interest the family of more than one
girl. Moreover, although there were clear individual differences in hunting ability among
the males, success at hunting did not make an individual a leader or allow him to have
large numbers of wives. As a result, marriage tended toward monogamy; polygyny,
however, although uncommon, did occur (Silberbauer, 1981). Polygyny was viewed as
appropriate in situations where sisters did not want to be separated and when women with
young children had lost their original husbands by divorce or death. In the former case,
the sisters are expected to be more cooperative and less jealous than are the unrelated co-
wives of the Gusii, and in the latter case the woman's value to other men is lowered since
she already has children fathered by other men. Thus, the women involved in polygynous
relationships may have benefited considerably, unlike the situation among the Gusii and
in polygynous societies generally (see Chapter 6). Consistent with the theory developed in
this chapter, Cashden (1980) notes that polygyny is much more common among the Gana,
who are closely related to the !Kung, but are more sedentary and have much greater
inequality of possessions.

Social controls on economic accumulation were a very salient feature of !Kung
society. These egalitarian social controls have the indirect effect of reinforcing monogamy
because they prevent the individual accumulation of resources that is the basis of sexual
competition. The most serious accusation one could make against another person was that
of arrogance. One's skills and the values of another's gifts were constantly being derided
by others to prevent an individual from feeling too important. Individuals, such as hunters, who were successful were expected to be modest about their accomplishments and
could expect their success to be derided and minimized by others, an assessment with
which the hunter was expected to agree.

2. *Kinship based on close genetic relationships was important with the !Kung.* !Kung
bands were based on close genetic and affinal relationships. At the core of each group
were individuals who were first-degree relatives of each other (Lee, 1979), and the
nuclear family household group was the most stable and enduring social unit (Silberbauer,
1981). Typically a group of siblings of both sexes was at the core of the band, and the

group was filled out with their spouses, the siblings of their spouses, and the spouses of the siblings of the spouses of the core spouses. The children of the group thus tended to be cousins of each other, and cross-cousins (e.g., child of mother's brother or father's sister) were considered ideal marriage partners (see also Silberbauer, 1981).

From an evolutionary perspective this high degree of genetic commonality should facilitate altruism and sharing. One of the salient features of !Kung society was the extent of generalized reciprocity among its members. Lee (1982) likens the level of sharing in a band of 15–30 !Kung to what would occur in a Western nuclear family around the dinner table. Stinginess was one of the most serious charges that !Kung could make against an individual and there were constant attempts to make individuals more generous. Thus, sharing did not come easily among the !Kung, and Lee (1979) notes that when conflicts broke out in the camp, sharing broke down. Bringing back an animal from a successful hunt was a source of tension and there were elaborate methods to diffuse the prestige of killing and the responsibility for sharing. For example, men traded arrows with each other so that if a man killed an animal with another man's arrow he would be obligated to share the kill with the other man and the other man would be viewed as having directly participated in the successful hunt. Successful men would sometimes stop hunting, partly to prevent others from becoming envious, but also to prevent a situation in which their own efforts were unreciprocated by other men.

Indeed, anticipated reciprocity would appear to be the basis of sharing, especially as individuals interacted with increasingly distant individuals. Silberbauer (1981) notes that within the band and within closely related cliques within the band reciprocity and cooperation were the rule, and reciprocity also characterized relationships with nonband !Kung. *Hraxo* trading, consisting of long-distance networks in which individuals gave an item to another and received something in return, clearly involved anticipated reciprocity, even though the return might take many months or even years. On the other hand, within the immediate family reciprocity was not expected and individuals accepted negative balances of resource flow. These patterns fit well with research on moral reasoning and altruism described in Chapters 7 and 8. It is argued there that self-interest is a very robust tendency in humans and it would appear that the !Kung are no exception. Clearly, however, the !Kung have developed a very highly elaborated socialization process that facilitates sharing and reciprocity rather than exploitation. In Chapter 8, it is argued that one aspect of this socialization process is the warm affective relations characteristic of !Kung familial relationships.

Another aspect of !Kung sharing and reciprocity that is highly congruent with evolutionary theory was that conflict and fighting occurred much more frequently when large groups of !Kung gathered during the dry season. These larger groups contained more distantly related individuals and conflicts of interest were thus much more common. This conflict was exacerbated because larger groups required more work per capita as individuals were forced to forage for longer distances from the camp.

3. *Military defense and aggression were not important among the !Kung.* !Kung groups were not typically engaged in warfare or feuding, but rather were based on mutually beneficial reciprocal relationships. Individuals did not have exclusive rights to land, and Lee (1982) comments that:

> The maintenance of *flexibility* to adapt to changing ecological circumstances is far more important in hunter–gatherer group structure than is the maintenance of exclusive rights to land. (p. 53)

Rather than excluding individuals, every effort was made to recruit individuals, particularly sons-in-law. However, access to resources was under considerable control of resident groups, so that distantly related groups had to ask permission to use the resources around a water hole and incurred a reciprocal obligation when they did so. Moreover, a visiting group was not able to overstay its welcome. In general, the degree to which other groups were tolerated was a direct function of the distance from which they came, presumably a direct function of genetic overlap between the groups as well.

4. *!Kung society was relatively egalitarian.* There were no headmen or chiefs among the !Kung. In the words of one informant, "Of course we have headmen! . . . We are all headmen . . . each one of us is headman over himself" (Lee, 1982, p. 50). Some people spoke out more than others during group discussions, but no one had formal authority over anyone else and personal qualities were very important in being able to influence others. A desire for personal wealth was not at all characteristic of leaders, and there were none of the economic differences between leaders and followers so common among the Gusii.

5. *Familial relationships were warm and not characterized by the provision of aversive events during socialization.* Based on the discussion of this chapter, it is expected that a hunter–gatherer group such as the !Kung would be characterized by monogamous nuclear families and by warm, intimate personal relationships. The !Kung did indeed have an essentially nuclear family social structure, although, as indicated above, low-level polygyny did occur. Personal relationships were also much warmer. Part of the marriage ceremony involved a pledge of conjugal affection, and, although not publicly affectionate, there was often an intense affective bond between spouses (Silberbauer, 1981). The relationship between husband and parents-in-law was also expected to be warm and affectionate. Although mothers and other young women had responsibility for over 90% of the child care, !Kung fathers were described as attentive and loving toward their children, and often spent leisure time playing with them (Lee, 1982). Silberbauer (1981) notes that mothers and fathers were equally emotionally attached to their children. Infants had a great deal of physical contact with their mothers in the first 2 years of life, far surpassing American norms (Draper, 1976; Konner, 1976): "When a baby wakes, he or she is played with, fondled, and kissed by anybody in the immediate vicinity" (Silberbauer, 1981, p. 163), including nonfamilial male and female members of the band. Parent–child relationships were characterized by parental control "in an atmosphere of affection and kindness" (Silberbauer, 1981, p. 162). Parents were demonstrably affectionate with children, but the intensity of affectionate displays was inversely proportional to the child's age. Consistent with the sex differences in socialization described in Chapter 6, however, Lee (1979) notes that males received less of this contact than females and females tended in general to be more often in the presence of adults.

6. *Sexual relationships were much more egalitarian among the !Kung than among the Gusii.* Among the !Kung, women had an important role in production and their role as core group members gave them considerable power. Women participated in discussions and decision making, but at a lower rate than did the men. Lee (1982) states that !Kung women appeared to have more power than women of other hunter–gatherer groups, but in any case the status of women among hunter–gatherer groups was far higher than among the Gusii. Silberbauer notes that spouses were expected to be mutually dependent with complementary roles and no institutionalized dominance of either partner.

7. *!Kung initiation rites conform to evolutionary expectations.* Assumption of adult

status as a hunter occurred when the boy succeeded in his first hunt, and after the ceremony the boy was considered to be a potential son-in-law. The ceremony involved a series of small cuts on various parts of the body into which medicines and fat from the boy's kill were rubbed. The atmosphere was casual and celebratory and the ritualistic purpose was to make the boy a better hunter. For example, an informant stated that the arm was cut in order to make the boy's aim better. Although the procedure is presumably somewhat painful, it is far less so than circumcision or clitoridectomy and there was none of the severe hazing and adversarial tone characteristic of the initiation rites among the Gusii. *Chomas,* or initiation rites, occurred when the boy was 15–20 years old in larger camps during the winter dry season and involved feasting and celebration and presumably introduction to the wider network of !Kung groups.

Girls' initiation rites often occurred after marriage, since girls were married before puberty (Silberbauer, 1981). Following seclusion and tatooing, the girl and her husband participated in a ceremony symbolizing their entrance into the adult world. The ceremony was a very affectively positive occasion and the father played a role by symbolically introducing her to other members of the band. The mother participated by caring for the girl during the menarcheal seclusion, by symbolically showing the girl the resources available to the band, and by being present during the ceremony when the conjugal virtues were impressed on the couple. Contrary to the theory of Paige and Paige (1981), there is no suggestion here that the menarcheal rite involved political maneuvering by the father to ensure a good marriage for the daughter, prevent seduction, etc. Girls were already married, and the exclusivity of the sexual rights of the husband was recognized and defended by the band as a whole. In the case of the !Kung the early age of marriage reflected the scarcity of females, and thus the ability of parents to expect long periods of bride service from sons-in-law. This departure from the generalizations proposed by Paige and Paige indicates the flexibility of human strategizing and adaptation rather than any departure from expectations based on evolutionary theory.

CHAPTER 6

Topics in the Development of Aggression, Peer Relations, and Sex Differences

This chapter continues the themes developed in the previous chapters by applying these ideas to some of the central issues in the area of social development. In particular, I will attempt to place these data in a cross-cultural and historical context, a context shaped by the sociobiologically predicted central tendencies described previously. Moreover, as in previous chapters, I will emphasize the environment-expectant affective systems and their roles in the socialization of behavior, as well as temperament as a ubiquitously important set of epigenetic rules that bias social behavior in a variety of domains. I will not attempt to review all of the research in the areas of aggression, peer relations, and sex differences, but instead select some of the central issues where an evolutionary analysis seems most appropriate and where there is already sufficient research to enable an assessment of this theoretical perspective.

I. ISSUES IN THE DEVELOPMENT OF AGGRESSION

A. An Evolutionary Perspective on the Development of Aggression

Aggression has assumed a central place in recent evolutionary thinking about humans. Alexander (1979) in particular has argued that aggression is the prime mover of human evolution. Alexander notes that humans evolved as group hunters with a social ecology similar to group-hunting canids and felids. The sizes of these groups were quite small, and Alexander proposes that the force necessary to change from the ecology of small-group hunters to much larger groupings, such as the nation state, is intergroup competition. This "balance-of-power" hypothesis proposes that at some point in human history the prime function of human groups was protection from the predatory effects of other human groups. Thus, intergroup competition and particularly warfare is viewed as resulting in increasingly larger human groupings.

Alexander views human evolutionary history as composed of three phases. In the first phase human groups are characterized by small, multimale polygynous bands whose main function is to ward off predators. In the second phase human groups are similarly composed, but function also to hunt large game. In the third phase, these groups function to protect their members from other human groups. It is crucial to Alexander's argument that this last phase is viewed as by far the most important: "I also suppose that we have been in the third stage so long that the influence of the first two stages is relatively minor" (Alexander, 1979, p. 224).

This thesis indicates the degree to which aggression and intergroup competition have assumed a central place in evolutionary thinking about humans. It is an important thesis and its acceptance would go a long way toward correcting a tendency for historians and anthropologists to ignore the Darwinian aspects of aggression and war. There has also been a tendency within developmental psychology to pathologize aggression, as when psychologists write of the deficits of aggressive children and the incompetence of their parents. In agreement with Alexander, it is maintained here that no theory of aggression can ignore the adaptive consequences of aggression.

As an example, consider the Mongol invasions of Eurasia in the 13th and 14th centuries. The Mongols practiced unlimited polygyny, with Genghiz Khan having more than 500 wives, a situation made possible by his controlling vast amounts of resources made available by conquests characterized by unprecedented levels of massacre and violence. According to Fitzgerald:

> The outstanding characteristic of the Mongols was their inhuman cruelty, or rather their total lack of any human feeling of pity. Genghiz himself expressed the Mongol idea of happiness: "The greatest joy is to conquer one's enemies, to pursue them, to seize their property, to see their families in tears, to ride their horses, and to possess their daughters and wives." (1938, p. 428)

Genghis Khan practiced nepotism, so that his male relatives and especially his sons were able to command very large harems of females and hold onto power in various parts of Eurasia for several centuries. Chagnon (1979) also speaks of the role of violence among males for the purpose of acquiring females among the Yanomamo in South America, and many other examples could be described (see, e.g., Appendix to Chapter 5).

If indeed intergroup aggression has been such a prominent force in human evolution for such a long period as proposed by Alexander, we would expect the evolution of proximate epigenetic mechanisms that would bias individuals toward aggressive phenotypes, and there is indeed evidence, described on pp. 187–197, that this is the case. Nevertheless, the fact that aggression is an important phenotype in human evolution does not imply the very elevated status bestowed on it by Alexander. Several writers have questioned the balance-of-power hypothesis for the emergence of large human groups. Thus, Flannery (1972) points out that warfare has been continually present in many parts of the world without the emergence of very large human groupings such as nation states. In order to defend his thesis against this argument, Alexander proposes that there may be a variety of extrinsic environmental circumstances that prevent balance-of-power relationships.

More important for the discussion here is the idea that aggression, although apparently existing throughout human history, became a major political force only with the rise of agriculture in the Neolithic period, approximately 12,000 years ago. Carneiro (1978) points out that by far the longest period of human evolution took place in the Paleolithic period, which lasted for some 3 million years prior to the Neolithic. During this period competition for resources was relatively less intense, and, as is the case among present-day simple societies, warfare existed mainly for noneconomic reasons, such as avenging a murder. However, with the rise of agriculture at the beginning of the Neolithic period, competition for resources increased dramatically and warfare became the prime moving force behind the creation of ever larger political units.

The perspective developed by Carneiro is thus consistent with that of Alexander, except that Carneiro deemphasizes the importance of war until the beginning of the Paleolithic, while Alexander seems to argue that the prewarfare phase of human evolution is inconsequential. Carneiro's perspective is consistent with the role of economic production as a contextual variable in a sociobiological analysis, as emphasized in Chapter 5 (see also MacDonald, 1983a, 1987a, in press). As described more fully there, increased productivity increases competition for fertile land and allows for the possibility that increased "surplus" production can be used to support a governing class whose consumption is based ultimately on agricultural production.

This idea derives directly from basic ecological theory. The fundamental argument is implicit in Chapter 5 and can be phrased as follows. Early human evolution involved natural selection for increased paternal investment and its concomitant proximal affective bonding mechanisms, which resulted in the nuclear family being the primeval human social structure. With increased production, and especially with the highly intensive production characteristic of societies with advanced agriculture, societies became no longer characterized by subsistence economies, but rather by economics in which individuals could produce more than they needed to consume. This "surplus value", as Marx termed it, then made possible predatory human relationships in which some individuals were able to control the "excess" production of others.

The situation is exactly analogous to the theory of predation in ecology. Predators exist at the top of the food chain by preying on the energy provided by animals or plants lower in the food chain than themselves. Predators as a group are thus typically forced to have a lower total biomass than their prey because the energy available to them is necessarily less than that available to their prey. As an obvious example, the total biomass of plants must be greater than that of animals because animals must eat plants and cannot ever completely convert all of the energy available in the plants for their own use. Typically, organisms are able to convert approximately 10% of the energy available to them from the energy level immediately below them, so that herbivores convert 10% of the plant material into their own energy and carnivores are able to convert 10% of the herbivores into their own energy needs.

It is proposed, then, that increased production, and especially advanced agriculture, provided increased energy, which was able to be utilized by other humans. Aggression and predatory human relationships thus became ecologically and economically feasible in a way that was previously not possible. This increase in production provides aggression with a new ecological rationale. Advanced agriculture is particularly important, for it is the increased economic production made possible by agriculture that makes possible the exploitation of others' production and the achievement of a large differential among males in Darwinian fitness. On the positive side, advanced civilizations characterized by great specialization of social roles become possible, but oppression and exploitation also become highly profitable enterprises, especially for males.

In agreement with Carneiro, then, one can see that the ecological rationale for aggression changes enormously with the rise of agriculture approximetely 12,000 years ago, a relatively short time compared to the previous 3 million years of the Paleolithic period. With increased economic production made possible by technological and agricultural advances, group size increased and the conflict between what Sahlins (1974) calls the domestic mode of production characterized by the independent nuclear family and the larger social organization is made possible. At this stage of human evolution, organized aggression, intergroup conflict, and war are far more likely, since the rewards of conquest are great. The story is told of Genghiz Khan that after the conquest of China he intended to massacre the inhabitants and turn the cultivated land into pasture for his horses. It was pointed out to him by one Yelu Chu-tśai, perhaps the greatest of Chinese heroes, that this would destroy the economic base of the country and that by preserving the cultivated land he could derive great revenue from it. It is this enormous wealth and the reproductive advantage that accrues from its control that makes aggression so attractive from an evolutionary perspective.

Such a perspective is also consistent with the views of the great majority of anthropologists, who regard contemporary hunter–gatherer societies as prototypes of later forms of human social organization and as characteristic of the vast majority of the human evolutionary experience. In order to defend his thesis, Alexander must argue that such contemporary groups are not typical of the great majority of human evolution, but are ecologically marginal groups forced by the success of larger human societies to the ecological peripheries of the earth. Rather than representing an ecological prototype, Alexander is forced to argue that they are evolutionary sideshows; that is, they are groups that have been forced by ecological contingencies to adopt a more pacific lifestyle characterized by less intergroup and intragroup competition. The counterargument is that these ecological contingencies existed for over 99% of our evolution, right up until the Neolithic agricultural revolution.

The difference between the account of Alexander and the mainstream view of anthropologists is vital to thinking about the epigenetic rules underlying human social organization. If, as I have argued, the mainstream view is correct, then these epigenetic rules would bias individuals toward increased cohesiveness of the primary human social organization built around the nuclear family and other close genetic relatives. They would consist of the positive bonding mechanisms discussed in previous chapters as well as the emotion of empathy discussed in Chapter 8. In this view, the epigenetic rules underlying aggression, exploitation, and violence would be in competition with these forces of social cohesion, and systematic natural selection and socialization of aggressive phenotypes a relatively recent phenomenon.

At present the conceptualization of the epigenetic rules underlying aggression is rudimentary to say the least, but in the following I will concentrate on two probable sources, familial affective relationships and temperament, and defer a discussion of sex differences and the role of hormones to a later section.

B. Environment-Expectant Affective Systems and the Development of Aggression

In the following several propositions regarding aggression are derived from the general approach suggested in earlier chapters. In attempting to find evidence for these hypotheses, it is necessary to consider the literature on what has been termed face-to-face aggression. This is the type of aggression studied most often by psychologists and it need not intersect with some of the broader issues that must be raised in a sociobiological discussion of aggression. Thus, in a sociobiological account warfare between societies is at least as interesting as face-to-face aggression within societies and scientific accounts of these two types of aggression may not intersect at all. However, it is argued here that the anthropological evidence suggests that the same forces that result in aggression within modern societies have been utilized as elements of socialization in societies where warlike aggression is an important aspect of public policy. If this is indeed the case, there are strong links between aggression at the societal and individual levels.

1. Aggression and the Positive Social Reward System

In this section, I examine the thesis that aggression is facilitated by promoting affective relations within the family and within larger social groups that are essentially the opposite of those promoting cohesive nuclear family structure and emphasized in Chapter 5. The thesis is that these positive affective mechanisms of bonding operate to maximize the cohesion of the family group and promote adaptive imbalances of resource exchange and altruism (see Chapter 8) by making such interactions highly intrinsically reinforcing. In order to overcome these centripetal tendencies and thereby promote exploitative relationships, lack of empathy, and altruism, and in general adapt to an environment with much lower average degrees of genetic relatedness, the hypothesis is that these goals are facilitated by socializing individuals in a manner that prevents the elaboration of what we have termed the positive social reward system. By preventing the elaboration of the positive social reward system, such socialization facilitates exploitative, impersonal relationships. As indicated by Carneiro and certainly by Alexander, aggression has presumably always been an aspect of the human behavioral repertoire. It is argued here that in order to facilitate aggression in a new ecological situation in which intensified inter- and intragroup competition are highly adaptive, methods of socialization that deemphasize the elaboration of the positive social reward system are introduced.

As indicated in Chapter 2, the elaboration of the positive social reward system via socialization results in the individual's being more responsive to the nurturant, warm behavior in others; that is, such an individual would find these behaviors more rewarding than would an individual socialized in a hostile, impersonal environment. The result of such socialization then is hypothesized to be an increased sensitivity to the reward value of these environments. In physiological terms, such hostile, impersonal socialization results in a lack of elaboration of the the the social reward centers of the brain. This argument stops short of proposing that the hostile, rejecting behaviors of parents facilitate the elaboration of a social reward system in which these behaviors on the part of parents are evaluated positively by the child. It has been argued in the previous chapters that the set of parental behaviors that appear to be intrinsically rewarding to children are those classified as warm and nurturant, not hostile and rejecting.

This perspective is consistent with the evolutionary history of aggression presented above as well as the discussion of the cross-cultural literature on family relationships presented in Chapter 5. In this perspective, the positive social reward system underlying human family functioning is viewed as dominant throughout most of human evolution.

However, with increasing production and the concomitant increase in sexual competition and competition for resources, the mechanisms underlying cohesive, nuclear family social organization become less adaptive and there is a shift to more extensive kinship networks and socialization for distant and hostile interpersonal relationships. These relationships predispose individuals to aggression, since such individuals are relatively unconcerned about receiving positive social rewards from others. As indicated in Chapter 2, children who are aggressive are indeed relatively unconcerned with positive social rewards, and correlational data within Western societies, described below, indicate that socialization in hostile, rejecting environments is associated with aggression. Finally, although for the reasons presented in Chapter 5 it is proposed that cross-cultural variation and a significant amount of within-cultural variation is environmental in origin, it is also possible that there has been natural selection in some cultures for insensitivity to positive social rewards. This natural selection would be reflected in the genetic variation for Eysenck's (1982) trait of psychoticism described in Chapter 2.

Developmental data on the role of the affective systems in the development of aggression give ample support for the idea that minimal elaboration of the positive social reward system is an aspect of the socialization of aggression. As Parke and Slaby (1983) point out, however, the socialization influences on aggression are multifaceted, and include such factors as television and peer influences. Television influences are a good example of a contextual influence on development that is difficult to conceptualize in evolutionary terms. An evolutionary analysis in these cases would presumably be quite indirect. In Chapter 9 I attempt to place some of the larger societal influences on human development in an evolutionary perspective.

Several recent reviews have concluded that there is evidence for an association between parental rejection and aggression (Martin, 1975; Hetherington & Martin, 1979, 1986; Parke & Slaby, 1983). For example, Hetherington, Stouwie, and Ridberg (1971) studied three types of delinquents characterized by conduct disorder, anxiety withdrawal, and socialized aggression, respectively. Parental rejection was found in all three groups, although in the case of socialized aggressive children there was more acceptance of the child. Olweus (1980) found that among the predictors of adolescent aggression was mother's negativism, a combination of hostility, rejection, and coldness. In addition, studies of the effects of divorce on children show that one the of sequelae of divorce is an increase in aggression shortly after the divorce and that this pattern continues over the first 2 years for boys (Hetherington et al., 1982). Mother–son relations during this period are characterized as negative and hostile, consistent with a link between this affective configuration and aggression. Conflict-ridden nuclear families were also associated with aggression in boys.

It is hypothesized above that parental rejection may result in individuals who are relatively unresponsive to social rewards, since parental rejection entails a relative lack of stimulation and elaboration of the social reward system. Congruent with this perspective, Parke and Slaby (1983) summarize data indicating that aggressive children are less responsive to social feedback and social rewards such as adult attention and approval, although there is no evidence that they are hyporesponsive to material reinforcers such as money and food. (Indeed, I argue on pp. 195–197 that they tend to be quite sensitive to the rewards involved in sensation seeking.) Mothers of antisocial children use fewer positive social rewards and in the present context this deficit would be seen as tending to result in the relative lack of elaboration of the environment-expectant social reward system.

In addition, however, Martin (1975) also points out that parental rejection may involve a variety of events that are perceived as aversive to the child, including frustrations resulting from lack of nurturance and nonalleviation of discomfort. Thus, parental rejection may consist of more than simply failure to provide evolutionarily expected environments, but in addition may facilitate aggression because of the provision of aversive events as described in the next section. In any case, the cross-cultural and historical evidence described in Chapter 5 (see also Chapters 8 and 9) points to similar correlations between distant, hostile parenting and socialization for aggression.

2. The Role of Aversive Environmental Stimulation in the Socialization of Aggression

The previous hypothesis essentially states that a facilitating condition for the maximization of aggression is the failure to elaborate the positive social reward system that evolved to underlie primitive human social organization. However, this hypothesis is insufficient to account for the data on aggression. The second factor proposed to facilitate the development of aggression in individuals derives from the idea that aggression has always been part of the human ethogram. As Cairns (1986) states, "The capacity for the developmental emergence of hurtful patterns of interchange is inherent in all mammalian species, including human beings. Accordingly, no specific learning experiences are required for the establishment of the behavior, although the interchanges may be learnable" (pp. 74–75). Given this primitive capability to engage in aggressive behavior, it is proposed that aggression is an evolutionarily derived response to aversive environmental events.

In the following, support will be provided for several propositions on the relationship between aversive stimulation and aggression. Much of the analysis follows that of Berkowitz (1982, 1983, 1984).

Both complex interpretive processes as well as natural clues result in individuals viewing events as aversive. An evolutionary perspective would suggest that aversive arousal occurs as the result of cognitive processes or natural clues in which the event is evaluated negatively as a threat to oneself or one's resources. If the aversive event is one's own fault, one feels disappointment. If it is another's fault, one feels anger or fear, depending on the situation.

In agreement with this evolutionary perspective on the relation between cognition and the emotions involved in aggression, Berkowitz (1982), relying on the work of Leventhal (1974, 1980) and Bower (1981), proposes that a person's emotional experience of anger or fear grows directly out of an interpretational process. Individuals receive information from the environment and evaluate it in terms of their interests and goals, their own responsibility or that of others, etc., and the emotions of anger or fear emerge as a result of this process. Such a perspective contrasts strongly with that deriving from Schacter's (1964) approach, in which emotions are viewed as the result of attributional processes in which one interprets one's arousal in terms of one's present environmental circumstances and one's own behavior.

In support of his contention, Berkowitz (1982; see also Berkowitz, 1983, 1984) notes that experiments purporting to show that anger is produced as a result of situationally induced labeling of a feeling of general arousal are equivocal and that indeed several of the experiments that originally provided support for the cognitivist viewpoint, particularly those of Schacter, have not been replicated (e.g., Marshall & Zimbardo, 1979). These results indicate that it is not as easy to manipulate a subjects subjective feelings as Schacter had contended. The perspective on arousal presented in the Appendix to Chapter 2 is highly consistent with this criticism, since it is argued that there are two very different kinds of arousal with very different subjective feelings. As a result, if an individual was in a state of high tense arousal as the result of some event, it would be difficult to alter this subjective feeling to result in a positive evaluation simply by presenting him or her with positive possibilities for these feelings. If anything, one would suppose that the individual would scan the environment for negative events responsible for the negative feeling of tense arousal and would ignore the positive possibilites. However, this formulation also appears to overrepresent the importance of being aware of one's feelings in order to have an emotion.

Berkowitz also notes that the findings of investigators such as Izard (see Chapter 3) indicate that there are very strong associations between particular facial expressions and discrete emotional feelings. Berkowitz suggests that individuals react to their interpretation of events with particular emotional expressions and that these expressions then facilitate the production of particular internal feelings. The awareness of the emotion of anger is a different process that is parallel to the emotion of anger itself, so that:

> A person does not have to think of himself as having a particular emotion if he is to experience the specific feelings or exhibit the kind of behavior that is consistent with this emotion. The label a person applies to his sensations does not in and of itself produce his differentiated feelings and actions. (Berkowitz, 1983, p. 111)

Finally, as Zillman (1983) notes, the labeling theory leaves the original source of arousal unexplained. The result is a highly counterintuitive theory of anger in which an individual who is originally unaware of why he or she is aroused searches the environment for cues as to what emotion he or she is feeling. Berkowitz' commonsense viewpoint suggests that anger often results from a very conscious interpretation of events and occurs whether or not we are aware of our anger. Our anger is quite consistent with all those around us being as happy as can be and even with attempts to make us feel happy. These considerations illustrate the total lack of fit between an evolutionary theory of emotions and the Schacterian attributional theory. In the attributional account the function of emotions is to give meaning to undifferentiated subjective arousal. In the evolutionary perspective the arousal itself is differentiated and the function of the emotions is to energize adaptive behavior. Moreover, the evolutionary perspective implies that self-consciousness of feeling a particular emotion is not critical, and thus offers an account that is far more intuitively appealing as an account of animal emotion. The attributional theory makes no sense at all as an evolutionary account of the origin of the universal emotions described by Izard and apparent in many mammals. The attributional process emphasized by Schacter would be expected to be a rare event, occurring only when there was no other obvious reason for one's arousal. Thus, Schacter's paradigm, even if the results are as he maintains, is viewed as completely unrepresentative of the context in which the vast majority of emotions occur.

In opposition to this perspective, Berkowitz maintains that labeling processes can influence attributions of which emotion one is feeling, but that they are not all-powerful. He also agrees with research indicating that general arousal produced by some other means (e.g., sexually stimulating materials) can facilitate aggression in a situation that elicits it, but there is no reason to claim that this facilitation is the result of relabeled feelings. The interpretational perspective is that arousal energizes any ongoing behavior, so that if one interprets events in such a way as to result in anger, one's reactions to these events will be correspondingly more intense if one is already aroused.

In keeping with this interpretational perspective, Berkowitz notes several studies which indicate that if one interprets the aversive behavior of others as due to circumstances beyond their control, it is less likely to result in aggression (e.g., Burnstein & Worchel, 1962). Several developmental studies have shown that aggressive boys tend to have social-cognitive biases that result in their interpreting the behavior of others as hostile. In terms of the present discussion, these boys are viewed as having a predisposition to view the actions of others not only as aversive, but also as blameworthy. For example, Dodge (1986) summarizes data indicating that aggressive boys tend to attribute hostility to ambiguous provocation situations. This interpretation influenced their views of what they expected others to do in the situation. Moreover, one aspect that affects the interpretational process is the reputation of the provocateur: Boys with aggressive reputations are more often viewed as intentionally causing harm.

Although the aversiveness of many events is the outcome of complex interpretive processes and past learning in many cases, some environmental cues for aggression can be viewed as "natural clues" for aggressive response in the sense of Bowlby. The idea here is that there is a biologically based disposition to view certain classes of environmental events as aversive. Such events appear to include environmental events such as physical abuse, hostility, rejection, the infliction of pain, and uncomfortable ambient temperatures. The theoretical status of this biological predisposition is the same as that of Bowlby's natural clues: They are stimuli that children are biologically primed to view in a negative manner and to which aggression is one possible and even prepotent response. Indeed, many of Bowlby's examples of natural clues are environmental events with negative affective consequences, such as fear of snakes and the absence of the attachment figure. Aggression is thus seen as an evolutionarily ancient system in humans for which there are natural eliciting stimuli.

There is considerable evidence that certain types of aversive events are reliable elicitors of aggression in a variety of animal species (Ulrich, Hutchinson, & Azrin, 1965) as well as humans (Berkowitz, 1982). These events include foot shocks, tail pinches, loud noises, and intense heat. The evolutionarily derived response to these events appears to be not merely negative evaluation and arousal, but also a tendency to respond with aggression or flight, depending on the situation. Whether flight or fight occurs depends on the animal's evaluation of the situation and its prior learning history. Thus, animals are more likely to fight if they do not know how to escape (Azrin, Hutchinson, & Hake, 1966).

Negative reinforcement of aggression has been shown in the animal literature (Knutson, Fordyce, & Anderson, 1980). Nevertheless, the animal literature indicates that negative reinforcement is not necessary to maintain aversively stimulated aggression. Ulrich and Craine (1964) found that aversively stimulated aggression persisted even when the fighting failed to remove the aversive stimulation and did not decrease when the aversive stimulus was removed contingent on nonaggressive responses. Moreover, there is evidence that painfully shocked animals will work to obtain suitable targets for their aggression (Azrin *et al.*, 1966) and that having a suitable target for aggression reduces gastric lesions resulting from repeatedly being subjected to painful stimulation (Weiss, Pohorecky, Salman, & Gruenthal, 1976).

On the basis of data such as these, Berkowitz (1982, 1983) argues that the aggression elicited by aversive stimulation is appetitive, not simply defensive aggression. The pained animal or person seeks not just to escape, but to find a target for aggression. Therefore, it would appear that aggression is a very prepotent response in reaction to some types of aversive stimulation, particularly physical pain. Berkowitz (1982) summarizes evidence indicating that unpleasant odors, high temperatures, and physical pain reliably increase aggression in humans, and that individuals subjected to aversive stimulation actively seek out others as targets of aggression, especially a person believed to be responsible for the pain. In addition, the literature on child abuse indicates that aversive environmental events such as economic instability, having a "bad day," and aversive behavior from children are important correlates of child abuse (Burgess, Kurland, & Pensky, 1988).

Whether aggression or flight occurs in response to stimulation interpreted as aversive depends on a variety of contextual features. From an evolutionary perspective individuals are expected to analyze situations in terms of potential costs and benefits. Thus, in a situation where fight or flight is called for, it is expected that past learning as well as one's present analysis will be crucial to which strategy one adopts. One responds quite differently to an insult from an armed stranger than one from a child. Consistent with the cost–benefit interpretation, Berkowitz (1983) suggests that aggression is more common at moderate levels of aversive stimulation and lower when extreme pain occurs. Aggression is thus not a stereotypical response, but a very flexible, adaptive response.

In conclusion, through a variety of cognitive processes and by means of biologically prepared affective responses, some environmental events are labeled as aversive. As Berkowitz (1982) suggests, this set of events then "gives rise to two instigations: one to escape from the unpleasant occurrence and the other to strike at a suitable target (preferably, but not only, the perceived source of unpleasantness)" (p. 283). Given the sociobiologically predicted tendency to manipulate cognitions in accord with self-interest (Krebs *et al.*, 1988; MacDonald, 1988b), it is expected that if individuals cannot find an acceptable target (such as would occur if the target was too dangerous or powerful), they will rationalize the situation in a way that legitimizes aggression against a more harmless target, perhaps a child. Such behavior would perhaps even have a positive effect on physical health if the study by Weiss *et al.* (1976) on rats is any indication of a similar effect in humans, and in some cases at least the successful aggression toward an alternative target might result in increased self-esteem. Nonetheless, such redirected aggression may well also be an index of pathology rather than an adaptive response, as in the case of child abuse (see Chapter 1).

Finally, although social psychological research indicates that aggression can be strongly influenced by manipulations of an individual's interpretation of the situation, it is expected from an evolutionary perspective that individuals are not infinitely malleable by others who attempt to manipulate their interpretations of events. Individuals are expected to be reasonably keen observers of events and to generally attempt to develop veridical theories about the sources of the aversive events in their environment. Such veridical beliefs are presumably often adaptive in redressing wrongs and in generally getting rid of the aversive events. In some cases such verdical beliefs may be maladaptive, however, and one is better off rationalizing an attack on someone else. As Krebs *et al.* (1988) point out, both rational as well as self-deceptive ideas about the world are expected from an evolutionary perspective and both processes can be adaptive in particular situations.

3. Socialization of Aggression with Aversive Events

Socialization in an environment rich in aversive events is hypothesized to result in aggressive response on the part of the child and over time a generalized tendency for aggressive response to others would be the expected developmental outcome. In addition, or as an aspect of this phenomenon, aggression can be negatively reinforced by its ability to terminate aversive stimulation.

Based on the animal literature, there are at least two mechanisms for expecting this result. The first, mentioned above, is that aggression can result from negative reinforcement resulting from the termination of aversive stimulation. Second, there is evidence that prolonged shock-induced aggression in rats results in extremely aggressive animals (Ulrich *et al.*, 1965) independent of its success in achieving any goal of the organism, including the removal of the aversive stimulation. This suggests that one way of socializing animals or children to be aggressive is to subject them continually to aversive environments, independent of whether the aggression provoked by these environments is instrumentally effective in lowering the incidence of aversive events or for any other goal.

In conformity to these findings in the animal literature, there is evidence deriving from the literature on parental control techniques that socialization for aggression involves the parental and societal provision of aversive events during childhood. Parke and Slaby (1983) state that the best evidence for an association comes from the more extreme examples such as child abuse, a finding that is consistent with the theoretical perspective developed in Chapter 1 suggesting that the intensity of an environmental variable is importantly related to its effect on development. Viewed in the present theoretical perspective, child abuse is an extreme example of parental provision of aversive environmental stimulation and is viewed as a "natural clue" for aggression in the sense of Bowlby. George and Main (1979) found that abused toddlers assaulted their peers twice as often as did control children, and Reid, Taplin, and Lorber (1981) similarly found higher rates of physical and verbal aggression in abused children. Finally, Patterson (1982) found that parents of antisocial boys are more than twice as likely to react aversively to their children's behavior than are the parents of nonproblem boys. These parents punish more often and use more extreme punishment, often including physical punishment.

Interestingly, infant abuse in rhesus monkeys is also associated with aggression: "Male infants of brutal mothers are among the most hostile animals raised in captivity, and they are particularly hostile toward infants" (Mitchell & Brandt, 1975). As is emphasized in Section III of this chapter, male monkeys are socialized with much more hostility and brutality than are female infants, a situation which in the present theoretical framework is hypothesized to be causally related to their greater aggressiveness.

Reproductive rituals associated with the socialization of aggression often appear to involve societal provision of aversive socialization events. It has already been shown that the cross-cultural distribution of these rituals conforms well to the sociobiologically expected patterns (see Chapter 5). Particularly striking examples come from the cross-cultural literature on circumcision and reproductive rituals and the brutal hazings that often accompany them. Paige and Paige (1981) show that societies characterized by moderately high levels of economic production are based on strong male lineage groups and that circumcision and brutal hazing operate to show the allegiance of the father and son to these larger groups. As the individual male is pulled away from the nuclear family social organization into the larger society characterized by greater levels of inter- and intragroup competition, socialization practices become increasingly aversive to the child and conducive to the development of aggression. Not surprisingly, these societies are characterized by high levels of military activity on the part of the males (see Appendix to Chapter 5). In addition, highly militaristic nation states, such as ancient Sparta (see Chapter 9), often have very brutal hazing practices directed especially at young males.

In addition to its general role in facilitating aggression, some of the effects of aversive stimulation on the development of aggression may be due to negative reinforcement. This aspect of the socialization of aggression has been emphasized particularly by Gerald Patterson. Patterson (1982) found that antisocial children were successful in approximately 40% of their coercive attempts to eliminate aversive stimulation. Patterson, Dishion, and Bank (1984) show connections between parental discipline encounters involving negative reinforcement with peer rejection and fighting at school, suggesting that negative reinforcement may contribute to a generalized tendency for negative interchanges away from the family. These results are consistent with the data indicating that the provision of aversive events facilitates aggression independent of its role in negative reinforcement: As noted above, Patterson (1982) also finds that the parents of aggressive children provide very high levels of aversive stimulation.

4. Conclusion

The research reviewed here indicates that humans can be reliably programmed to have a generalized tendency for aggression as a result of failure in the elaboration of the positive social reward system, providing high levels of aversive environmental events, and by negative reinforcement. Although studied mostly in contemporary societies, the cross-cultural literature is highly consistent with the view that cultures are able to use these methods in order to program adaptively a general tendency to be aggressive. This cross-cultural evidence is highly compatible with the analysis of Chapter 5, which indicates that negative familial interactions occur in situations where aggression, sexual competition, extended rather than nuclear family relationships, and war are highly adaptive. Societies that are able to effectively program individuals for high levels of aggression often use this aggression for obtaining resources and thereby increase their reproductive success both individually and collectively. This is the point of the first section of this chapter. Although the question of the adaptiveness of aggression in contemporary societies is far from clear, there is no question that in traditional societies it has often been a prime mechanism for achieving evolutionary goals.

Finally, it might be said that the foregoing pays too little attention to positive reinforcement and social learning in the development of aggression. Although I am not persuaded that these influences are nearly as important in the development of aggression in contemporary Western societies as temperament and the socialization mechanisms described above, these influences undoubtedly exist. The evolutionary theory of social learning stresses that individuals adopt behaviors that they observe to result in obtaining resources. Thus, it would not be at all surprising for individuals to imitate the aggressive behavior of highly successful individuals, and this may be a prime mechanism for developing aggression in delinquent subcultures where resources are obtained through physical aggression. From the perspective developed here, individuals who are low on their sensitivity to positive social rewards, who are temperamentally high in sensation seeking and perhaps emotionality (see below), and who have been socialized with a high level of aversive stimulation are much more likely to be attracted to successful models who are aggressive. An individual who is highly sensitive to positive social stimulation and rather cautious would find it difficult to imitate physically aggressive behavior even if there were obvious rewards in doing so.

One of the breakthroughs in the attempt to integrate evolutionary theory with data indicating environmental influences has been to realize that human behavior is quite flexible and can be quickly tailored to respond adaptively to new situations. Humans are "flexible strategizers" (Alexander, 1987, p. 9) rather than stereotypical robots. One of the repeated findings of social learning studies is the effectiveness of models who control resources or are powerful and these results are eminently reasonable in terms of evolutionary theory. Individuals who successfully obtain resources with aggression are then more likely to repeat this behavior in the future; that is, they are positively reinforced. It is perfectly reasonable to suppose then that in societies where highly aggressive warriors were highly successful in obtaining resources, power, and females other males would be attracted to this lifestyle and females would be attracted to these males as good providers for them and their children. The evidence reviewed above, however, suggests that societies intent on developing aggressive children do so in a "fail-safe" manner; that is, they rely not simply on social learning, but also on aversive stimulation and the lack of elaboration of the positive social reward system.

C. Temperament and Aggression

In Chapter 2, I presented evidence that one important aspect of temperament involved seeking high levels of rewards and being very insensitive to punishment—the dimension of sensation seeking or impulsivity. There is considerable evidence that aggression is characterized by these traits. First, Patterson (1982) found that aggressive children are extremely impulsive. They seek to maximize short-term profits and ignore possible punishments—the essence of this temperamental dimension. Many studies have shown that aggressive children are unable to delay gratification (e.g., Quay, 1965). Quay (1965, 1977, 1979) has also shown that aggressive adolescents seek very high levels of stimulation, interpreted here as attraction to rewards (see Chapter 2):

> What we are suggesting is that the psychopath . . . frequently finds himself in a state of stimulus deprivation. Since this condition is affectively unpleasant, he is motivated to change this affective state by the seeking of stimulation. In a highly organized environment such as that in which modern man resides this seeking of either added intensity or added variability of stimulation may on occasion involve transgressions of both law and the moral code. (Quay, 1965, p. 182)

Supporting this perspective, Skrzypek (1969) found that "psychopathic" delinquents tended to prefer novelty and complexity and increased these preferences after perceptual isolation. Conduct disorder groups were greatly affected by a perceptual isolation condition in which the subject was required to lie quietly on a bed while wearing gloves and translucent goggles and listening to white noise. After this manipulation, their preference for stimulation increased more than did that of the other group of delinquents. In addition, Orris (1969) found that conduct disorder delinquents performed worse in a vigilance task and engaged in more self-stimulating behavior, such as singing and talking to themselves, than did other types of delinquents.

Further evidence comes from the extensive overlap between hyperactive and aggressive children. In Chapter 3 evidence was reviewed indicating that hyperactive children are also high on the temperamental trait of sensation seeking, so that the extensive overlap between hyperactivity and aggression may well involve this temperamental trait. Hinshaw (1987) summarizes evidence indicating that hyperactivity and aggression are independent clinical entities despite large overlaps between the two syndromes. For example, Prinz, Connor, and Wilson (1981) found that whereas 32% of the hyperactive sample was aggressive, 92% of the aggressive children were hyperactive. Similarly, Loney and Milich (1982) found that 75% of the hyperactive boys in their sample were classified as aggressive, and Milich and Landau (in press) found that children who were both aggressive and hyperactive had more negative sociometric nominations than did children who were only aggressive. In addition, McGee, Williams, and Silva (1984a,b) found that approximately 42% of the children classified as hyperactive were classified as aggressive.

There is also evidence that aggression is linked to the reactivity (emotionality) dimension of temperament described in Chapter 2. Such a link is expected because of the link between emotionality and the fight-or-flight biological system. The behavior of individuals who are high on emotionality is highly energized and extreme individuals have difficulty controlling themselves. Thomas, Chess, and Birch (1968) found that behavior problems (including aggressiveness) were associated with low sensory thresholds, intensity, and distractibility. Olweus (1980) used the retrospective reports of mothers to find that "hot-headed" as opposed to calm temperament was associated with aggression in adolescents. Cairns (1986) notes that aggression is facilitated if animals are isolated, and that the mechanism involves increased reactivity and arousibility under these circumstances. The hypothesis that a high level of emotionality is linked with aggression is consistent with the finding that emotionality increases during adolescence (Rothbart & Posner, 1985), an increase corresponding to a large increase in aggression (Cairns, 1986). Consistent with these studies, MacDonald (1987d; see also Chapter 3) found that hyperactive children, a group that is clearly prone to aggression, tended to overreact to stimulation occurring during physical play sessions, often becoming overstimulated and attempting to control the level of stimulation provided by the parents.

Quite possibly the major means by which emotionality affects aggression is by making individuals irritable. Irritable individuals by definition have a low threshold for negative affective arousal. Thus, even fairly innocuous events are perceived as aversive by an irritable child, and the probability of aggression is increased in individuals who are otherwise predisposed to an aggressive response. Supporting this, Olweus, Mattson, Schalling, and Low (1980) found that aggression was associated with irritability as well as with testosterone levels in adolescents (see section on sex differences below). Berkowitz (1982) also notes that aversive events such as high temperatures make people irritable and this facilitates aggression.

These considerations strongly suggest that the temperamental dimensions of emotionality and sensation seeking described in Chapter 2 are important for hyperactivity and are predisposing factors in the development of aggression. As indicated there, however, children diagnosed as Undersocialized Aggressive Conduct Disorder appear to be extreme in the third temperamental dimension as well, that is, positive social reward. I have already described data showing that aggression is associated with lack of sensitivity to positive social rewards and with parental provision of hostile, rejecting environments. These data are consistent with evidence showing that family interactions are an important factor in whether aggression develops in hyperactive children. Hinshaw (1987) reviews data indicating that there is a large overlap between hyperactivity and aggression, but that they are nevertheless distinct clinical entities. Moreover, negative family interactions appear to be characteristic of the subgroup of hyperactive–aggressive children. Thus, Loney, Prinz, Mishalow, and Joad (1978), Paternite and Loney (1980), and Loney, Kramer, and Milich (1981) found that family hostility and negative family interactions were associated with aggression and hyperactivity–aggression, whereas children who were hyperactive without being aggressive were not consistently characterized by such family variables. Other studies have linked aggression and aggressiveness–hyperactivity to antisocial distubances in the parents, but these associations were not found in children diagnosed as having hyperactivity without aggression. Again, the families with aggressive children appear to have negative affective interactions (August & Stewart, 1983; Stewart, DeBlois, & Cummings, 1980). Finally, several studies have shown that aggressive and aggressive–hyperactive children, but not hyperactive–nonaggressive children, tend to come from broken homes and single-parent families (August & Stewart, 1983; McGee et al., 1984a).

D. Conclusion

Although by no means a complete model of the development of aggression, the above model is an attempt to capture some of the essential elements of an evolutionary theory of aggression. In this model temperament is an important predisposing factor in the development of aggression, but family factors operating on the social reward system and perhaps the other dimensions of temperament, as well as biologically based predispositions to respond to aversive events with aggressive responses, are crucial in determining whether aggression actually develops. In further sections of this chapter the topic of sex differences in aggression is discussed, and in Chapter 9 societal influences on aggression are emphasized, leading to a more complete picture of aggression.

The view developed here clearly implies a great deal of plasticity in the development of aggression and implies that cultures can program individual development in ways that maximize or minimize aggression and can do so in an adaptive manner. In our present culture the types of aggression studied by clinical psychologists appear to be maladaptive and pathological, at least in the sense that they appear to prevent upward mobility (see Chapter 5). However, a detailed study of the reproductive history of aggressive adolescents and adults might well reveal that such individuals are not being strongly selected against in contemporary societies and may in fact be doing quite well in terms of Darwinian fitness. Indeed, Draper and Harpending (1988), while not providing any data on the reproductive success of their subjects, suggest that sociopathy is highly adaptive under circumstances in which reciprocity is not an issue. Sociopaths are viewed as cheaters who exploit others and quickly move on to different surroundings in order to avoid detection and retaliation from their prey due to the sociopath's lack of reciprocity. In addition to showing such charactistics as childhood aggression, hyperactivity, impulsivity, stimulus seeking, and lack of sensitivity to social rewards (low guilt and empathy) discussed in this chapter, sociopaths have been found to move often and to be highly sexually promiscuous. This low-investment style of parenting may well result in high Darwinian fitness in circumstances in which other individuals or the society as a whole can be persuaded to care for their children. As predicted by an evolutionary theory (see section on sex differences below), this style of behavior is overwhelmingly a male phenomenon, exhibiting a 20 : 1 sex ratio.

II. ISSUES IN THE DEVELOPMENT OF PEER RELATIONS

A. *Introduction*

There are reasons for supposing that the topic of peer relations is an unpromising area for an evolutionary theory of development. The theoretical perspective developed thus far suggests that the epigenetic rules underlying human behavior resulted from evolutionary pressures to form small family groupings. In such circumstances significant numbers of children of roughly the same age would be an unlikely occurrence (Konner, 1976). Moreover, resources would be controlled by adults, so that access to resources would generally be mediated by relationships with adults, not by interactions among peers. Nevertheless, peer relationships are certainly an important aspect of contemporary human societies and these relationships will necessarily be influenced by many of the evolutionarily derived proximal mechanisms and ultimate evolutionary causes discussed here.

In the present section, children's friendships and social status differences will be emphasized because these topics have been analyzed successfully from an evolutionary perspective. There are several other aspects of peer relationships that will be better illuminated by future research within an evolutionary framework. For example, there are some preliminary indications that temperament and the regulation of affect (see Chapters 2 and 3) may be an important factor in sociometric status: There is a large overlap between hyperactivity and rejected sociometric status, and, as described above, there is good evidence for the role of temperament in hyperactivity. In addition, MacDonald (1987d) finds that both hyperactive and rejected children tend to engage in high levels of affectively arousing styles of parent–child physical play and that they tend to become overaroused and lose control in highly affectively arousing circumstances. Neglected children tend to have low levels of affectively arousing physical play with their parents and correspondingly low levels of overarousal and loss of control. Popular children tend to have quite high levels of affectively arousing physical play with their parents, but there was much less overstimulation in these play sessions. Although the issue of the direction of effects is still unsettled, it is clear from both the attachment literature and the literature on concurrent associations between the parent–child system and the peer system that these systems are linked: Behavior in the parent–child system is a strong predictor of behavior in the peer realm (see Parke *et al.*, 1988, in press). Moreover, an important aspect of this linkage appears to involve the regulation of affect. As indicated in Chapter 3, the regulation of affect is a fundamental social skill.

Further support for an evolutionary view of peer relations comes from cross-cultural evidence that the affective atmosphere of peer groups reflects the affective atmosphere of the family and the wider society and thus represents an aspect of development that is strongly affected by contextual influences (see Chapter 9 for a detailed discussion of contextual influences). Thus, Rohner (1975) found that peer groups in societies with warm parent–child interactions tended to be less hostile. As indicated in Chapter 5 (see also Chapter 8 and the discussion of aggression in this chapter), variation in the affective valence of family interactions is associated in theoretically derived ways with variation in economic production and sexual and resource competition. It is clear from the work of Youniss (1986) and Ginsberg, Gottman, and Parker (1986), described below, that one important aspect of friendship is an affective relation: friends are individuals who engage in positive interactions with one another. In terms of the theory of aggression described above, in societies where socialization or other sources of individual differences result in the lack of elaboration of the positive social reward system, peer relationships would be expected to be much more negative and hostile, perhaps not even corresponding at all to what we think of as friendship. On the other hand, individuals who are highly sensitive to social rewards would tend to be very sensitive to the rewarding behaviors of others and seek them out. Their behaviors would be characterized by affective reciprocity, in which each provides positive social rewards for the other. Positive affective reciprocity is thus an aspect of the general reciprocity found in friendships discussed below and its existence is crucially influenced by the sociobiologically predicted central tendencies and contextual variables emphasized throughout this volume.

B. Friendship as Reciprocity

From an evolutionary perspective one important aspect of any human relationship is the flow of resources between the participants (Charlesworth, 1988). In the case of parents and children it is expected that this flow will be highly imbalanced, while in other relationships individuals are expected to behave in a self-interested manner, which implies that individuals will at the very least attempt to give no more than they receive. Exploitative and asymmetrical relationships certainly exist, and will be discussed more fully later in this chapter and in Chapter 8, but the idea of friendship implies a certain reciprocity, or in the terms of evolutionary biology (Trivers, 1971), reciprocal altruism. Unlike true altruism, in which negative imbalances of resource flow are engaged in to the detriment of biological fitness, there are no conceptual difficulties posed by reciprocity, since the organisms involved do not incur any long-term net imbalance in resource flow. Trivers noted that friendship was particularly likely to be an example where reciprocity figures prominently, since the parties are of roughly equal status and can terminate the relationship voluntarily, thereby avoiding the possibility of cheating.

Youniss (1986) discusses the development of friendship in the context of reciprocity and notes the relevance of the evolutionary theory of reciprocal altruism as delineated by Trivers (1971). Several studies have shown that infants aged 12–24 months exhibited behaviors such as toy (resource) sharing, turn taking, and mutual imitation (Lewis,

Young, Brooks, & Michalson, 1975). Youniss notes that these elementary types of reciprocity do not involve a strict accounting of like for like, but appear to involve the mutual construction of ideas that are the outcome of both of the participants. As children get older, they become more efficient at producing a joint sense of reality.

Youniss (1986) also describes data indicating that the great majority of children aged 6–7 years consider acts of symmetrical reciprocity with other children as indicating that they are friends. Examples include trading opportunities to play with each other's toys or agreeing to play with dolls together. Moreover, these acts tend to be viewed positively by the participants, and negative symmetrical interactions are indications of nonfriendship. Youniss sums up this literature as indicating that:

> 1. Children are consistent in saying that their interactions follow the symmetrical reciprocal form.
> 2. The form bespeaks of an equality between children since whichever act one child initiates, the other child returns in kind.
> 3. In estimating the results of interactions, one cannot distinguish the interactants. Both get in the end the same benefit (or cost).
> 4. The participants are obviously described as equipotential agents because each is capable of duplicating the other's action.
> 5. The accounts seem to derive from the initial act since, once it occurs, subsequent acts follow in sequence. These features conform to Hinde's (1976, 1979) formal definition of symmetrical reciprocity and fit Piaget's (1965) depiction of reciprocity as the constituting rule of peer relations. (Youniss, 1986, p. 97)

Youniss also notes that as children get older they are able to sustain an essentially reciprocal friendship relationship despite cases of negative or omitted reciprocity. Children do not have to reciprocate immediately or in identical terms. The data on friendship are said to fit the predictions of Trivers' model quite well:

> 1. The content of children's interactions corresponds to the content of the list of altruistic domains proposed by Trivers; helping when in danger, sharing food, helping the more helpless, sharing implements, and sharing knowledge. The match may not be incidental. In our own research, children were free to give accounts of whichever interactions they thought fit our specification of partners and end result. It was the subjects who chose to describe friends as sharing food, sharing toys and school supplies (children's implements), helping in time of physical weakness, offering emotional support, and working together on the construction of knowledge.
> 2. Trivers suggests that a low dispersal rate promotes reciprocal altruism. It is interesting that children not only draw their friendships from classmates, whom they regularly see, but spend considerable time with their friends outside class hours. Time spent together and the wide variety of incidents that friends encounter together make for altruistic opportunities that non-friends do not have.
> 3. A check for cheating occurs when individuals are mutually dependent on one another. Mutual dependence increases the likelihood that the need to be the recipient of another's altruism will shift back and forth between friends. After about 9 or 10 years of age, children recognize this condition in their friendships. They also see that friends are individuals with different strengths and weaknesses; mutual dependence comes from the repeated experience of one's strengths compensating for the other's weaknesses, and vice versa.
> 4. Trivers notes that reciprocal altruism is unlikely between the young and their adult caretakers because the former generally have little to offer to the latter, due to huge differences in capacities as well as possession of resources. This asymmetry is not the case in friendship despite the fact that children appreciate the importance of individual differences, which they handle by constructing the principle of fair and equal treatment. Moreover, since any friendship covers so many different instances and domains of living, a balance can be achieved between giving and receiving with symmetry obtaining across instances within the friendship.

5. Trivers proposes that reciprocal altruism is enhanced when individuals maintain contact over long-periods of time. As was seen after about 10 years of age, children claim that their frendship is an enduring relationship . . . This may be more than wishful musing on their part. Fischer (1977) reports that friendships established at that time are, in fact, likely to endure. Adult men report that many of the friendships they now have began in childhood or early adolescence.

6. Trivers considers the number of reciprocal relationships important to altruism. The fewer in number, the more exclusive and the greater the opportunity for reciprocity. Unquestionably, after about 12 years of age, children consider friendship an exclusive relationship . . . For example, acts of omission are unkind only within the context of friendship wherein the principle of reciprocity applies. For another example, mutual self-disclosure not only occurs within the context of friendship but is unlikely to occur elsewhere, since outside its reciprocal boundaries disclosures entail risks, while within friendship reciprocity protects the partners and even draws them closer together. (Youniss, 1986, pp. 101–102)

The data and theoretical integration of Youniss (1986) are an excellent example in which recent evolutionary theory is able to incorporate a large area of developmental research. The fit between the theory and the data as well as the fact that the data were collected without reference to the theory indicate clearly the power of the evolutionary approach. Evolutionary theory may also shed light on the converse of the development of friendship—the development of social rejection. Rejected children are highly disliked by other children and in addition are not highly liked (Coie, Dodge, & Coppotelli, 1982). Evolutionary theory predicts that children become rejected if their behaviors are perceived as exploitative and aversive; that is, if their behaviors lack reciprocity. Rejected children score low on cooperation and high on aggression (Cole et al., 1982). Despite being aggressive, they are not leaders of the group, and indeed in some ways they may be considered to be ostracized. Barner-Barry (1986) presents a case study of a preschool boy whose aggressive, nonreciprocating behavior led to ostracism from the group. The boy, in addition to getting into a large number of aggressive interactions with his peers, did things such as taking a ball from a child and resisting efforts by the child and others to get it back. Or once:

When some men in military uniform walked by, he said to another child, "See those men over there? They're going to kill you. They'll suck your head off." Then he threatened the child using hitting and kicking movements. The child said "I'm sorry," although he had no reason to be sorry. Finally Rob kicked a ball out of another child's hands and that child retreated from him. (Barner-Barry, 1986, p. 286)

The fights and other aversive, nonreciprocating behavior (including taking away other children's toys and hoarding toys so that other children could not play with them) continued until gradually he became ostracized from the group. Coinciding with the rejection was a decrease in aggressive episodes, since the other children no longer interacted with him.

C. How Young Children Get What They Want

The title of this section mimics that of an article by Parkhurst and Gottman (1986), which studies strategies of resource acquisition among children. This literature is placed within Brown and Levinson's (1978) theory of politeness, a theory of the form of adult requests that is very compatible with evolutionary theory. First, Brown and Levinson assume that individuals are rationally self-interested and that in order to obtain a resource from another person one must take account of the other person's interests and his or her ability and willingness to protect those interests. Thus, the form of requests is powerfully influenced by whether there are large status differences between the individuals or a more reciprocal relationship. Familiarity is also expected to be important because lack of familiarity introduces some uncertainty into a relationship, resulting in more politeness than might occur just on the basis of status differences.

This theory can be readily seen to be quite compatible with an evolutionary account, since it stresses the importance of resources, self-interest, and status differences. The data for adults fit these predictions quite well, and in conformity with the general predictions of the Brown–Levinson model, Parkhurst and Gottman found that compliance with requests within dyads of young children was a function of the degree to which the child making the request could retaliate against noncompliance. Younger children failed to use politeness to get what they wanted, but by age 5 years politeness occurred and in general it was used by children when they were at a disadvantage in the relationship. Thus, for example, it was more commonly used by a child who was a stranger to another child and a guest in that other child's house. Several other strategies were noted in the study, including references to the commonality of interests in the situation, coercion and threats, humorous requests, and "assertions of validity," which are attempts to show the other person the validity of one's request.

Parkhurst and Gottman also reviewed other findings indicating clear developmental trends indicating that children become increasingly skilled at taking account of the other person's interests as they get older. When a request is refused, young children are relatively inflexible, often simply repeating the requests. They are relatively less able to take account of status differences and other aspects of the context. Thereafter there is a developmental progression in which children first rely on telling others their own desires and later become more polite, that is, take into account the fact that the other person is not likely to want to be imposed upon. Between the ages of 7 and 12 years, children are able to use deference as a strategy (Mitchell-Kernan & Mitchell, 1977) when refusal or retaliation is a possibility. When requesting a resource from someone of lower status, they will instead use the imperative grammatical form.

Parkhurst and Gottman note that the results for children over age 5 years conform well to the Brown–Levinson theory, but this is not the case for those under age 5 years, since children under this age, despite acting in their self-interest, are certainly less effective in doing so than are older children. These results pose a problem for an adaptationist theory as well, since the behavior of young children appears to be far from ideally adaptive. Indeed, the adaptive niche of the child is not well specified in evolutionary theory. Since parents form a buffer between the child and the world, the behavior of children need not be maximally efficient at obtaining resources from the world at large, and the adaptationist analysis of developing behavior must take account of the familial context of development. Similarly, in the study of moral reasoning (Chapter 7), there are indications that as children get older they are better able to produce reasons for their actions that appeal to disinterested parties. The results of Parkhurst and Gottman are exactly congruent with this, since the more sophisticated framing of requests is presumably better able to get positive results. The developmentally earlier strategy of simply stating one's desires is presumably quite adequate in dealing with one's parents, since they are predisposed to provide resources to their children. There are clearly limits to this beneficence, however, so that the later strategy of politeness is probably more effective with parents and certainly with strangers and peers.

The results indicate that children always have needs and behave in a self-interested manner, but with increasing cognitive sophistication they become more adept at meeting those needs by influencing other people as they get older. Parkhurst and Gottman note that this increased sophistication involves greater role-playing ability, since this would allow one to see the situation from the other's point of view and anticipate the probable response to one's behavior.

D. Affective Reciprocity in Friendship

Up to this point I have emphasized the role of reciprocity of resource flow in friendship and social rejection without discussing the role of affect in friendship. Clearly the affective aspect of friendship is an essential function of friendship. Ginsberg et al. (1986) note the intimate/affectionate aspect of friendship, and note that it is this quality that most clearly distinguishes it from other relationships, such as acquaintanceship.

The following discussion will stress several key points:

1. Since reciprocity is a key element of friendship within an evolutionary perspective, we expect that friendships will be characterized by affective reciprocity. Affection and intimacy are thus viewed as resources (needs) in the sense of Charlesworth (1988).

2. In terms of our model of affective relationships, it is expected that friends provide stimulation that is positively reinforcing to each other because it stimulates the positive social reward system.

3. The model proposes that the elaboration of the positive social reward system during early development, as, for example, in early parent–child relations (Chapter 4), results in a heightened sensitivity to such socially rewarding stimulation. Other individuals thus become potential sources of positive social rewards. In Chapter 5 it was emphasized that this reward system is one of the cohesive forces underlying the marriage relationship, but the affective side of friendship can also be seen as providing the same types of stimulation and satisfying the same needs.

4. It was noted in Chapter 3 that the positive social reward system was a self-regulatory system, that is, that it has strong self-motivating properties. The affective side of friendship thus implies motivation to seek out sources of positive social stimulation.

5. In Chapter 4 I noted a tendency for the positive social reward system to become centered around particular individuals (i.e., attachment objects). Friendship also clearly involves a highly discriminating relationship, which, once established, contains the potential for a great deal of pleasure, but whose termination is thus likely to result in great dysphoria.

I have suggested that the positive social reward system underlies both the cohesive ties of marriage (Chapter 5) and friendship. Consistent with this perspective, there is evidence that marriage and friendship serve some of the same affective functions. Mueller (1980) stressed that if an individual has a set of alternative relationships, he or she is less likely to be devastated by a single loss, whereas an individual without such alternatives is particularly likely to be devastated by a loss. Such a proposal is consistent with the finding that men tend to be much more devastated by the loss of a spouse than are women, because women more often have intimate relationships outside of marriage, whereas men rely on their spouse as a confidant (Booth & Hess, 1947; Fischer & Phillips, 1979, as cited in Ginsberg et al., 1986). Further evidence consistent with this hypothesis comes from White and Asher (1976 as described in Ginsberg et al., 1986), who found that men who adjusted successfully after divorce tended to have a good social life apart from marriage. Finally, even though men are generally more susceptible to the loss of a spouse than are women, if a widowed male does have a close confiding relationship, he tends to be happier than a married man without such a relationship (Lowenthal & Haven, 1968).

There is also clear evidence for the importance of peer relations for later psychiatric disorders, evidence here interpreted as due to an inadequacy of affective resources in the person's environment. Children without friends appear to be at risk for later psychiatric disturbance (Cowen, Pederson, Babijian. Izzo, & Trost, 1973; see Ginsberg et al., 1986, for a review). These studies do not clearly implicate the affective side of friendship in later psychiatric difficulties, since the measures tend to involve global characteristics of peer interaction available from clinic and school records, such as "failed to get along with other children" (Janes, Hesselbrock, Myers, & Penniman, 1979). Nevertheless, such children presumably do not have friends and thus do not exist in an environment high in positive social rewards. Moreover, evidence from studies on friendship in adulthood strongly implicate the affective side of friendship in psychiatric disorders. In their review of the literature, Ginsberg et al. (1986) conclude that there are positive correlations between close personal relationships and successful social involvement with emotional and physical well-being, with the latter qualities presumably resulting from finding the social environment to be rewarding.

Since friendships consist of highly rewarding social interactions, which individuals are therefore highly motivated to retain, it is not surprising that loss of a friend is a highly negative event, which, like the loss of a relative, often leads to depression.

Although these studies suggest that the lack of friends is linked to later psychiatric disturbance, the theory presented here is that sensitivity to positive social rewards as well as the skills involved in the regulation of affect are importantly influenced by the parent–child relationship and these in turn underlie interest and competence in friendship making (see Chapters 3–5). Within this perspective, then, inadequate peer relations are more a symptom of the problem than a cause of later psychiatric difficulties.

E. The Similarity of Friends in Evolutionary Perspective

Another finding that is highly compatible with an evolutionary account of friendship is that friends tend to be similar to one another. Genetic similarity theory (Rushton et al., 1984), described in greater detail in Chapter 8, suggests that individuals should have greater commonality of interests with other individuals who are likely to share copies of their genes. Relationships between similar individuals should thus be more reciprocating and more like friendship as compared to relationships between nonsimilar individuals. As indicated below, children of a similar dominance rank tend to form friendships, and it has been found that friends are similar on a large number of other phenotypic characteristics. Rushton et al. note that perceived similarity is a very powerful experimental manipulation, with results indicating that individuals perceived as similar are perceived as bene-volent (Sole, Marton, & Hornstein, 1975), compatible (Sussman & Davis, 1975), and rewarding (Brickman, Meyer, & Fredd, 1975). Friends also tend to be of similar height (Berkowitz, 1969). Rushton *et al.* predict that friendship should be associated with altruism, since similar individuals are willing to incur negative imbalances in resource flow because of the genetic benefits. The importance of similarity for altruism will be discussed in Chapter 8, but the data reviewed above certainly indicate minimally that reciprocity is characteristic of friends.

Segal (1988) also provides data indicating that genetic relatedness affects social preference and friendship. An evolutionary theory predicts that individuals with a greater degree of genetic relatedness will prefer each other socially and will become friends more easily. Consistent with this prediction, monozygotic twins tended to remain nearer to each other in a school playground situation than did dizygotic twins: "The greater preference that MZ twins showed for the company of the co-twin than DZ twins showed for their co-twin is testimony to the social and, possibly, emotional gains available from the company of a very close relative" (Segal, 1988, p. 184). Data from reunited twins also show that MZ twins quickly form a strong relationship despite the absence of previous familiarity. Reunited MZ twins are much more likely to live together, become professionally associated, and maintain close contact than are DZ twins.

F. Social Status Differences among Peers

The previous discussion shows that reciprocity in resource flow is characteristic of many of the friendship relations in which children are engaged. Friendships are typically dyadic relationships, but children are often thrown into larger groups and in these larger groups asymmetries of rank and resource control occur. There is evidence that within these larger groups individual children associate most with children close to themselves in the dominance hierarchy (Savin-Williams, 1987), suggesting that children tend to gravitate to relationships with a relatively high degree of reciprocity, even if in the structure of the group as a whole they rank relatively low. The relations between children of similar rank are thus more likely to be what we would call friendships, while those with other children in a group are less reciprocal and less symmetrical.

In the present section the human develomental data on dominance are discussed. The intellectual basis of this research is rooted in the animal literature and it is hypothesized that dominance translates into access to resources and eventually into reproductive advantages (Charlesworth, 1988; Rowell, 1966; Wilson, 1975). Reflecting the theoretical imperative of finding individually advantageous reasons for behavior, subordinate animals are thought to benefit from remaining in the dominance hierarchy because they avoid the costs of competing (McGuire, 1974), because they have higher chances of survival and reproduction within the group, even as a subordinate, than outside the group as a "loner"; because they might eventually inherit the top position if another animal dies or migrates; and because they can increase their own inclusive fitness by helping their relatives raise their offspring (Wilson, 1975). Moreover, there may be collective benefits to dominance hierarchies, including the reduction of aggression (Carpenter, 1942) and the coordination of affiliative behavior (Chance, 1967; Seyfarth, 1980).

Dominance interactions are a ubiquitous feature of many highly social species and have been extensively studied by ethologists (Wilson, 1975). For example, dominance relations develop early among wolf cubs and remain quite stable over time (Fox, 1972; MacDonald, 1983b, 1987b). Moreover, the characteristics that result in dominance among the wolf cubs appear to be characteristics of the animal, rather than situationally dependent characteristics of a relationship: Major disruptions of the group housing arrangements did not affect the dominance hierarchy, and measurements of the animals independent of the group were associated with dominance behaviors within the group (MacDonald, 1983b). Dominance in wolf cubs is associated with access to scarce resources such as a bone (MacDonald, 1983b, 1987b), and in adults it "functions to regulate the reproductive activities of the pack" (Ginsburg, 1987, p. 405). Ginsburg notes that stable wolf packs are characterized by the ability of dominant individuals to control their reproductive possibilities and they use a variety of techniques to do so. For example, the dominant female was much more likely to mate than were the other females and actively inhibited others from mating. Jenks and Ginsburg (1987) conclude that "There is a positively correlated, though not rigid, relationship between mate preference, breeding privilege and dominance" (p. 397).

Regarding dominance in human relationships, it should be noted that dominance relationships based on personal characteristics are probably most important in societies without institutionalized social structure. Indeed, one might propose that the institutionalization of social structure in many traditional societies is an attempt to regulate access to resources in a manner that deemphasizes the personal characteristics of individuals that otherwise would give rise to a dominance hierarchy. Anthropological studies are replete with examples of societies at the middle level of economic production (e.g., the Melanesian "big man" societies) in which the success of an individual male depends almost exclusively on his personal qualities, which enable him to amass resources and females. However, at a more advanced level individuals can inherit office as well as other resources, such as money or land, so that the role of personal qualities in variations in biological fitness, such as those resulting in dominance, is less (MacDonald, 1983a). From a more general perspective these institutional effects on control of resources can be viewed as an aspect of social controls described in several chapters of this volume. In our own society the existence of a vast array of niches suited to virtually every personality type, the complex market and nonmarket forces that determine the value of jobs, the continued inheritance of resources and social status by some, social controls on marriage and reproduction, which result in minimizing or removing any association between the control of resources and reproductive success, and possible discontinuities in development as one moves from the world of school to the world of work all make it unlikely that dominance behaviors in childhood can be simply mapped onto later biological fitness or resource control.

Nevertheless, there is evidence that children's groups are characterized by dominance rankings and that these relationships are remarkably stable and dependent on highly heritable physiognomic characteristics of individuals. The perspective developed above suggests that the associations between such individual characteristics and reproductive success will be strongest when these characteristics are themselves intimately tied to later resource control and when institutional controls are minimized, but, whatever the ultimate role of these characteristics of children, it is clear that symmetries and asymmetries of resource control during childhood are importantly influenced by these traits.

The developmental literature on dominance indicates that social dominance hierarchies are an organizational feature of preschool groups (e.g., Abramovitch, 1980; Strayer & Strayer, 1976) and that they function to reduce aggression within the group (LaFreniere & Charlesworth, 1983). Recently, Strayer and Trudel (1984) reported a decrease in antagonistic status differences and an increase in positive affiliative behaviors coinciding with the emergence of a stable linear dominance hierarchy in children in the age range of 1–5 years. Within the group of 5-year-old children there was a positive association between social dominance and receiving affiliative behavior from other children, and there was a general age trend in this direction over the age range from 1 to 5 years. Moreover, at the older ages there is an increasing number of unreciprocated social choices (i.e., preference as playmates) directed toward higher status children.

These results are consistent with the idea that affiliative skills rather than merely skill in dyadic conflict may become increasingly important to dominance interactions as children become older. This idea is supported by results of a study on triadic conflict reported by Strayer and Noel (1986). Here it was found that children who came to the aid of a child who was being aggressed against (*Defensive Conflict*) tended to be the recipient of affiliative behavior in others. There were other links between the affiliative system among peers and roles in triadic conflict: Both the aggressor and the ally in an *Alliance* conflict were often the recipient of and initiator of affiliative behavior with peers, as was the aggressor in a *Generalization* conflict (i.e., a conflict in which a child aggressed first against one child and then against another). These findings suggest complex relations between affiliation and dominance in children and indicate that children's social interactions cannot be analyzed solely by noting dyadic conflicts. Moreover, simple aggression is not the key to being dominant (Hartup, 1983), but in fact often leads to social rejection and ostracism (Barner-Barry, 1986).

Considerable research on dominance interactions has focused on adolescence, and this body of research has indicated substantial continuity from early childhood to early adulthood. Savin-Williams (1987) studied children from age 10 to 17 years who were housed in age-homogeneous, sexually segregated cabins during a summer camp. Sex differences in dominance behavior were ubiquitous. Approximately one-quarter of the encounters of the girls involved compliments, asking favors, imitation and seeking advice, compared to a rate of only 1/16 for the boys. Boys were much more direct in asserting their status than were girls, and this directness increased over the course of the camp, whereas girls became more indirect in status assertions. Thus, by the end of the camp the interactions of the boys were characterized by overt acts such as teasing, ordering, and arguing, while girls resorted to shunning, gossiping, and giving unsolicited advice or information. Conflict among the boys was more likely to be potentially physically injurious, but it tended to be relatively brief, while with girls interpersonal conflicts were long-lasting and actually became more entrenched in time.

Indeed, the sex differences were so pervasive that Savin-Williams concludes that the girls for the most part did not really establish a stable, linear hierarchy at all. Their dominance interactions were less salient both to themselves and to observers. They were less likely than boys to rank themselves correctly and tended to rank themselves lower than they actually were. Boys, on the other hand, were very concerned about their dominance status and consistently overranked themselves on this dimension. Moreover, structured group activities were voluntarily chosen by boys, while girls in their free time chose to interact in small groups in unstructured, unorganized activities such as talking and walking. Girls also described the ideal leader as relating to others' problems, friendly, patient, and considerate, whereas boys were much more likely to idealize an honest leader who can organize things and make the right decisions. Clearly the qualities the girls admire are socioemotional and would be ideal in dyadic relations where one wanted sympathy and kindness, whereas those idealized by boys would be good for a leader of a larger group, where making the correct decision and organizing the behavior of others was of paramount concern. Girls tended to conflate the ideas of an ideal friend and an ideal leader, whereas boys had two quite different concepts for these roles.

Dyadic combinations within cabin groups were overwhelmingly directional (approximately 85%), indicating dominance, and there were relatively few reversals within the dyadic interactions (between 17% and 34%). Further, there was a tendency toward stability as camp progressed, and nondirectional relationships tended to become directional. The dominance relationships were linear and transitive; that is, if A dominated B and B dominated C, then A dominated C. In seven of the eight cabins studied the dominance order remained stable. Among the boys, changes tended to involve low-ranking members, while with girls the most frequent shifts occurred between the top two positions. Dominant children of both sexes were athletic, physically mature, and leaders, and in addition, dominant girls were also popular with their cabin mates, while dominant boys were quite indirect in their methods of dominance.

The dominance interactions reflect the importance of resources in understanding human relationships (Charlesworth, 1988). Dominant children received a number of "personal benefits" from their status, including large portions of food and the best sitting and sleeping places. Dominant status also was associated with high self-esteem and confidence, and dominant individuals had a much larger than average input into the decision-making process of the group. However, low-ranking boys appeared to identify with the group and took part in activities, even when relegated by the dominant child to relatively unrewarding activities, such as playing right field in a baseball game. Theoretically, individuals should continue to perform activities that maintain the group until their own interests no longer benefit from group membership (Alexander, 1974). The fact that the boys continued to participate suggests that they were still receiving something from group participation.

Studies by Charlesworth and his colleagues (Charlesworth, 1988; Charlesworth & LaFreniere, 1983; Charlesworth & Dzur, 1987) indicate an association between resource control and rank in the preschool dominance hierarchy in young (3.5–5 years old) children as well. In addition, in randomly selected groups of four girls Charlesworth and Dzur (1987) found that girls who managed a high level of resource utilization issued more commands and showed more physically assertive behavior did than girls with less utilization. High-resource-utilization girls spent more time cooperating than the other girls, indicating that cooperation is not necessarily opposed to competition, but can often be an effective competitive strategy (see Charlesworth, 1988, for a discussion). Groups of boys, on the other hand, tended to be more homogeneous for dominance behaviors.

The study by Savin-Williams (1987) raises the question of the extent to which dominance is a trait versus a situationally determined set of behaviors. A crucial finding was that dominance rank was independent of setting within the various camp activities. This finding, along with the findings that the children agreed on who was dominant, the correlations between dominance rank and observed behavior, and the high stability of dominance, indicates that a trait approach to dominance is the best explanation of the data: "I believe that there is ample evidence . . . to suggest a trait conception of dominance. That is, some adolescents consistently win or are recognized by peers as winners; others consistently lose, and this is a secret to few" (Savin-Williams, 1987, p. 186). Savin-Williams argues, however, that the expression of this trait is context dependent, since the same individual might have a quite different status in a group of musicians or in a group of younger or older children: "dominance is both an individual trait and a relationship; I view the dominance trait as an orientation, a predisposition dependent on social conditions" (p. 186).

Another way of saying this is to claim that the evidence indicates that some individuals are likely to assume high (or low) rank in an average, expectable group of age-mates, depending on their personal characteristics. If the group is radically changed to include much older children or children with specific talents (such as music or intellectual ability), then the personal characteristics important in these average expectable groups would be relatively unimportant for status. Such a conception is similar to the idea of breeding value in biometrical genetics: An individual with a high breeding value is likely to have an influence on a trait given the average genetic background of the species. In particular matings the effect may not occur, but its general importance as a characteristic of the individual is clear. Thus, even though dominance is a relationship and may or may not occur in a given set of circumstances, the characteristics that result in dominance are traits of the individual. Similarly, a person's height is a characteristic of the person and, even though "taller than" is a relation, a tall boy will tend to be taller than most other children of his age due his personal characteristic. If placed with older children or a selected group of very tall children, he will no longer be taller than anyone. Nevertheless, his height is still a personal characteristic, a characteristic that tends to make him taller than most children in randomly selected groups of children of the same age. And so it is with dominance. Although this "main effect" of personal traits on dominance in unselected groups of children is clear, I have already commented that in a society such as our own with a huge diversity of niches, in adulthood the main effects may be of less importance than the multitude of interactions that ensure that a great many combinations of personal characteristics can achieve high status.

Another thrust of recent research on dominance has been to attempt to determine the long-term stability of dominance behavior and the origins of adolescent dominance in early childhood. Weisfeld, Muczenski, Weisfeld, and Omark (in press; see also Weisfeld & Billings, 1988) studied a small sample of boys from nursery school to late adolescence. Ratings of dominance stabilized in the first grade and the follow-ups at high school attempted to assess individuals who had remained together over the intervening period. Ratings by classmates on athletic ability, dominance, alertness in crisis, popularity, sociability, leadership, competitiveness, and self-confidence in grade 12 were very strongly correlated with ratings of "toughness" in first and second grades: Correlations between the second-grade and 12th-grade measures ranged from .84 to .93 for two cohorts, and the overall stability of dominance was .71 for four cohorts studied.

The authors conclude that "very stable determinants of social success were operating" with these groups of children" (Weisfeld et al., in press) and indicate that early puberty per se is not a determining factor in children's social success, but that "certain physiognomic traits, later abetted by pubertal maturation, are valued by peers from childhood to adulthood'' (Weisfeld *et al.,* in press). As with the results of Savin-Williams (1987) described above, dominance in boys was associated with athletic ability and attractiveness as well as early maturation, and the authors provide evidence indicating that these characteristics are highly heritable. Moreover, Weisfeld, Weisfeld, and Callaghan (1984) found that physical attractiveness and athletic ability were correlated with social success among African and Native American groups, suggesting a panhuman phenomenon. The authors also point out that the results would be expected to be even more striking in cultures where males typically engage in war or other activities demanding high levels of physical skill.

Finally, the authors place these phenomena in an evolutionary framework by noting that muscular, athletic males are attractive to females because such qualities would be correlated with economic success in hunter–gatherer societies. Such males would thus be attractive mates and there would be evolution for epigenetic rules in which these physiognomic features would be appraised positively (the biological basis of the aesthetic of human physiognomic features).

The phylogeny of our ideas of human attractiveness thus stems from the our prehistory, but Weisfeld *et al.* note that women in our culture also value the earning prospects of potential marriage partners. This analysis clearly implicates the importance of reproduction and control of resources in human social success. The findings suggest, however, that in our society the effects of personal attractiveness and athletic ability may still exist among adults (Adams, 1977), but that their influence will be relatively minimal compared to societies where these qualities are intimately tied to economic success. In the end an evolutionary analysis must speak the language of resources (Charlesworth, 1988), and the behavior of women in contemporary industrial societies apparently conforms quite well to this prediction. Female mate choice is discussed further in the following section on the development of sex differences in behavior.

In our own society, older, wealthy males are able to attract females of reproductive age as mates and sexual partners, presumably fairly independently of their physical appearance. To the extent that control of resources is independent of physical appearance and athletic ability (the traits associated with dominance in children and adults in our prehistory), dominance will be freed from the epigenetic rules associated with these traits and shifted to resource control. In a society such as ours where sexual behavior is becoming more unregulated, sociobiological theory predicts that male sexual competition for physically attractive females of reproductive age will be intensified and that males who command large resources will be able to have maximum access to this resource. Unless polygyny becomes socially acceptable, however, this access will not be strongly associated with reproductive success, especially if a long-term commitment of resources is not made by the male. Without such long-term commitment females are unlikely to have children (Essock-Vitale & McGuire, 1985). However, even without polygyny, successful males will be able to command females of reproductive age as mates even when they themselves are quite old, leading to the possibility of serial polygyny and higher lifetime fertility than for males without similar resources. The consequence to females will be an increasing number of older females who will be unable to find males willing to marry them, since their reproductive value is minimal or zero. The consequences to children will be increased levels of rearing by mothers alone as males opt for divorce of older women and marriage with younger women (see Chapter 5 for a discussion of the effects of divorce on children). Thus, dominance based on resource control will undoubtedly increase in importance in our society to the extent that human relationships are unregulated by institutional structures such as controls on divorce, fornication, and adultery. Since at present our society is going in the direction of deregulating sexual relationships, the prediction is that dominance behavior among males for access to young females will be an increasingly salient feature of our society.

III. SEX DIFFERENCES IN DEVELOPMENT

A. Evolutionary Theory and Sex Differences

In Chapter 5 there was a brief discussion of the evolutionary theory of sex differences. Essentially the evolutionary theory of sex differences, like all modern evolutionary theory, is a theory of the costs and benefits of behavior and morphology (see Daly & Wilson, 1983, for a discussion). Biologists propose that sex evolved because it provided the ability to produce large numbers of genetic combinations. During meiosis random subsets of the total genetic complement are used to form the gametes, and crossing-over further reshuffles the genetic cards. Sexual species thus retain more variability and are able to respond better to changing environments. They are able to evolve faster because new combinations are constantly being formed. Species that do not reproduce sexually are unable to get rid of deleterious genes: A parthenogenic female will transmit all of her deleterious genes to her offspring while a sexual species effectively edits the genetic script at each generation because some progeny will be without the mutation.

Sexual reproduction appears to be individually adaptive as well. Williams (1975) has shown that animals or plants that can reproduce with or without sex turn to sexual reproduction in situations of uncertainty. Thus parasites often reproduce asexually in the early stages of infestation in a host animal. At this time resources are plentiful, but later, when resources become scarce, sexual reproduction occurs, ensuring a large variability in the remaining animals as they disperse.

The foregoing explains the origin of sex, but not the origin of two morphologically distinctive gametes characteristic of male and female organisms. The main characteristic differentiating these two types of gametes is size: Evolution has resulted in a dichotomous distribution of gamete size, with the male having the smaller of the two gametes, and Parker, Baker, and Smith (1972) have shown that natural selection against intermediate sizes and in favor of a bimodal distribution of gamete sizes is likely to have taken place. In any case, from whatever evolutionary pressures, the consistent size difference among the gametes in sexually reproducing organisms biases the two sexes toward very different levels of parental investment. The egg itself represents an enormous investment in offspring compared to that of the male gamete, and internal fertilization, gestation, lactation, and the nurturance of the young have typically also tended to evolve in the female sex. As a basic result of this very large investment, the reproductive capacity of females tends to be severely restricted compared to that of the male. With few exceptions (see Hrdy,

1981), females benefit from further matings only at relatively long intervals, corresponding to the period of time it takes to rear young animals.

Males, on the other hand, can benefit from a much larger number of copulations. Whereas female reproduction is typically limited by the time and energy required to produce gametes and/or nurture the young, male reproduction is typically limited by the necessity of competing with other males for this relatively scarce resource. As indicated in Chapter 5, in human societies this essential sex difference is reflected in the fact that polygyny is a common human mating system, while polyandry is vanishingly rare in human societies and apparently confined to cases where the males are close biological relatives. Viewed another way, these results suggest that there will tend to be greater variance in male reproductive success than in female reproductive success. Daly and Wilson (1983) summarize data from the Xavante of Brazil showing that virtually all females mate and there is relatively little variance among the females. Seventy-four of 184 males had more than one wife and the variance in reproductive success among the males was correspondingly greater. In highly productive societies such as classical China, the variance in male reproductive success can be extremely high, as individual males are able to control large amounts of resources and control large numbers of females.

The foregoing suggests that male–female differences resulting from fundamental differences in investment will be a pervasive feature of animal behavior. However, natural selection can act to minimize differences between the sexes. For example, most bird species are monogamous and the male often contributes a great deal toward reproduction by providing food and other resources toward the reproductive effort. Daly and Wilson (1983) point out that this equalization tends to occur most often in species with external fertilization or in species such as birds where the embryo is externalized at an early age. In such cases parental care by the male can be selected for relatively easily.

Internal fertilization and female lactation among the mammals have resulted in a greater skewing toward male–female differences in this group than in many vertebrate groups. These adaptations have resulted in relatively large female investment, which is not easily overcome. Nevertheless, monogamy occurs among mammals. Kleiman (1981) describes two extreme forms of monogamy in mammals. *Facultative* monogamy occurs as the result of ecological pressures, such as the distribution of resources in an environment, that prevent a male from defending the territory of more than one female. Such animals tend to be asocial and have low levels of paternal care. *Obligate* monogamy, on the other hand, is the result of the need for higher levels of paternal investment in offspring and is associated with strong pair bonding, high levels of high-quality parental (including paternal) care of offspring, and prolonged juvenile development.

In monogamous species generally, morphological and behavioral differences between the sexes are minimized, whereas in polygynous species *sexual selection* operates within each sex to result in differences in secondary sexual characteristics, including possible behavioral differences. Among males the origin of many secondary sexual characteristics is the necessity to compete with other males for access to females, but in addition, female choice of male characteristics may operate. As an example of the latter, Darwin believed that the bright colors of many male birds were the result of female choice. Since females are the scarce resource in many species, they are expected to be highly discriminating and to mate only with males who are able to provide adequate resources. As Kevles (1986) points out, "measuring or comparing courting males is what female choice is all about" (p. 12), and there are a number of examples where it appears likely that females choose males with attributes that make the males less likely to survive. In general, however, females are presumed to choose males with the best possible genetic contribution to their offspring and do so by choosing males who are able to defeat other males in combat (e.g., elephant seals), provide a good nest (e.g., Siamese fighting fish, weaver birds), food (e.g., roadrunners and katydids), and territory (e.g., African bush-babies) (Kevles, 1986).

Among humans there are a large number of secondary sexual characteristics, such as larger body size and facial hair, but in general the magnitude of male–female differences is intermediate between exclusively monogamous species and extremely polygynous species (Alexander, 1979). Throughout this volume the importance of the epigenetic rules resulting in the possibility of pair bonding among adults and affective ties between parents and offspring have been emphasized. These characteristics, as well as the prolonged development of children and their prolonged need for resources, suggest evolution in the direction of obligate monogamy among humans, and in Chapter 5 and the section on aggression in this chapter, prolonged evolution for nuclear family social structure has been presented as a key feature of human evolution. This scenario leads to the expectation of minimal sex differences in behavior.

Nevertheless, this is an incomplete picture at best. Chapter 5 describes contextual variables that tend to break down nuclear family social structure. Increased economic production results in higher stakes in the game of sexual competition, as it results in individual males being able to provide economically for larger numbers of wives and offspring. In intermediate-level societies individual males are forced to integrate themselves with larger groups of kin, and polygyny is quite common. At even higher levels of social organization individual males can control very large numbers of females by mean of their control over immense productive resources. Such behavior by males can be very adaptive: Daly and Wilson (1983) note that the Sharifan emperor of Morocco, Moulay Ismail the Bloodthirsty, sired 888 offspring. Thus, human males must be seen as being pulled in two quite different directions as a result of our evolutionary history. Moreover, it is probable that natural selection in favor of pair bonding, monogamy, and high levels of paternal investment was never complete in humans, since males would always benefit from simultaneously adopting a strategy in which they invested heavily in the offspring of one female but attempted to mate as often as possible with other females without providing their offspring with a comparable level of support. This dual strategy would clearly be superior to a strategy of pure monogamy for a male, and when economic conditions changed so that intense polygyny was a possibility, males were predisposed by their evolutionary history to pursue this strategy.

Indeed, it is a consistent theme of the present treatment of altruism and family interactions that evolution has often resulted in contradictory pulls. In the area of sex differences in reproductive behavior and family relations generally, evolutionary theory is consistent with the existence of epigenetic rules that can bias individuals in ways that tend to generate conflict. For males there is the conflict between the epigenetic rules that facilitate pair bonding, monogamy, and high levels of paternal investment and those that facilitate sexual promiscuity, polygyny, and lack of paternal investment. For the theoretical reasons already given there is no reason to depict females as pulled both in the directions of monogamy and polyandry. However, females may have their own set of epigenetic rules that can result in conflict. For example, the epigenetic rules facilitating family cohesiveness might conflict with epigenetic rules biasing females to be attracted to males with large resource control. It is not a coincidence that the female sexual fantasy that is played out in the immensely popular romance novels involves an intense, reciprocated emotional attachment to a very wealthy male. The male sexual fantasy of unlimited sexual relationships with a large number of women is much more difficult to reconcile with the epigenetic rules tending toward pair bonding and high levels of paternal investment.

I have presented the evolutionary argument that females tend to be the choosers and discriminators in the evolutionary game. One aspect of female choice in humans may well have been to choose males who appeared to make an emotional commitment to the relationship. Females who were able to discriminate a true emotional commitment in a male would thereby choose a male who would be more likely to make a long-term commitment to her children. Thus, females are expected to attempt to minimize male attempts at low-investment parenting and this, in addition to the male's self-interest in high levels of paternal investment, could well be the evolutionary impetus for epigenetic rules biasing males toward affective bonding within the family.

As a further point on female discrimination and control of mating, it should be noted that these phenomena will be most clearly evident where males are unable to control females. Because of the asymmetrical levels of investment, it is always in the interest of the male to control as many females as possible, and indeed Kleiman (1981) notes that polygyny among mammals is associated with male ability to control large numbers of females. Among humans, female choice is most powerful where males are prevented from controlling large numbers of females. Historically, the rise of more advanced means of economic production and methods of political control have often resulted in males being able to control large numbers of females. Females have thus often become pawns in political battles among males, with little choice. Thus, the institution of bridewealth, described in Chapter 5, involves economic payments to the family of the woman, so that wealthy males could accumulate wives. As Hrdy (1981) points out, however, this arrangement is beneficial also to the female, since it results in the woman mating with a successful male. Similarly, by means of the institution of dowry a man was able to purchase inheritance rights for his grandchildren in another wealthy family, an arrangement also in the interests of the woman involved.

B. Predictions from Evolutionary Theory and Their Rationale

The evolutionary theory of sex differences is very powerful in explaining many of the patterns of human sexual behavior. Daly and Wilson (1983) and Symons (1979) summarize the great wealth of data on human behavior and its relation to evolutionary principles, including marriage patterns, sexual jealousy, the loss of estrus, female orgasm, female choice patterns, pornography, the double standard of sexual behavior, and the behavior of male and female homosexuals. The present section will describe several hypotheses related to human development that can be derived from this theoretical perspective, and the following section will describe various proximal mechanisms for these sex differences. As indicated in Chapters 1 and 5, evolutionary theory is an integral part of the ultimate explanation of human behavior patterns, but does not indicate the proximal mechanisms involved. These mechanisms may include hormonal differences due ultimately to genetic variation, other biological sources, or various types of purely cultural transmission.

Hypothesis 1. Males will tend to be more aggressive than females, their aggression will tend to be directed toward other males, and will be highest during their peak reproductive years. There are evolutionary reasons for both sexes to be aggressive, but under quite different circumstances. From an evolutionary perspective, females might be expected to be aggressive in obtaining resources, defending their young, and warding off unwanted male suitors. In the latter two cases, aggression is instrumental as a defensive technique, and in all three cases aggression is not a necessary technique. Females may achieve these evolutionary aims not by aggression, but by using the female power of choice to find male mates who will perform these functions. Males, on the other hand, are expected to use aggression as a means of controlling other males and in obtaining resources to attract and support females. The evolutionary theory of sex, particularly the possibility of a large variance in reproductive success for males compared to females, predicts that the stakes will always be much higher for males. Because all reproductively competent females are able to mate, whereas for males reproduction is a risky enterprise, interpersonal conflict between males thus tends to have much greater potential evolutionary consequences for males than for females. Aggression is thus always a possible means of increasing a male's fitness compared to other males, and in previous sections of this chapter the importance of aggression in male reproductive success has been discussed. As Wilson and Daly (1985) point out, female competition and aggression are expected to occur from an evolutionary perspective, "but there is a straightforward logic according to which males compete *more intensely*" (p. 60; italics in the original). Indeed, anyone reading about the competition among the wives in polygynous households, a competition focused on advancing the interests of themselves and their biological children, must be impressed with the female potential for aggression and competitiveness. The sex difference is one of degree, and there is no implication here that females are not expected to be aggressive.

The evidence that males are indeed more aggressive than females is overwhelming. This conclusion has been reached by every major review of the literature on sex differences, including Maccoby and Jacklin (1974), Parke and Slaby (1983), and Hyde (1986). This robust sex difference occurs "not just under a restricted set of conditions but in a wide variety of settings and using a wide variety of behavioral indexes" (Maccoby & Jacklin, 1974, p. 228). Thus, boys are more verbally and more physically aggressive (Maccoby & Jacklin, 1974; Parke & Slaby, 1983; Hyde, 1986), engage in more fantasy aggression, are more willing to shock and hurt others, engage in more imitative aggression, and score higher on hostility scales (Hyde, 1986). Moreover, boys are more aggressive in experimental and naturalistic research designs, in studies using direct observation, self-reports, and peer reports (Hyde, 1986). In her meta-analysis of studies of sex differences in aggression, Hyde (1986) notes that the magnitude of the observed difference between males and females is larger in naturalistic/correlational studies than in experimental studies, and suggests that this may be due to the spontaneous nature of aggression in the former type of study, while in the latter type the demand characteristics of the experiment or the presence of adult experimenters may result in lessening the difference between boys and girls. Boys are also more aggressive than girls in studies of non-Western cultures (Whiting & Edwards, 1973).

There is also evidence that most of boys' aggression is directed toward other boys. Smith and Green (1974) found that aggression was much higher in boy–boy dyads than in boy–girl dyads or girl–girl dyads, and McGrew (1972) found more aggression in dyads involving boys than in girl–girl dyads. Barrett (1979) found that boys were much more likely to retaliate with physical aggression against other boys than when provoked by girls, and in general found that both verbal and physical aggression was much more common if the target was another boy. These patterns are even more apparent when one examines violence among adolescents and young adults. Adolescent boys are five times as likely to be arrested for violent crime as are females (Gibbons, 1976; Johnson, 1979). Wilson and Daly (1985) found that males are much more likely than females to be both the perpetrator and the victim of homicide in their analysis of data from 1972 in Detroit. Thus, there were 348 homicides in which a male murdered a male, compared to only 16 in which a female murdered a female, a ratio of greater than 21 : 1. Males were almost five times more likely to murder another male than to murder a female, and one of the primary motives for males murdering females was sexual jealousy. Wilson and Daly (1985) also describe data indicating that "disputes of honor" are much more common among males and that serious injuries and homicide are often precipitated by status confrontations between males. Such behavior is rare among females.

The findings on age differences in aggression are not uniformly supportive of the prediction that the difference between boys and girls will increase as boys reach puberty and sexual competition intensifies. Hyde's (1986) meta-analysis of developmental sex differences in aggression finds evidence for a decline in aggression with age, but the basis for this conclusion is a sample of studies of college students, a highly nonrepresentative population. Other studies and reviews give overwhelming support to the idea that aggression and violence sharply increase around the onset of sexual maturation in both animals and humans. Thus, male mice exhibit a sharp increase in aggression around the time of sexual maturation (Cairns, MacCombie, & Hood, 1983). For humans, Wilson and Daly (1985) show census data indicating a steep rise in homicide for males during adolescence, which peaks in the mid-20s and declines thereafter, and Cairns (1986) notes that the most aggressive people in the United States are males aged 17–19 years. Even in a noncriminal sample, Cairns, Cairns, and Ferguson (1984) noted an increase among males in self-reported aggressive acts, whereas girls reported increases in social ostracism and alienation.

Finally, it should be pointed out that sex differences in general increase over development (Block, 1976) at least until the postreproductive years. This makes evolutionary sense, since it is at the point of sexual maturation that the sex-differentiated behavior discussed here becomes critical to successful adaptation. Weisfeld and Berger (1983) point to some lack of continuity between childhood and adolescence and placed these in an adaptationist context. The tendency for sex differences to increase as children approach adolescence may be an aspect of this phenomenon. The point of sexual maturation is a watershed age for an evolutionary theory, and the evidence points to an apex in sexual differentiation at this time. Interestingly, there is evidence that sex differences decline after the reproductive years. Reseach on aging has shown that older males tend to be less aggressive and more affiliative, while older females become more tolerant of their aggressive impulses (Gutmann, 1977). The developmental data thus conform remarkably to the predictions made by evolutionary theory.

Hypothesis 2. Males will tend to be risk takers and sensation seekers. The evolutionary scenario described above clearly suggests that for males mating is a relatively risky enterprise and suggests that males will tend to be the gamblers and risk takers. As Williams (1975) notes, "at every moment in the game of life the masculine sex is playing for higher stakes" (p. 138). Males are thus the unnecessary sex, and in the poker game of life this effectively ups the ante for every member of the sex. Every male is forced to play a game that much more approximates an all-or-none situation, whereas risky behavior for the female is relatively unlikely to have a very large payoff. For the female the best bet is to accept an average level of success.

These considerations lead to the predictions that males will be more impulsive than females (i.e., tend to ignore or underestimate the possible negative consequencs of their behavior) and seek higher levels of danger and excitement than will females. Since the mating prospects of males are highly precarious, males are expected to be relatively prone to exploring new environments. Thus, they would be expected to be innovators more often and to exhibit more curiosity toward the new. These characteristics are expected to be a general feature of male behavior, but one that is heightened in males whose present prospects are precarious and doubtful, whereas high-ranking members of an established social situation would be expected to be more prone to resist change and uphold the established order. Females, on the other hand, are expected to have much more confidence in their ability to mate successfully than males on the average, so that they are expected to generally gain less from adopting risky, untried behaviors. Finally, the age distribution of these behaviors should indicate a peak in late adolescence and early adulthood, corresponding to the age where sexual competition is most intense.

Zuckerman (1979) defines sensation seeking as "a trait defined by the need for varied, novel, and complex sensations and experiences and the willingness to take physical and social risks for the sake of such experiences" (p. 10). In Chapter 2, evidence was provided that sensation seeking (impulsivity) was a temperamental trait with a genetic basis and it was argued that individuals high on sensation seeking are highly sensitive to the reward value of these stimuli. There is considerable evidence for sex differences in sensation seeking that accord with the evolutionary predictions. Zuckerman (1979) reported that research has consistently shown that males score higher than females in sensation seeking. In Form IV of the Sensation Seeking Scale, research on late adolescents indicates that males are higher on the General scale and on all four subscales, including Thrill and Adventure Seeking (TAS), Disinhibition (Dis), Boredom Susceptibility (BS), and Experience Seeking (ES). An individual high on the TAS subscale endorses items such as "I enjoy many of the rides in amusement parks," "I often wish I could be a mountain climber," and "I would like to try parachute jumping." Individuals high on the Dis subscale endorse items such as "I like to gamble," "I like 'wild' uninhibited parties," "It is normal to get bored after a time with the same sexual partner," "Most adultery happens because of sheer boredom," "Keeping the drinks full is the key to a good party," and "Almost everything enjoyable is either illegal or immoral." Individuals high on the ES subscale endorse items such as "I have tried marijuana or I would like to" and ''I would like to travel to strange, out of the way places like the upper Amazon or Antarctica.'' Finally, individuals high on the BS subscale endorse items such as ''Although sometimes it is necessary, I usually dislike routine kinds of work'' and ''I would have preferred living in the unsettled days of our history'' (Zuckerman, 1979, pp. 388–394).

Clearly, the higher endorsement of these items and other similar items by males is consistent with the evolutionary predictions. Particularly interesting is the finding that the sex differences, while impressive for all the subscales, are most robust for the Dis subscale, which taps promiscuous sexual behavior. Females are generally expected to take fewer risks than males, but sexual behavior is expected to be an area where females exercise extremely close scrutiny and discrimination, so that uninhibited sexual behavior is particularly likely to show the effects of sexual selection.

It should also be noted that the Sensation Seeking Scale is associated with social dominance and aggression. Ozeran (1973, as cited in Zuckerman, 1979) found that high sensation seekers more frequently began conversations, spoke more, and became group leaders more often, and Zuckerman (1979) reports that high sensation seekers talked more and dominated the situation when paired with low sensation seekers in a study of behavior in close confinement. Zuckerman (1983) also reports that aggression is correlated with the Dis subscale. This pattern of correlations is consistent with the pattern of sex differences described above and suggests an intimate connection relating social dominance, aggression, and sensation seeking, perhaps indicative of a common mechanism.

Other evidence consistent with the idea that males are greater risk takers and sensation seekers comes from studies of younger children. Several cross-cultural studies of sex differences in approach–withdrawal have found that males tend to approach more than females (Carey & McDevitt, 1978; Hsu, Soong, Stigler, Hong, & Liang, 1981; Maziade, Boudreault, Thivierge, Caperaa, & Cote, 1984). In addition, there is evidence that girls tend to be higher on behavioral inhibition than boys (Rothbart, in press-a). Rothbart notes that several studies have shown that girls are more compliant than boys and suggests that sex differences in aggressive behavior may be in part due to boys' relative inability to inhibit reward-directed behavior. Girls also tend to be more fearful than boys (Buss & Plomin, 1984; Rothbart, in press-a), suggestive of higher levels of behavioral inhibition in girls than boys. These results fit well with the theory of temperament presented in Chapter 2 and the evidence on sex differences in aggression, conduct disorder, and hyperactivity described in this chapter. The theory of temperament described in Chapter 2, like that of Rothbart (in press-a), proposes two independent dimensions of approach (sensation-seeking impulsivity and behavioral inhibition). The evidence presented here indicates that boys are higher on the former and lower on the latter than girls—results highly congruent with the evolutionary theory of sex.

Wilson and Daly (1985) also discuss the phenomenon of risk taking, including drug use, gambling, and group versus individual decision-making, from an evolutionary perspective, noting particularly the relatively high levels of these behaviors in young males. They also note the increased level of mortality in young males that occurs due to these risk-taking behaviors. Accidental death is more common among males throughout life, but the difference peaks in late adolescence at a ratio of over 4 : 1. Death in motor vehicle accidents is also much higher among males than among females, and this difference is due to speeding and reckless driving. Interestingly, male drivers take more risks when other males are present than with females or alone (Jackson & Gray, 1976), consistent with the idea that risky behavior confers high prestige within male groups.

Zuckerman (1979) finds that males are more impulsive than females, a view that agrees with that of Block (1976) based on a review of the developmental literature. Block also finds evidence that boys are more dominant, have a stronger self concept, and are more curious, exploratory, and active, while girls are more fearful, more susceptible to anxiety, and maintain greater proximity to their friends. In terms of the discussion of temperament in Chapter 2, females are thus prone to caution, behavioral inhibition, and tense arousal in the presence of novelty and danger, while males are prone to impulsivity and energetic arousal.

Another aspect of sex differences in sensation seeking that is highly relevant to social development is the finding that males engage in much higher levels of rough and tumble play than do females with their parents and peers. Thus, fathers engage in more intense physical games with their sons than with their daughters (MacDonald & Parke, 1984, 1986; Parke & Suomi, 1982) and Blurton Jones (1972) and DiPietro (1981) showed that boys engage in rough and tumble play much more frequently than do girls. Whiting and Edwards (1974) found this sex difference in a cross-cultural sample, and several studies of other primate species have found this sex difference as well (Goy, 1966; Harlow & Lauersdorf, 1974; Mitchell, 1979). Indeed, Mitchell (1981) comments that this sex difference becomes increasingly robust as one ascends the primate evolutionary ladder, and becomes quite apparent in the Old World monkeys and apes. Males of these species "play more frequently, initiate more play, play rougher, and play longer than do females" (p. 17). As Blurton Jones (1972) and DiPietro (1981) note regarding children, rough and tumble play is quite different from aggression in these animals, although such play may function as a form of practice for aggression (see Chapter 3).

As described in Chapter 3, rough and tumble play involves very high levels of stimulation, and the findings that boys engage in these behaviors more than girls is consistent with the general sex difference in which males seek out higher levels of stimulation than do females. Zuckerman (1979) also notes that "Play in animals and children is considered to be an expression of the sensation-seeking trait" (p. 152), and states that high-sensation seekers "are assumed to have high information (change of input) needs," and lows to have an "intolerance for ambiguity" (p. 152). Physical play is just one aspect of the desire for high-stimulus environments characteristic of boys and the discussion of temperament in Chapter 2 suggests that this is because boys are highly sensitive to the reward value of such stimulation. Consistent with these differences, advertisers who attempt to appeal to boys make commercials with more variation in scenes, rapid cuts, loud music, and more sound effects than when attempting to appeal to girls (Welch, Huston-Stein, Wright, & Plehal, 1979).

There is also evidence that the clinical categories of conduct disorder and hyperactivity, which are overwhelmingly male (Rutter & Garmezy, 1983), are characterized by very high levels of sensation seeking. As indicated in the section on aggression in this chapter and Chapter 3, both hyperactivity and conduct disorder are characterized by abnormal levels of sensation seeking and are strongly associated with aggression.

Another biological basis of the greater risk-taking behavior of males is that males are the less buffered sex. Data summarized by Juraska (1986) indicate that males are more vulnerable throughout development and more susceptible to developmental disorders such as autism, dyslexia, stuttering, seizures, and cerebral palsy. The behavior of males shows more variability than that of females, and males are more often represented on both the high and low extremes of distributions such as IQ and mathematical ability. Stress has more negative effects on males, including miscarriage, separation from caretakers, the effect of divorce, and father absence.

In addition to the human data, Juraska (1986) summarizes literature from animal studies indicating that the phenomenon of greater plasticity in males exists in other mammalian species as well. Indeed, the evolutionary theory of sex would predict that such differences would be greatest in species that were most highly sexually dimorphic. Animal studies have shown that males are more susceptible to the effects of malnutrition, environmental enrichment or stress, isolation rearing, and parity of mother. Moreover, it would appear that the behaviors affected are varied and strongly related to adaptation, and include such behaviors as mating behavior, response to stress, learning, play behavior, self-aggression, exploration of novel environments, and appropriate social behavior. Females are indeed the more buffered sex.

These data show with great clarity that plasticity is indeed a two-edged sword (see Chapter 1). It is as if the biology of males is geared to more openness to environmental influences, good as well as bad, whereas the safer strategy of buffering is pursued by females. Males also develop more slowly and achieve adult levels of brain weight at a later age. In terms of the age-graded theory of plasticity discussed in Chapters 1 and 4, they are thus expected to be more open to experience at later ages. But to be open to the environment is to be open to good as well as bad influences, and clearly represents a more risky developmental strategy.

Hypothesis 3. Males will be more concerned with their status relative to other males whereas females will be concerned with their status relative to other females. Male groups will thus be more hierarchical and these status differences will be of more importance to males than females. Moreover, male peer groups will tend to be more extensive than female groups. The evolutionary logic sketched above makes it clear that for males the greatest threat necessarily comes from other males. The control of other males and access to resources, including females, is thus much more likely to be a male concern than a female one. The data from Savin-Williams (1987), described above, clearly conform well to this prediction. While male adolescent peer groups tend to be hierarchical and based at least partly on agonistic conflict, Savin-Williams questions whether female adolescents even have a real dominance hierarchy. Dominant females tend to be socioemotional resources for the other members of the group, whereas dominant males are disproportionately involved in decision making and resource apportionment.

Hypothesis 4. Girls will be more able to develop close, intimate confiding relationships with a variety of others, while such relationships among males will tend to be confined to a relationship with a female, usually the wife. As indicated above, the theory of sex differences implies that relationships among males are much more likely to be hierarchical, competitive, and concerned with resource acquisition and distribution. Given the overriding importance of such issues, the affective, self-disclosure side of friendship is expected to be less salient among males and, if such relationships occur at all, they are much more likely to occur between a male and a female, especially a spouse.

This theoretical perspective gives a very straightforward interpretation of the literature on sex differences in intimacy and self-disclosure described in the section on peer relationships above. The point there is not so much that males fail to have such relationships, but that they tend to occur with females rather than with other males. The data of Savin-Williams (1987), described above, is also consistent with this prediction, since he found that high-ranking females tend to be affective resources for other females. There is presumably an important developmental shift in intimacy. An evolutionary theory is consistent with the idea that at puberty there is an increasing role for the competitive, resource acquisition and distribution function of relationships among males and a lowering of the intimate, confiding nature of these relationships. At puberty and increasingly thereafter males tend to turn to females for intimate, self-disclosing relationships. There is no reason why males could not perform such a function, especially if the males were not in a competitive relationship to one another, but the status-graded nature of male groups makes it less likely that this will be the case.

Hypothesis 5. Females will be characterized by epigenetic rules that facilitate appropriate mate choice. One aspect of these rules is hypothesized to be affective relationships with the opposite sex; that is, affective relationships will be more important to female adolescents as a motivator for sexual relationships than for males. The evolutionary logic presented above suggests that females will develop epigenetic rules that aid in discriminating males who will make a major investment in parenting. Males, on the other hand, are expected to be opportunistic maters with less of a bias toward monogamous emotional involvement. Loving and being loved appear to function in this manner in regulating human courtship patterns, and the prediction is that females will be more sensitive than males to the rewards of giving and receiving love, while males will be more sensitive to erotic stimuli that is divorced from these affective connotations.

Hypothesis 5 is amply supported by empirical data. Weisfeld and Billings (1988) summarize data on adolescence indicating that girls devote much time to assessing males and attempt to attract them in a subtle, nonpromiscuous manner. Chastity in a female is a sign to a prospective male that he could be confident in his paternity, so that sexual restraint in females is predicted. Thus, females are less likely to brag about their sexual activity, their discussions often focusing on the need to assuage guilt.

Consistent with these findings, I have already noted that females score much lower than males on the Disinhibition subscale of Zuckerman's (1979) Sensation Seeking Scale. Moreover, females tend generally to have more conservative attitudes regarding premarital sex, the importance of love in a sexual relationship, avoidance of promiscuity, and respect for parental wishes: "For most girls, the overall relationship with the individual boy whom she loves—the extent to which the relationship is characterized by trust, concern, and a mutual sharing of life experiences—takes precedence over specific sexual release. Consequently, control of impulses is likely to constitute a considerably less urgent problem for girls" (Douvan & Adelson, 1966, p. 635). This dramatic sex difference remains even in the age of sexual permissiveness. For example, among American college freshmen in 1980, two-thirds of the males compared to only one-third of the females endorsed the statement "Sex is okay if people like each other" (Astin, 1981).

Predictably, differences in endorsement of premarital sex diminish if the proviso is added that the partners have a deep involvement (Norman & Harris, 1981). As another indication of this phenomenon, recently Haas (1979) found that among adolescents aged

15 to 18 years, 68% of the girls agreed that "you have to be romantically involved with a girl (boy) before you have sexual contact with her (him), compared to only 41% for the boys." Miller and Simon conclude:

> The investment of erotic meaning in both explicitly sexual and nonsexual symbols appears to be contingent on the emotional context. The two genders evaluate the meaning of potentially erotic symbols using distinctive sets of criteria. For males, the explicitly sexual is endowed with erotic meaning regardless of the emotional context. For females, the emotional context is endowed with erotic meaning without regard for the presence or absence of explicitly sexual symbols. (Miller & Simon, 1980, p. 403)

Finally, adolescent boys are much more likely than girls to fantasize about sexual activity with strangers (79% versus 22%) (Miller & Simon, 1980). In some ways these findings testify to the resilience of these epigenetic rules in the face of considerable media, academic, and peer pressure to adopt more permissive attitudes toward sex.

The findings indicating a greater importance of affective aspects of sexual relationships for females do not imply that this is the only issue of importance. Weisfeld and Billings (1988) note that girls also take into account the earning prospects of potential mates and value these more highly as they approach marriage, so that such attributes as physical attractiveness and athletic ability are of relatively less importance. This of course makes excellent evolutionary sense, since the acquisition of resources is of vital importance for a successful marriage. In Chapter 9, the data of Elder (1974) showing the stresses on marriage resulting from lack of resources are discussed. For a girl, the ideal marriage partner is someone with whom she can have a romantic emotional relationship, someone who can provide a high level of material resources, and someone who is physically attractive. Such male figures are the very essence of the romance novel genre which is so attractive to females in our society.

Hypothesis 6. Parental investment patterns will differ depending on the sex of the child, and this difference will be most pronounced in societies with large sex differences in the variance in reproductive success. Trivers and Willard (1973) used basic evolutionary logic to conclude that in species where males could achieve much higher levels of reproductive success than females, parents who are in good condition should preferentially invest more in male children than in female children, while parents in poor condition should be more inclined to invest in daughters. Translated to human terms, this hypothesis predicts that in societies with high levels of sexual competition (high polygyny possible), wealthy parents should invest more in sons than in daughters. If there is little prospect that a son could attain wealth and a high level of polygyny, parents would be better off investing in daughters. In Chapter 5, data on discriminative parenting that supports these predictions were discussed.

Another aspect of parental investment that has involved discrimination between the sexes is the practice of infanticide. Dickemann (1979, 1981) notes the tendency for high levels of female infanticide in preindustrial Old World stratified societies and places these data in evolutionary perspective. She notes that these stratified societies are characterized by intense levels of sexual competition among the males (see also Chapter 5) and an increasing benefit of female marriage to high-status males. In such societies there is an excess of females to the total number of high-status males and families compete by means of the institution of the dowry for female access to high-status males. Wives whose position was purchased for them by means of a dowry could expect to bequeath inheritance rights to their children, whereas the children of lower ranking wives and concubines would inherit much less or nothing at all. She notes that in situations of such intense reproductive competition raising female offspring becomes a high-risk strategy, since there are fewer and fewer higher status males and an excess of females. Female infanticide thus becomes a common practice in these societies.

Less extreme forms of parental discrimination in the allocation of resources to children have been historically quite common. In Chapter 5 it was noted that parents discriminate between children in their patterns of investment and that sex is often an important criterion of discrimination. Illustrations of this phenomena are the practices of primogeniture, the dowry, and contemporary inheritance patterns. Parents also provide more than economic resources to their children, however. Betzig and Turke (1986) showed that among the Ifaluk, a contemporary group living on a Pacific archipelago, there are patterns of differential psychological investment in the two sexes. Within this group, wealthy, high-status males have relatively high reproductive success compared to men who lack wealth or status. It was found that parents, and especially fathers, of high-status families tended to associate more with sons than with daughters, while the reverse was the case for the low-status, low-wealth group.

The following four hypotheses concern the differential socialization of the two sexes:

Hypothesis 7a. Parents will more closely supervise and monitor the sexual behavior of their daughters than that of their sons. Parents are expected to monitor the behavior of their daughters because there is a tendency for males to make attempts at low-investment parenting at the expense of females. These attempts can be countered by monitoring behavior on the part of the parent and are expected to be most intense as a girl approaches the age of reproductive competence. In addition, confidence in paternity is an important issue in male–female relationships, so that virginity is a prized commodity, especially in highly sexually competitive societies. By monitoring and secluding females, families are able to ensure the virginity of daughters.

There is overwhelming evidence both within contemporary Western societies and cross-culturally and historically that the behavior of women and girls is monitored by adult relatives much more closely than is the behavior of boys and men. This is also the case with rhesus monkeys (Mitchell, 1968). In the discussion of the reproductive rituals of adolescence in Chapter 5 evidence was presented that one of the main functions of fathers and other male relatives is to monitor the sexual behavior of daughters and thereby ensure an optimal marriage. In societies with low means of production this is accomplished by providing a ceremony that essentially buys the good will of the community toward the father and enlists cooperation to ensure an appropriate marriage and discourage seduction. In more advanced societies, kin groups and elaborate methods of social control have been practiced to monitor the behavior of girls (Paige & Paige, 1983). An excellent case study is the discussion by Dickemann (1981) of the practice of female claustration and veiling in Arab Muslim cultures. Dickemann notes that "the *seclusion* of females is in fact the *exclusion* of males" (p. 418). Sexual segregation is virtually complete in many such societies, and similar practices occurred in traditional Japanese, Chinese, and Indian societies:

> (C)laustration is supported by customary and legal sanctions: penalties for the loss of virginity may be inability to find a husband, rejection by the suitor, or even murder of the girl or her violator by her kinsmen; adulterous wives may suffer similar penalties. Murder of the violated

woman or her violator is generally treated with less severity in law than are other homicides, and often with approval in fact. This is the "crime of honor," a concept recognized throughout the Mediterranean basin. (Dickemann, 1981, pp. 418–419)

In conformity with the hypothesis regarding the likely age trends for monitoring female behavior, Dickemann also provides evidence that these practices of sexual segregation and monitoring are much less pervasive for young girls. (Interestingly, there is evidence that postmenopausal women are also less closely monitored.) Practices of sexual segregation and monitoring occur prior to or at puberty, but reach their height with the ritual veiling of the wedding. The monitoring of women and girls also is highest in the upper classes of society. For example, Cooper notes:

There is a saying [in Northern India] that you can tell the degree of a family's aristocracy by the height of the windows in the home. The higher the rank, the smaller and higher are the windows and the more secluded the women. An ordinary lady may walk in the garden and hear the birds sing and see the flowers. The higher grade lady may only look at them from her windows, and if she is a very great lady indeed, this even is forbidden her, as the windows are high up near the ceiling, merely slits in the wall for the lighting and ventilation of the room. (Cooper, 1915, p. 121, quoted in Dickemann, 1981, p. 419)

There is evidence from contemporary societies that parents monitor the behavior of daughters more than that of sons after early childhood and there is some suggestion that this sex difference increases at later ages. Newson and Newson (1976) found that sex differences in parental restrictiveness first emerged at age 7 years, with daughters receiving more "chaperonage." The authors make it clear that it is the whereabouts of the girl and whether she will have an adult present that are of paramount importance, not the ability to decide where to go. Girls play closer to home, are more often picked up at school, and generally have more restrictive rules about where they can go when away from home. Block (1978) also reports that parents are more concerned about the whereabouts of daughters than of sons. In discussing the Newson and Newson study, Maccoby and Jacklin (1974) suggest that this increased interest in chaperonage presages the monitoring of adolescent girls by their parents. By beginning these practices well prior to adolescence, parents may well internalize the attitude within girls that adult monitoring of their activities is a natural part of growing up so that the increased surveillance of adolescence is accepted by the girls. Dickemann (1981) notes that upper-class families especially were motivated to provide assurance of female chastity to prospective mates, since they attempted to marry these girls into good families. Wealthier families therefore tended to engage in restrictive practices for girls well before menarche.

Hypothesis 7b. Parents will attempt to facilitate the positive social reward system more in girls than in boys by socializing girls with more warmth and affection. This socialization hypothesis follows because, as indicated above, sensitivity to the social rewards of affection is hypothesized to be an epigenetic rule that facilitates mate discrimination in females. A second and perhaps even more important evolutionary reason for supposing that females will be socialized in a manner that makes them more sensitive to the reward value of affection is due to the role of affection in nurturance. Clearly one aspect of the mammalian female's parental investment involves a disproportionate responsibility for the physical and psychological nurturance of the young after birth. From a theoretical perspective these behaviors involve adaptive imbalances of resource flow, and these imbalances are facilitated by epigenetic rules that bias mothers toward the development of positive affective interactions with offspring (see Chapters 4 and 8). In accord with this perspective, the socialization of girls (and boys) with warmth is expected to be conducive to strong adult male–female affective attachments, monogamy, relative lack of aggression, and high level of paternal investment when they become adults.

Mitchell (1968) found that rhesus macaque mothers embrace and clasp their daughters more often than they do their sons and generally treat them less aversively (see below). Moreover, Mitchell and Brandt (1975) summarize data indicating that this pattern is common among a variety of primate species. In reviewing the ethnographic literature from a sample of 33 preliterate cultures, Barry, Bacon, and Child (1957) found that 82% socialized girls with more nurturance, none showed the reverse bias, and 18% showed no evidence of sex differences. No differences were reported for infancy, a pattern replicated by later research (Maccoby & Jacklin, 1974; Block, 1978). In discussing the data reviewed by Maccoby and Jacklin (1974), Block (1978) finds a tendency for father–daughter relationships to be characterized by more warmth than father–son relationships. In a study of parenting practices in the United States and five northern European countries, Block (1978) found that parent reports of practices with children aged 3 to 18 years as well as retrospective reports of young adults on the practices of their parents indicated that females exceeded males in receiving warmth, affection, and physical closeness. The socialization emphasis was on developing and maintaining close interpersonal relationships. Sex differences in socialization increased with development, reaching an apex in the high school years, and were consistenly present independent of socioeconomic level, education level, and cultural origin.

Regarding the effects of high levels of parental warmth on boys, the cross-cultural literature on familial affective relationships is consistent with the idea that these behaviors would facilitate monogamy and relative lack of aggressiveness in males (see Chapter 5 and section on aggression in this chapter). Such males would be more sensitive to the affective rewards of close personal relationships that would facilitate the bonding process. The attachment theory of Bowlby is also consistent with this perspective. In this view, boys (or girls) who are treated in a warm, loving manner as infants and children would be securely attached and would be more likely to form emotionally bonded relationships as adults. Ricks (1985) reviewed evidence consistent with this hypothesis, and, although the evidence tends to come from studies of women, there is no reason to suppose that similar results would not also be found for boys. Thus, Frommer and O'Shea (1973a,b) found that mothers who were poor parents and had poor marital relationships tended to have been separated from their parents prior to age 11 years. Hall, Pawlby, and Wolkind (1979) found that women from families disrupted by divorce, death, or separation were less likely to be warm, affectionate mothers and were more likely to be teenage mothers. Quinton and Rutter (1986) found that institution-reared women tended to have poor relationships with their partners and tended to be unmarried more often. Finally, Ricks (1985) found that mothers of secure babies tended to recall more acceptance as babies by their own mothers. These data are highly congruent with the data on the importance of early attachment experience on later behavior reviewed in Chapter 4.

Hypothesis 7c. In conformity with the discussion of the proximal mechanisms underlying the development of aggression, the socialization of boys in sexually competitive societies will more often be characterized by parental provision of aversive events than will the socialization of girls. The evolutionary theory presented above suggests that the socialization of males will be more conducive to the development of aggression, that is, in addition to less emphasis on the positive social reward system, there will be greater provision of aversive events during development.

There is considerable evidence in favor of this hypothesis. Mitchell (1968; see also Mitchell & Brandt, 1975) found that mother rhesus monkeys more often bit their sons than their daughters and mother–son interactions were generally rougher than mother–daughter interactions. Mitchell, Arling, and Moller (1967) reported that mothers punish males more than females and that the more punishing mothers have more aggressive offspring. Chamove, Harlow, and Mitchell (1967) also found that brutal mothering resulted in highly aggressive offspring. Among humans some of the best evidence for the provision of aversive events during the development of males comes from the intermediate-level societies characterized by sexual competition, aggression, and familial relationships typified by low warmth and high levels of hostility (see also MacDonald, 1987a, Chapter 5, and section on aggression in this chapter). Male initiation ceremonies tend to be quite hostile in these societies, often involving brutal hazing and severe beatings, practices that result in an "affective social response" (Young, 1962). The circumcision rites characteristic of many male initiation rites are also quite painful and dangerous to the child (Paige & Paige, 1981). Brutal rites of passage are also characteristic of some economically advanced societies. For example, ancient Sparta was known for a number of brutal tests of boys, some of which involved flogging (see also Chapter 9). In the present perspective the fact that Sparta was intensively militaristic is no surprise, and the negative affective character of the male rites in all of these societies contrasts strongly with the practices regarding females in these societies. As indicated in Chapter 5 and above, rather than subject girls to similarly harsh treatment, the tendency is to provide increasing strictures on the movement of girls and for increased monitoring of their behavior around puberty. Pubertal ceremonies tend to be absent.

There is some evidence that boys in contemporary society are socialized more aversively than girls. Thus, Block (1978) in her summary of data from six industrial societies reports that boys are subjected to more suppressed anger than girls, and are threatened more often with punishment and encouraged to suppress their emotions. Fathers are more authoritarian with boys, are strict and firm, believe in physical punishment, and are intolerant of aggression directed toward them by their sons. It was also noted in the section on the development of aggression that parents of aggressive children more often subject these children to aversive disciplinary practices. Since boys are much more likely to be aggressive than are girls, it may well be that this style of socialization is more common among boys.

Hypothesis 7d. Boys will be socialized in a manner that emphasizes the importance of competition and achievement striving. This hypothesis follows because, since evolution is a higher stakes game for boys, the control and acquisition of resources are expected to be of far more importance to boys. For girls the dynamics of sexual competition yield the expectation that they will select boys with good prospects of controlling resources; this logic implies that boys must seek to control resources.

Consistent with this prediction, Block (1978) reports that boys in industrial societies are socialized to be competitive and achievement-oriented to a greater extent than are girls. These differences hold up independent of socioeconomic level, education level, cultural origins, and the health status and age levels of children. Similarly Barry *et al.*

(1957) in their cross-cultural study of sex differences in child rearing found that socialization for achievement and self-reliance was much more characteristic of boys than of girls.

Hypothesis 8. Sex differences in the development and socialization of behavior generally will be greater in cultures with higher levels of sexual competition. The evolutionary logic described above predicts that one ultimate-level source for cross-cultural variation in the degree of sex differences is the level of sexual competition in the society and this will be reflected in the degree of economic production and the extent to which there are egalitarian controls on human sexual behavior. High levels of sexual competition typified by high levels of polygyny and enforced bachelorhood for some males should intensify the general expectation of sex differences in behavior. This prediction is in accord with the animal literature indicating that male–female morphological and behavioral differences are greatest where intramale sexual competition is most intense (see, e.g., Wilson, 1975). Translated into an hypothesis about human society, it predicts that male–female differences will be greatest in cultures characterized by polygyny and least in societies characterized by monogamy.

There is again ample evidence to support these predictions. Indeed, feminists (e.g., Blumberg, 1978), contemplating the pervasiveness of sex differences in human societies, have often noted this pattern and struggled to avoid an interpretation that included any consideration of evolutionary biology. Thus, in the most primitive human societies male–female relationships are more egalitarian and the division of labor involves less of a male–female status difference than in more economically advanced societies. Since high levels of aggression in the males are unnecessary and altruism more adaptive (see section on aggression, this chapter, and Chapter 8), there are fewer sex differences in the socialization process, with more emphasis in both sexes on warm, accepting parent–child interactions. Supporting these predictions, the report by Barry *et al.* (1957) on cross-cultural patterns in sex differences in socialization supports the present hypothesis by showing that there are greater sex differences in socialization patterns as a function of increased economic production and polygyny. Barry *et al.* find strong correlations between large sex differences in socialization with the presence of grain rather than root crops and with the presence of polygyny and extended family social organization rather than monogamy and nuclear family social organization. Thus, the patterns of sex differences in socialization stressed above (i.e., those related to nurturance, self-reliance, and achievement) are predictably strongest where sexual competition is most intense.

In traditional societies at the highest level of economic production in which there are no egalitarian social controls on male reproductive success we expect the apex of the cultural imposition of sex differences, and this seems to be the case. Dickemann (1981) describes the social structures of these societies as consisting of two almost completely different worlds for men and women. Women, except for the very poor, were (and still are in many areas) almost completely hidden, veiled, and cloistered from public view. Women in many of these societies were not seen at all in public places, and often wealthy women would never leave their homes at all except for occasional visits to temples or palaces under military escort. In classical China for many centuries the feet of women were bound so that as adults they could scarcely walk and had to be carried for all but the shortest distances. Interestingly, Dickemann (1981) notes that these practices were far less intense in Europe and especially in northern Europe. I have noted the historical importance of social controls on reproductive success in Europe (see Chapter 5) and, as expected, these social controls result in less intense forms of sexual segregation and differential treatment of women. Dickemann also notes that southern Europe continued the practices of slavery and concubinage much longer than the north, suggesting that within Europe the status of women was intimately associated with the level of sexual competition among males.

Before proceeding to a discussion of the mechanisms underlying this elaborate set of phenomena, we might pause to consider the possible effects of recent trends in our own society. From an evolutionary perspective it is not surprising that the movement for greater rights for women has occurred in a society with elaborate social controls on sexual competition among males, controls that result in the cultural imposition of monogamy and a strong damper on sexual competition. From an evolutionary perspective these social controls are a necessary condition for female emancipation. Consistent with this, the general finding of an association between sexual competition and differential treatment of women, one aspect of feminism has been to deemphasize sex differences by advocating androgyny and attempting to "desexualize" society by, for example, opposing pornography and the idea of separate male and female roles. A goal has been for egalitarian sexual relationships within marriage as seen by more equal roles in decision making, contribution to household tasks, child rearing, and in obtaining economic resources for the family.

Part of this program has clearly involved the advocacy of an elaborate series of social controls on behavior that facilitate these goals by giving preferential treatment to women in the job market, enjoining sexual harassment, etc. As I have indicated throughout, social controls have been very effective ways of altering human behavior throughout history and a biological theory predicts that social controls are necessary to produce egalitarian intra- (among males) and intersexual relationships. That is, a biological theory predicts that without social controls on sexual relationships there will be a strong tendency for males to compete with other males for access to young, fertile females and that wealthy males will be most successful in this endeavor. To the extent that there are differences in wealth in the society, it is expected that without social controls there will be large differences in access to this resource. Indeed, a biological theory predicts that, if females have freedom of choice, they will choose such wealthy, powerful males as mates and lovers, so that the ensuing large differences in male success will be due at least as much to female behavior as to male behavior. Weisfeld and Billings (1988) note that indeed females in industrial societies, although attracted to physical attractiveness and athletic ability in high school, tend to choose males who have high earning prospects as marriage partners.

Although feminists have seen the necessity for social controls on some aspects of behavior, they have generally not been in the forefront of movements attempting to restrict sexual competition among males. (These latter movements have historically been led and continue to be led by traditional Christian sects.) Indeed, recent developments have largely deregulated sexual behavior, so that divorce is much more easily obtained (see Chapter 5) and individual wealthy and powerful males (e.g., movie stars) are able to have extensive sexual relationships and/or serial polygyny with large numbers of young females. In this unregulated sexual world it is expected that older females will be increasingly rejected as mates by men and competition for younger women will be intensified, with the result that older women will be increasingly found to be forced to live alone or with their children but without their children's father, often under straitened economic circumstances (see Chapter 5). It is also predicted that overall reproduction will decline if sexual relationships are deregulated because women will be less willing to commit themselves to reproduction if there is a strong prospect of later divorce in which they would suffer more economically with the presence of children. The biological theory predicts that eventually a coalition of older females and less wealthy males will attempt to reinstate social controls on sexual behavior, that is, egalitarian social controls that are in their interest, although many younger females would also be expected to advocate such controls because they would provide more of a guarantee of long-term investment in children. One cannot easily change the different reproductive strategies that characterize the two sexes, but there is every reason to suppose that social controls are able to have a profound influence on these patterns.

C. Proximal Mechanisms in the Development of Sex Differences

1. Biological Sources of Sex Differences in Behavior

In 1974 Maccoby and Jacklin gave several reasons for believing that biological factors predispose males to be more aggressive than females:

> (1) Males are more aggressive than females in all human societies for which evidence is available. (2) The sex differences are found early in life, at a time when there is no evidence that differential socialization has been brought to bear by adults to "shape" aggression differently in the two sexes. . . (3) Similar sex differences are found in man and subhuman primates. (4) Aggression is related to levels of sex hormones, and can be changed by experimental administrations of these hormones." (Maccoby & Jacklin, 1974, pp. 242–243)

These reasons remain valid today. In the following, aspects of two (nonindependent) biological sources of variation in sex differences will be discussed, temperament and the role of hormones.

In Chapter 2, a theory of temperament was presented that described a group of self-regulatory aspects of temperament. Chief among the temperamental traits that show strong sex differences is that of sensation seeking, and I have proposed that sex differences in this trait are related to sex differences in aggression, sexual behavior, Zuckerman's (1979) "disinhibition," novelty preference, impulsivity, social dominance, and risk taking. In addition, it was suggested in Chapter 2 that the positive social reward system is a third dimension of temperament, which encompasses a variety of other social reinforcers, including empathy and the rewards of loving and being loved. Thus, the sex differences in sensitivity to positive social reward may quite possibly be due in part to genetic variation conceived as operating on the sensitivity to these social rewards. In Chapter 2, however, it was argued that environmental variation that elaborates the positive social reward system is also crucial.

There is evidence that the sex difference in sensation seeking and impulsivity is mediated by variation in brain biochemicals and testosterone production. Zuckerman (1983) reviews evidence showing a negative correlation between monoamine oxidase (MAO) and sensation seeking (see also Chapter 2) and that females have higher levels of MAO at all ages than males. Zuckerman notes that these results suggest that sensation seeking is affected by the levels of catecholamines in the brain, since the physiological function of MAO is to degrade monoamine neurotransitters.

Zuckerman (1983) also provides evidence that variation in testosterone is positively correlated with sensation seeking and differs between the sexes. In addition, both testosterone levels and sensation seeking decline with age, and animal studies show that castration, which decreases testosterone levels, increases MAO levels. Testosterone is a pharmacological antagonist of MAO, and Zuckerman proposes that relatively high levels of testosterone in males results in lowering MAO, which in turn results in increased sensitivity of the monoamine reward systems underlying sensation-seeking behaviors.

The role of gonadal hormones as the ultimate biological basis of sex differences has received a vast amount of attention at both the human level and the subhuman level. Androgens administered during sensitive periods to females or castrated male subhuman animals inhibit female behavior and result in increased levels of male sexual and nonsexual behavior, indicating an effect on brain organization, as well as male genital morphology. Similar results have been found in the rat (Barraclough & Gorski, 1961), guinea pig (Phoenix, Goy, Gerall, & Young, 1959), mouse (Edwards, 1968), hamster (Paup, Coniglio, & Clemens (1972), rabbit (Beyer, de la Torre, Larsson, & Perez-Palacio, 1975), dog (Beach, 1975), rhesus monkey (Goy, 1970), and ferret (Baum, 1987). There is substantial variation in the timing of the sensitive periods, with those of rhesus monkeys and guinea pigs occurring entirely prenatally and those of the rat and ferret extending beyond the time of birth.

A great deal of work has been performed on the rhesus monkey and the review by Mitchell (1979) will be briefly summarized here. The sensitive period for masculinization occurs between the 46th and 73rd days of pregnancy. If a female fetus is given androgens during this period it will be born with a graded mixture of male and female morphological and behavioral characteristics, depending on the dosage of androgen and its timing. These animals are termed pseudohermaphrodites and show intermediate levels of male sex-typed behaviors, such as rough and tumble play, social threat, and the double-foot-clasp mount essential for male reproductive behavior. These differences in behavior are due to hormonal differences occurring prenatally during the sensitive period, not to androgens occurring after the second trimester of prenatal development or postnatally prior to puberty. If males are castrated after birth they show typical male behavior during the juvenile period, but at puberty they do not show aggression, yawning, or erections as frequently as normal males. The results then implicate two distinct periods during which circulating androgens affect behavior in the rhesus: prenatally and during puberty and adulthood.

Mitchell (1979) summarizes data indicating that humans are less sexually dimorphic than the other primate groups, but show more different types of sex differences. Rhesus monkeys, the species on which most of the work has been done, are highly sexually dimorphic, so that the results from this species and subhuman species generally may not be entirely applicable to humans, especially since hormone differences between the rhesus monkey and the human have been shown. Nevertheless, the human brain has similar areas that have been shown to be affected by circulating androgens and there is an accumulating body of evidence suggesting a similar picture for the development of sexual dimorphisms in humans as with rhesus and other subhuman species, that is, a prenatal period during which the brain is masculinized and genital morphology determined, and a later period beginning at puberty during which circulating androgens affect aggression and other sex-typical behaviors. However, these biological mechanisms are not immune from environmental influences, and these latter influences will be discussed in the next section.

Much of the evidence on the importance of prenatal hormones for human sexual and behavioral differentiation comes from various experiments in nature in which abnormal

hormonal events take place. John Money and his colleagues pioneered this area of research and concluded that there was a critical period for the acquisition of sexual identity
prior to age 2½ years, so that socialization as a boy or a girl that was begun prior to this
time would result in normal sexual orientation according to the sex of rearing (Money,
Hampson, & Hampson, 1955). This model was not essentially altered by the finding that
genetic females exposed to abnormal levels of androgens during fetal development (the
adrenogenital syndrome) exhibited higher levels of rough-and-tumble play, intense energy
expenditure, and less fantasy about doll play and interest in infants, motherhood, and
marriage (Money & Ehrhardt, 1972; Ehrhardt & Baker, 1974). Later follow-up of these
girls indicates that as teenagers they had an undeveloped romantic and dating life, reached
puberty later, had greater interest in careers and less in nurturance, and as young adults
were far more likely than a normal sample to be bisexual or lesbian (Money, 1987).

The conclusion that these sex differences were the result of androgens has been
extensively criticized. For example, it has been pointed out that the cortisone replacement
therapy given these girls might result in higher activity levels (Archer, 1976), but this
could scarcely account for the other characteristics of these girls. Huston (1983) suggests
that the girls may have been exposed to androgen influences after beginning cortisone
therapy, presumably suggesting that the effects of the androgens might not be restricted to
the prenatal and early postnatal period. However, similar results indicating masculinization of behavior were obtained with a group of girls whose mothers received masculiniz-
ing doses of progestogens during pregnancy (Money & Ehrhardt, 1972). These girls
needed no subsequent hormonal treatment and only very minor surgical corrections.
Moreover, there is also no evidence from the Baker and Ehrhardt data that these girls were
raised as more boylike because of their history. Indeed, Ehrhardt and Meyer-Bahlberg
(1981) report that parents tended to be unconcerned with the issue or encouraged femininity. Boys with the adrenogenital syndrome also display higher energy play behavior than
male siblings as well as a slight increase in aggression. Finally, studies of boys exposed
prenatally to pharmacological doses of estrogen and progesterone showed less aggressive
play behavior and girls showed an increase in doll play and infant care and a lowered level
of physically energetic play (Ehrhardt & Meyer-Bahlberg, 1981).

Other data also argue convincingly that prenatal androgen has long-range effects on
sexual behavior and identity, but cast doubt on the idea of a critical period for sexual
socialization in the first 2½ years of life during which sexual reassignment is unproblem-
atic. Much of the support for the idea of a postnatal critical period for the socialization of
sex differences derived from data on hermaphrodites who tended to successfully adjust to
the sex of their rearing. However, Diamond (1965; see also Imperato-McGinley, Peterson, Gauthier, & Sturla, 1985) pointed out that hermaphrodites are not at all typical of
normal children and, in particular, their prenatal hormonal environment may not have
been typically masculine at all, thus facilitating feminine identification. Thus, the flexibility of hermaphrodites may not be present in normal children.

Recently, one of the cases advanced by Money and his associates (Money & Ehrhardt, 1972) as indicating the complete plasticity of early sexual identity has been called
into question, and the results suggest a stronger role for early prenatal environment. A
member of a pair of identical twins lost his penis during a circumcision accident and was
reassigned as a girl at 17 months of age. At age 4½ years the child was described as quite
feminine and very neat and tidy, and as enjoying dressing as a girl. However, a more

recent follow-up after puberty indicates a different story. As reported in Diamond (1982), the child has a very masculine gait and wants to become a mechanic. She has not adjusted well to the world of peers, and is teased by the other children as a "cavewoman."

Other data obtained by Imperato-McGinley and her colleagues also support the critical role of male hormones in the development of sex identity and behavior. Imperato-McGinley *et al.* (1985) studied 33 male pseudohermaphrodites who have a deficiency in a hormone (5a-reductase) that affects genital morphology at birth. These individuals are exposed to normal levels of testosterone prenatally, but the deficiency results in an effect on the peripheral sexual organs resulting in their being reared as females. However, at puberty they develop male secondary sexual characteristics and a more normal male genital morphology, and they commence living as a male. Nineteen of the 33 subjects were reared unambiguously as females and did not realize that they were different from other girls until they failed to develop breasts. The authors conclude that biological sex prevails if normal testosterone activation occurs at puberty, and that "the extent of testosterone exposure of the brain *in utero,* in the early postnatal period, and at puberty has greater impact in determining male gender identity than the female sex of rearing" (p. 132). The authors thus reject the idea of an early critical period for the socialization of gender identity, since their data indicate that individuals can change their gender identity at adolescence in response to their current hormonal milieu.

There is also evidence that postnatal testosterone has important effects on sex-differentiated behavior. Long-term testosterone treatment of adult ovariectomized female rhesus monkeys results in some malelike behaviors (Rubin, Reinisch, & Haskett, 1980). In humans the effects of castration postnatally but prior to puberty are a much lowered aggressiveness and sexual appetite. These effects of castration were highly prized by despotic males in many Eurasian cultures, who used eunuchs as personal servants without fear that they would be sexually interested in or impregnate their females. Males with Klinefelter syndrome (caused by an XXY sex-chromosomal abnormality) have small testes and lack of sperm production and concomitant lack of aggressiveness and sex drive. Treatment with testosterone results in increased male secondary sexual characteristics as well as male sexual behavior.

With the onset of puberty there is an increase in aggression (Weisfeld & Berger, 1983; see also above) and evidence has been mounting that this increase is caused by higher levels of androgens. In a study of a normal population of adolescent boys, Olweus *et al.* (1980) found a positive correlation among the level of circulating androgens and pubertal development, physical and verbal aggression, and lack of frustration tolerance. The findings indicated that high levels of testosterone were associated with aggressive response to provocation (threat or unfair treatment), as well as impatience and irritability. After correcting for the reliability of the measurements, the authors conclude that 40% of the variation in measures of testosterone levels can be predicted by the scores on the measures of aggression and frustration tolerance. Consistent with the above, Scaramella and Brown (1978) found correlations between testosterone level and responsiveness to threat in a sample of hockey players. In addition, analogous findings have been reported for women: Purifoy and Koopmans (1979) found higher levels of some androgens in women in traditionally masculine occupations than in those in traditionally feminine occupations.

Recently Susman, Inoff-Germain, Nottelmann, Loriaux, Cutler, and Chousos (1987) in a study of children aged 9–14 years found a direct association between measures of aggression and the levels of a variety of hormones associated with pubertal development in boys but not in girls, with the latter finding possibly due to error variance due to lack of control over time of menstrual cycle. Higher scores on measures of delinquency were related to lower levels of estradiol and higher levels of androstenedione, while rebelliousness was associated with higher levels of luteinizing hormone and dihydroepiandrosterone and lower levels of follicle stimulating hormone. When entered with several emotional variables in a series of regression analyses, it was found that hormone levels, in addition to the emotional trait of nervousness, were associated with the measure of delinquent behavior. These findings offer further support for a connection between concurrent measures of hormones and aggression.

Finally, data on early maturing versus later maturing girls are consistent with hormonal influences on sex-typed behavior (see Weisfeld & Billings, 1988, for a review). As noted above, in addition to a variety of effects on sex-typed behaviors, late onset of puberty is characteristic of fetally androgenized females. Among normal girls there appear to also be similar effects of early versus late puberty. Early maturing girls tend to be more feminine than later maturing girls. They are less achievement-oriented despite having slightly higher IQs and appear to be less competitive. They are more nurturant and romantic than late maturers, and begin dating earlier and value child-rearing as of greater importance. Weisfeld and Billings (1988) suggest that hormonal influences operate directly to influence these behaviors, a view that is strongly suggested by the totality of the evidence reviewed here.

2. Environmental Influences on Sex Differences

Sex differences are clearly at the heart of recent evolutionary thought and I have already indicated that there are epigenetic rules involving temperament and hormone levels that bias the two sexes toward behaviors that were adaptive in human evolutionary history. However, it has been a theme of this volume that many of the epigenetic rules underlying human social development are environment-expectant and are thus subject to important environmental influences. If sex differences are indeed an important evolutionary adaptation, we expect that human cultures will take advantage of human plasticity and environment-expectant mechanisms to shape these differences by providing different socialization environments for the two sexes. As suggested in Chapter 5, by providing extreme environments cultures are able to produce large main effects on behavior.

In the present chapter several socialization mechanisms have already been described that distinguish between boys and girls. Particularly important in the present context are the epigenetic rules influencing affective relationships in the family. I have already provided evidence for the differential socialization of the sexes regarding parental provision of warmth and suggested that such socialization results in differences in the elaboration of the positive social reward system. One could speculate in accordance with the theory of the development of aggression described earlier in this chapter that females are biased toward being relatively sensitive to positive social rewards and that this sensitivity and the differential socialization that it elicits from parents tends to inhibit aggression. This bias toward increased sensitivity of the social reward system as well as the differential socialization that parents provide and the sensitivity itself elicits would facilitate choosing a male who would provide high levels of investment and would facilitate nurturance of offspring.

Another type of epigenetic rule involved in the differential socialization of the sexes involves the biologically primed aggressive response to aversive socialization events described earlier in this chapter, and I have described evidence that boys and girls experience quite different levels of aversive events during socialization as a result of practices by parents and society. In addition, the relative restriction of boys and girls is another socialization practice that varies cross-culturally in a manner predicted by sociobiological theory.

Besides these aspects of socialization, there is evidence that other types of environmental events during development can affect gender-related behavior. As expected (see Chapter 1), environments that deviate a great deal from normative environments are most likely have long-lasting effects on behavior (MacDonald, 1986b). For example, isolate-reared male rhesus monkeys will not develop the double-foot-clasp mount necessary for mating (Novak, 1979), and extensive efforts at rehabilitation have proved unsuccessful. This is, however, an extreme departure from a normal rearing environment and is presumably not relevant to individual differences in a normal population.

Recent studies of extremely feminine boys strongly implicate environmental influences in the etiology of this syndrome (Coates, 1985; Green, 1987), some of which are of interest from an adaptationist perspective. Boys with gender-identity disorder are characterized by preoccupation with female-stereotyped activities and often find their own sexual organs repulsive. Follow-up studies indicate a high rate of homosexuality and bisexuality as adults. Both Coates and Green find very high rates of father absence in their sample groups, with Coates reporting father absence in 85% of the sample and with none of the mothers remarrying. Mothers reported being under extreme stress in the first year and were more depressed than a control group. Forty-five percent of the mothers had severe trauma in the first 3 years of the child's life that resulted in depression. Several such cases involved reactions to their husband's having an affair with another woman and there was a very high rate of hostility toward men. Fathers are described as emotionally distant and violent, and are presumably not attractive models for their highly feminine sons.

The very negative reactions of these women to low levels of paternal support are expected within an evolutionary perspective. The existence of homosexuality has been a problem for evolutionary theory because these individuals are less likely to reproduce. Wilson (1978) suggested that homosexuality might evolve as an adaptation in which affected individuals are predisposed to help relatives but defer their own reproduction, and in Chapter 9 male bonding involving homosexual-like relationships between adult males and boys will be suggested as a mechanism of social cohesion. The data reviewed above suggest also that some homosexuality may be a pathological outcome of highly stressed familial interactions and hence be maladaptive. McGuire and Troisi (1987) present a general ethological theory of psychiatric disorder that emphasizes the need for certain types of social interactions for normal psychological functioning, that is, interactions such as being recognized, liked, respected, and helped, and I have noted the general importance of evolutionarily expected environments for adaptive behavior. In the present context the high levels of prenatal stress and very negative parent–parent and father–child interactions constitute very high levels of stress on the system, a major departure from a biologically expected environment both for the mother and the child.

The findings reviewed above strongly suggest environmental influences, but these environmental influences may act through hormonal mechanisms. Thus, high levels of maternal stress during pregnancy could result in decreased testosterone production by the fetus, which would result in less masculinization of the brain. Stressful environmental circumstances have been shown to have a variety of pathological effects on reproduction (e.g., Burgess, Kurland, & Pensky, 1988), results that can be construed as indicating pathology in the absence of important psychological or material resources (Charlesworth, 1988). Research with rats (Ward, 1972) has shown that male offspring of mothers who were stressed during pregnancy were feminized compared to the offspring of mothers not so treated. Further reserach (Ward & Weisz, 1980) indicated that stress resulted in a failure of the normal testosterone surge on days 18 and 19 of gestation. Comparable differences in humans resulting from stress during pregnancy would not be discovered by comparing levels of circulating androgens after birth. Finally, Wilson's (1978) hypothesis that homosexuality may be an adaptation for increased helping behavior is not without support. Coates (1985) finds that many of the mothers of extremely feminine boys strongly encouraged high levels of helping behavior in their sons, even encouraging them to adopt a maternal role toward the parent. These sons are described as being very neat and tidy and extraordinarily helpful to adults.

Moral and Altruistic Development I

The Roles of Cognition and Context

The subjects of altruism and moral development are closely linked and both topics can be treated in ways that emphasize cognitive processing or in ways that emphasize the importance of affect and socialization. Whereas in Chapter 8 the latter features will be emphasized, in the present chapter the cognitive aspects of these topics will be presented. Following a presentation of some of the principal perspectives in the cognitive-developmental approach to moral development and a brief sketch of a sociobiological perspective on these topics, the empirical literature derived from these approaches will be reviewed, with an emphasis on how the data fit with the evolutionary perspective.

I. THE COGNITIVE-DEVELOPMENTAL APPROACH TO MORAL REASONING

A. Piaget on Moral Development

As in so many areas of cognitive development, the primary influence has been Jean Piaget. Piaget, as with Kohlberg and other cognitive-developmentalists who followed, defined the central problem as how children evaluate moral situations. He was relatively unconcerned about moral behavior or the links between moral reasoning and moral behavior. Piaget (1965) proposed two levels of morality, a morality of constraint and a morality of cooperation. Rest (1983) characterizes these two levels of moral development not as stages in the strict sense, but as descriptions of two contrasting perspectives on morality, which change with development. The morality of constraint is the morality of the young child who submits to the commands and strictures of adults. Morally right behavior is that which conforms to these strictures, and morally wrong behavior fails to conform. Central to this stage of moral reasoning is the contention that the intention of the actor is of little importance in the young child's moral reasoning. In a classic study, Piaget asked which of two story characters was naughtier, one who was well-intentioned and did a large amount of damage, and one who did a small amount of damage, but had bad intentions. Prior to age 9 or 10 years, children tend to believe that the child who did the most damage was more morally reprehensible. During this *heteronomous* stage of morality children believe in the immutability of rules. Rules are simply handed down from adult authority figures and are not to be questioned. Because the child believes adults to be wiser and more powerful, the child becomes socialized according to the prescriptions of the adult. In addition, the young child believes in *immanent justice*, that is, that bad people will inevitably be punished. Accidents, misfortunes, and punishments occur to people because they are morally culpable.

The second stage of morality described by Piaget is that of *autonomous* morality. At this stage the child develops an ability to reason for itself regarding the morality of actions. Unlike the blind obedience that characterizes children's compliance with adult strictures, this autonomy is achieved by peer interaction through working out reciprocal arrangements that are agreeable to all parties. The autonomous child focuses much more on intentions than on consequences and takes a more conventionalistic view of moral rules.

Piaget's technique of asking children to evaluate the moral goodness or badness of story characters has led to a large body of research on the variables that affect moral evaluation in general. Rest (1983) notes that this body of research has found an enormous number of circumstances that influence moral evaluation, including whether the effects of the story character's actions are physical or psychological, accidental or intentional, provoked, pressured, etc. Recent research has found that even young children find intentionality to be an important consideration in moral evaluation if the amount of harm is controlled. As children get older they are better able to coordinate various types of information about a story character relevant to moral evaluation and this increasing ability is a general aspect of developing cognitive competence. Children at the concrete operational stage of cognitive development are able to take more than one dimension into account and are therefore able to perform so-called conservation problems correctly. For example, they are able to realize that the amount of water in a short, wide container is the same as one in a tall, thin container by simultaneously considering both the dimensions of width and height. Similarly, at the level of concrete operations children are better able to take into account both intentions and consequences and gradually are able to consider both simultaneously in making moral evaluations.

These developing cognitive competencies are clearly very important for any theory of moral reasoning, and Rest (1983) summarizes recent work from an information processing perspective on children's developing abilities in their understanding of hypothetical story information. Nevertheless, the Piagetian emphasis on moral evaluation will be of scant importance in the remainder of this chapter, since the main focus of an evolutionary approach, as described below, must be on the relationships of moral reasoning to the costs and benefits of moral behavior. As Rest (1983) points out, one of the paradoxes that Piaget must explain is why young children should ever be disobedient if they view the strictures given them by adults as divinely inspired and immutable. Rest suggests that the reason is that there is a gap even in young children between the morally ideal course of action advocated in a hypothetical story situation and what children actually decide to do. It is this gap that is the focus of an evolutionary analysis.

B. *Kohlberg on Moral Development*

Lawrence Kohlberg has been the main recent proponent of a Piagetian approach to moral reasoning and his theory contains very strong statements of the processes involved. According to Kohlberg (see, for example, Kohlberg, 1984), moral reasoning develops in a series of six stages. These stages parallel the stages of logical thought described by Piaget and these logical stages are viewed as necessary but not sufficient for the similar level of moral development. Besides the vertical movement of individuals through the logical and moral stages, there is horizontal movement from the attainment of a particular cognitive stage, through the attainment of new social perceptions and role taking, to a new stage of moral reasoning and finally moral behavior (Kohlberg, 1984, p. 172).

The stages of moral reasoning are divided into three major levels: preconventional (most children under 9 years, some adolescents, and many adolescent and adult criminal offenders), conventional (most adolescents and adults), and postconventional (a minority of adults). For preconventional individuals the rules and expectations of society are viewed as external to the self; the preconventional individual evaluates situations from the perspective of his or her self-interest or the interest of isolated individuals. At the conventional level these rules are internalized; the conventional individual subordinates the needs of a single individual to the group or a shared relationship. At the postconventional level these rules are seen as depending on moral principles that underlie them and the individual is free to choose his or her own moral principles. The viewpoint is that of a rational individual prior to the creation of a society.

Stage 1 is characterized by moral realism, the view that the goodness or badness of an action is an inherent property of the act. There is a lack of justification of the action beyond appeal to authority, and an egocentric lack of appreciation that there may be other perspectives on the moral significance of the act. Stage 2 individuals are aware that other individuals may have conflicting and equally valid thoughts on the moral significance of an action and reciprocity is achieved by making a deal with the other person, a deal that is to the mutual benefit of the individuals. Stage 3 individuals view morality as based on particular relationships with individuals rather than from the point of view of some social system such as the family in general or society in general. Paradigmatic cases are relationships with family members. At Stage 4, morality is centered within some social system, such as one's society or the family seen as a general social system. Stage 5 morality distinguishes between the legal or conventional and the moral, but regards both as on a more or less equal level. At the sixth stage, the priority of the moral to the legal is fully recognized. Systems of law are valid only if they reflect a morality that all rational individuals can accept. Recently, Kohlberg has stated that there is little empirical evidence for a sixth stage of moral reasoning, although this stage is retained as an ideal terminal endpoint in what Kohlberg regards as a rational reconstruction of development.

Regarding motivation, only the preconventional levels are truly self-interested. Stage 1 individuals simply avoid punishment and acknowledge the superior power of authorities, while Stage 2 individuals are motivated to serve their own interests by engaging in reciprocal relationships with others. Beyond these stages self-interest is submerged to various considerations, including the opinion of others (Stage 3), the good of society (Stage 4), the welfare of all individuals (Stage 5), and universal moral principles (Stage 6).

Kohlberg claims that the most essential defining feature of morality is that it is concerned with justice: "Moral situations are ones of conflict of perspectives or interest; justice principles are concepts for resolving these conflicts, for giving each his or her due. . . . the core of justice is the *distribution of rights and duties regulated by concepts of equality and reciprocity*" (Kohlberg, 1984, p. 184). This relation of morality to justice is viewed as a conceptual truth by Kohlberg. Moreover, it is an empirical question to determine what children say in response to moral dilemmas, but the logical connections among these ideas are what define a given stage. It is a matter of logical analysis whether the ideas of children cohere in a stagelike manner and whether later stages include and presuppose previous stages.

Stages are ways of thinking that can be characterized as structured wholes or patterns of thought rather than specific responses. Stages are culturally universal and form an invariant sequence. As with Piaget, the proposition of cultural universality is consistent with a major role for the environment. Moral reasoning reflects cognitive ability, so that general cognitive stimulation is important. Role-taking opportunity is also viewed as important. Children who socialize with peers and who have higher socioeconomic status have more opportunities to take the roles of others or to take the point of view of the society's basic institutions. Exposure to situations resulting in cognitive-moral conflict is also important, because movement to a higher stage results from sensing the contradictions in one's current stage structure.

Kohlberg (1981) also posits a seventh "soft stage" of moral development, which answers the question "Why be moral?" by "constructing a sense of identity or unity with being, with life, or with God" (Kohlberg, 1984, p. 249). Such a stage is said to occur in adults after the consolidation of postconventional moral reasoning. Such principles are viewed as part of a natural law framework, which posits that principles of justice are in harmony with "broader laws regulating the evolution of human nature and the cosmic order" (p. 250).

C. A Sociobiological Perspective

Sociobiologists have made specific proposals regarding the importance of self-interest versus self-sacrifice in human behavior (see, e.g., Alexander, 1979, 1987). It is easy to see why self-interest should emerge as a fundamental evolutionary principle. Evolutionary success is defined in terms of reproductive success. Organisms that are able to leave more offspring than other organisms of the same species have by definition a greater genetic representation in the next generation. Natural selection occurs when some genes are favored over other genes, as would occur if a gene that facilitated parental care or competition for mates appeared in the population. Individuals with these genes would have a greater likelihood of reproducing than individuals without the gene. But what would happen if the gene resulted in the organism giving altruistic aid to another individual? Assume that such an altruistic animal provides resources for another animal so that the latter animal can raise more offspring, but the altruist now must restrict its own reproduction. In the extreme case the altruist leaves no progeny, while the animal benefiting from the altruism is quite successful. In such a case the altruistic genes are not passed on to the next generation, so altruism cannot evolve. Even if the altruistic gene causes only a relatively mild burden to the altruist, there will be natural selection against the gene: Compared to animals who behave in a selfish manner, the animal carrying the altruistic gene will tend to lose out.

As a result of this simple evolutionary logic, there has been considerable theoretical interest in explaining instances when in fact animals do exhibit behavior that benefits another. One clear example where animals benefit other animals is parental behavior. As described in Chapters 5 and 6, mothers and often the fathers in many species go to great lengths to provide resources and protection for their offspring. Among mammals internal fertilization and the resulting prolonged pregnancy, as well as lactation, constitute a major investment in resources. The most important aspect of this example from an evolutionary perspective, however, is that the parents of an animal have a very close genetic connection with their offspring. One-half of the offspring's genes come from each of its parents, so that in helping their offspring, parents in fact are ensuring that their own genes will be represented in the next generation. Hamilton (1964) was the first to extend this line of reasoning to more distant relatives: Individuals can improve the representation of their genes in the next generation not only by helping their own offspring, but also by helping the offspring of relatives, especially close relatives. For example, uncles and nephews share one-quarter of their genes, so that helping a nephew is a good strategy for increasing one's genes in the next generation.

As an illustration, in classical China it was quite common for the emperor to have eunuchs as servants. These individuals were incapable of sexual intercourse and could not themselves reproduce. Since the emperor had a very large harem, this arrangement served to ensure that the offspring sired in the imperial household were in fact the children of the emperor. The eunuchs often came from very humble families and it was not uncommon for these individuals to attain considerable wealth, which they often then used to help their relatives. By providing enough money for a nephew to purchase a wife and start a household, the eunuch would be able to provide for his own representation in the next generation.

The term for such an arrangement is kin selection, and is used by sociobiologists to describe instances where help is provided to relatives. I noted in Chapter 5 the importance of extended kinship relationships in many societies, particularly those in the middle level of economic productivity. From a sociobiological perspective these societies are based on genetic relationships, and Paige and Paige (1981) note that an essential part of these societies is the "fraternal interest group," a group of genetically related males which functions as a source of power and authority within the society.

Although kin selection is an example where individuals help others, it is clearly also an example of self-interest. From a sociobiological perspective, then, it is expected roughly that humans, as "survival mechanisms" (Dawkins, 1976), will in fact generally act in order to maximize their self-interest. When confronting the literature on helping behavior, it is expected minimally that in studies manipulating self-interest versus the interest of others there will be an important and powerful main effect of self-interest. Regarding the relation of moral beliefs, moral reasoning, and other ideological factors to behavior, evolutionary theory suggests that individuals generally believe what is in their self-interest (e.g., Wilson, 1978), but they would also emphasize the role of deception, both of others and of themselves, in moral action (see, e.g., Krebs *et al.*, 1988, for a sociobiological perspective on deception and self-deception). From an evolutionary perspective, moral reasoning thus emerges essentially as an epiphenomenon masking self-interest. Perhaps ironically, such a view of the epiphenomenal nature of moral reasoning is characteristic of the behaviorist tradition in moral reasoning (see Staub, 1978, for a review).

Prior to reviewing the literature on moral reasoning from a sociobiological perspective, it is relevant to describe the results of research on the question of self-interest. In a sense there is no literature on the development of self-interest, since research questions have been framed in terms of describing developmental changes in prosocial and altruistic behavior and showing environmental effects on these behaviors. One of the contributions of an evolutionary perspective will be to develop experimental paradigms in which the role of self-interest is studied in relation to competition and cooperation for resources. For example, the paradigm used by Charlesworth and his colleagues (e.g., Charlesworth & Dzur, 1987) studies the behavior of children in a situation in which there is a limited resource (movie viewing time) and in which competition and cooperation are intimately intertwined. In order for one child to view the movie, another child must turn a crank and a third child must push a button. The studies are constructed ''on the assumption that the vast majority of social interactions involve the pursuit of resources (broadly categorized as either material, social or informational), and that this pursuit usually requires engaging in both cooperative and directly self-serving behaviors'' (p. 192). Research with this paradigm, described in Chapter 6, has shown important sex differences and associations with position in the dominance hierarchy, and by using paradigms such as this it will be possible to explore developmental differences in competition and cooperation for resources. Thus, as suggested by the work of Parkhurst and Gottman (1986) (see Chapter 6), older children may well use far more sophisticated strategies of manipulating other children in order to obtain resources.

Studies conducted within the social learning tradition support the evolutionary idea that self-interest is an important aspect of children's behavior. In the hundreds of studies focused on these issues, self-interest is apparent in the baseline conditions and still present after the treatments have been performed. Many of these studies have shown that sharing and helping can be increased with appropriate reinforcement (see, e.g., Fischer, 1963; Rushton & Teachman, 1978; see Rushton, 1980, for a review). These studies therefore indicate that one means of increasing these behaviors is to provide contingencies such that the behavior is in the subject's self-interest. Reflecting these findings and a general behaviorist predisposition, many theorists reject the use of the word ''altruism'' for sharing and helping behaviors because the connotations of this word preclude the importance of external reinforcement in maintaining these behaviors (e.g., Gelfand & Hartmann, 1982).

Damon's (1977) work may be considered as a paradigm showing the importance of self-interest in children. The experimental task involved the distribution of candy bars following performance on a task, presumably a situation of considerable importance from the point of view of the children. One of the children was hypothetically designated as having made the most and the prettiest bracelets, one as being the biggest child, and one as being the nicest, and in addition there was one younger child whose performance on the bracelet-making task was inferior to the others. The principal findings were that children tended to give more to their own hypothetical position than to the other positions and there was no tendency for older children to give more to the younger, less competent child.

This finding of an important main effect of self-interest is also typical of laboratory studies. Usually the focus of social learning studies is to show the effects of treatments on subjects' behavior, but here the baseline rates of donating are of interest, since they show the importance of self-interest prior to treatment. For example, White (1972) found that control children who had won 12 nickels donated an average of only 0.57 nickels to charity. Similarly Rice and Grusec (1975) found that control children donated less than 10% of the marbles they had won to other children, while Eisenberg-Berg and Gersheker (1979) found that control children donated on the average less than 1% of the nickels they had won to needy children. Sometimes the controls make no contributions at all: Thus, Bryan and Walbek (1970) found that 41–69% of their subjects in the various treatment and baseline conditions made no contribution at all, and Grusec, Saas-Kortsaak, and Simutis (1978) and White and Burnham (1975) found that subjects in the control condition made no donations at all.

These results indicate that a high level of donation to others is not a normative characteristic of young children. The purpose of these experiments is, however, to raise the level of donating, and a great variety of means have been used in this effort, including modeling and moral exhortation. Staub (1978) summarizes the results of laboratory studies on the influence of modeling as showing that "Although . . . the effect of modeling was usually significant, often it was not substantial" (p. 201). For example, in the study by Grusec et al. (1978) described above it was found that modeling and moral exhortation, the most effective of the experimental treatments, resulted in average donations of about 30% of the children's winnings. Eisenberg-Berg and Gersheker (1979) found that a competent, generous model increased donations from near 0 nickels to an average of 2.64 out of the 10 that had been won. Several other studies have shown that treatment leads to gains in donations up to approximately 30% (Bryan & Walbek, 1970; White, 1972), but in other cases modeling has been shown to increase donations up to approximately 50% (Rice & Grusec, 1975; Rushton, 1975).

These results clearly indicate an important main effect of self-interest, even after experimental manipulations that somewhat reduce this effect. These is also often considerable resistance to modeling, so that subjects rarely, if ever, donate as much as the model, and the effect of the treatment generally declines on retesting (e.g., White, 1972; Rushton & Littlefield, 1979), although the effect may not entirely disappear. Moreover, it may well be that there is a great deal of situational pull for donating in a laboratory situation where it is made subtly clear that donating is the appropriate behavior. This pull of the situation may be particularly important for older subjects (Zarbatany, Hartmann, & Gelfand, 1985).

One might argue that the low baseline rates typical of these studies are peculiar to a Western, capitalist culture. However, the anthropological and historical data reviewed in Chapters 8 and 9 indicate that self-interest is a robust finding cross-culturally as well, although in some cases extremely self-sacrificing behavior has been produced via intensive socialization techniques. The data reviewed above indicate that self-interest is an important phenomenon even in seemingly trivial behaviors involving material resources whose value is so small that it could not possibly affect biological fitness. When more costly behavior is considered, the effects of self-interest are even more apparent.

II. REST'S COMPONENT MODEL OF MORAL BEHAVIOR

James Rest (1983) has proposed a framework for representing the interactions among the cognitive, affective, and behavioral processes involved in morality. In this section these components will be defined and related to an evolutionary perspective. The framework consists of four components, involving (I) interpreting the situation, (II) reasoning about the ideal moral course of action, (III) selecting among alternative actions to form an intention regarding the moral course of action, and (IV) executing this intention.

Component I, interpreting the situation, involves identifying how the welfare of the various individuals in the situation could be affected by one's actions. For example, individuals appear to engage in a variety of defensive maneuvers in order to deny responsibility to act in morally relevant situations. These maneuvers can result in a reappraisal of the moral nature of the situation and therefore affect the applicability of the moral reasoning process, which is the second component of the model. Schwartz and Howard (1984) describe four types of defensive methods, which reduce decisional conflict in situations where altruism is a possibility: denial of need, denial of the effectiveness of actions, denial of personal ability, and denial of responsibility. Denial of need refers to a person "seeking cues that permit denial of the need or at least a reduction in its severity (e.g., 'That's not an assault, its a lover's quarrel')" (p. 236). Denial of effectiveness of action refers to reconceptualizing the situation by denying that the action would really help "(e.g., 'No point intervening, they'll just start up again as soon as I leave')" (p. 236). Denial of personal ability refers to reconceptualizing the situation by denying one's competence to perform the contemplated action. Finally, denial of responsibility refers to reconceptualizing the situation by finding particular circumstances in the present case that render moral action unnecessary, such as illness, provocation, or external pressure. Other researchers have noted that exploiters rationalize exploitation by derogating the victim (Glass, 1964) and minimizing the victim's suffering (Brock & Buss, 1962).

These findings indicate important individual differences in how people interpret moral situations. Moreover, there are clear developmental trends in the ability of children to make inferences about moral situations. Young children are less able to comprehend the motives of others and often ignore relevant events and cues, abilities that develop with age (Shantz, 1983). Nevertheless, more than simply cognitive sophistication is involved in interpreting the situation. The above defensive maneuvers described by Schwartz and Howard (1984) suggest that individuals often interpret morally relevant situations in ways that serve their own self-interest. In the present perspective, self-interest emerges as an important aspect of moral reasoning, but these findings clearly indicate that self-interest often assumes considerable importance prior to moral reasoning.

The second component of morality involves moral reasoning, integrating the needs of the various parties involved and coming up with the morally ideal course of action. The principal research traditions addressing Component II derive from the cognitive-developmental tradition of Piaget and Kohlberg described above and research involving social norms, which derives from social psychology. Social norms are general rules that one applies to particular situations. For example, the norm of reciprocity states that one should attempt to repay favors. Research in these traditions will be considered from an evolutionary perspective in the following sections.

Component III involves deciding what one actually intends to do in the situation.

One need not perform the morally ideal course of action, and in many situations there are competing sources of motivation, such as affiliation and self-interest. In the following section, several examples will be described where actual behavior departs quite radically from morally ideal action as determined by the subject and does so in the direction of self-interest, as predicted by evolutionary theory. Also congruent with the evolutionary approach is Rest's point (based on the work of theorists such as Schwartz, 1977), that moral decision making often involves defensive evaluations of the situation, so that situations are appraised in such a way as to devalue persons in need or to deny responsibility to act. Rest also suggests that moral decision making may depart from decision making in other areas in that quite often people respond to moral situations rather impulsively, without a detailed calculation of costs and benefits. The issue of the impulsivity of moral behavior is addressed within an evolutionary perspective in the following chapter.

Component IV involves actually carrying out the planned course of behavior. Rest states that there is important variation in the degree to which individuals execute a plan of action, with personal qualitites such as persistence and competence coming strongly into play: "Weakness of the flesh is Biblical terminology for failures of Component IV processes" (Rest, 1983, p. 569). Being high in these qualities is in itself amoral: individuals can use these qualities for good or for evil deeds. The evolutionary perspective predicts neither good nor evil, but only that self-interest will be a salient feature of moral behavior.

III. A REVIEW OF THE LITERATURE ON MORAL REASONING FROM THE PERSPECTIVE OF SOCIOBIOLOGICAL THEORY

We have seen that sociobiological theory emphasizes the role of self-interest in moral behavior and moral cognition. The emphasis on self-interest in behavior is consistent with helping others, especially relatives, and even with biological predispositions to help others. In Chapter 8, I review evidence that affective relations within the family are important in the socialization of altruism and helping behaviors. Thus, strong tendencies toward self-interest as well as biologically based predispositions toward altruism are posited by sociobiological theory to be present in humans. The latter are expected to be the result of natural selection to exhibit altruism within the family grouping. The former tendency will be the focus of the following, and in Chapter 8 I will try to reconcile these two strands of sociobiological thinking.

Before beginning this section, it should be emphasized that a sociobiological perspective need not question the appropriateness of some sort of cognitive-developmental mechanism for moral development. Children may indeed develop in such a way that there are large average differences in how children of different ages reason about moral issues, and these differences may well reflect structural limitations on children's thought processes which prevent them from articulating high levels of moral reasoning. However, a sociobiological perspective is inconsistent with some of the substantive claims made by Kohlberg and others in the cognitive-developmental tradition. The principal inconsistency is that Kohlberg proposes universal tendencies to achieve both advanced levels of moral reasoning as well as a strong connection between moral reasoning and moral behavior.

Individuals at higher moral stages are expected to act in a manner that is objectively more just, that is, less self-interested and more able to give equal weight to the claims of others, than at previous stages. Thus, in the following, one of the principal concerns will be with the connections between moral reasoning and moral behavior, since it is here that the two theoretical approaches give different predictions.

Prior to addressing these issues, some points of definition should be addressed. Since this discussion will be heavily influenced by evolutionary theory, it is important to define what we mean by altruism and prosocial behavior. From an evolutionary perspective the theoretically interesting phenomena to be considered are behaviors that benefit some individual other than the self and are costly to the self. The implication is that an individual is giving up some tangible resource for another individual without the prospect of any sort of tangible reciprocity. Regarding motivation, altruistic acts do not include instances of exploitation, that is, where one is forced to be altruistic. However, there is no evolutionary requirement that the act be consciously intended to benefit another person. The behaviors of even very simple organisms can be altruistic without being consciously so. Nevertheless, since we are attempting to describe human altruism, the most interesting examples will come from situations in which the behavior is intended to benefit others. From an evolutionary perspective a person losing his wallet accidentally or becoming enslaved so that someone else benefited would be formally identical to a person voluntarily giving others all his or her money, but there is a clear psychological difference.

The emphasis on tangible rewards results in a deemphasis on psychological rewards to oneself, such as feeling good about oneself, unless these psychological rewards somehow result in tangible material benefits. Material benefits could conceivably result from psychological rewards if, for example, individuals who felt good about benefiting someone else actually became more attractive to others and received tangible rewards as a result. The emphasis on tangible rewards is necessary because an evolutionary theory must be principally concerned with material, economic benefits of the type that can be turned into differences in biological or cultural fitness. The psychological rewards of altruism are viewed within evolutionary theory as motivators that facilitate altruism (see Chapter 8), but there is no reason to suppose that triggering of this reward system in itself would increase one's fitness.

Thus we are concerned with altruism defined as behavior that the actor intentionally carries out in order to benefit another person and that results in a net loss of tangible benefits. Prosocial behavior, on the other hand, can then be defined (with Eisenberg, 1986) as including helping, sharing, and other seemingly intentional and voluntary positive behaviors for which the motive is not altruistic. Prosocial behaviors thus would include a variety of positive behaviors that are engaged in as a result of reciprocity or even exploitation. A good example would be helping behaviors one performs as part of one's job (e.g., a nurse or doctor). Prosocial behaviors do not raise any theoretical problems for evolutionary theory, since they are in the self-interest of those who perform them, and they will not be considered further.

A. The Importance of Cost–Benefit Analysis in Moral Reasoning

One of the difficulties of applying an evolutionary approach to human behavior is that it was often tacitly assumed that evolutionary accounts assume rigid, stereotyped behavior. Such approaches clearly ignore human cognitive abilities and in particular the human ability to make fine discriminations regarding the context of moral decision making. A sociobiological approach is thus necessarily contextual because it must emphasize features of the context that are important for making an adaptive choice, and especially relevant is a cost–benefit analysis of the behavioral alternatives available in the situation. The concern with cost–benefit analysis reflects the essentially economic nature of much of the fundamental theory within evolutionary biology and behavioral ecology (Wilson, 1975). From a sociobiological perspective these costs and benefits must be weighted by the relationships of the potential benefactor to the potential recipient. Rather than focusing on abstract principles of justice, the context of moral decision making is thus profoundly influenced by whether subjects' situations involve themselves and their relatives or hypothetical story characters, strangers, or enemies.

Damon's (1977) data, described above, also indicate that reasoning about real-life situations in which an individual has a stake in the outcome tends to be more self-interested than does purely hypothetical reasoning. After partialling out age, the correlation between hypothetical reasoning in which no resources were at stake and moral reasoning that affected actual resource acquisition was rather minimal, $r = .26$, and the author suggests methodological reasons for supposing that even this correlation is somewhat inflated.

Haan (1978, 1985) also clearly shows the importance of emphasizing potential costs and benefits in real-life moral reasoning. Haan (1978) contrasted formal (Kohlbergian) and interpersonal types of moral reasoning. Interpersonal styles of reasoning are focused on obtaining resources in face-to-face interactions with others, and she found that this type of reasoning is particularly salient in hypothetical games which resulted in divisiveness due to producing competition for status and power among the participants. Formal reasoning, on the other hand, was highly sensitive to situational demand: In situations that represented a threat to an individual's self-interest, it dropped precipitously, but was quite high "in pleasant situations in which verbalizations could be cheaply produced" (p. 297). In contrast, "Undoubtedly the stress evoked by the unjust and oligarchical structure of Starpower, which determined which individual teenagers were to control or be controlled by others, especially disrupted the relationships between interview- and action-based levels" (p. 300). She concludes that:

> Formal morality is an attempt to rise above the details of the occasion, discern the general rule, and then apply this rule, logically, impersonally, and ideally. Thus we can see that the formal system is remote from situations and that it results in less impressive predictions of action levels but more impressive predictions within interviews, where this kind of strategy is probably more functional. (Haan, 1978, pp. 300–301)

Anticipating the discussion of self-deception below, she states that "Probably no other kind of human functioning is as easily and frequently disrupted by self-deceptiveness" (Haan, 1978, pp. 302–303). Moral reasoning emerges as often involving defensive strategies such as intellectualizing and denial, suggesting that "formal reasoning can be an intellectualized exercise that is quite removed from the situation and the special needs of the persons involved" (Haan, 1978, p. 303). Consistent with an evolutionary perspective, she views Kohlbergian moral reasoning as being the result of a formal education that emphasizes abstract, intersubjective meanings.

Several other writers have described the contextual sensitivity of moral reasoning to personal cost–benefit decisions. Thus, Sobesky (1983) found that when severe consequences were said to occur to a hypothetical story character if the altruistic path was chosen, subjects tended to reason at a lower level than if the consequences for altruistic behavior were mild. Specifying severe consequences to the potential altruist resulted in subjects' choosing preconventional ways of resolving the moral dilemma. Similarly, Leming (1978) found that adolescents reasoned at a lower level if the subject was named as the protagonist than if the protagonist was a stranger. A further trend toward preconventional types of moral reasoning was noted when subjects reasoned about moral situations drawn from their actual lives. Finally, Levine (1976) found that if subjects were told that the protagonist was the subject's mother or the subject's best friend, there was an increase in Stage 3 reasoning and a corresponding decrease in Stage 4 reasoning compared to the reasoning for hypothetical story characters.

The results of these studies clearly show the importance of cost–benefit considerations and self-interest in moral reasoning. Further, the predicted importance of family and friends as variables that modify moral reasoning in the direction of greater self-interest is apparent. Reasoning about oneself, one's relatives, and significant others is done with a different calculus than is reasoning about hypothetical situations. Phrased differently, the results show that when the possible costs in the dilemma are increased by specifying negative consequences to self, relatives, or friends, children's moral reasoning responds to these cues by becoming more self-interested. When costs are low, individuals can afford to appear altruistic. The hypothetical story situation is thus an ideal, painless way to facilitate the appearance of altruism in children.

B. Moral Reasoning as Justification of Self-Interest

Kohlberg's theory implies that there is a built-in gap between the structure of moral reasoning (an aspect of a person's stage) and the content of the person's moral choice (e.g., should Heinz steal the drug). Thus, two Stage 5 individuals could advocate quite different courses of action in the same hypothetical dilemma. This split between the structure of moral reasoning and the content of moral reasoning leaves open the possibility that individuals will in fact rationalize self-interested behavior with whatever level of reasoning is open to them: If Stage 5 individuals can easily disagree on what is the moral course of action in real-life dilemmas, the sociobiological hypothesis that moral reasoning is often simply a rationalization for self-interested behavior becomes a real possibility. Although Kohlberg (1984) finds that for some dilemmas there is near unanimity of moral choice for individuals of a given stage, for other dilemmas there is much less universality of agreement, even at the most advanced stages.

Another reason to suppose that moral reasoning may be utilized in the service of self-interest is that higher stages of moral reasoning are associated with greater verbal comprehension, IQ (Rest, 1979), and education (Rest & Thoma, 1985). Moreover, there is a consistent finding of strong associations between IQ, postconventional moral reasoning, and opposition to conservative–authoritarian political values (Rest, 1979). These results suggest that to some extent advanced moral reasoning is the prerogative of the intelligent, the educated, and the verbally fluent, results that are quite consistent with the idea that moral reasoning represents little more than the justification of self-interest.

The most interesting data on the question of self-interest and moral reasoning will come from situations that are of high potential cost to the reasoner. Such a situation has been examined in the work of Carol Gilligan (1982) and the results of this work are an excellent illustration of the importance of rationalization and self-deception in moral reasoning. Gilligan studied the decision process of women contemplating abortion, clearly a situation with great implications for the woman's life as well as one that has instigated a great deal of moral controversy.

The dilemma as posed by the subjects tends to revolve around conflicting demands of self-interest, as reflected by concern of the subjects regarding the impact of the decision on career opportunities and relationships with boyfriends, husbands, and parents. These demands are sometimes contrasted with abstract moral principles, but in general the reasoning tends to be related to concrete issues in the person's life, and the course of behavior that is in the perceived self-interest of the woman is invariably chosen.

The importance of self-interest can be seen by the fact that survival is often mentioned as a motive for abortion. Thus, Betty (age 16 years) states that "preservation of oneself, I think, is the most important thing. It comes before anything in life" (Gilligan, 1982, p. 76). Josie states, "I see myself as becoming more mature in ways of making decisions and taking care of myself, doing something for myself." The importance of survival and self-interest is part of a dialectic in which subjects progress from what Gilligan terms a selfish mode to a responsible mode and back again to selfish mode, a mode that Gilligan describes as "not only honest but fair" (p. 85). In the end, "survival returns as the paramount concern" (p. 87).

The goal of self-interest is often reached with a great deal of rationalization and even self-deception. For example, Ellen ends up rejecting her married boyfriend's idea that she should have the child and raise it herself without his support. She struggles to find a method to justify the decision and realizes that she is able to argue for or against the morality of abortion "with a philosophical logic." Sarah reconstructs the dilemma in such a way as to justify her decision, rejecting self-sacrifice and self-abnegation as "immoral in their power to hurt." She claims that the factors against abortion are the admiration she would receive as a single mother (presumably an example of adaptive self-deception) and not having to face up to the guilt involved, and she balances this with the bad effects on her relationship with the father and her parents. The abortion is justified and, as an extra benefit, the subject is able to retain a positive self-image of herself as being honest and direct.

Martha also engages in self-deception. She realistically realizes that having a baby will cut into her time and entail a lot of responsibility and she rejects her previous idea that having a baby would make her feel happy as "selfish." By counterfactually suggesting that having the baby would make her happy and then engaging in self-deception by providing a negative label such as "selfish" to this false idea, she is free to choose what in fact is the self-interested course.

Moral reasoning emerges as a contextually sensitive, creative process rather than as a matter of invoking universal moral principles. Gilligan is correct in her criticism of the hypothetical dilemma approach to studying moral reasoning:

> Hypothetical dilemmas, in the abstraction of their presentation, divest moral actors from the history and psychology of their individual lives and separate the moral problem from the social contingencies of its possible occurrence. In doing so, these dilemmas are useful for the distillation and refinement of objective principles of justice and for measuring the formal logic of equality

> and reciprocity. However, the reconstruction of the dilemma in its contextual particularity allows
> the understanding of cause and consequence which engages the compassion and tolerance repeat-
> edly noted to distinguish the moral judgments of women. (Gilligan, 1982, p. 100)

These data coincide well with a sociobiological approach. The behavior of the subjects is self-interested and is rationalized with moral reasoning that results in a positive self-image and often a feeling of moral rectitude. Consistent with the discussion of self-esteem in Chapter 3, the self is engaged in manipulating information, and truth and reality are minor concerns. An evolutionary perspective also illuminates several of the variables seen to be important in the decision-making process. One common reason for choosing abortion in these cases had to do with a lack of economic and emotional support from the father. Essock-Vitale and McGuire (1985) have shown that economic support is an important factor in a woman's decision to bear a child, a finding congruent with the fundamental importance of resources in evolutionary theory (Charlesworth, 1988). Second, many of these women were very concerned with the impact their decision would have on affective relationships with boyfriends, husbands, and parents. I have repeatedly noted the importance of affective relationships in human behavior. Fear of losing an affective relationship is thus a strong motivator of behavior and is expected to result in rationalizations designed to validate behavior that maintains these relationships.

The finding that affective relationships are important considerations in moral decision making brings up the question of sex differences. Gilligan maintains that the decision making of men is hierarchical, logical, and aggressive, whereas that of women focuses on networks, communication, and relationships. This issue of sex differences in moral reasoning is controversial, with several studies and reviews finding little or no difference (Kohlberg, 1984; Rest, 1983; Walker, 1984, 1986). The results of this work indicate that even if there are sex differences in moral reasoning they are not very large, but it should be remembered that the vast majority of the studies on moral reasoning have been performed with hypothetical dilemmas. If more studies like that of Gilligan were performed with both men and women, it would not be at all surprising to find differences as hypothesized by Gilligan. The evolutionary analysis of the epigenetic rules involving the affective relationships in the family provided in Chapter 6 indicated that females are more sensitive to the reward value of nurturant, affectively warm interactions, probably as a result of both genetic variation and socialization patterns. It is expected therefore that females would weight affective relationships more heavily in moral decision making than would men and that they would thus tend to score lower in Kohlberg's stage scheme of moral reasoning. Females would fear the loss of an affective relationship more and their behavior would thus be more motivated by such considerations. Clearly, research on sex differences in moral reasoning in potentially very costly circumstances is needed. Recently Eisenberg, Shell, Pasternack, Beller, Lennon, and Mathy (1987) found that girls, but not boys, developed patterns of prosocial moral reasoning characterized by sympathy and role playing in early adolescence, a time when the evolutionary theory predicts an increase in the importance of affective relationships for girls relative to boys.

Finally, the foregoing indicates that moral reasoning often involves rationalization. However, there also appear to be cases where an individual cynically attempts to deceive others by rationalizing his or her behavior with the reasoning of an advanced moral stage. These cases differ from the preceding because the moral reasoning would be carried out only for the benefit of others, not to convince oneself of the morality of one's actions.

This issue has not been well studied, but Rest (1979) notes that politicians may hire speechwriters to find ideas that appeal to voters and certainly many businesses and individuals go to great lengths to develop a good public image. Part of having a good image is to convince others that one's behavior conforms to the highest type of moral reasoning. By definition, such reasoning appeals to rational, disinterested observers: "Regardless of one's stage . . . a person can fake great concern for moral values" (Rest, 1979).

C. The Link between Moral Reasoning and Moral Behavior

An evolutionary theory must propose that links between moral reasoning and moral behavior will be complex. In this perspective one's actual resource-directed behavior is of central importance, but the manner of one's reasoning can significantly alter the perceptions of oneself and others toward that behavior. An evolutionary theory need not question that in many cases there will be a strong connection between moral reasoning and moral behavior. A strong connection is expected because, as described above, moral reasoning appears to be a highly fluid, contextually sensitive process in which self-interest can be justified. As a result of the gap between the structure and content of moral reasoning, one's stage of moral reasoning does not imply any particular behavior and the justification of self-interest becomes the expected strategy.

There are two possibilities in which this expectation is not met. The first is that there is a conflict between moral reasoning and self-interested behavior and individuals ignore their own moral reasoning. The second is that individuals sometimes engage in behavior that is not self-interested and do so as the result of moral reasoning that favors this course of action. The former possibility is highly compatible with an evolutionary approach, while the latter requires some discussion.

1. Conflicts between Behavior and Moral Reasoning

Regarding the first possibility, there is some evidence that individuals at times ignore their own moral reasoning. One of Gilligan's (1982) subjects, Janet, has a conflict among Catholic religious ideology regarding abortion, financial self-interest, and her husband's affection. Although she decides to have an abortion for reasons she admits are self-interested, she does not reject the general principle that abortion is morally wrong. She thus is able to say to herself that what she is doing is morally wrong, but she will do it anyway. Similarly, Ugurel-Semin (1952) found that some of the children who distributed a reward in a selfish manner expressed disapproval of their own behavior.

This potential gap between moral reasoning and moral behavior is implicit in Rest's (1983) component model of moral reasoning described above. Deciding what one actually intends to do (Component III) can conflict with the morally ideal course of action (Component II), and Rest notes that moral reasoning is often rejected in the interest of other considerations. Prime among these considerations is self-interest. Thus, Rest cites the case of John Dean, who stated in his book *Blind Ambition* that questions of morality and justice were overridden by more pressing concerns.

These examples are particularly interesting because they indicate that it is not always possible for individuals to justify and rationalize their behavior in a moral manner. In a sense this might be termed a failure of ideology, since the individual is not able to rationalize his or her behavior with any available ideology. Unlike rationalization, in which persons can successfully justify their behavior to themselves and experience a feeling of moral rectitude as a result, this failure of ideology may well result in the individual experiencing a negative affective state (guilt). Unlike the other subjects studied by Gilligan, Janet is thus likely to undergo abortion with much more conflict and negative feelings. In Chapter 3, data were summarized indicating that one important component of self-esteem is a feeling of moral rectitude. In the present context these results can be said to indicate that successful rationalization leads to a feeling of moral rectitude and high self-esteem, while unsuccessful rationalization leads to guilt and a lowering of self-esteem. An evolutionary analysis of guilt is presented in Chapter 8.

2. Moral Reasoning as the Justification of Self-Sacrificing Behavior

The second possibility in which the rationalization mode of moral reasoning does not occur envisions the possibility that individuals actually perform behavior that is opposed to self-interest, behavior that conforms to a particular pattern of moral reasoning and may even result from it. The evolutionary perspective predicts that such reasoning will be relatively infrequent and that when it occurs it should involve relatively low-cost behaviors. In situations of low cost it may benefit individuals to both behave in the morally correct manner and reason at a high-stage level. Individuals who provide low-cost aid to others lose little or nothing and gain the respect and admiration of others. People tend to reward individuals who engage in altruistic actions, and indeed Trivers (1971; see also Alexander, 1987) noted that a variety of long-term benefits may accrue to individuals who accept negative imbalances in resource flow, so that altruistic behavior can often be better characterized as anticipated future reciprocity. If such behavior is accompanied by advanced levels of moral reasoning, we are more apt to ascribe this behavior to non-self-interested motives.

The present section will be confined to an attempt to show that the cases described in the literature that purport to show that moral reasoning is a cause of altruistic behavior involve low-cost behavior. In agreement with this perspective, several writers have noted that the best examples of a link between moral reasoning and non-self-interested behavior involve low costs. For example, Rest (1983) notes that some of the behaviors studied in attempts to discover the relationship between moral reasoning and moral behavior are of questionable moral significance, since they do not involve questions of justice or the rights of others. Such behaviors include being a virgin and smoking marijuana. In addition, he points out there there is no assurance that the verbal schemes a person uses in a hypothetical situation are operative in real situations. Many of the studies assess attitudes on public policy questions, for which there is no cost, rather than behaviors. And, as predicted, many of the behaviors studied are low in cost, such as providing help to a drugged student, voting, or simply accepting responsibility. Even in studies involving low-cost behaviors, the relationship between moral reasoning and moral behavior is quite weak and often insignificant. Blasi (1980) found that only 57 of 75 studies assessing these relationships reported significant results, and many of these studies were unpublished doctoral dissertations of unknown quality.

These conclusions apply to the studies reviewed by Kohlberg and Candee (1984). In the Helkema (1979) study, for example, the behavior studied is a judgment of responsibility on the part of subjects in a hypothetical situation. Despite the fact that no costs are involved, at Stage 5 only 67% think Heinz should steal the drug, only 53% think that Heinz is responsible if he steals the drug and the wife dies, and 50% of those who advocate stealing the drug also hold him responsible. These results show that even individuals with advanced stages of moral reasoning often show a lack of consistency between moral judgments and judgments of responsibility. Kohlberg and Candee also describe a study by McNamee (1978) where the costs of helping are minimal, involving either providing information or helping an apparently drugged student by taking the individual to a medical facility. Only 20% of the Stage 5 individuals offered the more costly helping behavior, and none of the previous three stages did. The less costly behavior of providing information was shown by 73% of the Stage 5 subjects. As predicted, therefore, by increasing the costs of the helping behavior, there was a decrease in helping behavior, even among Stage 5 individuals.

The other studies reviewed by Kohlberg and Candee (1984) also use low-cost helping behaviors: The Blasi (1983) study involved a cost-free acceptance of responsibility in a hypothetical situation, and Kohlberg and Candee (1984) discuss their own data on student protestors. No costs are specified for the protest behaviors, and the fact that the behaviors were done as part of a large peer movement suggests that the students may even have gained by such behavior.

In general these results indicate that high-stage moral reasoning justifies altruistic behavior for some people some of the time, but in general the behaviors involved are of minimal or (more often) no cost to the helper. These results fit well with evolutionary theory and in Chapter 8 further data supporting the importance of costs and benefits for helping behavior will be described. Such a perspective need not suppose that high-cost, low-benefit behaviors that are justified by a form of moral reasoning never occur, but need only claim that if they do occur, they are maladaptive to the individual and that there will be continuing selection against such individuals. As indicated in Chapter 1, the adaptiveness of behavior is a central tendency, not a law of nature, and fundamental evolutionary theory supposes not that maladaptive behavior will not occur, but only that it will be selected against. Thus, celibate religious personnel, Iranian suicide bombers, and individuals who accept their own exploitation are constantly being selected against, assuming of course that their behavior does not help their relatives in some way. It is interesting to note that the personal ideology or the manner of moral reasoning that motivates such selfless behavior may not be selected against at all, even if it leads individual proponents to maladaptive behavior. In Chapter 9 examples of highly successful ideologies that result in individually maladaptive, self-sacrificing behavior will be described, but in these cases a great many other people benefit from such ideologies and the ideology may be a part of a very successful culture.

D. Cross-Cultural Data: The Primacy of Self-Interest, Reciprocity, and Social Relationships

As indicated above, Kohlberg has taken a strong cognitive-developmental position regarding the status of stages of moral development. As a result of this perspective, Kohlberg was driven to find support for the cross-cultural universality of his proposed stages. The data provide evidence that the earliest of Kohlberg's stages occur in all cultures, while the more advanced stages, those past Stage 3, appear to require exposure to more formal education and perhaps participation in a centralized society rather than one based on kinship relations. For example, Kohlberg (1984) found that both rural and urban Turkish subjects advanced in their levels of moral reasoning, but that the former did so more slowly and stabilized at Stage 3. Reasoning at Stage 4 or higher was rare in both samples. Edwards (1975) and Tietjen and Walker (1985) found similar patterns in traditional societies.

These results fit well with a sociobiological viewpoint. Stage 3 moral judgments are made at the level of particular relationships. In societies without centralized political control, familial and kinship relations predominate (MacDonald, 1984, 1987a). Self-interest, reciprocity, and the affective relations built up with particular individuals are expected to be of great importance and weigh heavily in moral decision making. Just as the subjects in Gilligan's study were heavily influenced by the context of the moral decision and especially by affectively tinged relationships and unconcerned about the society as a whole or about the rights of individuals existing prior to society, the subjects of the studies discussed here are able to look no further than their own particular relationships in finding a rationale for their behavior. An individual in a contemporary industrial society easily sees himself or herself as embedded in this larger context and can resort to Stage 4 and Stage 5 reasoning to rationalize his or her behavior. Indeed, Kohlberg (1984) attributes the more advanced moral reasoning skills of middle-class children compared to children of lower socioeconomic status as due to their being able to see themselves as embedded in a larger insitutional framework required for Stage 4 and Stage 5 reasoning. These results are consistent with a large gap between moral reasoning and moral behavior, as previously argued: Unless one is prepared to argue that people in more advanced societies generally behave in a more moral manner, it is reasonable to suppose that what changes in the shift to more advanced, centralized societies is the style of reasoning, not the morality of actual behavior. Reasons appealing to the need for laws and social order, as well as appeals to human rights that transcend laws, become a possibility in these more advanced societies, and, because of their appeal to disinterested individuals, become important tools in justifying self-interested behavior. Indeed, it might be said that such appeals are more than a possibility; they are often a necessity, since at this level very intense forms of social control become a possibility and the interests of the individual can become completely submerged. The discussion in Chapter 9 will address the issues raised by the social control of altruism.

It should be pointed out that the patterns of altruistic behavior observed cross-culturally correspond well with sociobiological theory. Sahlins (1965) found that individuals tended to engage in generalized reciprocity (denoting indefinite reciprocation or lack of need for reciprocation) within the family and among close relatives. Indeed, Alexander (1979) notes that generalized reciprocity is really nepotism—the giving of resources to relatives. Balanced reciprocity refers to direct exchange and cannot tolerate one-way flow of resources. This type of reciprocity occurs among associates and friends, individuals who must be dealt with in the future and who are therefore unlikely to cheat. Balanced reciprocity thus tends to occur among individuals who have a large number of face-to-face encounters and who are not close enough relatives to warrant nepotism.

Sahlin's third category of reciprocity, negative reciprocity, refers to individuals attempting to cheat and exploit others; that is, to get something for nothing. This type of behavior tends to occur outside tribal boundaries. As Alexander (1979) points out, evolutionary theory predicts that such behavior is not likely to occur among individuals who have to continually interact with one another, since cheaters are quickly recognized. Moreover, the lack of genetic relatedness makes such persons ideal targets of exploitation.

The cross-cultural data thus illustrate the importance of genetic relatedness and the costs and benefits of behavior as guides to real-life behavior and deemphasize the importance of abstract moral principles. These results are amplified by a recent study by Tietjen (1986) on altruistic reasoning among the Maisin of New Guinea. The lowest percentage of helping responses occurred with regard to two stories, one involving a conflict between helping and delaying the protagonist's studies, the other a conflict over whether villagers who have only enough for their own needs should help a needy neighboring village whose fields have been flooded. In the former story, self-interest enters in because the principal means for obtaining money among the Maisin is from the remittances of their people who work away from home, and many Maisin noted that the protagonist should not help individuals not related to her when this would delay the ability of the individual to help her own relatives. In the second example, the conflict between the needs of one's own village and relatives versus a group of nonrelatives is resolved in favor of one's own village.

IV. RESEARCH ON NORMS RELATED TO ALTRUISM AND MORALITY

Another cognitive approach to morality and altruistic behavior postulates norms that guide people in the appropriate course of action in particular circumstances. Norms are of the general form "If I am in situation X, I ought to do Y" and refer to courses of action that are socially expected. For example, the norm of social responsibility (Berkowitz & Daniels, 1964) states that one should help an individual who is dependent without consideration of external reward. When, for example, an adult sees a child in need of help, the norm of social responsibility is triggered and the adult helps the child. Berkowitz and Daniels show that as the need or dependency increases there a greater tendency to help, and Eisenberg-Berg (1979) finds that the importance of need as a modifier of helping increases as children get older. However, a change in the external circumstances surrounding the situation may well change the applicable norm. Thus, if the child in fact had a highly infectious disease such that helping the child would endanger the life of the adult, the appropriate norm would be altered.

Various social norms have been proposed in addition to the norm of social responsibility. The norm of reciprocity (Gouldner, 1960) states that individuals should return favors and help those who have helped them. Gouldner describes the importance of reciprocity in human societies and states that self-interest is the motivating force behind this norm. Reciprocity has also received considerable attention from evolutionary biologists as an explanation for behavior in which there are temporary imbalances in resource flow (Trivers, 1971). Behavior performed on the expectation that future benefits will occur for the altruist presents no theoretical problems, since self-interest is paramount. Trivers proposes that reciprocal altruism should be most common in species, such as humans, where individuals can recognize each other and are able to remember altruistic acts long after their occurrence. The anthropological literature described above indicates quite clearly that reciprocity is a key feature of human social relationships: Individuals attempt to avoid exploitation by nonrelatives by attempting to obtain reciprocal benefits. Reciprocity becomes less important within close familial relationships. From a sociobiological perspective these findings occur because individuals are willing to tolerate greater imbalance in social relationships when it is in their genetic self-interest to do so.

Peterson (1980) contrasted the norm of social responsibility with the norm of reciprocity by comparing a situation in which children in kindergarten and grades 3 and 6 could help others who needed help and one in which children of this age could donate to others who could in turn help them. There was a clear tendency for children to donate more in the reciprocating condition and this tendency increased with age. However, when simply asked whether the children preferred a reciprocating donor to one who donated without hope of reciprocation, only a minority favored the reciprocal donors, a tendency that also decreased with age. The results point to the difference between verbal and behavioral allegiance to a norm and also indicate two quite different norms, depending on whether self-interest is involved: In cases of self-interest there is an increase in endorsement of a reciprocity norm, while in cases where self-interest is not involved there is a decrease in such endorsement.

Consistent with the above, Dreman (1976) found that knowledge of the recipient increased donating behavior in kindergarten children. If the subject is anonymous to the recipient, donation decreases from a high level if the recipient donated to the subject, to medium if the recipient donated to someone else, to low if the recipient made no donation. There appear, however, to be socioeconomic status and sex differences in the importance of reciprocity. Dreman and Greenbaum (1973) found that middle-class boys donated more when the recipient would find out who had donated to them, but this was not found for boys or girls of lower socioeconomic status. Children of professional families were more affected by reciprocity. In addition, Berkowitz and Friedman (1967) found that children with entrepreneurial fathers were more influenced by reciprocity considerations.

Another set of norms revolves around the idea of distributive justice. A typical experiment involves children being asked to divide up some resource among a group of subjects who obtained the resource as a reward for performing a task. Members of the group differ in their contribution to the performance of the task. Preschool children utilize a norm of self-interest, giving themselves a greater proportion whether or not they made an important contribution (Damon, 1977; Masters, 1971). Around the age of 5 years, however, children divide rewards either according to a norm of equality, in which each child gets an equal share, or a norm of equity, in which each child is given a reward in proportion to the contribution it made. As indicated in the discussions of Damon (1977) (see pp. 242–243), self-interest plays an important role in influencing behavior in these situations.

Self-interest also influences whether the norm of equity or equality is used. Streator and Chertkoff (1976) found that children who contributed more to a task suggested a division of reward based on equity, while children who contributed less or an average amount opted for an equal division. In addition, they found that if children are told they are supervisors they tend to use equity divisions. Barnett and Andrews (1977) found that boys tended to give proportional rewards to themselves when they were more productive, but tended to give fewer rewards to a group they were in competition with even when this other group was more productive. Possible reciprocity also enters into the decision process: Children who are told they will have future interactions with other group members have a greater tendency to divide resources more equally (Graziano, Brody, & Bernstein, 1980). Indeed Graziano *et al.* (1980) found that the prospect of future interaction resulted in third-grade children discounting the fact that poor performance was caused by the child being aggressive. In the absence of information on possible future interactions, children gave less to individuals whose poor performance was the result of being aggressive and more to individuals whose poor performance was the result of altruism. Possible reciprocity may also be the reason that being told that the group members are part of a team results in a tendency for an equal division of rewards compared to a nonteam situation (Barnett & Andrews, 1977).

It should be noted that these findings implicating the importance of self-interest in distributive justice are less clear in girls. Barnett and Andrews (1977) found that boys gave proportional rewards to themselves when they were more productive than a competitor, but fewer rewards to the competititor when the competitor was more productive. Girls awarded fewer rewards to themselves when they were more productive than they awarded to a competitor when the competitor was more productive. However, in both cases the girls departed from an equal distribution toward giving rewards on the basis of performance (i.e., equity). The authors suggest that this sex difference is the result of socialization differences which emphasize competitive, instrumental behavior for boys and group welfare for girls, but it should be noted that the girls' distribution did reflect a strong influence of equity considerations. In a situation where self-interest was not involved, Leventhal, Popp, and Sawyer (1973) found no difference between kindergarten boys and girls in the tendency to reward equitably. However, in a study with first and second graders, boys' distributions reflected equity more than did those of girls. But when told that an adult would evaluate their performance, the boys' allocations became less equitable (i.e., more equal) and did not differ from girls' allocations.

Although the norm approach to moral and altruistic behavior has been an important research tradition, it has not been without its critics. Krebs (1970) noted that there was a danger that social norms were little more than tautologies, since they can be used as an *ex post facto* explanation of any behavior. If the behavior does not occur in a particular situation, one can simply state that the norm does not apply and invent a new norm. Rest (1983) notes that social norms are really an inference to an individual's thought patterns on the basis of behavior. If one is able to show that a slightly different situation gives rise to different behavior, one has also discovered an additional factor supposedly taken into account in moral situations. Typically, however, researchers do not attempt to actually discover the person's real thinking processes. In addition, the number of moral norms is unknown, so that the result is a sort of piecemeal, *post hoc* theory.

Perhaps the most extended critique of the social norm approach is that of Darley and Latane (1970), who point out that social norms are often contradictory. For example, there are norms for giving help to others and norms stating that it is demeaning to accept help from others. Norms for helping sometimes conflict with norms for respecting the privacy of others. Norms are also quite vague and general. In order to be really useful in providing guidelines for behavior, norms would have to be qualified with an extensive list of exceptions, some of which arise only infrequently. They provide data from an experiment on helping that indicated that subjects provided strangers with change for a quarter, time of day, or directions, but not money. These data can be explained by invoking the norm of helping for the former findings and the norm of "looking out for oneself" in the latter. In addition, the findings that subjects did not give their names indicates a norm against invading privacy, but providing one's name to the subject along with the request for help increased helping, perhaps because it triggered the norm of reciprocity. Sex differences between males and females are explained by other norms, such as helping the weak and being gallant. The result is a proliferation of norms that is used to explain every significant variable in the experiment. As Krebs (1970) and Rest (1983) would agree, the result is a very *ad hoc* set of explanations. Congruent with this criticism is the statement of Piliavin, Dovidio, Gaertner, and Clark (1981) that the normative approach to altruistic behavior has fallen into disrepute because "it was too general to provide for accurate behavioral predictions" (p. 29).

In addition, Darley and Latane (1970) point out that there is no evidence that people actually use norms to guide their behavior. People often decide to help in a very short period of time, almost impulsively, and do not appear to make a complicated decision based on a choice among norms. In their own work they were unable to elicit any indication from subjects that they actually made any explicit reference to a norm. Therefore, as Rest (1983) also suggested, the link between behavior and social norms as an underlying cognitive process is quite weak. Indeed, Darley and Latane (1970) suggest that quite often individuals cite socially acceptable normative explanations for behavior that is actually determined by cost–benefit considerations. Their example is a particularly good one: When a child sees its parents giving money (presumably a relatively small amount) to the Salvation Army, the child learns the norm of giving to the less fortunate. However, if the child then gives away a very costly family possession, it quickly learns that one has to take cost into account and not be too swayed by a simple application of norms. Consistent with the previous discussion of moral reasoning, the authors conclude that applying norms is often a matter of rationalizing the rightness of actions.

Finally, Darley and Latane point out that the social norm approach is difficult to reconcile with some empirical findings. One would expect that the presence of bystanders would increase the salience of social norms for helping and even provide negative sanctions for not helping. However, the presence of bystanders has been seen consistently to lessen the tendency to help.

As an alternative analysis, Darley and Latane propose that the findings can be more simply interpreted in terms of subjects behaving in terms of their estimates of the costs and benefits in the situation. Although found from work with adults, the experimental results used to support this point of view fit well with much of the literature on children's altruism and moral behavior. An experimenter asked a confederate for directions and was misinformed, putting pressure on the naive subject to provide correct directions. When the misinformer behaved in a threatening way or behaved in an embarrassing manner, subjects were much less likely to correct him, presumably assessing this behavior as a potential risk. Having the question-asker dressed as a tourist or behave in an altruistic manner did not increase correct direction giving, even though these manipulations would be expected to arouse helping norms. Costs and benefits also figure in their previous results: Subjects were much less likely to give an individual a dime than they were to give change, tell the time, or provide directions.

These considerations suggest that the literature on social norms in children be regarded as indicating that children fundamentally approach situations in which rewards are allocated or help is provided by viewing the situation in terms of costs and benefits. Thus, reciprocity is a fundamental feature of behavior in these situations, and we have seen that self-interest influences the application of equitable versus equal allocations of resources. Peterson's (1980) results indicate that cost–benefit considerations strongly affect whether social responsibility or reciprocity is paramount, and the results of other studies reviewed above (e.g., Streator & Chertkoff, 1976) indicate that cost–benefit considerations also influence whether the norm of equity or equality is utilized. This tradition of research also shows that there are modifiers of the cost–benefit considerations which tip the balance one way or the other, but probably never completely render these considerations irrelevant. Thus, whether or not a person is deserving of his or her situation and whether the motives of the person in the situation are laudable or not affect the degree of generosity of subjects. Sex differences, perhaps due to socialization, also occur, but we have seen that they do not entirely erase cost–benefit considerations. Such an analysis is consistent with the view of Darley and Latane (1970) described above, as well as with theories of helping behavior in adults: As described in Chapter 8 in greater detail, cost and reward considerations are central to the theories of Piliavin et al. (1981) and Schwartz and Howard (1984; see also Epstein & Hornstein, 1969, and Wagner & Wheeler, 1969).

V. Reasoning about Altruistic Events

Eisenberg and her colleagues (see Eisenberg, Lennon, & Pasternack, 1986, for a review) have studied reasoning about altruistic situations. Whereas Kohlberg's dilemmas have focused on questions of justice (i.e., fairness) and the violation of prohibitions, the dilemmas constructed by Eisenberg focus on responsibility and caring. Typically, the self-interest of a story character is pitted against helping another individual in a situation in which the role of laws and other types of formal obligations are minimized. A typical example of an altruistic moral dilemma is as follows:

> One day a girl (boy) named Mary (Eric) was going to a friend's birthday party. On her (his) way she (he) saw a girl (boy) who had fallen down and hurt her (his) leg. The girl asked Mary to go to her house and get her parents so the parents could come and take her to the doctor. But if Mary did run and get the child's parents, she would be late for the birthday party and miss the ice cream, cake and all the games. What should Mary do? Why?

On the basis of cross-sectional and longitudinal studies of children's interview material, Eisenberg found evidence for a variety of types of altruistic reasoning. Trend analysis of the cross-sectional data indicated that children who suggested that the protagonist help the other person tended to use less stereotypic categorical reasoning and less approval/interpersonal orientation reasoning as they got older. In addition, they used more self-reflective and internalized affect categories at later ages. In general hedonistic reasoning was used less by older children whether or not they said that the protagonist should assist. Longitudinal data indicated in addition that needs-oriented reasoning occurred increasingly with age and that the use of both hedonistic and needs-oriented reasoning leveled off at approximately age 9 years (see also Eisenberg et al., 1987). More sophisticated self-reflective and empathic types of reasoning increased into the high school years.

Based on these data, Eisenberg proposes five levels of altruistic reasoning. These levels are not conceived as stages in Kohlberg's sense, and thus are not viewed as universal, sequentially invariant, homogeneous hierarchical structures. The highest levels are reached by only a minority of high school students, and even students who use advanced types of altruistic reasoning will sometimes use hedonistic reasoning when deciding that a protagonist should not assist. Thus, Eisenberg-Berg (1979) found that 73 of 125 sixth- to 12th-grade subjects chose at least one nonaltruistic response, and the great majority of these (69 of 73) did so for hedonstic reasons.

As in the case of moral reasoning, there is evidence that increasing the costs of the hypothetical behavior increases the frequency of nonaltruistic choices. Bar-Tal, Raviv, and Shavit (1981) found that all of their 4- to 5-year-old and 7- to 8-year-old subjects gave an altruistic response to situations in which a child could help another. In these hypothetical stories there were relatively low costs to the altruist, whereas in the study by Eisenberg-Berg (1979) the costs were rather high, for example, donating blood over a prolonged period in a situation where this behavior would result in weakness, loss of job, and disruption of studies, and there was a correspondingly lower endorsement of altruistic choices. In addition, Eisenberg-Berg and Neal (1981) found that when the cost of the altruistic act in the story was high, there was more hedonistic reasoning and less needs-oriented reasoning. These authors also found that subjects asked to imagine themselves as central characters in a story used significantly more hedonistic reasoning and less needs-oriented reasoning than when told that the subject of the story was a same-sex person. These results clearly implicate the importance of self-interest in altruistic reasoning.

Regarding the relationship between altruistic reasoning and altruistic behavior, there is again evidence for the importance of cost–benefit considerations. Eisenberg (1986) summarizes evidence indicating that for very low-cost behaviors there is no relation between level of altruistic reasoning and altruistic behavior. Such behaviors are performed in the manner of a social script, that is, automatically. As the task becomes more costly however, there is a moderate correlation, suggesting that children are engaged in a more extended cognitive appraisal of the situation. For example, Eisenberg, Pasternak, Cameron, and Tryon (1984) found a correlation of $-.53$ between hedonistic reasoning and spontaneous sharing, described as a relatively high-cost behavior.

These results can be interpreted to indicate that in situations of moderate cost individuals who engage in altruistic behavior are less likely to reason in a hedonistic manner. These results are analogous to the results from moral reasoning research, discussed above, indicating that sometimes moral reasoning acts to justify self-sacrificing behavior, and they are consistent with the proposition that as the costs of an action increase beyond a moderate level there will again be no correlation between high levels of altruistic moral reasoning in hypothetical situations and the actual altruistic behavior. This suggests a curvilinear relationship between hypothetical altruistic reasoning and altruism: At very low costs there is no relationship because the activities are automatic social scripts. At moderate costs there is a moderate relationship, and at high costs there is again no association.

Consistent with this perspective, the acts that are characterized as "high cost" in these studies are really of very low cost. For example, the "high-cost" manipulation in Eisenberg et al. (1987) involves donating to UNICEF from the eight nickels the children are given. Although the absolute levels of donations are not given here, this is clearly not an enormously costly activity, especially for the early adolescent subjects in the study, who, compared to the younger subjects, showed the most generosity and the least hedonistic reasoning. In this case there may well have also been demand characteristics of the situation that encouraged donating and were more salient to the older children, as found by Zarbatany *et al.* (1985; see also Chapter 8).

VI. SUMMARY AND CONCLUSION

Overall the data on the cognitive aspects of moral reasoning conform quite well to the predictions made by evolutionary theory. There is strong evidence for the importance of cost–benefit considerations in all of these data and in general the data as interpreted here challenge the central cognitive-developmental postulate of a rational observer who is progressively better able to take account of the objective interests of others and behave accordingly. Instead, there is evidence that the observer is a highly creative agent capable of reinterpreting situations and deceiving himself or herself (and others) in ways that generally promote self-interested behavior.

The foregoing provides strong support for the propositions derived from sociobiological theory. However, the importance of self-interest in moral and altruistic reasoning and behavior discussed in this chapter does not imply that humans or their societies are inevitably or invariably characterized by exploitation and inhumanity. In Chapter 8 it will be argued that familial socialization practices can have a significant effect on altruism even if they generally fail to eradicate self-interest completely. These results may be interpreted as a significant qualification of the perspective described above, since some individuals are apparently more altruistic than others, they are socialized differently, and they may well reason in a more advanced manner.

Moreover, whatever the tendencies for humans to be selfish, social controls on human behavior are possible and indeed have a demonstrable importance in human societies. These methods of control will be discussed extensively in Chapter 9. As indicated there, intense methods of socialization are able to make individuals extraordinarily self-sacrificing, and although these methods are not commonly found, they are of great theoretical importance. The results of this chapter must therefore be viewed in a larger context. From the perspective developed in Chapter 9, the data reviewed in this chapter must be qualified because they have been gathered in Western liberal democracies, a context that emphasizes the decentralizing influences of socialization within the family. Such influences are also present in the cross-cultural data reviewed here, but we shall see that the family can be completely circumvented as an agent of socialization and very high levels of self-sacrifice are indeed possible.

It should be pointed out that the emphasis here on self-interest in moral development is consistent with several other influential traditions. For example, Freudians regarded individuals as subject to strong instinctual tendencies of a selfish and aggressive nature and it is the role of society and especially the family to overcome these tendencies and instill a strong superego to combat these tendencies (see MacDonald, 1986c, for a discussion of the Freudian viewpoint on these matters from a sociobiological perspective). Behaviorists have also recognized the importance of controls on self-interest in developing morality and these controls and methods of socialization will be discussed in the following chapters. The behaviorist perspective regards self-interest as fundamental to human behavior and is therefore quite compatible with a sociobiological approach. Self-interest appears to be a very resilient and robust tendency in humans and it is only by invoking an ultimate-level theory such as sociobiology that this state of affairs is understandable.

Finally, the data described in this chapter might be said to support the basic premise of a cognitive-developmental perspective on moral reasoning. This premise is that as children become more sophisticated cognitively they are better able to reason in a manner that is more objective in the sense that it appeals to disinterested observers. The finding that young children apparently cannot be taught to reason at a Stage 5 or Stage 6 level is an important developmental fact and attests to the importance of the central tendencies of human development rather than an exclusive concern with individual differences between children at a particular age. This is the strength of the cognitive-developmental approach and the findings described above attest to the importance of structural factors as constraining the moral reasoning of children. As indicated in Chapter 1, such developmental constraints are an important source of departure from an adaptive optimum of behavior. An evolutionary perspective must suppose that these departures from optimum behavior are not truly maladaptive, since young children are shielded by adults from the consequences of many of their actions, but even more importantly, the evolutionary perspective implies that children will attempt to act in their self-interest and justify their actions to the best of their ability. Younger children are simply not as good at this game as are older children.

CHAPTER 8

Moral and Altruistic Development II

The Importance of Socialization and Affect

In Chapter 7, the roles of self-interest and cost–benefit analysis in moral decision-making and altruistic behavior were emphasized. Consistent with cognitive-developmental theory, the chapter stressed cognitive processing to the complete exclusion of affective responses to situations and people. In the present chapter, the other side of these issues is emphasized and an attempt is made to integrate these two approaches. No discussion of moral and altruistic behavior and cognition can be complete without a consideration of affect. As described in Chapter 3, the emotions are often important sources of motivation in human behavior. Whereas the previous chapter might give the impression that humans are passionless computers that cold-bloodedly calculate cost and benefit considerations, the present chapter will describe the evolutionary and ecological contexts of altruism and morality. In these contexts, affect must play a central role.

In many ways, the central theme of this chapter will be a familiar one. I have noted that sociobiological theory posits self-interest and cost–benefit analysis as central to human behavior. However, evolutionary theory is quite consistent with individuals accepting very high negative imbalances of resource flow in cases where the recipients of those resources are genetically related to them. The paradigmatic case is that of the human family. It was noted in Chapter 5 that there appear to be proximate affective mechanisms that function as centripetal forces in family life. These affective mechanisms create bonds of connectedness between individuals, and in the present chapter I explore the role of these bonds in biasing cost–benefit analyses in the direction of accepting a more negative balance in human relationships

In the following, I will examine the literature in order to assess the status of the following three hypotheses suggested by an evolutionary perspective: (a) Affective responses will bias cost–benefit considerations, but will not in general rule them out, and will in general be of less importance than cost–benefit considerations. (b) The affective responses will be most intense and thus most motivating when the consequences are important for the person's reproductive future, (that is, where the situation could have important positive or negative consequences to oneself or a close relative or other individual from whom one benefits. (c) Socialization within the family is an important vehicle for influencing the degree to which affective considerations are important, and this will be reflected in the cross-cultural literature on socialization and social structure.

These propositions will be examined following a discussion of the descriptive data on the development of emotions and their role as motivators of altruism.

I. DESCRIPTIVE STUDIES OF EMOTIONS AND THEIR ROLE IN MOTIVATING ALTRUISM

Apart from the Freudian perspective, socialization theories of altruism and moral development have only recently emphasized the role of affect. Traditional behaviorists such as Skinner (1971) viewed altruism and moral behavior as like any other behavior in being controlled by its consequences. Individuals behave in what we term a moral manner because other people and society have arranged the appropriate effective social contingencies. Clearly such behavior does not meet our definition of altruism. Recently, however, theorists have emphasized the role of affect in motivating altruistic and moral behavior. Particularly prominent have been the emotions of sympathy/empathy and self-evaluative emotions such as guilt and pride.

Regarding the origins of these emotions, Hoffman (1981, 1982) provides evidence that the primitive emotion of empathy "is a universal human response for which there is a constitutional basis" (Hoffman, 1981, p. 128). He describes results indicating that even 2- and 3-day old infants show empathic responses to others' distress. However, learning and increased cognitive sophistication regarding self and others result in important developmental influences on the eliciting conditions for empathy as well as on the subjective experience of empathy. Thus, the infant has no awareness of persons existing as separate physical entities. Later, children develop person permanence and perspective-taking abilities, and finally a sense of a person's plight extending beyond the immediate perceivable situation. Paralleling these four social-cognitive stages and dependent on them are four developmental levels of empathy ranging from the diffuse, global empathy of the infant up to empathy for another's general condition.

Although there is no question that the emotion of empathy exists and develops in children, the evidence for its role in motivating altruistic behavior is equivocal. Underwood and Moore (1982) state that there is little evidence for such a relationship in children. Their meta-analysis of published studies finding a positive relation between affective perspective taking and altruism suggested a correlation of approximately .25 between these measures. However, they also review several studies that show no relationships between these measures. Radke-Yarrow, Zahn-Waxler, and Chapman (1983) also note the inconsistent results in the developmental literature and suggest that the findings may be due, among other things, to poor measures of empathy, especially the use of techniques that attempt to induce empathy with stories or measure empathy by measuring the ability of the child to match the affect shown in stimulus materials.

Eisenberg (1986) notes the inconsistent findings on the relation between measures of empathy and altruism for children and suggests that the relationship is more consistently found when the measures of empathy are nonverbal. This suggestion fits well with the methodological suggestions of Radke-Yarrow et al. (1983) as well as the generally positive findings of a significant relation between empathy and altruism in the adult literature described below. In this literature the measures of empathy include measures of physiological arousal in response to highly salient, emotionally arousing stimuli. In the great majority of the studies on children there is little attempt to provide affectively arousing stimuli that would tend to elicit empathy in subjects. Research with adults has indicated several variables that affect the degree of arousal occurring in situations, such as the severity of the situation, the clarity of the cues emitted by the victim, and the physical distance between the victim and the potential helper (Piliavin et al., 1981).

Moreover, in the developmental literature the tasks measuring altruism are typically of very low cost to the child, often involving little more than politeness and common courtesy. For example, Eisenberg-Berg and Lennon (1980) measured altruism by observing naturally occurring instances of sharing, helping, and offering comfort. Many of these behaviors may well have involved simple reciprocity or anticipated future reciprocity. Reflecting the importance of costs so basic to an evolutionary analysis, Eisenberg et al. (1987) found a moderate correlation ($r = .38$) between a measure of empathy and donating behavior that was viewed as a relatively high-cost behavior, while the association between empathy and a low-cost helping behavior was nonsignificant. As we will see with the adult literature described below and as predicted by an evolutionary theory, the costs and benefits arising in a situation are important variables affecting whether the altruistic act will be performed and whether empathy motivates altruism or some substitute for altruism.

Given the strong possibility that the inconsistency of the developmental findings on the relation between empathy and altruism is due to methodological limitations, it is worthwhile describing research with adults that strongly implicates such a relationship. Indeed, the model presented by Piliavin et al. (1981; see also Dovidio, 1984) is remarkably similar to a model one would develop a priori on the basis of evolutionary theory and will be discussed in detail in the sections to follow. First, the authors focus on emergency situations. This focus on emergency situations is appropriate because such situations by definition involve fairly high potential costs to the victim. From an evolutionary perspective one would expect such situations to elicit the most motivation and hence the highest levels of arousal. From a methodological perspective it is these highly arousing situations that would be most likely to reveal the proposed relationship between empathy and altruism.

Second, the authors provide evidence that witnessing emergency situations involving other people results in arousal. For example, Gaertner, Dovidio, and Johnson (1979, discussed in Piliavin et al., 1981) presented an emergency over closed-circuit television in such a manner that the subjects were led to believe that the events they were watching were really happening. Heart-rate recordings of the subjects indicated a significant decrease in heart rate as the subjects oriented to the situation, followed by emotional activation and increased heart rate when the subjects believed they were seeing a real emergency. Piliavin et al. (1981) present further data indicating a linear increase in arousal as a result of length of time the subject is exposed to the emergency.

Third, there is evidence that emotional arousal in emergency situations motivates helping behavior, at least in situations that have low cost for the helper. Piliavin et al. (1981) summarize data from low-cost situations indicating a correlation of up to $-.77$

between latency to engage in helping behavior and levels of subjective and physiological arousal. This arousal is interpreted in a negative manner, as "being upset," presumably like the tense arousal discussed in Chapter 2. A further study by Gaertner and Dovidio (1977) indicated that subjects given a placebo that was said to increase arousal had longer latencies to intervene in an ambiguous helping situation than subjects who were told that the placebo would have nonarousing effects. These results are interpreted to indicate that subjects who are able to attribute their arousal to some other source take longer to intervene, while those who believe their arousal is due to the emergency help relatively quickly. If the emergency is made unambiguous by presenting extremely salient cues of pain and suffering, there is no difference due to the instructions accompanying the placebo, suggesting that in this case the subjects had no alternative but to attribute their arousal to the emergency. Separate analyses indicated that these findings were not due to differing cognitive interpretations of the emergency, such as how much help the victim needed, so that the results appear to be due to differences in the attribution of arousal.

II. THREE SOCIOBIOLOGICAL HYPOTHESES

A. Sociobiological Hypothesis 1

Affective responses will bias cost–benefit considerations, but will not in general rule them out, and will in general be of less importance than cost–benefit considerations.

As predicted by sociobiological theory, human helping behavior is not solely determined by emotional responses to victims in the helping situation. Unless emotional responses to events were in general programmed to covary with differences in self-interest, acting solely on the basis of arousal would often result in maladaptive behavior. However, with humans the costs and benefits of engaging in actions are often quite complex and emotions seem to offer a rather poor guide for action. Piliavin *et al.* (1981) have shown that the costs and benefits of helping are extremely important in influencing whether the emotions aroused in a helping situation lead to helping behavior or some substitute. Basic to their theory is the idea that individuals in a helping situation become emotionally aroused in a negative manner and seek to lower their arousal by incurring as few net costs (costs minus rewards) as possible. Piliavin *et al.* define costs and benefits as being subjective assessments by individuals in a helping situation, not "objectively" present costs and benefits. Thus, the individual is assumed to be acting on his or her own best estimates of the costs and benefits involved, and can clearly make mistakes in these assessments. Emotional arousal is crucial in motivating behavior in the the helping situation, but the behavior actually undertaken depends on the assessment of the costs and benefits involved.

This approach is consistent with an evolutionary perspective. The evolutionary approach suggests, however, that it is the real, objective costs and benefits resulting from the decision that will be the true measure of adaptiveness. Thus, an individual can seriously underestimate the costs of his or her behavior, so that helping results in far more losses than anticipated. Such an individual has made an evolutionary mistake and will suffer the consequences in terms of loss of fitness. Nevertheless, the decision to act was made on the basis of his or her subjective evaluation, and it is this proximal mechanism that must be studied by psychologists and understood by evolutionary biologists.

Piliavin *et al.* describe a variety of types of costs to the helper, such as the costs of foregone rewards and negative outcomes such as physical danger, effort expenditure, exposure to disgusting experiences, proximity to disliked groups, and embarrassment and feelings of inadequacy if one fails. In some of these the potential costs are clearly objectively present, such as physical danger, while in others, the costs, from an evolutionary perspective, may tend to be inflated by the potential helper, for example, being exposed to disgusting experiences such as the sight of blood or a person with a physical stigma. Other costs include costs of not helping the victim, such as self-blame, public censure, and possible prosecution, as well as empathy costs of not helping a victim who continues to suffer. Again, some of these costs may be quite real, while others, such as empathy costs, may only exist in the mind of the potential helper and be irrelevant or possibly deleterious to fitness. Indeed, if an individual is overwhelmed by empathy and acts without proper consideration of other objectively present costs of helping, the result may be quite maladaptive for the helper.

These considerations illustrate the challenge and difficulty of applying evolutionary theory to behavior. From an evolutionary perspective it would be ideal if people were equipped with unfailingly accurate cognitive/affective devices which would enable them to objectively assess the consequences of their behavior. Such a device would fit the adaptationist logic of evolutionary theory very well, but the devices that actually exist are quite complicated and, as suggested below, are prone to being influenced by such poorly behaved variables as emotion and temperament. If, for example, the temperamental trait of emotionality influences the degree of empathy one feels in a situation and/or the degree of impulsivity affects behavior in a helping situation, and if temperament is influenced by a polygenic biological trait is argued in Chapter 2, then individuals extreme on these dimensions may have a biologically based tendency to exhibit maladaptive behavior due to being overwhelmed by empathy to the exclusion of objectively present costs and/or due to acting impulsively without proper consideration of the costs.

As a minimal derivation from evolutionary theory, however, we would expect that there will be a strong central tendency to assess the costs in helping situations in a reasonably objective manner and to act in a manner that is reasonably viewed as objectively adaptive. Piliavin *et al.* (1981) summarize several studies showing that possible physical harm to the helper depresses helping behavior. For example, they summarize data indicating that potential helpers are far less likely to intervene in a robbery attempt than in a situation in which a woman has fallen. In addition, increasing costs lowers helping in situations where helping is incompatible with making an appointment on time or incompatible with common social expectations. As a developmental example of the latter possibility, Staub (1971) found that seventh graders who were explicitly told they could enter a room were more likely to help a victim in that room than other subjects who were given no instructions or instructions prohibiting entry. As a further developmental example, Pavlos (1971) found that children were more likely to respond to a teacher's feigned heart attack if they were explicitly told that such behavior would not interfere with their winning candy bar rewards.

Regarding the role of costs to the victim, Piliavin *et al.* (1981) find that, congruent with evolutionary theory, helping increases with increasing severity of costs to the victim, but only where there are low or moderate costs to the helper. In situations of high cost to the helper there will be a tendency to reinterpret the situation in such a manner as to render aid unnecessary or unjustified: Evidence is provided that in such situations potential helpers reinterpret the situation in a manner that justifies not helping ("She's not really suffering") or derogate the victim ("He never should have gone there in the first place"), or diffuse responsibility ("Someone else will take care of things").

Actually, increasing the costs to the victim of not intervening often results in increased costs to the potential helper for not intervening. For example, an individual who fails to aid another person who is seriously injured will be subject to severe public sanctions, including legal prosecution in some countries. Thus, there tends to be more help in low-cost situations where the potential helper is under public scrutiny or has personal responsibility in the situation. Schwartz and Gottlieb (1976, 1980) found that individuals who were slow to respond or failed to respond when they were anonymous were especially likely to respond when they knew their actions could be observed by others. Such behavior is consistent with the view that helping is often motivated by the possibility of future rewards and is hence a form of reciprocity (see, e.g., Alexander, 1987, for a detailed discussion of such a view). These results are consistent with the developmental literature described in Chapter 7 indicating increased helping behavior in situations where individuals would have future interactions compared to when the helper and person helped are anonymous. Once again, possible future reciprocity or other social rewards accruing to individuals who are known to have helped others appear to be a reasonable explanation.

As indicated above, assignment of personal responsibility increases helping behavior, presumably because this increases the potential costs to the helper for not helping: A nonhelping individual in such circumstances will be subject to increased possibility of public sanctions if there is a bad outcome. For example, Moriarty (1975) found that individuals who were asked to watch another person's belongings in a public place while the owner was absent were much more likely to intervene in a faked robbery attempt than individuals not so requested, even though these latter individuals were aware of the possessions and their rightful owner. In addition, individuals who are assigned responsibility and who do not help are much more likely to redefine the situation in a way that frees them of the necessity to do anything. Thus, Staub (1970) found that responsible individuals who failed to help were more likely to claim that nothing had really happened to warrant helping, while the nonresponsible nonhelpers engaged in much less distortion of the situation. These results are reminiscent of the self-serving distortions of moral reasoning described in Chapter 7, and Krebs et al. (1988), in their evolutionary account of the self-esteem, noted similar attempts to distort reality in favor of self-justification and high self-esteem (see also Chapter 3).

Finally, mention should be made of so-called impulsive helping behavior. Piliavin et al. (1981) describe studies indicating that in some cases individuals seem to be relatively unconcerned with costs and help without any very complicated or conscious cognitive processes. They define impulsive helping as occurring in studies in which at least 85% of the subjects respond within an average of 15 seconds to the emergency. Subjects in such studies often report that they intervene without thinking of the possible consequences, and from an evolutionary perspective such behavior is therefore potentially maladaptive.

However, the behavior of the individuals in these studies was far from being completely irrational. Only two of the published studies reviewed by Piliavin *et al.* are said to involve situations of potentially high cost to the helper, one the study by Moriarty, described above, in which responsible subjects prevented theft of others' belongings, and a study by Clark and Word (1974) in which subjects saw a staged accident in which a victim was apparently severely shocked and where most subjects (79% in one study) interpreted the situation to be dangerous for themselves. In situations where the emergency was unambiguous approximately 90% of subjects tested alone helped the victim, but 71% of those helping did so in a way that would reduce or eliminate their risk of injury. The authors note that possible severe consequences to the bystander increased the degree of indirect, less risky helping to 29% of the subjects compared to none of the subjects in a different study where there was no danger to the helper. Second, impulsive helping was more common where the subject had the appropriate knowledge and skills in the helping situation, so that there is really less perceived or actual danger to the helper. Clark and Word (1974) found that individuals who knew something about electricity were more likely to help and did so with less risk to themselves than did less skilled individuals.

Another variable strongly related to helping behavior in "impulsive" helping is prior contact with the victim, and Piliavin *et al.* propose that friendship or a love relationship increases the probability of impulsive helping by increasing arousal in the helping situation. The intense emotional response of an individual to the plight of a relative or loved one in fact may well have a very rational result despite being based primarily on emotional arousal in the helping situation. Thus, although impulsive helping appears to exist in some cases, it tends to occur more often where affective or genetic ties between individuals make such helping in one's self-interest. In terms of an evolutionary approach, anticipated future reciprocity or direct genetic benefits facilitate impulsive helping behavior. Moreover, the study by Clark and Word makes it clear that even "impulsive" helping is facilitated by having appropriate skills that minimize the risk of injury, and the great majority of people in fact take steps to minimize their risk of injury. These results are anticipated on the basis of evolutionary theory and indeed one can easily imagine circumstances under which the rate of direct helping would be far lower than the 90% rate found in the Clark and Word study, even under circumstances of maximum clarity. No one would expect a stranger to attempt to save an individual in a building with a raging fire, and few individuals would attempt to do so. Indirect means of helping, such as phoning the fire department, would be utilized instead. This is not to say that impulsive, maladaptive helping behavior does not occur. Individuals who are not professionally trained to provide rescues and who die attempting to save others are rare but not unknown (see Huston, Geis, & Wright, 1976, for an example). The point here is to claim that such behavior is maladaptive and an evolutionary mistake. For these individuals, a better thought-out plan of action or no action at all would have been the better course of action. Such impulsivity is an evolutionary dead end.

Nevertheless, I have described temperamental traits (see Chapter 2) that may well influence the extent to which individuals incur costs in helping and their impulsiveness in doing so. The trait of emotionality might well predispose some people to have much more intense emotional responses to the plight of another individual than would others. As we have seen, there is evidence that empathy motivates helping behavior and that individual differences in arousal in helping situations are correlated with latencies to intervene. These individual differences may be mediated in part by the temperamental trait of emotionality.

In addition, the temperamental trait of impulsivity, which is correlated with sensation seeking and extraversion (see Chapter 2), may well affect the extent to which one ignores costs in a helping situation. An individual high on this trait would be attracted to the danger and risk inherent in some helping situations and tend to underestimate his or her personal potential costs. Since males are higher on this trait than females, the influence of temperament would result in males behaving more impulsively in helping situations. There is indeed evidence that males are more likely to help than females in emergency situations (Deaux, 1976). However, the data can also be explained as being due to lower costs for helping for males as a result of larger physical size or more expertise (Piliavin *et al.*, 1981). A better test of the impulsivity theory would be to find personality correlates of individuals who help in highly dangerous situations. Some anecdotal evidence that temperament is important is given by Huston *et al.* (1976). They studied men who had been injured in the course of intervening in the commission of a crime, and state that "most of our Samaritans are risk-takers, men on familiar and rather amiable terms with violence." Moreover, the Samaritans had a "low-boiling point" and were much more easily provoked into aggression than a random sample of college men. These results suggest that, in addition to impulsivity, these individuals were high in emotionality, but that rather than empathy or sympathy mediating helping behavior, the emotion was more like anger: The men seemed more intent on attacking the criminal than helping the victim.

B. Sociobiological Hypothesis 2

The affective responses will be most intense and thus most motivating when the consequences are important for the person's reproductive future, that is, the situation could have important positive or negative consequences to oneself or a close relative or other individual from whom one benefits.

This hypothesis states essentially that people will become more emotionally aroused in a helping situation depending on who the potential recipient of help is and on how serious the consequences to the person are. The hypothesis reflects the discussion in Chapter 3 on the importance of resources and possible costs in affecting emotional intensity in general. From a sociobiological perspective, we would expect that, all things being equal, people would become more aroused (and thus more motivated to act in a helping situation) in cases where relatives and friends are experiencing distress, and most aroused when confronted with a direct threat to the self. In the case of relatives, the theory of kin selection predicts that people will have a very large affective investment in the welfare of their relatives and much less in the case of nonrelatives.

The affective investment one has in another individual, including relatives, will also be moderated by the reproductive value of the relative. (See Chapter 5 for a definition of reproductive value.) Sociobiological theory predicts people will have a tendency to discriminate between individuals of differing reproductive value in assessing the costs and benefits in a helping situation: All things being equal, it would be better to help the adolescent female than to help the postmenopausal woman. From the perspective of the present chapter, this results in the hypothesis that individuals in a helping situation would tend to become more affectively aroused (and thus motivated to help) when individuals with relatively high reproductive value need help compared to individuals with low reproductive value.

The category of friends defines a group of nonrelatives who are expected to have an increased tendency to help each other. The idea of friendship implies some affective investment between the friends and suggests that in a helping situation a friend would become more affectively aroused and thus more motivated to act than in the case of a nonfriend. From an evolutionary perspective the basis of friendship is likely to involve reciprocity, and the findings of Youniss (1986) reviewed in Chapter 6 strongly support this view. Thus, the increased affective investment in a friendship facilitates helping behavior and occurs in the context of a reciprocal relationship in which the helper can expect similar treatment if he or she should need help in the future.

In addition, it should be mentioned that there may be other characteristics of non-relatives besides friendship that are particularly likely to facilitate helping behavior in others. One that comes to mind is simply variation in wealth. Individuals who are wealthy are expected to be ideal targets of helping behavior because they are better able to reciprocate in a very generous manner. The theory would predict that in an experimental situation individuals would be much more likely to offer high-cost helping behavior to wealthy-appearing individuals than to individuals who appear to be impoverished.

Finally, another characteristic expected to influence whether helping occurs is the similarity of the helper to the person helped. Genetic similarity theory (Rushton et al., 1984) predicts that individuals will preferentially help others who resemble themselves on the assumption that the same genes may possibly be involved, even if these genes are not identical as a result of common descent (i.e., identical because of familial relationships). Thus, one is expected to preferentially help others from the same racial-ethnic group or one with the same physical appearance or other personal characteristics as oneself. Genetic similarity theory is a very powerful explanation of a wide variety of phenomena, including assortative mating, correlations of phenotypic characteristics among friends (Chapter 6), discriminative parenting (Chapter 5), and ethnic nepotism (see Rushton et al., 1984, for a review).

Thus, evolutionary theory predicts that the ideal beneficiary of high-cost helping behavior would be a close relative with high reproductive value in whom one has previously invested a great deal. One should be least likely to help an impoverished stranger from a different racial-ethnic group whose physical appearance is quite unlike one's own.

1. Data on Empathy, Costs/Benefits, and the Bystander–Victim Relationship

Piliavin et al. (1981) provide an "extreme example" which confirms the fundamental logic of an evolutionary approach: "it is difficult to deny that an emergency occurring to one's own child would be more arousing and failure to intervene more costly than the same emergency involving a total stranger" (p. 144). Further, "we seem more likely to put ourselves in the place of a victim we perceive to be like us, or one whom we know and have ties with than to do so with a stranger or with a person perceived to be different" (p. 144). These statements fit well with kinship and/or genetic similarity theory and are amply supported by experimental findings. The work of Segal (1988) comparing a variety of cooperative and competitive situations in monozygotic (MZ) and dizygotic (DZ) twin children documents the importance of biological relatedness in altruism and is consistent with the idea that affective ties between closely related individuals mediates this relationship. Compared to DZ twin pairs, MZ twins more often completed a puzzle task and their behavior during the task was generally more cooperative rather than individualistic. In a test of cooperation, MZ twins worked harder for their co-twin than did DZ twins. Naturalistic observations of twins revealed that MZ twins tended to interact with each other more than DZ twins and be physically nearer each other, while DZ twins socialized outside the twinship. Segal also provides evidence that MZ twins have a greater affective investment in the twinship than DZ twins, as indicated by bereavement reactions and reactions to reunion episodes for twins reared apart. Further evidence that genetic relatedness affects altruism or, in this case, its opposite, comes from studies of discriminative parenting. For example, Daly and Wilson (1981) show that parents are much more likely to abuse children who are not biologically related to them, that is, stepchildren, rather than biological children (see Chapter 5 for further examples).

Regarding the similarity of the potential recipient of help, Stotland (1969) and Krebs (1975) found that similarity to the victim resulted in increased empathic arousal as measured by a variety of physiological indicators, including heart rate, vasoconstriction, and skin conductance as well as self-report measures of arousal. Krebs (1975) also found that subjects who were led to feel that the potential victim was similar to themselves were more likely to take electric shocks in place of the potential victim than were subjects not so manipulated. Moreover, Coke, Batson, and McDavis (1978) found that telling subjects to imagine themselves in place of the victim resulted in higher levels of empathic arousal and helping. Another example of similarity is membership in an ethnic group, and there is evidence that such membership affects helping behavior. For example, Hornstein, Masor, Sole, and Heilman (1971) found that pedestrians in a Jewish section of New York City were much more likely to return lost envelopes if they contained pro-Israeli material rather than pro-Arab material (69% versus 30%). Finally, there is evidence that parents grieve more for dead children when the child resembles their side of the family (Smith, 1988).

The data on discriminative parenting described in Chapter 5 support the predictions of greater affective investment depending on the reproductive value of the expected recipient. As described more fully in Chapter 5, there is evidence that parents show more grief for an older child dying shortly before his or her reproductive years than for a younger child or a fetus (Littlefield & Rushton, 1986), and the the evidence on child abuse and abandonment described there (e.g., Daly & Wilson, 1981) also indicate that parents of defective infants often have less of an affective investment in their offspring.

Finally, sociobiologists such as Alexander (1979, 1987) have often emphasized that one factor that promotes cooperation and altruistic behavior is the perception of a common external threat. Experimental results support this idea and in addition suggest that affective responses aroused in such threatening circumstances play a motivational role. Thus, several studies have indicated that an external threat increases awareness of in-group identity and that this is especially true when the threat is highly stressful and thus arousing. For example, Dovidio and Morris (1975) found that subjects with a common fate in a stressful experiment involving shock were more likely to help than were subjects in a nonstressful experiment. Sharing a stressful experience appears to increase identification with the group and from an evolutionary perspective results in increased helping due to increased need for reciprocation in a stressful situation. Similarly, in a military situation high levels of cooperation and self-sacrifice are promoted and engaged in because these behaviors result in increased confidence of reciprocity among the group as a whole in a situation where the lack of these behaviors will be individually as well as collectively disastrous. These results are consistent with the discussion of the highly stressful socialization methods of ancient Sparta described in Chapter 9. One consequence of these very brutal methods was an intense loyalty to the group and an extreme willingness to engage in self-sacrificing behavior.

Interestingly, while the prediction of increased helping depending on similarity to the victim follows naturally from evolutionary theory, purely psychological theories are forced to explain such data in a highly contrived manner. Thus, Piliavin *et al.* (1981) propose that individuals help similar others or members of an in-group because as these attributes increase, both the benefits for helping and the costs for not helping increase monotonically. This formulation does not do justice to the experimental procedure used, where often there is no reasonable expectation that helping simliar individuals will be associated with greater rewards (other than those proposed by evolutionary theory) for helping or greater losses for not helping. For example, in the Krebs (1975) study similarity was manipulated by telling the subject that he or she had a similar field of study in college as the confederate. However, if one includes self-interest and expected genetic benefits obtained by helping similar others and especially biological relatives, even very costly helping behavior can be explained. Without the biological theory one must remain puzzled as to why similarity and relatedness should be important at all, and their existence a sort of scientific curiosity.

Furthermore, Piliavin *et al.* (1981) claim that the costs for helping similar victims should be lower "if only because the bystander would be more confident of the consequences associated with interacting with a similar victim" (p. 149). This appears to be a rather *ad hoc* explanation and seems to state that similar individuals are more predictable than dissimilar individuals. The statement is not based on empirical evidence, but to the extent that it is true, it is perhaps based on the idea that similar individuals are more likely to reciprocate helping behaviors than are dissimilar individuals. This formulation would, of course, be quite compatible with evolutionary theory. Moreover, they claim empathic costs for not helping disimilar victims should be lower "because the bystander may be less concerned for the victim's well-being, while personal costs for not helping might also be lower since the social censure for not intervening may be expected to be less" (p. 149). These statements are undoubtedly true and reflect the fact that proximal mechanisms such as empathy generally act in an adaptive manner and that the social expectations that we have regarding helping situations reflect an understanding that helping in some sense *ought* to be more generous in cases where there is a strong biological motive for helping, that is, we do not expect people to behave in a maladaptively self-sacrificing manner. There would be little public censure for a man who refused to risk his life for an unrelated stranger, but failure to do so for one's own child would be cause for censure. On the other hand, it is fascinating that we often give great rewards to people who do perform very costly or potentially costly behaviors with no clear biological motive. A person who risks his or her life to save someone else's child is highly praised, but similar behavior in saving one's own child is expected. From an evolutionary perspective the act of the former individual may result in an evolutionary mistake, but it may also be a risky gamble that could pay off in the form of public acclaim for such behavior. Such "self-sacrificing" behavior is often very highly valued in society, presumably because we implicitly understand that without extensive social rewards for such acts they would not occur. Congruent with this perspective, Alexander (1987) has argued that moral systems are systems of indirect reciprocity: The beneficent individual may gain by: (1) engaging in profitable interactions with others who notice his or her behavior, (2) receiving direct rewards as a result of his or her behavior, and (3) strengthening the group itself in such a manner as to benefit his or her own long-term interests in the group's success.

C. Sociobiological Hypothesis 3

The socialization of altruistic affect within the family is an important vehicle for influencing the degree of altruism, and this will be reflected in the cross-cultural literature on socialization and social structure.

One of the fascinating and challenging aspects of applying evolutionary theory to behavior is the presence of mechanisms that appear to pull in opposite directions. In the discussion of the evolution of the human family in Chapter 5, I described evolutionary forces that tend to pull in opposite directions, some tending to promote family cohesion and some promoting the dissolution of the family unit. There is an analogous situation with respect to moral development. On one hand there is the strong central tendency for self-interest. This prediction of a main effect of self-interest flows naturally from evolutionary theory, where natural selection is conceived as operating most efficiently at the individual level rather than at higher levels such as the group or the species (see Alexander, 1987, for a recent discussion). The result of this conclusion is the idea that the interests of individual organisms are maximally divergent and that cohesive social structure is a difficult evolutionary achievement.

On the other hand is the reality of human social organization and the complex mechanisms that modify this primitive atomism in ways that are individually adaptive. That human behavior should be analyzable in terms of these opposing forces is testimony to the power of the central theoretical problem of evolutionary biology: the relationship between the individual and the group. Social evolution, as Wilson (1975) has emphasized, is not very common among animals. Most animals live their lives apart from their conspecifics and the evolution of social structure is accomplished only by balancing the genetic interests of individuals with the benefits of cooperation. Affect appears to be one of the prime mechanisms which, in conjunction with cost–benefit analysis, facilitates adaptive imbalances in resource flow among humans.

The thesis presented here is that the affective mechanisms promoting negative imbalances of resource flow developed within the nuclear family system. We have already seen that the nuclear family system is the primeval form of human social structure and was characteristic of the vast majority of human evolutionary history. It is therefore likely that the epigenetic rules that facilitate this cohesiveness evolved during this time. In addition, one of the fundamental tasks of the family group is to care for offspring. This system essentially involves the transfer of resources to other, related individuals, and since the recipients of this flow of resources are related to the donor, the behavior is highly adaptive. Although it is conceivable that the elaboration of human parenting would involve purely cognitive appraisals of costs and benefits, it is clear from the discussions of

Chapters 4 and 5 that affective mechanisms have assumed a prominent place in motivating the resource flow that is characteristic of parenting. In the present chapter the developmental literature on the associations between warm parent–child interactions and altruistic behavior will be emphasized.

1. Warm Parent–Child Interactions: The Affective Basis of Human Connectedness

There has been much research into the associations between measures of parent–child warmth and measures of prosocial behavior and altruism. This literature has been reviewed several times recently (Staub, 1979; Mussen & Eisenberg-Berg, 1977; Radke-Yarrow et al., 1983). There appears to be some relation between measures of these behaviors, but the relationships are not particularly robust. Radke-Yarrow et al. (1983) point out that there have been problems measuring the construct of parental warmth, and, as is usual in the developmental literature in these areas, the cost of the measured altruistic and prosocial behaviors is generally quite low.

Nevertheless, the thesis that warm parent–child relations facilitate altruism is a defensible one, for three reasons:

1. It is consistent with the evolutionary view of the family described in Chapters 4 and 5 and the data on helping behavior described in the first section of this chapter indicating that close affective relationships tend to result in greater and quicker helping behavior. From an evolutionary perspective the intense affective relations occurring within the family would be expected to foster a maximal amount of negative imbalances of resource flow and helping behaviors. The affective relationships would foster a cohesive social structure, one in which individuals would be biased to aid other individuals and in which strict reciprocity would not be necessary. As described more fully below, these affective relationships would not make cost–benefit analysis irrelevant, but would tend to bias the cost–benefit analysis toward accepting a more negative balance of resource flow.

It is an important corollary of this thesis that the effect of warm parent–child relationships may extend far beyond the family. The mechanism by which warm parent–child relationships would foster helping and altruism beyond the family is still a matter of speculation, but the mechanism may well involve simple generalization to others (Staub, 1979). In this view, affect is blind in the sense that once warm relationships are established within the family, they tend to bias other relationships by making individuals who have been socialized in this manner less likely to engage in highly exploitative interactions with others. We have seen in Chapter 6 that there is evidence for the converse of this proposition: Hostile and rejecting parenting is associated with aggressive behavior in children.

In conjunction with the theory of temperament described in Chapter 2, and especially the theory described there of possible environmental influences on the social reward systems, one might speculate that the neural systems underlying the reward system that is responsive to the behaviors of parents classified as warm becomes elaborated when children are socialized by warm parents. Such individuals would be expected to be more sensitive as adults to the rewarding aspects of the nurturant behaviors of others, and hence attracted to warm, nurturant people. Conversely, the neural systems underlying hostility and aggression would be relatively less elaborated and such individuals would have a high threshold for aggressive, exploitative response. Moreover, such exploitative, aggressive responses would be incompatible with receiving responses from the victims of these responses that would be socially reinforcing to them; i.e., an exploited, victimized person is unlikely to respond with warmth to the person responsible for these acts. Thus, if an individual becomes highly sensitive to signals of warmth in others, he or she is unlikely to respond to others with hostility, since this is incompatible with receiving what he or she highly values. In a sense, therefore, this theory proposes a sort of affective reciprocity underlying the effects of parental warmth: Much like the subjects in Aronfreed's (1968) classic experiments, if someone makes someone else happy, the recipient of this gesture feels compelled to respond in kind.

It should be noted that such a mechanism may lead to maladaptive behavior. This is especially so in situations where the ecological context is far removed from the environment of evolutionary adaptedness. Thus, Alexander (1979) suggests that children in a contemporary industrial society may form attachments to nonrelatives with whom they are socialized and these attachments may make them more altruistic than would be predicted by evolutionary theory. Correspondingly, warm parent–child interactions may bias children toward altruism not only within the family, but also toward people far removed from the close biological relationships occurring within the family. On this view, which I find quite plausible, children subjected to warm parent–child interactions might still distinguish between close relatives and friends with whom they have specific close attachments and others with little or no such specific attachments. However, there would still remain a tendency to bias all human relationships toward helping and altruism compared to individuals reared by hostile, rejecting parents. Although there is the possibility that such a mechanism could lead to maladaptive behavior within contemporary societies, the data described in Chapter 7 and the first section of this chapter indicate that in general cognition is able to keep this affective biasing mechanism "on a leash" so that extremely self-sacrificing behavior is a rarity even in a society where warm parent–child interactions are the norm.

2. The thesis that warm parent–child relationships facilitate altruism is consistent with the cross-cultural and historical evidence. Despite the modest support for the importance of warm family relationships in the developmental literature within contemporary Western societies, a different picture emerges when we turn to the anthropological and historical record. As indicated in Chapter 5, cross-cultural and historical data are likely to reflect far greater extremes of environmental variation than within-cultural studies. If indeed altruism is affected by environmental influences involving environment-expectant familial affective systems, these relationships should be more obvious in the cross-cultural and historical record, and this is indeed the case.

As indicated above, the generalization theory of warm parent–child relationships implies that maladaptive behaviors could occur in situations where the nuclear family social structure gives way to larger forms characterized by lower average degrees of genetic relatedness. The prediction then would be that warm parent–child interactions, nuclear family social structure, and socialization for altruism would be co-occurring phenomena. As indicated in Chapter 5, this does in fact appear to be the case. It was seen there that as economic production increases, there is a tendency to form larger social groups based on the cooperation of related males. Sexual competition increases, as indicated by the presence of polygyny and the practice of bridewealth, and males, in order to be evolutionarily successful, are forced to establish themselves in larger social group-ings with a much lower average degree of genetic relatedness than that found in the nuclear family. Even within close familial relationships conflicts of interest assume much greater importance, as indicated by the discussion of father–son and brother–brother conflict described there.

Under these circumstances a generalized altruism is quite maladaptive and this type of social organization is characterized by distant, rejecting parent–child interactions. Individuals in these societies are thus socialized in a manner that will tend to bias them against helping and altruism and toward exploitative, antagonistic interactions. The work of Paige and Paige (1981), described more fully in Chapter 5, indicates quite clearly that these societies are characterized by fissioning and constant feuding and warfare. The thesis here is that the type of socialization that is adaptive in these circumstances includes the patterns of hostile, rejecting parenting actually found there. Moreover, the cross-cultural survey of Rohner (1975) indicates that in cultures where parental rejection is the norm adults tend to be "less generous and liberal in their giving" (p. 103). In conformity with the discussions in previous chapters of the relationships between patterns of family interaction and aggression and altruism, adults from societies characterized by parental rejection "are inclined to view the world, life, the very universe itself, as being an unfriendly, uncertain, insecure and often hostile place in which to live" (p. 103). (See Appendix to Chapter 5, pp. 169–177, for a compelling anthropological case study il-lustrating these relationships.)

As we turn to historical data from Western Europe, the prediction is that as warm parent–child interactions and the nuclear family become dominant, one should find evi-dence for less hostile and exploitative human relationships. The evidence for and against this prediction is complex and difficult to interpret, but there is some indication that this is the case.[1]

Thus, Daly and Wilson (1987) reported data indicating a long-term decrease in homicide in England over the period spanning from the Middle Ages to the present: Individuals are much less likely to be murdered in contemporary England than they were in past times. One could also point to the abolition of the ancient institution of slavery, the improved treatment of criminals, the elderly, and the disabled, the imposition of social controls on the excesses of 19th century capitalism, and the rise of egalitarian social movements, such as Marxism, as indications that the modern world is far less likely to condone extreme forms of exploitation than in times past.

This suggestion of a causal relationship between affective relationships within the family and increased altruism agrees essentially with that of Stone (1977), who notes the existence of extremely harsh, repressive child-rearing practices in 16th and 17th century England. Typical practices of the time included flogging and the deliberate breaking of affectional bonds by the practices of wet nursing and fostering children at early ages to live as servants for the wealthy or as apprentices. Wealthy children were also removed from the family at an early age to be placed in boarding schools, where harsh discipline and flogging prevailed. There was also a conscious attempt to break the will of the child

---

[1]The importance of this hypothesis is by no means restricted to a sociobiological account. Any theory that claims that warm parent–child interactions facilitate altruism must also claim that the historical trends in Western culture for increasingly warm parent–child relationships would be associated with increases in altruism.

and a pattern of generally cool and distant parent–child relationships, one that emphasized deference to parental authority. In agreement with the developmental literature, Stone (1977) writes that adults in the society were "cold, suspicious, distrustful and cruel, unable to form close emotional relationships and liable to sudden outbursts of aggressive hostility" (pp. 194–195). Clearly, the socialization patterns of the society were not geared for producing altruistic individuals, and they seem to have succeeded quite well. The decline in this pattern of child rearing coincided with the decline in the importance of extended kinship relationships and the rise of the independent nuclear family. Hareven (1985) reviews evidence indicating the lessening of extended kinship ties in the period following the 17th century and the increasing importance of affective ties as the basis of marriage. In conformity with the generalization view of affective relationships, these affective ties within marriage were associated with increasingly warm parent–child relations.

Clearly the socialization patterns typical of early modern England would fall into what contemporary developmental psychologists term the authoritarian pattern of child rearing. As indicated in Chapter 5, this pattern is characterized by very high levels of control of children and low levels of parental warmth. Several theorists have suggested that the methods used by parents to control their children may have a direct effect on altruism, especially in situations where children are disciplined for transgressions against others. The best example of this perspective is the work of Hoffman (1983), who emphasizes the importance of parental discipline as affecting the process of moral internalization. Parents who use "inductive" disciplinary techniques, that is, techniques that emphasize the negative effects of the child's behavior on others, tend to have children who behave in a moral manner independent of the threat of external sanctions and who show high levels of guilt. This is contrasted with children who are exposed consistently to "power assertive" discipline by parents, which tends to result in moral behavior only when external sanctions are present.

Hoffman suggests that the importance of the disciplinary encounter is mediated partly by an affective component. By exerting their power or withdrawing their love as a result of the child's behavior, the parent gets the attention of the child and is then able to provide an inductive censuring of the child's behavior. If the child becomes overly aroused in this situation it may not be able to apprehend cognitively the inductive components of the disciplinary encounter, while if arousal is too low, the child will not pay attention. The inductive explanation of the parents, while focusing on the victim, achieves its effect partly by resulting in an affective concern for the victim, that is, empathy as well as guilt, and this emotion motivates helping behaviors.

Later, in a situation where the parents are not present and the child is confronted with temptations and moral dilemmas, the norm of helping others will be triggered and viewed by the child as its own. This occurs because the child remembers the association between its previous actions and their negative effects on others. However, since the original encounters with the parent deemphasized the importance of the parent, but focused instead on the results to the victim, the child forgets the original importance of the parent in producing its attitude. Moreover, the cognitive process of remembering influences and/or is influenced by the strong affective associations of empathy and guilt that were aroused in the original disciplinary encounters. Thus, affective and cognitive processes are intimately intertwined in their effects on moral internalization.

Hoffman's theory reflects an important correlate of altruistic behavior in children and is consistent with a major role for familial affective relationships in the socialization of altruism: Hoffman (1983) points out that inductive parents also tend to have warm relationships with their children. However, the correlational data, both within contemporary society as well as historically and cross-culturally, are consistent with the view that parental control techniques make an independent contribution to individual, cross-cultural, and historical variation in altruism. Harsh, external methods of control by definition are responded to negatively by children, and constitute aversive events, events that are associated with the development of aggression rather than the development of altruism (see Chapter 6).

In any case, the historical record does not indicate a linear trend in familial affective relationships: The 19th century saw a return to many of the repressive practices of earlier centuries, whereas the 20th century has been characterized by increasingly warm parent–child relations. As indicated in Chapter 5, these data indicating that historical change can occur quite quickly show that the historical variation in familial relationships is not due to natural selection acting on genetic variation.

It is important from an adaptationist perspective to note that the pattern of warm parent–child interactions was most characteristic of the middle classes in England and was associated with upward social mobility. Patterns of child rearing in the upper classes lagged behind, perhaps because position was inherited and there was no need for upward social mobility. Kagan (1979) suggests that more child-oriented ways of child rearing facilitate instumental competence and thus also facilitate upward social mobility. This perspective fits well with the data from the attachment literature indicating a variety of beneficial effects of secure attachment not only on social popularity, but on aspects of cognitive style, such as ego resiliency and persistence in the face of difficulties, which are adaptive in modern society (see Chapter 4). Attachment theorists (e.g., Sroufe, 1979a) have generally argued that secure attachment, presumably a reflection of warm parenting, produces optimal development in contemporary society.

3. The thesis that warm parent–child relationships facilitate altruism is consistent with some important data sets where, in addition to the importance of affective relationships, the role of parent as model appears to be of importance. I have noted that one of the drawbacks to studies of altruism in children has been that researchers have generally studied relatively low-cost behaviors. The virtue of the research described here is that the behaviors are clearly of considerable cost to those performing them and, not coincidentally, these studies offer the strongest support for the facilitating role of warm parent–child interactions.

The classic study in this area is that of Rosenhan (1970), who studied former civil rights workers. The subjects were divided into two groups, the fully committed activists, who had worked for over 1 year in the movement, and the partially committed activists, who had participated in only one or two activities of the civil rights movement. The former group reported warm, positive relationships with at least one of their parents and in addition reported that these parents themselves were fully committed activists. The partially committed acitivists, on the other hand, tended to have negative or ambivalent relationships with their parents, and their parents had preached but not practiced altruism. Rosenhan distinguished the motivation of the fully committed group from that of the partially committed group by noting that the former appeared motivated by empathic concern for others, while the motivation of the latter was more the result of self-interested concern with the rewards for helping.

These relationships have been replicated and extended by Clary and Miller (1986). These researchers studied volunteers for a telephone crisis-counseling center. The costs of the behavior were relatively high compared to that studied in most reports: Subjects were required to work one 4-hour shift each week for 6 months and the dependent measure used was whether the subject fulfilled this agreement. It was found that subjects who were above the median on measures of parental modeling of altruism and measures of parental warmth were roughly twice as likely to complete their commitment as individuals below the median. This finding held only for members of groups low in cohesiveness. In such groups only highly autonomous altruists were likely to persist with their commitment. In groups with high cohesiveness, the attractions of group participation resulted in canceling out the influence of the socialization measures. These results indicate that the effect of parental warmth and modeling, although significant, is not extremely robust and can be overcome with situational variables. The lack of strength of the results can also be seen in the fact that over one-third of the subjects with both warm parent–child relations and modeling of altruism failed to fulfill their commitment.

The authors interpret their data as indicating independent influences of modeling and parental warmth. These conclusions are consistent with the above discussion in which the independent effect of parental warmth is emphasized. According to this perspective, social learning gives an extra boost to the facilitative effects of warm parent–child relationships, but both influences can operate independently. However, much developmental data indicate that the warmth of the model facilitates the effectiveness of the model (e.g., Bandura, 1969), so that an interactive, synergistic effect is an important possibility. Such a perspective would imply close connections between the social learning system and the biologically based affective systems within the family. Chapter 5 described how these systems interact in order to influence the transmission of culture from parents to children.

As emphasized throughout this chapter, there is no implication here that affective considerations, in this case warm family relationships, overwhelm self-interest. Rather, affective variables bias cost–benefit decisions away from extreme exploitation and toward what one might term moderate imbalances of resource flow. In both the study by Rosenhan and that of Clary and Miller there is no evidence that the self-sacrifice involved produced enormous detriments to the biological or cultural fitness of the subjects. Four hours per week for 6 months involves a sacrifice in time, but it is not comparable to foregoing reproduction or voluntarily becoming someone else's slave. Moreover, there may well have been considerable social benefits for the subjects in both of these studies, such as increased companionship, more friends, or a purpose and identity that were made possible by the volunteer effort. Nevertheless, these results, in conjunction with the cross-cultural and historical data described above, indicate that socialization methods can be an important source of individual differences in helping and altruism. The evidence indicates that individuals who are socialized by warm parents who use inductive disciplinary techniques and are attractive, altruistic models are less likely to engage in exploitative relationships, and that each of these aspects of socialization may have an independent effect on altruism. Persons socialized in this manner do not come close to completely losing their self-interest, but these methods of socialization may well be responsible for some of the major historical shifts in public policy and conscience that have occurred in recent times as well as be an important source of variation in the cross-cultural data.

III. CONCLUSION

A. Integration of the Socialization-Affective and the Cognitive-Developmental Approaches to Morality and Prosocial Behavior

It was noted in Chapter 1 that one of the goals of this essay is to develop an integrated view of the social development of the child. This theoretical convergence is the result expected by the philosophical realist approach to the issues of social development. Chapters 7 and 8 demonstrated two quite different approaches to prosocial and moral development and it is the purpose of this section to attempt an integration of these perspectives.

Gibbs and Schnell (1985) provided a critique of the postulated incompatibility of the cognitive-developmental and socialization-affective views of prosocial and moral development. They point out that these two schools have very different historical roots. While the cognitive-developmental tradition begins with Piaget and came to its fruition with Kohlberg's work, the societalist perspective goes back to Durkheim's (1961) view that morality is essentially a matter of the impression of moral values upon the individual by society. This perspective puts society first and the individual is seen as the relatively passive recipient of societal pressures. The socialization of affect is crucial for this process. Moral behavior is engaged in because individuals are socialized to engage in moral behavior either for the affective rewards of morally correct behavior or to avoid the affective punishments of failure to engage in morally correct behavior. The developmentally earlier morality of external sanctions is replaced by an internalized morality based on affective motivation. As we have seen, the cognitive-developmental perspective stresses the rational, structural aspects of morality. Kohlberg's rational reconstruction of morality is an attempt to see moral reasoning as a universal developmental phenomenon.

Thus stated, these two perspectives are examples of the mechanistic and organismic world views described in Chapter 1. Gibbs and Schnell (1985) propose an integration of these two perspectives by emphasizing both the importance of socialization as well as the cognitive contributions of the child. The theory of Hoffman (1983), which includes variables such as parental warmth described above, is presented as an integrated hybrid theory that is able to incorporate both of these influences. Thus, Hoffman's emphasis on parental socialization techniques and the internalization of societal norms is compatible with a developmental account of the child's contribution to the socialization process that features the child's developing cognitive competencies. One must understand the "cognitive and affective capacities that young children bring to the disciplinary encounters" (Hoffman, 1983, p. 264).

In their integration of the theoretical perspectives, Gibbs and Schnell (1985) emphasize the structural and affective aspects of moral cognition. They propose that, in addition to affective sources of motivation, moral motivation may derive from purely cognitive considerations, such as social nonreciprocity. Indeed, they propose that a negatively balanced lack of reciprocity may be an intrinsically motivating situation that results from a cognitive appraisal of a situation. However, motivation may also be primarily affective and in general a complex fusion of affect and cognition will motivate behavior.

The proposed integration need not dispense with a truly structuralist account of moral cognition and the result is a true integration between these two historical rivals. It should be clear that this account is consistent with a sociobiological perspective. I have already noted that there are structural and developmental aspects of moral reasoning that affect children's responses to moral dilemmas. Developmental-structural limitations on children's reasoning abilities prevent high-level moral reasoning in young children. In addition, unlike many of the emotional responses occurring in the parent–child relationship and emphasized in Chapters 3 and 4, emotions occurring in moral and prosocial situations are undoubtedly much more likely to be the result of cognitive appraisals of the situation. As emphasized throughout, prime among these cognitive appraisals must be a consideration of the costs and benefits to the individual that will accrue as a result of alternative courses of action.

Within this essentially cognitivist framework, socialization and the emotions act principally as modifier variables. The great bulk of evidence reviewed above indicates that prosocial and morally correct behavior occurs in the vast majority of cases in situations of low or moderate cost to the individual. Whether an individual helps in these situations is influenced strongly by his or her affective reactions and is importantly influenced by his or her socialization. There are persons, such as the contemporary religious suicide bombers, who completely throw caution to the winds and assist others at great cost to themselves in an impulsive manner as a result of intense emotion. However, such events, in which individuals perform very costly behaviors as a result of intense emotional commitments, are relatively rare and presumably examples of negative selection for excessive altruism. As argued above, being inordinately swayed by emotional considerations would be an evolutionary dead end.

Indeed, from an evolutionary perspective, the very presence of a strong influence of the emotions is difficult to conceptualize. One would suppose that the totally rational, self-interested individual would be favored by natural selection. Such an individual, proposed by classical sociobiology, would calculate the most adaptive behavior with a ruthless cost–benefit analysis modified by the appropriate coefficients of relatedness of the recipients of the behavior. There is indeed a main effect of such behavior in the literature reviewed above, but it is also clear that emotions play a prominent role in motivating moral behavior. In attempting to provide an adaptationist account of moral and altruistic emotions, one could emphasize, as in the present chapter, that such emotions would be quite adaptive within the family and promote adaptive imbalances in resource flow. In addition, however, it may be that pure cognition is ineffectual as a proximate mechanism underlying all of moral behavior because it lacks sufficient motivating properties. Thus, Gibbs and Schnell (1985) propose that nonreciprocated altruistic behavior is intrinsically motivating, and Haan (1985) makes a similar suggestion. However, the mere knowledge that one is being exploited may not be sufficient motivation to end the situation. The intense emotions aroused when a situation is appraised as exploitative strongly motivate individuals to terminate the situation. The computer can come up with the correct course of action, but without the intense motivation provided by the emotions it would be relatively inefficient at overcoming obstacles and persisting until reciprocity or a positive balance was restored.

From this latter perspective, departures from the theoretically expected maximization of self-interest can occur because of cognitive mistakes, as would occur when one incorrectly perceives the costs and benefits of a situation, as well as when individuals allow emotional considerations to overwhelm rational considerations. Emotions emerge as a necessary but poorly behaved variable—necessary because of their motivating properties, but poorly behaved because they can result in behavior that deviates from self-interest. In general, however, emotions probably serve to motivate self-interested behavior. I have already noted that the strongest emotions will center around family members and generally bias individuals in favor of interpreting situations and behaving in ways that will benefit these individuals.

B. An Evolutionary Analysis of Guilt and Moral Rectitude

In this chapter I have emphasized the role of the positive emotion of empathy in motivating moral behavior. However, the negative emotion of guilt has also been proposed as a motivator of moral behavior. As Eisenberg (1986) points out, guilt differs from empathy in being a self-evaluative emotion, whereas empathy is a vicarious response based on one's appraisal of another's situation. Guilt has been regarded as an important source of prosocial motivation and behavior. Thus, Hoffman (1982) summarizes data indicating that guilt resulting from immoral or egoistic action can be a motive for altruistic behavior, and Piliavin et al. (1981) report similar findings. Hoffman proposes that early in life guilt occurs when one feels empathy for someone in distress and accepts one's own responsibility for the other's situation, but that later in life guilt and empathy can be separated, so that simply being aware of being responsible for another's plight is sufficient to trigger guilt: "Empathy and guilt may thus be the quintessential prosocial motives, since they may transform another's pain into one's own discomfort and make one feel partly responsible for the other's plight whether or not one has actually done anything to cause it" (Hoffman, 1982, p. 304).

In the prototypical case, an individual performs an act that harms another in a situation where the individual bears some responsibility for the act, that is, it involves intentional harm or or at least negligence on the part of the perpetrator. As noted in Chapter 7, guilt can arise because of a gap between one's self-interested behavior and one's moral reasoning. Guilt need not involve empathy for another, since one can feel guilt over even nonmoral acts, such as eating too much or violating a religious prohibition, but one usual source of guilt is behavior that harms another, and empathy for the victim may, as Hoffman (1982) argues, result in guilt. Guilt appears to involve standards or norms of behavior (Staub, 1978; Schwartz & Howard, 1984), deviation from those norms, and a resulting negative affective reaction: a "painful feeling of dis-esteem for the self" (Hoffman, 1982, p. 298).

Guilt appears to be the opposite of a feeling of moral rectitude. In Chapter 3, moral rectitude was described as a component of self-esteem. Individuals with a feeling of moral rectitude adhere to their own personal standards and this adherence is accompanied by a positive affective tone. It was noted in Chapter 3 that self-evaluative emotions can involve self-deception and that individuals often go to great lengths to preserve a positive self-image, including that of moral rectitude. It was also shown in Chapter 7 that individuals will engage in moral reasoning characterized by rationalization and self-deception in order to picture themselves and their own actions in a positive light. In addition, individuals can avoid helping behavior by devaluing victims or reinterpreting situations, actions consistent with maintaining a feeling of moral rectitude even in the face of objectively callous and self-interested behavior. This does not mean that feelings of moral rectitude always involve self-deception or rationalization, as they may arise from some truly altruistic act. However, such acts tend to be of low cost and often involve anticipated future reciprocity. Moral rectitude seems to offer few puzzles from an evolutionary perspective.

Guilt, however, raises some interesting theoretical problems for an adaptationist account. Guilt often occurs as a result of self-censure for egoistic behavior, so if we suppose in general that egoistic behavior is adaptive, we must ask why individuals should often feel so negative after performing it. From an evolutionary perspective the interesting questions are whether a convincing adaptationist account of guilt can be given and whether these internal standards are an adequate guide to self-interested behavior. Regarding the first question, Trivers (1971) proposed that guilt could evolve as a means of indicating that individuals would provide compensation for their (presumably self-interested) misdeeds and refrain from such behavior in the future. In this view guilt thus performs a communicative function.

The description of moral rectitude presented above, however, suggests in addition that guilt may also have evolved as the opposite of this positive affective component of self-esteem. Whereas self-esteem is triggered when individuals are (roughly) getting on well in life (see Chapter 3), guilt would be interpreted as having evolved as a negative affective cue that motivates adaptive restructuring of one's situation, as, for example, with recompense. In this view, the only difference between guilt and other negative emotions resulting from, for example, exploitation by another or loss of resources via someone else's behavior, would be that in the case of guilt there would be the attribution of personal responsibility for the act. As a result of the fact that guilt involves personal responsibility, it can often be relieved by personal action, often of what we would term a prosocial nature. In this theory guilt need not arise in a social nexus, but can serve to motivate adaptive restucturing of nonsocial situations as well, as when one develops guilt over one's work habits or personal appearance. The link with the previous section on the motivating function of emotions surrounding morally relevant behavior is that guilt serves a motivating function that a purely cognitive appraisal lacks.

Such a view could be summarized by the statement that the emotions surrounding positive and negative self-esteem, as well as moral rectitude and guilt, have evolved to motivate adaptive behavior. The positive emotions will be triggered when one behaves in a competent manner, acquires resources, and is accepted by others. Ignoring instances of high-cost maladaptive altruism, moral rectitude results from rationalized self-interested behavior or low-cost altruism (itself often performed with the anticipation of future reciprocity; see Chapter 7). Negative self-evaluative emotions occur when one is deficient in competence, resources, and acceptance, and guilt in particular results when one feels personally responsible for this deficiency. Guilt, like pride, thus involves the attribution of causality and, in particular, personal agency, one of Roseman's (1979) dimensions of emotions. This negative affective response then motivates adaptive restructuring of one's situation, whether by recompense to a victim, improving one's work habits, adhering to one's religious practices, or perhaps behaving in an altruistic manner to nonvictims in order to restore one's self-image as a good person.

The foregoing account of guilt implicates the importance of internal standards of behavior in generating guilt and the question arises as to whether these internal standards tend to guide adaptive behavior. The evidence presented in this chapter and the previous one must be said to imply that an individual's internal standards of morally appropriate behavior, what one might term a personal ideology, do not in general conflict with adaptive self-interested behavior. Nevertheless, there are significant exceptions to this general perspective. In Chapter 9, the role of ideology will be discussed from an evolutionary perspective. Since internal standards of appropriate behavior appear to be crucial for motivating behavior via the affective mechanism proposed here, the inculcation of these personal standards becomes of immense political importance. It is an important thesis of Chapter 9 that these internal standards are manipulable to a significant degree by the social environment and that in modern societies the ability and the right to influence these internal standards of behavior become a battleground among forces such as governments, religious organizations, the family, the media, the school, and peers. In Chapter 9, it is argued that these contextual influences often result in personal ideologies that are individually maladaptive. The ideologies propagated by these institutions thus have profound effects on personal ideologies in ways that may be adaptive or maladaptive, and institutional ideology itself becomes a contextual variable influencing personal ideology.

C. The Proximal Mechanisms Underlying Self-Interest

The foregoing indicates the appropriateness of a sociobiological account of moral and prosocial development, but does not really suggest what, if anything, is influenced by the genes. We have seen that both Gibbs and Schnell (1985) and Haan (1985) propose that there is an inherent human propensity to view one's own exploitation in negative terms (see also MacDonald, 1984). In addition to these proposals, Hoffman (1982) views empathy as a primitive human emotion, the rudiments of which are present at birth, and Zahn-Waxler and Radke-Yarrow (1982) propose that the altruistic tendencies of children are innate.

These proposed tendencies all result in an individual either restoring a balance to a relationship from a state of negative imbalance or in an individual incurring negative imbalances. As such, they might be said to be incompatible with each other, and indeed some types of prosocial behavior can be viewed as simply the other side of the coin of exploitation (MacDonald, 1984). There is a great reluctance in all of these writers to propose an innate tendency for individuals to attain a net positive imbalance in social relationships (see especially Haan, 1985). However, such imbalances do occur with great regularity in human history and can hardly be ignored. Indeed, one might note a tendency for recent writers in the social sciences to ascribe all the "good" features of humans to innate tendencies and the "bad" features to environmental influence. It takes little imagination to see that positive imbalances of resource control can have great benefits in terms of biological fitness, especially in societies where polygyny is possible: Males who have been able to control large amounts of resources, often via highly imbalanced relationships, have been able to control large numbers of females (see Chapter 5). From an evolutionary-ecological perspective these imbalances are most likely to occur at fairly high levels of economic production and are often enforced by social controls on individual behavior.

We have seen that there is a strong main effect in the literature on moral and prosocial development for individuals to analyze situations in terms of costs and benefits. The thesis put forward by the writers described above proposes innate tendencies for individuals to attempt to achieve complete reciprocity in their interactions—costs minus benefits equals zero. The alternative hyposthesis, that individuals attempt to maximize the costs-minus-benefits relationship, would be consistent with imbalances favoring one individual at the expense of another. This latter hypothesis is much more congruent with evolutionary theory and there are indications in the literature reviewed above that favor this hypothesis.

Thus, the anthropological evidence indicates that as individuals deal with people who are progressively more distantly related to them there is a tendency to attempt to exploit them rather than simply maintain reciprocity (see Chapter 7). The literature on reciprocity suggests that individuals are more likely to maximize their own rewards when reciprocity is not possible. Judged simply in terms of ubiquity, the hypothesis that individuals attempt to have a positive balance of costs and benefits is at least as plausible as the thesis that striving to attain a balanced reciprocity or incurring negative balances is innate. Whether or not this tendency is innate is another question, one not answered by evolutionary biology. It may be that there is individual variation resulting from both biological and environmental influences in the degree to which imbalances in either direction are associated with positive or negative emotions, and in the present chapter I have emphasized the importance of socialization practices that affect this balance. Recent behavioral genetic research on altruism supports the idea of some genetic influence on individual differences in altruism (Rushton et al., 1986; Segal, 1988).

Whatever the status of the proximate mechanisms underlying resource balance in human relationships, it is quite probable that there are developmental shifts in this balance as well as important contextual factors. Regarding the latter point, the genetic program, if such a program exists, cannot simply prescribe an appropriate balance that would serve all situations. Among animals it is not uncommon to find specific mechanisms that prevent exploitation in particularly common situations. For example, the mother goat is prevented from caring for the young of another animal by the operation of a critical period during which the mother learns to direct her resources to her offspring and will not care for any other. The high level of information processing characteristic of humans allows for much less reliance on this type of stereotypic response. The program can make fine distinctions between situations, calculate the probability of future reciprocity, distinguish between relatives and nonrelatives, etc. Some sociobiologists (e.g., Wilson, 1975) have proposed proximate mechanisms that would influence this process, such as biologically based tendencies toward xenophobia, which would bias individuals in favor of establishing net positive balances with individuals outside one's group. I have already commented on the possibility that familial affective relationships will bias individuals toward greater negative imbalances.

Developmentally one would expect that young children would be biased in favor of obtaining net positive imbalances from their social environment. This is the case because children are selected to be net beneficiaries of resource flow from parents to offspring. There is indeed evidence that this is the case: For example, Froming, Allen, and Underwood (1983) term the linear relationship between generosity and age "one of the most frequently cited findings in the prosocial behavior literature" (p. 585). Froming et al. (1983) also find a nonlinear age trend, which consists of an increase in grade 1 followed by a decrease in grade 2 and then further increases. The work of Kohlberg and Eisenberg would also suggest such a linear age trend, given the evidence they provide for more advanced moral and altruistic reasoning as children become older and for a positive relationship between advanced moral reasoning and altruistic behavior. This age trend is quite consistent with a large main effect of self-interest: For example, Froming et al. (1983) found that the mean amount of candy or pennies donated increased from 2.57/23 to 6.21/25 over the age span from kindergarten to grade 5, indicating that the children kept the great majority of the reward for themselves. At grade 5, 20.5% of the children made no donations at all.

The proximal mechanisms proposed to underlie the linear age trend include a decrease in the subjective value of the items donated and an increase in the positive affective consequences of donating behavior (Froming et al., 1983). However, Zarbatany et al. (1985) find that in situations where there is no experimenter demand for generosity there is no tendency for older children to be more generous. They present evidence that older children are more sensitive to the demand characteristics of the experimental setting and are thus better able to infer that generosity is the socially expected behavior. In addition, younger children more often expressed the belief that charitable behavior is the responsibility of adults and, consistent with Froming et al. (1983), had systematically different subjective evaluations of the generosity involved in the various alternatives than the older children. The correct proximal mechanisms affecting the positive or negative balance in human relationships remain uncertain and will be an important area of future research. The literature indicates a strong central tendency for self-interest independent of age, and the work of Rushton et al. (1986) and Segal (1988) indicates that there will be an important influence of genetic variation on at least some of the proximal mechanisms.

CHAPTER 9

Development in a Wider Context
Evolutionary Considerations

Evolutionary treatments of development have tended to emphasize topics such as the parent–child relationship or dominance among peers because these topics have clear parallels in the animal literature and because the proximal mechanisms may be similar. Missing has been an evolutionary treatment of influences on the context of development—influences that affect development by their effects on the microenvironments in which the great majority of psychological research is performed. The key to a theoretical integration of these larger influences is to provide an evolutionary analysis of classes of contextual variables that have broad effects on the contexts of development.

The emphasis on contextual variables is a recent phenomenon in developmental psychology. Bronfenbrenner (1970, 1979, 1986) pioneered the ecological approach to development, an approach that emphasizes external systems that affect the context of development, particularly the family system. This approach is also essential to the contextualist world view as elaborated by Lerner (1986). In the present chapter, examples of contextual influences on the family that in turn affect socialization will be discussed, as well as examples in which larger social institutions attempt to socialize children independent of the family and in conflict with it.

Previous chapters introduced two such contextual variables: economic production and social controls. Thus, for example, in Chapter 5 the effects of these variables on family structure both cross-culturally and historically were explored and proposals were made regarding how these contextual variables interface with the central tendencies of human behavior as proposed by evolutionary theory, as well as how they interface with some of the proximal mechanisms proposed by developmental psychologists.

The present chapter will have two purposes. First, ideology and resource availability will be added to and integrated with the other contextual variables, central tendencies and proximal mechanisms. There will be no attempt to describe all of the contextual variables influencing human development, but rather to concentrate on those that offer the best hope of an evolutionary analysis. However, the variables considered here appear to be of central importance, since they are able to integrate evolutionary considerations with contextual influences on large areas of the cross-cultural and historical literature on human development. As a second objective, historically important examples where political entities beyond the immediate family have made efforts to socialize children will be examined. The discussion here will differ from the discussion in Chapter 5 because, whereas in Chapter 5 the discussion emphasized the influence of contextual variables on family structure and thereby on the socialization process, the present chapter will examine attempts to circumvent the family process entirely.

I. EVOLUTION AND IDEOLOGY

A. More on Economic Production and Social Controls as Contextual Variables

I have emphasized two contextual variables, economic production and social controls, that have had pervasive effects on development both cross-culturally and historically. These variables provide the context in which the evolutionarily expected central tendencies of human behavior and the proximal mechanisms proposed by psychologists are expressed. Social controls can range from subtle effects of group pressure on modes of dressing to the threats of physical force required to achieve large negative imbalances of resource flow such has occurred in the institution of slavery. In terms of human evolution, at more advanced stages of economic production there is an increased possibility of strong, centralized social controls on individual behavior. Economically primitive societies tend to be relatively egalitarian and informal, and centralizing forces, such as the need for cooperation, are insufficient to overcome an array of decentralizing forces represented by the nuclear family as the fundamental social unit (Sahlins, 1974). At intermediate levels of economic production the larger kin group is able to impose considerable control over individual behavior and the main goal of the individual male must be to integrate himself into these larger political units. However, intense social controls imposed by centralized political entities really become an issue only at the most advanced level of economic production, a level characterized by the political institution of the nation state. The discussion in this chapter will concentrate exclusively on societies at the nation state level of political and economic organization.

A crucial issue regarding social controls is the extent to which they are egalitarian or antiegalitarian. Egalitarian social controls limit the extent to which individuals differ in their control of resources, while antiegalitarian social controls facilitate an increase in the variance of control of resources. Examples of the former would be socialistic controls on wealth or sexual controls on individuals that institute monogamy as the only legitimate mating arrangement. Examples of the latter would be laws that forced some individuals to give their resources to others, such as in slavery. These social controls may be quite insensitive to genotypic or phenotypic characteristics of the individuals to whom they apply and cannot be analyzed reductionistically (i.e., as a genetic characteristic of individuals): Thus, whether or not one supports the idea of welfare payments to poor people or war in Indochina, there may be strong constraints on avoiding payment of taxes or the military draft, respectively. As another example, the children of slaves remained slaves independent of their intelligence, their personality, or any other phenotypic characteristic.

A second issue is the extent of social controls. In a *deregulated system* there are a minimum of social controls, whether of an egalitarian or antiegalitarian nature, on individual behavior. While there are no extant examples in which a state has no social controls at all on its citizens (for reasons that are obvious to an evolutionary biologist), it is possible to describe the directions that such a state might tend toward. Such a system would be consistent with large variances in the control of resources, since there would be no social controls on resource accumulation. More importantly for the present discussion, it would tend to leave the issues of family structure and the socialization of children more in the hands of individuals than the state. The state not only would be prevented from taking a major role in determining family structure and socialization, but it would be inhibited from controlling other potential socializing agents, such as the media and religious entities. In the present chapter the United States will be viewed as an example of an (albeitly imperfectly) deregulated socialization system.

A third issue regarding social controls is another aspect of their irreducibility. In addition to being insensitive to genetic variation, it is not possible to predict their existence or the extent to which they are egalitarian or antiegalitarian on the basis of any biological theory. For example, issues in our society such as the rights of women are resolved by a complex process involving popular beliefs, institutions such as the Supreme Court, the rules of legislative bodies, and so on. No biological theory can predict the result of this process. An evolutionary theory can describe and predict behavior within a system of social controls or their absence, but it cannot predict the form of these controls. As a result, it is incorrect to describe sociobiology as leading inevitably to racism, sexism, etc. Social controls are underdetermined by biological theory.

B. Production, Social Controls, and Ideology

Before providing an evolutionary analysis of how various types of egalitarian, antiegalitarian, and deregulated systems influence the socialization process, it is necessary to introduce the variable of ideology. While social controls emphasize the idea that behavior is often controlled from outside the individual, personal ideologies emphasize the idea that factors internal to the individual, such as an individual's personal beliefs, norms, and attitudes, often motivate and rationalize behavior. An evolutionary analysis proposes that individuals tend to believe what is in their self-interest (Wilson, 1978), and it was shown in Chapter 7 that in fact a compelling argument can be made that research in the area of moral reasoning reveals a strong element of such self-interest and rationalization.

However, that chapter also noted that individuals may hold morally relevant beliefs that are maladaptive, that is, beliefs that lead them to perform behavior that is against their self-interest. This phenomenon of individuals holding beliefs that are not in their own self-interest is quite probably common. Personal ideologies appear to be a potent force in motivating behavior, and since these ideologies are relatively plastic, they are the target of attempts at manipulation by others. It was seen in Chapter 8 that when behavior conflicts with personally held standards and norms there is a tendency for the person to feel guilty. Guilt and anticipatory guilt can serve to motivate self-interested behavior, but can also motivate behavior that is not in one's self-interest if one's standards fail to reflect that self-interest. Personal ideology is thus viewed as a third type of contextual variable: Like social controls, it can be relatively insensitive to individual self-interest and is underdetermined by biological theory.

The main reasons for supposing that ideology often acts as a contextual variable are that ideologies often characterize an entire society and are often intimately intertwined with various social controls. To the extent that an ideology characterizes an entire society it becomes insensitive to individual self-interest, and to the extent that it is reinforced by social controls it is possible that individuals who do not benefit from adopting the ideology will be socialized to do so. In the present chapter, case studies of the effects of ideologies on the education and behavior of children will be examined. In the cases examined, the ideologies are promulgated by a larger political and institutional structure, which is dominated by adults whose aims are to control the behavior of these children. Coincident to the imposition of these social controls is the inculcation of an ideology that justifies not only the behavior of the children, but also the structures of social control that facilitate this indoctrination. Thus, for example, Marxist ideology justifies strong social controls on individual behavior, and the pervasive teaching of Marxist ideology in Marxist societies is supported by these social controls, and similarly for the Nazi ideology and social controls operating in Germany from 1933 to 1945. As another example, Christian ideology, which has traditionally included beliefs in strong restraints on sexual behavior and attitudes that support monogamy, is a prominent part of the teaching of children and historically has been backed up with a variety of social controls reinforcing these beliefs and behavior. Thus, Stone (1977) describes the ecclesiastical courts as well as public opinion as reinforcing monogamy and sexual rectitude in England in the modern era, and he describes the fear of God as a powerful motivator of individual behavior.

In all of these cases, the individual self-interest of those who are pressured to adopt the ideology may not be served. Thus, in the case of Christian ideology, the self-interest of a wealthy male would not be served by adopting an ideology of sexual restraint and monogamy, yet there is abundant historical evidence that in fact this was quite common historically in Western Europe (MacDonald, 1983a; Herlihy, 1985). Similarly, a poor male who adopts an ideology in which it is the natural state of affairs that the emperor have many wives while he has one or none may not be behaving adaptively. Ideology therefore often appears to function to motivate fitness-decreasing behaviors and may facilitate the imposition of social controls on behavior by providing an internal source of motivation that renders the use of force unnecessary. If a man is motivated by the fear of God to engage in monogamy, there is less need of invoking explicit social controls such as incarceration to enforce these restrictions on behavior.

As in the case of social controls and also because ideologies are so often intricately bound up with social controls, it is not possible to predict which ideology will prevail in a particular society. Ideologies may be egalitarian or antiegalitarian. They may promote the deregulation of human behavior or they may foster strong social controls on behavior. Like social controls, personal ideologies are strongly influenced by complex, group-level political processes and are thus not analyzable in a reductionistic manner as solely the property of an individual.

Moreover, although intricately intertwined with social controls, ideologies are apparently somewhat independent of social controls: First, I have noted that ideology provides an internal source of motivation for fitness-decreasing (or -increasing) behavior, so that social controls can be less salient or even perhaps disappear if the ideology is effective enough. In addition, individuals often hold ideologies that are in conflict with official ideologies and the social controls they justify, as occurs among revolutionaries. Finally, I have noted that ideology can justify the deregulation of human behavior as well as its regulation, as in the libertarian ideology common in our own society. Thus, it is theoretically possible for ideology to act fairly independently of social controls, and to this extent it must be viewed as an independent, nonreducible variable in an evolutionary analysis of human culture.

The above analysis implies that individual ideologies are not genetically determined. There is in fact evidence for genetic variation for attitudes in modern democracies. For example, Martin, Eaves, Heath, Jardine, and Feingold (1986) found genetic variation for attitudes toward the death penalty, although the great majority of attitudes were strongly influenced by common environment, and some attitudes, such as religious preference (Eaves, 1986), show no evidence of genetic influence. However, there is apparently much less ideological variation in traditional societies (see discussion of identity formation in Chapter 5) or modern totalitarian societies (Eysenck & Wilson, 1978). Reflecting these contextual constraints, Eysenck and Wilson (1978) restrict their claim for genetic influences on ideology to Western democracies and explicitly exclude totalitarian societies. These considerations indicate an important effect of context on behavioral genetic studies (see also below and Bronfenbrenner, 1986). Moreover, independent of the importance of context, a large literature on attitude change (e.g., Eagly & Chaiken, 1984; Zimbardo, Ebbeson, & Maslach, 1977) indicates that attitudes are a relatively plastic characteristic of humans.

It would appear that the principal mechanism by which ideology influences behavior is the mechanism of guilt described in Chapter 8. As a result of a complex process of socialization, individuals develop internal standards of conduct (personal ideologies), which arouse negative emotions in situations where those standards are violated. In the case studies described below, institutional structures above the level of the family attempt to control this process via their control of the schools, the media, and other institutions. Other contexts provide more opportunity for family influences on these internal standards, and it will be argued that in these contexts the social learning environment of the family becomes an important consideration for determining which personal ideology is adopted.

C. Resource Availability as a Contextual Variable: Theory

Up to this point I have spoken of economic production from the point of view of an anthropologist, i.e., as a rather gross characteristic of a society that characterizes its basic level of economic development. On this scale human societies range from hunter–gatherer societies through intermediate types of production up to advanced agricultural and industrial societies. However, there may also be important variation historically within a society in the availability of resources and these may have important effects on development. Following Charlesworth (1988) and as emphasized throughout this volume, resources and resource acquisition are fundamental human activities from an evolutionary ecological perspective, so it is expected that large, society-wide historical changes in resource availability will be accompanied by major shifts in human behavior. In the present chapter the examples of child maltreatment (Burgess et al., 1987) and the changes in development and socialization brought about by the Great Depression (Elder, 1974) are discussed in the context of the general importance of resource availability during development.

D. *Evolutionary Models of Cultural Variation*

Figures 6–8 are attempts to visualize evolutionary models of the determinants of cultural variation in family and social structure and socialization practices discussed in Chapters 5, 6, and 8 of this volume. Model 1 (Figure 6) is suggested by the work of Lumsden and Wilson (1981). It attempts to explain this variation as a function of variation in epigenetic rules that bias individuals toward adopting particular cultural variants that vary in their relative fitness. Model 2 (Figure 7) explains variation as being influenced by the central tendencies of human behavior as well as social controls and ideology viewed as irreducible variables as described above. Among the central tendencies relevant here are the sociobiologically predicted tendencies toward selfishness, different male and female reproductive strategies, and a tendency to aid genetic relatives. In addition, the theory requires human cognitive abilities needed to maximize production within a particular environment. These cognitive abilities (as well as the sociobiologically predicted central tendencies) are conceived as well-buffered behavioral systems in the sense of Waddington (1957; see Chapter 1), without significant cross-cultural genetic or phenotypic variation. Within developmental psychology such a conceptualization of cognition is provided by Piagetian theory and its modern derivatives as well as by information processing models of intelligence. In this perspective the universal endpoints of cognitive development are viewed as sufficient to ensure the ability to profit from experience and to generally evolve, via cultural evolution, toward higher levels of economic production.

Variation in economic production is also an independent variable in Model 2 and is conceived as being influenced by exogenous ecological factors. Such exogenous variables include the type of soil and the availability of water and appropriate animals to domesticate. Advanced agriculture could not evolve in the tropical rain forests or in a waterless desert (Goody, 1976), and as a result the societies living in such areas would not be able to utilize such methods and would be forced to live at a lower level of economic production.

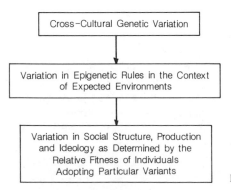

FIGURE 6. Diagrammatic representation of Model 1.

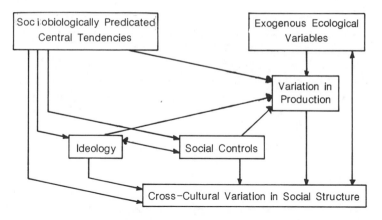

FIGURE 7. Diagrammatic representation of Model 2.

Even today intensive agriculture is extremely difficult in many parts of the world and requires the very high technology that has only recently become available.

Moreover, human societies are able to influence their environments by, for example, altering the productive capacities of the land, and this is reflected in the line connecting variation in social structure with exogenous ecological variables. Exogenous ecological variables can also have a rather direct effect on families and human development, as indicated by the discussion of environmental instability above. Finally, ideology and social controls also have an independent influence on economic production, as seen, for example, by the contrasting results of adopting capitalist versus socialist economic philosophies.

Model 3 (see Figure 8) is similar to Model 2, except that genetic variation is included as an influence on the variables. This variation could be conceived along the lines proposed by Lumsden and Wilson (1981), but includes in addition the contextual vari-

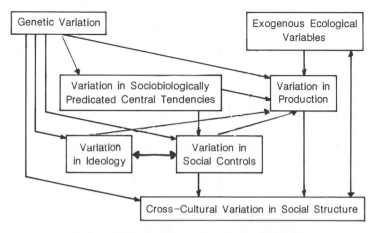

FIGURE 8. Diagrammatic representation of Model 3.

ables described here. The difference between Models 2 and 3 is similar to the difference between models of central tendencies and models of individual differences (see Chapter 1). Rather than thinking in terms of well-buffered central tendencies toward universal cognitive abilities, this approach emphasizes the role of genetic variation in producing differences in cognitive ability, which would in turn affect variation in economic production by, for example, enabling some cultures to be better able to exploit the environment. Such an approach is consistent with independent influences from both genetic and non-genetic sources of variation. Thus, for example, production might be influenced by genetic variation, but also by ecological constraints. For both Models 2 and 3, and in contrast to Model 1, there is an important role to be played by central tendencies and by contextual variables.

In terms of evaluating the models, Model 1 is clearly deficient in its disregard for these central tendencies and contextual variables. The data discussed throughout this volume make a persuasive case for the existence of important human central tendencies as predicted by sociobiological theory. These data also strongly implicate contextual variables as irreducible elements of a sociobiological analysis. Distinguishing between Models 2 and 3 is more difficult and must await empirical verification of the role of genetic variation in producing cross-cultural variation. Clearly, most of the changes in economic production and the socialization practices influenced by these changes have occurred too quickly to be explainable by genetic variation alone (see Chapter 5). Nevertheless, there is *prima facie* support for some aspects of Model 3 from the increasingly influential behavioral genetic literature indicating important genetic variation for virtually every human behavior. Cross-cultural and within-culture genetic variation may thus be of considerable importance in producing the variation in socialization practices and developmental outcomes discussed here. However, I have discussed several reasons why behavior genetic models are misleading when attempting to conceptualize environmental influences on development (see below, and especially Chapter 5).

II. SOCIALIZATION BEYOND THE FAMILY AND PEER SYSTEMS

In this section several historical examples of socialization in which institutions above the family play a prominent role will be discussed. The purpose will be to provide examples of societies with strong social controls as well as a society that is largely deregulated.

A. *The Case of the Soviet Union*

Bronfenbrenner (1970) notes that in the Soviet Union socialization is viewed as the responsibility of the state, with the family socialization process geared to the demands of society rather than the interests of the individual family. In the words of Anton Semyonovitch Makarenko, an eminent Soviet educator:

> Our family is not a closed-in body, like the bourgeois family. It is an organic part of Soviet society, and every attempt it makes to build up its own experience independently of the moral demands of society is bound to result in a disproportion, discordant as an alarm bell.

> Our parents are not without authority either, but this authority is only the reflection of social authority. In our country the duty of a father toward his children is a particular form of his duty toward society. It is as if our society says to parents:
> You have joined together in goodwill and love, rejoice in your children. . . . A time will come when these people will cease to be only a joy to you and become independent members of society. It is not at all a matter of indifference to society what kind of people they will be. In handing over to you a certain measure of social authority, the Soviet state demands from you correct upbringing of future citizens. (Quoted in Bronfenbrenner, 1970, p. 3)

One of the main foci of socialization within the collective environment is the discouragement of selfishness and the encouragement of sharing and communal attitudes such as the communal nature of property. Toys are designed that require the cooperation of a group to make them work. These emphases, presumably deriving from socialist ideology, are also reflected in the encouragement of individuals to criticize others from the standpoint of group goals and values. The leading Soviet educator Makarenko, quoted above, advocates work, group competitiveness, and collective discipline in the educational process. Competition is stressed, but it is competition between collectives, and peer evaluation and group sanctions are stressed. Altruism is stressed as a goal, and children must adopt younger children to care for and help with their schoolwork. As Makarenko states, the child is brought up "in the collective, by the collective, and for the collective" (quoted in Bronfenbrenner, 1970, p. 51).

However, the methods for socializing altruism involve the manipulation of the child's own self-interest. By engaging in collectively oriented behavior the child avoids the criticism of others and possible expulsion from the group. Moreover, one's status as an individual is influenced by the performance of the collective, so it is in the individual's best interest to further the aims of the collective. Teachers do not ask that individuals sit straight, but ask to see which row can sit straightest, a process that encourages evaluation of others in one's group. Rewards are given to the group, not the individual, and the teacher encourages the entire class to criticize recalcitrant individuals whose behavior is seen as an affront to the entire group. Row monitors from among the children are appointed in order to formally evaluate the performance of the row to the teacher.

Bronfenbrenner (1970) provides evidence that indeed Soviet children are less antisocial than are Western children and more influenced by the possibility of negative peer evaluation. The experiment involved the children's reactions to moral dilemmas under several conditions in which the knowledge by others of the children's actions was manipulated. If the children were told that others in the group would be told of their behavior, there were fewer antisocial choices, whereas in Western samples this manipulation increased antisocial behavior. Soviet children were also much more willing to correct the behavior of classmates than were Western children.

Bronfenbrenner points out that the role of the family in socialization remains in flux in the Soviet Union, so that the research described above may be dated. Nevertheless, the attempt to shape behavior toward less individualistic goals is important and apparently has had some effect. Unfortunately, it is difficult to determine to what extent the behavior involved is truly self-sacrificing. As indicated in Chapter 7, it is quite possible to design social controls that facilitate altruism, and in our own society taxpayers are forced to support the welfare system. Essentially these controls make it in the self-interest of the individual to accept negative imbalances in resource flow, and a similar engineering of contingencies is apparent in the socialization practices in the Soviet Union. The data then do not show that self-interest can be socialized out of children, but rather that contingencies can be constructed that assure that enlightened individuals will act in the interests of the group. By performing well, the individual helps himself or herself and the group. Indeed, the system relies on the fact that the individual wants to better his or her own situation by elevating group performance. Nevertheless, it is quite possible, though as yet unsubstantiated, that such socialization could result in a general disposition to accept more negative imbalances of resource flow than would be predicted by assuming complete self-interest.

In the Soviet Union as well as in the case of Nazi Germany, described below, there is a clear conflict between the state and the family. Families are viewed as decentralizing influences, which must be overcome with appropriate socialization directed by the state. In many ways this reflects the fundamental conflict between the family and the larger social unit described by Sahlins (1974) and emphasized in Chapter 5. Centralizing tendencies arising either out of the need to integrate oneself with a larger kinship group or from attempts by larger political entities to control individual behavior inevitably weaken the family's influence in the socialization process. Modern societies, especially totalitarian societies, since they lack the evolutionarily based binding forces of kinship, resort to other means based on social controls and ideology to cement disparate, genetically very distantly related groups into a cohesive social unit. In some cases, these forces quite possibly result in individuals voluntarily performing self-sacrificing acts that would not be expected if they simply followed their own self-interest. In a sense, the rather extreme methods used to facilitate a sort of group selection mentality attest to the robustness of individual self-interest in human behavior and the decentralizing, fragmenting influence of family relationships on human behavior.

B. The Case of Nazi Germany

In his treatment of the Hitler Youth movement Koch (1976) notes that youth groups were a prominent feature of the Nazi party from its inception. When Hitler came to power in 1933 the Hitler Youth was able to assume a monopoly position and was an important institution in the state's attempt to eliminate the individual's private sphere and for superceding such traditional socialization influences as the family and church. Other youth groups were quickly absorbed by the Hitler Youth under the leadership of Baldur von Schirach and the basic organization of separate male and female groups with two age categories established. Children aged 10–14 years formed the younger of the two groups, and children aged 14–18 years the older. However, the control of the state extended even beyond age 18 and below age 10, since the children were typically recruited into the army and/or other Nazi party organizations after age 18 and the elementary school system was tightly controlled by the government. Leadership schools were set up throughout Germany with instruction in racial ideology, leadership, history, and physical fitness, and the leadership itself became increasingly middle-class and educated. As an example of how the Hitler Youth attempted to supercede the influence of the churches, the Protestant church was forced to agree that the Protestant Youth movements would accept political instruction from the state and the Hitler Youth, and all members under the age of 18 were integrated into the Hitler Youth. In 1936, a law was passed making membership in the

Hitler Youth compulsory for children from their 10th birthday on and placing the Hitler Youth on a coequal position with the family and school as socializing influences for the physical, spiritual, and ethical education of Germany's youth. Koch (1976) shows also that the school was tightly controlled by the Nazis, with particular emphasis being placed on the teaching of history and literature as ideological orientation. Indeed, the entire teaching profession was purged after the Nazis came to power in 1933 and the entire purpose of the schools was "the education of youth for the service of *Volk* and state in the National Socialist spirit" (Koch, 1976, p. 168).

Thus, the entire institutional power of the state was attempting to socialize children independent of what individual families may have wanted. The values of the Hitler Youth were often quite different than the values of the family: "for the Hitler Youth stood for a fundamentally different model of society from that of many of the parents of its members, whose values were still mainly those of an age gone by" (Koch, 1976, p. 130). Socialization in the Hitler Youth was also specifically anticlerical, but the power of the churches and their independence, particularly the Catholic church, resulted in a complex association between these institutions. In the words of Gottfried Been, a poet and Army doctor during the war, "already in peace-time they were far removed from those still educated in the old traditions, from parents, educators, clergymen, and humanistic circles" (quoted in Koch, 1976, p. 239). In the early years of the Nazi rule attempts were made to win the loyalty of the parents, but after 1936, when membership in the Hitler Youth became compulsory, these endeavors were stopped. Parents no longer had any choice in the matter.

One of the primary emphases in the Hitler Youth was the molding of the young mind. The inculcation of ideology, in this case the ideology of nationalistic tribalism, antirationalism, the organic unity of the state, blind faith in Hitler, and anti-Semitism, became of supreme importance and there was a never-ending attempt at total control over the thinking of young people. Physical courage and a warlike mentality were encouraged, and "Faithfulness and loyalty irrespective of the consequences were an article of faith shared among wide sections of Germany's youth" (Koch, 1976, p. 119). An ideology of socialism was taken very seriously, albeit a nationalistic socialism in which social controls favoring economic leveling were absent. However, class divisions and social barriers were broken down within the Hitler Youth movement to some extent, a process that resulted in increased opportunities for lower and working class children to move into positions of leadership.

Socialization for competition was strongly stressed, and, as in the Soviet Union, it was competition between groups rather than between individuals, "all the emphasis centering on obedience, duty to the group, and helping within the group" (Koch, 1976, p. 128). A constant refrain of the propaganda and literature of the Hitler Youth was the idea of the individual sacrificing himself for the leader:

> The basic idea is . . . that of a group of heroes inseparably tied to one another by an oath of faithfulness who, surrounded by physically and numerically superior foes, stand their ground. The man who represents the centre of the small band is the *Fuhrer* who is the strongest and boldest in the fight, yet at the same time not a rash man but one who thinks clearly about what he does. Either the band of heroes is reduced to the last man, who is the leader himself defending the corpses of his followers—the grand finale of the *Nibelungenlied*, or through its unparalleled heroism brings about some favourable change in its fortune. (Koch, 1976, p. 143)

Socialization was also directed at making children more aggressive and warlike. Hitler was a strong advocate of physical fitness and championed the sport of boxing, and these preferences were reflected in the training provided by the Hitler Youth: "There is hardly any sport, so Hitler declared, which advances the aggressive spirit more, and which demands lightning power of decision in a greater degree than boxing" (Koch, 1976, p. 163). The emphasis on physical fitness was intended to deemphasize rationality and to "develop man's innate aggressive spirit" (p. 165). The purpose was to produce ultimately the "eternally enthusiastic fighter" (p. 166). A British teacher who visited an elite school for future leaders in 1938 commented that "boys are taught to develop a soldierly attitude towards life." For a sport to be included in the curriculum it must "be a form of *Kampf* sport—that is to say, it must give ample scope for the fighting spirit" (quoted in Koch, 1976, pp. 188–189).

Viewed from an evolutionary perspective, this method of socialization is an attempt to make the child more self-sacrificing than would be in its interest. Indeed, the racial ideology of National Socialism may be viewed as an attempt to make the child view the entire society as a large kinship group in which very high levels of individual self-sacrifice are warranted. If the individual is led to view himself or herself as an interchangeable part in a large organic kinship with strong ties of biological relatedness, it is expected that the individual will be more willing to engage in self-sacrificing behavior.

Clearly, and for obvious evolutionary reasons, the ideology of kinship is a very powerful one, and the anthropological literature suggests that individuals have often manipulated kinship ideology to their advantage. Thus, Chagnon (1982) notes that among the Yanomamo, individuals redefine kinship relations in order to obtain resources, including better marriages, and Sahlins (1963) gives many instances where individuals manipulate kinship terms in order to further their self-interest. Firth (1926) reports that the Maori have a saying "a relative in winter, a son in summer," meaning that at harvest time people are more inclined to view themselves as close relatives. As indicated in the discussion of the Soviet Union above, in a modern industrial society where there are very low average levels of biological relatedness, the absence of state controls would result in a fragmented social structure centered around the family. By inculcating the racial ideology of National Socialism and by means of an elaborate system of social controls, it was possible largely to overcome these decentralizing forces. One's duty was not to oneself or one's family, but to the race.

That the results were maladaptive for a great many individuals is quite clear, since the Second World War resulted in the decimation of the Hitler Youth. Hitler Youth were enlisted in a great many support activities during the war and the older ones were drafted. As the war continued military service began at younger ages, so that by 1943 antiaircraft batteries were manned by Hitler Youth from the age of 15 years and older, and later in the war grammar school children were often used as soldiers. Koch notes their enthusiasm and selfless behavior both as soldiers and as support personnel in the war effort, and quotes from individual youth clearly indicate that the indoctrination of young people with Nazi ideology was often quite successful and often appears to be causally responsible for individuals engaging in extremely self-sacrificing behavior. In the case of Nazi Germany, then, socialization that stressed the value of sacrificing the individual for the sake of the group and the leader clearly resulted in biologically maladaptive behavior.

C. The Case of Ancient Sparta

Ancient Sparta was a Greek state known for its military prowess as well as several other characteristics that make it of interest from an evolutionary perspective. It should be noted, however, that the data on Sparta are quite sparse and unreliable, partly because the Spartans themselves were extremely secretive and because they discouraged all of the "civilized arts" such as writing history (Hooker, 1980). As a result, what has come down to us is from a variety of second-hand sources. Nevertheless, this legend of Sparta describes a state that had a major role in the socialization of children, a role that would have minimized family influences. However, given the intense communality of interest produced by the Spartan system (see below) it is quite possible that whatever socialization occurred within the family was congruent with the aims of the state educational system.

Children were viewed as the property of the state, and each infant was examined by the authorities shortly after birth and destroyed if it appeared weak or deformed (Hooker, 1980). At age 8 years boys were taken away from home and educated by the state "according to a rigorous discipline of quasi-military type" (Hooker, 1980, p. 137). The boys were in the charge of the Warden of the Boys, whose authority was absolute, as well as the "whip-bearers," who apparently lived up to their name (Hooker, 1980). The training was athletic and military, the main focus being to inculcate obedience, physical fitness, and preparedness for a military life. Indeed, the classical view of Spartan education was that it brutalized the children:

> The boys lived very hard—they slept in dormatories on rushes which they had to cut themselves without knives, received one garment a year, and very meagre rations. They were not allowed baths. . . To supplement their meagre diet they were encouraged to steal food and punished if they were caught for being so clumsy. . . Girls received similar athletic and musical training and like the boys held public competitions. . . Some of the tests to which the boys were put were very brutal. Notorious was the game of stealing cheeses from the altar of Artemis Orthia; the boys had to run a gauntlet of flogging under which not a few died. (Jones, 1967, p. 35)

Atkinson (1949) also mentions the prevalence of boxing in the training of young Spartans, as well as the extreme barbarity of a contest in which two groups of boys would viciously fight on a bridge attempting to push the others into the water: "the fighting itself, though done without weapons, was of the most violent and barbarous character; the lads fought and kicked and bit those on the opposing side and 'tore each others' eyes out' " (Atkinson, 1949, p. 118). Consistent with the discussion of proximal mechanisms in the development of aggression (see Chapter 6), these socialization practices are seen as consisting of the provision of aversive events and a lack of elaboration of the positive social reward system.

The Spartans were also known for their self-sacrifice and willingness to give their lives for the state:

> The Spartan, from his childhood on, has learnt to give his life for his country, without any hesitation. Not only the state, the laws, the leaders, and the comrades expect this of him, even his own mother finds it natural that her son should be either victorious or dead. . . Nor does she grieve at his death, provided that he has fought valiantly and that Sparta has won victory, for this is why she gave birth to him, and she knows that Sparta has other valiant men. (Tigerstedt, 1974, p. 20)

Hooker (1980) comments that all activities such as the civilized arts and commerce were prohibited in favor of activities that promoted political cohesion and military prowess. Clearly the highest form of political cohesion is one in which an individual is willing to give his or her life for the group—a true group-selection mentality.

Sparta did in fact achieve great military success and at its height was able to extend its influence over much of the ancient world. At the time of its greatest influence in the affairs of Greece it had developed a social system that made it quite unlike other Greek cities (Hooker, 1980). Interestingly, despite the fact that Sparta was a slave state, within the group of Spartan free citizens there appear to have been a number of egalitarian social controls. Marriage was monogamous and adultery and divorce were rare (Hooker, 1980; Tigerstedt, 1974). Spartan women were famous for their fidelity (Tigerstedt, 1974). Although the state was a monarchy, there were a number of institutional controls on the kings, such as the institution of the ephorate, which dispersed political power, so that despotism by one individual was not characteristic of Sparta. In fact, Sparta was unique in having two kings descending from two separate clans, thus providing two legitimate sources of power.

Further evidence of egalitarian social controls derives from Plutarch (see Hooker, 1980), who claimed that the great Spartan lawmaker Lycurgus originally made all Spartans equal by dividing the land up equally into 9000 estates with one citizen for each estate. In any event, it appears that all citizen were landowners, although later in its history large inequalities in land ownership occurred (Hooker, 1980). Nevertheless, "the common education . . . and the common meals produced a genuine equality, and poor and obscure Spartiates could readily rise by merit" (Jones, 1967, p. 37). The status of women in Sparta was also much higher than in other cities of Greece (Hooker, 1980), so that marriage was presumably more egalitarian. Finally, Lycurgus is also reputed to have attempted to discourage sexual jealousy:

> Accordingly he proclaimed that it was perfectly honourable for a Spartiate to share the begetting of children with worthy fellow-citizens. Thus if an elderly man have a young wife, he might introduce her to a younger man of whom he approved and adopt any offspring of their union. Again, a citizen might admire another man's spouse for the splendid children she bore her husband and for her own wifely virtues; then, if he had the husband's consent, he could beget children upon her. (Plutarch, quoted in Hooker, 1980, p. 136)

The passage is said to illustrate the idea that children are the property of the state, not the property of the individual.

From a sociobiological perspective, this is egalitarianism and a group-selectionist ideology with a vengeance. As Alexander (1987) has suggested, by deescalating sexual competition, these practices quite possibly made it much easier to engage in highly altruistic behavior on behalf of the group and improve political cohesion.

It is interesting to speculate that the practice in Sparta of encouraging "spiritual" homosexual relationships in boys of the age of 12 years and over (Hooker, 1980) may also have been a practice that improved the bonding and cohesion among the males and, in addition, may have led to the deemphasis of heterosexual sex and thus also lowered heterosexual competition among the males. Weisfeld and Billings (1988) note that strong male bonding appears in a number of primate species and review data indicating that such bonds improve group cohesion and the transmission of appropriate male behavior to boys. Practices such as very intense group initiation, certainly typical of Sparta, are expected to facilitate a sense of group identity and social cohesion among cohorts of young males—the "common fate" syndrome (Berkowitz, 1982).

Although the reasons for the decline of Sparta remain a source of controversy, it is an interesting question as to whether some or all of these egalitarian aspects of Sparta did indeed cause its downfall. One theory for the downfall is a sharp decline in available Spartan manpower in the later years (e.g., Hooker, 1980). The Spartans may well have had a quite low birth rate, since marriage occurred later than in other parts of Greece (Hooker, 1980). Moreover, the emphasis on monogamy prevented males from maximizing their reproductive potential. As an example indicating the extent to which males accepted the ideology of monogamy, a king is said to have refused a second wife even after his first was barren and even after pressure from the other Spartiates to produce a legitimate heir. To refuse a second wife under the circumstances is manifestly maladaptive. A far better strategy for a nation as powerful as Sparta would have been for the males to practice polygyny with females made available as a result of their superior political and military power. Such a strategy would avoid any population problems as well as be highly individually adaptive. Perhaps pervasive egalitarianism proved maladaptive in the end.

The evidence on socialization in Nazi Germany, Sparta, and to some extent the Soviet Union is of relevance to the theoretical debate within evolutionary biology on individual versus group selection. With the vast majority of writers on this topic (e.g., Alexander, 1979, 1987), I have developed a position based on natural selection at the individual level. Opponents of this position have seen in group selection a mechanism for the evolution of selflessness and altruism, and have often evaluated this possibility as morally superior to selection at the individual level. In the examples described above, however, we see intense pressure to overcome individual self-interest in the interests of the entire group. Indeed, the best examples of a group selection ideology in human societies are societies such as Nazi Germany and Sparta where intense pressure is used at an early age to inculcate selflessness. Unfortunately, the history of these societies indicates that this selflessness can easily be used to conquer and oppress other groups. The decentralizing tendencies, such as the nuclear family and individual self-interest, that figure so prominently in the present treatment should not be seen as necessarily leading to morally inferior social systems, any more than the imposition of a group selection ideology leads to a good and just social system.

These considerations apply not only to modern industrial societies: Stone (1977) points out that individuals quickly leave the extended kinship group when they feel that their interests can be safeguarded by the state, further evidence for the decentralizing effects of the nuclear family and individual self-interest. I have repeatedly noted that aggression and war are characteristic of societies based on the extended family, so that the decentralizing forces of self-interest and the nuclear family are again arrayed against a social system that facilitates war and aggression. The theory of selection at the individual level predicts that individuals will resist exploitation by others and that enormous time and effort must be used in order to make individuals extremely self-sacrificing. Enlightened self-interest and nuclear family social structure would appear to be much more "in tune" with our biologically based tendencies and perhaps even constitute a morally superior alternative.

Finally, in Chapter 1 the importance of the intensity of environmental stimulation for producing change in behavior was stressed, and in Chapter 5 it was suggested that cultures are able to program development successfully by utilizing intensive environmental stimulation to produce large average effects on the phenotype. The results described here are excellent examples which fit this model. By using intensive methods of socialization directed toward producing aggressive, self-sacrificing individuals, and by bypassing influences such as the family that would tend to increase variation and respond to a multiplicity of interests and influences, these cultures are able to produce very large average environmental effects on socialization. Thus, the intensive methods of socialization typical of male reproductive rites in sexually competitive societies (see Chapter 5) are an attempt to produce ideological solidarity and political cohesion (Young, 1962, 1965; see MacDonald, 1987a). Cultures take advantage of human plasticity and the effectiveness of intensive environmental stimulation to produce adaptive (and sometimes maladaptive) phenotypes.

It was emphasized in Chapter 5 that these large average effects of socialization occurring because of cultural adoption of extreme methods of socialization would remain unanalyzed by a behavioral genetic study conducted within a particular society. This indicates a large effect of context on the results of behavioral genetic research, a point emphasized by Bronfenbrenner (1986) and noted above with respect to ideology. Another aspect of the importance of context on behavior genetic studies is the idea that as children become older, genetic differences become more important as a source of variation in behavior (Scarr & McCartney, 1983). This finding is also quite possibly limited to particular contexts. In the examples of Nazi Germany and Sparta there is every reason to suppose that these societies would continue to restrict the access of individuals to environments in a continuing effort to influence socialization. In the case of Sparta, there is every reason to suppose that early rearing efforts would be consistent with the production of individuals who would be prepared for a self-sacrificing life of military service and that they would also have a profound influence on the choice of later environments even if these environments were not rigidly socially controlled. Choice of environment is thus a highly contextually sensitive feature of development and one likely to be controlled by a society intent on a particular method of socialization.

D. Contextual Influences on Development in a Contemporary Liberal Democracy

The previous examples have described societies where the state has a major influence on the socialization process in direct competition with the family. Contextual influences exist in any society at the level of the nation state, even those where these influences are more diverse and controversial. For example, in the United States the role of governmental institutions in the control of individual behavior and the socialization of children is a chronic political issue. One of the themes in this volume is the conflict between the family and larger forms of social organization. In a liberal democracy this conflict can be seen in attempts by parents to influence the context of their children's development so that this context more closely resembles the socialization influences that occur within the family. Because different families have different ideas about what this context should be, and because liberal democratic ideals limit the extent to which governments can socialize children, the issues of determining the contextual influences on children remain a source of controversy.

At the present time issues such as prayer in public schools, the teaching of "creation science," racial integration, sex education, school-supported birth control policies, courses on human sociobiology at universities, and public support for religious schools are examples in which various interest groups differ in their attempts to socialize children through the institutional structure of the state. In addition to schools, there are influences of the media on children, and in democratic societies in which free speech is protected, there are minimal controls on the media, so that parents often have little control over the influences to which their children are subjected. Recent efforts by adults to censor the lyrics of rock music and the sexual content of movies are an indication of the vitality of the issues involved in the control of the context of socialization. Peers also influence the socialization process, often in ways that parents disapprove (Bronfenbrenner, 1986). Thus, parents clearly recognize the importance of contextual influences in development and try to alter them in what they perceive to be a self-interested manner in order to produce a context of development that is in conformity with their own view of appropriate socialization influences, that is, in conformity with the environment they would provide in the absence of these contextual influences.

It is clear, however, that in a society such as that of the United States that accepts the legitimacy of family influences, there will be strong interactions between these family influences and the contextual socialization influences of the schools, media, and peers. Presumably these interactions are much stronger in a society such as the United States compared with those in the societies discussed previously. In these societies every effort is made by the state to reduce the variation due to family influences and substitute socialization according to the unitary ideology of the state. The state makes every effort to control all the possible sources of socialization, including the media, the schools, and peer groups, and the result from a scientific perspective is that a very large main effect is produced with relatively small interactions. Socialization in a liberal democracy becomes more complicated as a much larger number of fairly independent forces operate on the child. For example, Bronfenbrenner (1986) reviews research showing a large number of contextual influences in the family, including parental employment, day care, the hospital, the peer group, and the school, and Brook, Whiteman, and Gordon (1983) find evidence that the child's personality, peer influences, and family influences all make independent contributions to variation in drug usage.

In Chapter 5, I made an effort to show how the proximal epigenetic mechanisms underlying family functioning operate to influence a variety of adaptive behaviors, including teenage pregnancy and juvenile delinquency. In the present chapter evidence will be provided that these epigenetic rules of family functioning have an important role in moderating contextual influences. These effects are most likely to occur in societies such as that of the United States in which family influences are viewed as legitimate and in which considerable individual choice is possible. Reflecting our discussion of identity formation in Chapter 5, in a pluralistic society in which a great degree of individual choice of environments is possible and in which there is a high degree of freedom of association and occupational niche, the epigenetic rules underlying family functioning may be far more important in influencing development than in traditional societies with few choices available or in societies such as Nazi Germany where the state has an enormous influence on development. In the following, two large studies examining the relationships between the influences of family and peers will be discussed in this context.

In their study of large samples of adolescents and their parents in Denmark and the United States, Kandel and Lesser (1972) reported a consistent and strong association between parent–child relationships and orientation to peers. Children who reported being close to their parents were relatively unlikely to rely on peers for advice, and conversely, children who were quite distant from their parents were much more peer-oriented, particularly if the parents were permissive, interpreted here as a lack of parental concern or limit setting. Reflecting the discussion on social learning, the transmission of culture, and identity formation in Chapter 5, children who report a distant relationship with their parents are less likely to want to be like them. Similar effects were found for both sexes of children and parents, and in both countries. These findings apply only to reliance on peers for advice and decision making, not for contact with peers. Indeed, there was some evidence for a positive association between contact with peers and close association with parents, a pattern also found by Stone (1960) in a large study of high school children in the United States.

Another study showing strong connections between the evolutionarily derived epigenetic rules underlying family functioning and the contextual variable of peer influence is that of Elder (1980), who analyzed data from a large sample of adolescents and their parents gathered in the late 1950s and early 1960s. Elder found that autocratic styles of parenting strengthened the normative shift away from associations with the parents, so that over 90% of the older boys with rejecting parents felt very little association with either parent. On the other hand, well over half the older boys and girls from egalitarian families still felt close to their parents. The shift to relying on peers for value orientation was much more pronounced in children with poor relationships with their parents. Adolescents with good relationships with their parents tended to choose friends with values similar to those of the parent. Motivation in the school context was also markedly lower in autocratically reared adolescents and such individuals tended to rely more on peer values, while those who retained a good relationship with their parents accepted parental values more readily and performed well in school.

Finally, as indicated in Chapter 5, Steinberg (1987) found that adolescents reared by single parents or in reconstituted families are more susceptible to antisocial peer influences than are children reared in intact families. Boys particularly were more susceptible, and these results remained after controlling for a variety of variables, such as socioeconomic and maternal employment status.

These last findings are consistent with the perspective developed in Chapter 5 that decrements in parental investment provide a context in which family influences are less important and peer influences increase. Taken together, the studies reviewed above are also congruent with the perspective developed in Chapter 5 suggesting the importance of interactions between social learning and the biologically based affective systems as well as parental control in influencing adaptive behavior and as moderating the influence of contextual variables. These mechanisms undoubtedly play an important role in moderating the influence of mass media on adolescent behavior as well as, for example, in moderating permissive media influences in the areas of sexual behavior and drug use when these influences conflict with parental values. In terms of the discussion of guilt in Chapter 7, the epigenetic rules underlying family functioning affect individuals' social learning by resulting in internal standards of behavior. Effective methods of socialization result in parents being able to have a major effect on these internal standards and thus on the behavior of their children.

The evolutionary basis of family influences on behavior has been emphasized here, but it should also be pointed out that media influences on behavior are also mediated by epigenetic rules. The wealth and prestige of media personalities presumably are effective in making those individuals attractive because of the evolutionarily derived responses to individuals who are physically attractive and/or are able to control large amounts of resources and control the behavior of others. Advertisements and movies directed to young males often stress female nudity and the fulfillment of the male fantasy of sexual attractiveness and success with large numbers of women, while the romance genre appeals to females by featuring an intense, emotionally fulfilling relationship between a woman and a wealthy man. The media also take advantage of personality differences in boys and girls in designing advertising campaigns, with ads for boys containing fast-paced action sequences and quick cuts and often glorifying aggression (see Huston, 1983, for a discussion). Quite often these influences can be maladaptive for individuals who do not possess the resources of the models, as when individuals imitate movie stars who become pregnant without marriage or flagrantly use drugs. In a pluralistic society in which families cannot control the media, the moderating influence of the family system on contextual variables becomes extremely important. Rather than being less important for producing adaptive behavior than in "the environment of evolutionary adaptedness," the primeval epigenetic rules of family functioning are quite possibly more important than ever.

III. Resource Availability as a Contextual Variable: Empirical Data

Resources are of fundamental importance from an evolutionary-ecological perspective (Charlesworth, 1988) and one expects that major disruptions in resource availability to the family unit will have major effects on child rearing. Burgess et al. (1988) develop the concept of ecological instability as referring to "circumstances in which the balance of resources to stress is weighted in favor of stress" (pp. 306–307). They argue that animals with adequate cognitive abilities to adjust their response to the environment should be especially sensitive to fluctuations in the resource availability of the environment. Thus, among monkeys the likelihood of infanticide increases with increasing population density, decreased parental control over resources, and disruptions in habitat (Hrdy, 1979). Burgess et al. (1988) point out that many of the marker variables associated with child abuse can be interpreted as indicators of ecological instability. Thus, lack of social support, low income, joblessness, large family size, single-parent status, and the presence of step-relatives are all associated with higher rates of child abuse. Such families live in relatively high-stress environments, have poorer diets, live in more disorganized neighborhoods, and must put up with creditors and a relatively high risk of victimization by criminals. Moreover, their personal interactions with others tend to be aversive because they are surrounded by other people similarly under stress. They integrate the research of Dumas and Wahler (1984) into this perspective by noting that abuse is particularly likely when the parent has had a "bad day," that is, the parent is particularly irritable as a result of recently occurring negative interactions with neighbors, relatives, or social agencies.

Consistent with the perspective on aggression developed in Chapter 6, aversive, frustrating events are particularly likely to give rise to aggressive outbursts, and perhaps the relative defenselessness of young children makes them particularly attractive victims.

Child abuse in the context of environmental instability is presumably an index of pathology rather than an adaptive response to the environment. The resources involved are quite clearly not only economic, but may also involve affective resources, such as concern and interest which would normally be provided by family members. The environment-expectant genetic systems emphasized throughout this volume imply that human needs go well beyond the merely economic. Recently McGuire and Troisi (1987) developed an ethological theory of needs, such as being respected, valued, and loved, which fits well with this perspective and clearly indicates that the resource environment that responds to human needs is quite varied and complex.

This is not to deemphasize the importance of economic resources. To the extent that the inadequacy of economic resources is due to social controls imposed by others, as, for example, in a slave society, it would be another example of state manipulation of the socialization environment of children. The state manipulation of socialization environment via economic resource inadequacy is theoretically quite analogous to the cases of Sparta and Nazi Germany discussed above, except that it involves a different type of state control. In all of these cases the state controls the affective environment and other aspects of socialization, but the actual mechanism is different in the two cases. Whether by means of a monolithic state educational system or by imposing an environment inadequate in resources for families, the result in both cases is a strong influence on the socialization environment and, quite possibly, the facilitation of behavior that is maladaptive for the individual.

Another work that indicates the importance of resources as a context for development is Elder's (1974) book, *Children of the Great Depression*. Perhaps one of the reasons for ignoring the importance of resources in developmental science is the fact that the vast majority of data have been collected during a period of economic abundance. The Depression caused an enormous upheaval in the lives of many families and downward social mobility for many. The direct association between resources and reproduction best seen in traditional societies and a cornerstone of the evolutionary-ecological approach is illustrated by census data showing that the cohort born between 1930 and 1940 is considerably smaller than the preceding or following cohort (U.S. Department of Commerce, (1979, pp. 8–9). This effect of resource availability on reproduction resulted in a large contextual effect on this cohort, as they had less competition for resources such as jobs, education, and promotions.

Elder studied families with children born in 1921–1922 and found that the Depression forced adaptations in two main areas: the division of labor within the family and family relationships. Regarding the division of labor, economic hardship resulted in great demands placed on children to fulfill economic roles formerly filled by adults. Households became labor-intensive in an effort to obtain goods and services formerly purchased from others. As a result, adolescence as a period of preadult dependency was replaced by the imposition of important economic responsibilities, especially for boys. Parent–child relationships became more reciprocal instead of being a one-sided transfer of resources from parent to child. Children who were employed outside the home were more adult-oriented and those from economically deprived families more often aspired to adult status.

Regarding family relationships, Elder assumes that families attempt to maximize resources and social status and that the economic conditions of the Depression led to disparities between income before and after the depression, and between income and occupational status. These disparities provoke a negative affective evaluation by the parents and result in a variety of effects on parent–child and parent–parent relationships and the effectiveness of parents as models. For example, children of formerly middle-class parents wished their parents were happier and perceived their parents to be of lower social status. This loss in status often resulted in the mother being ashamed of the father's status and in negative effects on the children's evaluations of the father. Loss of status and unemployment in general also favored wives becoming dominant to husbands. Financial difficulties led to higher rates of marital conflict, particularly in mother-dominated homes. Any weakness or shortcoming in the husband was seized on as a cause of the husband's failure as a provider and the marriage tended to become a battleground for scarce resources. Moreover, loss of status was associated with increasing emotional distance and detachment between fathers and their families.

Loss of father's status and an increase in the dominance of the mother resulted in the father being a less effective model and in children meeting their needs for guidance and affection outside the family, particularly with the peer group and nonfamilial adults. In addition, the mother gained in importance as someone to rely on and as someone who was sided with in conflict situations. Boys had more freedom and tended to resist parental authority more, while girls were more constrained, perhaps due to the increased status of the mother. As economic conditions improved, the father increased in popularity.

As indicated in Chapter 3, economic deprivation and loss of social status also had consequences for the self-image of children, leading to hypersensitivity and self-consciousness regarding their social status and the elitist behavior of others. Girls particularly were conscious of the effects of economic deprivation on dress and grooming. Boys whose families lost most during the Depression scored highest on desiring status and power in social relationships. Family background was not an important source of social success or elite status in schools, but children who became prominent despite an economically deprived background were more highly motivated and had social aspirations that exceeded their perceived achievements. One factor in the success of economically deprived children may have been social controls occurring at the school, which were aimed at minimizing the effects of socioeconomic inequalities, another example of egalitarian social controls. Teachers and deprived students, particularly the girls, were highly critical of "elitist" behavior on the part of nondeprived students, an attempt at social control. However, whereas economic deprivation often occurred fairly independently of the personal characteristics of individuals, these social controls apparently had the purpose of making social success independent of the economic background of the child and more dependent on personal characteristics.

The above results suggest the importance of control of resources for affecting the salience of the parent as a model and as a source of guidance. In Chapter 5, the importance of the affective relationship between parent and children was emphasized. These two influences on modeling are highly congruent with the results of social learning experiments (Bandura, 1969) and they may actually be intertwined here. As indicated above, economic deprivation is associated with increasing emotional distance of the father from the family and therefore in increasingly negative affective relations. The fact that Elder found that some of the families who suffered economic deprivation did not also suffer the typical affective and modeling consequences indicates that economic hardship itself may not be a sufficient condition for impairment of modeling in this study, but has its greatest effect when combined with emotional distance, as suggested by the results of Chapter 5.

There is some indication that these contextual environmental influences may have had adaptive consequences, especially for deprived middle-class boys. This group in later life achieved slightly higher social status than the nondeprived middle-class group and had fewer psychiatric symptoms. They appeared to take life more seriously, as indicated by their being much less interested in leisure activities and self-indulgence, perhaps as a result of their early work experiences. In marriage the men were less interested in companionship and sexual relations than in their children, and their marriages were more egalitarian, reflecting the heightened role of the mother in their adolescence. These findings are consistent with the idea that their negative family affective environment and their intimate exposure to the economic basis of marriage relationships may have made them find positive husband–wife relationships less important, and perhaps their interest in children stems from the fact that for this generation being able to reproduce successfully was the ultimate sign of cultural success. In later life they remained interested in economic and political issues rather than foreign affairs, and valued job security, testimony to their sensitization for a heightened concern for resources resulting from their early experiences.

The success of these boys later in life indicates that the methods of socialization resulting from scarcity of resources often resulted in adaptive resource acquisition behavior later in life. In theoretical terms one might view the Depression as a moderate stress, which acted during a period of relatively high plasticity and sensitized that generation to the importance of resources and had a strong influence on other areas of adaptive functioning, such as affective relationships and familial dominance interactions, long after resources ceased being scarce. As such, these findings may be incorporated into the general model of the effects of early experience described in Chapter 1.

IV. CONCLUSION AND INTEGRATION

The foregoing indicates that contextual variables can be integrated into an evolutionary account of development. Human behavior is infinitely complex and subtle, and much of this complexity and subtlety provides for finely graded responses to rapidly changing environments. This plasticity is not limitless, however, and I have noted several examples where contextual and other environmental influences result in maladaptive behavior for individuals. Humans are constrained by their evolutionarily derived needs, including needs for economic and affective resources (Charlesworth, 1988); they are constrained by the nature of epigenetic rules, which developed in quite different environments and are relatively susceptible to influence at some periods in development and relatively unsusceptible at other times; they are constrained by some very powerful central tendencies, such as that of self-interest. Paradoxically, a belief in the complete plasticity of human behavior would lead to the idea that individuals could be happy in any environment, no matter how oppressive and exploitative.

Human behavior is quite malleable, however, and it is instructive to compare the results of Chapter 8 and the present chapter on the question of the development of altruism. In Chapter 8 a proximal mechanism for the development of altruism was described which emphasized familial affective relations. It was pointed out, however, that this system does not result in complete selflessness. Indeed, family-based altruistic tendencies are insufficient to develop a high level of altruism beyond the family, so that a basic message of this book is that the family is a decentralizing influence in human societies. The forces necessary to overcome these decentralizing influences require high levels of social control and indoctrination of the ideology of the group, and the result is a completely different mechanism for the production of altruism. Whereas in Chapter 8 it was proposed that an elaboration of the positive social reward system was an important part of socialization for altruism, here we see examples where very high levels of self-sacrifice are produced in the presence of very brutal methods of socialization, methods that are here proposed to facilitate aggression and are presumably quite incompatible with an elaboration of the positive social reward system. The result represents a triumph of the malleability of human behavior and at the same time shows the extreme pressures that have existed on human societies in the course of their recent evolution. In the cases described in this chapter it is fascinating that examples of extreme altruism coexist with socialization for extreme cruelty to individuals outside of the group. Sparta, after all, was a slave state, and their interactions with their slaves and their opponents in war is quite consistent with the idea that there was no attempt at all to facilitate the positive social reward system, which was emphasized as important for the socialization of altruism in Chapter 8. This is an example of two quite different mechanisms for the production of altruism—perhaps one should say, two quite different types of altruism.

Although these phenomena indicate the malleability of human behavior, I have also stressed various sources of inertia in human behavior. Selflessness is not easily created in humans, and I have pointed to other sources of variation in developmental plasticity throughout the volume, particularly Chapter 4. It should also be pointed out that the context of development often displays considerable inertia and quite often it is beyond the ability of the individual to influence it. Historical changes have often come quite slowly, and the context that allows a group to achieve superiority is not necessarily one that will allow it to retain superiority for a long period. Perhaps this is the lesson of Sparta. The context of development at the nation-state level is inevitably a political question and political systems are more or less open to change and more or less able to make adaptive decisions regarding the context of development. As indicated above, the context of development remains a chronic political issue in the United States.

While this chapter and the previous one point to very different mechanisms for producing altruism, the methods are, of course, conceptually compatible with each other. These results indicate that contextual variables can be meaningfully integrated with the proximal mechanisms of developmental psychology and again show the inadequacy of the "incommensurable world view" perspective criticized throughout this volume. In some cases, such as that of Sparta or Nazi Germany, contextual variables result in a huge main effect on development, while in others they are importantly moderated by family influences, and in some cases disappear completely, as would happen if someone had a strong genetic predisposition for a debilitating psychiatric condition that is expressed in any known environment. As in the case of the attempt to pit internal organizational factors against external shaping contingencies, the answer to the question of which is important is not an article of scientific faith, but a matter of realizing that sometimes they are all important, whereas at other times interactions are important, and at still other times one or the other influence dominates the development of an individual. There are no general laws of development and there will never be any, but there are mechanisms, and there are contexts, and there are a very, very large number of potential developmental pathways.

References

Abernathy, V. (1974). Illegitimate conception among teenagers. *American Journal of Public Health, 64,* 662–665.

Abramovitch, R. (1980). Attention structures in hierarchically organized groups. In D. R. Omark, F. F. Strayer, & D. G. Freedman (Eds.), *Dominance Relations: An Ethological View of Human Social Conflict and Social Interaction.* New York: Garland.

Adams, G. R. (1977). Physical attractiveness research: Toward a developmental social psychology of beauty. *Human Development, 20,* 217–239.

Adams, P. L., Milner, J. R., & Schreph, N. A. (1984). *Fatherless Children.* New York: Wiley.

Ainsworth, M. D. S. (1963). The development of mother–infant interaction among the Ganda. In D. M. Foss (Ed.), *Determinants of Infant Behavior* (Vol. 2). New York: Wiley.

Ainsworth, M. D. S. (1974). Infant–mother attachment and social development: Socialization as a product of reciprocal responsiveness to signals. In M. Richard (Ed.), *The Integration of the Child into the Social World.* Cambridge: Cambridge University Press.

Ainsworth, M. D. S., & Bell, S. M. (1970). Attachment, exploration and separation: Illustrated by the behavior of one-year-olds in a strange situation. *Child Development, 41,* 49–67.

Ainsworth, M. D. S., & Wittig, B. A. (1969). Attachment and exploratory behavior of infants in a strange situation. In B. M. Foss (Ed.), *Determinants of Infant Behavior, Vol. 4.* London: Methuen.

Ainsworth, M. D. S., Blehar, M. C., Waters, E., & Wall, S. (1978). *Patterns of Attachment.* Hillsdale, NJ: Erlbaum.

Alexander, R. (1974). The evolution of social behavior. *Annual Review of Ecology and Systematics, 5,* 325–383.

Alexander, R. (1979). *Darwinism and Human Affairs.* Seattle: University of Washington Press.

Alexander, R. D. (1987). *The Biology of Moral Systems.* New York: Aldine.

Alfred, B. M. (1970). Blood pressure changes among male Navajo migrants to an urban environment. *Canadian Review of Sociology and Anthropology, 7,* 289–300.

Alloy, L. B., & Abrahamson, L. Y. (1982). Learned helplessness, depression, and the illusion of control. *Journal of Personality and Social Psychology, 42,* 1114–1126.

Allport, G. W. (1961). *Pattern and Growth in Personality.* New York: Holt, Reinhart and Winston.

American Psychiatric Association (1980). *Diagnostic and Statistical Manual of Mental Disorders,* 3rd ed. Washington, DC. Author.

Archer, J. (1976). Biological explanations of psychological sex differences. In B. B. Lloyd & J. Archer (Eds.), *Exploring Sex Differences.* New York: Academic.

Arend, R., Gove, F. L., & Sroufe, L. A. (1979). Continuity of individual adaptation from infancy to kindergarten: A predictive study of ego-resiliency and curiosity in preschoolers. *Child Development, 50,* 950–959.

Arnold, M. (1960). *Emotions and Personality.* New York: Columbia University Press.

Aronfreed, J. (1968). *Conduct and Conscience: The Socialization of Internalized Control over Behavior.* New York: Academic.

Aronson, J. L. (1984). *A Realist Philosophy of Science.* New York: St. Martins.

Astin, A. W. (1981). *The American Freshman: National Norms for Fall 1980.* Los Angeles: American Council on Education and Graduate School of Education, University of California, Los Angeles.

Atkinson, K. M. T. (1949). *Ancient Sparta.* Manchester: Manchester University Press.

August, G. J., & Stewart, M. A. (1983). Familial subtypes of childhood hyperactivity. *Journal of Nervous and Mental Disease, 171,* 362–368.

Azrin, N. H., Hutchinson, R. R., & Hake, D. F. (1966). Extinction-induced aggression. *Journal of the Experimental Analysis of Behavior, 9,* 191–204.

Bacon, W. E., & Stanley, W. C. (1963). Effect of deprivation level in puppies on performance maintained by a passive person reinforcer. *Journal of Comparative and Physiological Psychology, 56,* 783–785.

Bacon, M. K., Child, I. L., & Berry, K. (1963). A cross-cultural study of the correlates of crime. *Journal of Abnormal and Social Psychology 66,* 291–300.

Baldwin, A. L. (1948). Socialization and the parent–child relationship. *Child Development, 19,* 437–447.

Baldwin, A. L. (1949). The effect of home environment on nursery school behavior. *Child Development, 20,* 49–62.

Baldwin, A. L. (1955). *Behavior and Development in Childhood.* New York: Dryden.

Bandura, A. (1969). Social learning theory of identificatory processes. In D. A. Goslin (Ed.), *Handbook of Socialization Theory and Research.* New York: Rand-McNally.

Bandura, A. (1977). *Social Learning Theory.* Englewood-Cliffs, NJ: Prentice-Hall.

Bandura, A., & Huston, A. C. (1961). Identification as a process of incidental learning. *Journal of Abnormal and Social Psychology, 63,* 311–318.

Barash, D. P. (1977). *Sociobiology and Behavior.* New York: Elsevier/North-Holland.

Barglow, P., Bornstein, M., Exum, D. B., Wright, M. K., & Visotsky, H. M. (1981). Some psychiatric aspects of illegitimate pregnancy in early adolescence. *American Journal of Orthopsychiatry, 38,* 672–687.

Barker, P., & Gholson, B. (1984). The history of the psychology of learning as a rational process: Lakatos versus Kuhn. *Advances in Child Development and Behavior, 18,* 227–244.

Barkow, J. (1986). The elastic between genes and culture. Paper presented at a conference entitled "Evolved Constraints on Culture," UCLA, May 19–20, 1986.

Barkow, J., & Burley, N. (1980). Human fertility, evolutionary biology and the demographic transition. *Ethology and Sociobiology, 1,* 163–180.

Barner-Barry, C. (1986). Rob: Children's tacit use of peer ostracism to control aggressive behavior. *Ethology and Sociobiology, 7,* 281–294.

Barnett, M. A., & Andrews, J. A. (1977). Sex differences in children's reward allocation under competitive and cooperative instructional sets. *Developmental Psychology, 13,* 85–86.

Barraclough, C. A., & Gorski, R. A. (1961). Evidence that the hypothalamus is responsible for androgen induced sterility in the female rat. *Endocrinology, 68,* 68–79.

Barrett, D. E. (1979). Naturalistic study of sex differences in children's aggression. *Merrill-Palmer Quarterly, 25,* 193–203.

Barry, H., Bacon, M. K., & Child, I. L. (1957). A cross-cultural survey of some sex differences in socialization. *Journal of Abnormal and Social Psychology, 55,* 327–332.

Bar-Tal, D., Raviv, A., & Shavit, N. (1981). Motives for helping behavior: Kibbutz and city children in kindergarten and school. *Developmental Psychology, 17,* 766–772.

Bateson, G. (1956). A theory of play and fantasy. *Psychiatric Research, 2,* 39–59.

Baum, M. J. (1987). Hormonal control of sex differences in the brain and behavior of mammals. In D. Crews (Ed.), *Psychobiology of Reproductive Behavior.* Englewood Cliffs, NJ: Prentice-Hall.

Baumrind, D. (1967). Child care practices anteceding 3 patterns of preschool behavior. *Genetic Psychology Monographs, 75,* 43–88.

Baumrind, D. (1971). Current patterns of parental authority. *Developmental Psychology Monograph, 4*(1, Pt. 2).

Baumrind, D. (1977). Socialization determinants of personal agency. Paper presented at the meeting of the Society for Research in Child Development, New Orleans, March 27–30, 1977.

Beach, F. A. (1975). Hormonal modification of sexually dimorphic behavior. *Psychoneuroendocrinology, 1,* 3–32.

Becker, W. C. (1964). Consequences of different kinds of parental discipline. In M. L. Hoffman & L. W. Hoffman (Eds.), *Review of Child Development Research* (Vol. 1). New York: Russel Sage Foundation.

Beilin, H. (1984). Functionalist and structuralist research programs in developmental psychology: Incommensurability or synthesis? *Advances in Child Development and Behavior, 18,* 245–257.

Bell, R. Q. (1968). A reinterpretation of the direction of effects in studies of socialization. *Psychological Review, 75,* 81–95.

Belsky, J., & Rovine, M. (1987). Temperament and attachment security in the strange situation: An empirical rapprochement. *Child Development, 58,* 787–795.

Belsky, J., Rovine, M., & Taylor, D. (1984). The Pennsylvania Infant and Family Development Project, III: Mother and infant contributions. *Child Development, 55,* 718–728.

Bennett, E. L. (1976). Cerebral effects of differential experience and training. In M. R. Rosenzweig & E. L. Bennett (Eds.), *Neural Mechanisms of Learning and Memory.* Cambridge: MIT Press.

Berkowitz, L. (1982). Aversive conditions as stimuli to aggression. In L. Berkowitz (Ed.), *Advances in Experimental Social Psychology* (Vol. 15). New York: Academic Press.

Berkowitz, L. (1983). The experience of anger as a parallel process in the display of impulsive "angry" aggression. In R. G. Geen & E. I. Donnerstein (Eds.), *Aggression: Theoretical and Empirical Reviews: Vol. 1: Theoretical and Methodological Issues.* New York: Academic Press.

Berkowitz, L. (1984). Physical pain and the inclination to aggression. In K. J. Flannery, R. J. Blanchard, & D. C. Blanchard (Eds.), *Biological Perspectives on Aggression.* New York: Liss.

Berkowitz, L., & Daniels, L. (1964). Affecting the salience of the social responsibility norm: Effects of past help on the response to dependency relationships. *Journal of Personality and Social Psychology, 68,* 275–281.

Berkowitz, L., & Friedman, P. (1967). Some social class differences in helping behavior. *Journal of Personality and Social Psychology, 5,* 217–224.

Berkowitz, W. R. (1969). Perceived height, personality and friendship choice. *Psychological Reports, 24,* 373–374.

Berlyne, D. E. (1960). *Conflict, Arousal, and Curiosity.* New York: McGraw-Hill.

Berlyne, D. E. (1966). Curiosity and exploration. *Science, 153,* 25–33.

Berlyne, D. E. (1971). *Aesthetics and Psychobiology.* New York: Appleton-Century-Crofts.

Berndt, T. (1979). Developmental changes in conformity to peers and parents. *Developmental Psychology, 15,* 608–616.

Betzig, L. L. (1986). *Despotism and Differential Reproduction: A Darwinian View of History.* Hawthorne, NY: Aldine.

Betzig, L. L., & Turke, P. W. (1986). Parental investment by sex on Ifaluk. *Ethology and Sociobiology, 7,* 29–38.

Beyer, C., de la Torre, L., Larsson, L., & Perez-Palacio, G. (1975). Synergistic actions of estrogen and androgen on the sexual behavior of the castrated male rabbit. *Hormones and Behavior, 6,* 301–313.

Blain, J., & Barkow, J. (1988). Father involvement, reproductive strategies and the sensitive period. In K. MacDonald (Ed.), *Sociobiological Perspectives on Human Development.* New York: Springer-Verlag.

Blasi, A. (1980). Bridging moral cognition and moral action: A critical review. *Psychological Bulletin, 88,* 1–45.

Blasi, A. (1983). Bridging moral cognition and action: A theoretical view. *Developmental Review, 3,* 178–210.

Block, J. H. (1976). Issues, problems and pitfalls in assessing sex differences: A critical review of *The Psychology of Sex Differences. Merrill-Palmer Quarterly, 22,* 257–282.

Block, J. H. (1978). Another look at sex differentiation in the socialization behaviors of mothers and fathers. In J. Sherman & F. L. Denmark (Eds.), *The Psychology of Women: Future Directions of Research.* New York: Psychological Dimensions.

Blumberg, R. L. (1978). *Stratification: Socioeconomic and Sexual Inequality.* Dubuque, IA: Brown.

Blurton Jones, N. (1972). *Ethological Studies of Child Behavior.* Cambridge: Cambridge University Press.

Booth, A., & Hess, C. (1947). Cross-sex friendship. *Journal of Marriage and the Family, 36,* 38–47.

Bornstein, M., & Sigman, M. (1986). Continuity in mental development from infancy. *Child Development, 57,* 251–274.

Borstelmann, L. J. (1983). Children before psychology: Ideas about children from antiquity to the late 1800's. In W. Kessen (Ed.), *Handbook of Child Psychology: Vol. 1. History, Theories and Methods.* New York: Wiley.

Bower, T. G. R. (1981). Mood and memory. *American Psychologist, 36,* 129–148.

Bowlby, J. (1969). *Attachment and Loss: Vol. 1. Attachment.* New York: Basic Books.

Bowlby, J. (1973). *Attachment and Loss: Vol. 2. Separation, Anxiety, and Anger.* New York: Basic Books.

Bowlby, J. (1982). Attachment and loss: Retrospect and prospect. *American Journal of Orthopsychiatry, 52,* 664–678.

Brackbill, Y. (1979). Obstetrical medication and infant behavior. In J. Osofsky (Ed.), *Handbook of Infant Development.* New York: Wiley.

Brazelton, T. B., Koslowski, B., & Main, M. M. (1974). The origin of reciprocity: The early mother–infant interaction. In M. Lewis & L. Rosenblum (Eds.), *The Development of Affect.* New York: Plenum Press.

Bretherton, I. (1985). Attachment Theory: Retrospect and prospect. In I. Bretherton & E. Waters (Eds.), *Growing Points of Attachment Theory and Research. Monographs of the Society for Research in Child Development, 50*(1–2, Serial No. 209), 3–35.

Brickman, P., Meyer, P., & Fredd, S. (1975). Effects of varying exposure to another person with familiar or unfamiliar thought processes. *Journal of Experimental and Social Psychology, 11,* 261–270.

Brimer, E., & Levine, F. M. (1983). Stimulus-seeking behavior in hyperactive and nonhyperactive children. *Journal of Abnormal Child Psychology, 11,* 131–140.

Brock, T. C., & Buss, A. H. (1962). Dissonance, aggression and the evaluation of pain. *Journal of Abnormal and Social Psychology, 65,* 197–202.

Bronfenbrenner, U. (1970). *Two Worlds of Childhood: U.S. and U.S.S.R.* New York: Russell Sage.

Bronfenbrenner, U. (1979). *The Ecology of Human Development.* Cambridge: Harvard University Press.

Bronfenbrenner, U. (1986). Ecology of the family as a context for human development: Research perspectives. *Developmental Psychology, 22,* 723–742.

Brook, J. S., Whiteman, M., & Gordon, A. S. (1983). Stages of drug use in adolescence: Personality, peer, and family correlates. *Developmental Psychology, 19,* 269–277.

Brown, P., & Levinson, S. (1978). Universals in language usage: Politeness phenomena. In E. N. Goody (Ed.), *Questions and Politeness: Strategies in Social Interaction.* New York: Cambridge University Press.

Bryan, J. H., & Walbeck, N. H. (1970). Preaching and practicing generosity: Children's actions and reactions. *Child Development, 41,* 329–354.

Burgess, R. L., Garbarino, J., & Gilstrap, B. (1983). Doing what comes naturally? An evolutionary perspective on child abuse. In E. J. Callahan & K. McCluskey (Eds.), *Life-Span Developmental Psychology: Non-Normative Life Events.* New York: Academic.

Burgess, R., Kurland, J., & Pensky, E. (1988). Ultimate and proximate determinants of child maltreatment: Natural selection, ecological instability and coercive interpersonal contingencies. In K. MacDonald (Ed.), *Sociobiological Perspectives on Human Development.* New York: Springer-Verlag.

Burnstein, E., & Worchel, P. (1962). Arbitrariness of frustration and its consequences for aggression in a social situation. *Journal of Personality, 30,* 528–541.

Buss, D. M. (1987). Evolutionary hypotheses and behavioral genetic methods: Hopes for a union of two disparate disciplines. *Behavioral and Brain Sciences, 10,* 20–21.

Buss, A. H., & Plomin, R. (1984). *Temperament: Early Developing Personality Traits.* Hillsdale, NJ: Erlbaum.

Cairns, R. B. (1986). An evolutionary and developmental perspective on aggressive patterns. In C. Zahn-Waxler, E. M. Cummings, & R. Iannotti (Eds.), *Altruism and Aggression: Biological and Social Origins.* Cambridge: Cambridge University Press.

Cairns, R. B., MacCombie, D. M., & Hood, K. E. (1983). A developmental-genetic analysis of aggressive behavior in mice. *Journal of Comparative and Physiological Psychology, 97,* 69–89.

Cairns, R. B., Cairns, B. D., & Ferguson, L. D. (1984). Aggressive behavior in elementary school children: Gender similarities, differences, and developmental continuities. Paper presented at the Eighth Biennial Meeting of the Southeastern Conference on Human Development, Athens, GA, April 1984.

Campos, J. J., & Barrett, K. C. (1984). Toward a new understanding of emotions and their development. In C. E. Izard, J. Kagan, & R. B. Zajonc (Eds.), *Emotions, Cognitions and Behavior.* New York: Cambridge University Press.

Campos, J. J., Barrett, K. C., Lamb, M. E., Goldsmith, H. H., & Stenberg, C. (1983). Socioemotional development. In M. M. Haith & J. J. Campos (Eds.), *Handbook of Child Psychology: Vol. 2. Infancy and Developmental Psychobiology.* New York: Wiley.

Carey, W. B., & McDevitt, S. C. (1978). Revision of the Infant Temperament Questionnaire. *Pediatrics, 61,* 735–739.

Carlson, N. R. (1986). *Physiology of Behavior* (3rd ed.). Boston: Allyn & Bacon.

Carniero, R. L. (1978). Political expansion as an expression of the principle of competitive exclusion. In R. Cohen & E. R. Service (Eds.), *Origins of the State: The Anthropology of Political Evolution*. Philadelphia: Institute for the Study of Human Issues.

Carpenter, C. R. (1942). Sexual behavior of free ranging rhesus monkeys. Periodicity of estrus, homo- and autoerotic and nonconformist behavior. *Journal of Comparative Psychology, 33,* 147–162.

Carrol, E. N., Zuckerman, M., & Vogel, W. H. (1982). A test of the optimal level of arousal theory of sensation seeking. *Journal of Personality and Social Psychology, 11,* 572–575.

Cashden, E. A. (1980). *American Anthropologist, 80,* 163–180.

Casler, L. (1968). Perceptual deprivation in institutional settings. In G. Newton & S. Levine (Eds.), *Early Experience and Behavior*. Springfield, IL: Charles C Thomas.

Chagnon, N. (1979). Is reproductive success equal in egalitarian societies? In N. Chagnon & W. Irons (Eds.), *Evolutionary Biology and Human Social Behavior*. North Scituate, MA: Duxbury.

Chagnon, N. (1982). Paper presented at the Human Sociobiology Symposium, Midwest Regional Animal Behavior Meeting, University of Illinois, Champaign, IL, February 1982.

Chamove, A., Harlow, H. F., & Mitchell, G. (1967). Sex differences in the infant-directed behavior of rhesus monkeys. *Child Development, 38,* 329–335.

Chance, M. R. A. (1967). Attention structure as the basis of primate rank orders. *Man, 2,* 503–518.

Charlesworth, W. (1988). Resources and resource acquisition during ontogeny. In K. MacDonald (Ed.), *Sociobiological Perspectives on Human Development*. New York: Springer-Verlag.

Charlesworth, W., & Dzur, C. (1987). Gender comparisons of preschoolers' behavior and resource utilization. *Child Development, 58,* 191–200.

Charlesworth, W., & LaFreniere, P. (1983). Dominance, friendship, and resource utilization in preschool children's groups. *Ethology and Sociobiology, 4,* 175–186.

Chess, S., & Thomas, A. (1984). *Origins and Evolution of Behavior Disorders: Infancy to Early Adult Life.* New York: Brunner/Mazel.

Chisholm, J. (1983). *Navaho Infancy*. Chicago: Aldine.

Cichetti, D., & Sroufe, L. A. (1978). An organizational view of affect: Illustration from the study of Down's syndrome infants. In M. Lewis & I. A. Rosenblum (Eds.), *The Development of Affect* New York: Plenum Press.

Clark, R. D. III, & Word, L. E. (1974). Where is the apathetic bystander? Situational characteristics of the emergency. *Journal of Personality and Social Psychology, 29,* 279–287.

Clarke-Stewart, K. A. (1978). And daddy makes three: The father's impact on mother and young child. *Child Development, 49,* 466–477.

Clary, E. G., & Miller, J. (1986). Socialization and situational influences on sustained altruism. *Child Development, 57,* 1358–1369.

Cloninger, C. R. (1987). A systematic method for clinical description and classification of personality variants. *Archives of General Psychiatry, 44,* 573–588.

Coates, S. (1985). Extreme boyhood femininity: Overview and new research findings. In Z. DeFries, R. C. Friedman, & R. Corn (Eds.), *Sexuality*. Westport, CT: Greenwood.

Cohn, J. F., & Tronick, E. Z. (1982). Communicative rules and the sequential structure of infant behavior during normal and depressed interaction. In E. Z. Tronick (Ed.), *Social Interchange in Infancy*. Baltimore: University Park Press.

Coie, J., Dodge, K., & Coppotelli, H. (1982). Dimensions and types of social status: A cross-age perspective. *Developmental Psychology, 18,* 557–570.

Coke, J. S., Batson, C. D., & McDavis, K. (1978). Empathic mediation of helping: A two-stage model. *Journal of Personality and Social Psychology, 36,* 752–766.

Conger, I I, & Petersen, A. C. (1984). *Adolescence and Youth*. New York: Harper & Row.

Connell, J. P., & Thompson, R. (1986). Emotion and social interaction in the strange situation: Consistencies and asymmetric influences in the second year. *Child Development, 57,* 733–745.

Conners, C. K. (1973). Rating scales for use in drug studies with children. *Psychopharmacology Bulletin* [Special Issue: Psychopharmacology of Children] *1973,* 24–84.

Cooper, E. (1915). *The Harem and the Purdah: Studies of Oriental Women*. New York: Century.

Coopersmith, S. (1967). *The Antecedents of Self-Esteem*. San Francisco: Freeman.

Costa, P. T., Jr., & McCrae, R. R. (1980). Still stable after all these years: Personality as a key to some issues in aging. In P. B. Baltes & O. G. Brim (Eds.), *Life-Span Development and Behavior* (Vol. 3). New York: Academic.

Cowen, E. L., Pederson, A., Babijian, H., Izzo, L. D., & Trost, M. A. (1973). Long term follow-up of early detected vulnerable children. *Journal of Consulting and Clinical Psychology, 41*, 438–446.

Crnic, K. A., Greenberg, M. T., Ragozin, A. S., Robinson, N. M., & Basham, R. B. (1983). Effects of stress and social support on mothers and premature and full-term infants. *Child Development, 54*, 209–217.

Cummins, M. S., & Suomi, S. J. (1976). Long term effects of social rehabilitation in rhesus monkeys. *Primates, 17*, 43–52.

Daly, M., & Wilson, M. I. (1980). Discriminative parental solicitude: A biological perspective. *Journal of Marriage and the Family, 42*, 277–288.

Daly, M., & Wilson, M. I. (1981). Abuse and neglect of children in evolutionary perspective. In R. D. Alexander & D. W. Tinkle (Eds.), *Natural Selection and Social Behavior*. New York: Chiron Press.

Daly, M., & Wilson, M. (1983). *Sex, Evolution and Behavior* (2nd ed.) Boston: PWS.

Daly, M., & Wilson, M. I. (1984). A sociobiological analysis of human infanticide. In G. Hausfater & S. B. Hrdy (Eds.), *Infanticide: Comparative and Evolutionary Perspectives*. New York: Aldine.

Daly, M., & Wilson, M. I. (1987). *Homicide*. New York: Aldine de Gruyter.

Damon, W. (1977). *The Social World of the Child*. San Francisco: Jossey-Bass.

Damon, W., and Hart, D. (1982). The development of self-understanding from infancy through adolescence. *Child Development, 51*, 831–857.

Daniels, D., Dunn, J., Furstenberg, F. F., & Plomin, R. (1985). Environmental differences within the family and adjustment differences within pairs of adolescent siblings. *Child Development, 56*, 764–774.

Darley, J. M., & Latane, B. (1970). Norms and normative behavior: Field studies of social interdependence. In J. Macaulay & L. Berkowitz (Eds.), *Altruism and Helping Behavior*. New York: Academic.

Dawkins, R. *The Selfish Gene* (1976). Oxford, U. K.: Oxford University Press.

Deaux, K. (1976). *The Behavior of Women and Men*. Monterey, CA: Brooks-Cole.

DeFries, J. C., Hegmann, J. P., & Weir, M. W. (1966). Open-field in mice: Evidence for a major gene effect mediated by the visual system. *Science, 154*, 1577–1579.

Dennis, W. (1940). Does culture appreciably affect patterns of infant behavior? *Journal of Social Psychology, 12*, 305–317.

Dennis, W. (1973). *Children of the Creche*. New York: Appleton.

Diamond, M. (1965). A critical evaluation of the ontogeny of human sexual behavior. *Quarterly Review of Biology, 40*, 147–175.

Diamond, M. (1982). Sexual identity, monozygotic twins reared in discordant sex roles and a BBC follow-up. *Archives of Sexual Behavior, 11*, 181–186.

Dickemann, M. (1979). Female infanticide, reproductive strategies, and social stratification: A preliminary analysis. In N. A. Chagnon & W. Irons (Eds.), *Evolutionary Biology and Human Social Behavior*. North Scituate, MA: Duxbury.

Dickemann, M. (1981). Paternal confidence and dowry competition: A biocultural analysis of Purdah. In R. D. Alexander & D. W. Tinkle (Eds.), *Natural Selection and Social Behavior: Recent Research and New Theory*. New York: Chiron Press.

DiPietro, J. A. (1981). Rough and tumble play: A function of gender. *Developmental Psychology, 17*, 50–58.

Dodge, K. A. (1986). Social information processing variables in the development of aggression and altruism in children. In C. Zahn-Waxler & M. Radke-Yarrow (Eds.), *The Development of Altruism and Aggression: Biological and Social Origins*. Cambridge: Cambridge University Press.

Dornbusch, S. M., Carlsmith, J. M., Bushwall, S. J., Ritter, P. L., Leiderman, H., Hastorf, A. H., & Gross, R. T. (1985). Single parents, extended households, and the control of adolescents. *Child Development, 56*, 326–341.

Douglas, J. W. B. (1975). Early hospitalization and later disturbances of behavior. *Developmental Medicine and Child Neurology, 17*, 456–480.

Douglas, J. W. B., Ross, J. M., & Simpson, H. R. (1968). *All Our Future*. London: Peter Davies.

Douglas, V. I. (1985). The response of ADD children to reinforcement: Theoretical and clinical implications. In L. M. Bloomingdale (Ed.), *Attention Deficit Disorder: Identification, Course, and Rationale*. New York: Spectrum.

Douvan, E. A., & Adelson, J. (1966). *The Adolescent Experience*. New York: Wiley.

Dovidio, J. F. (1984). Helping behavior and altruism: An empirical and conceptual overview. *Advances in Experimental Social Psychology, 17,* 362–427.

Dovidio, J. F., & Morris, W. N. (1975). Effects of stress and commonality of fate on helping behavior. *Journal of Personality and Social Psychology, 31,* 145–149.

Draper, P. (1976). Social and economic constraints on child life among the !Kung. In R. B. Lee & I. DeVore (Eds.) *Kalihari Hunter–Gatherers.* Cambridge: Cambridge University Press.

Draper, P., & Harpending, H. (1988). A sociobiological perspective on human reproductive strategies. In K. MacDonald (Ed.), *Sociobiological Perspectives on Human Development.* New York: Springer-Verlag.

Dreman, S. B. (1976). Sharing behavior in Israeli schoolchildren: Cognitive and social learning factors. *Child Development, 47,* 186–194.

Dreman, S. B., & Greenbaum, C. W. (1973). Altruism or reciprocity: Sharing behavior in Israeli kindergarten children. *Child Development, 44,* 61–68.

Duffy, E. (1962). *Activation and Behavior.* New York: Wiley.

Duffy, E. (1972). Activation. In N. S. Greenfield & R. A. Sternbach (Eds.), *Handbook of Psychophysiology.* New York: Holt, Rinehart & Winston.

Dumas, J. E., & Wahler, R. G. (1984). Indiscriminate mothering as a contextual factor in aggressive-oppositional child behavior: Damned if you do and damned if you don't. *Journal of Abnormal Child Psychology, 13,* 1–17.

Dunham, H. W. (1965). *Community and Schizophrenia.* Detroit: Wayne State University Press.

Durkheim, E. (1961). *Moral Education: A Study in the Theory and Application of the Sociology of Moral Education,* (M. K. Wilson & H. Schnurer, Trans.). New York: Free Press. (Originally published in 1925)

Eagly, A. H., & Chaiken, S. (1984). Cognitive theories of persuasion. In L. Berkowitz (Ed.), *Advances in Experimental Social Psychology,* Vol. 17. Orlando, FL: Academic.

Eaves, L. J. (1986). The transmission and reporting of religious affiliation in twins and their parents. *Behavior Genetics, 16,* 616–617 (Abstract).

Edwards, C. P. (1975). Societal complexity and moral development. *Ethos, 3,* 505–527.

Edwards, C. P. (1982). Moral development in comparative cross-cultural perspective. In D. A. Wagner & H. W. Stevenson (Eds.), *Cultural Perspectives on Child Development.* San Francisco: Freeman.

Edwards, D. A. (1968). Mice: Fighting by neonatally androgenized females. *Science, 161,* 1027–1028.

Egeland, B., & Sroufe, L. A. (1981a). Attachment and early maltreatment. *Child Development, 52,* 44–52.

Egeland, B., & Sroufe, L. A. (1981b). Developmental sequelae of maltreatment in infancy. *New Directions for Child Development, 11,* 77–92.

Ehrhardt, A. A., & Baker, S. W. (1974). Fetal androgens, human central nervous system differentiation, and behavior sex differences. In R. C. Friedman, R. M. Richart, & R. L. VandeWiele (Eds.), *Sex Differences in Behavior.* New York: Wiley.

Ehrhardt, A. A., & Meyer-Bahlberg, H. F. L. (1981). Effects of prenatal sex hormones on gender-related behavior. *Science, 211,* 1312–1318.

Eisenberg, N. (1986). *Altruistic Emotion, Cognition, and Behavior.* Hillsdale, NJ: Erlbaum.

Eisenberg, N., Pasternack, J. F., Cameron, E., & Tryon, K. (1984). The relations of quantity and mode of prosocial behavior to moral cognitions and social style. *Child Development, 55,* 1479–1485.

Eisenberg, N., Lennon, R., & Pasternack, J. L. (1986). Altruistic values and moral judgment. In N. Eisenberg (Ed.), *Altruistic Emotion, Cognition, and Behavior.* Hillsdale, NJ: Erlbaum.

Eisenberg, N., Shell, R., Pasternack, J., Beller, R., Lennon, R., & Mathy, R. M. (1987). Prosocial development in middle childhood: A longitudinal study. *Developmental Psychology, 23,* 712–718.

Eisenberg-Berg, N. (1979). Development of children's prosocial moral judgment. *Developmental Psychology, 15,* 87–89.

Eisenberg-Berg, N., & Gersheker, E. (1979). Content of preachings and power of the model/preacher: The effects on children's generosity. *Developmental Psychology, 15,* 168–175.

Eisenberg-Berg, N., & Lennon, R. (1980). Altruism and the assessment of empathy in the preschool years. *Child Development, 51,* 552–557.

Eisenberg-Berg, N., & Neal, C. (1981). Children's moral reasoning about self and others: Effects of identity of the story character and cost of helping. *Personality and Social Psychology Bulletin, 7,* 17–23.

Ekman, P., Sorenson, E., & Friesen, W. (1969). Pancultural elements in the facial expression of emotion. *Science, 164,* 86–88.

Elder, G. (1974). *Children of the Great Depression*. Chicago: University of Chicago Press.

Elder, G. (1980). *Family Structure and Socialization*. New York: Arno Press.

Ellis, M. J. (1973). *Why People Play*. Englewood Cliffs, NJ: Prentice-Hall.

Emde, R. N., Gaensbauer, T. J., & Harmon, R. J. (1976). *Emotional Expression in Infancy: A Biobehavioral Study*. New York: International Universities Press.

Epstein, Y. M., & Hornstein, H. A., (1969). Penalty and interpersonal attraction as factors influencing the decision to help another person. *Journal of Experimental Social Psychology, 5,* 272–282.

Erickson, E. (1968). *Identity: Youth and Crisis*. New York: Norton.

Eriksson, B. (1972). Physical training, oxygen supply and muscle metabolism in 11–13 year old boys. *Acta Physiologica Scandinavia Supplement 384.*

Essock-Vitale, S. (1984). The reproductive success of wealthy Americans. *Ethology and Sociobiology, 5,* 45–50.

Essock-Vitale, S., & McGuire, M. T. (1985). Women's lives from an evolutionary perspective. I. Sexual histories, reproductive success, and demographic characteristics of a random sample of American women. *Ethology and Sociobiology, 6,* 137–154.

Eysenck, H. J. (1982). Development of a theory. In H. J. Eysenck (Ed.), *Personality, Genetics, and Behavior*. New York: Praeger.

Eysenck, H. J. (1983). A biometrical-genetical analysis of impulsive and sensation seeking behavior. In M. Zuckerman (Ed.), *Biological Bases of Sensation Seeking, Impulsivity, and Anxiety*. Hillsdale, NJ: Erlbaum.

Eysenck, H. J., & Eysenck, S. B. G. (1976). *Psychoticism as a Dimension of Personality*. New York: Crane, Russak.

Eysenck, H. J., & Wilson, G. D. (1978). Conclusion: Ideology and the Study of Social Attitudes. In H. J. Eysenck & G. D. Wilson (Eds.), *The Psychological Basis of Ideology*. Lancaster, UK: MTP.

Eysenck, H. J. (1967). *The Biological Basis of Personality*. Springfield, IL: Charles C Thomas.

Fagen, R. (1981). *Animal Play Behavior*. New York: Oxford University Press.

Falk, J. L. (1972). The nature and determinants of adjunctive behavior. In R. M. Gilbert & J. D. Keehn (Eds.), *Schedule Effects: Drugs, Drinking, and Aggression*. Toronto: University of Toronto Press.

Fein, G. (1981). Pretend play in childhood. An integrative overview. *Child Development, 52,* 1095–1118.

Fiedler, N. L., & Ullman, D. G. (1983). The effects of stimulant drugs on the curiosity behavior of hyperactive boys. *Journal of Abnormal Child Psychology, 11,* 193–206.

Field, T. (1982). Affective displays of high-risk infants during early interactions. In T. Field (Ed.), *Emotion and Early Interaction*. Hilsdale, NJ: Erlbaum.

Field, T. (1985). Attachment as psychobiological attunement: Being on the same wavelength. In M. Reite & T. Field (Eds.), *The Psychobiology of Attachment and Separation*. New York: Academic Press.

Field, T., & Reite, M. (1984). Children's responses to separation from mother during birth of another child. *Child Development, 55,* 1308–1316.

Firth, R. (1926). Proverbs in native life. *Folklore, 37,* 135–153.

Fischer, C. S. (1977). *Networks and Places: Relations in the Urban Setting*. New York: Free Press.

Fischer, C. S., & Phillips, S. L. (1979). Who is alone? Social characteristics of people with small networks. Paper presented in a conference on loneliness, UCLA California at Los Angeles.

Fischer, W. F. (1963). Sharing in pre-school children as a function of amount and type of reinforcement. *Genetic Psychology Monographs, 68,* 215–245.

Fitzgerald, C. (1938). *A Short Cultural History of China*. New York: Appleton-Century.

Flannery, K. (1972). The cultural evolution of civilizations. *Annual Review of Ecology and Systematics, 3,* 399–426.

Flavell, J. (1985). *Cognitive Development* (2nd ed.). Englewood-Cliffs, NJ: Prentice-Hall.

Flint, B. B. M. (1968). *New Hope for Deprived Children*. Toronto: Toronto University Press.

Fogel, A. (1982). Affect dynamics in early infancy: Affective tolerance. In T. Field (Ed.), *Emotion and Early Interaction*. Hillsdale, NJ: Erlbaum.

Forgays, D. G., & Forgays, J. W. (1952). The nature of the effect of free environment experience in the rat. *Journal of Comparative and Physiological Psychology, 45,* 322–328.

Forgays, D. G., & Read, V. M. (1962). Crucial periods for free environment experience in the rat. *Journal of Comparative and Physiological Psychology, 55,* 816–818.

Fox, G. L. (1981). The family's role in adolescent sexual behavior. In T. Ooms (Ed.), *Teenage Pregnancy in a Family Context*. Philadelphia: Temple University Press.

Fox, M. W. (1972). Socioecological implications of individual differences in wolf litters: A developmental and evolutionary perspective. *Behaviour, 41*, 298–313.

Freedman, D. G. (1974). *Human Infancy: An Evolutionary Perspective*. Hillsdale, NJ: Erlbaum.

Freedman, D. G., & Freedman, N. A. (1969). Differences in behavior between Chinese-American and European-American newborns. *Nature, 224*, 1227.

Freedman, D. G., King, J. A., & Elliot, O. (1961). Critical period in the social development of the dog. *Science, 133*, 1016–1017.

Freud, S. (1961). *Civilization and Its Discontents*. In J. Strachey & A. Freud (Eds.), *The Standard Edition of the Complete Psychological Works of Sigmund Freud*, Vol. 13. London: Hogarth Press and Institute of Psychoanalysis. (Original work published 1930)

Froming, W. J., Allen, L., & Underwood, B. (1983). Age and generosity reconsidered: Cross-sectional and longitudinal evidence. *Child Development, 54*, 585–593.

Frommer, E., & O'Shea, G. (1973a). Antenatal identification of women liable to have problems in managing their infants. *British Journal of Psychiatry, 123*, 149–156.

Frommer, E., & O'Shea, G. (1973b). The importance of childhood experience in relation to problems of marriage and family building. *British Journal of Psychiatry, 123*, 161–167.

Fulker, D. W. (1981). The genetic and environmental architecture of psychoticism, extraversion and neuroticism. In H. J. Eysenck (Ed.), *A Model for Personality*. Munich: Springer-Verlag.

Gaertner, S. L., & Dovidio, J. F. (1977). The subtlety of white racism, arousal and helping behavior. *Journal of Personality and Social Psychology, 35*, 691–707.

Gaertner, S. L., Dovidio, J. F., & Johnson, G. (1979). The subtlety of white racism: The effects of the race of prevailing authority, opportunity for diffusion of responsibility, and race of victim on helping behavior. Unpublished manuscript, University of Delaware.

Garcia, J., Hankins, W. G., & Rusiniak, K. W. (1976). Flavor aversion studies. *Science 192*, 265–266.

Garcia-Coll, C., Kagan, J., & Reznick, J. S. (1984). Behavioral inhibition in young children. *Child Development, 55*, 1005–1019.

Gelfand, D., & Hartmann, D. P. (1982). Response consequences and attributions: Two contributors to prosocial behavior. In N. Eisenberg (Ed.), *The Development of Prosocial Behavior*. New York: Academic.

Gelman, R., and Baillargeon, R. (1983). A review of some Piagetian concepts. In J. Flavell & E. M. Markman (Eds.), *Handbook of Child Psychology: Vol. 3. Cognitive Development*. New York: Wiley.

George, C., & Main, M. (1979). Social interactions of young abused children: Approach, avoidance and aggression. *Child Development, 50*, 306–318.

Gibbons, D. C. (1976). *Delinquent Behavior* (2nd ed.). Englewood Cliffs, NJ: Prentice-Hall.

Gibbs, J. C., & Schnell, S. V. (1985). Moral development "versus" socialization: A critique. *American Psychologist, 40*, 1071–1080.

Gies, F., & Gies, J. (1987). *Marriage and the Family in the Middle Ages*. New York: Harper & Row.

Gilligan, C. (1977). In a different voice: Women's conception of the self and of morality. *Harvard Educational Review, 47*, 481–517.

Gilligan, C. (1982). *In a Different Voice: Psychological Theory and Women's Development*. Cambridge: Harvard University Press.

Gillis, J. R. (1981). *Youth and History*. New York: Academic.

Ginsberg, D., Gottman, J., & Parker, J. (1986). The importance of friendship. In J. Gottman (Ed.), *Conversations of Friends: Speculations on Affective Development*. Cambridge: Cambridge University Press.

Ginsberg, B. E. (1987). The wolf pack as a socio-genetic unit. In H. Frank (Ed.), *Man and Wolf*. The Hague: Junk.

Glass, D. C. (1964). Changes in liking as a means of reducing cognitive discrepancies between self-esteem and aggression. *Journal of Personality, 32*, 531–549.

Goldberg, E. M., & Morrison, S. L. (1963). Schizophrenia and social class. *British Journal of Psychiatry, 109*, 785–802.

Goldberg, S., & DiVitto, B. (1982). *Born Too Soon: Preterm Birth and Psychological Development*. San Francisco: Freeman.

Goldman, D., Kohn, P. M., & Hunt, R. W. (1983). Sensation seeking, augmenting-reducing and absolute auditory threshold: A strength-of-the-nervous-system perspective. *Journal of Personality and Social Psychology, 45*, 405–411.

Goldsmith, H. H., & Campos, J. J. (1982). Toward a theory of infant temperament. In R. N. Emde & J. J.

Harmon (Eds.), *The Development of Attachment and Affiliative Systems: Psychobiological Aspects*. New York: Plenum Press.

Goleman, D. (1986). *Vital Lies, Simple Truths*. Oregon: Touchstone.

Goleman, D. (1987). Who are you kidding? *Psychology Today, 21* (3), 24–30.

Goody, J. (1976). *Production and Reproduction*. New York: Cambridge University Press.

Gottesman, I. I., & Schields, J. (1982). *Schizophrenia: The Epigenetic Puzzle*. New York: Cambridge University Press.

Gould, S. J. (1977). *Ontogeny and Phylogeny*. Cambridge: Harvard University Press.

Gouldner, A. (1960). The norm of reciprocity: A preliminary statement. *American Sociological Review, 25*, 161–178.

Goy, R. W. (1966). Role of androgens in the establishment and regulation of behavioral sex differences in mammals. *Journal of Animal Science, 25*, 21–35.

Goy, R. W. (1970). Experimental control of psychosexuality. *Philosophical Transactions of the Royal Society London, Series B, 259*, 149–162.

Gray, J. (1971). *The Psychology of Fear and Stress*. New York: McGraw-Hill.

Gray, J. (1981). A critique of Eysenck's theory of personality. In H. Eysenck (Ed.), *A Model for Personality*. Berlin, Springer-Verlag.

Gray, J. (1982). *The Neuropsychology of Anxiety*. New York: Oxford University Press.

Gray, J., Owen, S., Davis, N., & Tsaltas, E. (1983). Psychological and physiological relations between anxiety and impulsivity. In M. Zuckerman (Ed.), *The Biological Bases of Sensations Seeking, Impulsivity, and Anxiety*. Hillsdale, NJ: Erlbaum.

Graziano, W. G., Brody, G. H., & Bernstein, S. (1980). Effects of information about future interaction and peer's motivation on peer reward allocation. *Developmental Psychology, 16*, 475–482.

Green, R. (1987). *The "Sissy Boy Syndrome" and the Development of Homosexuality*. New Haven, CT: Yale University Press.

Grossman, K. E., Schwan, A., & Grossman, K. (1986). Infants' communications after brief separation: A reanalysis of Ainsworth's Strange Situation. In P. B. Read & C. E. Izard (Eds.), *Measuring Emotions in Infants and Children* (Vol. 2). New York: Cambridge University Press.

Grusec, J. E., Saas-Kortsaak, P., & Simutis, Z. M. (1978). The role of example and moral exhortation in the training of altruism. *Child Development, 49*, 920–923.

Guidubaldi, J., Cleminshaw, H. K., Perry, J. D., & Mcloughlin, C. S. (1983). *School Psychology Review, 12*, 300–323.

Gutmann, D. L. (1977). The cross-cultural perspective: Notes toward a comparative psychology of aging. In J. E. Birren & K. W. Schaie (Eds.), *Handbook of the Psychology of Aging*. New York: Van Nostrand Reinhold.

Haan, N. (1978). Two moralities in action contexts: Relationships to thought, ego regulation and development. *Journal of Personality and Social Psychology, 36*, 286–305.

Haan, N. (1985). *On Moral Grounds*. New York: New York University Press.

Haas, A. (1979). *Teenage Sexuality: A Survey of Teenage Sexual Behavior*. New York: MacMillan.

Hall, F., Pawlby, S., & Wolkind, S. (1979). Early life experiences and later mothering behaviors: A study of mothers and their 20-week-old babies. In R. Shaffer & J. Dunn (Eds.), *The First Year of Life*. New York: Wiley.

Hamilton, W. D. (1964). The genetical evolution of social behavior, I, II. *Journal of Theoretical Biology, 7*, 27–52.

Hareven, T. (1985). Historical changes in the family and the life course: Implications for child development. *Monographs of the Society for Research in Child Development, 50*(4–5, Serial No. 211), 8–23.

Harlow, H. F., & Harlow, M. K. (1965). The affectional systems. In A. M. Schrier, H. F. Harlow, & F. Stolnitz (Eds.), *The Behavior of Non-Human Primates*. New York: Academic.

Harlow, H. F., & Harlow, M. K. (1969). Effects of various mother–infant relationships on rhesus monkey behavior. In B. M. Foss (Ed.), *Early Experience and Early Behavior* (Vol. 4). New York: Academic.

Harlow, H. F., & Lauersdorf, H. E. (1974). Sex differences in passion and play. *Perspectives in Biology and Medicine, 17*, 348–360.

Harter, S. (1983). Developmental perspectives on the self-system. In P. H. Mussen & E. M. Hetherington, (Eds.), *Handbook of Child Psychology, Vol. 4: Socialization, Personality and Social Development*. New York: Wiley.

Hartung, J. (1976). Natural selection and the inheritance of wealth. *Current Anthropology, 17,* 607–622.

Hartup, W. (1983). Peer relations. In P. Mussen & E. M. Hetherington (Eds.), *Handbook of Child Psychology: Vol. 4. Socialization, Personality and Social Development.* New York: Wiley.

Hatfield, J. S., Ferguson, L. R., & Alpert, R. (1967). Mother–child interaction and the socialization process. *Child Development, 38,* 365–414.

Havighurst, R. J. (1972). *Developmental Tasks and Education.* New York: Longman.

Hebb, D. O. (1946). On the nature of fear. *Psychological Review, 53,* 250–275.

Helkama, K. (1979). The development of the attribution of responsibility: A critical survey of empirical research and a theoretical outline. *Research Reports of the Department of Social Psychology,* No. 3, University of Helsinki.

Henderson, N. D. (1970). Genetic influences on the behavior of mice can be obscured by laboratory rearing. *Journal of Comparative and Physiological Psychology, 72,* 505–511.

Herlihy, D. (1985). *Medieval Households.* Cambridge: Harvard University Press.

Hetherington, E. M. (1966). Effects of paternal absence on sex-typed behaviors in negro and white preadolescent males. *Journal of Personality and Social Psychology, 4,* 87–91.

Hetherington, E. M., & Frankie, C. (1965). Effects of parental dominance, warmth, and conflict on imitation in children. *Journal of Personality and Social Psychology, 2,* 188–194.

Hetherington, E. M. (1972). Effects of father absence on personality development in adolescent daughters. *Developmental Psychology, 7,* 313–326.

Hetherington, E. M. (1979). Divorce: A child's perspective. *American Psychologist, 34,* 851–858.

Hetherington, E. M. (1987). Presidential address. Paper presented at the meetings of the Society for Research in Child Development, April 25, Baltimore, MD.

Hetherington, E. M., & Martin, B. (1979). Family interaction. In H. C. Quay & J. S. Werry (Eds.), *Psychopathological Disorders of Childhood* (2nd ed.). New York: Wiley.

Hetherington, E. M., & Martin, B. (1986). Family interaction. In H. C. Quay & J. C. Werry (Eds.), *Psychopathological Disorders of Childhood,* (3d ed.). New York: Wiley.

Hetherington, M., Stouwie, R., & Ridberg, E. H. (1971). Patterns of family interaction and child rearing attitudes related to three dimensions of juvenile delinquency. *Journal of Abnormal Child Psychology, 77,* 160–176.

Hetherington, E. M., Cox, M., & Cox, R. (1982). Effects of divorce on parents and children. In M. Lamb (Ed.), *Non-Traditional Families.* Hillsdale: Erlbaum.

Hetherington, E. M., Camara, K. A., & Featherman, D. L. (1983). Achievement and intellectual functioning of children from one-parent households. In J. Spence (Ed.), *Achievement and Achievement Motives.* San Francisco: Freeman.

Hill, J. (1984). Prestige and reproductive success in man. *Ethology and Sociobiology, 5,* 77–95.

Hinde, R. A. (1976). On describing relationships. *Journal of Child Psychology and Psychiatry, 17,* 1–19.

Hinde, R. A. (1979). *Toward Understanding Relationships.* London: Academic.

Hinde, R. A. (1987). *Individuals, Relationships, and Culture: Links between Ethology and the Social Sciences.* Cambridge: Cambridge University Press.

Hinshaw, S. P. (1987). On the distinction between attentional deficits/hyperactivity and conduct problems/aggression in child psychopathology. *Psychological Bulletin, 101,* 443–463.

Hirsch, H. V. B., & Spinelli, D. N. (1971). Modification of the distribution of receptive field orientation in cats by selective visual exposure during development. *Experimental Brain Research, 13,* 509–527.

Hodges, W. F., & Bloom, B. L. (1984). Parents' report of children's adjustment to marital separation: A longitudinal study. *Journal of Divorce, 8,* 33–50.

Hodges, W. F., Wechsler, R. C., & Ballantine, C. (1979). Divorce and the preschool child: Cumulative stress. *Journal of Divorce, 3,* 55–67.

Hodges, W. F., Buchsbaum, H. K., & Tierney, C. W. (1983). Parent child relationships and adjustment in preschool children in divorced and intact families. *Journal of Divorce, 7,* 43–58.

Hofer, M. (1987). Early social relationships: A psychobiologist's viewpoint. *Child Development, 58,* 633–647.

Hoffman, M. L. (1981). Is altruism part of human nature? *Journal of Personality and Social Psychology, 40,* 121–137.

Hoffman, M. L. (1982). Development of prosocial motivation: Empathy and guilt. In N. Eisenberg (Ed.), *The Development of Prosocial Behavior.* New York: Academic.

Hoffman, M. L. (1983). Affective and cognitive processes in moral internalization. In E. T. Higgins, D. N.

Ruble, & W. W. Hartup, (Eds.), *Social Cognition and Social Development: A Sociocultural Perspective.* Cambridge: Cambridge University Press.

Hogan, D. P., & Kitagawa, E. M. (1985). The impact of social status, family structure, and neighborhood on the fertility of black adolescents. *American Journal of Sociology, 90,* 825–855.

Hooker, J. T. (1980). *The Ancient Spartans.* London: Dent.

Hornstein, H. A., Masor, H. N., Sole, K., & Heilman, M. (1971). Effects of sentiment and completion of a helping act on observer helping: A case study for socially mediated Ziegarnik effects. *Journal of Personality and Social Psychology, 17,* 107–112.

Hrdy, S. B. (1979). Infanticide among animals: A review, classification, and examination of the implications for the reproductive strategies of females. *Ethology and Sociobiology, 1,* 13–40.

Hrdy, S. B. (1981). *The Woman That Never Evolved.* Cambridge: Harvard University Press.

Hsu, C. C., Soong, W. T., Stigler, J. W., Hong, C. C., & Liang, C. C. (1981). The temperamental characteristics of Chinese babies. *Child Development, 52,* 1337–1340.

Humphreys, A. P., & Smith, P. K. (1987). Rough and tumble, friendship, and dominance in schoolchildren: Evidence for continuity and change with age. *Child Development, 58,* 201–212.

Huston, A. C. (1983). Sex-typing. In P. Mussen & E. M. Hetherington (Eds.), *Handbook of Child Psychology: Vol. 4. Socialization, Personality and Social Development.* New York: Wiley.

Huston, T. L., Geis, G., & Wright, R. (1976). The angry Samaritans. *Psychology Today, 1976* (June), 61–64.

Hutchings, D. E. (1963). Early "experience" and its effects on later behavioral processes in rats: III. Effects of infantile handling and body temperature reduction on later emotionality. *Transactions of the New York Academy of Science, 25,* 890–901.

Hyde, J. S. (1986). Gender differences in aggression. In J. S. Hyde & M. C. Linn (Eds.), *The Psychology of Gender.* Baltimore: Johns Hopkins University Press.

Igel, G. J., & Calvin, A. D. (1960). The development of affectional responses in infant dogs. *Journal of Comparative and Physiological Psychology, 53,* 302–305.

Immelmann, K. (1972). Sexual and other long-term effects of imprinting in birds and other species. In D. Lehrman, R. Hinde, & E. Shaw (Eds.), *Advances in the Study of Behavior,* (Vol. 4). New York: Academic Press.

Imperato-McGinley, J., Peterson, R. E., Gautier, R., & Sturla, E. (1985). The impact of androgens on the evolution of male gender identity. In Z. DeFries, R. C. Friedman, & R. Corn (Eds.), *Sexuality: New Perspectives* Westport, CT: Greenwood Press.

Inazu, J. K., & Fox, G. L. (1980). Maternal influence on the sexual behavior of teenage daughters. *Journal of Family Issues, 1,* 81–102.

Irons, W. (1979). Cultural and biological success. In N. A. Chagnon & W. Irons (Eds.). *Evolutionary Biology and Human Social Behavior.* North Scituate, MA: Duxbury Press.

Izard, C. E. (1971). *The Face of Emotion.* New York: Appleton-Century-Crofts.

Izard, C. E. (1972). *Patterns of Emotion.* New York: Academic.

Izard, C. E. (1977). *Human Emotions.* New York: Plenum Press.

Izard, C. E. (1978). On the ontogenesis of emotions and emotion–cognition relationships in infancy. In M. Lewis & L. Rosenblum (Eds.), *The Development of Affect.* New York: Plenum Press.

Izard, C. E. (1984). Emotion–cognition relationships in human development. In C. E. Izard, J. Kagan, & R. B. Zajonc (Eds.), *Emotions, Cognition and Behavior.* Cambridge: Cambridge University Press.

Jackson, T. T., & Gray, M. (1976). Field study of risk-taking behavior of automobile drivers. *Perceptual and Motor Skills, 43,* 471–474.

Janes, C. L., Hesselbrock, V. M., Myers, D. G., & Penniman, J. H. (1979). Problem boys in young adulthood: Teachers' ratings and twelve-year follow-up. *Journal of Youth and Adolescence, 8,* 453–472.

Jenks, S. M., & Ginsburg, B. E. (1987). Socio-sexual dynamics in a captive wolf pack. In H. Frank (Ed.), *Man and Wolf.* The Hague: Junk.

Jessor, S. L., & Jessor, R. (1974). Maternal ideology and adolescent problem behavior. *Developmental Psychology, 10,* 246–254.

Johnson, R. E. (1979). *Juvenile Delinquency and Its Origins.* New York: Cambridge University Press.

Jones, A. H. M. (1967). *Sparta.* Oxford: Basil Blackwell.

Juraska, J. M. (1986). Sex differences in developmental plasticity of behavior and the brain. In W. T. Greenough & J. M. Juraska (Eds.), *Developmental Neuropsychobiology.* Orlando, FL: Academic.

Kadushin, A. (1970). *Adopting Older Children.* New York: Columbia University Press.

Kagan, J. (1971). *Change and Continuity in Infancy.* New York: Wiley.

Kagan, J. (1974). Discrepancy, temperament and infant distress. In M. Lewis & L. Rosenblum (Eds.), *The Development of Affect.* New York: Plenum Press.

Kagan, J. (1979). Overview. In J. Osofsky (Ed.), *Handbook of Infant Development.* New York: Wiley.

Kagan, J. (1980). Perspectives on continuity. In J. Kagan & O. Brim (Eds.), *Constancy and Change in Human Development.* Cambridge: Harvard University Press.

Kagan, J. (1983). Developmental categories and the premise of connectivity. In R. M. Lerner (Ed.), *Developmental Psychology: Historical and Philosophical Perspectives.* NJ: Erlbaum.

Kagan, J. (1984a). The idea of emotion in human development. In C. E. Izard, J. Kagan, & R. B. Zajonc (Eds.), *Emotions, Cognition, and Behavior.* Cambridge: Cambridge University Press.

Kagan, J. (1984b). *The Nature of the Child.* Cambridge: Harvard University Press.

Kagan, J. (1986). Rates of change in psychological processes. *Journal of Applied Developmental Psychology, 7,* 125–130.

Kagan, J., & Klein, R. (1973). Cross-cultural perspectives in early development. *American Psychologist, 28,* 947–961.

Kagan, J., Kearsley, R., & Zelazo, P. R. (1978). *Infancy: Its Place in Human Development.* Cambridge: Harvard University Press.

Kagan, J., Reznick, J. S., & Snidman, N. (1986). Temperamental inhibition in early childhood. In R. Plomin & J. Dunn (Eds.), *The Study of Temperament: Changes, Continuities and Challenges.* Hillsdale, NJ: Erlbaum.

Kagan, J., Reznick, J. S., and Snidman, N. (1987). The physiology and psychology of behavioral inhibition in children. *Child Development, 58,* 1459–1473.

Kandel, D. B., & Lesser, G. S. (1972). *Youth in Two Worlds.* San Francisco: Jossey-Bass.

Kantner, J. F., & Zelnick, M. (1973). Contraception and pregnancy: Experience of young unmarried women in the United States. *Family Planning Perspectives, 5,* 11–25.

Kasper, J. C., Millichap, J. G., Backus, D. C., Child, D., & Schulman, J. L. (1971). A study of the relationship between neurological evidence of brain damage in children and activity and distractibility. *Journal of Consulting and Clinical Psychology, 36,* 329–337.

Kass, E. M., Rosner, B., Zinner, S. H., Margolius, H. S., & Lee, Y.-H. (1977). Studies on the origin of human hypertension. In D. Aarltrop (Ed.), *Pediatric Implications for Some Adult Disorders.* London: Fellowship of Postgraduate Medicine.

Katz, M. M., and Konner, M. J. (1981). The role of the father: An anthropological perspective. In M. E. Lamb (Ed.), *The Role of the Father in Child Development* (2nd ed.). New York: Wiley.

Kevles, B. (1986). *Females of the Species: Sex and Survival in the Animal Kingdom.* Cambridge, MA: Harvard University Press.

Kleiman, D. G. (1981). Correlations among life history characteristics of mammalian species exhibiting two extreme forms of monogamy. In R. Alexander & D. W. Tinkle (Eds.), *Natural Selection and Social Behavior.* New York: Chiron Press.

Kleinman, A. (1982). Neurasthenia and depression. *Culture, Medicine, and Psychiatry, 6,* 117–190.

Klein, M., & Stern, L. (1971). Low birth weight and the battered child syndrome. *American Journal of Diseases of Childhood, 122,* 15–18.

Klinnert, M., Campos, J. J., Sorce, J., Emde, R., & Svedja, M. (1983). Emotions as behavior regulators: Social referencing in infancy. In R. Plutchik & H. Kellerman (Eds.), *Emotions in Early Development: Vol. 2. The Emotions.* New York: Academic Press.

Knutson, J. F., Fordyce, D. J., & Anderson, D. J. (1980). Escalation of irritable aggression: Control by consequences and antecedents. *Aggressive Behavior, 6,* 347–359.

Koch, H. W. (1976). *The Hitler Youth: Origins and Development 1922–45.* New York: Stein & Day.

Kohlberg, L. (1969). Stage and sequence: The cognitive-developmental approach to socialization. In D. A. Goslin (Ed.), *Handbook of Socialization Theory and Research.* Chicago: Rand McNally.

Kohlberg, L. (1981). *Essays on Moral Development: Vol. 1. The Philosophy of Moral Development.* San Francisco: Harper & Row.

Kohlberg, L. (1984). *Essays on Moral Development: Vol. 2. The Psychology of Moral Development.* San Francisco: Harper & Row.

Kohlberg, L., & Candee, D. (1984). The relationship of moral judgment to moral behavior. In L. Kohlberg, *Essays on Moral Development: Vol. 1. The Psychology of Moral Development.* San Francisco: Harper & Row.

Konner, M. J. (1976). Maternal care, infant behavior and development among the !Kung. In R. B. Lee & I. DeVore (Eds.), *Kalahari Hunter–Gatherers*. Cambridge: Harvard University Press.

Konner, M. J. (1981). Evolution of human behavior development. In R. H. Monroe, R. L. Monroe, & B. B. Whiting (Eds.), *Handbook of Cross-Cultural Human Development*, New York: Garland Press.

Koob, G. F., Fray, P. J., & Iversen, S. D. (1976). Tail-pinch stimulation: Sufficient motivation for learning. *Science, 194*, 637–639.

Korner, A. (1971). Individual differences at birth. Implications for early experience and later development. *American Journal of Orthopsychiatry, 41*, 608–619.

Korner, A., Gabby, T., & Kraemer, H. C. (1980). Relation between prenatal maternal blood pressure and infant irritability. *Early Human Development, 4*, 35–39.

Krebs, D. L. (1970). Altruism: An examination of the concept and a review of the literature. *Psychological Bulletin, 73*, 258–302.

Krebs, D. L. (1975). Empathy and altruism. *Journal of Personality and Social Psychology, 32*, 1134–1146.

Krebs, D. L., Denton, K., and Higgins, N. C. (1988). On the evolution of self-knowledge and self-deception. In K. B. MacDonald (Ed.), *Sociobiological Perspectives on Human Development*. New York: Springer-Verlag.

Kuhn, T. S. (1962). *The Structure of Scientific Revolutions* (2nd ed.). Chicago: University of Chicago Press.

LaFreniere, P. J., & Charlesworth, W. R. (1983). Dominance, affiliation and attention in a preschool group: A nine-month longitudinal study. *Ethology and Sociobiology, 4*, 55–67.

Laird, J. D., Wagener, J. J., Halal, M., & Szedja, M. (1982). Remembering what you feel: The effects of emotion on memory. *Journal of Personality and Social Psychology, 42*, 646–657.

Lakatos, I. (1970). Falsification and the methodology of scientific research programmes. In I. Lakotos & J. Musgrave (Eds.), *Criticism and the Growth of Knowledge*. London: Cambridge University Press.

Lamb, M. E. (1977a). Father–infant and mother–infant interaction in the first year of life. *Child Development, 50*, 167–181.

Lamb, M. E. (1977b). The development of mother–infant and father–infant attachments in the second year of life. *Developmental Psychology, 13*, 637–648.

Lamb, M. E., Thompson, R. A., Gardner, W., & Charnov, E. L. (1985). *Infant–Mother Attachment*. Hillsdale, NJ: Erlbaum.

Langer, J. (1970). Werner's comparative organismic theory. In P. Mussen (Ed.), *Carmichael's Manual of Child Psychology* (Vol. 1). New York: Wiley.

Laudan, L. (1977). *Progress and its problems: Towards a theory of scientific growth*. Berkeley: University of California Press.

Lazarus, R. S. (1982). Thoughts on the relation between emotion and cognition. *American Psychologist, 37*, 1019–1024.

Lee, R. B. (1979). *The !Kung San: Men Women, and Work in a Foraging Society*. Cambridge: Cambridge University Press.

Lee, R. B. (1982). Politics, sexual and non-sexual in an egalitarian society. In E. Leacock & R. B. Lee (Eds.), *Politics and History in Band Societies*. Cambridge: Cambridge University Press.

Leming, J. (1978). Interpersonal variations in stage of moral reasoning among adolescents as a function of situational context. *Journal of Youth and Adolescence, 7*, 405–416.

Lepper, M. R. (1981). Intrinsic and extrinsic motivation in children: Detrimental effects of superfluous social controls. In W. A. Collins (Ed.), *Minnesota Symposia on Child Psychology* (Vol. 14). Minneapolis: University of Minnesota Press.

Lepper, M. R., Greene, D., & Nisbet, R. E. (1973). Undermining children's intrinsic interest with extrinsic reward: A test of the "overjustification" hypothesis. *Journal of Personality and Social Psychology, 28*, 129–137.

Lerner, R. M. (1984). *On Human Plasticity*. Cambridge: Cambridge University Press.

Lerner, R. M. (1986). *Concepts and Theories in Human Development*. New York: Random House.

Lerner, R., & Busch-Rossnagel, N. (Eds.) (1981). *Individuals As Producers of Their Development*. Hillsdale, NJ: Erlbaum.

Lerner, R. M., & Kauffman, M. B. (1986). The concept of development in contextualism. *Developmental Review, 6*, 309–333.

Lerner, R. M., Lerner, J. V., Windle, M., Hooker, K., Lenerz, K., & East, P. L. (1986). Children and adolescents in their contexts: Tests of a goodness of fit model. In R. Plomin & J. Dunn (Eds.), *The Study of Temperament: Changes, Continuities and Challenges*. Hillsdale, NJ: Erlbaum.

Leventhal, G. S., Popp, A. L., & Sawyer, L. (1973). Equity or equality in children's allocation of reward to other persons? *Child Development, 44,* 753–763.

Leventhal, H. (1974). Emotions: A basic problem in social psychology. In C. Nemeth (Ed.), *Social Psychology.* Chicago: Rand-McNally.

Leventhal, H. (1980). Toward a comprehensive theory of emotion. In L. Berkowitz (Ed.), *Advances in Experimental Social Psychology* (Vol. 13). New York: Academic.

Levine, C. (1976). Role-taking standpoint and adolescent usage of Kohlberg's conventional stages of moral reasoning. *Journal of Personality and Social Psychology, 34,* 41–47.

Levine, R. A., & Levine, B. B. (1966). *Nyansongo: A Gusii Community in Kenya.* New York: Wiley.

Lewis, M., & Goldberg, B. (1969). The acquisition and violation of expectancy: An experimental paradigm. *Journal of Experimental Child Psychology, 7,* 70–80.

Lewis, M., & Michalson, L. (1983). *Children's Emotions and Moods.* New York: Plenum Press.

Lewis, M., & Saarni, C. (1985). Culture and emotions. In M. Lewis & C. Saarni (Eds.), *The Socialization of Emotions.* New York: Plenum Press.

Lewis, M., Young, G., Brooks, J., & Michalson, L. (1975). The beginning of friendship. In M. Lewis & L. Rosenblum (Eds.), *Friendship and Peer Relations.* New York: Plenum Press.

Lewis, M., Sullivan, M. W., & Michalson, L. (1984). The cognitive-emotional fugue. In C. E. Izard, J. Kagan, & R. B. Zajonc (Eds.), *Emotions, Cognition, and Behavior.* York: Cambridge University Press.

Lewis, R. A. (1973). Parents and peers: Socialization agents in the coital behavior of young adults. *Journal of Sex Research, 9,* 156–170.

Littlefield, C. H., and Rushton, J. P. (1986). When a child dies: The sociobiology of bereavement. *Journal of Personality and Social Psychology, 51,* 797–802.

Loehlin, J. C., Horn, J. M., & Willerman, L. (1981). Personality resemblances in adoptive families. *Behavior Genetics, 11,* 309–330.

Loney, J., & Milich, R. (1982). Hyperactivity, inattention, and aggression in clinical practice In M. Wolraich & D. Routh (Eds.), *Advances in Behavioral Pediatrics* (Vol. 3), Greenwich, CT: JAI.

Loney, J., Prinz, R. J., Mishalow, J., & Joad, J. (1978). Hyperkinetic/aggressive boys in treatment: Predictors of clinical response to methylphenidate. *American Journal of Psychiatry, 135,* 1487–1491.

Loney, J., Kramer, J., & Milich, R. (1981). The hyperactive child grows up: Predictors of symptoms, delinquency and achievement at follow-up. In K. D. Gadow & J. Loney (Eds.), *Psychosocial Aspects of Drug Treatment for Hyperactivity.* Boulder, CO: Westview.

Lovejoy, C. O. (1981). The origin of man. *Science, 211,* 341–350.

Lowenthal, M. F., & Haven, C. (1968). Interaction and adaptation: Intimacy as a critical variable. *American Sociological Review, 33,* 20–30.

Lumsden, C. J. (1988). Psychological development: Epigenetic rules and gene-culture coevolution. In K. B. MacDonald (Ed.), *Sociobiological Perspectives on Human Development.* New York: Springer-Verlag.

Lumsden, C., & Wilson, E. O. (1981). *Genes, Mind, and Culture.* Cambridge: Harvard University Press.

Lykken, D. T. (1987). An alternative explanation for low or zero sib correlations. *Behavioral and Brain Sciences, 10,* 31.

Maccoby, E. E., & Jacklin, C. N. (1974). *The Psychology of Sex Differences.* Stanford, CA: Stanford University Press.

Maccoby, E., & Martin, J. (1983). Socialization in the context of the family: Parent–child interaction. In P. Mussen & M. Hetherington (Eds.), *Handbook of Child Psychology: Vol. 4. Socialization and Personality Development.* New York: Wiley.

MacDonald, K. B. (1983a). Production, social controls and ideology: Toward a sociobiology of the phenotype. *Journal of Social and Biological Structures, 6,* 297–317.

MacDonald, K. B. (1983b). Development and stability of personality characteristics in prepubertal wolves. *Journal of Comparative Psychology, 97,* 99–106.

MacDonald, K. B. (1984). An ethological social learning theory of the development of altruism: Implications for human sociobiology. *Ethology and Sociobiology 5,* 97–109.

MacDonald, K. B. (1985). Early experience, relative plasticity and social development. *Developmental Review 5,* 99–121.

MacDonald, K. B. (1986a). Early experience, relative plasticity and cognitive development. *Journal of Applied Developmental Psychology, 9,* 101–124.

MacDonald, K. B. (1986b). Developmental models and early experience. *International Journal of Behavioral Development, 9,* 175–190.

MacDonald, K. B. (1986c). *Civilization and Its Discontents* revisited: Freud as an evolutionary biologist. *Journal of Social and Biological Structures, 9,* 307–318.

MacDonald, K. B. (1987a). Biological and psychosocial interactions in early adolescence: A sociobiological perspective. In R. M. Lerner & T. T. Foch (Eds.), *Biological and Psychosocial Interactions in Early Adolescence: A Lifespan Perspective.* Hillsdale, NJ: Erlbaum.

MacDonald, K. B. (1987b). Development and stability of personality characteristics in prepubertal wolves: Implications for pack organization and behavior. In H. Frank (Ed.), *Man and Wolf.* The Hague: Junk.

MacDonald, K. B. (1987c). Parent-child physical play with rejected, neglected, and popular boys. *Developmental Psychology, 23,* 705–711.

MacDonald, K. B. (1987d). The regulation of affect in parent-child interactions with hyperactive children and children of differing sociometric status. Paper presented at the meetings of the Society for Research in Child Development, Baltimore, MD, April 24, 1987.

MacDonald, K. B. (1988a). Overview: The interfaces of developmental psychology and sociobiology. In K. MacDonald (Ed.), *Sociobiological Perspectives on Human Development.* New York: Springer-Verlag.

MacDonald, K. B. (1988b). Sociobiology and the cognitive-developmental tradition in moral development research. In K. MacDonald (Ed.), *Sociobiological Perspectives on Human Development.* New York: Springer-Verlag.

MacDonald, K. B. (1988c). Socialization in the context of the family: A sociobiological perspective. In K. B. MacDonald (Ed.) *Sociobiological Perspectives on Human Development.* New York: Springer-Verlag.

MacDonald, K. B. (In press). The plasticity of human social organization and behavior: Contextual variables and proximal mechanisms. *Ethology and Sociobiology, 9*(4).

MacDonald, K. B., & Ginsburg, B. E. (1983). Induction of normal behavior in wolves with restricted rearing. *Behavioral and Neural Biology, 33,* 133–162.

MacDonald, K. B., & Parke, R. D. (1984). Bridging the gap: Parent–child interactions and peer interactive competence. *Child Development, 55,* 1155–1167 (1984).

MacDonald, K. B., & Parke, R. D. (1986). Parent–child physical play: The effects of sex and age of parents and children. *Sex Roles, 9,* 367–378.

MacFarlane, A. (1986). *Marriage and Love in England: Modes of Reproduction 1300–1840.* London: Blackwell.

Mackey, W. C. (1980). A sociobiological perspective on divorce patterns of men in the United States. *Journal of Anthropological Research, 36,* 419–430.

Main, M., Kaplan, N., & Cassidy, J. (1985). Security in infancy, childhood, and adulthood. In I. Bretherton & E. Waters (Eds.), *Growing Points of Attachment Theory and Research. Monographs of the Society for Research in Child Development, 50*(1–2, Serial No. 209), 66–104.

Mandler, G. (1975). *Mind and Emotion.* New York: Wiley.

Mandler, G. (1980). The generation of emotion: A psychological theory. In R. Plutchik & H. Kellerman (Eds.), *Emotion: Theory, Research, and Experience: Vol. 1. Theories of Emotion,* New York: Academic Press.

Mandler, J. H. (1979). Categorical and schematic organization in memory. In C. R. Puff (Ed.), *Memory Organization and Structure.* New York: Academic.

Marcia, J. E. (1966). Development and validation of ego-identity status. *Journal of Personality and Social Psychology, 20,* 551–558.

Marcia, J. E. (1967). Ego identity status: Relationship to change in self-esteem, "general maladjustment", and authoritarianism. *Journal of Personality, 35,* 119–133.

Marcia, J. E. (1980). Identity in adolescence. In J. Adelson (Ed.), *Handbook of Adolescent Psychology.* New York: Wiley.

Marcia, J. E., & Friedman, M. L. (1970). Ego identity in college women. *Journal of Personality, 38,* 249–263.

Marshall, G. D., & Zimbardo, P. G. (1979). Affective consequences of inadequately explained physiological arousal. *Journal of Personality and Social Psychology, 37,* 970–985.

Martin, B. (1975). Parent–child relations. In F. D. Horowitz (Ed.), *Review of Child Development Research* (Vol. 4). Chicago: University of Chicago Press.

Martin, J. A. (1981). A longitudinal study of the consequences of early mother–infant interaction. *Monographs of the Society for Research in Child Development, 46*(3, Serial No. 190).

Martin, N. G., Eaves, L. J., Heath, A. C., Jardine, R., & Feingold, L. M. (1986). Transmission of social attitudes. *Proceedings of the National Academy of Science USA, 83,* 4364–4368.

Massie, H. N. (1982). Affective development and the organization of mother–infant behavior from the perspective of psychopathology. In E. Z. Tronick (Ed.), *Social Interchange in Infancy*. Baltimore: University Park Press.

Masters, J. C. (1971). Effects of social comparison upon children's self-reinforcement and altruism toward competitors and friends. *Developmental Psychology, 5*, 64–72.

Matheny, A. P. (1983). A longitudinal twin study of stability of components of Bayley's Infant Behavior Record. *Child Development, 51*, 1157–1167.

Matheny, A. P., Dolan, A. B., & Wilson, R. S. (1976). Within-pair similarity on Bayley's Infant Behavior Record. *Journal of Genetic Psychology, 128*, 263–270.

Matteson, D. R. (1974). Alienation versus exploration and commitment: Personality and family correlaries of adolescent identity statuses. Report from the Project for Youth Research, Royal Danish School of Educational Studies, Copenhagen.

Maziade, M., Boudreault, M., Thivierge, J., Caperaa, P., & Cote, R. (1984). Infant temperament: SES and gender differences and reliability of measurement in a large Quebec sample. *Merrill-Palmer Quarterly, 30*, 213–216.

McCall, R. (1981). Nature–nurture and the two realms of development: A proposed integration with respect to mental development. *Child Development, 52*, 1–12.

McDevitt, S. C. (1986). Continuity and discontinuity of temperament in infancy and early childhood: A psychometric perspective. In R. Plomin & J. Dunn (Eds.), *The Study of Temperament: Changes, Continuities and Challenges*. Hillsdale, NJ: Erlbaum.

McGee, R., Williams, S., & Silva, P. A. (1984a). Background characteristics of aggressive, hyperactive, and aggressive–hyperactive boys. *Journal of the American Academy of Child Psychiatry, 23*, 280–284.

McGee, R., Williams, S., & Silva, P. A. (1984b). Behavioral and developmental characteristics of aggressive, hyperactive, and aggressive–hyperactive boys. *Journal of the American Academy of Child Psychiatry, 23*, 270–279.

McGrew, W. C. (1972). *An Ethological Study of Children's Behavior*. New York: Academic Press.

McGuire, M. T. (1974). The St. Kitts vervet. *Contributions to Primatology, 1*, 1–199.

McGuire, M. T., & Troisi, A. (1987). Physiological regulation–deregulation and psychiatric disorders. *Ethology and Sociobiology, 8*, 9S–25S.

McKay, H., Sinisterra, L., McKay, A., Gomez, H., & Floreda, P. (1978). Improving cognitive ability in cognitively deprived children. *Science, 200*, 270–278.

McNamee, S. (1978). Moral behavior, moral development and motivation. *Journal of Moral Education, 7*, 27–31.

Milich, R. S., & Landau, S. (In press). The role of social status variables in differentiating groups of hyperactive children. In J. M. Swanson & L. Bloomingdale (Eds.), *Attention Deficit Disorders IV: Emerging Trends in the Treatment of Attention in Behavior Problems of Children*. Monograph supplement to the *Journal of Child Psychology and Psychiatry*.

Miller, P. Y., & Simon, W. (1980). The development of sexuality in adolescence. In J. Adelson (Ed.), *Handbook of Adolescent Psychology*. New York: Wiley.

Minde, K., Lewin, D., Weiss, G., Lavigueur, H., Douglas, V. I., & Sykes, E. (1971). The hyperactive child in elementary school: A 5-year controlled follow-up. *Exceptional Children, 38*, 215–221.

Mischel, W. (1976). *Introduction to Personality* (2nd ed.). New York: Holt, Rinehart, & Winston.

Mitchell, G. (1968). Attachment differences in male and female infant monkeys. *Child Development, 39*, 611–620.

Mitchell, G. (1979). *Behavioral Sex Differences in Nonhuman Primates*. New York: Van Nostrand Reinhold.

Mitchell, G. (1981). *Human Sex Differences: A Primatologist's Perspective*. New York: Van Nostrand Reinhold.

Mitchell, G., & Brandt, E. M. (1975). Behavior of the female rhesus monkey during birth. In G. H. Bourne (Ed.), *The Rhesus Monkey* (Vol. 2). New York: Academic Press.

Mitchell, G., Arling, G. L., & Moller, G. W. (1967). Long-term effects of maternal punishment on the behavior of monkeys. *Psychonomic Science, 8*, 209–210.

Mitchell-Kernan, C., & Mitchell, K. T. (1977). Pragmatics of directive choice among children. In S. Ervin-Tripp & C. Mitchell-Kernan (Eds.), *Child Discourse*. New York: Academic.

Miyake, K., Chen, S., & Campos, J. J. (1985). Infant temperament, mother's mode of interaction, and attachment in Japan: An interim report. *Monographs of the Society for Research in Child Development, 50*, (1–2, Serial No. 209).

Money, J. (1987). Human sexology and psychoneuroendocrinology. In D. Crews (Ed.), *Psychobiology of Reproductive Behavior: An Evolutionary Perspective*. Englewood-Cliffs, NJ: Prentice-Hall.

Money, J., & Ehrhardt, A. A. (1972). *Man, Woman, Boy, Girl*. Baltimore: Johns Hopkins University Press.

Money, J., Hampson, J. G., & Hampson, J. L. (1955). An examination of some basic sexual concepts: The evidence of human hermaphroditism. *Bulletin of the Johns Hopkins Hospital, 97*, 301–319.

Moriarty, T. (1975). Crime, punishment and the responsive bystander: Two field experiments. *Journal of Personality and Social Psychology, 31*, 370–376.

Mortimer, J. T. (1976). Social class, work, and the family: Some implications of the father's career for familial relationships and son's career decisions. *Journal of Marriage and the Family, 1976* (May), 241–256.

Mortimer, J. T., Lorence, J., & Kumka, D. (1982). Work and family linkages in the transition to adulthood: A panel study of highly educated men. *Western Psychological Review, 13*, 50–68.

Moss, H. A., & Susman, E. J. (1980). Longitudinal study of personality development. In O. Brim & J. Kagan (Eds.), *Constancy and Change in Human Characteristics*. Cambridge: Harvard University Press.

Mueller, D. P. (1980). Social networks: A promising direction for research on the relationship of the environment to psychiatric disorder. *Social Science and Medicine, 14*, 147–161.

Mueller, E., & Lucas, T. (1975). A developmental analysis of peer interactions among toddlers. In M. Lewis & A. Rosenblum (Eds.), *Friendship and Peer Relations*. New York: Wiley.

Mussen, P., & Eisenberg-Berg, N. (1977). *Roots of Caring, Sharing and Helping*. San Francisco: Freeman.

Muuss, R. E. (1982). *Theories of Adolescence* (4th ed.). New York: Random House.

Neill, S. R. (1976). Aggressive and non-aggressive fighting in 12–13 year-old preadolescent boys. *Journal of Child Psychology and Psychiatry, 17*, 213–220.

Nelson, K., & Gruendel, J. (1981). Generalized event representations: Basic building blocks of cognitive development. *Advances in Developmental Psychology, 1*, 131–158.

Newson, J., & Newson, E. (1976). *Seven Years Old in the Home Environment*. London: Allen & Unwin.

Norman, J., & Harris, M. (1981). *The Private Life of the American Teenager*. New York: Rawson, Wade.

Novak, M. (1979). Social recovery of monkeys isolated for the first year of life: Long term assessment. *Developmental Psychology, 15*, 50–61.

Olweus, D. (1980). Familial and temperamental determinants of aggressive behavior in adolescent boys: A causal analysis. *Developmental Psychology, 16*, 644–666.

Olweus, D., Mattesson, A., Schalling, D., and Low, H. (1980). Testosterone, aggression physical and personality dimensions on normal adolescent males. *Psychosomatic Medicine, 42*, 253–269.

Ooms, T. (1981). Introduction. In T. Ooms (Ed.), *Teenage Pregnancy in a Family Context*. Philadelphia: Temple University Press.

Orlofsky, J. L. (1978). Identity formation: Achievement, and fear of success in college men and women. *Journal of Youth and Adolescence, 7*, 49–62.

Orlofsky, J. L., Marcia, J. E., & Lesser, I. M. (1973). Ego-identity status and the intimacy versus isolation crisis of young adulthood. *Journal of Personality and Social Psychology, 27*, 211–219.

Orris, J. B. (1969). Visual monitoring performance in the subgroups of male delinquents. *Journal of Abnormal Psychology, 74*, 227–229.

Overton, W. F. (1984). World views and their influence on psychological theory and research: Kuhn–Lakatos–Lauden. In H. W. Reese, Ed. *Advances in Child Development and Behavior* (Vol. 18o. New York: Academic Press.

Overton, W. F., & Reese, H. W. (1973). Models of development: Methodological implications. In J. R. Nesselroade & H. W. Reese (eds.), *Life-Span Developmental Psychology: Methodological Issues*. New York: Academic.

Ozeran, B. J. (1973). Sensation seeking as a predictor of leadership in leaderless, task-oriented groups. Unpublished master's thesis, University of Hawaii.

Paige, J. E., & Paige, J. M. (1981). *The Politics of Reproductive Ritual*. Berkeley: University of California Press.

Panksepp, J. (1986). The psychobiology of prosocial behaviors: Separation distress, play, and altruism. In C. Zahn-Waxler, E. M. Cummings, & R. Iannotti (Eds.), *Altruism and Aggression*. Cambridge: Cambridge University Press.

Panksepp, J., Siviy, S. M., & Normansell (1985). Brain opioids and social emotions. In M. Reite & T. Field (Eds.), *The psychobiology of attachment and separation*. New York: Academic.

Parke, R. D., & Collmer, C. W. (1975). Child abuse: An interdisciplinary analysis. In E. M. Hetherington (Ed.), *Review of Child Development Research* (Vol. 5). Chicago: University of Chicago Press.

Parke, R. D., & Slaby, R. G. (1983). The development of aggression. In P. Mussen & E. M. Hetherington (Eds.), *Handbook of Child Psychology, Vol. 4, Socialization and Personality Development*. New York: Wiley.

Parke, R. D., & Suomi, S. J. (1982). Adult male–infant relationships: Human and non-human primate evidence. In K. Immelmann, G. W. Barlow, L. Petrinovich, & M. Main (Eds.), *Behavioral Development*. Cambridge: Cambridge University Press.

Parke, R. D., MacDonald, K. B., Beitel, A., & Bhavnagri, N. (1988). The role of the family in the development of peer relationships. In R. D. Peters & R. J. McMahon (Eds.), *Social Learning and Systems Approaches to Marriage and the Family*. New York: Brunner/Mazel.

Parke, R. D., MacDonald, K. B., Burks, V. M., Carson, J., Beitel, A., Bhavnagri, N., & Barth, J. (In press). Family and peer systems: In search of the linkages. In K. Kreppner & R. M. Lerner (Eds.), *Family Systems and Life Span Development*. Hillsdale, NJ: Erlbaum.

Parker, G. A., Baker, R. R., & Smith, V. G. F. (1972). The origin and evolution of gamete dimorphism and the male–female phenomenon. *Journal of Theoretical Biology, 36*, 529–533.

Parkhurst, J., & Gottman, J. (1986). How young children get what they want. In J. Gottman & J. Parker (Eds.), *Conversations of Friends: Speculations on Affective Development*. Cambridge: Cambridge University Press.

Pastor, D. L. (1981). The quality of mother–infant attachment and its relationship to toddlers' initial sociability with peers. *Developmental Psychology, 17*, 326–335.

Paternite, C. E., & Loney, J. (1980). Childhood hyperkinesis: Relations between symptomatology and home environment. In C. K. Whalen and B. Henker (Eds.), *Hyperactive Children: The Social Ecology of Identification and Treatment*. New York: Academic Press.

Patterson, G. R. (1982). *Coercive Family Processes*. Eugene, OR: Castalia Press.

Patterson, G. R., Dishion, T. J., & Bank, L. (1984). Family interaction: A process model of deviancy training. *Aggressive Behavior, 10*, 253–267.

Paup, D. C., Coniglio, L. P., & Clemens, L. G. (1972). Masculinization of the female golden hamster by neonatal treatment with androgen or estrogen. *Hormones and Behavior, 2*, 49–63.

Pavlos, A. J. (1971). Effects of Machiavellianism, reward–cost outcomes, and modeling on altruistic behavior in a crisis. Paper presented at the Southern Society for Philosophy and Psychology, University of Georgia, Athens, GA, April 1971.

Pellegrini, A. D. (1987). Rough and tumble play: Developmental and educational significance. *Educational Psychologist, 22*, 23–43.

Perry, D. G., & Bussey, K. (1984) *Social Development*. Englewood Cliffs, NJ: Prentice-Hall.

Peterson, L. (1980). Developmental changes in verbal and behavioral sensitivity to cues of social norms of altruism. *Child Development, 51*, 830–838.

Phoenix, C. H., Goy, R. W., Gerall, A. A., & Young, W. C. (1959). Organizing action of prenatally administered testosterone propionate on tissues mediating mating behavior in the female guinea pig. *Endocrinology, 65*, 369–382.

Piaget, J. (1965). *The Moral Judgment of the Child* (M. Gabain, Trans.). New York: Free Press. (Originally published in 1932)

Piliavin, J. A., Dovidio, J. F., Gaertner, S. L., & Clark III, R. D. (1981). *Emergency Intervention*. New York: Academic.

Plomin, R., & Daniels, D. (1987). Why are children in the same family so different from one another? *Behavioral and Brain Sciences, 10*, 1–16.

Plomin, R., & DeFries, J. C. (1985). *The Origins of Individual Differences in Infancy*. New York: Academic Press.

Plomin, R., & Kuse, A. R. (1979). Genetic differences between humans and chimps and among humans *American Psychologist, 43*, 188–190.

Plomin, R., DeFries, J. C., & Loehlin, J. C. (1977). Genotype-environment interaction and correlation in the analysis of human behavior. *Psychological Bulletin, 84*, 309–322.

Power, T. G., & Parke, R. D. (1983). Play as a context for early learning: Lab and home analyses. In L. M. Laosa & I. B. Sigel (Eds.), *The Family As a Learning Environment*. New York: Plenum Press.

Price, J. S., Slater, E., & Hare, E. H. (1971). Marital status of first admissions to psychiatric beds in England and Wales in 1965 and 1966. *Social Biology, 18*, S74–S94.

Pringle, M. L. K., & Bossio, V. (1960). Early prolonged separation and emotional maladjustment. *Journal of Child Psychology and Psychiatry, 1*, 37–48.

Prinz, R. J., Conner, P. A., & Wilson, C. C. (1981). Hyperative and aggressive behaviors in childhood: Intertwined dimensions. *Journal of Abnormal Child Psychology, 9,* 191–202.

Pulkkinen, L. (1982). Self-control and continuity from childhood to adolescence. In P. B. Baltes & O. Brim (Eds.), *Life-Span Development and Behavior* (Vol. 4). New York: Academic.

Pulliam, H. R., & Dunford, C. (1980). *Programmed to Learn.* New York: Columbia University Press.

Purifoy, F. E., & Koopmans, L. H. (1979) Androstenedione, testosterone, and free testosterone in women of various occupations. *Social Biology, 26,* 179–188.

Quay, H. C. (1965). Psychopathic personality as pathological stimulus seeking. *American Journal of Psychiatry, 122,* 180–183.

Quay, H. C. (1977). Psychopathic behavior: Reflections on its nature, origins, and treatment. In F. Weizmann & I. Uzgiris (Eds.), *The Structuring of Experience.* New York: Plenum Press.

Quay, H. C. (1979). Classification. In H. C. Quay & J. S. Werry (Eds.), *Psychopathological Disorders of Childhood* (2nd ed.). New York: Wiley.

Quay, H. C. (1985). Aggression, conduct disorder, and attention problems. In L. M. Bloomingdale (Ed.), *Attention Deficit Disorder: Identification, Course, and Rationale.* New York: Spectrum.

Quay, H. C. (1986). Classification. In H. C. Quay & J. S. Werry (Eds.), *Psychopathological Disorders of Childhood* (3rd ed.). New York: Wiley.

Quinton, D., & Rutter, M. (1976). Early hospital admission and later disturbances in behavior: An attempted replication of Douglas' findings. *Developmental Medicine and Child Neurology, 18,* 447–459.

Radke-Yarrow, M., Zahn-Waxler, C., & Chapman, M. (1983). Prosocial dispositions and behavior. In P. Mussen & E. M. Hetherington (Eds.), *Handbook of Child Psychology: Vol. 4. Socialization and Personality and Social Development.* New York: Wiley.

Reed, S. (1971). Discussion: Mental illness and reproduction. *Social Biology, 18,* S95–S102 (1971).

Reese, H. W., & Overton, W. F. (1970). Models of development and theories of development. In L. R. Goulet & P. B. Baltes (Eds.), *Life-Span Developmental Psychology: Research and Theory.* New York: Academic Press.

Reid, J. B., Taplin, P. S., & Lorber, R. (1981). A social interactional approach to the treatment of abusive families. In R. B. Stuart (Ed.), *Violent Behavior: Social Learning Approaches to Prediction, Management and Treatment.* New York: Brunner/Mazel.

Reite, M., & Capitanio, J. P. (1985). On the nature of social separation and social attachment. In M. Reite & T. Field (Eds.), *The Psychobiology of Attachment and Separation.* New York: Academic Press.

Rest, J. R. (1979). *Development in Judging Moral Issues.* Minneapolis: University of Minnesota Press.

Rest, J. R. (1983). Morality. In J. H. Flavell & E. Markman (Eds.), *Handbook of Child Psychology: Vol. 3. Cognitive Development.* New York: Wiley.

Rest, J. R., & Thoma, S. J. (1985). Relation of moral judgment development to formal education. *Developmental Psychology, 21,* 709–714.

Reznick, J. S., Kagan, J., Snidman, N., Gersten, M., Baak, K., & Rosenberg, A. (1986). Inhibited and uninhibited children: A follow-up study. *Child Development, 57,* 660–680.

Rholes, W. S., & Lane, J. W. (1985). Consistency between cognitions and behavior: Cause and consequence of cognitive moral development. In J. B. Pryor & J. D. Day (Eds.), *The Development of Social Cognition.* New York: Springer-Verlag.

Rice, M., & Grusec, J. (1975). Saying and doing: Effects on observer performance. *Journal of Personality and Social Psychology, 32,* 584–593.

Ricks, M. H. (1985). The social transmission of parental behavior: Attachment across generations. In I. Bretherton & E. Waters (Eds.), *Growing Points of Attachment Theory and Research. Monographs of the Society for Research in Child Development, 50*(1–2, Serial No. 209).

Roebuck, J., & McGee, M. J. (1977). Attitudes toward premarital sex and sexual behavior among black high school girls. *Journal of Sex Research, 13,* 104–114.

Rohner, R. P. (1975). *They Love Me, They Love Me Not.* New Haven, CT: HRAF

Roseman, I. (1979). Cognitive aspects of emotion and emotional behavior. Paper presented at the meetings of the American Psychological Association, New York City, September 1979.

Rosenhan, D. (1970). The natural socialization of altruistic autonomy. In J. Macauley & L. Berkowitz (Eds.), *Altruism and Helping Behavior.* New York: Academic.

Ross, H. L., & Sawhill, I. V. (1975). *Time of Transition: The Growth of Families Headed by Women.* Washington, DC: Urban Institute.

Rothbart, M. K. (1986). Longitudinal observations of infant temperament. *Developmental Psychology, 22,* 356–365.

Rothbart, M. K. (1987). Roundtable: What is temperament? *Child Development, 58,* 505–529.

Rothbart, M. (in press-a). Behavioral approach and inhibition. In S. Reznick (Ed.), *Perspectives on Behavioral Inhibition.* Chicago: University of Chicago Press.

Rothbart, M. K. (in press-b). Temperament in childhood: A framework. In G. Kohnstamm, J. Bates, and M. K. Rothbart (Eds.), *Handbook of Temperament in Childhood.* London: Wiley.

Rothbart, M. K., & Derryberry, D. (1981). Development of individual differences in temperament. In M. E. Lamb & A. L. Brown (Eds.), *Advances in Developmental Psychology* (Vol. 1). Hillsdale, NJ: Erlbaum.

Rothbart, M. K., & Posner, M. I. (1985). Temperament and the development of self-regulation. In L. C. Hartlage & C. F. Telzrow (Eds.), *The Neuropsychology of Individual Differences.* New York: Plenum Press.

Rowell, T. E. (1966). Hierarchy in the organization of a captive baboon group. *Animal Behavior, 14,* 430–443.

Royce, J. R. (1973). The conceptual framework for a multi-factor theory of individuality. In J. R. Royce (Ed.), *Multivariate Analysis and Psychological Theory.* London: Academic Press.

Rubin, K. H., Fein, G. G., and Vandenberg, B. (1983). Play. In P. Mussen & E. M. Hetherington (Eds.), *Handbook of Child Psychology: Vol. 4. Socialization, Personality and Social Development.* New York: Wiley.

Rubin, R. T., Reinisch, J. M., & Haskett, R. F. (1980). Postnatal gonadal steroid effects on human behavior. *Science, 211,* 1318–1324.

Ruppenthal, G. C., Arling, G. A., Harlow, H. F., Sackett, G. P., & Suomi, S. J. (1976). A ten-year perspective on motherless-mother monkey behavior. *Journal of Abnormal Psychology, 85,* 341–349.

Rushton, J. P. (1975). Generosity in children: Immediate and long term effects of modeling, preaching, and moral judgment. *Journal of Personality and Social Psychology, 31,* 459–466.

Rushton, J. P. (1980). *Altruism, Socialization and Society.* Engelwood Cliffs, NJ: Prentice-Hall.

Rushton, J. P. (1982). Social learning theory and the development of prosocial behavior. In N. Eisenberg (Ed.), *The Development of Prosocial Behavior.* New York: Academic.

Rushton, J. P., & Littlefield, C. (1979). The effects of age, amount of modeling, and a success experience on seven-to-eleven-year-old children's generosity. *Journal of Moral Education, 9,* 55–56.

Rushton, J. P., & Teachman, G. (1978). The effects of positive reinforcement, attributions, and punishment on model induced altruism in children. *Personality and Social Psychology Bulletin, 4,* 322–325.

Rushton, J. P., Russell, R. J. H., & Wells, P. A. (1984). Genetic similarity theory: Beyond kin selection. *Behavior Genetics, 14,* 179–193.

Rushton, J. P., Fulker, D., Neale, M. C., Nias, D. K. B., & Eysenck, H. J. (1986). Altruism and aggression: The heritability of individual differences. *Journal of Personality and Social Psychology, 50,* 1192–1198.

Rutter, M., & Garmezy, N. (1983). Developmental psychopathology. In P. Mussen & E. M. Hetherington (Eds.), *Handbook of Child Psychology: Vol. 4. Socialization, Personality and Social Development.* New York: Wiley.

Sackett, G. P. (1966). Monkeys reared in visual isolation with pictures as visual input: Evidence for an innate releasing mechanism. *Science, 154,* 1468–1473.

Sackett, G. P., Ruppenthal, G. C., Fahrenbruch, C. E., Hold, R. A., & Greenough, W. T. (1980). Social isolation rearing effects in monkeys vary with genotype. *Developmental Psychology, 17,* 313–318.

Sackett, G. P., Sameroff, A. J., Cairns, R. B., & Suomi, S. J. (1982). Continuity in behavioral development: Theoretical and empirical issues. In K. Immelmann, G. W. Barlow, L. Petrinovich, & M. Main (Eds.), *Behavioral Development.* London: Cambridge University Press.

Sahlins, M. D. (1963). Poor man, rich man, big-man chief: Political types in Melanesia and Polynesia. *Comparative Studies in Society and History, 5,* 285–303.

Sahlins, M. D. (1965). On the sociology of primitive exchange. In M. Banton (Ed.), *The Relevance of Models for Social Anthropology.* London: Tavistock.

Sahlins, M. D. (1974). *Stone-Age Economics.* Chicago: Aldine.

Sales, S. M., Guydosh, R. M., & Iacono, W. (1974). Relationship between "strength of the nervous system" and the need for stimulation. *Journal of Personality and Social Psychology, 29,* 16–22.

Sameroff, A. J. (1975). Early influences: Fact or fancy? *Merrill-Palmer Quarterly, 20,* 275–301.

Savin-Williams, R. (1987). *Adolescence: An Ethological Perspective.* New York: Springer-Verlag.

Scaramella, T. C., & Brown, W. A. (1978). Serum testosterone and aggressiveness in hockey players. *Psychosomatic Medicine, 40,* 262–265.

Scarr, S. (1976). An evolutionary perspective on infant intelligence: Species patterns and individual variations. In M. Lewis (Ed.), *The Origins of Infant Intelligence.* New York: Plenum Press.

Scarr, S. (1985). Constructing psychology: Making facts and fables for our times. *American Psychologist, 40,* 499–512. Reprinted in S. Chess & A. Thomas (Eds.), *Annual Progress in Child Psychiatry and Child Development,* pp. 43–68. New York: Brunner/Mazel, Inc.

Scarr, S. (1987). Distinctive environments depend on genotypes. *Behavioral and Brain Science, 10,* 38–39.

Scarr, S., & Kidd, D. (1983). Developmental behavior genetics. In M. M. Haith & J. J. Campos (Eds.), *Handbook of Child Psychology: Vol. 2. Infancy and Developmental Psychobiology.* New York: Wiley.

Scarr, S., & McCartney, K. (1983). How people make their own environments: A theory of genotype–environment effects. *Child Development, 54,* 424–435.

Scarr, S., & Weinberg, R. A. (1976). IQ test performance of black children adopted by white families. *American Psychologist, 31,* 726–739.

Scarr, S., & Weinberg, R. A. (1978). The influence of "family background" on intellectual attainment. *American Sociological Review, 43,* 674–692.

Schacter, S. (1964). The interaction of cognitive and physiological determinants of emotional state. *Advances in Experimental Social Psychology,* Vol. *1,* New York: Academic.

Schacter, S., & Singer, J. (1962). Cognitive, social and physiological determinants of emotional state. *Psychological Review, 69,* 379–399.

Schaefer, E. S. (1959). A circumplex model for maternal behavior. *Journal of Abnormal and Social Psychology, 59,* 226–235.

Schmauk, F. J. (1970). Punishment, arousal, and avoidance learning in sociopaths. *Journal of Abnormal Psychology, 76,* 325–335.

Schneider-Rosen, K., & Cichetti, D. (1984). The relationship between affect and cognition in maltreated infants: Quality of attachment and the development of visual self-recognition. *Child Development, 55,* 648–658.

Schneider-Rosen, K., Braunwald, K. G., Carlson, V., & Cicchetti, D. (1985). Current perspectives in attachment theory: Illustration from the study of maltreated infants. In I. Bretherton & E. Waters (Eds.), *Growing Points of Attachment Theory and Research. Monographs of the Society for Research in Child Development, 50* (1–2, Serial No. 209).

Schnierla, T. C. (1957). The concept of development in comparative psychology. In D. B. Harris (Ed.), *The Concept of Development.* Minneapolis: University of Minnesota Press.

Schultz, T. R. (1979). Play as arousal modulation. In B. Sutton-Smith (Ed.), *Play and Learning.* New York: Gardner.

Schwartz, S. H. (1977). Normative influences on altruism. In L. Berkowitz (Ed.), *Advances in Experimental Social Psychology* (Vol. 10). New York: Academic.

Schwartz, S. H., & Gottlieb, A. (1976). Bystander reactions to a violent theft: Crime in Jerusalem. *Journal of Personality and Social Psychology, 34,* 1188–1199.

Schwartz, S. H., & Gottlieb, A. (1980). Bystander anonymity and reactions to emergencies. *Journal of Personality and Social Psychology, 39,* 418–430.

Schwartz, S. H., & Howard, J. A. (1984). Internalized values as motivators of altruism. In E. Staub, D. Bar-Tal, J. Karylowski, & J. Reykowski (Eds.), *Development and Maintenance of Prosocial Behavior.* New York: Plenum Press.

Segal, N. (1988). Cooperation, competition and altruism in human twinships: A sociobiological approach. In K. B. MacDonald (Ed.), *Sociobiological Perspectives on Human Development.* New York: Springer-Verlag.

Seyfarth, R. M. (1980). The distribution of grooming and related behaviors among adult female vervet monkeys. *Animal Behavior, 28,* 798–813.

Sigman, M., Cohen, S. E., and Forsythe, A. (1981). The relation of early infant measures to later development. In S. L. Friedman & M. Sigman (Eds.), *Preterm Birth and Psychological Development).* New York: Academic.

Silberbauer, G. B. (1981). *Hunter and Habitat in the Central Kalihari Desert.* Cambridge: Cambridge University Press.

Skinner, B. F. (1971). *Beyond Freedom and Dignity.* New York: Knopf.

Skolnick, E. K. (1986). Influences on plasticity: Problems of definition. *Journal of Applied Developmental Psychology, 7,* 131–138.

Skrzypek, G. J. (1969). Effect of perceptual isolation and arousal on anxiety, complexity preference, and novelty preference in psychopathic and neurotic delinquents. *Journal of Abnormal Psychology, 74,* 321–329.

Slater, E., Hare, E. H., & Price, J. S. (1971). Marriage and fertility of psychiatric patients compared with national data. *Social Biology, 18,* S60–S73.

Smith, M. S. (1988). Research in developmental sociobiology: Parenting and family behavior. In K. B. MacDonald (Ed.), *Sociobiological Perspectives on Human Development.* New York: Springer-Verlag.

Smith, M. K., Kish, B. J., & Crawford, C. B. (1987). Inheritance of wealth as human kin investment. *Ethology and Sociobiology, 8,* 171–182.

Smith, P. K., & Green, M. (1974). Aggressive behavior in English nurseries and playgrounds: Sex differences and responses of adults. *Child Development, 45,* 211–214.

Smith, P. K., & Noble, R. (1987). Factors affecting the development of caregiver–infant relationships. In L. W. C. Tavecchio & M. H. Van IJzendoorn (Eds.), *Attachment in Social Networks: Contributions to the Bowlby–Ainsworth Attachment Theory.* Amsterdam: North-Holland.

Snowdon, C. T., & Suomi, S. J. (1982). Paternal behavior in primates. In H. E. Fitzgerald, J. A. Mullins, & P. Gage (Eds.), *Child Nurturance. Studies of Development in Nonhuman Primates* (Vol. 3). New York: Plenum Press.

Sobesky, W. E. (1983). The effects of situational factors on moral judgments. *Child Development, 54,* 575–584.

Sole, L., Marton, J., & Hornstein, H. A. (1975). Opinion similarity in helping: Three field experiments investigating the bases of promotive tension. *Journal of Abnormal and Social Psychology, 11,* 1–13.

Sroufe, L. A. (1977). Wariness of strangers and the study of infant development. *Child Development, 48,* 731–746.

Sroufe, L. A. (1979a). The coherence of individual development: Early care, attachment and subsequent developmental issues. *American Psychologist, 34,* 834–842.

Sroufe, L. A. (1979b). Socio-emotional development. In J. Osofsky (Ed.), *Handbook of Infant Development.* New York: Wiley.

Sroufe, L. A. (1983). Infant–caregiver attachment and patterns of adaptation in preschool: The roots of maladaptation and competence. In M. Perlmutter (Ed.), *Minnesota Symposia on Child Psychology: Vol. 16. Development and Policy Concerning Children with Special Needs.* Hillsdale, NJ: Erlbaum.

Sroufe, L. A. (1985). Attachment classification from the perspective of infant–caregiver relationships and infant temperament. *Child Development, 56,* 1–14.

Sroufe, L. A., & Waters, E. (1977). The organizational construct of attachment. *Child Development, 48,* 1184–1199.

Sroufe, L. A., Schork, E., Motti, E., Lawroski, N., & LaFreniere, P. (1984). The role of affect in emerging social competence. In C. Izard, J. Kagan, & R. Zajonc (Eds.) *Emotion, Cognition, and Behavior.* New York: Cambridge University Press.

Stanley, W. C., & Elliot, O. (1962). Differential handling as reinforcing events and as treatments influencing later social behavior. *Psychological Reports, 10,* 775–788.

Staub, E. (1970). A child in distress: The effects of focusing responsibility on children on their attempts to help. *Developmental Psychology, 2,* 152–154.

Staub, E. (1971). Helping a person in distress: The influence of implicit and explicit "rules" of conduct on children and adults. *Journal of Personality and Social Psychology, 17,* 137–144.

Staub, E. (1978). *Positive Social Behavior and Morality: Vol. 1. Personal and Social Influences.* New York: Academic Press.

Staub, E. (1979). *Positive Social Behavior and Morality: Vol. 2. Socialization and Development.* New York: Academic Press.

Stein, L. (1983). The chemistry of positive reinforcement. In M. Zuckerman (Ed.), *Biological Bases of Sensation Seeking, Impulsivity and Anxiety.* Hillsdale, NJ: Erlbaum.

Steinberg, L. (1987). Single parents, stepparents, and the susceptibility of adolescents to antisocial peer pressure. *Child Development, 58,* 269–275.

Stern, D. (1977). *The First Relationship.* Cambridge: Harvard University Press.

Stewart, M. (1970). Hyperactive children. *Scientific American, 222,* 97–98.

Stewart, M. A., DeBlois, C. S., & Cummings, C. (1980). Psychiatric disorder in the parents of hyperactive boys and those with conduct disorder. *Journal of Child Psychology and Psychiatry, 21,* 283–292.

Stone, C. (1960). Some family characteristics of socially active and inactive teenagers. *Family Life Coordinator, 8,* 53–57.

Stone, L. (1977). *The Family, Sex and Marriage in England: 1500–1800*. New York: Harper & Row.

Stotland, E. (1969). Exploratory explorations of empathy. In L. Berkowitz (Ed.), *Advances in Experimental Social Psychology* (Vol. 4). New York: Academic.

Strayer, F. F., & Noel, J. M. (1986). The prosocial and antisocial foundations of preschool aggression: An ethological study of triadic conflict among young children. In C. Zahn-Waxler, E. M. Cummings, & R. Iannotti (Eds.), *Altruism and Aggression: Biological and Social Origins*. Cambridge: Cambridge University Press.

Strayer, F. F., & Strayer, J. (1976). An ethological analysis of social agonism and dominance relations among preschool children. *Child Development, 47,* 980–989.

Strayer, F. F., & Trudel, M. (1984). Developmental changes in the nature and function of social dominance among young children. *Ethology and Sociobiology, 5,* 279–295.

Streator, A. L., & Chertkoff, J. M. (1976). Distribution of rewards in a triad: A developmental test of equity theory. *Child Development, 47,* 800–805.

Suomi, S. (1987). Individual differences in rhesus monkey behavioral and adrenocortical responses to social challenge: Correlations with measures of heart rate variability. Paper presented at the meetings of the Society for Research in Child Development, Baltimore, MD, April 25, 1987.

Suomi, S. J., & Harlow, H. F. (1972). Social rehabilitation of isolate-reared monkeys. *Developmental Psychology, 6,* 487–496.

Super, C. M., & Harkness, S. (1981). Figure, ground and Gestalt: The cultural context of the active individual. In R. M. Lerner & N. A. Busch-Rossnagel (Eds.), *Individuals As Producers of Their Development: A Life-Span Perspective*. New York: Academic.

Super, C. M., & Harkness, S. (1986). Temperament, development, and culture. In R. Plomin & J. Dunn (Eds.), *The Study of Temperament: Changes, Continuities, and Challenges*. Hillsdale, NJ: Erlbaum

Surbey, K. (1987). Father absence and the timing of menarche. Unpublished manuscript, Brock University, London, Ontario.

Susman, E., Inoff-Germain, G., Nottelmann, E. D., Loriaux, D. L., Cutler, G. B., & Chousos, G. P. (1987). Hormones, emotional dispositions, and aggressive attributes in young adolescents. *Child Development, 58,* 1114–1134.

Sussman, M., & Davis, J. (1975). Balance theory and the negative interpersonal relationship: Attraction and agreement in dyads and triads. *Journal of Personality, 43,* 560–581.

Symons, D. (1979). *The Evolution of Human Sexuality*. New York: Oxford University Press.

Terman, L. M., & Tyler, L. E. (1954). Psychological sex differences. In L. Carmichael (Ed.), *Manual of Child Psychology* (2nd ed.). New York: Wiley.

Thayer, R. E. (1978). Toward a psychological theory of multidimensional activation (arousal). *Motivation and Emotion, 2,* 1–34.

Thayer, R. E. (1985). Activation (arousal): The shift from a single to a multidimensional perspective. In J. Strelau, F. H. Farley, & A. Gale (Eds.), *The Biological Bases of Personality and Behavior*. Washington, DC: Hemisphere.

Thayer, R. E. (1986). Activation–deactivation adjective checklist: Current overview and structural analysis. *Psychological Reports, 58,* 607–614.

Thayer, R. E. (1987). Energy, tiredness, and tension effects of a sugar snack versus moderate exercise. *Journal of Personality and Social Psychology, 52,* 119–125.

Thayer, R. E., Takahashi, P. J., & Pauli, J. A. (1988). Multidimensional arousal states, diurnal rhythms, cognitive and social processes, and extraversion. *Personality and Individual Differences, 9,* 15–24.

Thayer, R. E. (in press). *The Biopsychology of Mood and Arousal*. Oxford: Oxford University Press.

Thomas, A., & Chess, S. (1977). *Temperament and Development*. New York: Brunner/Mazel.

Thomas, A., & Chess, S. (1980). *The Dynamics of Psychological Development*. New York: Brunner/Mazel.

Thomas, A., & Chess, S. (1986). The New York longitudinal study: From infancy to early adolescence. In R. Plomin & J. Dunn (Eds.), *The Study of Temperament: Changes, Continuities and Challenges*. Hillsdale, NJ: Erlbaum.

Thomas, A., Chess, S., & Birch, H. (1968). *Temperament and Behavior Disorders in Children*. New York: New York University Press.

Thomas, A., Chess, S., Sillen, J., & Mendez, O. (1974). Cross-cultural study of behavior in children with special vulnerabilities to stress. In D. Ricks, A. Thomas, & M. Roff (Eds.), *Life History Research in Psychopathology* (Vol. 3). Minneapolis: University of Minnesota Press.

Thompson, R. A., & Lamb, M. E. (1984). Assessing qualitative dimensions of emotional responsiveness in infants: Separation reactions in the Strange Situation. *Infant Behavior and Development, 7,* 423–445.

Thompson, R. A., Lamb, M. E., & Estes, D. (1982). Harmonizing discordant notes: A reply to Waters. *Child Development, 54,* 521–524.

Tietjen, A. M. (1986). Prosocial reasoning among children and adults in a Papua New Guinea society. *Developmental Psychology, 21,* 982–992.

Tietjen, A. M., & Walker, L. (1985). Moral reasoning and leadership among men in a Papua New Guinea society. *Developmental Psychology, 21,* 982–992.

Tigerstedt, E. N. (1974). *The Legend of Sparta in Classical Antiquity,* Vol. II. Uppsala, Sweden: Almqvist & Wiksell.

Tizard, B. (1978). *Adoption: A Second Chance.* New York: Free Press.

Trivers, R. L. (1971). The evolution of reciprocal altruism. *Quarterly Review of Biology, 46,* 35–57.

Trivers, R. (1974). Parent–offspring conflict. *American Zoologist, 14,* 249–264.

Trivers, R. (1985). *Principles of Social Evolution.* Menlo Park, CA: Benjamin-Cummings.

Trivers, R. L., and Willard, D. E. (1973). Natural selection of parental ability to vary the sex ratio of offspring. *Science, 179,* 90–92.

Tronick, E. Z. (1982). Affectivity and sharing. In E. Z. Tronick (Ed.), *Social Interchange in Infancy.* Baltimore: University Park Press.

Turner, R. J., & Wagenfeld, M. O. (1967). Occupational mobility and schizophrenia: An assessment of the social causation and social selection hypotheses. *American Sociological Review, 32,* 104–113.

Ugerel-Semin, R. (1952). Moral behavior and moral judgment of children. *Journal of Abnormal and Social Psychology, 47,* 463–474.

Ulrich, R. E., & Craine, W. H. (1964). Persistence of shock-induced aggression. *Science, 143,* 971–973.

Underwood, B., & Moore, B. (1982). Perspective-taking and altruism. *Psychological Bulletin, 91,* 143–173.

U.S. Department of Commerce (1979). *Statistical Abstract of the United States: 1979,* 100th ed.

Van den Berghe, P. (1979). *Human Family Systems.* New York: Elsevier.

Van Lawick-Goodall, J. (1971). *In the Shadow of Man.* Boston: Houghton Mifflin.

Vaughn, B., Egeland, B., Sroufe, L. A., & Waters, E. (1979). Individual differences in mother–infant attachment at twelve and eighteen months: Stability and change in families under stress. *Child Development, 51,* 47–66.

Vining, D. R. (1986). Social versus reproductive success: The central theoretical problem of human sociobiology. *Behavioral and Brain Sciences, 9,* 167–216.

Wachs, T. (1986). Understanding early experience and development: The relevance of stages of inquiry. *Journal of Applied Developmental Psychology, 7,* 153–165.

Wachs, T., & Gruen, G. (1982). *Early Experience and Human Development.* New York: Plenum Press.

Waddington, C. H. (1957). *The Strategy of the Genes.* London: Allen.

Wagner, C., & Wheeler, L. (1969). Model, need, and cost effects in helping behavior. *Journal of Personality and Social Psychology, 12,* 111–116.

Walker, L. J. (1984). Sex differences in the development of moral reasoning: A critical review. *Child Development, 55,* 677–691.

Walker, L. J. (1986). Sex differences in the development of moral reasoning: A rejoinder to Baumrind. *Child Development, 57,* 522–526.

Wallerstein, J., & Kelly, J. B. (1980). *Surviving the Breakup.* New York: Basic Books.

Ward, I. C. (1972). Prenatal stress feminizes and demasculinizes the behavior of males. *Science, 175,* 82–84.

Ward, I. C., & Weisz, J. (1980). Maternal stress alters plasma testosterone in fetal males. *Science, 207,* 328–329.

Waters, E. (1978). The reliability and stability of individual differences in infant–mother attachment. *Child Development, 49,* 483–494.

Watson, D., & Tellegen, A. (1985). Toward a consensual structure of mood. *Psychological Bulletin, 98,* 219–235.

Weisfeld, G. E., & Berger, J. M. (1983). Some features of adolescence viewed in evolutionary perspective. *Human Development, 26,* 121–133.

Weisfeld, G. E., & Billings, R. L. (1988). Observations on adolescence. In K. B. MacDonald (Ed.), *Sociobiological Perspectives on Human Development.* New York: Springer-Verlag.

Weisfeld, G. E., Weisfeld, C. C., & Callaghan, J. W. (1984). Peer and self-perceptions of Hopi and Afro-American third and sixth graders. *Ethos, 12,* 64–84.

Weisfeld, G. E., Muczenski, I., Weisfeld, C., & Omark, D. R. (in press). Stability of boys' social success among peers over an eleven-year period. In J. A. Meacham (Ed.), *Interpersonal Relations: Family, Peers, Friends.* Basel: Karger.

Weisner, T. S. (1984). Ecocultural niches of middle-childhood: A cross-cultural perspective. In W. A. Collings (Ed.), *Development during Middle Childhood: The Years from Six to Twelve.* Washington, DC: National Academy Press.

Weiss, J. M., Pohorecky, L. A., Salman, S., & Gruenthal, M. (1976). Attenuation of gastric lesions by psychological aspects of aggression in rats. *Journal of Comparative and Physiological Psychology, 90,* 252–259.

Welch, R. L., Huston-Stein, A., Wright, J. C., & Plehal, R. (1979). Subtle sex-role cues in children's commercials. *Journal of Communication, 29,* 202–229.

Werner, E. E., & Smith, R. S. (1982). *Vulnerable but Invincible.* New York: McGraw-Hill.

Werner, H. (1957). The concept of development from a comparative and organismic point of view. In D. B. Harris (Ed.), *The Concept of Development.* Minneapolis: University of Minnesota.

Whimbey, A. E., & Denenberg, V. H. (1966). Two independent behavioral dimensions in open field performance. *Journal of Comparative and Physiological Psychology, 63,* 500–504.

White, G. M. (1972). Immediate and deferred effects of model observation and guided and unguided rehearsal of donation and stealing. *Journal of Personality and Social Psychology, 21,* 139–148.

White, G. M., & Burnham, M. A. (1975). Socially cued altruism: Effects of modeling, instructions, and age on public and private donations. *Child Development, 46,* 559–563.

White, S. W., & Asher, S. J. (1976). Separation and divorce: A study of the male perspective. Unpublished manuscript, University of Colorado, Boulder.

Whiting, B., & Edwards, C. P. (1973). A cross-cultural analysis of the behavior of children aged three to eleven. *Journal of Social Psychology, 91,* 171–188.

Whiting, J. W. M., & Whiting, B. B. (1975). Aloofness and intimacy between husbands and wives. *Ethos, 3,* 183–207.

Williams, G. C. (1966). *Adaptation and Natural Selection.* Princeton, NJ: Princeton University Press.

Williams, G. C. (1975). *Sex and Evolution.* Princeton, NJ. Princeton University Press.

Wilson, E. O. (1975). *Sociobiology: The New Synthesis.* Cambridge: Harvard University Press.

Wilson, E. O. (1978). *On Human Nature.* Cambridge: Harvard University Press.

Wilson, M., & Daly, M. (1985). Competitiveness, risk taking, and violence: The young male syndrome. *Ethology and Sociobiology, 6,* 59–73.

Winick, M. M., Meyer, K. K., & Harris, R. C. (1975). Malnutrition and environmental enrichment by adoption. *Science, 190,* 1173–1175.

Wolins, M. (1970). Young children in institutions. *Developmental Psychology, 2,* 99–109.

Wolkind, J. N. (1974). The components of affectionless psychopathy in institutionalized children. *Journal of Child Psychology and Psychiatry, 15,* 215–220.

Woodruff, D. S. (1985). Arousal, sleep, and aging. In J. E. Birren & K. W. Schaie (Eds.), *Handbook of the Psychology of Aging.* New York: Van Nostrand Reinhold.

Wundt, W. M. (1893). *Grundzuge der Physiologischen Psychologie.* Leipzig: Engleman.

Wynne-Edwards, V. C. (1962). *Animal Dispersion and Its Relation to Social Behavior.* Edinburgh: Olwen & Boyd.

Young, F. W. (1962). The function of male initiation ceremonies: A cross-cultural test of an alternative hypothesis. *American Journal of Sociology, 67,* 379–396.

Young, F. W. (1965). *Initiation Ceremonies: A Cross-Cultural Study of Status Dramatization.* New York: Bobbs-Merrill.

Youniss, J. (1986). Development in reciprocity through friendship. In C. Zahn-Waxler, E. M. Cummings, & R. Iannotti (Eds.), *Altruism and Aggression: Biological and Social Origins.* New York: Cambridge University Press.

Zahn-Waxler, C., & Radke-Yarrow, M. (1982). The development of altruism: Alternative research strategies. In N. Eisenberg (Ed.), *The Development of Prosocial Behavior.* New York: Academic.

Zajonc, R. (1980). Feeling and thinking: Preferences need no inferences. *American Psychologist, 35,* 151–175.

Zarbatany, L., Hartmann, D. P., & Gelfand, D. M. (1985). Why does children's generosity increase with age: Susceptibility to experimenter influence or altruism? *Child Development, 56,* 746–756.

Zentall, S. S. (1975). Optimal stimulation as theoretical basis of hyperactivity. *American Journal of Orthopsychiatry, 45,* 549–563.

Zentall, S. S. (1977). Environmental stimulation model. *Exceptional Children, 43,* 502–510.

Zentall, S. S. (1980). Behavioral comparisons of hyperactive and normally active children in natural settings. *Journal of Abnormal Child Psychology, 8,* 93–109.

Zentall, S. S., & Zentall, T. R. (1983). Optimal stimulation: A model of disordered activity and performance in normal and deviant children. *Psychological Bulletin, 94,* 446–471.

Zillman, D. (1983). Arousal and aggression. In R. G. Geen & E. I. Donnerstein (Eds.), *Aggression: Theoretical and Empirical Reviews: Vol. 1. Theoretical and Methodological Issues.* New York: Academic Press.

Zimbardo, P. G., Ebbesen, E. B., & Maslach, C. (1977). *Influencing Attitudes and Changing Behavior* (2nd ed.). Reading, MA: Addison-Wesley.

Zuckerman, M. (1979). *Sensation Seeking: Beyond the Optimal Level of Arousal.* Hillsdale, NJ: Erlbaum.

Zuckerman, M. (1983). A biological theory of sensation seeking. In M. Zuckerman (Ed.), *Biological Bases of Sensation Seeking, Impulsivity, and Anxiety.* Hillsdale, NJ: Erlbaum.

Index

341